The Servant of the Lord

H. H. Rowley

The Servant of the Lord

and other Essays on the Old Testament

SECOND EDITION, REVISED

Basil Blackwell
Oxford

First published 1952 by the Lutterworth Press
© Basil Blackwell & Mott Ltd., 1965

Printed in Great Britain by
Western Printing Services Ltd., Bristol

THIS VOLUME IS INSCRIBED
TO THE
SOCIETY FOR OLD TESTAMENT STUDY
IN WHOSE FELLOWSHIP AND SERVICE
MY UNDERSTANDING OF THE BIBLE
HAS BEEN DEEPENED AND ENRICHED

Contents

Preface

MOST of the essays collected in this volume have already appeared in journals or other publications in this country or abroad. Their republication now is in response to a number of requests for such a collection as is here made, though I have been unable to include some essays that were suggested for inclusion. All have been revised to a greater or less extent, and some of the more recent literature has been drawn on.

The opening study, which gives the main title to the volume, has not been published before. Like all the other essays, it is on a subject which has been much discussed, and on which a variety of opinions can be found in contemporary authors. It is too much to hope that I shall carry all scholars with me in every case—or, indeed, in any case—but since the same can be said of every treatment of every one of these subjects, this is not surprising. I can only offer a contribution to the study of the Old Testament, and any man who claims to do more is to be suspected.

It will be observed that the history of interpretation figures to no small extent in this volume. Such studies always seem to me to be particularly illuminating, and to give a perspective against which any given solution of problems should be seen. Many an author can make out a strong case for his own solution by presenting it in isolation, and can persuade himself and others that it is as clear as a pikestaff. He usually has to avoid mentioning those elements of the problem which have led to other solutions. It seems wiser to me to risk bewildering the reader with the variety of solutions that have been offered, in order that he may appreciate the complexity of the issues, and may be assured that the solutions he is offered have not been reached by ignoring what has been said in favour of others.

All of these studies are technical studies on Old Testament problems. Yet most of them may prove to have some interest for many who are not technical scholars. They will not be diverted from my argument by the footnotes, and may even wish they had been omitted. To them the only value of these footnotes will be their evidence that I have sought to compass an appreciable part of the literature that has been devoted to these subjects. To others they may have a greater value in stimulating further study and in directing the reader to the works in which he will find the subjects treated.

After each of the articles appeared in its earlier form I received many letters from other scholars pointing out gaps in the literature I had read. Alas! No man can read everything, or even remember all he has read; and while I always regret missing anything of importance, I make no claim to encyclopædic knowledge of the literature, but only to a reasonable effort to become acquainted with the various views that have been advanced. To those of my readers who will once more deplore the inadequacy of my documentation I present my apologies in advance. It has been impossible to take more than occasional notice of works which have appeared while the present volume has been in the press. I am especially sorry not to have been able to make fuller use of Mowinckel's great book *Han som kommer*.[1]

I have not thought it well to include collected lists of works consulted at the end of the volume. To list them separately for each essay would lead to much repetition, while to list them all together would yield some thirty pages of titles that would not provide a bibliography of any one subject, but that would read more like a library catalogue. In the footnotes I have endeavoured to give enough information to locate any book or article in which the reader may be interested.

Acknowledgments must be made to those who have made it possible for this volume to appear, or who have helped me in its preparation. I have to express my gratitude for permission to reissue articles to the Dutch Old Testament Society and its editor, Professor P. A. H. de Boer; to the editor of the *Harvard Theological Review*, Professor A. D. Nock; to the editors of the *Ignace Goldziher Memorial Volume*, Drs. J. Somogyi and S. Löwinger; to the Delegates of the Clarendon Press; to the Royal Asiatic Society; to the Governors of the Hebrew Union College, Cincinnati, and the Emeritus President, Dr. Julian Morgenstern; and to the Governors of the John Rylands Library and the Librarian, Professor Edward Robertson. To the Lutterworth Press for publishing the volume, and to its Editorial Secretary, the Rev. Gordon Hewitt, for the interest and assistance he has given

---

[1] Lindblom's book *The Servant Songs in Deutero-Isaiah*, 1951, appeared too late to be used at all.

to it, I would also express my thanks. In addition I have to thank my daughter, Margaret, for help in the preparation of my manuscript, and for preparing the Author and Scripture Indexes.

In sending the volume forth, I would express the hope that it will deepen interest in the Old Testament, which I love so well. Its problems are many and fascinating, and we do well to read it with our minds and seek to understand it. That its profoundest message is spiritual I know full well, and my published work sufficiently testifies that to this I render more than lip service. Yet the understanding of its spiritual message is not unrelated to the study of its problems. For the religious meaning of the Old Testament must be soundly based on the intelligent understanding of the literature through which it is given. Writers who find in the text what they bring to it, instead of first finding what the text was intended to mean and then perceiving what it has come to mean, are a peril to themselves and to their readers. The Bible is most honoured when it is studied for what it is, and not made the peg for the ideas we bring to it; and it is supremely worthy of the effort to read it with the understanding mind as well as with the eyes of faith.

H. H. ROWLEY

MANCHESTER UNIVERSITY
September 1950

Preface to the Second Edition

THE call for a reprint of this volume has given me the opportunity to revise these essays, and in particular to bring the bibliographical material up-to-date. The amount of further work I have been able to do on the various essays differs, and I can only hope I have missed nothing of outstanding importance. I have no doubt some of my readers will find the footnotes more than adequate, while others will complain that they are less complete than could be desired. It is hard to satisfy everyone, as I have long since discovered, and in this matter I prefer to take the middle way. I have sought only to help the reader who wishes to pursue any subject farther, and to make plain to every reader the variety of scholarly opinion on all of the questions discussed. To select only views that agree with my own, or that appear to support my thesis, could give a specious air of simplicity to all the problems, but could only tend to throw dust in the eyes of the reader. I have always preferred to let my reader see how far other scholars take different views from mine, and, while offering him all the guidance I can, to leave him to exercise his own judgement. It will be seen that in the years that have passed since this collection of essays was first issued, scholarly opinion has continued to be divided.

H. H. ROWLEY

STROUD, GLOS.
August 1964

xii

Abbreviations

A.A.S.O.R. = *Annual of the American Schools of Oriental Research*
A.f.O. = *Archiv für Orientforschung*
A.J.A. = *American Journal of Archæology*
A.J.S.L. = *American Journal of Semitic Languages and Literatures*
A.J.Th. = *American Journal of Theology*
A.N.E.T. = *Ancient Near Eastern Texts relating to the Old Testament*, ed. by
      J. B. Pritchard
A.P.A.W. = *Abhandlungen der preussischen Akademie der Wissenschaften*,
      Phil.-Hist. Klasse
A.R.W. = *Archiv für Religionswissenschaft*
A.T.D. = Das Alte Testament Deutsch
A.Th.R. = *Anglican Theological Review*
B.A. = *The Biblical Archæologist*
B.A.S.O.R. = *Bulletin of the American Schools of Oriental Research*
B.E.H.J. = *Bulletin des études historiques juives*
Bi.Or. = *Bibliotheca Orientalis*
B.J.R.L. = *Bulletin of the John Rylands Library*
B.K.A.T. = Biblischer Kommentar, Altes Testament
B.O.T. = De Boeken van het Oude Testament
B.Z.A.W. = Beihefte zur *Zeitschrift für die alttestamentliche Wissenschaft*
C.A.H. = *Cambridge Ancient History*
Camb. B. = Cambridge Bible
C.B.Q. = *Catholic Biblical Quarterly*
C.G.T. = Cambridge Greek Testament
C.I.S. = *Corpus Inscriptionum Semiticarum*
C.N.T. = Commentaire du Nouveau Testament
C.Q.R. = *Church Quarterly Review*
C.R.A.I. = *Comptes rendus de l'Académie des Inscriptions et Belles Lettres*
D.B. = *Dictionary of the Bible*, ed. by James Hastings
D.O.T. = *Documents from Old Testament Times*, ed. by D. Winton Thomas
E.B. = Études Bibliques
E.B. = *Encyclopædia Biblica*
Echt.B. = *Echter Bibel*
E.R.E. = *Encyclopædia of Religion and Ethics*, ed. by James Hastings
E.T. = *Expository Times*
E.Th.L. = *Ephemerides Theologicae Lovanienses*
E.Th.R. = *Études Théologiques et Religieuses*
E.Tr. = English translation
Exp. = *Expositor*
F.u.F. = *Forschungen und Fortschritte*
G.G.A. = *Göttingische gelehrte Anzeigen*
G.S.A.I. = *Giornale della Società Asiatica Italiana*
H.A.T. = Handbuch zum Alten Testament, ed. by O. Eissfeldt

H.S.A.T.=Kautzsch-Bertholet, *Die Heilige Schrift des Alten Testaments*
H.S.A.Tes.=Die Heilige Schrift des Alten Testamentes (Bonner Bibel)
H.T.R.=*Harvard Theological Review*
H.U.C.A.=*Hebrew Union College Annual*
I.B.=*Interpreter's Bible*
I.B.D.=*Interpreter's Bible Dictionary*
I.C.C.=The International Critical Commentary
J.A.=*Journal asiatique*
J.A.O.S.=*Journal of the American Oriental Society*
J.B.L.=*Journal of Biblical Literature*
J.B.R.=*Journal of Bible and Religion*
J.E.A.=*Journal of Egyptian Archæology*
J.E.O.L.=*Jaarbericht Ex Oriente Lux*
J.N.E.S.=*Journal of Near Eastern Studies*
J.P.O.S.=*Journal of the Palestine Oriental Society*
J.Q.R.=*Jewish Quarterly Review*
J.R.=*Journal of Religion*
J.R.A.S.=*Journal of the Royal Asiatic Society*
J.S.O.R.=*Journal of the Society for Oriental Research*
J.S.S.=*Journal of Semitic Studies*
J.T.S.=*Journal of Theological Studies*
K.A.T.=Kommentar zum Alten Testament, ed. by E. Sellin
K.A.T.=E. Schrader, *Die Keilinschriften und das Alte Testament*, 3rd ed., ed. by
    H. Zimmern and H. Winckler, 1903
K.H.A.T.=Kurzer Hand-Commentar zum Alten Testament, ed. by K. Marti
M.D.O.G.=Mitteilungen der deutschen Orient-Gesellschaft
M.J.U.P.=*Museum Journal* of the University of Pennsylvania
M.G.W.J.=*Monatsschrift für Geschichte und Wissenschaft des Judenthums*
M.V.A.G.=Mitteilungen der vorderasiatischen Gesellschaft
Ned.T.T.=*Nederlands Theologisch Tijdschrift*
N.K.Z.=*Neue kirchliche Zeitschrift*
N.T.D.=Das Neue Testament Deutsch
N.T.S.=*New Testament Studies*
N.T.T.=*Nieuw Theologisch Tijdschrift*
Nor.T.T.=*Norsk Teologisk Tidsskrift*
O.L.Z.=*Orientalistische Literaturzeitung*
O.T.M.S.=*The Old Testament and Modern Study*, ed. by H. H. Rowley
O.T.S.=*Oudtestamentische Studiën*
P.E.F.Q.S.=*Quarterly Statement of the Palestine Exploration Fund*
P.E.Q.=*Palestine Exploration Quarterly*
P.G.=*Patrologia Græca*, ed. by J. P. Migne
P.L.=*Patrologia Latina*, ed. by J. P. Migne
P.R.E.=Herzog-Hauck, *Realencyclopädie für protestantische Theologie und Kirche*,
    3rd ed.
R.Ass.=*Revue d'assyriologie et d'archéologie orientale*
R.B.=*Revue Biblique*
R.E.J.=*Revue des études juives*
R.E.S.=*Revue des études sémitiques*
R.E.S.-B.=*Revue des études sémitiques et Babyloniaca*
R.G.G.=*Die Religion in Geschichte und Gegenwart*
R.H.P.R.=*Revue d'histoire et de philosophie religieuses*
R.H.R.=*Revue de l'histoire des religions*
R.S.P.T.=*Revue des Sciences philosophiques et théologiques*

R.S.R.=*Recherches de science religieuse*
R.S.V.=Revised Standard Version
R.Th.Ph.=*Revue de théologie et de philosophie*
S.A.T.=*Die Schriften des Alten Testaments in Auswahl*
S.B.U.=*Svenskt Bibliskt Uppslagsverk*
S.D.B.=*Supplément au Dictionnaire de la Bible*, ed. by L. Pirot, A. Robert, H.
    Cazelles and A. Feuillet
S.E.Å.=*Svensk Exegetisk Årsbok*
St.*Th.*=*Studia Theologica*
S.V.T.=Supplements to *Vetus Testamentum*
TA=Tel el Amarna text
T.C.A.=*Transactions of the Connecticut Academy of Arts and Sciences*
T.G.O.S.=*Transactions of the Glasgow Oriental Society*
Th.L.Z.=*Theologische Literaturzeitung*
Th.R.=*Theologische Rundschau*
Th.Z.=*Theologische Zeitschrift*
T.S.K.=*Theologische Studien und Kritiken*
T.T.=*Theologisch Tijdschrift*
U.J.E.=*Universal Jewish Encyclopedia*
V.T.=*Vetus Testamentum*
Z.A.=*Zeitschrift für Assyriologie*
Z.A.W.=*Zeitschrift für die alttestamentliche Wissenschaft*
Z.D.M.G.=*Zeitschrift der deutschen morgenländischen Gesellschaft*
Z.D.P.V.=*Zeitschrift des deutschen Palästina Vereins*
Z.K.T.=*Zeitschrift für katholische Theologie*
Z.N.W.=*Zeitschrift für die neutestamentliche Wissenschaft*
Z.R.G.G.=*Zeitschrift für Religions- und Geistesgeschichte*
Z.S.T.=*Zeitschrift für systematische Theologie*
Z.Th.K.=*Zeitschrift für Theologie und Kirche*
Z.W.T.=*Zeitschrift für wissenschaftliche Theologie*

ABBREVIATIONS

THE SERVANT OF THE LORD
IN THE LIGHT OF
THREE DECADES OF CRITICISM

The Servant of the Lord
in the Light of Three Decades of Criticism[1]

Lecture One

INDIVIDUAL THEORIES

NO subject connected with the Old Testament has been more discussed than the question of the identity of the Suffering Servant
in Deutero-Isaiah.[2] Nor can it be said that we are any nearer to a consensus of opinion to-day than we have ever been since the era of critical
scholarship opened.[3] Professor C. R. North has published a masterly
review[4] of the history of interpretation of the Servant, together with
the statement of his own views on the question. In the present lectures
I propose to limit my survey to the work done during the last generation[5] and to offer my own modest contribution to the discussion of the
problem.[6] So far as the survey is concerned I have little to add to what
Professor North has said, and I cannot pretend to anything like the

[1] Two lectures delivered at King's College, London, in January 1950.

[2] Cf. T. H. Weir, *The Westminster Review*, clxix, 1908, p. 309: "The literature of the
subject has grown to such an extent that no one can boast of having fathomed all the
recesses of this sea."

[3] Cf. A. Causse, *Israël et la vision de l'humanité*, 1924, p. 54: "La question reste toujours
ouverte, et la variété des solutions proposées prouve l'extrême incertitude de la critique."

[4] *The Suffering Servant in Deutero-Isaiah*, 1948. Cf. also J. van der Ploeg, *Les Chants du
Serviteur de Jahvé*, 1936. North's view is further presented in *I.D.B.*, iv, 1962, pp. 292–294,
and Hastings's one-volume *D.B.*, revised ed., edited by F. C. Grant and H. H. Rowley,
1963, pp. 898 f.; van der Ploeg's is briefly presented in *Dictionnaire encyclopédique de la
Bible*, 1960, cols. 1729–1735.

[5] For an earlier survey of a generation's study of this question cf. C. Lindhagen, "De
tre sista decenniernas Ebed Jahveforskning", in *Svensk Teologisk Kvartalskrift*, viii, 1932,
pp. 350 ff. Cf. also A. Vaccari, "I carmi del 'Servo di Jahve': ultime risonanze e discus-
sioni", in *Miscellanea Biblica edita a Pontificio Instituto Biblico*, ii, 1934, pp. 216 ff., and
L. M. von Pákozdy, *Deuterojesajanische Studien*, i, 1940, where a number of Hungarian
writers, not easily accessible, are laid under contribution. Cf. also C. Kuhl, *Th.R.*, N.F. xix, 1951,
pp. 298 ff.; O. Eissfeldt, *Th.L.Z.*, lxviii, 1943, cols. 273–280 (reprinted in *Kleine Schriften*,
ii, 1963, pp. 443–452); C. Lindhagen, *E.T.*, lxvii, 1955–56, pp. 279–283, 300–302.

[6] I have briefly indicated my view in *Israel's Mission to the World*, 1939, pp. 10 ff.; *The
Missionary Message of the Old Testament*, 1945, pp. 51 ff.; *The Biblical Doctrine of Election*,
1950, pp. 111 ff. Cf. also *Interpretation*, viii, 1954, pp. 259–272, *The Faith of Israel*, 1956,
pp. 118 ff., and *R.G.G.*, 3rd ed., iii, 1959, cols. 1680–1683.

completeness of detail of his review. My purpose is but to emphasize how great is the variety of contemporary view, and to warn against the acceptance of mine or anyone else's view with an easy satisfaction. I should add that I can select only a few examples of the various theories that have been advanced or defended during the last generation, since a complete survey would require far more time than is at my disposal. So far as my own contribution to the discussion of the problem is concerned, let me say at the outset that I have much in common with the view of Professor North, though in certain respects I want to carry his view a little farther. For many years he and I have discussed aspects of this problem together, and my debt to him, and not merely to his book, must be acknowledged at the outset.

So far as Is. 53 is concerned, the traditional Christian view down to the end of the eighteenth century was that it was a messianic prophecy, and there were few who questioned it. With the advent of the critical era in Old Testament studies, and the recognition that from chapter 40 the book of Isaiah could not be regarded as the work of Isaiah of Jerusalem, but as the work of an exilic prophet in Babylonia, there came a growing tendency on the part of Christian scholars to accept the common Jewish view that the Suffering Servant was none other than the Israelite nation.[1] But this did not solve all the difficulties, and there soon developed several varieties of this view.[2] Then, towards the end of last century, came Duhm's commentary on the book of Isaiah,[3] which in two respects has profoundly influenced all succeeding work. Duhm first recognized not two, but three, main divisions of the book, and brought Trito-Isaiah into the field;[4] he also isolated the Servant Songs

[1] This view was still presented by K. Budde, "The so-called 'Ebed-Yahweh Songs' . . . in Isaiah", in *A.J.Th.*, iii, 1899, pp. 499 ff., or *Die sogenannten Ebed-Jahwe-Lieder*, 1900; K. Marti, *Das Buch Jesaja*, 1900, pp. 344 f., 360 f.; F. Giesebrecht, *Der Knecht Jahwes des Deuterojesaia*, 1902; and A. S. Peake, *The Problem of Suffering in the Old Testament*, 1904, pp. 34–72. A. Lods (*Annales de bibliographie théologique*, viii, 1900, p. 38) says: "Nous croyons que M. Budde a rendu un service signalé à la théologie en s'élevant contre une hypothèse qui mutile l'une des œuvres les plus puissantes de l'Ancien Testament, et réduit à n'être plus que l'ombre d'elle-même 'la création première, éblouissante, débordante de vie' du Deutéro-Esaïe". The theory against which Budde had erected this defence was that of Duhm (see below). C. F. Burney similarly praised Budde's work, and held it to amount to a thorough-going refutation of Duhm's theory (*C.Q.R.*, lxxv, 1912–13, p. 119).
[2] See North, *op. cit.*, pp. 28 ff.   [3] *Das Buch Jesaia*, 1892.
[4] Some earlier writers had found elements in Is. 56–66 later than Deutero-Isaiah. Cf. C. H. Cornill, *Th.R.*, iii, 1900, p. 416; R. H. Pfeiffer, *Introduction to the Old Testament*, 1941, p. 453. W. S. McCullough (*J.B.L.*, lxvii, 1948, pp. 27–36) holds that Trito-Isaiah is earlier than Deutero-Isaiah. Unlike most modern writers he finds a single hand in these chapters, and in this respect his view is shared by H. Odeberg (*Trito-Isaiah: a Literary and Linguistic Analysis*, 1931), and by K. Elliger (*Die Einheit der Tritojesaia*, 1928). L.

from their context and brought them together as a series of connected poems.[1]

In Duhm's view these four songs were not by the author of the rest of Deutero-Isaiah, and they portrayed the career of a historical individual earlier than the prophet or contemporary with him.[2] Many scholars, especially on the Continent, have followed him in general, save that some have thought of other historical individuals; and a long list of candidates for the honour of being the original of the portrait has been compiled by the efforts of succeeding scholars.[3] Moreover, there has been little agreement as to whether the songs were earlier than Deutero-Isaiah and incorporated by him in his work, or later than Deutero-Isaiah and inserted subsequently into his work, or whether they were actually by the same hand as the surrounding passages.[4] There has also been disagreement as to the precise delimitation of the

Glahn (in Glahn and Köhler, Der Prophet der Heimkehr, 1934) argues for the unity of Is. 40–66, while C. C. Torrey (The Second Isaiah, 1928) ascribed Is. 34 f., 40–66 to a single author who wrote circa 400 B.C.

[1] Already in Die Theologie der Propheten, 1875, p. 289, Duhm had brought together Is. 42: 1–7; 49: 1–6; 50: 4–9; and 52: 13–53: 12 as a connected series of songs, which perhaps came from a separate work; but in 1892 he limited the first song to 42: 1–4, and put forward his theory of the identity of the Servant. In the earlier work he had suggested that the career of Jeremiah formed the basis of the portrayal of the Servant, though he thought the Servant was intended to represent Israel.

[2] See Das Buch Jesaia, 1892, pp. xviii, 284 ff., 365 ff. In the first monograph on the Servant Songs, M. Schian (Die Ebed-Jahwe-Lieder in Jesaias 40–66, 1895) followed Duhm in identifying the Servant with an unknown martyr, but limited the fourth song to 53: 2–12 (pp. 34 f., 47), and assigned it to a different, and perhaps earlier, author (p. 59). while 42: 5–7; 50: 10 f.; 52: 13–15, and 53: 1 he held to be later additions (p. 60).

[3] Apart from some older interpretations of this kind (cf. North, op. cit., pp. 20 ff., 39 ff.), we may note the following: Jehoiachin [A. van Hoonacker, Exp., 8th series, xi, 1906, p. 210—where Jehoiachin is thought of as the model for the description of the future Messiah; cf. Sellin, Das Rätsel des deuterojesajanischen Buches, 1908, pp. 131 ff.; W. Staerk, Die Ebed Jahwe-Lieder in Jesaja 40 ff., 1913, pp. 137 f.—in the fourth song only, Jeremiah being suggested for the first three songs (p. 129)]; Ezekiel (R. Kraetzschmar, Das Buch Ezechiel, 1900, p. 46); Zerubbabel (E. Sellin, Serubbabel, 1898, pp. 148 ff.); Jehoiakim, the priest who figures in the book of Judith (W. Erbt, O.L.Z., xxi, 1918, col. 35); the Maccabaean hero Eleazar (A. Bertholet, Zu Jesaja 53, 1899, pp. 23 ff.).

[4] Into these questions there is no space to enter here, and for their discussion the reader is referred to J. van der Ploeg, Les Chants du Serviteur de Jahvé, 1936, pp. 16–26; C. R. North, op. cit., pp. 156–188. Professor North concludes (p. 188): "Songs and prophecy are nearly contemporary, the songs being rather later than the prophecy, and almost certainly by the same author. It is probable that they were not all composed at the same time." It will be noted below, p. 37, n. 2, that there is reason to think that the verses immediately following the first three songs were written with the songs in mind, and therefore after the songs. S. Mowinckel (He that Cometh), E.Tr. by G. W. Anderson, 1956, p. 253) rejects the idea that the Songs can be by Deutero-Isaiah, and so R. Press (Z.A.W., N.F. xxvi, 1955, p. 70). As those who have most carefully examined this question maintain unity of authorship, it would seem to be more reasonable to accept

four songs, and even as to their number. Most writers have found four songs, and have found them to consist of Is. 42 : 1–4; 49 : 1–6; 50 : 4–9; and 52 : 13–53 : 12. Others have attached some of the immediately following verses to some of these, while yet others have found additional songs in Deutero-Isaiah, or even in Trito-Isaiah, belonging to this cycle.[1]

the Songs as by Deutero-Isaiah until reasons which are generally accepted as convincing are advanced for the opposite view. The onus of proof is on those who would reject passages. Cf. O. Kaiser, *Der königliche Knecht*, 1959, p. 10: "Eine literarkritische Ausscheidung der Lieder aus dem eigentlichen Bestande dieses Buches erscheint uns daher ungerechtfertigt solange sich exegetisch noch eine Möglichkeit findet, sie im Zusammenhang mit ihrem Kontext zu interpretieren"; V. de Leeuw, *De Ebed Jahweh–Profetieën* 1956, p. 350: "Rien ne nous invite à les arracher à leur cadre littéraire pour composer en quelque sorte une œuvre unique qu'un rédacteur anonyme postérieur aurait démembrée." J. Muilenburg (*I.B.*, v, 1946, p. 406b) says: "The excision of the four servant poems, far from resolving difficulties, has only added to them" (cf. also pp. 407 f.).

[1] Many scholars have held the first songs to consist of 42: 1–7, as Duhm at first did, the second to extend to 49: 9, and the third to 50: 11. To the four songs as commonly delimited W. W. Cannon (*Z.A.W.*, N.F. vi, 1929, pp. 284 ff.), O. Procksch (*In piam memoriam A. von Bulmerincq*, 1938, p. 152), and W. A. L. Elmslie (*How Came our Faith*, 1948, p. 354 n.) would add 61: 1–3 (against this, however, cf. L. Glahn, *Der Prophet der Heimkehr*, 1934, pp. 78 f.; A. Vaccari, in *Miscellanea Biblica edita a Pontificio Instituto Biblico*, ii, 1934, p. 218; J. van der Ploeg, *Les chants du Serviteur de Jahvé*, 1936, p. 204; and C. R. North, *The Suffering Servant in Deutero-Isaiah*, 1948, pp. 137 f.); G. H. Box (*The Book of Isaiah*, 1916, pp. 317 f.) 61: 1–4; C. C. Torrey (*The Second Isaiah*, 1928, pp. 452 ff.) 61: 1–11, 62: 1–12 and 63: 7–14; P. Volz (*Jesaja II*, 1932, pp. 149 f.), J. Lindblom, (*Profetismen i Israel*, 1934, pp. 205 f.; but see below, pp. 37 f., for a modification of this), A. Weiser (*Einleitung in das Alte Testament*, 1939, p. 162, 2nd ed., 1949, p. 153), and J. Coppens [in *Pro regno pro sanctuario* (Festschrift for G. van der Leeuw), 1950, p. 117= *Nieuw Licht over de Ebed-Jahweh-Liederen* (Analecta Lovaniensia Biblica et Orientalia, II, 15), pp. 5, 12] 42: 5–9 (cf. however, *Sacra Pagina*, i, 1959, pp. 434 f.); A. van Hoonacker (*loc. cit.*, pp. 192, 197 f.; cf. *Het Boek Isaias*, 1932, pp. 245 f., 266 ff.) 51: 4 ff. and 61: 1–3; J. Begrich (*Studien zu Deuterojesaja*, 1938, pp. 73, 114, 141) and A. Bentzen (*Indledning til det Gamle Testamente*, I, i, 1941, p. 100; E. Tr. ii, 1949, p. 110) 51: 9–16; R. B. Y. Scott (*The Relevance of the Prophets*, 1944, p. 83 n.) 51: 4 f. and 48: 16 c.; W. H. Brownlee (*The Meaning of the Qumran Scrolls for the Bible*, 1964, p. 193 ff.) 51: 4 ff. and 62: 10 ff.; H. Gressmann (*Der Messias*, 1929, pp. 287 ff.) finds the following seven Servant Songs: 42: 1–4; 42: 5–9; 49: 1–6; 49: 7; 49: 8–13; 50: 4–10; 52: 13–53: 12; while J. Morgenstern (*U.J.E.*, x, 1943, p. 356b) delimits the four Servant Songs as follows: 42: 1–4; 49: 5–7; 50: 4–10; 53: 1–12. More recently Morgenstern has advanced the view that the Servant passages formed a drama (see below, pp. 19 f.) and arranged them in the following order: 42: 1–7; 61: 1; 49: 9a; 61: 1–4, 5c, 5ab, 6; 51: 10; 50: 4–8; 9aβ; 52: 13–53: 12 (*V.T.*, xi, 1961, pp. 293 ff.). It may be noted that long before it became customary to speak of the Servant Songs, Rosenmüller had brought the four passages together, though slightly differently delimited and associated with a few other isolated verses. Cf. *Scholia in Vetus Testamentum*, iii, *Iesaiæ vaticinia*, Part 3, 1793, p. v: "Non imprudenter quoque is, qui hunc librum sub Iesaiæ nomine composuit, quædam inseruit, quæ id agunt, ut vati auctoritatem concilient, eumque ut hominem a numine afflatum sistant; veluti XL, 6. XLII, 1–7. XLIV, 26. XLVIII, 16. XLIX, 1–9. L, 4–7. LII, 13–LIII, 12. LIX, 21. LXI, 1. cum quibus conferri possunt ex priori libri parte hæc loca: VI. VIII, 16.17.19." (This passage does not stand in the 3rd ed., 1834.)

Meanwhile, British scholars, speaking generally, were not much drawn to the individual theories, and continued to advocate the collective theory in some form or other. Instead of finding the Servant to be the whole nation Israel,[1] some thought rather of the spiritual core of the nation, the Israel within Israel,[2] and some of the ideal Israel as opposed to the actual Israel of experience.[3]

(1)

Such, in brief, was the position at the beginning of the period I wish to review. That period may begin with the work of Mowinckel, who in 1921 published his brief monograph of seventy pages,[4] of which Eissfeldt observes[5] that it has exercised an influence comparable with that of Duhm's commentary. Mowinckel held the first three songs to consist of Is. 42 : 1–7; 49 : 1–6; 50 : 4–11 (or possibly to verse 9 only), and drew a sharp contrast between the Servant in the four songs and in the surrounding passages. He maintained that while in the rest of Deutero-Isaiah the Servant is always passive, here the Servant is depicted as active,[6] and that while in the context the Servant is clearly Israel, in these songs the Servant is just as clearly an individual. As to the identification of that individual, he propounded the view that it was none other than the prophet himself.

For this, as for all the main types of view on the Servant, there is some *prima facie* justification. For the second and the third of these songs are written in the first person singular. The prophets naturally used the first person singular of themselves, and they also spoke in the first person in the name of God. For the prophet, as the mouthpiece of God, was an extension of the personality of God.[7] But the prophets do not commonly use the first person, in the manner of these songs, in the

[1] So G. W. Wade, *The Book of the Prophet Isaiah*, 1911, pp. 345 ff.

[2] So O. C. Whitehouse, *Isaiah xl–lxvi*, pp. 18 ff.; C. F. Burney, *C.Q.R.*, lxxv, 1912–13, p. 121.

[3] So J. Skinner, *Isaiah, Chapters 40–66*, rev. ed., 1917, pp. lvii ff., 263 ff. Similarly G. H. Box, *The Book of Isaiah*, 1916, pp. 194 ff., 265 ff., where, however, it is argued that in the fourth song there are conscious reminiscences of Jeremiah.

[4] *Der Knecht Jahwäs.* Cf. E. Balla, in *Eucharistērion* (Gunkel Festschrift), i, 1923, pp. 245 ff. S. A. Cook, "The Servant of the Lord", in *E.T.*, xxxiv, 1922–23, pp. 440 ff., says he had independently reached a view closely similar to Mowinckel's.

[5] See *Der Gottesknecht bei Deuterojesaja im Lichte der israelitischen Anschauung von Gemeinschaft und Individuum*, 1933, p. 7 (=*E.T.*, xliv, 1932–33, p. 262 b).

[6] Cf. Schian, *op. cit.*, pp. 13 f.

[7] Cf. A. R. Johnson, *The One and the Many in the Israelite Conception of God*, 1942, pp. 36 ff. (2nd ed., 1961, pp. 32 ff.).

name of any other. They did not regard themselves as the extension of the personality of any other in a comparable way. Hence, Mowinckel argued, since it is out of the question that the first person of these songs has reference to God, it must have reference to the prophet himself.[1]

Yet this by no means disposes of all the difficulties. For it is strange that the prophet should use so many expressions here of himself which he elsewhere uses of Israel. For there are many similarities of phraseology outside these four songs, where the reference is clearly and undeniably to Israel, closely parallel to phrases used of the Servant inside the songs.[2] Again, in Is. 49 : 3—i.e. in the second song, where the first person is held to mean the prophet—we read: "And he said unto me: Thou art my Servant, Israel, in whom I will be glorified." Here Mowinckel follows the simple device of all to whom the word *Israel* is inconvenient, and cuts it out of the text.[3] One Hebrew MS., and that not one of any special importance,[4] omits the word.[5] This is not very impressive evidence, and no one would take the slightest notice of it, unless on other grounds he thought there was reason to doubt the

---

[1] *Op. cit.*, p. 9.

[2] Cf. my *Israel's Mission to the World*, pp. 14, 16 f., 19 f. Also below, pp. 51 f.

[3] *Op cit.*, pp. 4 f. note. J. B. Koppe preferred to transfer the second part of this verse to the following verse. He says: "Ich trenne den ganzen Satz *Yiśrā'ēl* '*ašher b^ekhā 'ethpā'ēr* vom 3ten V. und verbinde ihn mit dem folgenden als Anrede des Propheten, des '*ebhedh YHWH*, an sein Volk. 'Israel! wie könnt' ich verherrlicht werden durch dich! Aber klagen muss ich: Umsonst bemüh' ich mich; um nichts, um eitel nichts verzehr' ich mein Kraft u.s.w.' " (*Robert Lowth's Jesaias neu übersetzt*, iv, 1781, p. 34).

[4] Kennicott (*Vetus Testamentum Hebraicum cum variis lectionibus*, ii, 1780, p. 79) observes that this MS. shows many variants. No special weight is given to its readings elsewhere. J. A. Bewer (*Jewish Studies in Memory of George A. Kohut*, 1935, pp. 86 ff.) studies this MS. and shows that most of its variations are clerical errors due to the inattention of the scribe. In Is. 42: 3 it omits the word *mishpāṭ*, but no one has claimed any authority for this. It is to be noted that the word *Yiśrā'ēl* is included in the text of Isaiah recovered amongst the Dead Sea Scrolls (cf. M. Burrows, *The Dead Sea Scrolls of St. Mark's Monastery*, i, 1950, plate xl). While the date of this MS. is disputed, it is probable that it is by far the oldest extant MS. of the Hebrew text.

[5] Mowinckel says the word is omitted from several LXX MSS., and this statement is repeated in *De senere profeter*, 1944, p. 233 n., and with emphasis in *Han som kommer*, 1951, p. 334 (cf. *He that Cometh*, E.Tr. by G. W. Anderson, 1956, pp. 462 ff., where Mowinckel repeatedly says several LXX MSS. omit the word, but prudently refrains from specifying them). Similarly L. Köhler, *Deuterojesaja (Jesaja 40–55) stilkritisch untersucht*, 1923, p. 37. J. Ziegler (*Isaias*, 1939, p. 305) merely records that two MSS. have *Iakōb* for *Israël*, but one of these corrects this in the margin (cf. Swete, *The Old Testament in Greek*, iii, 3rd ed., 1905, p. 192). Neither of these can be cited as authority for simple omission. Nor do Holmes and Parsons (*Vetus Testamentum græcum cum variis lectionibus*, iv, 1827, *ad loc.*) note any MS. which omits. Where so much weight is given to the alleged MSS. which omit the word, it is important that they should be specified. J. Morgenstern (*V.T.*, xi, 1961, pp. 306 ff.) claims that the word "Israel" is not only original here, but that it shows that the servant was a royal figure and that "Israel" means "King of Israel".

text. A second reason has therefore to be found to fortify this, and it is alleged that the word is metrically superfluous. Though this statement may be found in many authors, it is without the slightest foundation.[1] The poem is in 3 : 3 rhythm, and if Israel is omitted from the verse, it can only be read as 3 : 3 if *'asher b'khā* be given two accents. It is unusual for *'asher* to carry a separate accent, and wherever it does it incurs a certain amount of suspicion, unless the following word is sufficiently long to justify two accents for the whole group. But here the following word is itself very short, and it has no rhythmical weight to spare.[2] Once more, no one would dream of questioning the rhythm, unless he found something awkward in the text.[3] On the other hand, if Israel is omitted, there is much more ground for rhythmical dissatisfaction and it would then be more natural to read the line as 3 : 2, with catalexis.[4] There are no adequate reasons, on grounds of purely textual criticism, for the omission of the word.[5]

A yet greater difficulty for Mowinckel's view is provided by the fourth song. For here there is described the death and exaltation of the Servant. Mowinckel claimed, however, that it is difficult to distinguish

[1] Cf. F. Prätorius, in Z.A.W., xxxvi, 1916, pp. 9 f. Cf., too, P. Humbert, in La Bible du Centenaire, ii, 1947, p. 407: 'Le rhythme en demande le maintien"; R. Tournay, R.B., lix, 1952, pp. 374 f.: "Il n'y a aucune raison d'omettre ce mot, pas plus du point de vue de la critique textuelle que du point de vue rhythmique".

[2] It may be added that even if *'asher b'khā* be given two accents, it would not necessarily follow that the line was overweighted. For "and he said unto me" could be taken extra metrum, as Kennicott (op. cit., p. 63) takes this, as well as "and I said" in the following verse, with the transference of the verse division.

[3] Cf. A. S. Peake, The Problem of Suffering in the Old Testament, 1904, p. 46 n.: "There is no solid reason whatever for assuming it to be a gloss, unless we adopt the view that the Servant is an individual. The balance of clauses is disturbed by its removal." Cf. N. H. Snaith, Studies in Old Testament Prophecy (T. H. Robinson Festschrift), 1950, p. 198. Sellin (Mose und seine Bedeutung, 1922, p. 89) recognizes that some word is wanted here, and therefore arbitrarily substitutes "my chosen" for it.

[4] As it would most naturally be read on Kennicott's arrangement.

[5] Cf. C. C. Torrey, The Second Isaiah, 1928, p. 381: "The attempt to remove the word Yiśrā'ēl from this verse by some commentators . . . is inexcusable. Its presence in the original text is attested (1) by all the versions; (2) by numerous parallel passages (e.g., 41: 8; 43: 10; 44: 1, 2, 21); (3) by the rhythm of the verse, which is sadly impaired by its omission"; H. Birkeland, Zum hebräischen Traditionswesen, 1938, p. 36: "Dieses Wort steht textlich fest . . . Nach Lage der Sache muss eine solche textkritische Method gänzlich abgelehnt werden"; M. Buber, The Prophetic Faith, E.Tr. by C. Witton-Davies, 1949, p. 223: "These words are not to be regarded as proof of the truth of the corporate interpretation, nor is the word 'Israel' to be omitted as a late insertion." R. Press (Z.A.W., N.F. xxvi, 1955, p. 74 n.) retains the word "Israel", but thinks the parallelism of the verse is not synonymous, but that here the Servant and Israel are addressed. C. H. Giblin (C.B.Q., xxi, 1959, pp. 207–212) thinks that two originally separate poems have been combined in this Servant Song, giving rise to the divergence between v. 3 and v. 5.

with any certainty what is the precise significance of the tenses in this song. The perfects may be prophetic perfects, and the death as well as the exaltation of the Servant be in the future.[1] Here, it may be agreed, there is some substance in the claim.[2] It has failed to satisfy some of the followers of Mowinckel,[3] however; nor did it long satisfy Mowinckel himself. Some of those who adopted his autobiographical view of the Servant preferred to suppose that the fourth song was written by a disciple of the prophet after his death, or by a later writer. This was the view of Sellin[4] and of Volz.[5] The former had earlier proposed, in a succession of studies of the Servant problem, to identify the Servant with Zerubbabel,[6] Jehoiachin,[7] and Moses,[8] but in 1930 he returned to the subject and followed Mowinckel, save that he ascribed the fourth song to the author of Trito-Isaiah.[9] Volz, on the other hand, separated the fourth song entirely from the first three,[10] and held that while Deutero-Isaiah was the Servant of the first three,[11] the fourth was to be eschatologically interpreted and came from a much later age.[12]

---

[1] Op. cit., pp. 37 f. note.

[2] I cannot share the dogmatism of R. H. Kennett (The Composition of the Book of Isaiah, 1910, p. 72): "A careful study of the tenses of the verbs here used shows with absolute certainty that the suffering of the Lord's servant is an accomplished fact, and that this suffering has already issued in the deliverance of the nation."

[3] J. Begrich (Studien zu Deuterojesaja, 1938, pp. 131 ff.) still maintains Mowinckel's view that the songs are autobiographical and that in the fourth song the prophet anticipated his own death. So also A. Weiser (Einleitung in das Alte Testament, 1939, pp. 162 ff., 5th ed., 1963, pp. 178 ff.; E.Tr. by D. M. Barton, 1961, pp. 200 ff.).

[4] "Tritojesaja, Deuterojesaja und das Gottesknechts-problem", in N.K.Z., xli, 1930, pp. 73 ff., 145 ff. Cf. Einleitung in das Alte Testament, 6th ed., 1933, pp. 92 f.; 7th ed., 1935, pp. 90 f. Also "Die Lösung des deuterojesajanischen Gottesknechtsrätsels", in Z.A.W., N.F. xiv, 1937, pp. 177 ff. Cf. K. Elliger, Deuterojesaja in seinem Verhältnis zu Tritojesaja, 1933, pp. 75 ff., 267 ff.

[5] Jesaia II, 1932, pp. 149 ff.; Prophetengestalten des Alten Testaments, 1938, pp. 316 ff. Cf. C. Kuhl, The Old Testament: its Origin and Composition, E.Tr. by C. T. M. Herriot, 1961, pp. 181 f.

[6] Serubbabel, 1898, pp. 148 ff.

[7] Das Rätsel des deuterojesajanischen Buches, 1908, pp. 131 ff. Cf. L. H. K. Bleeker, in Z.A.W., xl, 1922, p. 156.

[8] Mose und seine Bedeutung für die israelitisch-jüdische Religionsgeschichte, 1922, pp. 81 ff.

[9] Cf. Z.A.W., N.F. xiv, 1937, p. 185.

[10] W. F. Lofthouse, who does not belong to the autobiographical school of interpretation, also finds a contrast between the fourth song and the first three, as well as a marked contrast between the first three and the rest of Deutero-Isaiah. Cf. J.T.S., xlviii, 1947, pp. 171 ff.

[11] So already in Beiträge zur alttestamentlichen Wissenschaft (Budde Festschrift), 1920, pp. 184 ff.

[12] J. Lindblom (Israels Religion i gammaltestamentlig tid, 1936, p. 196) agrees with Volz, holding the Servant of the fourth song to be a parallel figure to the Messiah. Cf. also his Profetismen i Israel, 1934, pp. 205 ff. N. Johansson (Parakletoi, 1940, p. 58) objects to Lind-

More recently, however, Mowinckel has himself changed his ground. In 1931[1] he propounded the view that the oracles of Deutero-Isaiah were collected by his disciples, who together make up Trito-Isaiah, and that the Servant songs were neither written by Deutero-Isaiah[2] nor included in the first edition of his oracles. They were all written by one of the Trito-Isaiah circle and inserted in Deutero-Isaiah.[3] Mowinckel no longer asserts that it is more than a possibility that Deutero-Isaiah is the Servant. Nevertheless it is, he holds, a possibility. The Servant was already dead, he maintains, before the songs were written, and here he is described in terms that were tinged with mythology.[4]

This, of course, is to abandon the first foundation on which his theory was built. For whereas he had said that the prophet could not use the first person singular, save of himself or of God, he now holds that the author of the second and third songs both could and did do so.[5]

blom's view, saying: "Eine solche Aufteilung ist indessen unrichtig. Kap. 42, 49 und 50 setzen 53 voraus und umgekehrt. Das Ebed-JHWH-Gedicht ohne Kap 53 wäre etwa dasselbe wie das Buch Hiob ohne die Gottesreden." M. Schmidt (*Prophet und Tempel*, 1948, p. 221) also rejects the separation of this song from the others.

[1] "Die Komposition des deuterojesajanischen Buches", in *Z.A.W.*, N.F. viii, 1931, pp. 87 ff., 242 ff., esp. pp. 245 ff. Cf. also "Neuere Forschungen zu Deuterojesaja, Tritojesaja und dem 'Äbäd-Jahwä-Problem", in *Acta Orientalia*, xvi, 1938, pp. 1 ff.

[2] Cf. *Acta Orientalia*, xvi, 1938, p. 40: "Denkt man sich aber genau in die geschichtliche, die literargeschichtliche und religionsgeschichtliche Seite der Sache hinein, so möchte ich behaupten, dass man es doch wohl bald als den zweiten festen Punkt betrachten könne, dass der Verfasser der vier Lieder nicht mit Dtjes identisch gewesen ist."

[3] *Ibid.*, p. 248. H. Odeberg, *Trito-Isaiah*, 1931, p. 27, dissents from this view, and declares that the author of Trito-Isaiah, which he holds to be a unity, cannot be identified with the writer of any of the Servant songs.

[4] In his more recent treatment of the subject (*De senere profeter*, 1944, pp. 192 ff.; cf. A. Bentzen, *Th.R.*, N.F. xvii, 1948–49, p. 302, and C. R. North, *Scottish Journal of Theology*, iii, 1950, pp. 363 ff.) Mowinckel adheres substantially to these positions. He holds that the Servant was a historical individual, prophet or missionary, who had lived among the Jews shortly before the author's time, and who was expected to rise again shortly. Since two of the songs are in the first person, the question arises whether the Servant is to be identified with Deutero-Isaiah. This view is rejected, however, on the ground that the Servant was already dead. As against the theory that the fourth song was by a different hand, he notes the similarity of style, and concludes that the Servant was an unknown historical person, who lived some time after Deutero-Isaiah (*ibid.*, p. 196), who is distinguished from the author of the songs (*ibid.*, pp. 198 f.). Into the conception of the Servant he maintains that many Israelite elements went, together with ancient Canaanite and oriental ideas associated with the dying and rising god (*ibid.*, p. 197). Yet more recently (*Han som kommer*, 1951, pp. 166 ff.; *He that Cometh*, 1956, pp. 246 ff.) Mowinckel recognizes the possibility that the Servant is a purely future figure, though not to be directly equated with Jesus. On this see below.

[5] Cf. *Z.A.W.*, N.F. viii, 1941, p. 256. Here Mowinckel explains the use of the pronoun as due to cultic influence.

In either of its forms, I find this theory unconvincing.[1] If the prophet really believed that he was destined to set judgement in the earth, and to see the isles wait for his law,[2] and that men would acknowledge that he was wounded for their transgressions and bruised for their iniquities,[3] and that his death was a sin-offering for their sins, whereby they should find justification,[4] he was only a misguided, self-opinionated dreamer,[5] and not in any sense the mouthpiece of God.[6] Happily the objective grounds for this view are so weak that Mowinckel himself abandoned it. It is even more incredible to me, however, that after the Servant's death one of his disciples should declare that he would not fail or be broken until he had achieved his world-wide mission, when his words were already known to be false before they were even written.

More recently again, Mowinckel has once more shifted his ground. He now says that the identification of the Servant with the prophet himself, while a natural one, is refuted by the fact that in ch. 53 the death of the Servant is described as having already taken place.[7] He now advances the view that the Servant was a prophet from the same circle as the author of the Songs—probably the Isaianic and Deutero-Isaianic circle—who lived some time after Deutero-Isaiah, and who held it to be his mission to win his countrymen to true conversion to Yahweh, which would lead to the spread of this religion to other nations.[8] He thinks the two Songs which are in the first person were written by the Servant himself,[9] and that after his death his disciples or perhaps one of them, idealized the portrait of him and gave expression to the faith that God would raise him from the dead.[10] So far from his being conceived of as the Messiah, his work was thought

---

[1] G. von Rad (*Theologie des Alten Testaments*, ii, 1960, pp. 272 f.) rejects the identification of the Servant with Deutero-Isaiah.

[2] Is. 42: 4. [3] Is. 53: 5. [4] Is. 53: 10.

[5] A. Bentzen (*Introduction to the Old Testament*, 2nd ed., 1952, Appendix, pp. 25 f.) replies to this by saying: "He who according to Church Theology fulfilled the prophecy . . . had the same ideas of himself. . . . Was he, then, 'a misguided, self-opinionated dreamer, and not in any sense the mouthpiece of God'?" But the two cases are not in any sense parallel. No one ever supposed that Deutero-Isaiah was bruised for their iniquities, whereas many through the centuries and still today acknowledge the claim of Christ to be justified, and humbly declare that the words of Isaiah 53: 5 express their faith and their experience. Cf. H. H. Rowley, *From Moses to Qumran*, 1963, p. 24: "Whatever explanation of the fact be offered, fact it is that the effect of His Cross on men has corresponded precisely with the anticipated effect of the sufferings of the Servant." There is a vital difference between an unjustified claim and a justified claim.

[6] Cf. Peake, *The Servant of Yahweh*, p. 44: "The language in which the Servant speaks would imply far too extravagant an egotism for us lightly to charge the prophet with it."

[7] Cf. *He that Cometh*, 1956, p. 248. [8] *Ibid.*, pp. 250, 254. [9] *Ibid.*, pp. 251 f.

[10] *Ibid.*, p. 250.

of as something surpassing that of the Messiah.[1] Yet both prophet and poet were mistaken, and the concept of the Servant was only fulfilled in Christ.[2] It will be seen that Mowinckel has tried to meet some of the objections that have been raised against his earlier formulations of his view. But the Servant, though no longer Deutero-Isaiah, is still presented as one who was woefully mistaken about his mission, and the poet is still presented as one who dreamed of a mission for the Servant after it had been demonstrated that his dreams were vain. It is surely a remarkable assumption that dreams which were so misguided in relation to the poet's contemporary, the Servant, should be so remarkably fulfilled centuries later in the person of another.

(2)

Passing over other varieties of the theory that Deutero-Isaiah is himself the Servant,[3] we may note some other theories which identify the Servant with a historical individual either contemporary with Deutero-Isaiah or of an earlier age. Amongst the candidates for the portrait, I have already mentioned that Sellin once put forward Jehoiachin.[4] Within the period under survey this was proposed, but in a different form, by Eric Burrows.[5] His view had elements in common also with the view of Rothstein,[6] published in 1902, though he had no

---

[1] Ibid., pp. 256 f. [2] Ibid., p. 257.

[3] H. W. Wolff, Jesaja 53 im Urchristentum, 1942, pp. 32 ff. (2nd ed., 1950, pp. 35 ff.), while holding that the Servant was in the first instance the prophet, finds that he was a Vorbild of Jesus, and so combines a messianic element in his interpretation. A similar view was taken by H. Gunkel, Ein Vorläufer Jesu, 1921, where Mowinckel's monograph was enthusiastically hailed.

[4] For our latest extra-Biblical knowledge of Jehoiachin, cf. E. F. Weidner, "Jojachin, König von Juda, in babylonischen Keilschrifttexten", in Mélanges Syriens (Dussaud Festschrift), ii, 1939, pp. 923 ff., W. F. Albright, "King Joiachin in Exile", in B.A., v, 1942, pp. 49–55, and A. Bea, 'König Jojachin in Keilschrifttexten', in Biblica, xxiii, 1942, pp. 78–82.

[5] The Gospel of the Infancy, 1940, pp. 59 ff. The paper here printed was read by Father Burrows to the Society for Old Testament Study in 1937, and printed posthumously.

[6] Review of Sellin's Studien zur Entstehungsgeschichte der jüdischen Gemeinde, in T.S.K., lxxv, 1902, pp. 282 ff., esp. pp. 292 f., 319 ff. Rothstein says (p. 321): "Dagegen halte ich so, um das nochmals zu betonen, nicht für unwahrscheinlich, dass das Geschick dieses Königs"—i.e. Jehoiachin—"den geschichtlichen Stoff für den Inhalt des letzten Stücks (52, 13–53, 12) gegeben hat, muss aber auch bis auf weiteres bezweifeln, ob, als das Stück schriftstellerisch in seinen gegenwärtigen Zusammenhang eingefügt wurde, der Verfasser dabei wirklich noch an Jojachin dachte oder auch nur noch denken konnte"; also "Nur muss ich es wenigstens vorläufig noch für sehr fraglich halten, ob der Verfasser wirklich nur an die Persönlichkeit dieses Königs gedacht hat, ob er nicht vielmehr in ihm zugleich an den königlichen Stamm, deren Repräsentant er war, gedacht wissen wollte."

knowledge of Rothstein's work when he advanced it.[1] Rothstein had suggested that the Servant was the Davidic dynasty, personified for the writer in its contemporary representative, Jehoiachin. This is substantially the view of Burrows, who summarizes his view by saying that the Servant is "the house of David, the messianic house in the past, or future as the case may be; his title of Servant of Yahweh being suggested by that of David himself; his vocation to give law to the nations being indicated by messianic prophecy; his history during the exile being that of Jehoiachin, the representative of the house of David at that time; his future being the messianic King."[2]

This view, again, seems to me to be quite improbable. Elsewhere the Davidic king is represented as ruling in the Golden Age. His kingdom is thought of as universal and as resting on foundations of righteousness and peace, and bringing blessings to the whole creation, animal as well as human. But the Servant is not thought of as a ruler, but as a sufferer, the organ of whose service is to be his suffering.[3] This is a fundamentally different conception,[4] and it is not surprising that there is no evidence that the concept of the Suffering Servant and that of the coming Davidic king were ever brought together until the time of our Lord, or that their confluence is not the result of His ministry.[5]

[1] In the discussion that followed the reading of Father Burrows' paper, Professor North drew attention to the points of similarity with the view of Rothstein.

[2] Op. cit., p. 60. Cf. the view of N. H. Snaith, who thinks the Servant is primarily Jehoiachin and the exiles of 597 B.C., but then extended to include the exiles of 586 B.C. See Studies in Old Testament Prophecy (T. H. Robinson Festschrift), 1950, p. 191.

[3] Cf. S. Mowinckel, De senere profeter, 1944, p. 195: "Tjeneren er derimot tenkt som profet, ikke som konge; som lidende og foraktet og utstøtt, ikke som hersker."

[4] This is not to deny that both had common roots, as will be said below.

[5] In recent years a number of scholars have held that the concepts of the Davidic Messiah and the Suffering Servant had been brought together before the time of Christ. Cf. J. Jeremias, Deutsche Theologie, ii, 1929, pp. 106 ff.; N. Johansson, Parakletoi, 1940, pp. 113 ff.; H. Riesenfeld, Jésus transfiguré, 1947, pp. 81 ff., 314 ff.; W. D. Davies, Paul and Rabbinic Judaism, 1948, pp. 274 ff. The last named refers with approval to W. Manson, Jesus the Messiah, 1943, pp. 171 ff., where it is shown that predicates of the Servant and of the Messiah have many details in common. What is not shown is that this had been noticed in any comparable way before the beginning of the Christian era, and that it had led to an equation, not of the predicates alone, but of the figures of the Messiah and the Servant. All that the evidence brought together by Manson establishes is that it was not without reason that the concepts were merged in the New Testament, and not that they had been already merged before the time of our Lord. It is sometimes held that 1 Enoch shows that the concept of a Suffering Messiah was current in pre-Christian days, since here we find the Servant equated with the Son of Man, and also the messianic title employed. But there is no evidence that 1 Enoch equates the Suffering Servant with the Son of Man. Enoch's Son of Man is clearly connected with the Son of Man of Dan. 7: 13, where the figure represents the saints as invested with authority (cf. my Darius the Mede and the Four World Empires in the Book of Daniel, 1935, pp. 62 ff. note), and in

The Gospels tell us that the disciples were always nonplussed when Jesus spoke to them of His mission in terms of suffering. Although they, as well as others, were thinking of Him in terms of the Davidic king, they regarded a mission of suffering as completely alien to that role. While the concept of the Davidic Messiah and that of the Suffering Servant both have reference to the Golden Age, they are such fundamentally different ideas about that age and the means whereby it should be brought about, that it seems quite gratuitous and inappropriate to suppose that the one was a form of the other.[1]

The verse I have already quoted may perhaps be brought against me, however. For in Is. 42 : 4 we read: "He shall not fail or be broken until he have set judgement in the earth; and the isles shall wait for his law." Is not the thought of the rule of the Servant in mind here? Scarcely. For it is probable that the word *mishpāṭ* here means *religion*,[2] and the parallel term *tôrāh* means instruction, rather than *royal edict*.[3] The thought here is then in harmony with that elsewhere in these

---

1 Enoch the Son of Man is invested with authority and power. It is sometimes pointed out that in Dan. 7 the element of suffering is not wanting, since the saints are persecuted before they are delivered and exalted; but the persecuted saints are not identified with the Son of Man. Their suffering ends when the Son of Man appears. This does not mean that the Son of Man is to be distinguished from the saints, but that this is a figure for *the kingdom of the saints*, or *the saints as invested with power*. For a full examination of this whole question, and for my reasons for adhering to the view which has been held by most of the experts in this field, and which alone does not reduce the evidence of the New Testament to nonsense, see my paper, "The Suffering Servant and the Davidic Messiah", in *O.T.S.*, viii, 1950, pp. 100–136 (reprinted in the present volume below, pp. 63 ff.).

1 L. Köhler, while using the term "Messiah" for the Servant, does not equate him with any other figure in the Old Testament (*Theologie des Alten Testaments*, 1936, pp. 229 f.; E.Tr. by A. S. Todd, 1957, p. 238). "The rest of the Old Testament knows nothing more about him," he says (*ibid.*). Cf. Mowinckel (*De senere profeter*, 1944, p. 195): "men han har sett en skikkelse som efterhvert skulde avløse den tradisjonelle Messias".

2 Cf. H. W. Hertzberg, *Z.A.W.*, xli, 1923, p. 41; R. Levy, *Deutero-Isaiah*, 1925, p. 144; J. van der Ploeg, in *O.T.S.*, ii, 1943, p. 155; C. R. North, *op. cit.*, pp. 140 f.; R. Koch, *Geist und Messias*, 1950, p. 111.

3 G. Östborn, (*Tōrā in the Old Testament*, 1945, p. 57) says: "in Is. 42: 4, therefore, *tōrā* probably denotes oral instruction". He goes on to maintain, however, that the Servant imparts the *tôrāh* in his capacity of king, while adding in a note that he might equally be thought of as a prophet, or a priest. The imparting of *tôrāh* is, indeed, much more characteristic of prophet and of priest than of king. Cf. A. S. Peake, *The Servant of Yahweh*, 1931, p. 28; "This is not an element in royal administration; it is entrusted to the teacher or the prophet." Östborn's view is very similar to that of H. Gressmann, who says: "Die hier gebrauchten Bilder passen nicht zu einem Propheten, wohl aber zu einem Könige, der die Pflicht hat, als oberster Richter *mishpāṭ* und als *summus episcopus tôrāh* zu verkünden" (*Der Messias*, 1929, p. 289). J. B. Koppe (*Robert Lowth's Jesaias neu übersetzt*, iii, 1780, pp. 228 f.) maintained that *tôrāh* here is not *religion* or *teaching*, but *Gesetze*.

songs, and the general conception behind the songs is of a mission of the Servant through suffering to bring the nations into a right relationship with God.[1]

Nor is it likely that the thought of Jehoiachin's sufferings would be linked with the world-wide destiny of the Davidic house. That his tragic sufferings would inspire infinite pity amongst his own people may well be true, but few could imagine that he was likely now so to impress the world by his sufferings that he would become the light of the nations. If these songs are from the pen of Deutero-Isaiah, by the time they were written he had already been released from his prison and his acuter sufferings were past. And if during the thirty-seven years they had lasted they had not impressed the nations, they were scarcely likely to do so now.[2] I could understand how one could believe that in spite of the low ebb of the fortunes of the Davidic house, and in spite of the miserable estate to which it had sunk in the person of the unfortunate Jehoiachin, it would yet rise again. But that is not the message of the Servant songs. That is the message of Ezek. 37 in relation to the national fortunes. But it is not the message here— which is that by the organ of the sufferings not merely the restoration of Israel's fortunes, but the service to the nations, would be effected.

This view has been advanced in a new form. J. Coppens has suggested that while the author thought of the Davidic dynasty, he especially had Jehoiachin in mind for the first three songs and Zedekiah for the fourth, but that he was really portraying the Messiah in terms inspired by the memory of these kings.[3] F. M. Th. de Liagre Böhl, however, has gone further and suggested that Jehoiachin may have been released by Evil-merodach, in order to be put to death as the royal substitute in the following year.[4] It is known that on occasion

[1] That there are kingly features in the characterization of the Servant is recognized by many scholars, and is not here denied. Such kingly features as are found, however, are other than those attaching to the concept of the Davidic Messiah. Both concepts may have some roots in the cult, but they are developments of different elements of that cult.

[2] M. Schmidt (Prophet und Tempel, 1948, p. 229) says: "Vielleicht verband er also (wenn Jojachin damals gestorben war) mit seinem sonstigen wunderbaren Hoffnungen des Kommenden auch diejenige auf einen Jojachin redivivus." It seems gratuitous to create such a legend today, in the absence of any evidence for it, and Jehoiachin was scarcely of such importance as to justify it.

[3] Cf. Pro regno pro sanctuario (Festschrift for G. van der Leeuw), 1950, pp. 118 ff.= Nieuw Licht over de Ebed-Jahweh-Liederen (Analecta Lovaniensia Biblica et Orientalia, II, 15), 1950, pp. 7 ff., 14 f.

[4] Cf. Ned. T.T., iv, 1949–50, pp. 161–176.

such a royal substitute was sacrificed,[1] and it is not therefore impossible that Jehoiachin should have been so sacrificed, and then have inspired the Servant songs. As against this, however, it is to be noted that there is no positive evidence for this assumption, and the Biblical statement that Jehoiachin was set free[2] would hardly have been expected if the author had known that such release was but the prelude to a more tragic fate.

Other varieties of individual historical interpretation can only be mentioned. In 1892 Duhm put forward the view that the Servant was an anonymous contemporary of Deutero-Isaiah, a leprous Rabbi.[3] In 1926, in a brief paper, A. Marmorstein revived a variety of the same view, when he argued that the Servant was a pious sufferer of that age.[4] A view which was advanced by the Jewish writer Sa'adia Gaon, who died more than a thousand years ago, was that the Servant was Jeremiah.[5] This has found some modern advocates, including some within

[1] Cf. R. Labat, "Le sort des substituts royaux en Assyrie au temps des Sargonides", in R. Ass., xl, 1945–46, pp. 123–142, and G. Goossens, Les substituts royaux en Babylonie (Analecta Lovaniensia Biblica et Oreintalia, II, 13), 1949. Cf. also H. Frankfort, Kingship and the Gods, 1948, pp. 262 ff.; S. H. Hooke, "The Theory and Practice of Substitution", V.T., ii, 1952, pp. 2–17.

[2] 2 Kings 25: 27 ff. Cf. esp. vv. 28 f.: "And he spake kindly to him, and set his throne above the throne of the kings that were with him in Babylon. And he changed his prison garments, and did eat bread before him continually all the days of his life." J. Morgenstern (V.T., xi, 1961, pp. 414 ff.) holds that Jehoiachin was not sacrificed as the royal substitute, but that another suffered this fate. He believes that two prisoners were selected for such an occasion, of whom one was put to death, while the other ever after received the royal favour. He brings into connexion with this Pharaoh's butler and baker, Mordecai and Haman, and Absalom, and associates the accounts of all of these with a similar ritual occasion.

[3] A. Guillaume (Theology, xii, 1926, p. 3) criticizes the view that the Servant was a leper. He says: "It is extraordinarily difficult to believe that a leprous figure could have been chosen as the ideal figure for a community wherein lepers were dreaded sources of infection, forbidden to associate with their fellows, and the object of a special section of the Law." Cf. W. Rudolph. Z.A.W., N.F. ii, 1925, pp. 92 f.; A.S. Peake, The Servant of Yahweh, 1931, pp. 13 f.; I. Engnell, B.J.R.L., xxxi, 1948, pp. 82 f. Engnell's objection is principally based on his linking of the Servant with Tammuz, and the fact that Tammuz is never visited with leprosy. M. Buber, however, follows the view that the Servant is depicted as a leper (The Prophetic Faith, 1949, pp. 227 f.). On Symmachus's rendering of Is. 53: 4, with its suggestion of leprosy, cf. H. J. Schoeps, Aus frühchristlicher Zeit, 1950, pp. 107 ff. Cf. also, for the same suggestion, Bab. Talmud, Sanhedrin, 98 b.

[4] "Zur Erklärung von Jes 53", in Z.A.W., N.F. iii, 1926, pp. 260 ff. Cf also W. E. Barnes, in The People and the Book (ed. A. S. Peake), 1925, p. 308.

[5] See P. Volz, Jesaia II, p. 188, where Sa'adia is cited for this interpretation of the fourth song. Cf. p. 167, where he is not mentioned for this view in connexion with the earlier songs. Cf. also H. A. Fischel, in H.U.C.A., xviii, 1943–44, p. 74. On the Suffering Servant in Jewish thought cf. also A. Médebielle, in S.D.B., iii, 1938, cols. 109 f.; J. J. Brierre-Narbonne, Le Messie souffrant dans la littérature rabbinique, 1940; and H. W. Wolff, Jesaja 53 im Urchristentum, 1942, pp. 35 ff. (2nd ed., 1950, pp. 38 ff.).

our period. F. A. Farley[1] in 1926 argued that the songs abound in reminiscences of the career of Jeremiah, and that the writer began with the idea that Israel was to be the world's Jeremiah, its mission being represented by the life and work of that prophet, but that he came to realize that the mission would not be fulfilled by the people as a whole, and hence perceived that the prophetic element in Israel would be the Servant. Very similarly, Sheldon Blank[2] argued that while the Servant was a collective figure, representing the nation Israel, the career of Jeremiah supplied some of the terms in which the personification was described. He was thus thought of as epitomizing in some measure the mission of the nation.[3]

I have already mentioned that amongst the abandoned views of Sellin was the view that the Servant was Moses. This was first put forward within our period, in the year following that in which Mowinckel's monograph saw the light. Sellin advanced the thesis that Moses had been martyred by his people, but that they were then so ashamed of what they had done that they suppressed the story from the Old Testament. He believed the story still lived on in prophetic circles, and by a forced and unnatural exegesis of emended texts in Hosea he found references to it, though without the mention of Moses. This is a slender basis on which to build the legend of Moses' martyrdom, and poor evidence for the connexion of the Servant songs with such a shadowy legend. Sellin's theory of the martyrdom of Moses has been adopted by Freud,[4] but is scarcely worthy of serious attention to-day. It will be seen later that in a very different way Bentzen thinks there is some connexion between Moses and the Servant, but his view does not belong here.

[1] "Jeremiah and 'The Suffering Servant of Jehovah' in Deutero-Isaiah", in E.T., xxxviii, 1926–27, pp. 521 ff. H. G. May (Z.A.W., N.F. xxv, 1954, p. 239) rejects Farley's view as undiscriminating.

[2] "Studies in Deutero-Isaiah", in H.U.C.A., xv, 1940, pp. 1 ff., esp. pp. 18 ff. Cf. also Prophetic Faith in Isaiah, 1958, pp. 100 ff.

[3] R. Kittel proposed the view that the Servant was an unspecified contemporary of the prophet, who was martyred but whose triumph was looked for in a resurrected state and in the political sphere. Cf. Geschichte des Volkes Israel, iii, 1927, pp. 222 ff. This led him to a most improbable explanation of the first person of the second and third songs. He says: "Ist aber Deutero-jesaja der Verfasser derjenigen Ebed Stücke, die vom Knecht Jahves in der dritten Person reden, und hat er die in der ersten Person redenden entweder im Namen seines Helden selbst gedichtet oder von jenen als eine Art Monologe des Knechts übernommen, so ist er auf diese Weise dessen Herold und der berufenste Verbreiter und Deuter seiner Gedanken, zugleich der Anwalt seiner Person geworden." C. R. North [in Studies in Old Testament Prophecy (T. H. Robinson Festschrift), 1950, p. 126] denies any political background to the fourth Servant song.

[4] Moses and Monotheism, 1939, pp. 59 f.

The identification of the Servant with Uzziah was proposed by K. Dietze,[1] but the extravagance of the author, to whom Uzziah was a sort of King Charles's head, to be found wherever he looked in the Old Testament, effectively ensured that he should have no followers. The composition of the songs was ascribed to the eighth-century Isaiah, and the Song of Songs, Job, and a number of Psalms were associated with Uzziah. The Tabeel of Is. 7 : 6 was held to be the name of a woman whom Uzziah married, the wedding being celebrated by the composition of the Song of Songs and Ps. 45.[2] Much significance was held to belong to the words $wē'lōhay\ hāyāh\ 'uzzî$,[3] which stand on the title-page of Dietze's work, and in which an allusion to Uzziah was found. That all this is highly subjective, and not the presentation of evidence subject to the ordinary canons of discussion, needs no demonstration, and the work will remain a curiosity of interpretation.[4]

In 1934 the Dutch Jew Palache propounded the view that the Servant was Meshullam.[5] This word occurs in Is 42 : 19—not in a Servant Song therefore—where it is rendered by the Revised Version "he that is at peace with me". Palache preferred to read it as a proper name, and to identify its holder with the son of Zerubbabel.[6] It is unnecessary to enlarge on the slenderness of this basis, or on our complete ignorance as to any suitability of the obscure Meshullam for the portrait of the Servant.

An original view of the Servant passages has been put forward by J. Morgenstern, who now thinks that they originally constituted a drama on the Greek pattern, complete with chorus.[7] He collects the passages and arranges them in the following way: 42 : 1–4, God speaks; 42 : 5, Chorus; 42 : 6–7, God addresses the Servant; 61 : 1, 49 : 4a,

---

[1] *Ussia, der Knecht Gottes, sein Leben und sein Leiden und seine Bedeutung für den Propheten Jesaja* (Abhandlungen und Vorträge herausgegeben von der Bremer Wissenschaftlichen Gesellschaft, Schriften der Bremer Wissenschaftlichen Gesellschaft, Reihe D, Jahrgang 4, Heft 1/2, September 1929). The author also published a *Nachwort zu "Ussia"*, 1930.

[2] *Ussia*, pp. 30 f.

[3] Is. 49: 5.

[4] Van der Ploeg (*Les chants du Serviteur de Jahvé*, 1936, p. 118) observes: "On est un peu stupéfait quand on lit tout ce que prétend Dietze dans son 'Ussia'. Son interprétation des textes n'a rien d'une saine exégèse, car au lieu de rechercher le véritable sens des textes, il leur en attribue un qu'ils *pourraient* peut-être avoir."

[5] *The 'Ebed-Jahveh Enigma in Pseudo-Isaiah.*

[6] 1 Chron. 3: 19.

[7] Cf. *V.T.*, xi, 1961, pp. 292–320, 406–431. H. Kruse had earlier put forward the view that the Songs formed a drama in six acts (*Verbum Domini*, xxix. 1951, pp. 193–205, 286–295, 334–340).

61 : 10, the Servant speaks; 49 : 1–5c, 5ab, 6, the Servant speaks; 50 : 10, Chorus; 50 : 4–8, 9aβ, the Servant speaks; 52 : 13–53 : 10, Chorus; 53 : 11–12, God speaks.[1] He assigns the composition of this drama to a disciple of Deutero-Isaiah[2] who belonged to a sectarian group and who wrote about 450 B.C.,[3] and believes that it was based on the fate of one Menahem, of the line of David,[4] who was associated with the rebellion of Jerusalem against Xerxes in the year 485 B.C. which Morgenstern postulates and reconstructs in a variety of publications.[5] The difficulties here are that there is no very solid evidence of the postulated rebellion,[6] and Menahem is so unsubstantial a historical figure, of whom we have no information outside Morgenstern's writings, that it is hard to ascribe to him the historical significance the author of the drama is credited with ascribing.[7]

What has been said already in criticism of the theory that the Servant is Deutero-Isaiah will apply in some degree against all the historical individual theories.[8] It is possible that memories of some person might furnish the writer with some of the terms in which he describes the suffering of the Servant, but it is not likely that he identified such a person with the Servant, or ascribed the mission of the Servant to that person.[9] An artist may have in his studio a model without making his picture a mere portrait of the model, and without ascribing to the model the experiences or the function his picture seeks to express. And in so far as any historical person entered into the picture

[1] Cf. V.T., xi, 1961, pp. 293 ff. R. Tournay (R.B., lix, 1952, p. 508), on the contrary, says we must retain every passage in its present place, and rejects any rearrangement.

[2] Morgenstern thinks the work of Deutero-Isaiah was limited to Isa. 40–48, and that Isa. 49–66 were the work of Trito-Isaiah, except potentially for the Servant passages in the whole of Isa. 40–66; see H.U.C.A., xxix, 1958, p. 18.

[3] V.T., xi, 1961, pp. 410, 429 ff., 428.

[4] Ibid., p. 427.

[5] Cf. J.A.O.S., lv, 1935, p. 364; A.J.S.L., lv, 1938, p. 56; H.U.C.A., xvi, 1941, pp. 25 n., 48 n.; xix, 1945–46, p. 494; xxi, 1948, p. 458; xxii, 1949, pp. 380, 399; xxiii, Part I, 1950–51, pp. 198 f.; xxiv, 1952–53, p. 63 n.; xxvii, 1956, pp. 101–179; xxviii, 1957, pp. 15–47; xxxi, 1960, pp. 1–29; U.J.E., x, 1943, p. 356. See also S. H. Blank, H.U.C.A., xi, 1936, pp. 172, 174, 182.

[6] Cf. H. H. Rowley, Men of God, 1963, pp. 238 ff.

[7] Cf. J. Muilenburg, I.B., v, 1956, p. 409a: "Scholars have repeatedly turned to historical characters about whom very little is known and for whom extant information gives little support."

[8] H. E. del Medico has suggested that the Servant is none other than the Danel of the Ras Shamra texts (La Bible Cananéenne, 1950, p. 120). That this Danel was known in the sixth century B.C. is probable enough from the references in Ezek. 14: 14, 20; 28: 3; but this proposed identification can scarcely be taken seriously.

[9] Cf. P. Auvray and J. Steinmann, Isaïe (Jerusalem Bible), 2nd ed., 1957, p. 17.

of the Servant, he fulfilled no higher role than that of the artist's model.[1]

(3)

The traditional messianic interpretation of the Servant is not without its modern advocates. These include some scholars of high standing, who are familiar with the whole range of modern literature on the subject, such as Johann Fischer,[2] F. Feldmann,[3] A. Vaccari,[4] J. van der Ploeg,[5] E. J. Young,[6] E. Power,[7] and Steinmueller-Sulli-

[1] A. Dupont-Sommer (Aperçus préliminaires sur les Manuscrits de la Mer Morte, 1950, p. 117; E.Tr. by E. M. Rowley, 1952, p. 96) has suggested that the Servant songs and certain other passages of the Old Testament, such as Dan. 9, Zech. 12: 10–14, Ps. 22, refer to one who was martyred by Aristobulus II in the first century B.C., and who is referred to as the 'Teacher of Righteousness' in the Zadokite Fragments and in some of the texts of the Dead Sea Scrolls. Apart from the speculative character of this identification of the 'Teacher of Righteousness'. it is very improbable that any of these passages is so late as this theory would require. S. Lassalle (Bulletin du Circle Ernest Renan, No. 73, June, 1960) thinks that Dupont-Sommer was carried away by his enthusiasm in this view, but himself proposes the scarcely less improbable view that the Servant was Onias III, who was martyred in 171 B.C. (cf. also Cahiers du Circle Ernest Renan, No. 30, 1961, pp. 1–11). It should be added that more recently Dupont-Sommer has modified his view and now agrees that the Servant Songs are older than the ministry of the Teacher of Righteousness. He now holds that the Teacher of Righteousness applied the Songs to himself (cf. The Essene Writings from Qumran, E.Tr. by G. Vermes, 1961, p. 361).

[2] See Isaias 40–55 und die Perikopen vom Gottesknecht, 1916; Wer ist der Ebed in den Perikopen Js 42, 1–7; 19, 1–9a; 50, 4–9; 52, 13–53, 12? 1922; Das Buch Isaias, II. Teil: Kap. 40–66, 1939. Cf. also E. Tobac, Les prophètes d'Israël, ii, 1921, pp. 171 ff.; M. J. Lagrange, Le judaïsme avant Jésus-Christ, 1931, pp. 368 ff.; P. Heinisch, Theologie des Alten Testamentes, 1940, pp. 316 ff.; Höpfl-Miller-Metzinger, Introductio specialis in Vetus Testamentum, 1946, pp. 427 f.; R. T. Murphy, "Second Isaias: the Servant of the Lord", in C.B.Q., ix, 1947, pp. 262 ff.; R. Koch, Geist und Messias, 1950, p. 109.

[3] Das Buch Isaias, ii, 1926, pp. 16 ff. Cf. the same writer's Der Knecht Gottes in Isaias Kap. 40–55, 1907.

[4] Cf. "I carmi del 'Servo di Jahve'," in Miscellanea Biblica edita a Pontificio Instituto Biblico, ii, 1934, pp. 241 ff.

[5] See Les Chants du Serviteur de Jahvé, 1936, E. J. Young, Westminster Theological Journal, x, 1947–48, p. 163, says: "Probably no one has investigated the problem quite as thoroughly as van der Ploeg. . . . The author has performed a service from which the entire church of Christ will reap benefit."

[6] See "The Study of Isaiah since the time of Joseph Addison Alexander", in Westminster Theological Journal, ix, 1946–47, pp. 1 ff.; x, 1947–48, pp. 23 ff., 139 ff. A. H. Edelkoort (De Christusverwachting in het Oude Testament, 1941, pp. 372 ff.) also adopts the messianic view, though he prefers to use the word Christ rather than Messiah, as is indicated by the title of his book. O. Procksch ("Jesus der Gottesknecht", in In piam memoriam A. von Bulmerincq, 1938, pp. 146 ff.), too, finds in the Servant a direct prophecy of our Lord. Cf. also U. E. Simon, A Theology of Salvation, 1953, where the view is presented that the Servant is a messianic figure (G. W. Anderson in E.T., lxv, 1953–54, p. 139b, complains that he does not clearly define what he means by "messianic"), and Cyrus is held to be a type of the Messiah (cf. the present writer's review in J.T.S., N.S. v, 1954, pp. 83–85).   [7] Cf. A Catholic Commentary on Holy Scripture, 1953, p. 542.

van.[1] For our present purpose we may confine ourselves to Fischer, who has published more than one work dealing with the subject, and who has brought to it a learning that is unsurpassed in any discussion of the subject.[2] The first of his works falls outside our period, while the other two fall within it. In the first work he discussed the relation of the songs to their context, and came to the conclusion that while they did not belong originally to the context, since the figure of the Servant in them is different from that of the Servant in the surrounding passages,[3] they can never have formed an independent and connected series, and therefore they must have been inserted into their present places by the author of Deutero-Isaiah, to set forth a later development of his thought.[4] In the second work he discusses the identity of the Servant, and criticizes in turn the various theories that have been advanced. The collective theory stands condemned, because it cannot be carried consistently through the songs, and almost every advocate of the collective theory has had to modify it in some way. On the other hand, the individual theories, that connect the poems with some past or contemporary figure of history, lead into inextricable difficulties, similar to those that have been noted. Since the rival theories are unsatisfactory, he returns to consider the traditional theory, and shows the remarkable correspondence between the experiences of the Servant

[1] Cf. J. E. Steinmueller and K. Sullivan, *Catholic Biblical Encyclopedia*, Old Testament, 1956, pp. 993 f.

[2] E. J. Young (*loc. cit.*, x, 1947–48, pp. 148 f.) says of the first of Fischer's three works: "It is the production of a master exegete. It is one of the few really great works on Isaiah which this century has seen, and in any serious study of the prophecy must be taken into account."

[3] W. Staerk, *Soter: die biblische Erlösererwartung als religionsgeschichtliche Problem* (Beiträge zur Förderung christlicher Theologie, 2. Reihe, 31), i, 1933, pp. 28 f., similarly contrasts the Servant of the Servant songs with the Servant of Deutero-Isaiah, from whom he separates the songs. So far as the Servant of the first three songs is concerned, he says (p. 33): "Hier wie dort (sc. Is. 55: 3–5) ist die messianische, an die Person des Heilbringers oder des Repräsentanten der Heilszeit geknüpfte Eschatologie radikal umgestaltet durch den beherrschenden theozentrischen Gedanken der Gottesherrschaft 'bis zu den Enden der Erde'. In der Glut dieses Glaubens sind sie alten Formen der christologischen Heilshoffnung, die mythische vom göttlichen Heilbringer und die geschichtliche vom Knechte David, dem rechten *einen* Hirten der *einen* Herde, aufgelöst worden." As for the fourth song, he thinks (pp. 33 ff.) it was originally independent, and says: "Ob rein als religiöse Idee, ob mythisch oder geschichtlich vorgebildet, vermögen wir nicht zu sagen."

[4] Cf. J. van der Ploeg, *op. cit.*, p. 25: "Les quatre chants du Serviteur de Jahvé ne dépendent pas de leur contexte. Ce sont des morceaux à part que nous sommes en droit de considérer et d'étudier sans nous préoccuper beaucoup du contexte (chapitres 40–55), encore que ce contexte puisse nous aider à mieux comprendre leur style et leur langue."

and those of Christ, and concludes that this correspondence cannot be due to chance.

Many of the advocates of other views of the original meaning of the songs would agree that they found their fulfilment in Christ in a unique degree, and that He alone of all the figures of history can be said to have realized in Himself what was predicated of the Servant. They would also agree that the correspondence is not due to chance. But this is not to say that the songs were a conscious prediction of the life and death of Christ, and that the writer had His figure and no other in mind when he wrote the songs.

It is not without significance that Fischer is at such pains to isolate the songs from their context, just as Duhm, who began the non-messianic individual interpretation, had been. He delimits the first two songs as Is. 42 : 1–7 and 49 : 1–9a, and he is embarrassed by the word *Israel* in 49 : 3. Here he suggests that it should either be struck out as an intrusion, or the verse should be rendered: "And he said unto me, Thou art my servant; an Israel in whom I will be glorified."[1] He then explains the choice of the word "Israel" here to mean "one who fights with God". But the Servant is not represented as one who struggles with God, and the interpretation is forced and unnatural. Outside the songs we read: "Remember these things, O Jacob; and Israel, for thou art my servant . . . for the Lord hath redeemed Jacob, and will glorify himself in Israel".[2] When two passages which are recognized as coming from the same writer's hand use such closely similar language, we are justified in asking for strong reasons before we interpret them so differently, and there is nothing whatever in the passage itself to suggest the unnatural interpretation. It is safe to say it would not have occurred to anyone whose view would not be embarrassed by the more natural interpretation.

Van der Ploeg, whose general position is closely similar to Fischer's, prefers to follow the usual way with *Israel* adopted by most of the

---

[1] Cf. *Das Buch Isaias II*, pp. 102 f.; also *Wer ist der Ebed?* pp. 4 f. E. Burrows retained the text, but somewhat similarly argued that it was not a vocative, but a title of honour, and claimed the support of the etymology of Gen. 32: 29 (*The Gospel of the Infancy*, 1940, pp. 62 f.). So, too, M. Buber (*The Prophetic Faith*, 1949, p. 223): "If the saying really was directed to Israel, there was no need to say: 'Thou art Israel.' If, however, what is meant by the servant is a person, but a person standing in a quite peculiarly close relationship to Israel, it is fairly evident that God speaks to him: '*Thou* art the Israel in whom I glorify myself.' " Ibn Ezra somewhat similarly gave an individual interpretation to this verse, taking *Israel* to be equivalent to *an Israelite* (cf. H. A. Fischel, in *H.U.C.A.* xviii, 1943–44, p. 69).

[2] Is. 44: 21, 23.

individual interpreters of the Servant, and strikes it out of the text. Instead of claiming any support from MSS., however, he bases himself on his interpretation of the Servant alone, and frankly says the word cannot be squared with it.[1]

Along a somewhat different way Professor North[2] reaches a similar conclusion to Fischer. In common with views to which we shall come later, he finds some fluidity in the writer's thought, and finds collective elements in the conception, which render it unnecessary for him to resort to such expedients as the one just noted. Instead of finding

---

[1] Op. cit., pp. 36 f., esp. p. 37: "M ajoute 'Israël', mot auquel tous les exégètes collectivistes font appel pour prouver leur théorie. . . . Condamin, van Hoonacker et Lagrange (pour nommer seulement des auteurs catholiques) considèrent le mot comme une glose et il nous semble que cela s'impose, si on n'identifie pas le Serviteur avec Israël. . . . On est donc autorisé à considérer dans 49.3 comme glose le mot 'Israel' dont la présence dans le texte est inconciliable avec l'explication certaine de celui-ci." The claim that one is authorized to make intractable evidence square with a disputed theory because one regards the theory as certain can hardly be allowed. Cf. L. Dennefeld, Les grands prophètes (in Pirot and Clamer's La Sainte Bible, vii), 1947, p. 179: "Du moment que dans le contexte le Serviteur désigne un individu, le mot Israël ne peut être qu'une glose fautive du texte hébreu;" A. Médebielle, in S.D.B., iii, 1938, col. 91; R. Kittel, Geschichte des Volkes Israel, iii, 1927, p. 228. So also Budde's introduction of Israel into the fourth song is to deprecated. He emended yaśkîl in Is. 52: 13 into Yiśrā'ēl (A.J.Th., iii, 1899, pp. 533 f.; Die sogenannten Ebed-Jahwe-Lieder, 1900, pp. 34 f.). In this he was followed by J. Montieth (E.T., xxxvi, 1924-25, pp. 499 f.) who propounded the strange theory that the fourth Servant song is a mosaic of two originally separate songs, of which one dealt with an individual leper, and the other with captive Israel (cf. "A New View of Isaiah liii", ibid., pp. 498 ff.). J. Morgenstern (V.T., xi, 1961, p. 313) emends yaśkîl to yiśśākēl, with the meaning "hangs suspended", but this again is wholly conjectural and without authority. I. Engnell (B.J.R.L., xxxi, 1948, pp. 75 ff.) connects the word yaśkîl with the word used in some Psalm headings maśkîl, which he connects with enthronement, and accordingly he renders "he will take the throne". Again it is improbable that we should read so much into the term. Engnell also adduces Dan. 12: 3, where we have the plural participle from this verb in maśkîlîm, "they that be wise", which he thinks may be a direct allusion to Is. 52: 13. This is no new view (cf. North, The Suffering Servant in Deutero-Isaiah, pp. 6 f., 10, 20), and it seems very probable that the author of the Daniel passage had the Fourth Servant Song in mind [cf. R. Press, Z.A.W., N.F. xxvi, 1955, p. 77, where the allusion is carried back to Dan. 11: 33 ff., as well as to 12: 1 ff.; cf. also W. H. Brownlee, B.A.S.O.R., No. 132, Dec. 1953, pp. 12 f.; H. L. Ginsberg, V.T., iii, 1953, p. 402 (who also carries the allusion back to Dan. 11: 33 ff.); A. Feuillet, R.B., lx, 1953, pp. 336 f.; A. Bentzen, King and Messiah, 1955, p. 55; V. de Leeuw, De Ebed Jahweh-Profetieën. 1956, pp. 6 f.; D. S. Russell, The Method and Message of Jewish Apocalyptic, 1964, p. 188]. If this is right, then the earliest interpretation of the Servant was in terms of the loyal in Israel, who suffered for their faith and looked for a glorious vindication (cf. The Faith of Israel, 1956, p. 198). H. Ringgren points out (Z.A.W., N.F., xxiii, 1952, p. 142 n.) that the same word yaśkîl is used in Jer. 23: 5 in a prophecy of the Davidic Messiah, where, however, we can hardly assume there is any reference to the Servant.

[2] Op. cit., pp. 207 ff.; cf. also "Who was the Servant of the Lord in Isaiah 53?" in E.T., lii, 1904-41, pp. 181 ff., 219 ff.

oscillation in the fluidity, however, he finds progress, the thought moving from Israel to an individual, pointing forward to Christ, in whom its expectation was realized.[1] Up to a point I am in agreement with this, as I shall say later; I am not convinced that the fluidity was of this character, however. A movement forward without return involves the abandonment of the positions from which movement is made, and I do not think there is evidence that the author first cherished a collective view of the Servant and then abandoned it. That there was development in his thought is, I think, certain; but I am not persuaded that it was a development that involved abandonment.

Gressmann, whose earlier view will be mentioned later, also came to adopt a messianic interpretation,[2] though one much farther from the traditional view than Professor North's. Denying that the Servant is Israel, or any group within Israel, or any figure of history prior to the age of the author, he finds kingly and prophetic traits in the conception, and holds that the exilic author drew on memories of king Josiah for his portrayal of a figure whose advent he expected in the near future.

(4)

Passing by theories like those of Rudolph,[3] Kittel,[4] and Oesterley,[5] that the Servant is both an unknown contemporary of the prophet and

[1] Cf. *The Suffering Servant in Deutero-Isaiah*, pp. 215 f.: "As I understand him"—i.e. Wheeler Robinson—"the 'ebb and flow' of Deutero-Isaiah's thought was from Israel to his own prophetic consciousness, *and back to Israel*. As I see it, the direction was rather from collective Israel to an individual who was neither himself nor anyone else who had lived hitherto." In the Preface to the 2nd edition, 1956, p.v., Professor North explained that he intended only to make clear that his view was of an oscillation of the prophet's thought between Israel and a future individual, as against Wheeler Robinson's view that it was an oscillation between Israel and the prophet himself. His choice of words to italicize suggested that he was rejecting the idea that Israel was still the Servant, and this he now repudiates, and explains that his view is really substantially the same as mine. He now italicizes the words *to his own prophetic consciousness*. A. Causse (*Israël et la Vision de l'humanité*, 1924, p. 54) adopts a linear view of the development of the prophet's thought, from a figure for the exiled people, through the loyal Jews to a hero analogous to the Messiah.

[2] *Der Messias*, 1929, pp. 287–339.

[3] "Der exilische Messias", in *Z.A.W.*, N.F. ii, 1925, pp. 90–114; and' 'Die Ebed-Jahwe-Lieder als geschichtliche Wirklichkeit", *ibid.*, N.F. v, 1928, pp. 156–166. In the latter article he replies to the views and criticisms of W. Staerk, "Zum Ebed Jahwe-Problem", *ibid.*, N.F. iii, 1926, pp. 242–260.

[4] *Geschichte des Volkes Israel*, iii, 1927, pp. 222–257.

[5] Oesterley and Robinson, *Hebrew Religion: its Origin and Development*, 1930, pp. 264 ff., 2nd ed., 1937, pp. 303 ff.

also an eschatological figure[1]—a reformer who attempted the moral and spiritual renewal of his people, whom the prophet mistakenly supposed to be about to fulfil the messianic prophecies—we may turn to the mythological view. Early in the present century it had been maintained that Is. 53 was to be interpreted in terms of the Adonis-Tammuz cult, and that it was based on one of the ritual songs of the cult of the dying and rising god. The chief exponents of this view were Gressmann[2] and Gunkel,[3] both of whom modified their view to a greater or less extent later. Gressmann denied that the Servant could be the nation Israel or any historical individual, and claimed that the implied resurrection of the Servant in the fourth song pointed to the myth of the dying and rising god as the source of the prophet's ideas.[4] Both he and Gunkel called attention to the vagueness in the description of the Servant and the element of mystery that surrounds his person.[5] Gunkel emphasized the transcendent quality of the Servant, who far surpassed any of the figures of Israel's history who may have supplied elements of the description we have.[6] None of this brought clear and tangible evidence for their theory of a connexion with Adonis-Tammuz, however, and it is not surprising that the view was criticized by Baudissin in his great work *Adonis und Esmun*, where all real basis for the theory is denied.[7] It is, indeed, hard to see how this theory ever came into being. For the Servant is not a figure of Nature myth, and the death of the god of the Nature myth had no atoning

[1] Mowinckel now allows that the Servant may be both eschatological and historical. Cf. *De senere profeter*, 1944, pp. 195 f. Cf. also Th. C. Vriezen, Copenhagen *Congress Volume*, 1953 (S.V.T. i) 1953, pp. 217 f.

[2] *Der Ursprung der israelitisch-jüdischen Eschatologie*, 1905, pp. 302 ff.

[3] "Knecht Jahves", in *R.G.G.*, iii, 1912, cols. 1540–1543.

[4] *Op. cit.*, pp. 328 ff.

[5] *Ibid.*, pp. 317 ff.; Gunkel, *loc. cit.*, iii, col. 1543.

[6] *Loc. cit.*, iii, col. 1541. In the second edition of *R.G.G.*, iii, 1929, cols. 1100–1103, Gunkel announced his acceptance of Mowinckel's autobiographical theory: "Diese Erklärung des 'K.s J.s' als des Propheten selber, zeigt ein so einheitliches, geschichtlich verständliches und ergreifendes Bild, dass man wohl annehmen darf, sie werde nach gewisser Zeit in weiten Kreisen anerkennt werden" (col. 1103).

[7] Cf. *Adonis und Esmun*, 1911, p. 424 n.: "Eine über den Gedanken des Wiederauflebens nach dem Tode hinausgehende Berührung zwischen dem Knechte Jahwe's bei Deutero-Jesaja und dem Adonismythos vermag ich nicht wahrzunehmen. Gressmann . . . sieht in dem sterbenden Adonis oder Tammuz das Urbild des sterbenden Knechtes Jahwe's, indem er für den Tod des Gottes eine sühnende Bedeutung vermutet. Diese Auffassung des Adonis- oder auch des Tammuzmythos scheint mir durch nichts nahe gelegt zu sein." Cf. S. Smith, *Isaiah, chapters xl–lv*, 1944, pp. 101 f., esp. p. 102: "The Tammuz laments as known to us in Sumerian texts contain nothing specifically comparable with Isaiah c. liii." Cf. also R. Kittel, *Geschichte des Volkes Israel*, iii, 1927, pp. 255 ff.; A. Weiser, *Introduction to the Old Testament*, E.Tr., 1961, p. 204.

significance. Moreover, Deutero-Isaiah, with his uncompromising monotheism, was hardly likely to have adopted one of the not-gods for this high role. For he had no place for syncretism. To him Yahweh alone was God, and all other gods were just non-existent. Their idols were symbols of nothing, and therefore just bits of wood and metal.

This is generally recognized to-day, and the mythological interpretation only survives in a modified form. I have already said that in 1931 Mowinckel suggested that the songs were tinged with mythology. He held that the dead Servant was celebrated as a cult-hero by his disciples, and described in terms borrowed from the Adonis cult.[1] In varying ways the idea that a mythological colouring has been given to the songs has been attached to different theories of the interpretation of the Servant. Thus, G. H. Dix[2] brought this idea to a variety of the messianic interpretation. He identified the Servant with the "Messianic Angel", and held that "the Babylonian Tammuz songs influenced the Jewish prophet's description of the Suffering Servant".[3] M. Haller[4] similarly found Tammuz elements in the terms of the songs, though he adopted a predominantly collective interpretation of the Servant. Böhl,[5] again, thought there were Tammuz features in the Servant, though he regarded the Servant as an ideal figure into which national elements entered, to be fused with the thought of the Davidic dynasty and of the coming Messiah. Up to a point, I think there may be an element of truth in this view, though I cannot accept it in any of these forms. The prophet's language might be reminiscent of the language of the Tammuz cult—as Milton's language is often reminiscent of classical mythology. But if so, he was applying the language of that cult to the Servant, and not conforming the Servant to the ideas of the Tammuz cult, for which he could have had nothing but contempt. For, as I have said, the conception of the Servant in its totality is quite different from the conception of the dying and rising Nature god. I therefore think that in so far as the prophet's language had any cultic background it is more likely to have been in the Yahwistic ritual of his own people.

[1] *Z.A.W.*, N.F. viii, 1931, pp. 256 f.

[2] "The Influence of Babylonian Ideas on Jewish Messianism", in *J.T.S.*, xxvi, 1925, pp. 241–256.

[3] *Ibid.*, p. 256.

[4] *Das Judentum* (in *S.A.T.*, II, iii,), 1914, pp. 51 ff., esp. p. 57: "Aber es hindert nichts, anzunehmen, dass eine solche Figur, wie die des Knechtes Jahves, nach dem Vorbild der sterbenden Götter der Nachbarvölker, neben dem Davids-Sohn in den Zukunftserwartungen Judas lebte."

[5] *De "Knecht des Heeren"* in *Jezaja* 53, 1923, pp. 24 ff.

The Roman Catholic scholar Dürr[1] turned rather to the Babylonian *akitu* festival, or New Year festival, for the source of the phraseology. In that festival the king was ritually struck by the high priest in the course of a ceremony which had expiatory significance. But, again, it is hard to concede much to this view.[2] Dürr himself holds the Servant to have been the Messiah,[3] and therefore only brings a mythological colouring to a fundamentally different view.[4] But since Is. 46 shows that the prophet took a poor view of the *akitu* festival, and made it the butt of his contempt, it is very doubtful how far he was influenced by it in the conception of the Servant. Moreover, the Servant was not ritually struck in any piece of dumb-show. The third and fourth songs show that he was smitten in earnest.[5]

(5)

Before turning to the recent varieties of collective theory, we may briefly examine some individual views which differ widely from those so far reviewed, and which, while differing considerably from one another, have yet something in common. All of the views so far examined interpret the songs without reference to their context. Mowinckel and some of his followers interpreted them partly in contrast to their context, but quite differently from the views I have here in mind.

Mowinckel himself was impressed by the points of connexion with the Cyrus prophecies. He pointed out[6] that both the Servant and Cyrus

---

[1] *Ursprung und Ausbau der israelitisch-jüdischen Heilanderwartung*, 1925, pp. 134 ff.

[2] R. Kittel (*Geschichtes des Volkes Israel*, iii, 1927, pp. 256 f.) allows that there may be some allusion to Babylonian rites in the fourth Servant song, but finds no evidence that the Servant is depicted as a king.

[3] Cf. *ibid.*, pp. 125 ff.; *Wollen und Wirken der alttestamentlichen Propheten*, 1926, p. 81.

[4] Cf. *Ursprung und Ausbau*, p. 152: "Wir haben auch im 'leidenden Gottesknechte' Jes. 53 denselben Tatbestand wie überhaupt in der ganzen orientalischen Entwicklung: den einzigartigen Gedanken der Sühne durch den erwarteten 'Heiland' in gemeiner, orientalischer Ausprägung. Das Heilandsbild selbst wie die ganze Erwartung ist urisraelitisch und ohne jede altorientalische Parallele, die Darstellungsmittel aber sind, wie man es bei Semiten nicht anders erwarten konnte, gemeinsemitisch, ja altorientalisch."

[5] Cf. J. van der Ploeg, *op. cit.*, p. 177. Cf. also M. J. Lagrange, *Le Judaïsme avant Jésus-Christ*, 1931, pp. 380 f.: "Si les rois de Babylone se soumettaient, (théoriquement) à ce rite humiliant, il y a cependant loin de ce symbolisme de commande à la tragédie qui plonge Isaïe dans la stupeur." Cf. also A. Feuillet, *S.D.B.*, iv, 1949, col. 711.

[6] *Der Knecht Jahwäs*, 1921, pp. 7 f. It will be remembered that Mowinckel held the first song to consist of Is. 42: 1–7, and hence he draws on verses which others do not regard as part of that song. Cf. J. Hontheim, *Z.K.T.*, xxx, 1906, pp. 760 f., where the parallels between Cyrus and the Servant had already been noted.

were called by name,[1] were called in righteousness,[2] were called to free the prisoners,[3] and were taken by the hand by Yahweh.[4] Hence he thought that Cyrus and the Servant were the obverse and the reverse of the divine means of deliverance. To Cyrus was assigned the political and to the Servant the spiritual side of the mission.[5] Hence the Servant of the songs stands in a sense over against the Cyrus of the context.[6] Haller, who had by now adopted Mowinckel's autobiographical theory of the Servant, developed this contrast in a different way.[7] In his view the prophet began by thinking of Cyrus as the divinely appointed instrument of deliverance, but later was disappointed in Cyrus,[8] and so substituted himself as the Servant in place of Cyrus in his expectations. For by now the conviction had grown within him that he was destined to be the instrument of the fulfilment of his own great hopes. In Haller's view, Is. 42 : 5–9, which is attached by some writers to the first Servant song, was a Cyrus song.[9] Hempel[10] disagreed as to this last point, but in general followed the same way. He

---

[1] Is. 49: 1; cf. 45: 3 f.　　　　　　　　　[2] Is. 42: 6; cf. 45: 13.
[3] Is. 42: 7; 49: 6; cf. 45: 13.　　　　　　[4] Is. 42: 6; cf. 45: 1.

[5] Cf. *Acta Orientalia*, xvi, 1938, p. 38: "Was Dtjes von Kyros erwartete, das, und viel mehr, erwartet hier der Verfasser in anderer Weise und von einer anderen religiösen Grundanschauung heraus von dem unschuldig leidenden und sterbenden 'Knecht' näher bestimmt." Cf. also F. Feldmann, *Der Knecht Gottes in Isaias Kap 40–55*, 1907, pp. 88, 91, 168 f.

[6] Cf. J. Hontheim, *Z.K.T.*, xxx, 1906, p. 751: "Der Messias wird in Gegensatz gestellt zu Cyrus, von dem im vorigen Kapitel die Rede war". Some writers have not hesitated to transfer the first song bodily out of a Cyrus context in order to get rid of its embarrassment. Thus A. Condamin transferred Is. 42: 1–9 to follow 49: 7 (*Le livre d'Isaïe*, 1905, pp. 298 f., and *R.B.*, N.S. v, 1908, pp. 163, 170 ff.; for a criticism of this cf. J. Hontheim, *Z.K.T.*, xxx, 1906, pp. 760 f.), while A. van Hoonacker transferred Is. 42: 1–7 to follow 52: 12 (*R.B.*, N.S. vi, 1909, pp. 518, 525; cf. *Het Boek Isaias*, 1932, pp. 252 ff.), and was followed by E. Tobac (*Les Prophètes d'Israël*, ii, 1921, pp. 161 ff., 169, and *Dictionnaire de Théologie catholique* viii, 1924, col. 22).

[7] Cf. "Die Kyros-Lieder Deuterojesajas", in *Eucharistērion* (Gunkel Festschrift), 1923, i, pp. 261–277; and *Das Judentum*, 2nd ed., 1925, pp. 31 ff., 51 ff., 57 f., 63 ff.

[8] Cf. M. Buber, *The Prophetic Faith*, 1949, pp. 221 f. Cf. also C. E. Simcox, "The Role of Cyrus in Deutero-Isaiah", in *J.A.O.S.*, lvii, 1937, pp. 158 ff. Here it is argued that Deutero-Isaiah shows much evidence of Persian influence (cf. A. von Gall, *Basileia tou Theou*, 1926, p. 187, where it is held that the Servant of Yahweh may have been so inspired), and that chaps. 40–48 must have been written before Cyrus's entry into Babylon, their author being concerned to transfer to Yahweh the triumph in the struggle of the gods and to transform the Messiah-kingship of the House of David into a Messiahship of œcumenical significance exercised through the person of Cyrus.

[9] W. Caspari (*Lieder und Gottesprüche der Rückwanderer*, 1934, p. 86) holds that Is. 42: 1–4 was originally the third Cyrus song, and opposes Mowinckel's view that this was not written with reference to Cyrus (*ibid.*, pp. 196 f.).

[10] "Vom irrenden Glauben", in *Z.S.T.*, vii, 1930, pp. 631–660 [reprinted in *Apoxysmata* (Hempel Festgabe), 1961, pp. 174–197]. Cf. Sellin, *Z.A.W.*, N.F. xiv, 1937, pp. 186 f.

thought Is. 42 : 5–9 was an adaptation of a Cyrus song, but held that in its present form it belongs to a Servant song. Like Haller, he argued that the Servant songs were composed at a time when the prophet was experiencing disillusionment, after Cyrus had entered Babylon and had failed to fulfil his expectations, Similarly Volz,[1] whose general view has been already noted, felt the contrast between Cyrus and the Servant, though apparently less acutely than these other writers.[2]

The two writers to whom I now turn, however, both regard the songs as intimately related to their context, and not to be read in contrast to that context. They therefore interpret the songs in accordance with their context. They also agree in holding that these four songs in no sense belong together as a connected series, needing to be interpreted in relation to one another. Hence they give a different interpretation to the Servant in the different songs. Here their agreement almost ends. The two writers in question are E. J. Kissane[3] and Sidney Smith.[4] To Kissane Is. 41 : 29–42 : 4 is just one stanza of a single poem that runs from 41 : 1–42 : 9; 49 : 1–7 forms a complete poem; and 50 : 4–11 forms a complete poem. In the first and second of these passages, he finds the Servant to be Israel; in the third he identifies the Servant with the prophet himself; while in the fourth song, Is. 52 : 13–53 : 12, he follows the traditional interpretation of the Messiah. Basing himself on the same principle of interpretation in relation to the immediate context, Sidney Smith finds the Servant of the first song to be Cyrus,[5] and of the other three to be the prophet himself, holding that the fourth song was written by another hand after the death of the prophet. It is clear that the application of the principle is as important as its formulation, since it yields such varied results in these two works.[6]

[1] *Jesaja II*, 1932, p. 167. A Vaccari, in *Miscellanea Biblica edita a Pontificio Instituto Biblico*, ii, 1934, p. 219, notes the contrast of Cyrus in Is. 42: 25 and 45: 1 ff. with the gentleness of the Servant in 42: 3.
[2] E. Jenni (*Th.Z.*, x, 1954, pp. 241–256) thinks this view is very questionable, and is doubtful if we should conclude from the fact that Cyrus and the Servant stand side by side in Deutero-Isaiah that they were successive centres of the prophet's hopes.
[3] *The Book of Isaiah*, ii, 1943.
[4] *Isaiah, Chapters xl–lv*, 1944.
[5] Cf. also W. E. Barnes, "Cyrus the 'Servant of Jehovah', Is. 42: 1–4 (7)", in *J.T.S.*, xxxii, 1931, pp. 32–39. He argued that there was progress in the teaching of the author, who first thought of Cyrus as the Servant, and then realized that a spiritual agent must take up the work.
[6] R. Tournay (*R.B.*, lix, 1952, pp. 355, 359, 508) similarly insists that the Songs should be interpreted in relation to their context. He finds in the first Song the promise of a new prophet, a second Moses (pp. 367, 371), who in the second Song is brought into association with the Messiah (p. 379) and in the third is presented as a persecuted prophet (p. 487), while in the fourth he is presented in unmistakably eschatological terms as one

Only in the case of the third song do they agree in their views.

So far as the principle itself is concerned, as an *a priori* principle, I think we may agree that the interpretation may not necessarily be the same in all four songs. We ought, however, to seek some principle of modification to account for the variation, if we differently interpret the songs. This Haller did by his view that the prophet first thought of Cyrus as the Servant, and then in disappointment turned to another. They should be interpreted both in relation to one another and to their context, unless they are denied to the author of the surrounding passages.[1] The whole strength of the collective interpretation of the songs has always been in its appeal to this principle of interpretation in relation to the context. For it is undeniable that in Deutero-Isaiah as a whole Israel is the Servant. One of the writers to protest most strongly against the isolation of the Servant songs from the rest of Deutero-

whose sufferings will have expiatory power (p. 505). He further links the messianic traits of the Servant with the oracles of Is. 9 and 11 (p. 409), and so with the Davidic Messiah. H. Cazelles (*R.S.R.*, xliii, 1955, p. 49) regards the Servant as a new David, and identifies him with Immanuel of the prophecies of First Isaiah and with the child of Is. 9. A. Bentzen, on the contrary, finds in the Servant a prophetic figure, a second Moses, beside whom the Davidic figure of Is. 55: 3 ff. stands (cf. *King and Messiah*, E.Tr. 1955, p. 67). S. Mowinckel, who starts from the opposite principle, that the Servant Songs must be studied in relation to one another, without any presuppositions of any relation to anything else in Deutero-Isaiah (*He that Cometh*, E.Tr., by G. W. Anderson, 1956, p. 188), rejects the view of Bentzen (pp. 228 ff.). It should be added that A. Feuillet (*S.D.B.*, iv, 1949, cols. 709–714) thinks of the Servant as a second Moses, a prophetic rather than a royal figure, whose mission is to be contrasted with that of the Servant Israel of the surrounding passages. G. von Rad (*Theologie des Alten Testaments*, ii, 1960, p. 270) also holds that the figure of the Servant is prophetic rather than kingly, and thinks it was based on the Deuteronomic promise of a prophet like Moses (pp. 273 f.). J. Kahmann (*Biblica*, xxxii, 1951, p. 172) finds links between Is. 53 and the patriarchal history, and finds in the Servant a new Abraham through whom the covenant with the patriarchs will be brought to its full achievement. W. Zimmerli (*The Servant of God*, E.Tr., 1957, pp. 24 ff.) also maintains that the Servant's office is prophetic, and thinks the traits which suggest kingship can also be understood from a prophetic point of view, while R. Press (*Z.A.W.*, N.F. xxvi, 1955, p. 98) says the Servant is more than a prophet, and brings the Songs into relation with a series of psalms (Pss. 22, 38, 69, 102, 118). It is interesting to note that J. Lindblom, who like Tournay holds that the Songs are related to their context, draws the very different conclusion that the Servant must have been thought by the compiler to stand for Israel. He says (*Prophecy in Ancient Israel*, 1962, pp. 268 f.): "If these Songs . . . deal with an individual personality . . ., it would be impossible to explain why these Songs were placed where they now stand. . . . The matter assumes a different aspect if we admit that at least *the collector* of the Deutero-Isaianic revelations thought that the Ebed of the Songs referred to Israel in some sense. If this is true, it can easily be shown that these Songs have been appropriately placed among the poems concerning the people of Israel."

[1] J. Coppens, who denies the Songs to Deutero-Isaiah (*Sacra Pagina*, i, 1959, p. 435) thinks they are inappropriately placed and unrelated to their context (*ibid.*, and *Studia Biblica et Orientalia*, i, 1959, pp. 114–124).

Isaiah is N. H. Snaith,[1] but he does so in the interest of the collective theory. It is, however, just as undeniable that we find the language of the Servant used in relation to Cyrus, and there is much *prima facie* ground for the view that the prophet at first thought of Cyrus as the Servant.

This view finds some support from the evidence of the Cyrus Cylinder.[2] After his entry into Babylon, we read that the conqueror ascribed his success to Marduk. It is this which is believed to have disillusioned a prophet who believed he would recognize that his success was due to Yahweh. But whereas the writers referred to above think the Servant cycle was a reaction from the Cyrus period, and all dissociate the first song from Cyrus, Smith makes the first song a Cyrus song. He notes that in the second song the prophet uses of himself the same epithets which he also used of Cyrus, but, rather after the manner of Mowinckel, Smith finds no contrast here. He explains by the simple statement that the prophet's own activities and those of Cyrus have become indistinguishable to him.[3] I must confess that I am baffled to know what this means. Smith objects to the view of Wheeler Robinson on the ground that it is esoteric,[4] and "one that could not possibly occur to anyone first hearing the words." The supposition that the prophet had ceased to be able to distinguish his own activities from Cyrus's seems to me highly esoteric, and one that would be unlikely to occur either to the prophet's contemporaries or to a modern reader. Moreover the necessity to ascribe the fourth song to another hand revives the difficulty we have already seen.

Kissane's view suffers from an obscurity that remains to be noted. He holds that the prophecies of Deutero-Isaiah came in substance from the eighth-century Isaiah of Jerusalem, but were handed down in the form of oral teaching from his own day to the time of the exile. Then in the age when these prophecies were finding their fulfilment, they were given form by one who edited the first part of the book. Who, then, is the person of whom Kissane interprets the third song? I must confess that I do not know whether he thinks it was Isaiah of Jeru-

---

[1] "The So-called Servant Songs", in *E.T.*, lvi, 1944–45, pp. 79–81.

[2] See R. W. Rogers, *Cuneiform Parallels to the Old Testament*, 1912, pp. 380 ff.

[3] *Op. cit.*, pp. 174 f.

[4] *Ibid.*, p. 100. Cf. T. H. Weir's observation on Delitzsch's "pyramid" theory, which had much in common with the fluidity of Wheeler Robinson's view: "Such elastic abstractions as these, however, may look well upon paper, but it may be doubted whether the oriental mind, at any rate, is capable of such abstruse thinking. . . . Such exegesis is its own refutation" (*The Westminster Review*, clxix, 1908, p. 309).

salem, or the exilic editor. If he thinks it was Isaiah, then we know of no special sufferings which he endured, save the tradition that he was sawn asunder with a wood saw, but this could have no special significance in the age of the exile. If he thinks it was the exilic editor, then we are asked to believe that Isaiah of Jerusalem taught that a disciple of his about a century and a half after his death would endure special sufferings, and that his teaching was nowhere written down until it turned out that the man who edited his works reaped the fulfilment. And when that exilic editor wrote it down, he wrote it in the first person of himself, as though it were his own original prophecy. Surely he would have been at pains to make it clear that Isaiah had so marvellously foretold what was being fulfilled before men's eyes, instead of completely obscuring the fact. Moreover, what special significance this suffering may have had is left unexplained by Kissane, or what purpose Isaiah's long foresight of what was so empty of meaning could have served. If the suffering of the third song and that of the fourth are linked together, a clear meaning can be given to it. But if the two songs are given a wholly different reference, the third lies useless.

There have been others within our period who have similarly held that the songs should be separately interpreted, and not linked together as a series,[1] but their results diverge widely from one another, as well as from those of the writers just mentioned. In a single paragraph Bruston[2] maintained that the first song lay within a section of Deutero-Isaiah that conceived of the Servant as Israel; the second and third songs, and also the song in Is. 61, lay within a section that presented the prophet himself as the Servant; while the fourth song thought of a future personage who would continue the same work. This view, like that already noted, assumes a linear development of the prophet's thought, though it gives a place to the prophet himself in the development from Israel to the future individual that Professor North would not give. I find it hard to believe that the prophet ascribed such significance to

---

[1] Of writers before our period who took a similar way we may note J. B. Koppe (*Robert Lowth's Jesaias neu übersetzt*, ii, 1780, pp. 228 f.; iv, 1781, pp. 31, 43, 62), who held that in the first song the Servant is Cyrus, in the second and third the prophet, and in the fourth "Unser Jesu"; and T. H. Weir (*The Westminster Review*, clxix, 1908, pp. 311 f., 314), who identified the Servant in the first song with Cyrus, in the second and third with the prophet, and in the fourth with Cyrus. In this last surprising identification he agreed with Servetus. See L. I. Newman, *Jewish Influence on Christian Reform Movements*, 1925, pp. 582 ff. For older Jewish writers, who identified the Servant with Cyrus in the first of the songs, cf. H. A. Fischel, in *H.U.C.A.*, xviii, 1943–44, pp. 74 f.

[2] "Le Serviteur de l'Éternel dans l'avenir", in *Vom Alten Testament* (Marti Festschrift), 1925, pp. 37–44, esp. p. 37.

his own sufferings, or thought of the future Servant as one who should continue his own sufferings.

In one of the few papers on the subject to which Professor North makes no reference, J. D. Smart[1] argued that the Servant in Is 42 : 1–7; 49 : 1–6; 52 : 13–15 is Israel, while in Is. 50 : 4–9 and 53 : 1–12 the Servant is the prophet himself. Here again unity of interpretation is abandoned, and the fourth song is divided into two parts,[2] with a quite different reference. It is particularly interesting to note that whereas Bruston linked the second and third songs together, Smart divides them, just as Kissane does. He differs from Kissane in his treatment of the fourth song, and particularly in interpreting most of it in relation to the prophet himself, where he runs against the difficulties which have been already noted. That the sufferings of any exilic prophet were of such unique significance as to justify the terms of Is. 53 is out of the question; that any such prophet had so false a sense of his own importance that he mistakenly exaggerated the significance of his own sufferings to such a degree is an unproved and improbable assumption.

With one other writer I must conclude this section of our survey. This is F. X. Pierce,[3] who is also unnoticed in Professor North's survey. Here the Servant of the first song is held to be the ideal Israel, while in the three remaining songs he is identified with the Messiah. Pierce says:[4] "The Songs of the Servant are not one poem which has been broken up and inserted in the text haphazardly, but four distinct, vital units of the very contexts in which we find them. And we must likewise conclude in the same spirit, that there are two distinct Servants to be considered, one the ideal Israel, in the first Song, and the other the Messias, in the remaining three." With this view it will appear later that I have a measure of sympathy, though it does not seem to me wholly satisfactory, in that it does not adequately relate the two conceptions to one another, and in that it is too linear in its development from the one to the other, in so far as it does relate them.

From this review of the various individual views of the Servant

---

[1] "A New Approach to the 'Ebed-Yahweh Problem", in *E.T.*, xlv, 1933–34, pp. 168–172.

[2] H. Jahnow (*Das hebräische Leichenlied im Rahmen der Völkerdichtung*, 1923, p. 256) similarly divided the fourth song into Is. 52: 13–15 and 53-1–12, but held them to be separate but parallel pieces. N. H. Snaith [*Studies in Old Testament Prophecy* (T. H. Robinson Festschrift), 1950, p. 199] also regards Is. 52: 13–15 and 53: 1–12 as separate pieces.

[3] "The Problem of the Servant in Is. 40–66", in *The Ecclesiastical Review*, xcii, 1935, pp. 83–95. [4] *Ibid.*, p. 95.

current within our period, it is clear that no one view can claim any consensus of opinion, and while the autobiographical view has found not a little following, the stream is scarcely running in its favour. Rather is there a tendency in the direction of the messianic view. Before we conclude that this, or any other of the views at which we have looked, is the true view, however, we must examine the case for the collective view, and see what following that has commanded within our period; and to that we shall turn in our next lecture.

Lecture Two

COLLECTIVE AND FLUID THEORIES

IN the previous lecture we examined the varieties of individual interpretation of the Servant from the time when Mowinckel propounded the autobiographical view down to the present. We found that in addition to the interpretation of the songs in relation to the prophet himself the interpretation in terms of those who from the point of view of the prophet were already figures of history continued to find support. The messianic view also continued to be held, and that not alone in circles that repudiated the whole modern critical method, but also in the thought of such an admittedly critical scholar as Professor North. We also found several varieties of the view that the Servant in all the poems need not be identified with the same individual figure, but that in one song he may point to one person, and in another to another.

(1)

We must now turn to the modern forms of the collective hypothesis that flourished during the nineteenth century and that continued to be widely held between the time when Duhm gave fresh vitality to the individual interpretation and the time when Mowinckel launched the autobiographical theory. During the period under review—that is, the period following the publication of Mowinckel's monograph—few have maintained this hypothesis in its older form.[1] There have,

[1] W. Rudolph observed in 1928 that the rejection of the collective view increasingly prevailed in Germany. Cf. *Z.A.W.*, N.F. v, 1928, p. 156.

however, been at least two writers[1] who have done so, both scholars of high eminence. They are A. S. Peake[2] and A. Lods.[3] Both maintained that the Servant is Israel, and Peake stoutly defended the view that it is not the ideal Israel, but the actual, empirical Israel, though regarded from an ideal point of view.[4] Similarly, Lods held that it was the actual Israel.[5] As for the passages that appear to distinguish the Servant from Israel, such as that in the second song which points to a mission to Israel, or that in the fourth which represents him as suffering for the sins of "my people", he suggested that here the thought might perhaps move to the minority that was conscious of the mission of Israel, or more probably the passages may be corrupt.[6] He was impressed by the representation of the Servant in the fourth song as active after his death, implying therefore his resurrection. If the prophet had risen to the conception of an individual resurrection in the age when he lived, Lods thinks he would surely have formulated it more explicitly. On the other hand, the idea of a national resurrection was quite familiar and could be referred to allusively or implicitly.[7] Nevertheless, Lods urges, we should not endeavour to interpret the songs *au pied de la lettre*.

[1] Cf. also W. L. Wardle in *Peake's Commentary on the Bible*, 1920, p. 460; G. Hölscher, *Geschichte der israelitischen und jüdischen Religion*, 1922, pp. 123 f.; J. M. Powis Smith, *The Prophets and their Times*, 1925, pp. 188 f.; F. James, *Personalities of the Old Testament*, 1939, pp. 383–387; R. H. Pfeiffer, *Introduction to the Old Testament*, 1941, pp. 478 f.; P. Humbert, in *La Bible du Centenaire*, ii, 1947, pp. 389, 416. Mention should be made of H. Birkeland, who holds that whereas for the original author the Servant was individual, for the collector who placed the songs in their present context the Servant was collective (*Zum hebräischen Traditionswesen*, 1938, p. 36).

[2] *The Servant of Yahweh*, 1931, pp. 1 ff. Cf. *The Problem of Suffering in the Old Testament*, 1904, pp. 34 ff.

[3] *Les Prophètes d'Israël*, 1935, pp. 275–280 (E.Tr., 1937, pp. 244–249). Cf. also the same author's *Histoire de la littérature hébraïque et juive*, 1950, pp. 472 ff.

[4] *The Servant of Yahweh*, p. 67. Cf. also *The People and the Book* (ed. by A. S. Peake), 1925, p. 287 n.

[5] H. Friedlaender (*Der Knecht Gottes, Schicksal, Aufgabe, Trost*, 1947) identifies the Servant with Israel, and sets him in a background of Old Testament passages, commencing with Exod. 19: 2–8, and including passages in Jeremiah and in Deutero-Isaiah other than the Servant songs. The songs proper are delimited as follows: Is. 42: 1–9; 49: 1–13; 50: 4–9; 50: 10–51: 8; 52: 13–53: 12. S. H. Blank (*Prophetic Faith in Isaiah*, 1958, pp. 77 ff.) identifies the Servant with Israel, and so P. A. H. de Boer [*Second Isaiah's Message* (O.T.S., xi), 1956, p. 115]. H. G. May (*Z.A.W.*, N.F. xxv, 1954, pp. 236–244) says the collective view of the Songs is the most plausible (p. 237), and interprets the fourth Song as collective (p. 238). He brings the Songs into comparison with Ps. 44 (pp. 241 ff.).

[6] *Op. cit.*, p. 277 (E.Tr., p. 246).

[7] *Ibid.*, p. 276 (E.Tr., p. 245); also *Histoire de la littérature hébraïque et juive*, 1950, p. 476. Cf. K. Budde, *A.J.Th.*, iii, 1899, p. 504; *Die sogenannten Ebed-Jahwe-Lieder*, 1900, p. 6; K. Marti, *Das Buch Jesaja*, 1900, p. 345.

Some at least of their traits should be recognized to be images of the sufferings of the Servant and not precise descriptions.

In a paper read to the Society for Old Testament Study,[1] Professor Lindblom presented what appears to be a variety of this view. He holds that the songs are to be related to their context and not merely to one another, and that we have in the context indications of the interpretation. The first song consists of Is. 42 : 1–4, but the immediately following verses offer the interpretation in the form of an oracle. Similarly the second song, which he limits to Is. 49 : 1–6, is followed by an oracular interpretation. The fourth song he limits to Is. 53 : 2–12,[2] but holds that the preceding verses are related to it, though standing outside it.[3] The Servant in all the songs he finds to be an allegorical figure, whose interpretation is not to be pressed in all details.[4] In the second and third songs the prophet may have drawn his terms in part from his own sufferings, but he did not think of himself as the Servant. It is, indeed, as foolish to ask "Who is the Servant?" as to ask "Who is the Prodigal

[1] At its meeting held at King's College Hostel, London, in January, 1950. This paper has been published in an expanded form under the title *The Servant Songs in Deutero-Isaiah*, 1951. Cf. also *Prophecy in Ancient Israel*, 1962, pp. 268 ff. Cf. further H. Kruse, *Verbum Domini*, xxx, 1952, pp. 341–347; J. Muilenburg, *J.B.L.*, lxxi, 1952, pp. 259–261.

[2] Lindblom's view as to the delimitation of the songs is closely similar to that of Schian. See above, p. 5 n. 2

[3] The difficulty of determining the end of the first three songs is manifest from the variety of views which have been held. Their beginning is generally agreed, and they can be separated from what precedes without uncertainty. But the verses that follow Duhm's first three songs have been included by many in the songs and excluded by others. That they have some relation to the songs seems clear, yet their introduction by the oracular formula separates them from the songs. It would seem probable that the writer of these verses was acquainted with the songs, whether he was himself their author or not. While I do not here discuss the question whether Deutero-Isaiah is the author of the songs, I may say that I hold the view of common authorship. Cf. W. E. Barnes, *J.T.S.*, xxxii, 1931, p. 33, where it is observed that there is no obvious boundary rounding off the first three songs; also I. Engnell, *B.J.R.L.*, xxxi, 1948, p. 62, who says: "The very difficulties in the attempts at distinguishing the songs as literary units and the very different results should be sufficient evidence for the fact that they are from the first at home in their environment." W. F. Lofthouse, who does not think the songs were by the author of the context, notes the same feature but draws a different conclusion from it. He says (*J.T.S.*, xlviii, 1947, p. 171): "The beginning of each is marked by a definite break with what immediately precedes, but an apparent attempt, in the case of I, II, and III, to fit them in with what follows makes the end of each somewhat doubtful." Cf. T. H. Robinson, *Prophecy and the Prophets in Ancient Israel*, 1923, p. 168: "Certain it is that whilst none of them is closely attached to what precedes it, each of them, except the last, runs smoothly—one might almost say dissolves—into what follows."

[4] Cf. *Acta Academiæ Aboensis*, Humaniora, xviii (Hyllningsskrift tillägnad Rolf Pipping), 1949, p. 223, where Lindblom poses the question whether the Servant is to be thought of as a figure of history or as an ideal figure.

Son?"[1] The Servant embodies an idea, and that idea is the mission of Israel to the world.[2]

L. Rignell, who follows Lindblom in dividing the fourth Song into a prophecy with commentary,[3] identifies the Servant with Israel personified,[4] but says "The prophet makes no distinction between that Israel which lives in the present and that Israel which includes the past as well as the future generations."[5] Nevertheless he holds that even in the fourth Song he is thinking of the generation which endured the plague and distress of the Babylonian captivity.[6]

The view that the Servant is an Israel within Israel has also not been unrepresented. This is the view still taken by E. König[7] and I. G. Matthews.[8] B. D. Eerdmans[9] identified the Servant with the Chasi-

---

[1] Cf. S. A. Cook, *C.A.H.*, iii, 1925, p. 492: "All this . . . seems . . . to remove the problem of the Servant's identity from the sphere of strictly historical inquiry."

[2] Cf. P. Volz, *Beiträge zur alttestamentlichen Wissenschaft* (Budde Festschrift), 1920, p. 184. Cf. also T. H. Robinson, *op. cit.*, p. 169: "The whole picture is no more that of an actual historical character than was Glaucon's sketch of the perfectly just man in Plato's *Republic*. What is brought before our eyes is the character of the ideal slave of Yahweh, of the man who is utterly and wholly devoted to his Divine Master."

[3] Cf. *V.T.*, iii, 1953, p. 90.

[4] Cf. *A Study of Isaiah Ch. 40–55*, 1956, pp. 31, 59, 68, 78.

[5] *V.T.*, iii, 1953, p. 88.　　　　　[6] *Ibid.*

[7] *Das Buch Jesaja*, 1926, pp. 444 ff. Cf. also "Die Ebed-Jahwe-Frage und die Hermeneutik", in *Z.A.W.*, N.F. vi, 1929, pp. 255 f., where he replies to Staerk and Rudolph. Of König's *Das Buch Jesaja* Mowinckel observes: "Sein Stil und seine Dartsellungsform gehören zu den schwierigsten, die man überhaupt lesen kann, und bedürften eigentlich eines authentischen Kommentars in einer nicht-delphischen Sprache" (*Acta Orientalia*, xvi, 1938, p. 15).

[8] *The Religious Pilgrimage of Israel*, 1947, pp. 174 ff. J. N. Schofield also adopts this view, but finds elements derived from past individual experience and from Nature woven into the conception. He says (*The Religious Background of the Bible*, 1944, pp. 159 f.): "Features taken from the characters of previous religious leaders, from the history of his nation, and from the writer's own experience, have been welded together to make a vivid personification of what Isaiah had called the righteous remnant. Humble and unobtrusive, the Servant carries the knowledge of Israel's God to the Gentiles . . . and though in the end he is killed . . . he will bear the sins of those who slay him, and, like the plants that every year die at summer time, he will rise again in ever greater glory." O. J. Baab, *The Theology of the Old Testament*, 1949, p. 197, says: "Viewed as the redeemed, chastened, and spiritualized Jewish community within the larger community of exiles, the Servant exemplifies to the world his *raison d'être*—the furtherance of the rule of God over the lives of men." P. A. H. de Boer similarly identifies the Servant with the true Israel, or the Remnant. He says (*O.T.S.*, iii, 1943, p. 196): "De '*ebed* is het 'ware Israël', de rest, die zich in het ordeel bekeerd heeft en die trouw betoont aan Jhwh, wardoor zij voor anderen heil bewerkt." Miss A. E. Skemp (*E.T.*, xliv, 1932–33, pp. 94 f.) combined the suggestion that the Servant is a personification of the Remnant with the suggestion that the Immanuel of Is. 7: 14 is a similar personification, and so proposed to see in the Servant Immanuel coming to his full stature.

[9] *The Religion of Israel*, 1947, pp. 216 f. Cf. *O.T.S.*, i, 1941–42, pp. 255 ff.

dim. While this is superficially in agreement with the view which R. H. Kennett[1] advanced many years ago, it is really not quite the same, since Eerdmans does not ascribe the composition of the songs to the Maccabaean age or think of the Chasidim of that period. He holds that they were to be found under this name even in the pre-exilic period, and therefore long before the time of Deutero-Isaiah.[2]

Other writers, while holding that if the songs are by the author of Deutero-Isaiah the presumption is that he will mean the same thing by the Servant of Yahweh within the songs and without, yet recognize a measure of fluidity in the meaning of the term. I may illustrate simply what I mean by the word "church". Here is a modern word with much fluidity. We use it of the building in which men worship, of the local congregation of Christians, of the totality of Christians of a particular variety—the Anglican or the Roman church—or we use it of the church universal. These meanings are all clearly distinguishable, yet they are all connected with one another, and we have not a purely fortuitous and arbitrary collection of meanings, as we have, say, with the word *cipher*, where the meanings *secret code* and *the figure* o have nothing in common and probably have quite independent derivations,[3] or the word *match*, where two separate derivations have again led to a common word in English. In the same way, then, as in the case of the word *church*, we need not be surprised if we find a variety of related meanings attaching to the word Servant, yet meanings which are distinct from one another and between which there may be some fluidity.[4] But it must in that case be fluidity, and the meaning must be able to flow understandably from one idea to another.

C. C. Torrey, that veteran of Old Testament scholarship who continued to write vigorously at an age when most are content to rest on their laurels, published some years ago his revolutionary work on Deutero-Isaiah,[5] in which he started from the same principle as Kissane

[1] *The "Servant of the Lord"*, 1911. Cf. the same writer's *The Composition of the Book of Isaiah*, 1910, p. 72. For a criticism of Kennett's view, cf. C. F. Burney, *C.Q.R.*, lxxv, 1912–13, pp. 125 ff.

[2] Cf. "The Chasidim", in *O.T.S.*, i, 1941–42, pp. 176 ff.

[3] Cf. my paper, "The Semitic Sources of 'Cipher' and its Cognates" in *Werden und Wesen des Alten Testaments* (ed. by J. Hempel), 1936, pp. 175–190.

[4] For a fluid view of the Servant, cf., earlier, I. Loeb, *La littérature des pauvres dans la Bible*, 1892. On this see below, p. 56, n. 2.

[5] *The Second Isaiah*, 1928. With Torrey's treatment of Is. 40–66 as a unity (Torrey also combines 34 f. with this), cf. L. Glahn and L. Köhler, *Der Prophet der Heimkehr*, 1934, and L. Glahn, "Quelques remarques sur la question du Trito-Ésaïe et son état actuel", in *R.H.P.R.*, xviii, 1938, pp. 34 ff. But whereas Torrey transferred this work to a date *circa* 400 B.C., Glahn stands firmly for the sixth-century date of this prophet.

and Sidney Smith, holding that the songs must be related to their context. That context leads him to the view[1] that the Servant is always the personified nation Israel, or Israel's representative. The particular representative varies in different contexts, but is always an individual considered not merely as an individual, but as the representative of the nation. The representative may be Abraham, Jacob, or the future Messiah. Similarly, when the Servant is the personification of the nation, it may be either the nation in the whole course of its history, or the nation of the prophet's own day, or the Israel within Israel. In essence this agrees with the view which is presented by Wheeler Robinson and Eissfeldt, with a close study of Hebrew thought processes. But Torrey's applications of the view would not be shared by them. For, surprisingly enough, he gives a collective interpretation to the fourth song, and an individual messianic interpretation to the first two songs. To most interpreters, if any of the songs has a messianic reference it is the fourth, and if any has a collective reference it is the first.

H. Wheeler Robinson[2] and O. Eissfeldt[3] independently travelled along similar lines in approaching the problem. Both[4] based themselves on the Lévy-Bruhl[5] and Durkheim[6] ideas on primitive psychology as applied to Hebrew psychology. It is sometimes supposed that their view stands or falls with the view of the French school on primitive psychology, but this is not quite true.[7] Their evidence was found in the Old Testament, and is quite independent of Lévy-Bruhl and Durkheim, and it must really be judged by its relevance to Old Testament evidence rather than by the soundness of Lévy-Bruhl's and Durkheim's interpretation of the thought forms of primitive peoples. For it is, in any case, quite certain that the Israelites were not primitive people in the technical sense of that term.[8]

Wheeler Robinson shows that in Old Testament thought there is a frequent transition from the individual to the corporate that is foreign

[1] Ibid., pp. 135 ff.   [2] The Cross of the Servant, 1926.
[3] Der Gottesknecht bei Deuterojesaja, 1933; or in English translation, without the notes, "The Ebed-Jahwe in Isaiah 40–55", in E.T., xliv, 1932–33, pp. 261–286. Cf. also N. Johansson, Parakletoi, 1940, pp. 49 ff. For a criticism of Eissfeldt's view cf. K. Budde, Th.L.Z., lviii, 1933, cols. 323 ff., or S. Mowinckel, Acta Orientalia, xvi, 1938, pp. 29 f.
[4] Cf. Eissfeldt, Der Gottesknecht bei Deuterojesaja, pp. 13 f., note; and Wheeler Robinson, "The Hebrew Conception of Corporate Personality", in Werden und Wesen des Alten Testaments (ed. by J. Hempel), 1936, pp. 49–62, esp. p. 53.
[5] Cf. How Natives Think, E.Tr., 1926.
[6] Cf. The Elementary Forms of the Religious Life, E.Tr., 1915.
[7] Cf. A. R. Johnson, The Vitality of the Individual in the Thought of Ancient Israel, 1949, p. 7.
[8] Cf. A. R. Johnson, ibid.

to our thought,[1] but that belongs to the concept of what he calls "corporate personality". He was not the first scholar to call attention to this, but amongst English-speaking persons his name is most closely associated with it, and he has been the most persistent advocate of this key to much Old Testament thought. "The whole group", he says, "including its past, present and future members, might function as a single individual through any one of those members conceived as representatives of it."[2] This gives rise to an oscillation in speech between the group and the individual, which does not rest on an antithesis between the individual and the group, but on an identification of the individual with the group which he represents. Hence, in discussing the Servant songs, Wheeler Robinson says: "The central issue, that between a collective and an individualistic interpretation, is being argued on an antithesis true to modern, but false to ancient modes of thought."[3] Or again: "The Hebrew conception of corporate personality can reconcile both, and pass without explanation or explicit indication from one to the other, in a fluidity of transition which seems to us unnatural. In the light of this conception the Servant can be both the prophet himself as representative of the nation, and the nation whose proper mission is actually being fulfilled only by the prophet and that group of followers who may share his views."[4]

In the light of this, we are free to recognize that there are some features in the Servant songs which clearly suggest that the Servant stands for the nation Israel, and also to recognize that there are other elements which equally clearly suggest that it is an actual individual which is in mind.[5] There is no need to quibble at the indication that

---

[1] *Loc. cit.*, pp. 49 ff. See also his essays on "The Social Life of the Psalmists", in *The Psalmists*, ed. by D. C. Simpson, 1926, pp. 67–86, esp. pp. 82 ff., and on "Hebrew Psychology", in *The People and the Book*, ed. by A. S. Peake, 1925, pp. 353–382, esp. pp. 375 ff. Cf. also J. Pedersen, *Israel, I–II*, 1926, pp. 275 ff.; S. A. Cook, *Cambridge Ancient History*, iii, 1925, p. 493; *The Old Testament: a Reinterpretation*, 1936, pp. 164 f.; S. Mowinckel, *The Psalms in Israel's Worship*, E.Tr. by D. R. Ap-Thomas, ii, 1963, pp. 42 ff.

[2] *Werden und Wesen*, p. 49.   [3] *Ibid.*, p. 58.

[4] *Ibid.*, p. 59. Cf. the same writer's *The Old Testament: its Making and Meaning*, 1937, pp. 110 f.

[5] Cf. K. H. Fahlgren, *Ṣᵉdāḳā*, 1932, p. 234; L. Gautier, *Introduction à l'Ancien Testament*, ii, 1914, reprinted 1939, pp. 362, 364 f., 365 ff. Cf. also W. F. Albright, *From the Stone Age to Christianity*, 2nd ed., 1946, p. 255 (= *Von der Steinzeit zum Christentum*, 1949, pp. 330 f.), where the author thinks the concept of the Servant is older than Deutero-Isaiah and is differently treated in the different poems. The fluidity of his interpretation is expressed in the following words: "The Servant is the people of Israel, which suffers poignantly in exile and affliction: he is also the pious individual who atones for the sins of the many by his uncomplaining agony; he is finally the coming Saviour of Israel." N. Dahl (*Das Volk Gottes*, 1941, p. 42) also finds fluidity in the conception of the Servant.

the second song ascribes to the Servant a mission to Israel, and Wheeler Robinson is so far from wishing to base himself on the occurrence of the word *Israel* in Is. 49 : 3 that he is prepared to let it go. I think, as I have said, that it is unsound textual criticism to cut it out, but I would agree that the collective interpretation of the Servant does not need to base itself on this word.

It will be seen that though to a point Wheeler Robinson is to be classed with the collective theorists, he is also to be classed with the individual theorists. "There is a fluidity of conception," he says, "a possibility of swift transition from the one to the many, and *vice versa*, to which our thought and language have no real parallel."[1] It is therefore possible for him to allow a measure of validity to the view of Mowinckel.[2] He says: "We are to think of the prophet's consciousness as capable of a systole and diastole, an ebb and flow, so that though he utters his own experience in the service of Yahweh, it is always with the sense implicit or explicit that these things are true of all the devout disciples of Yahweh, and that *they* are Israel. We cannot, however, be true to his conception as a whole without saying that for him the Servant *is* Israel."[3]

While, as will be seen, I have much in common with this view, I am not persuaded that the fluidity of the prophet's thought was between Israel and himself, passing through the thought of the devout

---

[1] *The Cross of the Servant*, pp. 33 f.

[2] Cf. M. Buber, *The Prophetic Faith*, 1949, p. 230: "It can never be proved that these two, the servant and his announcer, are one; but many sayings in the two songs written in the first person tell us the 'Deutero-Isaiah' felt himself as one of the figurations of the servant, and that he felt himself as the one among them before whom was uncovered the mystery of the servant's being concealed and of his future being revealed. We may assume that, after he had despaired of Cyrus, he recognized his own being as one of the temporal elements in the way of the person for whom the very work of the redemption of world history was reserved." Buber differs from Wheeler Robinson, however, in that while he assumes a fluidity in the thought of the writer, he excludes the collective view entirely. He says (p. 229): "The substance of the servant is more than a single human person without, however, having a corporate character." For Buber's view of the Servant cf. also *De godsdiensten der wereld*, i, 2nd ed., 1948, pp. 393 ff.

[3] *Op. cit.* p. 36. The view of Wheeler Robinson is followed by C. Ryder Smith, *The Biblical Doctrine of Salvation*, 1941, p. 72, and J. Paterson, *The Goodly Fellowship of the Prophets*, 1948, pp. 200 ff. Other holders of fluid views include J. Bright (*The Kingdom of God*, 1953, pp. 153 f.); E. Jacob (*Theology of the Old Testament*, E.Tr., by A. W. Heathcote and P. J. Allcock, 1958, pp. 340 f.); B. W. Anderson (*Understanding the Old Testament*, 1957, pp. 420 f.); A. Gelin (in *Introduction à la Bible*, Ancien Testament, ed. by A. Robert and A. Feuillet, 1957, pp. 555–560); N. K. Gottwald (*A Light to the Nations*, 1959, pp. 425 f.); J. W. L. Hoad (*The New Bible Dictionary*, ed. by J. D. Douglas, 1962, p. 1166); W. Harrelson (in Manson's *Companion to the Bible*, 2nd ed., edited by H. H. Rowley, 1963, p. 362).

in Israel. I think it included all of these in some measure, but also passed beyond them. I do not think he can have been thinking of himself in the fourth song, and as little can the collective view satisfy in relation to that song. That the fourth song found its perfect expression in the person and work of our Lord Wheeler Robinson agrees, as so many other writers of almost all schools have allowed. But I find it hard to think that that expression corresponded to the prophet's thought of himself, and as hard to eliminate the individual element of the fluidity from this song, where the individual element seems the strongest.

Eissfeldt, while having much in common with Wheeler Robinson, puts more emphasis on the collective side of the fluidity.[1] He delimits the first song as Is. 42 : 1–7,[2] whereas Wheeler Robinson delimited it as Duhm had done as Is. 42 : 1–4. Otherwise, however, the two views, while independently reached, have striking points of similarity. Eissfeldt thinks the balance of evidence suggests that the songs are by the author of the surrounding passages, and observes that until clear evidence against this is provided, "the assumption that the Servant Songs were the work of Deutero-Isaiah, and that the figure of the Ebed therein is to be understood as elsewhere in Deutero-Isaiah, has the right of precedence on its side."[3] Nevertheless, the personification of Israel is carried to an exaggerated extent, though not to an impossible extent, and therefore we are driven to recognize the fluidity of the concept of the Servant, which can be defined neither in purely collective nor in purely individual terms. Eissfeldt thinks that the parallels

[1] L. M. von Pákozdy is much influenced by the view of Eissfeldt. Cf. *Deuterojesaanische Studien*, i, 1940, pp. 83 f., and ii, 1942, pp. 243 ff. R. Marcus (*H.T.R.*, xxx, 1937, pp. 249 f.) commends Eissfeldt's presentation of the case for the shifting aspects of the Servant as a collective term, and observes that the conception of the Servant in the first Song is closer to that found in Deutero-Isaiah outside the Songs than it is to that of the last Song.

[2] *Der Gottesknecht bei Deuterojesaja*, p. 3; *E.T.*, *loc. cit.*, p. 261a.

[3] *E.T.*, *loc. cit.*, p. 264b. Cf. *Der Gottesknecht bei Deuterojesaja*, p. 12. Cf. M. Burrows, *An Outline of Biblical Theology*, 1946, p. 85: "The burden of proof is on those who maintain that the Servant of the Songs, including ch. 53, means anything else than Israel." Similarly N. H. Snaith, in *Studies in Old Testament Prophecy* (T. H. Robinson Festschrift), 1950, p. 188. In this article (pp. 187–200) Snaith argues against the universalistic outlook of Deutero-Isaiah and maintains that he was uniformly nationalistic in his thought. In this he is followed by P. A. H. de Boer, *Second Isaiah's Message* (*O.T.S.*, xi), 1956, pp. 80 ff., esp. pp. 89 f. Th. C. Vriezen (*An Outline of Old Testament Theology*, E.Tr., 1958, p. 362) rejects this view, saying: "This view does not, however, do full justice to Is. xlix. 5–6, where, for example, the deliverance of Israel is represented as an easy task in comparison with the greater and ultimate task that Israel should become a light to the Gentiles so that God's salvation might spread as far as the ends of the earth."

between the Servant and Jeremiah, which have led some to identify the Servant with Jeremiah, show how the prophet can have drawn on individual experience in conceiving the figure of the Servant.[1] Nevertheless, his view is predominantly a collective view, and Smart, in an article to which reference has already been made, imagined that Eissfeldt had "delivered a blow to the theory of an individual Servant . . . from which it is not likely to recover".[2]

(2)

Before I return to present my own modification of this view, I want to turn to some recent Scandinavian views in which we find a combination of elements of the views so far examined, together with some new emphases.[3]

In an important article H. S. Nyberg[4] stressed a temporal fluidity, as well as a fluidity as between the individual and the collective. He also found a number of streams of influence merging in the conception of the Servant. He maintained that the Servant belongs to the past, the present, and the future, and that elements derived from the Tammuz liturgy and from Israelite history, elements running back to the Ras Shamra ritual and having roots in Canaanite practice, were all fused in the concept. So far as the Israelite elements were concerned he found links with the patriarchs, with Moses, with David, and with the prophets.[5] He did not interpret the Servant in terms of the Messiah, however, or suppose that the songs were concerned with an actual king, since they were not written until the time of the exile, when Israel had no king.[6]

---

[1] *Der Gottesknecht bei Deuterojesaja*, p. 16; *E.T.*, *loc. cit.*, p. 265a.

[2] *E.T.*, xlv, 1933–34, p. 168a. With this contrast the observation of H. W. Wolff, *Jesaja 53 im Urchristentum*, 1942, p. 33: "Die Gründe, die für die Deutung auf das Volk Israel angeführt worden sind, fielen nach und nach dahin" (2nd ed., 1950, p. 35).

[3] Cf. C. R. North, "The Suffering Servant: Current Scandinavian Discussions", in *Scottish Journal of Theology*, iii, 1950, pp. 363–379.

[4] "Smärtornas man", in *S.E.Å.*, vii, 1942, pp. 5–82. Cf. the review by O. Eissfeldt in *Th.L.Z.*, lxviii, 1943, cols. 275 ff. (republished in Eissfeldt's *Kleine Schriften*, ii, 1963, pp. 445 ff.). For a summary of Nyberg's article in English, cf. C. R. North, *The Suffering Servant in Deutero-Isaiah*, pp. 220 ff. (2nd ed., 1956, pp. 223 ff.), and *Scottish Journal of Theology*, iii, 1950, pp. 366 ff., and A. Bentzen, *Introduction to the Old Testament*, ii, 1948, pp. 111 f. Cf. the view of W. A. Irwin, in Powis Smith-Irwin, *The Prophets and their Times*, 2nd ed., 1941, pp. 228 ff.

[5] Cf. the view of Böhl, noted above, p. 27.

[6] Cf. I. Engnell's citation of his view, without reference, but apparently from a source later than the above-mentioned article, in *B.J.R.L.*, xxxi, 1948, p. 93 n.

Nyberg was not the first to find points of connexion with Ras Shamra. Mowinckel[1] had already called attention to these, and Engnell[2] and Hyatt[3] did so somewhat later and independently. Others, too, as has been already said, claimed points of connexion with the Tammuz cult. I find it hard to suppose that Deutero-Isaiah took his material directly from the Tammuz cult as he saw it in Babylonia, since his attitude to Babylonian religion was one of scorn and contempt, though I see no reason why his language should not have points of connexion with Israelite cultic usage, running far back into the past, and embodying elements which once belonged to non-Israelite practice.[4] In particular, there is no reason why he should not use language which had been associated with the royal cultic acts. That there was no king at the moment would be no obstacle to this, since the memory of the kingship and of its ritual could hardly have passed away, and the prophet was not describing any actual king, but using the language to portray a figure who was other than a historical king.[5] Similarly, I see no reason to question that he could portray the Servant in terms that

---

[1] "Til uttrykket 'Jahvæs tjener' ", in Nor.T.T., xliii, 1942, pp. 24–26. Cf. also W. A. Irwin, in Powis Smith-Irwin, The Prophets and their Times, 2nd ed., 1941, pp. 234 f.

[2] Studies in Divine Kingship in the Ancient Near East, 1943, pp. 119 n., 130 n., 152 n., 170 n.

[3] "The Sources of the Suffering Servant Idea", in J.N.E.S., iii, 1943, pp. 79–86, esp. pp. 83 ff.

[4] Engnell makes it clear that despite his emphasis on the links with Tammuz ritual he does not think of any direct borrowing from Babylonia, but of influence which has come through a long Israelite tradition. He says (B.J.R.L., xxxi, 1948, p. 80): "It is not a question of a superficial influence from outside, from Babylonia, but of an idea autochthonic with the western Semites, too, inherently bound up with the sacred kingship pattern in Canaan, and taken over there by Israel." That much in Israel's ritual had a background of Canaanite and Semitic tradition is widely recognized, though I think it probable that it was not a simple borrowing, but a transformation of the borrowed elements, to make them the vehicle of Israel's religion. Cf. J. Pedersen (Israel III–IV, 1940, p. 709): "The parallels from foreign peoples cannot quite be made to fit Israel." I am not therefore persuaded that in Israel's ritual the dying and rising god has any place, though language which once may have had reference to that god could well have survived. Nor would I deny that some of Israel's kings may have followed Canaanite and other cultic rites, as they are declared in the Old Testament to have done. But the fact that they are said to have done this would seem to imply some real difference between the Israelite ritual and the Canaanite. Cf. J. Pedersen (ibid., p. 472): "The sexual rites constantly occurred in connexion with the lamentation over the dying God, which the Israelites, with their traditions from the nomadic period, always regarded as militating against the nature of their God. The utterances of the prophets would seem to indicate, however, that the sexual cult in itself struck them as un-Israelitish, and inimical to their traditions." We should neither over-emphasize the points of contact to the extent of obscuring the differences, nor be unwilling to allow points of contact in our desire to stress the differences.

[5] Cf. E. Jacob, Theology of the Old Testament, E.Tr., 1958, pp. 339 f.

were derived in part from the experience of Jeremiah or of another, or that he should think of the Servant as a new Moses. But I am persuaded that if his language was drawn from the history or cult of the past,[1] his thought was not of any contemporary individual, or of any individual of the past.[2]

Ivan Engnell, in an important paper which is available in English[3] as well as in Swedish,[4] has taken up some of the ideas of Nyberg and of others, and developed them in a way quite different from that of Nyberg. He too emphasizes the variety of strands combined in the concept of the Servant, and in particular the Tammuz strands and those that have links with Ras Shamra cultic usage. But more especially he stresses the royal ideology of the songs,[5] and claims that here we have a prophetic remodelling of a liturgical composition belonging to the annual festival.[6] In that festival he finds evidence of the ritual suffering of the king, of which we have traces in the Psalter in what he calls the "royal passion psalms". He thus links the songs with the conception of the dying and rising god[7] found in the Tammuz worship and in Ras Shamra. It may be noted in passing that Gordon[8] has stated that he fails

---

[1] Cf. J. Muilenburg, I.B., v, 1956, p. 412a: "That the prophet is influenced by the prevailing modes of Near Eastern thinking is highly probable. . . . The language may well · have been influenced by the liturgies of the Near East."

[2] E. J. Young has underlined the profound differences between his thought and that of the Ras Shamra texts. Cf. "The Origin of the Suffering Servant Idea", in *Westminster Theological Journal*, xiii, 1950–51, pp. 19–33.

[3] "The 'Ebed Yahweh Songs and the Suffering Messiah, in 'Deutero-Isaiah' ", in B.J.R.L., xxxi, 1948, pp. 54–93. This is a revised and expanded form of the Swedish article mentioned in the following note. Mowinckel (*He that Cometh*, E.Tr., 1956, pp. 224 ff.) offers criticism of Engnell's view.

[4] "Till frågan om Ebed Jahve-sångerna och den lidande Messias hos 'Deutero-jesaja' ", in S.E.Å., x, 1945, pp. 31–65.

[5] Cf. B.J.R.L., xxxi, 1948, pp. 56, 69. Engnell claims (*ibid.*, pp. 68 n., 69 n.) that Servant is a royal title. While it may be used of a king, it is scarcely an indication of a king, since the word *'ebhedh* has so many other uses. W. W. von Baudissin studied the religious use of the term in "Zur Entwicklung des Gebrauchs von 'ebed in religiösem Sinne", in *Beiträge zur alttestamentlichen Wissenschaft* (Budde Festschrift), 1920, pp. 1 ff. Cf. also S. A. Cook, C.A.H., iii, 1925, p. 490; and, above all, C. Lindhagen, *The Servant Motif in the Old Testament*, 1950.

[6] *Ibid.*, pp. 56 f.

[7] Cf. H. Jahnow, *Das hebräische Leichenlied im Rahmen der Völkerdichtung*, 1923, pp. 260 f.; G. H. Dix, J.T.S., xxvi, 1925, pp. 252 f.; W. A. Irwin, in Powis Smith-Irwin, *The Prophets and their Times*, 2nd ed., 1941, pp. 234 f.; S. Mowinckel, *De senere profeter*, 1944, p. 197.

[8] *Ugaritic Literature*, 1949, pp. 3 f. Cf. the note of caution in O. Eissfeldt, Th.L.Z., lxviii, 1943, col. 279. On the other hand, S. H. Hooke (*The Origins of Early Semitic Ritual*, 1938, p. 38) says this conception is characteristic of the myth and ritual of Ras Shamra.

to find any evidence of the dying and rising god in the Ras Shamra texts. Returning to Engnell, however, it is to be observed that he does not identify the Servant with the king or with a substitute for the god in the cultic acts, but holds that he is the Messiah depicted in these categories.[1]

So far it is possible to go at least part of the way with Engnell. Others have stressed the trait of kingship[2] in the Servant songs, and Professor A. R. Johnson in an oft-cited article noted passages in the Psalms in which the king is presented as humiliated.[3] Engnell observes[4] that he did not carry the link to the Servant songs or the Tammuz liturgies. Professor Johnson does not find evidence of the dying and rising god in Israelite ritual,[5] though he finds evidence of an Israelite ritual in which the king is annually delivered from death in the ritual combat.[6] So far as the Servant songs are concerned, he must clearly have had them in mind, since he referred to the Davidic king as the "Servant of

[1] B.J.R.L., loc. cit., p. 57. Cf. G. Widengren, J.S.S., ii, 1957, pp. 26 f.

[2] Cf. H. S. Nyberg, S.E.Å., vii, 1942, pp. 66 f.; G. Widengren, Religion och Bibel, ii, 1943, p. 71; G. Östborn, Tōrā in the Old Testament, 1945, pp. 56 ff.; H. Ringgren, in Ny Kyrklig Tidskrift, xviii, 1949, pp. 74 f., Z.A.W., N.F. xxiii, 1952, pp. 120–147, and Messias konungen, 1954 (E. Tr., The Messiah in the Old Testament, 1956); J. Coppens, in Pro regno pro sanctuario, 1950, pp. 116 f.=Nieuw Licht over de Ebed-Jahweh-Liederen, 1950, pp. 4 f., 13; O. Kaiser, Der königliche Knecht, 1959, pp. 18, 64 f.; W. Eichrodt, Theology of the Old Testament, E. Tr. by J. A. Baker, i, 1961, p. 483 n.; A. S. Kapelrud, Et folk på hjemferd, 1964, pp. 89 ff. Cf., however, S. Mowinckel, "Urmensch und 'Königs-ideologie' ", in Studia Theologica, ii, 1949, pp. 71 ff., for some criticism of this view. In He that Cometh, pp. 219 ff., Mowinckel denies that there are kingly traits in the Servant and notes that no political element enters into the concept of his work (p. 247). He maintains that he was a prophetic figure (pp. 218, 250, 254). In a series of publications V. de Leeuw has argued for the royal character of the Servant. Cf. De Koninklijke Verklaring van de Ebed-Jahweh-Zangen (Analecta Lovaniensia Biblica et Orientalia, Series II, Fasc. 33), 1952; "Le Serviteur de Jahvé; Figure royale ou prophétique", in L'Attente du Messie (Recherches Bibliques), 1954, pp. 51–56; De Ebed Jahweh-Profetieën, 1956. De Leeuw identifies the Servant with the Davidic Messiah; cf. L'Attente du Messie, p. 56, and De Ebed Jahweh-Profetieën, p. 353: "Les chants de l'Ebed envisagent pour l'avenir la venue d'un descendant idéal de la lignée davidique".

[3] "The Rôle of the King in the Jerusalem Cultus", in The Labyrinth, ed. by S. H. Hooke, 1935, pp. 73–111, esp. pp. 99 f. Cf. also Sacral Kingship in Ancient Israel, 1955, pp. 22 f.; also "Hebrew Conceptions of Kingship", in Myth, Ritual and Kingship, ed. by S. H. Hooke, 1958, pp. 204–235.

[4] B.J.R.L., loc. cit., p. 56 n.

[5] So, too, F. F. Hvidberg, who says (Weeping and Laughter in the Old Testament, 1962, p. 136=Graad og Latter i det Gamle Testamente, 1938, p. 118): "In the Old Testament Yahweh nowhere appears as a dying and rising deity." Cf. J. Pedersen, Israel III–IV, 1940, p. 442: "The idea of a dying and resurrected God entertained by agricultural peoples was incompatible with the nature of Yahweh."

[6] Cf. loc. cit., pp. 93 f.

Jahweh", and as the "Suffering Servant".[1] He would probably be willing to allow that the terminology of the Servant songs has been influenced by that of the ritual reflected in a number of Psalms. I think it is probable that he would hold—as seems to me most likely—that whatever cultic usages had supplied the author of the songs with ideas or terms, they had reached him through Israelite and Yahwistic sources, however much they might have been modelled on older usages far back in the past.[2]

Most significant, however, is Engnell's recognition that in so far as the Servant is an individual he is a figure of the future.[3] I say in so far as the Servant is an individual, for he recognizes an oscillation between the individual and the collective.[4] The Servant is described in kingly terms, but he finds him to be essentially a messianic figure. Engnell does not regard the Servant as a direct prediction of our Lord,[5] but he brings him into direct association with the Davidic Messiah of other passages,[6] and identifies the Davidic Messiah and the Suffering Messiah within the Old Testament. Here I am unwilling to go quite so far. The passages concerning the Davidic Messiah think of him only as ruling, though always as ruling in righteousness and not merely subduing to his own will; in the case of the Suffering Servant, such kingly

[1] Ibid., p. 100; also p. 111. G. Widengren rightly perceived this (Religionens värld, 1945, p. 223 n.), but was taken to task for this by Engnell (S.E.Å., x, 1945, pp. 32 f.; the reference to Widengren in this connexion is omitted from the English text of Engnell's article, above referred to) and Haldar (Bi. Or., iii, 1946, pp. 21 f.). Cf. A. Bentzen, Messias, Moses redivivus, Menschensohn, 1948, pp. 43 n., 80 n. C. R. North (The Suffering Servant in Deutero-Isaiah, p. 99) also observes that Johnson does not draw any parallels between the suffering king and the Suffering Servant, but he appears to be reflecting Engnell's view rather than stating his own.

[2] In a private letter Professor Johnson writes: "I should say that this"—sc. the annual deliverance of the king from 'Death' in the ritual combat—"is a variation on the old theme of the dying and rising god brought about by the modification of the old Canaanite ritual and mythology in terms of Yahwism." Professor A. Bentzen has argued for the Israelite "historification" of the myth which accompanied the ritual, whereby the mythological conflict of the Nature religion was converted into the terms of Yahweh's mighty acts in history on behalf of his people. Cf. "The Cultic Use of the Story of the Ark in Samuel", in J.B.L., lxvii, 1948, pp. 37–53; also Studia Theologica, i, 1948, pp. 186 f.

[3] Mowinckel (De senere profeter, 1944, p. 247) recognizes the possibility that the Servant is a future figure. Cf. Han som kommer, 1951, p. 167; He that Cometh, 1956, p. 249.

[4] Ibid., p. 62 n. Similarly G. A. Danell (Ny Kyrklig Tidskrift, xviii, 1949, p. 87) finds oscillation between the collective and the individual, between the true Israel, the Remnant, and the Messiah in whose person its mission is concentrated. H. Ringgren, whose general position is closely similar to Engnell's, also allows for oscillation between the individual and the collective (ibid., p. 75). Cf. also J. Coppens, in Pro regno pro sanctuario, 1950, p. 116=Nieuw Licht over de Ebed-Jahweh Liederen, 1950, pp. 4, 13.

[5] Ibid., p. 90.   [6] Ibid., p. 93.

features as are found are quite other. They may have been derived from the ritual,[1] but it is hard to believe that in the fourth song they are thought of as ritual sufferings but as real.[2] They go far beyond anything that may have suggested their terms, and in so far as the Servant emerges triumphant it is through the organ of his sufferings that he finds his success. In the royal passion psalms the king is rather delivered from his sufferings by the power of Yawheh and set on high —to be the type of the Davidic Messiah, perhaps, though not in virtue of his sufferings.

A view which has not a little in common with Engnell's, though differing from it fundamentally at other points, is that of S. H. Hooke.[3] This distinguishes the author of the Servant songs from the surrounding passages, and sets him in sharp contrast, indeed. Professor Hooke holds that while the author of Deutero-Isaiah as a whole looked forward to the restoration of Israel to Palestine, the author of the songs did not. He contemplated a permanent dispersion of Israel, and a continued suffering which would become the organ of Israel's mission. Professor Hooke therefore repudiates all messianic interpretation, and holds firmly to the collective interpretation of the Servant as Israel. Where he shares the view of Engnell is in tracing the origin of the conception to the cult of the dying and rising god. He says the prophet is here "transforming the central element of the ancient ritual pattern, the death of the representative individual upon whom the well-being of the community depended, into the vicarious death of the Servant —that is to say, the death of Israel in a political sense".[4]

Finally, the view of Aage Bentzen[5] calls for notice. He again finds

---

[1] W. A. Irwin (in Powis Smith-Irwin, *The Prophets and their Times*, 2nd ed., 1941, pp. 235 ff.) finds a basis for the songs in the ritual, but yet gives to them a collective interpretation.

[2] W. Staerk (*Z.A.W.*, N.F. iii, 1926, pp. 258 f.) thinks otherwise. He says: "Aber das ist ja gerade das Stilproblem dieses vierten Ebed-Liedes, ob die zur Beschreibung des Leidens des Ebed und des Leidens seiner Zeit- und Volksgenossen gebrauchten Ausdrücke eigentlich oder bildlich gemeint seien . . . Denn gibt es einen, wohl an alten Tammuzklagen gebildeten eigenen Stil solcher Poesie, in dem das subjektive Leid des Beters als Todesgefahr, Todesart oder sogar als leiblicher Tod plastisch vor Augen gestellt wird, dann ist dieser konventionelle Stil sicher nicht beschränkt geblieben auf wirkliche Gebetslieder von Kranken und Leidenden, sondern wurde auch, wie z. B. in Jes 53, in Liedern verwendet, die sich der Stilform des Krankenliedes bedienten zum Ausdruck der Klage über eigene und fremde Not." Against this cf. W. Rudolph (*ibid.*, N.F. v, 1928, p. 163 f.).

[3] *Prophets and Priests*, 1938, pp. 40 ff.   [4] *Ibid.*, p. 42.

[5] *Messias, Moses redivivus, Menschensohn*, 1948. Cf. also *Indledning til det Gamle Testamente*, I, i, 1941, pp. 98 ff., and, more especially, *Introduction to the Old Testament*, ii, 1949, pp. 110 ff.

messianic elements entering into the concept, but in a very different way. In part he follows Nyberg and in part Mowinckel. Like Nyberg, he finds links between the Servant and Moses, and holds that the Servant was a second Moses.[1] He does not accept Sellin's theory of the martyrdom of Moses, and indeed pronounces it a fantastic theory.[2] But he recalls the Biblical traditions of the vicarious suffering of Moses, who was ready to perish for the sake of the people he led, and who interceded for them.[3] He therefore combines this Mosaic strand in the concept of the Servant with the messianic strand, and to this, following Nyberg again, he adds a prophetic strand. Here, however, he brings in what he has learned from Mowinckel, and claims that the Servant is a historical person, whose historical character can no more be denied than can that of Cyrus.[4] He therefore identifies the Servant with the prophet himself, and proclaims his adhesion to the autobiographical theory "as it was propounded by Mowinckel in 1921".[5] It is interesting to find here reaffirmed the view of Mowinckel with which our survey began. It is also interesting to find that after Sellin had abandoned his view that the Servant was Moses, it should be revived in this form, and after Mowinckel had become at least hesitant about the autobiographical theory, it should be reaffirmed by Bentzen in this way. Nevertheless, it will be clear that neither theory is revived in quite the form it once had, if only because the two are brought into association with one another. With Bentzen the Servant is not the historical Moses, but a second Moses, who is an ideal messianic figure, whom the prophet believed to be actualized in his own person.[6]

All of these Scandinavian views are therefore in some measure eclectic, though they each differ from one another. In particular Bent-

---

[1] *Messias, Moses redivivus, Menschensohn*, pp. 64 ff. Many writers have noted the points of contact between the work of Moses and the mission of the Servant, and have seen the latter as a second Moses. Cf. G. Füllkrug, *Der Gottesknecht des Deuterojesaja*, 1899, pp. 82 ff.; J. Hontheim, *Z.K.T.*, xxx, 1906, pp. 751 ff.; J. Fischer, *Isaias 40–45 und die Perikopen vom Gottesknecht*, 1916, pp. 191, 193 ff., and *Wer ist der Ebed?* 1922, pp. 55, 81 ff.; E. Balla, in *Eucharistērion* (Gunkel Festschrift), i, 1923, p. 245; J. Jeremias, *Deutsche Theologie*, ii, 1929, pp. 112 f.; A. S. Peake, *The Servant of Yahweh*, 1931, pp. 32 f.; R. Koch, *Geist und Messias*, 1950, p. 109. On this view cf. Mowinckel, *Han som kommer*, 1951, p. 154; *He that Cometh*, 1956, pp. 228 f.

[2] *Introduction to the Old Testament*, ii, p. 112.

[3] *Messias, Moses redivivus, Menschensohn*, p. 65; *Introduction to the Old Testament*, ii, p. 112.

[4] *Introduction to the Old Testament*, ii, p. 112. Cf. also *Messias, Moses redivivus, Menschensohn*, p. 60.

[5] *Introduction to the Old Testament*, loc. cit.

[6] On Bentzen's view cf. C. R. North, *Scottish Journal of Theology*, iii, 1950, pp. 374 ff.

zen differs sharply from Engnell, in that he maintains that the fourth song speaks of the actual death of the Servant, and not of a royal representation of the dying and rising god. Common to all these writers is the view that behind the songs there is a cultic background, though it is somewhat differently conceived by them. Their views all contain a messianic element, though in Bentzen's view the prophet is thought to incarnate the messianic ideal, whereas in Engnell's view the Servant is an ideal figure of the future. Less definable is the messianic element in the thought of Nyberg, since with him the Servant belongs to the past, the present, and the future.

(3)

From all this multiplicity of view, what shall we conclude? Shall we merely say that the problem is insoluble, and refrain from formulating any view at all. That is impossible. The fourth Servant song is of such importance in the thought of the Old Testament and of the New that we must hold some view about it. At the same time, the fact that so many views have been propounded and are held in recent years, all presenting evidence which offers some support for their conclusions, of itself suggests that no one of the views is impregnably based. The individual and the collective view, the messianic and the view that looks to the past for elements of the thought, all have something on their side. No simple, clear-cut solution is likely to do justice to all the evidence, therefore. It is precisely for this reason that I think the views that emphasize the many strands that went into the thought and the fluidity that marks it in the Servant songs are likely to be in the right direction.[1] In particular, I think the "corporate personality" view holds the promise of a reasonable and intelligible interpretation of the whole problem. I am not able to subscribe to it, however, in quite the form given to it by Wheeler Robinson.

We may note first of all the collective traits. The first song begins: "Behold, my servant . . . my chosen one."[2] Outside the songs we find: "And thou Israel my servant, Jacob whom I have chosen";[3] "And I said: My servant art thou, I have chosen thee and have not rejected thee";[4] "Ye are my witnesses, saith Yahweh, and my servant whom I have chosen";[5] "And now hear, O Jacob my servant, Israel whom I have chosen".[6] Here, then, outside the songs we frequently find these terms used of Israel which are here used of the Servant.

[1] V. de Leeuw (De Ebed Jahweh-Profetieën, 1956, p. 352) rejects any form of fluid view.
[2] Is. 42: 1.   [3] Is. 41: 8.   [4] Is. 41: 9.   [5] Is. 43: 10.   [6] Is. 44: 1.

Again, in the first song we read: "(Thou art my servant) whom I uphold."[1] This, too, is predicated of Israel outside the songs: "I have upheld thee by the right hand of my righteousness."[2] In the first song also we read: "I have set my spirit upon him",[3] with which we may compare: "I will pour my spirit upon thy seed",[4] where the reference is clearly to Israel.

The second song declares: "Yahweh hath called me from the womb, from the birth made mention of my name."[5] Here we may compare: "Hearken unto me, O Jacob, and Israel, my called",[6] and: "who formed thee from the womb"[7] and: "I have called thee by name."[8] In all of these cases standing outside the songs, the reference is clearly to Israel. The following verse in the second song reads: "He made my mouth as a sharpened sword, In the shadow of his hand did he hide me."[9] Here again we may compare: "I have put my words in thy mouth, And in the shadow of my hand have I covered thee."[10] It must be noted here, however, that some writers suppose that this verse is a fragment of a Servant song,[11] and Van Hoonacker would transfer it to follow Is. 49 : 3.[12] There is no clear reason for this transference, however, and the majority of scholars of all schools leave it in a context which is referred to Israel.

All of these, and other examples that could be given, sufficiently illustrate that within the songs things are predicated of the Servant which outside them are predicated of Israel. Unless we deny the songs to the author of the surrounding oracles, all probability suggests the community of reference. If we deny the community of reference and ascribe the songs to a different author, it is hard to explain why songs which have so much in common and yet so little in common with the surrounding passages were placed just here.

Yet any simple identification of the Servant with Israel is out of the question to-day.[13] Its difficulties have given rise to all the welter of modern individual views of the Servant. For in the second song the Servant has a mission to Israel, which has to be got rid of on the collective view by some such exegesis as Budde's: "in that he brought

[1] Is. 42: 1.   [2] Is. 41: 10.   [3] Is. 42: 1.   [4] Is. 44: 3.   [5] Is. 49: 1.
[6] Is. 48: 12.   [7] Is. 44: 2, 24.   [8] Is. 43: 1.   [9] Is. 49: 2.   [10] Is. 51: 16.
[11] L. Laue (Die Ebed-Jahwe-Lieder im II. Teil des Jesaia, 1898, p. 16 n.) held that this verse was a fragment of a song or a gloss on one.
[12] R.B., N.S. vi, 1909, pp. 518 f.; Exp., 8th series, xi, 1916, pp. 190 f.; Het Boek Isaias, 1932, p. 237. A. Condamin (R.B., N.S. vii, 1910, p. 214) criticized this transfer, and Van Hoonacker then defended it (ibid., N.S. vii, 1910, pp. 560 ff.).
[13] A. Médebielle (S.D.B., iii, 1938, cols. 93 ff.) well summarizes the difficulties of the simple collective interpretation.

Jacob again (out of Egypt) to him, and drew Israel to him (in the desert)".[1] It is also to be observed that there are features in the fourth song which cannot naturally be interpreted of Israel. "It was our sufferings that he endured, And our pains were those that he bore. . . . But he was pierced by reason of our sins, By our evil deeds was he crushed . . . And Yahweh hath laid on him, The iniquity that we all have done . . . Although he had done no violence. And there was no deceit in his mouth."[2] It is impossible to suppose that Deutero-Isaiah believed that Israel's sufferings in the exile were innocent sufferings, which she had borne vicariously for the redemption of the nations.[3] The pre-exilic prophets had declared in no uncertain way that the sufferings of the exile were the instrument of God's discipline of His own people for their folly and neglect of His will, and there is every reason to believe that Deutero-Isaiah accepted this view. Indeed, he begins his prophecies with the observation that now Israel's iniquity was pardoned, and that she had received of the Lord's hand double for all her sins.[4] Clearly he did not suppose that she had suffered innocently and vicariously.[5] It was "for all her sins."

We may therefore reasonably ask whether there is not some development in his thought of the mission of the Servant, and whether what began as a personification did not become a person. The first song has the closest connexions with Israel passages outside the songs, and the author's thought here seems to have been dominantly of the collective Servant, Israel, destined to carry the light of true religion to all the world, in a mission of gentle persistence and unflagging zeal. In the second song the prophet realizes that only a purified Israel can fulfil this mission, and there is therefore a mission to Israel as well as through

---

[1] A.J.Th., iii, 1899, p. 521; cf. Die sogenannten Ebed-Jahwe-Lieder, 1900, p. 23, and Th.L.Z., lviii, 1933, cols. 324 ff. J. A. Bewer (Jewish Studies in memory of George A. Kohut, 1935, pp. 88 ff.; cf. Festschrift für Alfred Bertholet, 1950, pp. 67 f.) argues that the meaning is "And now Yhwh, who formed me from the womb to be his servant, has said that he would bring Jacob back to himself and that Israel should be gathered to him." This is followed by W. A. Irwin, in Powis Smith-Irwin, The Prophets and their Times, 2nd ed., 1941, p. 130, and R. H. Pfeiffer, Introduction to the Old Testament, 1941, p. 478 n.

[2] Is. 53: 4-6, 9.

[3] Cf. G. von Rad (Theologie des Alten Testaments, ii, 1960, p. 272: "Vor allem aber ist es unmöglich, das kleingläubige, unwillige Israel bei Deuterojesaja mit dem willigen und ganz ergebenen, glaubensstarken Knecht der Lieder zu identifizieren."

[4] Is. 40: 2.

[5] A. Guillaume (Theology, xii, 1926, p. 5) observes that the difference between the sufferings of the nation and the sufferings of the Servant is fundamental, in that the nation suffered because of its disobedience to Yahweh while the Servant suffered because of his obedience.

Israel. This may still have been thought of as a mission to Israel through the pure core or Remnant of the nation, a leavening of Israel as the prelude to Israel's leavening of the world. The third song deals with the suffering and shame which the Servant will experience in the execution of his mission. By this time the prophet realizes that the mission will be no easy one, but it is not unmistakably clear whether he is thinking of the collective Servant, or of an individual representative and leader, in whose person the mission of Israel would be both symbolized and supremely expressed. The fourth song is, in my opinion, unmistakably individual,[1] and it perceives that the suffering will not be merely incidental to the mission, but its organ. It contemplates an individual who will supremely fulfil the mission of Israel through the organ of his own innocent and vicarious suffering, and who will pass through shame and death to exaltation and triumph.[2]

That the language in which he expresses himself is drawn from a variety of sources and has links with ritual and with history is not surprising. Every writer draws on more than he knows when he puts pen to paper. All his past experience and knowledge supply the forms of his thought, and neither can be defined by himself or by any other. He may consciously or unconsciously use phrases which he has inherited through eye or ear. More important than the forms of his thought is its content, and that may easily transcend his own grasp. It may well be that the prophet himself would have been hard put to it to define with precision just how he conceived the Servant.[3] For he was carried by the dynamic of a thought which possessed him to the implications of his initial thought, which was more pregnant than he had realized.

In so far as the thought of these songs is of an individual Servant, in whom the mission of Israel reaches its supreme point, it seems incredible to me that it can be other than a future figure.[4] To describe

[1] Cf. J. Muilenburg, I.B., v, 1956, p. 408a: "There is a concreteness of detail and withal such a striking semblance to an actual person that a collective entity like Israel seems out of the question."

[2] Cf. A. Causse, Israël et la vision de l'humanité, 1925, p. 54: "Au point de départ, le serviteur représente le peuple exilé, puis la communauté yahviste, la minorité des anavim. Au point d'arrivée, c'est bien un héros personnel, le libérateur mystérieux, un héros analogue au Messie."

[3] Cf. my Israel's Mission to the World, 1939, p. 12: "I believe the writer would have found difficulty in defining with precision what was in his own mind." Cf. also J. Woods, The Old Testament in the Church, 1949, p. 19: "In all probability it goes beyond anything in its writer's consciousness." Cf. N. K. Gottwald, A Light to the Nations, 1959, p. 425.

[4] Cf. J. Coppens, Pro regno pro sanctuario, 1950, p. 121: "Het messians karakter, d.i. het verband van de zangen met de ideale koning-redder van de toekomst, is niet meer betwistbar" (=Nieuw Licht over de Ebed-Jahweh Liederen, 1950, p. 9).

in these terms any figure of earlier history of whom we have knowledge seems utterly out of the question; to suppose that some nameless
contemporary of the prophet was imagined to justify such language,
yet left no ripple on the course of history, is equally beyond belief. For
the mission of the Servant was not to fire with a vision, but to fulfil the
vision and to lead the nations to God. To suppose that the prophet
cherished the confidence that he himself was destined to achieve this
mission, yet died without even beginning it, is to ascribe these glorious
songs to empty egotism. Yet the mark of egotism is not upon them.
The writer is filled with the sense of the glory of God and not of his
own greatness. Similarly, it is impossible for me to suppose that any
disciples of the prophet should have imagined after his death that the
mission which he had certainly not achieved was the mission for which
he was destined, and should have written of him in the terms of the
fourth song which were so extravagantly at variance with truth. I can
understand how the prophet should perceive that Israel was called to a
mission to the world, and that that mission was the corollary to her
election by the only God to be His people. No prophet lays greater
emphasis on the election of Israel; no prophet stresses more clearly
the doctrine of monotheism. If God is the only God, then His worship
is for all men; and if He has chosen one people to receive His revelation, then it is for her to share it with all. The conception of Israel as
the Servant, charged with a mission to bring all men to the true
religion, is therefore intimately related to other elements of the
teaching of this prophet.[1]

Similarly I can understand how his thought could move from the
nation as a whole to one who should represent it, who should in himself embody its mission.[2] But I can find this intelligible only if it was
of a future individual that he thought.

Wherein does my view differ from that of Professor North? He
has declared that I am to be classed with the collective interpreters,[3]
while all readers of his book have classed him with the messianic
interpreters. Yet he recognizes some fluidity in the concept as I do,
and I find the songs to culminate in the thought of a future Servant,

[1] On the universalism of Deutero-Isaiah cf. S. Blank, "Studies in Deutero-Isaiah",
in *H.U.C.A.*, xv, 1940, pp. 1 ff., amd J. Morgenstern, "Deutero-Isaiah's Terminology
for 'Universal God' ", in *J.B.L.*, lxii, 1943, pp. 269 ff.

[2] Cf. T. W. Manson, *B.J.R.L.*, xxxii, 1949–50, p. 190: "Where the conception of
corporate personality is dominant there is often a tendency to see the corporate personality as embodied in a person."

[3] *E.T.*, lii, 1940–41, p. 220a.

as he does. It is true that I do not like the term "messianic", because it suggests the Davidic Messiah, and so prejudges some questions. Both the Davidic Messiah and the Servant were conceived of as agents in the establishment of the divine rule in all the earth, but they were different conceptions of the means whereby this should be accomplished. They were therefore not unrelated conceptions, and both may have had some roots in the ritual of Jerusalem, though they were not brought together in any vital way before the time of Christ, and we ought to beware of equating them.

The real difference of my view from that of Professor North, as he first propounded it, is not to be found in my greater reluctance to use the term "messianic". We are both thinking of a future figure who should embody the ideal of the Servant, and are fundamentally at one here. Our difference appeared to lie in our conception of the nature of the fluidity in the prophet's thought. Professor North appeared to find only linear progress and to reject the idea of oscillation,[1] whereas I find development from the thought of Israel as the Servant to the thought of an individual Servant *par excellence*, without abandoning the thought of Israel as still the Servant.[2] If the fourth song is dominantly individual, the mission which the Servant fulfils is still not merely his own, but Israel's,[3] and Israel is still called to enter in some measure into it, so that the Servant may really be Israel's representative.[4] I therefore find oscillation in the thought of the prophet, that links it much more closely to "corporate personality", as it has been above defined, than the view of Professor North appeared to do. He now defines his view in closer agreement with mine,[5] and says he accepts

[1] *The Suffering Servant in Deutero-Isaiah*, p. 216.
[2] J. Coppens has propounded a view which has many points of similarity with mine (*Sacra Pagina*, i, 1959, pp. 434–454). He holds (pp. 439 ff.) that in the first two Songs the Servant is Israel, in the third Song it is the prophet himself (pp. 437 ff.), and in the fourth Song the interpretation is fluid (pp. 443 ff.), with a *sensus plenior* (p. 453). It will be seen that it is in relation to the third Song that we differ most. Coppens draws attention to the similarity of my view to that of I. Loeb (*Revue des Études juives*, xxiii, 1891, pp. 1–31, 161–193), of which I was ignorant, save for a reference in Coppens' article in *Pro regno pro sanctuario* (van der Leeuw Festschrift), 1950, p. 116. Loeb argues (pp. 14 ff.) that the conception of the Servant is elastic and variable, and that it is best represented by a series of concentric circles, since the Servant is sometimes the whole Jewish nation, sometimes the faithful in Israel, but sometimes has such pronounced individual characteristics that he can only be thought of as a future miraculous person, or the Messiah.
[3] Cf. J. Pedersen, *Israel III–IV*, 1940, pp. 603 ff., where it is held that while the Servant has a mission to Israel, he is none the less Israel embodied in a person.
[4] Cf. N. A. Dahl, *Das Volk Gottes*, 1941, p. 42.
[5] See above, p. 25, n. 1.

the same oscillation. It is not clear, however, why he still classes my view as collective,[1] though I am no more a collectivist than he is.

It is not without interest to observe that the spiritual pilgrimage of our Lord was in some measure that of the author of the Servant songs. At the beginning of His ministry He preached that the Kingdom of God was at hand, with a gentleness like that of the Servant in the first song. Then He intensified His mission to Israel in the sending out of His disciples with an urgent call to Israel to be ready for the coming of the Kingdom. Then came the recognition that suffering and sorrow were before Him, and that suffering was to be the organ of His triumph.[2]

---

[1] Cf. *The Suffering Servant in Deutero-Isaiah*, 2nd ed., p. 207.

[2] The view has been held that the ascription to Jesus of an interpretation of His mission in terms of the Servant is an unhistorical creation of the post-resurrection church (cf. J. Weiss, *Die Schriften des Neuen Testaments*, 3rd ed., edited by W. Bousset and W. Heit-müller, i, 1917, pp. 174 f.; H. Rashdall, *The Idea of Atonement in Christian Theology*, 1919, pp. 49 ff.; B. W. Bacon, *J.B.L.*, xlviii, 1929, pp. 60 ff.; C. T. Craig, *J.R.*, xxiv, 1944, pp. 240 ff.; F. C. Grant, *The Earliest Gospel*, 1943, p. 179 n., and *I.B.*, vii, 1951, pp. 767 f.; R. Bultmann, *Theology of the New Testament*, i, 1952, p. 131; B. H. Branscomb, *The Gospel of Mark*, 5th imp., 1948, pp. 190 f.; also F. J. Foakes Jackson and K. Lake, *The Beginnings of Christianity*, i, 1942 ed., pp. 383 ff.). Against this cf. A. E. J. Rawlinson, *St. Mark*, 1925, pp. 146 ff.; H. Wheeler Robinson, *The Cross of the Servant*, 1926, pp. 64 ff.; A. M. Ramsey, *The Gospel and the Catholic Church*, 1936, p. 17; W. F. Howard, *E.T.*, l, 1938–39, pp. 107 ff.; R. Otto, *The Kingdom of God and the Son of Man*, E.Tr. by F. V. Filson and B. Lee-Woolf, 1943 ed., pp. 244 ff.; J. W. Bowman, *J.R.*, xxv, 1945, pp. 56 ff.; V. Taylor, *Jesus and His Sacrifice*, 1943 ed., pp. 39 ff., and *The Gospel according to St. Mark*, 1952, pp. 445 f.; C. J. Cadoux, *The Historic Mission of Jesus*, 1941, pp. 253 f.; H. W. Wolff, *Jesaja 53 im Urchristentum*, 1942, pp. 49 ff. (2nd ed., 1956, pp. 55 ff.); W. Manson, *Jesus the Messiah*, 1943, pp. 30 ff.; C. R. North, *The Suffering Servant in Deutero-Isaiah*, pp. 24 f.; J. Schniewind, *Das Evangelium nach Markus* (N.T.D.), 5th ed., 1949, p. 144; R. H. Fuller, *The Mission and Achievement of Jesus*, 1954, pp. 55 ff.; D. M. Stanley, *C.B.Q.*, xvi, 1957, pp. 393 ff., 410; J. Jeremias, *The Servant of God*, E.Tr., 1957, pp. 101 ff.; O. Cullmann, *Die Christologie des Neuen Testaments*, 1957, pp. 80 f.; C. E. B. Cranfield, *The Gospel according to St. Mark* (C.G.T.), 1959, pp. 343 f.; R. McL. Wilson in *Peake's Commentary*, rev. ed., edited by M. Black and H. H. Rowley, 1962, p. 811a.; P. Bonnard, *L'Évangile selon Matthieu* (C.N.T.), 1963, p. 262; also J. Moffatt, *The Theology of the Gospels*, 1912, p. 149: "The suffering Servant conception was organic to the consciousness of Jesus." G. Kittel, "Jesu Worte über sein Sterben", in *Deutsche Theologie*, 1936, pp. 166 ff., also argues that the ascription is genuine, and says (pp. 174 f.) that had it been otherwise, Is. 53 would have played a larger part in the sayings (similarly V. Taylor, *op. cit.*, p. 48; Th. Preiss, *E.Th.R.*, xxvi, 1951, p. 52). Cf. also M. Buber, "Jesus und der 'Knecht' ", in *Pro regno pro sanctuario* (van der Leeuw Festschrift), 1950, pp. 71 ff. M. D. Hooker (*Jesus and the Servant*, 1959, pp. 62–102) maintains that there is little in the Synoptics to support the view that Jesus identified His mission with that of the Servant. L. S. Mudge (*S.J.Th.*, xii, 1959, p. 115 n.) says he "cannot quite agree with her systematic elimination of Isaiah 53 from a position of doctrinal influence in the New Testament apart from a few late passages" (cf. also pp. 116 ff.). Cf. H. E. W. Turner, in *Manson's Companion to the Bible*, rev. ed., edited by H. H. Rowley, 1963, p. 470: "It is as difficult as it is unnecessary to maintain that it (i.e. the figure of the Servant) was not present to the mind of Jesus Himself." S. Mowinckel (*He that Cometh*, E.Tr., 1956, p. 449) observes:

Here it will be remembered that the second song draws attention to the mission to Israel that must precede the mission to the world, while the third song tells of the suffering of the Servant, and the fourth shows that the suffering is not merely the price of the mission but its organ. In a very real sense, therefore, the songs were fulfilled in Him, and there has certainly been no other of whom the language of the fourth song could be used with an appropriateness comparable with that found in its use of Him. Not every detail was fulfilled in Him, and there is no need to look for it. Yet the area of its fulfilment in Him is truly remarkable.

Moreover, we find the same fluidity in the fulfilment which we have found in the conception. For if our Lord is the supreme Suffering Servant, He gathers His church unto Himself that it may be His body, that He may so fill it with His own spirit that it may become the extension of His personality and the organ of the continuation of His mission to the world. The church believed that it had inherited the mission of Israel, and it is therefore called to be the Servant. It is true that it cannot attain the peak of service attained by its Lord, but it is called to enter into that service to the fullest degree possible, so that the Saviour and Lord of the church may be indeed its representative. The New Testament can talk of entering into the sufferings of Christ,[1] or even of making up that which was lacking in the sufferings of Christ.[2] In a profound sense the Church is called to agonize for the world's redemption, and to realize that it can never fulfil its mission in the world unless it is prepared to tread the path of suffering and sacrifice, and to know in its heart an agony that reflects the agony of the Cross.

Wheeler Robinson drew attention to this corresponding fluidity in the songs and in their fulfilment. He says: "If we are to think of the ancient idea of the Servant as being capable of contraction and expansion (which was the point of emphasis laid on corporate personality), then we may say that though the collective idea contracted into a primary reference to Jesus, yet its virtual presence is seen in the readiness with which it expanded into the doctrine of the Church."[3] To Wheeler Robinson I am more indebted than to any other who has

"There can be little doubt about the source from which Jesus derived this idea (i.e. of suffering, death and resurrection). It came from Scripture, from the Suffering Servant of the Lord." S. M. Gilmour (Hastings's one-volume *D.B.*, rev. ed., edited by F. C. Grant and H. H. Rowley, 1963, p. 496a) is non-committal.

[1] Phil. 3: 10; cf. Rom. 8: 17.   [2] Col. 1: 24.
[3] *The Cross of the Servant*, pp. 75 f.

discussed the Servant, though I am not convinced that in the thought of the prophet the oscillation was between the nation and himself. I think rather it was between the nation and a future representative who should in himself incarnate its mission without making it any less the mission of the nation, and that in the person of our Lord the mission was indeed incarnate, fulfilling the hope of the prophet, and lifting into that fulfilment all who are truly "in Christ", and who can say with Paul: "I have been crucified with Christ; nevertheless I live; and yet no longer I, but Christ liveth in me; and the life which I now live in the flesh I live by the faith of the Son of God, who loved me, and gave himself for me."[1] It is not alone in that there is fluidity as between the corporate and the individual that the vision and its fulfilment are bound together, but that the future individual in whom the mission was focused in the thought of the prophet and the Individual from whose focus of the mission in Himself the new expansion took place are to be identified.

Whether I am to be classed with the collective interpreters or not I leave you to judge, though I am not greatly concerned where I am classed. I would stress far more than most interpreters do the collective element in the fulfilment. For most are content to find an embodiment of the conception of the Servant in Christ, whatever thought they ascribe to the authors of the songs, and to leave any collective fulfilment without thought or word.[2] Yet with this collective element I stress the future individual element in the conception, and link it with the individual element in the fulfilment, so that though I approach the question along different lines from the traditional messianic view, I have much in common with its solution.

My purpose in these lectures is not primarily to offer a solution of the problem, but to survey the solutions that have been offered in our day, and I am aware that I am debtor to many and have little of my own to contribute. I may conclude by emphasizing once more the collective element in the fulfilment of the mission in words which I wrote some years ago: "If, then, the Church is called to carry to the world the message of the fulfilment of the prophecy of the Servant in

---

[1] Gal. 2: 20.
[2] L. M. von Pákozdy (*Deuterojesajanische Studien II: der Ebed Jahweh in der Theologie Deuterojesajas*, 1942) does, however, call attention to this. He says: "Eine individuell-messianische Erklärung der EJL auf Jesus ist nur dann möglich, wenn wir uns auf den Standpunkt der biblischen Anschauung über Gemeinschaft und Individuum stellen und das vom Volk erwartete in seiner vertretenden Spitze, in Jesus, erfüllt sehen. Sein 'Leib', die Kirche, ist dann die 'erfüllende' Gemeinschaft, das geistige Israel" (p. 246).

the Cross of Christ, it is also called to enter into the experience of the Cross, and to share in some measure in the fulfilment of the prophecy. We do not merely proclaim the love of God in Christ objectively; we enter into that love, and know its eager yearning of spirit; and feel the pangs of God's rejected love. Unless we feel that sympathy, in the proper sense of the word—that suffering with Christ and with God— we cannot enter into the world mission which the Church inherited from Judaism; but if we do, we are transported into that mission in no half-hearted and formal way. It becomes a part of our very life, laying upon us its imperious constraint, and filling our heart with an eager passion that fails not."[1]

[1] *The Missionary Message of the Old Testament*, 1944, p. 82. Cf. R. Tournay, *R.B.*, lix, 1952, pp. 509 f.

THE SUFFERING SERVANT AND THE DAVIDIC MESSIAH

2

The Suffering Servant and the Davidic Messiah[1]

IT has long been commonly held that amongst the Jews the concepts of the Davidic Messiah, the Son of Man, and the Servant of the Lord were separate and distinct before the time of Jesus, and that they were first brought together and fused into one in His thought.[2] This is not to say, of course, that the ideas were completely unrelated. It is but to say that while all had to do with the Golden Age, when evil should be finally overthrown and the eternal rule of righteousness in a world in which all would obey the law of Israel's God in sincerity and truth would be inaugurated, they represent different emphases in the thought of that age.[3] While the term Messiah, or Christ, does not appear to be actually used of the Davidic descendant in the Old Testament,[4] the concept of the Davidic Messiah is familiar enough. He is represented as the ruler and lord in that coming age,[5] whose power should be matched by his wisdom,[6] and who should give peace to the whole world because he should rule it in righteousness.[7] The Son of

---

[1] Paper read at the International Meeting of the Dutch Old Testament Society at Leiden, September 1950.

[2] This is the position which I took in *The Re-discovery of the Old Testament*, 1946, pp. 210 f. (American ed., 1946, pp. 296 ff.).

[3] Cf. W. Manson, *Jesus the Messiah*, 1943, p. 174: "The concepts of the Davidic Messiah, the Suffering Servant, and the pre-existent Heavenly Man . . . are to be recognized . . as successive phases of the Messianic idea, which connect respectively with Israel as nation, Israel as Church, and Israel as final, perfected elect of the supernatural Reign of God."

[4] The term *māshîaḥ* is used of kings of Israel, of priests, and also of Cyrus. It is found in some psalms which have been traditionally interpreted as messianic, but the interpretation is disputed, and the reference may be to actual kings. It stands also in Dan. 9: 25 f., where most scholars again think the reference is to a historical person, and the R.V. accordingly eliminates the technical use of the word *Messiah* here. Cf. W. O. E. Oesterley, *The Gospel Parables in the Light of their Jewish Background*, 1936, p. 24: "In the Old Testament the Messiah as a technical term does not occur." It is found unmistakably as a technical term in the Psalms of Solomon, though reference will be made below to occurrences in the older Ethiopic Enoch, where, however, many scholars doubt the originality of the text. It should be noted that C. C. Torrey (*J.B.L.*, lxvi, 1947, pp. 268 f.) gives a messianic interpretation to the above-mentioned passage from Daniel. On this see below.

[5] Mic. 5: 1 (E.V.2).   [6] Is. 11: 2.   [7] Is. 9: 6 (E.V.7), 11: 6 ff., Jer. 23: 5 f.

THE SERVANT OF THE LORD

Man, as the figure appears in the book of Daniel,[1] in relation to this
world of ideas, is a representation of the saints of the Most High,[2] as
invested with power,[3] for to them the dominion should be given in
the day of the overthrow of evil and the establishment of the enduring
kingdom of righteousness.[4] This is not to be understood to mean that

[1] Dan. 7: 13. W. A. Curtis has argued that the New Testament use of the title Son
of Man rests on the book of Ezekiel (cf. *Jesus Christ the Teacher*, 1943, pp. 127 ff.), but
against this T. W. Manson effectively says: "We are bound, I think, by the fact that
the one explicit reference by Jesus to the Old Testament in a Son of Man saying is a
reference to the Son of Man in Dan. 7: 13. We should therefore begin the study of the
term Son of Man in the Gospels by a consideration of its meaning in the one Old Testament passage to which we have an explicit reference" (*B.J.R.L.*, xxxii, 1949-50, p. 173).
P. Fiebig (*Der Menschensohn*, 1901, pp. 75 ff.) similarly held that we must begin from Dan.
7: 13, where, however, he identified the Son of Man with the Messiah. For earlier studies
of the connexions between the Gospels and Ezekiel, cf. E. A. Abbott, "*The Son of Man*",
or *Contributions to the Study of the Thoughts of Jesus*, 1910, pp. 82 ff., and D. Völter, *Die
Menschensohn-Frage neu untersucht*, 1916, pp. 27 ff. E. Sjöberg, "Uttrycket 'Människoson'
i Gamla Testamentet", in *Svensk Teologisk Kvartalskrift*, xxvi, 1950, pp. 35-54, studies
the expression "Son of Man" elsewhere in the Old Testament.

[2] In my *Darius the Mede and the Four World Empires in the Book of Daniel*, 1935, pp.
62 ff. note, I gave a summary review of the interpretation of this passage in a large number of works, and I have noted a few further views in *The Relevance of Apocalyptic*, 3rd
ed., 1963, pp. 31 ff. The subject has continued to be discussed, and the documentation
might be considerably extended; but few new points have emerged, and few fundamentally fresh views have been advanced. The paper of M. Noth (*Interpretationes ad Vetus
Testamentum Sigmundo Mowinckel missae*, 1955, pp. 146-161) may be mentioned for its
examination of the question whether the saints of the Most High are angelic beings or
a symbol for an eschatological kingdom (cf. L. Dequeker, in J. Coppens and L. Dequeker,
Le Fils de l'homme et les Saints du Très-Haut en Daniel vii, 1961, pp. 21 ff.), that of L.
Rost (*Festgabe für Erich Fascher*, 1958, pp. 41-43) for its view that ancient mythological
elements associated with Ras Shamra mythology have been fused with the conception
of four world empires to produce the figure of the Son of Man (cf. J. Muilenburg,
J.B.L., lxxix, 1960, pp. 197 ff.), and that of J. Morgenstern (*J.B.L.*, lxxx, 1961, pp.
65-77) for its argument that the passage is based on the conception of the aged Ba'al
Shamem handing over authority to the youthful Melkart, the god in human form
(Epiphanes) resurrected to replace him, and hence that the passage could not possibly
antedate the reign of Antiochus Epiphanes. J. A. Emerton (*J.T.S.*, N.S. ix, 1958, pp.
225-242) also stresses the links with Ras Shamra mythology [cf. also M. Pope, *El in the
Ugaritic Texts* (S.V.T.), 1955, pp. 32 ff.] in the effort to get behind Daniel 7 to the sources
of the idea, and finds its roots in the Israelite enthronement festival (cf. A. Bentzen,
King and Messiah, 1955, p. 75). See also A. J. B. Higgins, "Son of Man-*Forschung* since
'The Teaching of Jesus' ", in *New Testament Essays* (T. W. Manson Memorial Volume),
1959, pp. 119-135; A. Feuillet, "Le Fils de l'Homme de Daniel et la Tradition Biblique",
R.B., lx, 1953, pp. 170-202, 321-346.

[3] Dan. 7: 27. It is sometimes claimed that since in this chapter we read of the persecution of the saints, we have here the thought of the suffering of the Son of Man. This is
not so, however. The saints suffered before the appearance of the Son of Man, for this
is a figure for the saints only after they are invested with power. Cf. G. Kittel, *Deutsche
Theologie*, 1936, p. 173: "Niemals im Alten Testament ist von einem Leiden oder gar
Sterben des Menschensohnes die Rede."

[4] Dan. 7: 12 f.

the author of the chapter repudiated the idea of the Davidic Messiah. It is improbable that he thought of the kingdom of the saints as without any leader and head; but he was not concerned with the person of that head, but only with the thought of the kingdom, whose character he symbolized by this figure.[1] The Suffering Servant is presented in a very different setting from both of these other figures. No conquering king is he, and no intervention of God in judgement elevates him to power. Instead, he is a humble sufferer,[2] who by the organ of his suffering leads men to penitence before God,[3] and whose power springs from his sacrifice for men, which is described as a guilt offering.[4]

In recent years there has been some reaction against this view, and a tendency to claim that two, or even all three, of these terms were already equated in Jewish thought before the beginning of the Christian era.[5] The weight of scholarship is still against this tendency, and the names of scholars of such eminence in this field as Moore,[6] Lagrange,[7]

---

[1] T. W. Manson has presented as "not in doubt" the collective interpretation of this passage in his paper "The Son of Man in Daniel, Enoch and the Gospels" in *B.J.R.L.*, *loc. cit.*, pp. 171 ff. (see esp. pp. 173 ff.). On the other hand, W. F. Albright has interpreted the passage in terms of a pre-existent heavenly figure, destined to appear as Messiah (*From the Stone Age to Christianity*, 2nd ed., 1946, pp. 290 ff.= *Von der Steinzeit zum Christentum*, 1949, pp. 375 f.), and W. O. E. Oesterley has interpreted it individually in terms of one comparable with the Messiah (*The Jews and Judaism during the Greek Period*, 1941, pp. 152 ff.). Cf. H. Gressmann, *Der Messias*, 1929, pp. 343 ff., and P. Volz, *Die Eschatologie der jüdischen Gemeinde im neutestamentlichen Zeitalter*, 1934, p. 13. Manson (*loc. cit.*, p. 174) maintains that Daniel's Son of Man does not come from heaven, but goes to heaven to receive the kingdom. He identifies the Son of Man with the Remnant or with the Servant of Yahweh (*ibid.*, p. 175). In this he was anticipated by W. Staerk, *Soter: die biblische Erlösererwartung als religionsgeschichtliches Problem*, 1933, pp. 38 f.

[2] Is. 50: 6, 53: 7.

[3] Is. 53: 5 f.

[4] Is. 53: 8, 10.

[5] Cf. C. C. Torrey, *J.B.L.*, xlviii, 1929, p. 25: "These three conceptions had been combined, speculated upon, and fashioned into a many-sided doctrine, held and cherished by the Jewish people long before the beginning of the Common Era." On the other hand, many writers have denied that these conceptions were brought together until after the ministry of Jesus; cf. above, p. 57, n. 2. F. C. Grant (*An Introduction to New Testament Thought*, 1950, pp. 22 ff.) thinks the bringing of these concepts together reflects the varying types of Christology in the Early Church, and could not have been achieved in the mind of Christ.

[6] Cf. *Judaism in the First Centuries of the Christian Era*, i, 1927, pp. 551 f.; iii, 1930, p. 166.

[7] Cf. *Le judaïsme avant Jésus-Christ*, 1931, p. 385: "Nous devons insister seulement sur le Messie souffrant, précisément pour dire que nous ne l'avons pas rencontré. Si saississant qu'ait été le tableau du Serviteur, si poignante la lamentation de la maison de David, le judaïsme n'a pas songé un seul instant à attribuer la souffrance et la mort expiatrice au Sauveur attendu. Fait capital, abstention plus significative que des details pittoresques et multipliés."

and Strack-Billerbeck,[1] not to mention a number of other well-known scholars,[2] can scarcely be matched by those who are arrayed against them. Nevertheless, the challengers include several scholars who cannot be lightly brushed aside,[3] and the issue is to be decided by weighing arguments rather than by weighing names. It may not be amiss, therefore, to look anew at some of these in this paper.

In later Jewish sources we find references to a Messiah ben Ephraim, or ben Joseph, alongside a Messiah ben David.[4] Sometimes it is argued

[1] Cf. *Kommentar zum Neuen Testament aus Talmud und Midrasch*, ii, 1924, p. 274: "Aus dem NT erkennen wir, dass ein leidender Messias in Jesu Tagen den messianischen Hoffnungen des jüdischen Volks jedenfalls nicht entsprochen hat . . . Die Ablehnung eines leidenden Messias hat etwas Auffallendes, wenn man die hohe Bedeutung erwägt, die die alter Synagoge gerade den Leiden beigelegt hat." On the last point cf. H. A. Fischel, "Martyr and Prophet", in *J.Q.R.*, xxxvii, 1946–47, pp. 265 ff., 363 ff.

[2] Cf. G. H. Box, in *The People and the Book* (ed. by A. S. Peake), 1925, p. 454: "The application of the great passage in Is. 53 to the Messiah is something entirely new when it emerges in the New Testament"; P. Volz, *Die Eschatologie der jüdischen Gemeinde im neutestamentlichen Zeitalter*, 1934, p. 228: "Von einem Leiden des Messias ist in unserer Periode nicht oder kaum die Rede. Jes 53 hat man erst später mit dem Messias in Verbindung gebracht . . ., und in unserem Zeitraum verschiedenfach in nichtmessianischem Zusammenhang verwendet"; J. Héring, *R.H.P.R.*, xviii, 1938, p. 422, speaks of "l'impossibilité d'un rapprochement matérial entre le Ebed souffrant et le Messie. Les deux personnages s'excluent et s'opposent comme l'eau et le feu"; J. J. Brierre-Narbonne, *Le Messie souffrant dans la littérature rabbinique*, 1940, p. 133: "Il n'est pas question d'un Messie souffrant dans la littérature juive extrabiblique avant la mort du Christ Jésus"; C. J. Cadoux, *The Historic Mission of Jesus*, 1941, pp. 52 f.: "We have no evidence to show that these Servant-poems were in his (*sc.* our Lord's) time interpreted by the Jews messianically." Cf. also H. Wheeler Robinson, *Redemption and Revelation*, 1942, pp. 199, 251 f.; M. Burrows, *An Outline of Biblical Theology*, 1946, p. 86; T. W. Manson, *The Servant Messiah*, 1935. W. D. Davies (*Paul and Rabbinic Judaism*, 1948, p. 283 n.) claims that J. Bonsirven (*Le judaïsme palestinien*, i, 1934, pp. 380 ff., esp. p. 385) tends to accept his view (see below). I can find nothing in the pages mentioned which supports this claim. Bonsirven recognizes a Suffering Messiah in Jewish thought of the second century A.D., but does not project this back to a pre-Christian date.

[3] Cf. J. Jeremias, "Erlöser und Erlösung im Spätjudentum", in *Deutsche Theologie*, ii, 1929, pp. 106 ff. (cf. also "Zum Problem der Deutung von Jes. 53 im palästinischen Spätjudentum", in *Aux Sources de la Tradition Chrétienne* (Goguel Festschrift), 1950, pp. 113–119); W. Staerk, *Soter*, 1933, pp. 77 f.; N. Johansson, *Parakletoi*, 1940, pp. 113 ff.; H. Riesenfeld, *Jésus transfiguré*, 1947, pp. 81 ff., 314 ff.; W. D. Davies, *Paul and Rabbinic Judaism*, 1948, pp. 274 ff. I. Engnell goes so far as to say that the Servant of Yahweh in Deutero-Isaiah was from the start "the Messiah himself, the Saviour king of the dynasty of David waited for" (*The 'Ebed Yahweh Songs and the Suffering Messiah in "Deutero-Isaiah"*—reprinted from *B.J.R.L.*, xxxi, 1948—p. 7=*S.E.Å.*, x, 1945, p. 34; cf. also pp. 11 f., 42 of the English text=pp. 38 f. of the Swedish, the Swedish text lacking the last of these passages).

[4] Cf. J. Drummond, *The Jewish Messiah*, 1877, pp. 356 ff.; E. G. King, *The Yalkut on Zechariah*, 1882, pp. 85 ff.; G. H. Dalman, *Der leidende und der sterbende Messias der Synagoge*, 1888, pp. 1 ff.; M. J. Lagrange, *Le messianisme chez les juifs*, 1909, pp. 251 ff.; Strack-Billerbeck, *op. cit.*, ii, 1924, pp. 292 ff.; G. H. Dix, "The Messiah ben Joseph", in *J.T.S.*, xxvii, 1926, pp. 130 ff.; Bousset-Gressmann, *Die Religion des Judentums im späthellenistischen*

that these two concepts already co-existed in Jewish thought in pre-Christian days, and that the former of these was already the concept of a Suffering Messiah. Sometimes it is argued that the Davidic Messiah was identified with the Suffering Servant, and that the two figures were already fused into one. These are fundamentally different positions requiring separate examination.

Professor A. Guillaume holds[1] that the Jews expected a Suffering Messiah in pre-Christian days,[2] and declares that the Jews interpreted the Servant of Is. 53 as the Messiah "until Christian polemic forced them to abandon it in favour of the national theory; though the latter had its advocates from an early time, as the LXX show."[3] The only evidence which is adduced in support of this thesis is post-Christian, and lies in the fact that the Targum and both Talmuds find the Messiah in Is. 53. On the other hand, the only pre-Christian evidence which is cited is that of the Septuagint, and this, as Guillaume admits, is against him.[4]

The Septuagint equates the Servant in Is. 42 : 1 with the nation Israel, and in Is. 53 represents the sufferings of the Servant as past.[5]

Zeitalter, 3rd ed., 1926, pp. 230 ff.; G. F. Moore, *op. cit.*, ii, 1927, pp. 370 f.; J. Klausner, *Die messianischen Vorstellungen des jüdischen Volkes im Zeitalter der Tannaiten*, 1904, pp. 86 ff.= Hā-ra'yôn ham-meshîḥî be-Yiśrā'ēl, 1927, pp. 312 ff.; J. Bonsirven, *op. cit.*, i, 1934, pp. 380 ff.; C. C. Torrey, "The Messiah Son of Ephraim", in *J.B.L.*, lxvi, 1947, pp. 253 ff. A. Grabar, in the course of an article on "Le thème religieux des fresques de la Synagogue de Doura (245–256 après J.-C.)", in *R.H.R.*, cxxiii, 1941, pp. 142 ff., argues (pp. 168 f.) that there are evidences of the two Messiahs in these frescoes (cf. R. Wischnitzer, *The Messianic Theme in the Paintings of the Dura Synagogue*, 1948, pp. 13 ff., 24). He says: "En présence de cette doctrine des Targum, les deux *Bénédictions de Jacob* de la fresque reçoivent un sens précis et en rapport avec le théme eschatologique de l'ensemble du panneau central." The Messiah ben Ephraim figures also in 3 Enoch 45: 5 (cf. H. Odeberg, *3 Enoch, or The Hebrew Book of Enoch*, 1928, Part II, pp. 144 f.), which Odeberg dates in the second half of the third century A.D. (Part I, p. 41). See also B. J. Bamberger, *H.U.C.A.*, xv, 1940, pp. 425 ff., for the Suffering Messiah in a text of the seventh century A.D.

[1] Cf. "The Servant Poems in the Deutero-Isaiah", in *Theology*, xi, 1925, pp. 254 ff., 309 ff.; xii, 1926, pp. 2 ff., 63 ff.

[2] Cf. also C. Lattey, *C.B.Q.*, iv, 1942, pp. 16 ff., and my comments in *The Relevance of Apocalyptic*, 2nd ed., 1947, pp. 135 ff. (3rd ed., 1963, pp. 150 ff.).

[3] *Loc. cit.*, xii, 1926, p. 67. In *A New Commentary on Holy Scripture*, ed. by C. Gore, H. L. Goudge, and A. Guillaume, 1928, p. 468a, Guillaume withdraws his earlier view in favour of the collective view of the Servant.

[4] L. Gillet, *Communion in the Messiah*, 1942, p. 94, says: "The classical Jewish exegesis, in Targum and Talmud, interpreted Is. 53 as referring to Messiah himself." He completely ignores the LXX and gives a quite false idea that the Targum presents the Messiah as the Suffering Servant. Similarly, I. Abrahams, in *The People and the Book* (ed. by A. S. Peake), 1925, p. 408.

[5] Cf. K. F. Euler, *Die Verkündigung vom leidenden Gottesknecht aus Jes. 53 in der griechischen Bibel*, 1934, pp. 125 ff.; W. Staerk, "Zur Exegese von Jes 53 im Diasporajudentum", in *Z.N.W.*, xxxv, 1936, p. 308; N. S. Nyberg, *S.E.Å.*, vii, 1942, pp. 8 ff.; also H. W. Wolff, *Jesaja 53 im Urchristentum* 1942, pp. 37 f.

On the other hand, it is true that the Targum equates the Servant in the latter passage with the Messiah.[1] It does not, however, present a suffering Messiah.[2] It clearly has in mind the Davidic Messiah, and not the Messiah ben Ephraim, but the sufferings which are mentioned in the chapter are systematically transferred to Israel's foes, or to the disloyal Israelites.[3] There is no suffering Messiah.[4] It is gratuitous to assume that the Targum once interpreted the chapter in terms of a Suffering Messiah and that this was subsequently changed, since there is no evidence for the assumption,[5] and no evidence that the Davidic Messiah was thought of as a Suffering Messiah either then or later. In one verse the Targum failed to transfer the sufferings from the Messiah —viz., Is. 53 : 12—where Humbert argues[6] that the phrase $m^e sar$ $l^e m\hat{o}th\hat{a}$ $naphsh\hat{e}h$ means "risked his life", and claims the support of Jastrow's Dictionary.[7] In any case, this single expression in the Targum

[1] For the text of the Targum cf. J. F. Stenning, The Targum of Isaiah, 1949, pp. 179, 181; for a study of the Targumic treatment cf. P. Humbert, "Le Messie dans le Targum des Prophètes", in R.Th.Ph., xliii, 1910, pp. 420 ff.; xliv, 1911, pp. 5 ff.; R. A. Aytoun, "The Servant of the Lord in the Targum", in J.T.S., xxiii, 1922, pp. 172 ff.; P. Seidelin, "Der 'Ebed Jahwe und die Messiasgestalt im Jesajatargum", in Z.N.W., xxxv, 1936, pp. 194 ff.; P. Churgin, Targum Jonathan to the Prophets, 1927 (1907 on title-page), pp. 83 f.; G. Kittel, Deutsche Theologie, 1936, pp. 179 ff.; W. Manson, Jesus the Messiah, 1943, pp. 168 ff.; C. R. North, The Suffering Servant in Deutero-Isaiah, 1948, pp. 11 f.

[2] Cf. Humbert, loc. cit., xliv, 1911, p. 6: "Le traducteur fait des efforts désespérés pour échapper à l'idée d'un Messie souffrant"; Churgin, op. cit., p. 84: "The targumist reverses the simple meaning of the words, transforming the gloomy portraiture of the Messiah into an image of magnificence and splendour. . . . He actually rewrites ch. 53, replacing it by one bearing no resemblance to the original."

[3] Humbert, loc. cit., xliii, 1910, pp. 443 ff., notes that the sufferings are transferred to Israel, to impious Jews, to the heathen, or to the Temple.

[4] Cf. A. Médebielle, in S.D.B., iii, 1938, col. 109: "La paraphrase d'Isaïe, 52: 13–53: 12, nous révèle la totale incompréhension des Juifs en face du mystère de la rédemption par la souffrance."

[5] The Suffering Messiah, Messiah ben Ephraim, appears in the Targum of pseudo-Jonathan and in the Babylonian Talmud, but not in the Targums of Onkelos and Jonathan ben Uzziel. Cf. H. Riesenfeld, Jésus transfiguré, p. 81 n.; "La croyance en deux Messies est caractéristique du Targum de Ps.-Jonathan et du Talmud babylonien, tandis qu'elle ne se trouve pas dans les autres Targums ou dans le Talmud palestinien". (It may be noted that it is also found in the Targum to the Song of Songs, which is, however, late. Cf. C. C. Torrey, J.B.L., lxvi, 1947, p. 254.) Since the Suffering Messiah does not appear at all in the Targum of Jonathan ben Uzziel, there is no reason to suppose that the Targum of this passage ever contained such a conception, and if it did, it is hard to see why a Judaism which cherished the idea of a suffering Messiah should have eliminated it from the whole of this Targum, and not from this passage alone, unless it also went on to eliminate it from all its thought and ceased to cherish the idea altogether. If the suffering Messiah had never been associated with this passage, there would be every reason to impose an anti-Christian interpretation on a chapter to which the Church made such appeal.   [6] Loc. cit., xliv, 1911, pp. 5 f.

[7] Cf. Dictionary of the Targumim, ii, 1903, p. 810 b, s.v.

is quite insufficient to justify the conclusion that the Messiah and the Suffering Servant were identified long before it was prepared. The hand that prepared the Targum was at pains to avoid the idea of a suffering Messiah, and as Churgin says,[1] he "reverses the simple meaning of words", and "actually rewrites ch. 53, replacing it by one bearing no resemblance to the original." This may well have been due to the Christian use of this chapter, and the desire to repudiate it as strongly as possible.[2] It offers no evidence, however, of any pre-Christian interpretation of the chapter in a messianic sense, either in connexion with a Davidic Messiah or with any other messianic figure standing beside him. R. A. Aytoun, who argued that the chapter was recognized to be messianic at least as early as the time of our Lord, thought[3] the desire to represent the Messiah as triumphant would have been as natural then as later. In that case it could offer no ground for holding that the Suffering Servant and the Messiah were identified, but only for supposing that the Davidic Messiah had been associated with a distorted Servant, who was no longer thought of as a Suffering Servant.

Professor W. Manson has a valuable appendix[4] in his important work *Jesus the Messiah*, in which predicates of the Servant and of the Messiah are shown to have many details in common. W. D. Davies

---

[1] *Op. cit.*, p. 84.

[2] Cf. H. Riesenfeld, *op. cit.*, p. 86: "Que cette polémique ait été provoquée par le rôle important que jouait l'exégèse chrétienne de *Is.* LIII dans l'Église et dans sa mission ou qu'elle ait une autre origine, une telle modification du sens originaire du chapitre laisse supposer qu'il existait auparavant une autre interprétation juive et qui correspondait à celle adoptée par l'Église." It may be agreed that anti-Christian feeling would strengthen the diversity of the Synagogue's interpretation from that of the Church, but it is gratuitous to assume that the Church took its interpretation from the Synagogue. The oldest Jewish interpretations we have are at variance with the theory that the Jews cherished the idea of a suffering Messiah in connexion with this passage in pre-Christian days. For not only does the Septuagint interpret differently, but S. D. Luzzatto noted that in the days of the Tannaim the interpretation of the passage in terms of the Israelite nation was already found (cf. A. Neubauer and S. R. Driver, *The Fifty-third Chapter of Isaiah according to the Jewish Interpreters*, i, 1876, p. 351, translated in ii, 1877, p. 412). The evidence for this is found in Origen, who states that a Jew with whom he argued held ταῦτα πεπροφητεῦσθαι ὡς περὶ ἑνὸς τοῦ ὅλου λαοῦ, καὶ γενομένου ἐν τῇ διασπορᾷ καὶ πληγέντος, ἵνα πολλοὶ προσήλυτοι γένωνται τῇ προφάσει τοῦ ἐπεσπάρθαι Ἰουδαίους τοῖς λοιποῖς ἔθνεσι (*Contra Celsum*, i, 55, ed. P. Koetschau, *Origenes Werke* [in Die griechischen christlichen Schriftsteller der ersten drei Jahrhunderte], i, 1899, p. 106]. Cf. Dalman, *op. cit.*, pp. 34 f. In Numbers Rabbah xiii, 2 (Soncino edition of *Midrash Rabbah, Numbers*, ii, E.Tr. by J. J. Slotki, 1939, p. 5), we again find the interpretation in terms of the nation. This is a late source, but H. A. Fischel thinks it may go back to an older tradition (*J.Q.R.*, xxxvii, 1946–47, p. 278 n.).

[3] *Loc. cit*, p. 176.

[4] *Jesus the Messiah*, 1943, pp. 171 ff.

refers[1] with approval to this appendix, and appears to think that this is evidence for the thesis that the two concepts were associated in pre-Christian days. What is not shown is that this evidence for the bringing together of the two figures had been noticed by anyone in any comparable way before the beginning of the Christian era, and that it had led to an equation, not of *predicates* alone, but of the *figures* of the Messiah and the Servant. Many of the predicates are used of others, indeed. Others are called Servants of God,[2] and have His Spirit,[3] are called from the womb,[4] and suffer,[5] without being thought of as Messiah. All that the evidence collected by Manson establishes is that it was not without reason that the concepts were brought together in the New Testament, and not that they had been already brought together before the time of our Lord.

W. D. Davies imports into his discussion of the question a reference to the Messiah ben Joseph, but admits that he is unable to prove conclusively that the Messiah ben Joseph was expected in the first century A.D.[6] If he could this would only complicate the question, since he approves of the evidence collected by W. Manson, and thinks it is significant evidence for the bringing together of the concepts of Messiah and Servant. But the evidence would not be valid in relation to the Messiah ben Ephraim, since its messianic passages are concerned with the Davidic Messiah. To the equation of Servant and Davidic Messiah, therefore, Davies returns. Nor is he very sure of himself here. For after saying categorically:[7] "We have pointed out that the concept of the Servant of Yahweh of Deutero-Isaiah had become associated with that of the Messiah before the first century", he concludes more doubtfully[8] that "the assumption is at least possible that the conception of a Suffering Messiah was not unfamiliar to pre-Christian Judaism". Yet the only evidence he cites is of post-Christian

[1] *Op. cit.*, p. 280.

[2] E.g., Moses (Exod. 14: 31, Num. 12: 7, Deut. 34: 5), Caleb (Num. 14: 24), David (2 Sam. 7: 5, 8), Job (Job 1: 8), Isaiah (Is. 20: 3), Nebuchadrezzar (Jer. 25: 9), Zerubbabel (Hag. 2: 23). Cf. L. Dürr, *Wollen und Wirken der alttestamentlichen Propheten*, 1926, p. 4, where the following passages in which the prophets are referred to as Servants of Yahweh are mentioned: 2 Kings 9: 7, 17: 13, 23, 21: 10, 24: 2; Jer. 25: 4, 26: 5, 29: 19, 35: 15, 44: 4; Amos 3: 7; Zech. 1; 6 ; Dan. 9: 6, 10; Ezra 9: 11. Cf. C. Lindhagen, *The Servant Motif in the Old Testament*, 1950.

[3] E.g., Bezalel (Exod. 31: 3), Balaam (Num. 24: 2), Joshua (Deut. 34: 9), Gideon (Judges 6: 34), Jephthah (Judges 11: 29), Samson (Judges 14: 6), Saul (1 Sam. 11: 6), David (1 Sam. 16: 13).

[4] E.g., Israel (Is. 44: 2, 24), Jeremiah (Jer. 1: 5).

[5] Here it will suffice to refer to Jeremiah, Job and many Psalmists.

[6] *Op. cit.*, p. 280.   [7] *Ibid.*, p. 283.   [8] *Ibid.*

date, much of it from the second century or later, and it is of the kind that had been taken fully into account by Moore and others.[1]

Davies cites,[2] as others have done,[3] the arguments put into the mouth of Trypho in Justin Martyr's *Dialogue with Trypho*, and says that "Trypho does not know of any other possibility than that of a suffering Messiah. It is the *manner* of Christ's death, not His suffering, that is the stumbling-block." T. W. Manson cites[4] another passage, where Trypho falls back on the same argument that crucifixion involved the curse of the Law, but comments: "Justin himself has brought forward the passage and offered a Christian interpretation of it, claiming (a) that it prophesies the coming of the Messiah . . ., and (b) that it refers to Christ. Trypho replies that he finds (a) proved, but not (b). I doubt whether his words should be taken to mean, 'We Jews already hold (a); but we must reject (b)'. In any case, Justin here is only evidence for the second century A.D." Médebielle is doubtful if Trypho could have been sincere in his admissions, and thinks he had merely run out of arguments.[5] If that is true, his words can certainly not be taken to express the contemporary Jewish positions, let alone those of an earlier age.

Not a few writers claim that the concept of the Messiah ben Ephraim goes back to pre-Christian days.[6] Of this there is inadequate evidence, and even if it were established it would be irrelevant to the question of the Suffering Servant, since the two conceptions are quite different. The evidence on which the theory rests is found chiefly in the Old

---

[1] The earliest explicit references to the Messiah ben Ephraim which we have date from the second century A.D. Cf. J. Bonsirven, *Le judaïsme palestinien*, i, 1934, p. 385. For a collection of later references cf. Strack-Billerbeck, *op. cit.*, ii, 1924, pp. 294 ff. A. Edersheim (*The Life and Times of Jesus the Messiah*, 11th imp., ii, 1901, p. 435) thought the idea of this Messiah developed after the death of Bar-Kokhba. Cf. J. Levy, *Neuhebräisches und chaldäisches Wörterbuch über die Talmudim und Midraschim*, iii, 1883, p. 271a; J. Klausner, *Der messianischen Vorstellungen des jüdischen Volkes im Zeitalter der Tannaiten*, 1903, pp. 88 f., and *Hā-ra'yôn ham-m^eshîḥî b^e-Yiśrā'ēl*, 1927, pp. 315 ff.; H. Odeberg, *3 Enoch*, 1928, Part II, p. 145 n.; and G. Kittel, *Deutsche Theologie*, 1936, p. 177. G. Dalman, *op. cit.*, p. 21, rejects the view that this idea arose out of the death of Bar-Kokhba. For other theories of the source of the conception cf. Odeberg, *op. cit.*, pp. 144 ff. note.

[2] *Op. cit.*, pp. 280 f.

[3] Cf. J. Jeremias, *Deutsche Theologie*, ii, 1929, p. 115. H. Riesenfeld is here very cautious. He says: "Rappelons encore le fait qu'il y a quelques répliques qui lui sont relatives dans le 'Dialogue avec Tryphon' de Justin, auxquelles on doit certes se garder d'accorder une trop grande valeur probant, mais qui peuvent cependant servir à appuyer, dans une certaine mesure, une hypothèse née par ailleurs" (*op. cit.*, p. 84).

[4] *B.J.R.L.*, xxxii, 1949–50, pp. 175 f.

[5] *S.D.B.*, iii, col. 110.

[6] Cf. E. G. King, *loc. cit.*; G. H. Dix, *loc. cit.*; C. C. Torrey, *loc. cit.*

Testament. It consists of such passages as the cryptic Gen. 49 : 10,[1] Gen. 49 : 23 ff.,[2] Ezek. 21 : 30 ff. (E.V. 25 ff.),[3] together with a further

[1] Cf. Dix, *loc. cit.*, pp. 131 f. The much-discussed words (A. Posnanski, *Schiloh*, i, 1904, devotes over 600 pages to the history of the interpretation of this word) rendered in R.V. "until Shiloh come" he renders "until he come to Shiloh", and supposes the meaning is that the sceptre will not depart from Judah until "one" comes to the Ephraimite city of Shiloh and there takes over the rulership from Judah. If, as Dix supposes, this provided the starting-point for the idea of the Messiah ben Ephraim, it would seem to have lost all contact with it before it appears indubitably before us. J. Lindblom, who also renders "until he come to Shiloh", thinks the meaning is that the kingdom established in Judah through the election of David will be extended to the northern tribes [*Copenhagen Congress Volume* (S.V.T. i), 1953, pp. 78–87]. The Targum of Onkelos did not find the proper name Shiloh here, but rendered the word by "to whom", and it has been followed by many modern writers. L. Dennefeld (*Le Messianisme*, 1929, p. 28) adopts this view and supposes that the word *mishpāṭ* has fallen out of the text. He therefore renders "jusqu'à ce que vienne celui à qui (appartient) le gouvernement, et à qui (appartient) l'obéissance des peuples". It would carry us too far to discuss other views of this text, which in any case offers a precarious basis for any far-reaching theory. A common view has been that Shiloh is to be equated with Akkadian *šēlu*=ruler [so G. R. Driver, *J.T.S.*, xxiii, 1921–22, p. 70; R. Eisler, *E.T.*, xxxvi, 1924–25, p. 477; F. Nötscher, *Z.A.W.*, N.F. vi, 1929, pp. 323 ff., vii, 1930, p. 80; E. Sellin, *Z.A.W.*, N.F. xix, 1944, pp. 57 f.; S. Mowinckel, *He that Cometh*, E.Tr. by G. W. Anderson, 1956, p. 13 n.; J. Coppens, *Volume du Congrès de Strasbourg* (S.V.T. iv), 1957, pp. 112 f.; N. K. Gottwald (*I.D.B.*, iv, 1962, p. 330; J. Gray, in Hastings's one-volume *D.B.*, rev. ed., 1963, p. 908a]. Some ancient versions rendered "he to whom it belongs", and so R.S.V.; R. de Vaux, *Genèse* (Jerusalem Bible), 1951, p. 212; the Confraternity Version, i, *Genesis to Ruth*, 1952, p. 118; E. Dhorme, *La Bible de la Pléiade*, L'Ancien Testament, i, 1956, p. 169. The new Jewish version of the Bible (*The Torah*, 1962, p. 92) divides the word Shiloh and reads *shay lōh*, rendering "tribute shall come to him". C. Lattey (*C.B.Q.*, iv, 1942, pp. 17 f.), following A. Hausrath, (*Neutestamentliche Zeitgeschichte*, iv, 1877, p. 77 n.) argued that Taxo in Assumption of Moses 9 is to be equated with Shiloh in Gen. 49: 10, and that he was thought of as a suffering Messiah, combining in himself the concept of the Messiah—the Davidic Messiah in this case—and the Suffering Servant. On this cf. H. H. Rowley, *The Relevance of Apocalyptic*, 3rd ed., 1963, pp. 150 ff. There is a Dead Sea Scrolls fragment which interprets Gen. 49: 10 messianically, but in terms of the Davidic Messiah. Cf. J. M. Allegro, *J.B.L.*, lxxv, 1956, pp. 174 ff. Here the text is interpreted: "Until the Messiah of Righteousness come, the Shoot of David". This is valuable evidence for the pre-Christian messianic interpretation of this passage, but it does not favour the view that the Messiah ben Ephraim was a pre-Christian expectation. Cf. also W. H. Brownlee, *The Meaning of the Qumrân Scrolls for the Bible*, 1964, pp. 90 ff.

[2] Dix here (*loc. cit.*, pp. 132 f.) regards the verse rendered by R.V. "From thence is the Shepherd, the Stone of Israel" as an interpolation, predicting the Messiah ben Ephraim, whom he identifies with the one who will come to Shiloh. This can hardly be pronounced convincing evidence, or even clear evidence. Cf. E. G. King, *op. cit.*, p. 85.

[3] Cf. Dix, *loc. cit.*, pp. 140 ff. Here the words "Until he come whose right it is; And I will give it to him" are connected with Gen. 49: 10, and the interpretation of the Messiah ben Ephraim is then frankly read into them. Dix admits that there is nothing here to suggest any connexion with the tribe of Ephraim. It may be added that there is nothing whatever in this or the passages referred to in the preceding notes to suggest the death of the Messiah whom Dix reads into them, and they can in no sense be said to provide any evidence of the conception of a suffering Messiah.

passage which will be mentioned below.[1] All that this evidence could amount to, at the best, would be that the seeds of the idea of the Messiah ben Ephraim are to be found in the Old Testament,[2] and not that there was any formulated doctrine of a second Messiah beside the Davidic.[3] Still less could it establish that the figure of Is. 53 was in any way connected with Ephraim, or that the figure which is said to be referred to in these passages was that of a suffering Messiah.

In the later thought on the Messiah ben Ephraim, he is represented as slain in battle when defending Jerusalem in the war against Gog and Magog.[4] This clearly rested on Zech. 12 : 10: "They shall look on him[5] whom they have pierced." That the reference here is to one who suffered is undeniable, and the sequel makes it plain that he is thought of as dying, while the following chapter indicates that the events here referred to should inaugurate the age when evil should be exterminated, and all should be brought into harmony with the will of God.[6] There

---

[1] H. Riesenfeld, *op. cit.*, pp. 86 ff., notes the associations of the haggadic interpretations of the sacrifice of Isaac with the idea of a suffering Messiah, and concludes (p. 95): "Ainsi nous croyons avoir demontré que des concepts qui, en tous cas, sont très proches de l'idée d'un Messie souffrant, ont été associés au récit du sacrifice d'Isaac." These ideas were brought to the passage by late writers rather than derived from it. Cf. D. Lerch, *Isaaks Opferung christlich gedeutet*, 1905, pp. 19 f.; also H. J. Schoeps, *J.B.L.*, lxv, 1946, pp. 385 ff.

[2] J. Klausner traced the origin of the idea of the two Messiahs to the separation of the political and the ethical elements in the conception of the Messiah. In this case the political elements attached to the suffering Messiah, the Messiah ben Ephraim, and hence this could not have provided the preparation for the non-military conception of the Messiahship of Jesus. Cf. *Die messianischen Vorstellungen*, pp. 94 f., and *Hā-ra'yôn hammeshîḥî be-Yiśrā'ēl*, pp. 320 f. Cf. also G. Dalman, *op. cit.*, p. 23: "Das ganze Werk des Messias ben Joseph hat fast nur politische Bedeutung."

[3] A. Médebielle (*loc. cit.*, col. 111) says this conception does not in any case go back earlier than the time of Hadrian; and so J. Klausner (*The Messianic Idea in Israel*, 1956, pp. 400 f.). Cf. the view of Edersheim, cited above, that it arose from the death of Bar Kokhba.

[4] Cf. J. Klausner, *Die messianischen Vorstellungen*, pp. 86 ff., and *Hā-ra'yôn ham-meshîḥî be-Yiśrā'ēl*, pp. 313 ff.

[5] The reading of M.T. is "me", but most editors favour the change to "him". In the latter form it is cited in John 19: 37. M. Delcor (*R.B.*, lviii, 1951, pp. 189 ff.) and P. Lamarche [*Zacharie ix–xiv* (E.B.), 1961, pp. 82 ff.], however, favour the Massoretic text as the *lectio difficilior*. So also E. Dhorme, *La Bible de la Pléiade*, L'Ancien Testament, ii, 1959, p. 865. Here, however, the text is differently divided [following A. van Hoonacker, *Les douze Petits Prophètes* (E.B.), 1908, p. 683]: "et ils regarderont vers moi. Quant à celui qu'ils ont transpercé, ils feront sur lui une lamentation."

[6] Cf. F. Horst, in Robinson-Horst, *Die zwölf kleinen Propheten* (H.A.T.), 1938, pp. 247 f. L. Dennefeld (*Le Messianisme*, 1929, p. 153) thinks that Zech. 12: 10 is to be interpreted as a prophecy of the Servant of Yahweh of Deutero-Isaiah in another form. He does not, therefore, associate either passage with Messiah ben Ephraim. J. Morgenstern (*V.T.*, xi, 1961, p. 418) similarly holds that Zech. 12: 10 is another formulation of the

is, however, no reference whatever to Ephraim, and no evidence at all that in pre-Christian days this had been related to any idea of a Messiah ben Ephraim.[1] Still less is there any evidence that the Suffering Servant of Is. 53 had anything to do with the Messiah ben Ephraim.

Suffering Servant motif. He thinks the piercing of the divinely appointed saviour was a recent occurrence, and that the reference is to one of David's line (and, therefore, not Messiah ben Ephraim) who had been pierced and slain. M. J. Lagrange (Le judaïsme avant Jésus-Christ, 1931, p. 381) thought the reference was to the Servant of Yahweh, conceived as the Davidic Messiah, and P. Lamarche (op. cit., pp. 124 ff.) thinks the passage rests on Is. 53 and belongs to the same prophetic current. M. Delcor (R.B., loc. cit., p. 197), on the other hand, thinks the reference to the Servant is not solidly based. E. Dhorme (op. cit., p. 864) finds the reference to be to an unknown person who was pierced, while several scholars seek to identify him with some historical character. Thus O. Plöger (Theokratie und Eschatologie, 1959, pp. 105 f.) suggests the identification with the brother of Johanan, whom the latter murdered in the Temple; K. Marti [Dodekapropheton (K.H.A.T.), 1904, p. 447] thought of Onias III, whose death in 171 B.C. is commonly found alluded to in Dan. 9: 26, and similarly E. Sellin [Das Zwölfprophetenbuch (K.A.T.), ii, 1930, p. 545], who however adds: "Aber Deuterosacharja ist in seiner Auffassung von dessen Schicksal beeinflusst durch die Gottesknechtsstücke Deuterojesajas"; Oesterley and Robinson (History of Israel, ii, 1932, pp. 269 ff., and Introduction to the Books of the Old Testament, 1934, pp. 424 f.) identify the pierced one with Simon the Maccabee. F. F. Hvidberg (Weeping and Laughter in the Old Testament, E.Tr., 1952, p. 119) suggested that the passage is based on an old tradition in which the term "they have pierced" referred to the killing of a deity. Cf. B. Otzen, Studien über Deuterosacharja, 1964, pp. 173 ff., where it is argued that the reference is not simply cultic, but rests on the historification of the cultic motif in a concrete person. A. Dupont-Sommer (Aperçus préliminaires sur les manuscrits de la Mer Morte, 1950, p. 117, E.Tr. by E. M. Rowley, The Dead Sea Scrolls, 1952, p. 96) suggested that the reference in Zech. 12: 10 was to the martyrdom of the Teacher of Righteousness, which he placed in the 1st century B.C. M. Treves (V.T., xiii, 1963, pp. 196–207) would assign the composition of most or the whole of Zech. 9–14 to the Maccabaean age, and part of it, at least, to the authorship of Judas Maccabaeus.

[1] C. C. Torrey, J.B.L., lxvi, 1947, pp. 272 f., connects this passage with the Messiah ben Ephraim, and quotes in support the interpretation of Rabbi Dosa as recorded in T. B. Sukkah 52 a (cf. L. Goldschmidt, Der babylonische Talmud mit Einschluss der vollständigen Mišnah, iii, 1899, p. 146), observing that this interpretation ought not to be questioned. M. J. Lagrange, however, observes of this passage: "Cependant Zacharie suggère plus clairement que celui qui a été tué, dont la mort est une source de grâce, appartient à la maison de David, ce qui revient presque à le designer comme le Messie, le plus grann des fils de David" (Le judaïsme avant Jésus-Christ, 1931, p. 381). Cf. also J. Jeremias, Deutsche Theologie, ii, p. 116. In The Servant of God, E.Tr., 1957, p. 74, Jeremias says the first reference in rabbinic literature to this passage for the slaying of Messiah ben Ephraim comes from a disciple of Rabbi Akiba. A. McCaul (Rabbi David Kimchi's Commentary upon the Prophecies of Zechariah, 1837, pp. 159 f.) rejects the view that Zech. 12: 10 can refer to the Messiah ben Ephraim, saying: "Why should the house of David and the inhabitants of Jerusalem mourn so bitterly for a son of Joseph, especially as, according to Abarbanel, his death is to make way for the object of their hopes and prayers, Messiah, the son of David?" S. Mowinckel connects the passage with the ritual of the Enthronement Festival (Psalmenstudien, ii, 1922, pp. 231 f.), while Beek (Inleiding in de Joodse Apocalyptiek van het Oud- en Nieuw-testamentisch tijdvak, 1950, p. 28) thinks the reference is to a historical figure who cannot, however, be identified.

For neither in this Servant song nor in the others is there any suggestion of the Servant engaging in warfare, or dying in battle.[1] In the
third song the Servant gives his back to the smiters and his cheek to
them that plucked out his beard,[2] while in the fourth he is led as a lamb
to the slaughter.[3] The conception here is quite unrelated to that of the
later thought on the Messiah ben Ephraim, and there is once more not
the slightest suggestion of any association of the Servant with the tribe
or territory of Ephraim. What is wanted, but what has not yet been
produced, is clear evidence (a) that the Messiah ben Ephraim was a
formulated conception in pre-Christian days, (b) that Is. 53 was either
then or later associated with the Messiah ben Ephraim, (c) that the
Davidic Messiah was identified with either the Messiah ben Ephraim
or with the Suffering Servant in Jewish thought, either in pre-Christian
or in post-Christian days, or (d) that the conception of the Messiah
ben Ephraim is a relevant background for the Gospels, which are at
pains to connect Jesus with the line of David. That a suffering deliverer
was expected in pre-Christian days may be established from Is. 53,
and that the piercing of a sufferer should herald the dawn of the
expected age may be established from Zech. 12 : 10. What remains to
be shown, however, is that Jewish thought had been concentrated on
these passages in relation to the messianic hope in the way it had been
concentrated on the Davidic Messiah, and that there had been any serious
integration of these passages along with the others in a single whole.

G. H. Dix makes appeal[4] to a passage in the Testaments of the
Twelve Patriarchs, where reference is made to the sinless one dying
for ungodly men,[5] to support his view of the early expectation of the
suffering Messiah. Here, however, he confesses that there is nothing to
show that the writer had a messianic figure in mind, and agrees that
the Testaments as a whole look for a Messiah ben Levi.[6] It may also

---

[1] Cf. V. H. Stanton, *The Jewish and the Christian Messiah*, 1886, p. 124: "Messiah Ben-
Joseph, . . . who prepares the way for Messiah Ben-David, is not according to the original
conception of his character a sufferer, but a warrior. Though he falls, there is nothing
specifically atoning in his death." A. Médebielle, *loc. cit.*, col. 111: "Le Talmud de Babylone parle cependant d'un Messie qui sera mis à mort . . . ; mais ce n'est pas le vrai Messie.
Il est fils de Joseph, de la tribu d'Ephraïm, et non descendant de David; il n'est pas lui-
même le sauveur du peuple, il prépare seulement les voies au Messie, fils de David; enfin,
il n'est pas le serviteur-victime, mais un guerrier qui succombe glorieusement dans sa
victoire." Cf. also C. Guignebert, *Le monde juif vers le temps de Jésus*, 1935, p. 191 (E.Tr.
by S. H. Hooke, 1939, p. 145).

[2] Is. 50: 6.   [3] Is. 53: 7.   [4] *Loc. cit.*, pp. 135 f.   [5] T. Benj. 3: 8.

[6] G. R. Beasley-Murray, "The Two Messiahs in the Testaments of the Twelve Patriarchs", in *J.T.S.*, xlviii, 1947, pp. 1 ff., argues that the Messiah ben Judah, as well as
the Messiah ben Levi, figures in the Testaments.

be noted that whereas the death of this sinless one is apparently vicarious, there is nothing to suggest that the death of the Messiah ben Ephraim was vicarious.[1] As Dix himself summarizes the expectation,[2] "it would seem that the Messiah ben Joseph would gather a great army from the reunited tribes and set up his kingdom in Palestine with Jerusalem as his capital. Then the hosts of the heathen nations would come to make war against the Holy City, as Ezekiel and some of his predecessors had predicted, and slay the Messiah ben Joseph with many of his followers. Thereafter the Messiah ben David would appear, raise the Messiah ben Joseph and his faithful followers from the dead, and establish the final kingdom which should last for ever." None of this would seem to be relevant to the discussion of Is. 53.

C. C. Torrey thinks the speculation on the Messiah ben Ephraim started from Is. 53.[3] In the development of the thought, as he traces it, however, there is little evidence of the influence of this chapter in pre-Christian times. He brings Dan. 9 : 24–27 into the story, and claims that the "anointed one" who was cut off was no other than the Messiah ben Ephraim.[4] The whole picture here is quite other than that in Is. 53, in that it is clearly set in a context of war and conquest, and in that there is nothing to suggest that the cutting off of the anointed one was in any way vicarious.[5] The fundamental idea of Is. 53 is therefore lacking here. Torrey also claims[6] that in its original form Zech. 4 contained a reference to the two Messiahs, but since he finds in these the Messiah anointed for war and the Messiah anointed to rule, there is again nothing which could naturally be said to have its roots in Is. 53, since the vicarious element so important there is missing here. Similarly, when he finds[7] in 1 Enoch 90 : 38 a reference to the Messiah ben Ephraim in the buffalo with great black horns on its head, he carries us once more to a world of thought quite different from that of Is. 53. The fact that this is generally regarded as an allusion to Deut. 33 : 16 f., and that later speculation interpreted that Biblical passage of

---

[1] Dix surprisingly claims support for his view by arguing that the words of Caiaphas, "It is expedient that one man should die for the people, and that the whole nation perish not" (John 11: 50), are an allusion to the doctrine of the suffering Messiah (loc. cit., pp. 136 f.). It is surely manifest that Caiaphas had no such idea in mind, and the Evangelist declares it to be an unwitting prophecy, and not an allusion to current expectations.

[2] Op. cit., p. 130.   [3] J.B.L., loc. cit., p. 256.   [4] Ibid., pp. 268 ff.

[5] Cf. Dalman, op. cit., p. 22: "Keine der mit ihm (sc. the Messiah ben Joseph) sich beschäftigenden Stellen gibt seinem Tode einen Sühnwert, keine redet von einem demselben vorangehenden Leiden."   [6] Loc. cit., pp. 273 ff.

[7] Ibid., pp. 266 ff. Cf. also the same writer in J.A.O.S., lxii, 1942, p. 57 and The Apocryphal Literature, 1945, pp. 111 f.

the warrior Messiah, is not very clear evidence that the writer of I Enoch was thinking of the Messiah ben Ephraim, and offers no vestige of evidence for the connexion of Is. 53 either with this passage or with the whole concept of the Messiah ben Ephraim.[1]

Other writers have claimed that in I Enoch we have evidence for the bringing together of the three concepts of the Son of Man, the Messiah, and the Suffering Servant.[2] It is undeniable that the terms Son of Man[3] and Anointed One, or Messiah, are found here, and that some of the language of the Servant songs is echoed in this work.[4] It is frequently held that the work has been interpolated,[5] and the references to the Son of Man are regarded as secondary accretions.[6] Even if we give these passages the benefit of the doubt,[7] several questions

[1] Cf. G. Dalman, *op. cit.*, p. 19: Strack-Billerbeck, *op. cit.*, ii, pp. 293 f.; Bousset-Gressmann, *op. cit.*, pp. 230 f.

[2] Cf. I. Engnell, *The 'Ebed Yahweh Songs and the Suffering Messiah*, p. 4 n.: "The idea of the suffering Messiah still stands out quite clearly in the circle behind I Enoch."

[3] On the Son of Man in Enoch cf. especially E. Sjöberg, "Känner I Henok och 4 Esra tanken på den lidande Människosonen?" in *S.E.Å.*, v. 1940, pp. 163 ff.; "Ville Jesus vara Messias?" *ibid.*, x, 1945, pp. 82 ff.; and *Der Menschensohn im äthiopischen Henochbuch*, 1946; S. Mowinckel, "Henok og 'Menneskesønnen' ", in *Nor.T.T.*, xlv, 1944, pp. 57 ff.; "Ophavet til den senjødiske forestilling om Menneskesønnen", *ibid.*, pp. 189 ff.; and *He that Cometh*, E.Tr. by G. W. Anderson, 1956, pp. 385 ff.

[4] Cf. J. Jeremias, *Deutsche Theologie*, ii, pp. 109 f.; N. Johansson, *Parakletoi*, pp. 109 ff. Cf., however, E. Sjöberg, *Der Menschensohn im äthiopischen Henochbuch*, pp. 120 ff., esp. p. 128: "Die festgestellten, sehr begrenzten Beziehungen zwischen dem Menschensohn und den Ebed-Jahve-Liedern geben also keinen hinreichenden Grund für die Annahme, dass die Bilderreden den Menschensohn mit der Vorstellung des leidenden Ebed Jahve verbunden haben."

[5] Cf. Bruno Bauer, *Kritik der evangelischen Geschichte der Synoptiker*, 2nd ed., i, 1846, p. 402.

[6] Cf. J. Drummond, *op. cit.*, pp. 49 ff.; E. de Faye, *Les apocalypses juives*, 1892, pp. 215 f.; W. Bousset, *Jesu Predigt im ihrem Gegensatz zum Judentum*, 1892, pp. 105 ff. (contrast however, *Die Religion des Judentums im neutestamentlichen Zeitalter*, 2nd ed., 1906, p. 301); N. Schmidt, in *Encyclopædia Biblica*, iv, 1907, col. 4711. Cf. also O. Pfleiderer, *Das Urchristenthum: seine Schriften und Lehren*, 1887, p. 315; M. J. Lagrange, *Le messianisme chez les juifs*, 1909, pp. 89 f., 93 n., and *R.B.*, xxxi, 1922, p. 624; J. B. Frey, in *Supplément au Dictionnaire de la Bible*, i, 1928, col. 359. It has been pointed out that the oldest MS. of the Similitudes of Enoch now extant is not older than the fifteenth century, and that although the early Fathers knew the work, none of them cite any of these passages, which may not have belonged to the work in their time (J. B. Frey, *loc. cit.*,; cf. L. Gry, *R.B.*, N.S. vi, 1909, p. 464).

[7] Among those who have rejected the interpolation hypothesis are M. Goguel, *R.H.P.R.*, v, 1925, p. 526; E. Sjöberg, *Der Menschensohn im äthiopischen Henochbuch*, 1946, pp. 11 ff.; J. Bowman, *E.T.*, lix, 1947–48, p. 287a. Cf. also S. Mathews, *The Messianic Hope in the New Testament*, 1906, p. 104: "Recent criticism has shown conclusively the impossibility of attributing these sections to Christian influences. There is in them absolutely nothing that can reasonably argue Christian origin; but, on the contrary, they are thoroughly pharisaic in spirit." For an analysis of the sources of the Similitudes cf. F. Stier, "Zur Komposition und Literarkritik der Bilderreden des äthiopischen Henoch (Kap. 37–69)",

have to be faced before we can rely on this work to establish the thesis that the three terms had run together before the time of our Lord.[1] It is well known that T. W. Manson holds the view that the Son of Man is a collective figure here, as in the book of Daniel.[2] He also maintains

in *Orientalistische Studien* (Littmann Festschrift), 1935, pp. 70 ff. Like many other critics, Stier rejects chapters 70 f. from the original Similitudes (cf. H. Gressmann, *Der Messias*, 1929, p. 377 n.); others regard these chapters as the climax of the section.

[1] In *The Relevance of Apocalyptic*, 1944, p. 56, I observed: "Even though we accept all these passages and equate all of these terms, and treat them all as individual in their reference, that does not involve the equating of the Son of Man with the Messiah, in the individual sense of that term." For this W. D. Davies (*Paul and Rabbinic Judaism*, 1948, p. 279) takes me to task, and declares that "already before the Christian era the ideas of the Messiah and of the Son of Man had been merged, although it would be incorrect to think of this merging as a precise identification." What Professor Davies fails to show is why Jesus should deprecate the use of the term Messiah in relation to Himself and yet use the term Son of Man, if these two concepts had merged, or why Peter's confession at Caesarea Philippi (Matt. 16: 16) should have been in any way remarkable if our Lord's use of the term Son of Man had so clearly pointed to it.

[2] Cf. *The Teaching of Jesus*, 2nd ed., 1935, pp. 228 f. Against Manson cf. V. Taylor, *Jesus and His Sacrifice*, 1943 ed., pp. 24 f. A. Feuillet (*R.B.*, lx, 1953, p. 344) dismisses Manson's view by saying it "relève de la haute fantaisie". Manson returned to this subject in *B.J.R.L.*, xxxii, 1949–50, pp. 178 ff., where he argued convincingly that the Son of Man is not here a pre-existent being as commonly held (cf. Sjöberg, *op. cit.*, pp. 83 ff.), but one who existed in the purpose of God from the beginning of time, but was now about to be given reality in the community of the saints (p. 186), and that he could more properly be described as unborn than as pre-existent (p. 185). M. Black, *E.T.*, lx, 1948–49, p. 14, presented a view very similar to that of Manson, to whom he acknowledged his indebtedness for private suggestions. Such a view was already rejected by L. Gry, *Le Muséon*, N.S. ix, 1908, pp. 335 f., though with arguments that can scarcely stand against Manson's. Cf. also J. Bowman, *loc. cit.*, p. 288a. Cf. further M. A. Beek, *Inleiding in de Joodse apocalyptiek van het Oud- en Nieuw-testamentisch tijdvak*, 1950, p. 105: "De mensen-zoon naar de voorstelling van Henoch is dus prae-existent, waarbij het niet veel zin heeft om te twisten over een reële of ideële prae-existentie, want deze onderscheiding kent de Joodse apocalyptiek nauwelijks". W. Staerk follows the common view which rests on the work of Bousset, Reitzenstein, and Gressmann (see below, p. 81, n. 1), and identifies the Son of Man with the *Urmensch* (cf. *Soter*, 1933, pp. 72 ff., and *Die Erlö-sererwartung in den östlichen Religionen*, 1938, pp. 438 ff.). Cf. J. M. Creed, "The Heavenly Man", in *J.T.S.*, xxvi, 1925, pp. 113 ff. A. H. Edelkoort, though holding that the Son of Man in 1 Enoch was pre-existent, rejects any influence from Persian religion or any idea of the *Urmensch*. He says: "De Messias een prae-existent wezen is, dat het paradijs beheerscht, tot dat hij aan het einde der dagen komen zal. . . . Maar het is niet noodig die herkomst te zoeken in het Parsisme en aan den oer-mensch te denken" (*De Christus-verwachting in het Oude Testament*, 1941, p. 500). Cf. S. Mowinckel, "Urmensch und Königsideologie'", in *Studia Theologica*, ii, 1948, pp. 71–89. J. Schniewind goes so far as to suggest that the pre-existence of Jesus, which is presupposed by some sayings in the Gospels, rests on the pre-existence of the Son of Man in Enoch (*Das Evangelium nach Markus*, 5th ed., 1949, p. 163). B. D. Eerdmans held that the Son of Man is not here a title, but should be rendered "man" (*T.T.*, xxviii, 1894, pp. 168 ff.), and so, too, H. Lietzmann (*Der Menschensohn*, 1896, pp. 42 ff.). On the Son of Man in 1 Enoch cf. also J. Coppens, in J. Coppens and L. Dequeker, *Le Fils de l'homme et les Saints du Très-Haut en Daniel vii, dans les Apocryphes et dans le Nouveau Testament*, 1961, pp. 73 ff.

that the term Anointed One, or Messiah, is collective in this work.[1] Messel eliminates the term "Son of Man" in all but two passages, where he similarly offers a collective interpretation,[2] and the term "Anointed One" he declares to be secondary.[3] If we hold to the commoner view that the terms are individual in their reference, an equation of the figures indicated with either of the two Messiahs of later Jewish thought is not simple.[4] For this is no Messiah ben David or Messiah ben Ephraim, but rather a transcendental figure who should be the leader and head of the kingdom, the crystallization of the Danielic personification in a concrete person, who should come from above.[5] In his latest treatment of the subject, T. W. Manson recognizes both an individual and a collective element in the conception, and notes the parallel with the oscillation that always marks the idea of "corporate personality" in Hebrew thought.[6] This simplifies the

[1] Cf. *The Teaching of Jesus, loc. cit.*

[2] Cf. *Der Menschensohn in den Bilderreden des Henoch*, 1922, pp. 3 ff. The two passages where it is allowed to stand are I Enoch 46: 2 ff. and 48: 2. A. von Gall, *Basileia tou Theou*, 1926, p. 420 n., says: "Messels schon angeführtes Buch 'Der Menschensohn' ist als ganzes verfehlt, in dem er den 'Menschensohn' und den 'Auserwählten' mit der Gemeinde der Heiligen identifiziert."

[3] *Ibid.*, p. 31. Cf. M. J. Lagrange, *R.B.*, xxxi, 1922, p. 624. G. Dalman (*Die Worte Jesu*, 1898, p. 221) regards the references to the Messiah in I Enoch 48: 10, 52: 4 as secondary, while L. Gry (*Le Muséon*, N.S. ix, 1908, pp. 329 f.) retains them as original. On the former of these passages, cf. J. Héring, *R.H.P.R.*, xviii, 1938, p. 419: "Si ce texte est ancien il constitue une tentative d'innovation sans lendemain. Il est en effet très curieux qu'aucun autre parmi les nombreux textes concernant le Sauveur hénochien ne fasse la moindre allusion au Roi d'Israël." Cf. also J. Y. Campbell, *J.T.S.*, xlviii, 1947, pp. 146 ff. M. Black, however, is "inclined to be doubtful of a hypothesis which depends on a process of such extensive obelizing" as Messel's (*E.T.*, lx, 1948–49, p. 12a).

[4] Cf. C. Guignebert, *Le monde juif vers le temps de Jésus*, 1935, p. 185 (E. Tr., by S. H. Hooke, 1939, p. 140), apodictically states that the identification of the Son of Man and the Messiah was effected in the book of Enoch. Cf. P. Fiebig, *Der Menschensohn*, 1901, pp. 85 ff.; also C. H. Kraeling, *Anthropos and Son of Man*, 1927, p. 137: "The Son of Man of Enoch is the pre-existent Messiah."

[5] Cf. W. Bousset, *Die Religion des Judentums im neutestamentlichen Zeitalter*, 2nd ed., 1906, p. 301: "Er ist überhaupt *keine irdische Erscheinung mehr*, er wird nicht wie der Messias aus Davids Stamm auf Erden geboren, er ist ein engelartiges Wesen, dessen Wohnung sich im Himmel (Paradies) unter den Fittichen des Herrn der Geister befindet. Er ist *präexistent*." J. Schniewind, on the contrary, claims that in I Enoch the Davidic Messiah and the transcendental Son of Man are identified, but adds "Wie kann beides zugleich bestehen? Im Henoch-Buch stehen beide Überlieferungen unausgeglichen nebeneinander" (*Das Evangelium nach Markus*, 5th ed., 1949, p. 163).

[6] Cf. *B.J.R.L., loc. cit.*, pp. 188 ff. Manson observes: "The group idea finds expression in the concept of the elect and righteous ones, i.e. the Israel within Israel, the Remnant. The individual finds expression in two personalities: at the beginning of the course of events in Enoch, who is regarded as the first human individual to embody the Son of Man idea, the nucleus of the group of the elect and righteous ones; at the end it finds

problem created by the passage in which the Son of Man is identified with Enoch.[1] Charles emended this passage in order to eliminate the equation,[2] while Otto retained the text,[3] but resorted to the very difficult idea that a preacher of righteousness should become the one

expression again in the figure of the Messiah who is to carry out the final vindication of the saints. But whether it be in Enoch, who is as it were the first-born of many brethren, or in the Messiah, or in the corporate body of the elect and righteous, it is the same idea that is embodied, an idea that formed part of the divine purpose before the creation of the world." Here I would question the use of the word Messiah, since it implies an identification of the second of these personalities that goes beyond the evidence. It is possible, indeed, that the author thought of the return of Enoch rather than of a second individual. E. Sjöberg ("Människosonen och Israel i Dan. 7", in *Religion och Bibel*, vii, 1948, pp. 1–16) finds this same fluidity in the conception of the Son of Man in Dan. 7. So also A. Bertholet, in *Oriental Studies in Honour of Cursetji Erachji Pavry*, 1934, pp. 37 f.; A. Bentzen, *Daniel* (H.A.T.), 1937, pp. 33 f.; and J. Coppens, in J. Coppens and L. Dequeker, *Le Fils de l'homme et les Saints du Très-Haut en Daniel vii, dans les Apocryphes et dans le Nouveau Testament*, 1961, p. 67.

[1] 1 Enoch 71: 14: "Thou art the Son of Man." F. Martin (*Le livre d'Hénoch*, 1906, p. 161) renders "Toi, tu es le fils de l'homme", thus distinguishing the reference from 46: 3, where he has "le Fils de l'homme", with F. This, however, is difficult to sustain, since the context in both cases has similar predicates of the Son of Man as Martin agrees (p. 161 n.). H. Lietzmann (*Der Menschensohn*, 1896, p. 46) treated both passages as Martin treated 71: 14, finding 46: 3 to mean "dies ist ein Mensch", and 71: 14 to mean "du bist ein Mensch". Cf. also S. Mowinckel, *Nor. T.T.*, xlv, 1944, pp. 59 ff., where the expression is said to be used in 71: 14 "i sin 'dagligdagse', uterminologiske mening" (cf. R. Laurence, *The Book of Enoch the Prophet*, 3rd ed., 1838, p. 46: "Thou art the offspring of man"), and *He that Cometh*, E.Tr., 1956, pp. 442 f.; E. Sjöberg, *Der Menschensohn im äthiopischen Henochbuch*, pp. 149 ff. N. Dahl (*Das Volk Gottes*, 1941, p. 91) on the contrary, says: "So müsste man an eine 'Einverleitung' des Henoch in diese 'Gesamtperson' des Menschensohnes denken." H. Gressmann (*Der Messias*, 1929, p. 378) thinks this passage originally had reference to Noah, and not Enoch.

[2] Cf. *The Book of Enoch*, 2nd ed., 1912, pp. 144 f., where Charles reads "This is the Son of Man", assimilating the passage to 1 Enoch 46: 3. So, too, P. Riessler, *Altjüdisches Schrifttum ausserhalb der Bibel*, 1928, p. 403.

[3] Cf. *The Kingdom of God and the Son of Man*, E.Tr., 2nd ed., 1943, p. 208. Otto holds that 1 Enoch expressed the idea "that a powerful preacher alike of righteousness, the coming judgment, and the blessed new age, a prophet of the eschatological Son of Man, would be transported at the end of his earthly career to God; that he would be exalted to become the one whom he had proclaimed, in the literal sense that he himself would become the very one whom he had proclaimed" (p. 213), and that 1 Enoch 71: 14 is associated with this hope. I have elsewhere observed that Otto's view raises more questions than it solves (cf. *The Relevance of Apocalyptic*, 3rd ed., 1963, p. 62 n.). With Otto's view cf. Sjöberg's (*op. cit.*, p. 187), and T. W. Manson's criticism (*B.J.R.L.*, *loc. cit.*, p. 188). Amongst the many who retain the text in 71: 14 are G. Beer, in *Die Apokryphen und Pseudepigraphen des Alten Testaments*, ed. by E. Kautzsch, ii, 1900, p. 277; J. Flemming and L. Radermacher, *Das Buch Henoch* (in Die griechischen christlichen Schriftsteller der ersten drei Jahrhunderte), 1901, p. 91; C. H. Kraeling, *Anthropos and Son of Man*, 1927, pp. 162 f.; L. Jansen, *Die Henochgestalt*, 1939, p. 125; M. A. Beek, *Nationale en transcendente motieven in de Joodse apocalyptiek van de laatste eeuwen voor Christus*, 1941, pp. 14 f.; J. Bowman, *E.T.*, lix, 1947–48, p. 287 a, note. L. Gry, *Le Muséon*, N.S. ix, 1908, pp. 63 f. note, allows that there may be interpolation in this verse.

whom he had proclaimed.[1] This would carry us far from either of the two Messiahs, and in any case there is nothing to connect the Son of Man with either David or Ephraim, or to suggest that he should be killed.[2]

Nor can we readily conclude that the Son of Man is here identified with the Suffering Servant.[3] Some of the language used of the Son of Man had undoubted links with the language used of the Suffering Servant. Yet here, as so constantly, we must be careful to avoid confusion of thought. The fact that something is predicated of the one figure which is predicated of the other does not involve the conclusion that the two are to be identified.[4] Johansson has noted[5] some verbal links between Gen. 5 : 24, which refers to Enoch, and Is. 53 : 8. Many have drawn attention to the points of connexion between Moses and the Servant.[6] Few would propose any simple identification of the

[1] L. Jansen (*Die Henochgestalt*, 1939, pp. 86 ff.) basing himself on the work of W. Bousset (*Hauptprobleme der Gnosis*, 1907, pp. 160 ff.), H. Reitzenstein (*Das iranische Erlösungsmysterium*, 1921, pp. 115 ff.), A. von Gall (*Basileia tou Theou*, 1926, pp. 409 ff.), C. H. Kraeling (*Anthropos and Son of Man*, 1927), and H. Gressmann (*Der Messias*, 1929, pp. 343 ff.), traced the figure of the Son of Man partly to foreign sources. He similarly held that the figure of Enoch combined native and foreign elements. Both Enoch and the Son of Man are connected with the Babylonian Ea-Oannes, while the earthly Enoch is a combination of Israelite prophet and Chaldæan wise man. N. Dahl justly observes, however, that on the difficult question of the relation between Enoch and the Son of Man Jansen does not shed any clear light (*Das Volk Gottes*, 1941, p. 297, n. 64).

[2] J. Y. Campbell, who is doubtful if the Similitudes of Enoch are of pre-Christian origin (*J.T.S.*, xlviii, 1947, p. 147), concludes "that the Book of Enoch affords not the slightest trustworthy evidence for the existence of 'the Son of Man' as a Messianic title in pre-Christian times" (p. 148). M. Black (*S.J.Th.*, vi, 1953, p. 10) observes: "One fact stands out: nowhere in 1 Enoch is the main function of the Servant, his vicarious and redemptive suffering, ascribed to the Son of Man." G. H. P. Thompson (*J.T.S.*, N.S. xii, 1961, pp. 201–209) maintains that before the time of Jesus there had developed the expectation of the coming of a heavenly Son of Man, who was "more or less equivalent to the Messiah", and that Jesus adopted this title, "perhaps because it had fewer political associations than the title Messiah".

[3] On the one side cf. J. Jeremias, *Deutsche Theologie*, ii, pp. 109 f.; E. Lohmeyer, *Das Evangelium des Markus* (Meyer's Kritisch-exegetischer Kommentar über das Neue Testament, 10th ed.), 1937, pp. 5 f., and N. Johansson, *Parakletoi*, pp. 113 ff.; on the other side cf. E. Sjöberg, *S.E.Å.*, v, 1940, pp. 162 ff., vii, 1942, pp. 141 ff., and *Der Menschensohn im äthiopischen Henochbuch*, pp. 116 ff.; H. W. Wolff, *Jesaja 53 in Urchristentum*, 1942, pp. 38 f. (2nd ed., 1950, pp. 42 f.).

[4] Cf. Sjöberg, *op. cit.*, p. 132: "Der Menschensohn der Bilderreden ist nicht ein leidender Erlöser." Similarly, J. Bowman, *E.T.*, *loc. cit.*, p. 286a: "We have absolutely nothing on the suffering and death of the 'son of Man'."

[5] *Op. cit.*, pp. 117 ff. Cf. E. Sjöberg, *op. cit.*, pp. 131 f., and *S.E.Å.*, vii, 1942, pp. 142 f.

[6] Cf. G. Füllkrug, *Der Gottesknecht des Deuterojesaja*, 1899, pp. 82 ff.; J. Hontheim, *Z.K.T.*, xxx, 1906, pp. 751 ff.; J. Fischer, *Isaias 40–55 und die Perikopen vom Gottesknecht*, 1916, pp. 191, 193 ff., and *Wer ist der Ebed?* 1922, pp, 55, 81 ff.; E. Balla, in *Eucharistērion* (Gunkel Festschrift), i, 1923, p. 245; J. Jeremias, *Deutsche Theologie*, ii, 1929, pp. 112 f.;

Servant with Enoch or with Moses, though Sellin did propose the latter identification in one phase of his long pilgrimage of interpretation of the Servant.[1] Most have been content to say that the Servant is thought of as a second Moses.[2] In the same way, we must beware of reading too much into a common predication here, and the salutary warning of Moore should be remembered. That excellent scholar deprecated the carrying of rabbinic application beyond the words actually cited to their context, and said:[3] "In view of such utterances as have been quoted above about the fathers and the prophets, it would be neither strange nor especially significant, if among the many and diverse homiletical applications of Scripture to the Messiah, something of a similar kind should have been said about him. Such application would, however, be no evidence that the Jews had a doctrine of a suffering Messiah."[4]

This warning is especially appropriate here. W. Manson,[5] who is followed by W. D. Davies,[6] adduces a number of verbal links which are no more convincing than those adduced to link the Servant with the Davidic Messiah. In 1 Enoch 46 : 3, 48 : 4, 62 : 2, 71 : 14, the Son of Man is endowed with righteousness, and here Is. 9 : 6 (E.V. 7), 11 : 4 f., Jer. 23 : 5 f., and Zech. 9 : 9 are cited for the Davidic Messiah, and Is. 42 : 6 and 53 : 11 for the Servant. In 1 Enoch 46 : 3 the Son of Man is said to be chosen, and here Ps. 2 : 6 f. and 89 : 28 (E.V. 27) are brought forward for the Messiah and Is. 42 : 1 for the Servant. In 1 Enoch 46 : 4, 62 : 3, 9, the Son of Man is said to raise up kings and to see kings fall down before him, while comparable things are produced for the Messiah from Ps. 2 : 2 f., 10–12, 72 : 10 f., 89 : 28 (E.V. 27), and for the Servant from Is. 49 : 7 and 52 : 15. It is unnecessary

---

A. S. Peake, *The Servant of Yahweh*, 1931, pp. 32 f.; A. Bentzen, *Messias, Moses redivivus, Menschensohn*, 1948, pp. 64 ff. Jeremias also draws attention to some links between Moses and the Messiah.

[1] Cf. *Mose und seine Bedeutung für die israelitisch-jüdische Religionsgeschichte*, 1922, pp. 77 ff.

[2] Cf. A. Bentzen, *op. cit.*, p. 68, where Moses is treated as "Modell" for the Servant.

[3] *Judaism*, iii, 1931, p. 166.

[4] Cf. F. J. Foakes Jackson and Kirsopp Lake, *The Beginnings of Christianity*, i, 1942 ed., p. 355 n.: "Interpreters of the apocalypses, not being familiar with the methods and mental habits of Jewish students of the Bible, do not recognize the midrashic character of such associations of texts"; also J. Bowman, *E.T.*, lix, 1947–48, p. 285a: "Midrashic interpretation cares nothing for the original meaning, nor does it read statements in their contexts; it seizes a word, a phrase, and utilizes it as a peg for extraneous ideas."

[5] *Jesus the Messiah*, 1943, pp. 173 f.

[6] *Paul and Rabbinic Judaism*, 1948, pp. 279 f.

to pursue this argument further. None of this goes beyond a certain community of predicates, and none requires the identification of the persons. There is not the slightest suggestion that the Son of Man is of Davidic descent,[1] and in so far as he has appropriated the attributes of the Davidic Messiah he may be said to have supplanted him, as the Messiah ben Levi is held to have supplanted the Messiah ben David under the Hasmonaeans, rather than to be identified with him. There is not the slightest suggestion of any suffering of the Son of Man comparable with the suffering which is the most notable feature of the Servant,[2] and the claim that they are to be identified involves the assumption that the conception of the Servant has been as violently transformed as it has in the Targum of Jonathan.

Similarly, when Jeremias draws attention[3] to the intercession of the Son of Man for the righteous in 1 Enoch 47 : 1–4 as the counterpart of the intercession of the Servant in Is. 53, this does not provide any evidence for the identification of the two figures, since the context in the one case is of the victorious might of the Son of Man, who puts down kings and breaks the teeth of sinners, while in the other it is of shameful suffering and death as a guilt offering for men.[4]

---

[1] If he is identified with Enoch, this is definitely ruled out; while if the common view that he is a transcendental and pre-existent being is correct, he could just as little be thought of as a descendant of David.

[2] Cf., however, the claim of J. Jeremias to find some evidence that the exaltation of the Son of Man in 1 Enoch is through death (*loc. cit.*, p. 110), and the reply of Sjöberg, *Der Menschensohn im äthiopischen Henochbuch*, pp. 130 ff. Cf., too, G. Kittel, *Deutsche Theologie*, 1936, pp. 175 f., where it is noted that while 1 Enoch uses Servant language of the Son of Man, it does not speak of the Son of Man as suffering or dying. Cf. S. Mowinckel, *He that Cometh*, E.Tr., 1956, pp. 410 ff.

[3] Cf. Johannson, *Parakletoi*, pp. 115 ff., and Sjöberg's criticism, *op. cit.*, pp. 128 ff.

[4] It would carry us beyond our present purpose to examine passages in 4 Ezra (2 Esdras) and 2 Baruch, which have been adduced to show the antiquity of the concept of the suffering Messiah in Judaism, since they are in any case later than the ministry of Jesus, and therefore not relevant for the purpose of this paper. On these passages cf. H. Gressmann, *Der Messias*, 1929, pp. 379 ff.; J. Jeremias, *loc. cit.*, pp. 110 f.; W. Staerk, *Soter*, 1933, pp. 76 f., and *Die Erlöserwartung in den östlichen Religionen*, 1938, pp. 448 ff.; H. Riesenfeld, *op. cit.*, p. 317; C. C. Torrey, *loc. cit.*, p. 259 ff.; and on the other side, H. W. Wolff, *op. cit.*, pp. 40 f., and E. Sjöberg, *op. cit.*, pp. 134 ff. Cf also L. Gry, "La 'Mort du Messie' en IV Esdras, VII, 29 [III, V, 4]", in *Mémorial Lagrange*, 1940, pp. 133 ff., and the observation of P. Volz on this passage: "So ist darin nicht die geringste Spur von der Idee des Sühnleidens enthalten, nicht einmal wahrscheinlich auf Jes 53 angespielt" (*Jesaja II*, in Sellin's K.A.T., 1932, p. 186 n.). H. W. Wolff denies the presence of any suffering Messiah in the Apocrypha (*op. cit.*, pp. 39 ff.; 2nd ed., pp. 43 ff.).

Moreover, the evidence of the New Testament is not to be ignored. The Gospels tell us that the disciples were always confused and bewildered when Jesus spoke of His mission in terms of suffering. They were thinking in terms of the Davidic Messiah, and it is clear that they did not bring the idea of suffering and death into relation with that concept.[1] It is equally clear that they did not equate the terms Son of Man and Davidic Messiah,[2] or our Lord's express disapproval of any reference to Himself as Messiah would have been quite futile in view of His use of the term Son of Man.[3] And if it be held, as some have held,[4]

[1] Cf. J. W. Bowman, *The Intention of Jesus*, 1945, p. 10: "Jesus and he alone was responsible for the fusion of the two prophetic concepts noted" (i.e. the Suffering Servant and the Davidic Messiah).

[2] W. F. Albright, *From the Stone Age to Christianity*, 2nd ed., 1946, p. 292 (= *Von der Steinzeit zum Christentum*, 1949, p. 376), thinks the terms Son of Man and Messiah had been already fused before the time of our Lord. Cf. S. Mowinckel, *Nor.T.T.*, xlv, 1944, pp. 191 ff., where the separateness of the terms is maintained. J. Bowman, *E.T.*, lix, 1947–48, p. 285b, cites a passage from Numbers Rabba (xiii. 14, translated by J. J. Slotki in the Soncino edition of the *Midrash Rabbah, Numbers*, ii, 1939, pp. 527 f.), which he declares to offer evidence coming from no later than *circa* A.D. 200 for the identification of the Son of Man of Dan. 7: 13 with the Messiah. He does not give his reasons for this dating of the passage, but H. L. Strack (*Introduction to the Talmud and Midrash*, E.Tr., 1931, pp. 214 f.) says that this section is not older than the twelfth century, while J. J. Slotki (*op. cit.*, i, 1939, pp. vii f.) says that the work rests on an older framework derived from Midrash Tanḥuma, which seems to have had three successive editions, of which the earliest dated from the fifth century A.D.

[3] Cf. W. A. Curtis, *Jesus Christ the Teacher*, 1943, p. 135: "If 'the Son of Man' was a not unfamiliar name for the Christ in popular expectancy, drawn from current apocalyptic, then His repeated use of it was utterly inconsistent with His attitude towards the latter title."

[4] So J. Wellhausen, *Skizzen und Vorarbeiten*, vi, 1899, pp. 187 ff.; C. S. Patton, "Did Jesus call Himself the Son of Man?", in *J.R.*, ii, 1922, pp. 501 ff.; S. J. Case, "The Alleged Messianic Consciousness of Jesus", in *J.B.L.*, xlvi, 1927, pp. 1 ff. Cf. B. W. Bacon, *ibid.*, xli, 1922, p. 143: "To students accustomed to think of 'meekness and lowliness' as typical traits in the personal character of Jesus there was distinct relief in the authoritative declaration of eminent philologians some twenty years ago, that the self-designation 'the Son of Man' would be unintelligible in the Palestinian Aramaic of Jesus' time, so that the title with all its connotations of superhuman authority and dignity must be ascribed to the period after the development of the resurrection faith, and could not be an embodiment of Jesus' thought concerning himself." P. Parker ("The Meaning of 'Son of Man' ", *ibid.*, lx, 1941, pp. 151 ff.) maintains that save in three unauthentic passages the term Son of Man is never found on the lips of our Lord in a messianic or apocalyptic setting. Against this cf. G. Kittel, *Deutsche Theologie*, 1936, p. 173; "Es hat allen Bestreitungen zum Trotz dabei zu bleiben, dass wir in diesem Namen (*sc.* Menschensohn) die wichtigste Selbst-bezeichnung Jesu vor uns haben; denn alle Versuche den Namen aus dem Munde Jesu zu entfernen und als sekundäre Gemeinde-Dogmatik zu erklären, geben nicht eine Erklärung des hochst eigentümlichen Überlieferungsbefundes, sondern machen ihn vielmehr endgültig rätselhaft und unerklärbar." S. Mowinckel (*He that Cometh*, E.Tr., 1956, p. 445), says it is "quite certain that Jesus actually used this title by preference in referring to Himself".

that Jesus did not use the term Son of Man of Himself,[1] the attribution to Him of the term alongside the attribution to Him of reluctance to have the term Messiah used would have appeared ridiculous to people who equated the terms.[2] It is equally clear that the disciples knew nothing of any equation of the terms Son of Man and Suffering Servant, since though Jesus is said to have spoken of Himself as Son of Man from the outset of His ministry, at its end they were completely unprepared for the idea of His suffering.[3] All this is quite definite and positive evidence against the theories which can offer no better evidence than the reading back into an earlier age of ideas which are well attested later, but which are not really relevant to the conclusions drawn from them.

There is a further variety of the view that would carry back to a pre-Christian date the thought of a suffering Messiah, which remains to be considered. This is the theory that an esoteric group cherished such an idea, while the generality of men looked for the nationalistic

[1] T. W. Manson, *The Teaching of Jesus*, 2nd ed., p. 227, maintained that on the lips of Jesus the expression Son of Man stood "for the manifestation of the Kingdom of God on earth in a people wholly devoted to their heavenly King", precisely as in Daniel, and that the individualizing of the figure and equation with Jesus was the outcome of His ministry. Cf. also "Mark 2: 27 f.", in *Coniectanea Neotestamentica*, xi (Fridrichsen Festskrift), 1947, pp. 138 ff., and *B.J.R.L.*, xxxii, 1949–50, pp. 190 ff. Cf. H. Lietzmann, *Der Menschensohn*, 1896, pp. 81 ff., and N. Schmidt, *J.B.L.*, xlv, 1926, pp. 326 ff.; J. R. Coates, *The Coming of the Church*, 1929, pp. 30 ff.; C. J. Cadoux, *The Historic Mission of Jesus*, 1941, p. 100; W. E. Wilson, "The Coming of the Son of Man", in *The Modern Churchman*, xxxvi, 1946, pp. 56 ff. In his latest treatment of the subject Manson recognizes that he allowed too little weight to the oscillation between the individual and the collective in his earlier treatment, and is now "prepared to find that this corporate entity is embodied *par excellence* in Jesus Himself in such a way that His followers, who together with Him constitute the Son of Man as a group, may be thought of as extensions of His personality." He observes that "the best reason for calling Jesus Son of Man *par excellence* is the fact that his Ministry reveals perfectly the true meaning of the term" (*loc. cit.*, p. 191). Cf. what I have written in *The Biblical Doctrine of Election*, 1950, p. 157: "It seems to me probable that there was a measure of fluidity in the significance of the term . . . so that it could stand as a symbol for the kingdom or as a term for the representative of the Kingdom." Cf. also S. Hanson, *The Unity of the Church in the New Testament*, 1946, p. 11, where the Son of Man is defined as a corporate personality having individual traits. J. Y. Campbell ("The Origin and Meaning of the Term Son of Man", in *J.T.S.*, lxviii, 1947, pp. 145 ff.) holds that the original Aramaic which lies behind the term "Son of Man", on the lips of Jesus was simply an unusual periphrasis for the first personal pronoun.

[2] Cf. J. B. Frey, "Le conflit entre le Messianisme de Jésus et le Messianisme des Juifs de son temps", in *Biblica*, xiv, 1933, pp. 133 ff., 269 ff.

[3] E. Lohmeyer (*Gottesknecht und Davidsohn*, 1945) thinks the title Christ was applied to Jesus by the disciples with reference to the anointing of the Servant of Yahweh, and not with reference to the Davidic Messiah. This seems most improbable in view of Matt. 16, where, following Peter's acknowledgment of Him as Christ, He speaks of His sufferings to Peter's utter surprise.

Messiah. This is the view which has been advanced by J. Jeremias,[1] N. Johansson,[2] and more recently by W. D. Davies[3] and J. Jocz.[4] But again no positive evidence of the existence of such a group can be produced,[5] and it leaves the New Testament evidence still completely unaccounted for. Jeremias thinks this esoteric view was crushed by anti-Christian polemic.[6] Had this been the case we should have expected the Church to appeal to it, and to preserve the memory of it. Yet is it as completely without trace in the New Testament as in Judaism.[7] If there existed a small group of people who awaited a suffering

---

[1] Cf. *Deutsche Theologie*, ii, pp. 106 ff. Against Jeremias cf. P. Volz, *Jesaja II*, 1932, pp. 185 f. note; J. Héring, *R.H.P.R.*, xviii, 1938, pp. 419 ff.; E. Sjöberg, *S.E.Å.*, v, 1940, pp. 163 ff., and *Der Menschensohn im äthiopischen Henochbuch*, pp. 116 ff.

[2] Cf. *Parakletoi*, 1940, pp. 113 ff.

[3] Cf. *Paul and Rabbinic Judaism*, 1948, pp. 274 ff.

[4] *The Jewish People and Jesus Christ*, 1949, p. 162. Cf. also W. Staerk, *Soter*, 1933, pp. 37 ff., 77 ff.; *Die Erlösererwartung in den östlichen Religionen*, 1938, p. 407. K. Barth, (*The Knowledge of God and the Service of God according to the Teaching of the Reformation*, 1938, p. 61) says that in the Old Testament there is the hope of a deliverer who should be a prophet like Moses, a priest like Aaron, a King like David, and the Servant of God in Deutero-Isaiah, but offers no evidence of the equation of these various forms of Old Testament hope.

[5] The theses of Jeremias, whereby he seeks to establish the view that the teaching of a suffering Messiah was not strange to Judaism in the time of Jesus are: "1. Der Bar *'enāshā* der pseudepigraphischen Literatur geht durch eine Leidenszeit vor seiner Parusie. 2. Der Messias als zweiter Moses wird als Leidensgestalt geschildert. 3. Jes. 53 ist bereits in vorchristlicher Zeit messianisch gedeutet worden, ebenso wahrscheinlich Psalmen wie 22, 31, 69, die vom Leiden des Frommen handeln und andere alttestamentliche Stellen wie Sach. 12, 10 ff. 4. Dass die Lehre von dem durch Leiden verherrlichten Erlöser im Talmud nur einen kleinen Raum annimmt, hat zwei Gründe: (*a*) es war eine esoterische Lehre; (*b*) sie wurde durch antichristliche Polemik unterdrückt. 5. Zu dem Zeugnis der Texte kommt das Zeugnis der Geschichte; dass von Gestalten der Geschichte und der Zeitgeschichte trotz ihres Todes erwartet wurde, dass sie als Messias wiederkehren würden, zeigt die Kraft der Lehre im Leben. 6. Bei seinem Auftreten fand Jesus also eine doppelte Erlösererwartung vor: die herrschende eines nationalen Befreiers und die esoterische des leidenden Elösers" (*loc. cit.*, pp. 106 f.). Cf. also his *Jesus als Weltvollender*, 1930, pp. 55 f., where he maintains that before the time of our Lord there was already the expectation of an Urmensch who should be a redeemer through suffering, and that this expectation was much more widely spread than in Palestine alone. He says (p. 56): "Wenn Jesus diese messianische Bezeichnung auf sich selbst anwendet und sich als den neuen Menschen bezeichnet, so lehnt er damit alle nationalpolitischen Erwartungen ab, die an den Davidssohn geknüpft waren, und bezeichnet sich als den Welterneuerer, der durch Leiden hindurch zur Herrlichkeit eingeht und den neuen Åon herbeiführt."

[6] *Deutsche Theologie*, loc. cit., p. 116.

[7] A. Dupont-Sommer has recently propounded the view that the leader of the heretical sect of the Essenes was martyred in the middle of the first century B.C., and that this event gave rise to "toute une théologie du Messie souffrant, du Messie rédempteur du monde" (*Aperçus préliminaires sur les Manuscrits de la Mer Morte*, 1950, p. 116). He declares that Jesus appeared as a surprising reincarnation of this martyr (p. 121), and that we have here light on the origin of the Christian church (p. 122). All this is more than doubtful,

Messiah, from whom Jesus received the idea, is it not surprising that not one of His disciples should have come from that group? For it is clear that none of the disciples did come from such a group, since no exception to the bewilderment that reference to His sufferings produced is recorded. When the evidence of the Gospels is that our Lord found no one to understand Him when He spoke in such terms, and when no traces of the supposed group can be found, it is surely gratuitous to assume that our Lord's bringing of these concepts together rested on the thinking of people who stood right outside His following,[1] and whose ideas were completely strange to those who did follow Him.[2] If Jesus accepted the teaching of a group which existed before

and it rests on Dupont-Sommer's view of the origin of the non-Biblical texts among the Dead Sea Scrolls, and assumption of a martyrdom which has left but little trace. If, as Dupont-Sommer holds, the Essenes were expecting the return of such a Master as Jesus was, it is surprising that they did not follow Him. Yet there is no evidence that His disciples were drawn from their ranks. It is less surprising that those who were expecting a different kind of Messiah turned from Him, though some of these appear to have followed Him. Moreover, when Dupont-Sommer ascribes many passages of the Old Testament to a date later than the supposed martyrdom, and holds that Dan. 9, Zech. 12: 10–14, Ps. 22, and the Servant songs of Deutero-Isaiah, all refer to the death of the martyr, he makes still stronger the improbability of his view (cf. above, p. 21, n. 1). For it is quite incredible that at so late a date passages which emanated from a heretical sect should have been incorporated in the Scriptures of those who had martyred its leader. More recently Dupont-Sommer agrees that the Servant Songs antedated the Ministry of the Teacher of Righteousness (cf. *The Essene Writings from Qumran*, E.Tr. by G. Vermes, 1961, p. 362). There is no evidence that the Teacher of Righteousness was regarded as the Messiah, or was expected to return from the dead (cf. H. H. Rowley, *From Moses to Qumran*, 1963, pp. 245 f.), and the fact that he is unmentioned in the text that is held to describe the Messianic Banquet makes this absolutely clear. That text refers to the coming of the Davidic Messiah, who could not be the Teacher of Righteousness, since the latter was a priest, and refers to the priest who shall be in those days, who shall have precedence over the Messiah, in accordance with the view of the sect that priests should always have precedence over the laity, but gives no remote hint that the priest should be the resurrected Teacher of Righteousness (cf. *ibid.*, pp. 267 f.).

[1] Cf. E. O. James, *Origins of Sacrifice*, 1937, ed. p. 212: "Taken together these two figures constitute the background of the Messianic thought in the Gospel narrative, and whatever may have been the precise evaluation put upon them by Jesus Himself, that He first realized the Messianic import of the prophecies is suggested by the reluctance of His followers to look upon His death as anything but a catastrophe and the death-blow to all their hopes and aspirations."

[2] J. Héring criticizes the view of Jeremias in the strongest terms. He says: "Ce n'est que parce que Jeremias, grâce à un abus de langage que nous ne cessons de dénoncer, juge bon d'appeler les espérances eschatologiques de Dan. et Hén. '*une autre espérance messianique*' (comme si l'espérance messianique *politique* n'était pas la seule attestée par les textes) qu'il peut faire naître *l'illusion* d'un Messie souffrant dans la religion juive, et ce à condition qu'on se décide au surplus à confondre l'Homme céleste de l'Apocalyptique avec un autre Homme qui s'incarne et qui souffre (dont l'existence est également tout à fait hypothétique). Nous ignorons si on peut encore qualifier d'hypothèse scientifique, ce qui n'est que l'ombre d'un reflet d'une illusion" (*loc. cit.*, p. 420). P. Volz is similarly

His time, this might have been expected to be made clear from the beginning of His ministry. Yet actually, while there is some evidence that from the beginning of His ministry He was aware of the road He must tread,[1] His references to His sufferings in His conversations with His disciples belong especially to the later part of His ministry, and particularly after Caesarea Philippi.[2] It is true that in the Fourth Gospel we read that John the Baptist, at the outset of the ministry of Jesus, referred to Him as the Lamb of God.[3] Here, however, it is to be noted that we cannot be sure that this is not a reading back into the story of the ideas of the Evangelist, and that even though it should be a verbatim report of what John the Baptist said, it would still not involve the conclusion that there was any group which expected a suffering Messiah. It would carry us no further than the conclusion that John, in a moment of illumination, had some perception of the truth. The words of John are said to have influenced some to follow Jesus, but it is plain from the Gospel story as a whole that they did not lead them to expect a suffering Messiah. They passed as unheeded as the words of Jesus Himself on this subject. We cannot find here any evidence, therefore, that an element of the fundamental teaching of John or of any contemporary group had relation to a suffering Messiah.[4]

The view that the bringing together of the Messianic concept and the concept of the Suffering Servant antedated the Christian era has taken a new turn since the discovery of the Dead Sea Scrolls. The view has been advanced that a reading *mšḥty* in the Dead Sea Scrolls MS. of Is. 52 : 14, giving the meaning "I anointed" instead of "marred" proves the bringing together of the two concepts.[5] This understanding

---

unsparing in his terms. He says: "Auf alle Fälle ist an den Ausführungen von Jeremias zu beanstanden, dass er die Quellen nicht sorgfältig genug liest, die nicht mit der notwendigen chronologischen Genauigkeit bucht und dass er zu weitgehende Schlüsse aus dem Vorhandenen zieht" (*Jesaja II*, p. 186 n.). Cf. also S. Mowinckel, *He that Cometh*, E.Tr., 1956, pp. 327 ff. (p. 327: "In spite of statements to the contrary, Judaism knows nothing of a suffering, dying and rising Messiah").

[1] Cf. W. Manson, *Jesus the Messiah*, pp. 30 ff.; also J. Jeremias, *Deutsche Theologie*, ii, p. 118.

[2] Cf. Matt. 16: 21; Mark 8: 31.

[3] John 1: 29.

[4] Jeremias argues that suffering and triumph are not mutually exclusive, and adduces the belief recorded in the New Testament (Mark 6: 14) that John the Baptist had been raised from the dead (*loc. cit.*, p. 117). This is not evidence of any antecedent expectation that the Messiah would reach his triumph through death, and since John is said to have announced himself as the Forerunner and not as the Messiah, it is not obvious that popular comment about him after his death is relevant evidence of belief about the Messiah.

[5] Cf. W. H. Brownlee, *B.A.S.O.R.*, No. 132, Dec. 1953, pp. 10 ff. Cf. also D. Barthélemy, *R.B.*, lvii, 1950, pp. 546 ff.; F. Nötscher, *V.T.*, i, 1951, p. 301.

of the reading is by no means certain, however.[1] Still more question-able is the assumption that the Teacher of Righteousness was identified with the Suffering Servant[2] and the supposition that the teacher was thought to be the Messiah,[3] so that the two concepts met in his person. Millar Burrows has declared the idea that the Teacher of Righteous-ness was identified with the Suffering Servant unconvincing,[4] and there can be no evidence that the Teacher was identified with the Davidic Messiah, since he was a priest.[5] He could not possibly have been responsible for bringing together the concepts of the Davidic Messiah and the Suffering Servant, therefore, and neither Jesus nor the New Testament writers can have owed this combination to him. It is often said that the Qumran community expected two Messiahs,[6] a priestly and a lay Messiah, and in that case the Teacher of Righteous-ness would have been the priestly Messiah.[7] There is no mention of the Teacher of Righteousness in the text which is held to describe the Messianic Banquet,[8] where there is mention only of the lay Messiah

---

[1] Cf. J. Reider, *B.A.S.O.R.*, No. 134, April, 1954, pp. 27 f. and Brownlee's replies; also A. Rubinstein, *Biblica*, xxxv, 1954, pp. 475–479; M. Burrows, *The Dead Sea Scrolls*, 1955, p. 314. Cf. also Brownlee's further discussion of this passage in *The Meaning of the Qumran Scrolls for the Bible*, 1964, pp. 204 ff. A. Guillaume (*J.B.L.*, lxxvi, 1957, pp. 41 f.) connects the Scroll reading with the Arabic *masakha*, and renders "I marred".

[2] Cf. above, p. 21, n. 1, for Dupont-Sommer's earlier suggestion that the Teacher of Righteousness was the source of the Servant Songs and his later view that he applied the Songs to himself, and the view of S. Lassalle that the Servant was Onias III, who is generally held to be referred to in Dan. 9: 25 f. as an anointed one. Cf. also W. H. Brown-lee, *N.T.S.*, iii, 1956–57, p. 26.

[3] Cf. *From Moses to Qumran*, 1963, p. 245. M. Black (*S.J.Th.*, vi, 1953, p. 5) says the passage in the Zadokite Work referring to the period between the gathering in of the Unique Teacher until the Messiah from Aaron and Israel should arise alone makes it difficult to maintain that the Teacher of Righteousness and the Messiah were believed to be one.

[4] Cf. *More Light on the Dead Sea Scrolls*, 1958, pp. 66, 336.

[5] Cf. J. M. Allegro, *P.E.Q.*, lxxxvi, 1954, pp. 69 ff. (Commentary on Ps. 37, col. 2, line 15). The superior status of priests in the sect should also be borne in mind.

[6] Cf. M. Burrows, *A.Th.R.*, xxxiv, 1952, pp. 202 ff., and *The Dead Sea Scrolls*, 1955, pp. 264 f.; A. S. van der Woude, in *La Secte de Qumrân et les origines du Christianisme* (Recherches Bibliques, iv), 1959, pp. 121 ff.; J. Liver, *H.T.R.*, lii, 1959, pp. 149 ff. In this connection the phrase found in the Manual of Discipline, col. ix, line 11, "the Mes-siahs of Aaron and Israel" plays a considerable part. On this phrase and its meaning cf. *From Moses to Qumrân*, 1963, p. 243 n., and the literature there cited.

[7] Cf. M. Burrows, *More Light on the Dead Sea Scrolls*, 1958, p. 69; "If the Teacher of Righteousness was expected to return as Messiah in any sense, it would obviously be as the priestly Messiah of Aaron."

[8] The Rule of the Congregation, col. ii. Whether it is rightly thought of as a Messianic Banquet is uncertain; cf. M. Burrows, *More Light on the Dead Sea Scrolls*, 1958, p. 101; T. H. Gaster, *The Scriptures of the Dead Sea Sect*, 1957, p. 29; J. van der Ploeg, *The Excava-tions at Qumran*, E.Tr. by K. Smyth, 1958, p. 213.

and a presiding priest. If that priest were conceived of as the Teacher of Righteousness resurrected to messianic glory, it would be quite astonishing for this fact to be unmentioned and left to modern imagination to supply.[1] There is, therefore, no evidence that the concepts of a priestly Messiah and the Suffering Servant were brought together in the Qumran community, and if there were, this would have no relevance for New Testament usage. For Jesus was thought of as the Davidic Messiah, and not a priestly Messiah.[2]

There is no serious evidence, then, of the bringing together of the concepts of the Suffering Servant and the Davidic Messiah before the Christian era,[3] or of the formulation of the doctrine of the Messiah ben Ephraim at so early a date, and the opinions of the leading authorities in this field cannot be overturned by any tangible evidence. On the other hand, there is tangible and positive evidence in the New Testament which is fatal to such a view. Nevertheless, it is insufficient to adopt a merely negative position and to maintain the separateness of the two ideas. For it must be recognized that it was not without reason that the two concepts were brought together in the thought and teaching of Jesus. As has been already said, the passage dealing with the Davidic Messiah and those treating of the Suffering Servant are eschatological in their reference, in that they deal with the bringing in of the age when God's will should prevail within Israel and beyond. While they are different conceptions of the way in which the awaited age would be introduced, they alike think of that age. Moreover, as

[1] Cf. *From Moses to Qumran*, pp. 267 f.

[2] In the Epistle to the Hebrews Jesus is presented as a priest. But his priesthood is after the order of Melchizedek, and he is no Aaronite or Zadokite priest (cf. F. F. Bruce, *N.T.S.*, ii, 1955–56, pp. 180 ff.), whereas in the Qumran sect it was the latter priesthood which was exalted to honour (cf. *From Moses to Qumran*, p. 246 n.). J. M. Allegro (*The Dead Sea Scrolls*, 1956, p. 153) says: "There seems to be nothing which would preclude the acceptance by the Qumran Sect of Jesus as the expected Messiah of David's line." On this M. Burrows (*More Light on the Dead Sea Scrolls*, 1958, p. 68) says: "This is an astonishing statement. Jesus was so unlike what all Jews expected the son of David to be that his own disciples found it almost impossible to connect the idea of the Messiah with him."

[3] Cf. S. Mowinckel, *He that Cometh*, E.Tr., 1956, p. 449: "No one in Judaism had really connected the Servant with the Messiah, the mediator of the Kingdom of God, and of the new relationship between God and men . . The essential and decisive way in which Jesus transformed the idea of the Messiah was that He combined the thought of the suffering, dying, and exalted Servant of the Lord with that of the Son of Man;" J. Klausner, *The Messianic Idea in Israel*, 1956, p. 405: "In the whole Jewish Messianic literature of the Tannaitic period there is no trace of the 'suffering Messiah'."

W. Manson has so well emphasized,[1] some of the predicates of the Davidic Messiah and of the Suffering Servant are common to both figures. While they are not identical conceptions, they would therefore seem to be related conceptions.[2] We may go farther and say that probably both are drawn from common roots. Several writers have noted the kingly traits in the figure of the Servant,[3] and while these traits do not belong so much to the regnant side of the king's office, they may well have their origin in other sides of his office. For there is evidence that the king played a part in the ritual usage of Israel,[4] and that in some of its elements he was humiliated.[5] Part of the evidence for this is drawn from non-Israelite sources,[6] whose relevance to the discussion of Israelite usage is disputed by some writers. But part of the evidence is found in the Psalter, and is not so easily dismissed. In his first published paper, still often referred to, A. R. Johnson[7] directed

[1] Cf. op. cit., p. 99: "Apart from this common pattern of thought it will be seen that all three figures are invested with the same attributes of wisdom, judgement, righteousness, and the possession of the Spirit of God. All three are 'a light to the Gentiles', all three are associated with a 'covenant' which God makes with His people, all three receive the homage of 'kings' and raise the mighty from their seats."

[2] Cf. what I have written in The Re-discovery of the Old Testament, 1946, p. 197 (American ed., p. 279): "Beneath all the varying forms and emphases of these eschatological hopes of Israel there is a deep underlying unity of conception." Cf. also T. K. Cheyne, The Prophecies of Isaiah, ii, 1889, pp. 221 f.

[3] Cf. H. S. Nyberg, S.E.Å., vii, 1942, pp. 66 f.; G. Widengren, Religion och Bibel, ii, 1943, pp. 61, 71; I. Engnell, The 'Ebed Yahweh Songs and the Suffering Messiah, p. 3; G. Östborn, Tōrā in the Old Testament, 1945, pp. 56 ff.; H. Riesenfeld, The Resurrection in Ezekiel xxxvii and in the Dura-Europos Paintings, 1948, p. 9; J. Hempel, Worte der Profeten, 1949, p. 298; H. Ringgren, Ny kyrklig tidskrift, xviii, 1949, pp. 74 f.; J. Coppens, Pro regno pro sanctuario (van der Leeuw Festschrift), 1950, pp. 116 f. [=Nieuw Licht over de Ebed-Jahweh-Liederen (Analecta Lovaniensia Biblica et Orientalia, II, 15), 1950, pp. 4 f., 13]. Against this cf. A. Bentzen, Jesaja, ii, 1943, p. 100, and Messias, Moses redivivus, Menschensohn, pp. 69 f. Cf. also M. Buber, Pro regno pro sanctuario, p. 73, where it is observed that the royal and the Davidic in the Messiah concept gives place to the prophetic in the Servant songs.

[4] Cf. S. Mowinckel, Psalmenstudien, ii, 1922, and the considerable literature of discussion provoked by this study—much too considerable to be recorded here.

[5] Cf. R. Labat, Le caractère religieux de la royauté assyro-babylonienne, 1939, pp. 323 ff.; I.Engnell, Studies in Divine Kingship in the Ancient Near East, 1943, pp. 33 ff., 112 f.

[6] In addition to the works mentioned in the two preceding and the following notes, cf. S. H. Hooke, The Origins of Early Semitic Ritual, 1938; G. Widengren, "Det sakrale kungadömet bland öst- och västsemiter", in Religion och Bibel, ii, 1943, pp. 49 ff., "Konungens vistelse i dödsriket", in S.E.Å., x, 1945, pp. 66 ff., and "Til det sakrale kungadömets historia i Israel", in Horae Soederblomianae, i: Mélanges Johs. Pedersen, Fasc. iii, 1947; A. Bentzen, Det sakrale kongedømme, 1945; A. Lauha, "Några randanmärkningar till diskussionen om kungaideologien i Gamla Testamentet", in S.E.Å., xii, 1947, pp. 182 ff.; C. J. Gadd, Ideas of Divine Rule in the Ancient East, 1948. Cf. also A. Médebielle, in S.D.B., iii, cols. 8 ff.

[7] "The Rôle of the King in the Jerusalem Cultus", in The Labyrinth, ed. by S. H. Hooke, 1935, pp. 73 ff.

attention to this evidence, and used the terms "Messiah of Yahweh" and "Suffering Servant" of the king in this connexion.[1] This evidence would seem to justify the inference that the concepts of the Davidic Messiah and of the Suffering Servant alike had their roots in the royal cultic rites,[2] though they developed separate elements of those rites. H. Riesenfeld is therefore probably right when he speaks[3] of the disintegration of the ancient concept of the king, and we have a forking out of thought along two separate lines.

If this view is right, it may be acknowledged that the bringing together of these two lines and reintegration of them in the thought of our Lord was not without reason. It is not necessary to resort to the unsupported assumption that the reintegration had been already effected before His time, or to miss the significance of His penetration. H. Wheeler Robinson has well observed: "It is no exaggeration to say that this is the most original and daring of all the characteristic features of the teaching of Jesus, and it led to the most important element in His work. There has been no success in all the endeavours made to find previous or contemporary identification of the Messiah with the suffering servant of Yahweh."[4] The merely negative position

[1] *Ibid.*, p. III. G. Widengren, *Religionens värld*, 1945, p. 223 n., observed: "Den som såsom en av de första klart uttalat liknande synpunkter och sett sambandet mellan vissa psalmer och Jes 53 är A. R. Johnson" (cf. also *S.E.Å.*, x, 1945, p. 68). I. Engnell, *S.E.Å.*, x, 1945, pp. 32 f. note, takes exception to this, and says: "Johnson uppvisar, att i vissa psalmer, främst 89, 18 och 118, *den davidiske konungen* framträder såsom i kulten ödmjukad och lidande. Däremot är linjen icke dragen vare sig till Ebed Jahve i Jes 53 eller till Tammuz, vars namn ej nämnes" (cf. *The 'Ebed Yahweh Songs and the Suffering Messiah*, p. 5 n.). Since Johnson's words were "it is the sign that the suffering Servant and humble Messiah is adopted once more as the 'Son' of Jahweh", it is surely beyond question that he was drawing the line to the Servant of Yahweh in Is. 53, even though the passage is not mentioned. His whole point, though it was undeveloped, was that the Davidic Messiah and the Suffering Servant had common roots in the ritual of the cult. See also p. 100, where he says: "The Davidic King is the Servant of Jahweh; but, as we see from the above lines, at the New Year Festival he is the Suffering Servant. He is the Messiah of Jahweh; but on this occasion he is the humiliated Messiah." Cf. A. Bentzen, *Messias, Moses redivivus, Menschensohn*, p. 43 n., and Appendix. Cf. also L. Gillet (*Communion in the Messiah*, 1942, p. 95), who rightly perceived that Johnson had the Suffering Servant of Deutero-Isaiah in mind, but who imperfectly understood other elements of his view.

[2] Cf. Bentzen, *op. cit.*, pp. 76 f.

[3] *Jésus transfiguré*, pp. 81 f. Cf. also p. 83 n.; "Dès l'origine il n'est pas question de deux types différentes de Messie, mais le Messie de David est en même temps le Messie de la passion."

[4] *Redemption and Revelation*, 1942, p. 109; cf. also pp. 251 f. Cf. W. F. Howard, *E.T.*, I, 1938–39, p. 108b: "The more we study the primitive Christian tradition and the earlier Christian preaching the more we must acknowledge that the creative mind in the Church was that of Jesus Himself. . . . The outstanding assertion made by Jesus in the whole tenor of His teaching and example is that the Messiah must be interpreted in the light of the Servant of Jehovah."

of the second of these sentences is insufficient, however, since it fails to recognize that those efforts have contributed something to carry forward the debate. They have made much clearer the relations between these conceptions, and also their relations with the conception of the Son of Man, and enabled us more clearly to perceive that in our Lord's bringing of them together He was doing no violence to them, but was uniting ideas that had a common root and had many points of connexion with one another.

THE NATURE OF OLD TESTAMENT PROPHECY
IN THE LIGHT OF RECENT STUDY

The Nature of Old Testament Prophecy in the Light of Recent Study[1]

"THE central place in the field of Old Testament religion", says H. W. Hertzberg,[2] "is undoubtedly occupied by the prophets. It is therefore little wonder that research and investigation have concentrated ever more directly on this point: What are the prophets, and what is their significance for the spiritual development of men?" For a generation now the most keenly discussed question in this connexion has been that of "ecstasy" and the extent to which the prophets were subject to abnormal experiences.[3] It has been held that "ecstasy" is of the *esse* of prophecy, and that it provided a criterion without which neither the prophet nor his audience would be satisfied. Yet at best the "ecstatic theory" could tell us only the How? rather than the What? of prophecy.[4]

---

[1] Paper read to the Oxford Society of Historical Theology on 28 January 1943. For a valuable review of recent studies on the prophets up to 1952, cf. E. Jacob, "Le prophétisme israélite d'après les recherches récentes", *R.H.P.R.*, xxxii, 1952, pp. 59–69.

[2] *Prophet und Gott*, 1923, p. 7.

[3] H. Wheeler Robinson holds that it is better to speak of abnormal experiences than of ecstatic experiences, since there were many elements besides ecstasy proper, and since ecstasy corresponds with Greek psychology rather than with Hebrew (*Z.A.W.*, xli, 1923, p. 2=*Redemption and Revelation*, 1942, p. 140). "The term properly applies," he says, "only to a psychology which sharply distinguishes the soul from the body, as in the Greek dualism. It ought not to be used of the phenomena of Hebrew prophecy, which is based on a very different psychology" (*ibid.*, p. 135). Cf., however, A. R. Johnson, *The Cultic Prophet in Ancient Israel*, 1944, pp. 19 f. note (2nd ed., 1962, pp. 18 f. note). In the present writer's judgement the use of the term "ecstasy" has brought much confusion into the discussion of prophecy, but it must necessarily be used in this paper, in a discussion of the "ecstatic theory". E. Jacob (*Theology of the Old Testament*, E.Tr. by A. W. Heathcote and P. J. Allcock, 1958, p. 242 n.) says: "All depends obviously on the sense that is given to the word 'ecstasy'. If by the word the disappearance or the absorption of the subject by a superior power is understood, it is not suitable for defining the prophet's experience; but if one understands by ecstasy the concentration of a subject on an object, to a point where that object alone impinges upon him to the exclusion of all others, the use of the term seems legitimate."

[4] Cf. J. Lindblom, *Z.A.W.*, N.F. xvi, 1939, p. 66: "Wenn wir sagen, dass die israelitischen Propheten Ekstatiker waren, haben wir also damit gar nichts über ihre Religion ausgesagt."

(1)

It was with the publication of G. Hölscher's *Die Profeten* in 1914 that the "ecstatic" view came into prominence, though earlier writers had long recognized an "ecstatic" element in prophecy.[1] Hölscher analysed the abnormal factors in the prophetic consciousness, and found "ecstasy" to be characteristic of the prophets from first to last.[2] In this he has been followed by a long line of scholars of high eminence, including H. Gunkel,[3] W. Jacobi,[4] L. P. Horst,[5] T. H. Robinson,[6] J. Lindblom,[7] H. W. Hertzberg,[8] A. Lods,[9] H. Hackmann,[10] and H.

---

[1] S. Mowinckel (*Psalmenstudien*, iii, 1923, p. 14 n.) observes that much of the material assembled by Hölscher he had himself used, and that he had drawn the same conclusions as Hölscher, in his paper "Om nebiisme og profeti", in *Nor.T.T.*, 1909, pp. 217–224, 358–360 (to which I have been unable to get access). R. Kraetzschmar (*Prophet und Seher im alten Israel*, 1901, p. 7) had already described the earlier prophets as "ecstatics". Cf. also F. Giesebrecht, *Die Berufsbegabung der alttestamentlichen Propheten*, 1897, pp. 38 ff.; B. Stade, *Biblische Theologie des Alten Testaments*, i, 1905, pp. 131 f. A. W. Knobel (*Der Prophetismus der Hebräer*, i, 1837, pp. 155 f.) had used the term "ecstasy" of the prophets, but in a different sense. For him it meant not the lowest element in prophecy, the "dancing dervish" element, but inner rapture of spirit. He says: "Diese ist die höchste Stufe derselben und überhaupt der höchste Grad der Geistesregsamkeit; sie ist die Steigerung der geistigen Lebendigkeit zur höchsten Potenz." He was therefore using the word "ecstasy" in its proper, etymological sense. Its looser use is apparently found in the Early Church, however. Cf. A. Lods, *R.H.R.*, civ, 1931, pp. 279 f.

[2] For some parallels gathered from a wider field than usual, cf. A. F. Puukko, "Ekstatische Propheten mit besonderer Berücksichtigung der finnisch-ugrischen Parallelen", in *Z.A.W.*, N.F. xii, 1935, pp. 23–35, and W. E. Peuckert, "Deutsche Volkspropheten", *ibid.*, pp. 35–54. Cf. also J. Lindblom, *Prophecy in Ancient Israel*, E.Tr., 1962, pp. 1 ff.

[3] "The Secret Experiences of the Prophets", in *Exp.*, 9th series, i, 1924, pp. 356–366, 427–435; ii, 1924, pp. 23–32= *S.A.T.*, II, ii, 1923, pp. xvii–xxxiv; also *Die Propheten*, 1917.

[4] *Die Ekstase der alttestamentlichen Propheten*, 1920.

[5] "L'extase chez les prophètes d'Israël d'après les travaux de Hölscher et de Gunkel", in *R.H.P.R.*, ii, 1922, pp. 337–348.

[6] "The Ecstatic Element in Old Testament Prophecy", in *Exp.*, 8th series, xxi, 1921, pp. 217–238, and *Prophecy and the Prophets in Ancient Israel*, 1923. Cf. also "Die prophetischen Bücher im Lichte neuer Entdeckungen", in *Z.A.W.*, N.F. iv, 1927, pp. 3–9, and "Neuere Propheten-Forschung", in *Th.R.*, N.F. iii, 1931, pp. 75–103. Professor Robinson is the most notable exponent of the "ecstatic theory" in English, and therefore figures largely in this paper. It will be seen below that I do not go so far in this theory as he does, while sharing it in a measure. I should like to take this opportunity of recognizing that no living British scholar has done more for the understanding of the prophets than Professor Robinson, and the measure of my debt to him greatly exceeds the measure of my disagreement.

[7] *Die literarische Gattung der prophetischen Literatur*, 1924. It is, however, with some modification that Lindblom follows Hölscher and Gunkel. He says: "Nur Eins möchte ich hier betonen, nämlich dass es nicht angeht, sich den psychischen Zustand der Propheten als durchaus einheitlich und gleichartig vorzustellen. Das Wort 'Ekstase' scheint in manchen Fällen dafür ein zu starkes Wort zu sein" (p. 43). Cf. *id.*, *Hosea literarisch untersucht*, 1928, p. 148: "Weil alles das für die prophetische *Frommigkeit* nicht das Wesentliche war,

Knight.[1] "The fundamental experience of all types of prophecy is ecstasy," says Gunkel,[2] and Jacobi similarly, "Ecstasy is of the essence of prophecy."[3] "In its extremest form," says Theodore Robinson,[4] "this view holds that every prophetic oracle arose out of an ecstatic experience."

It is to be observed, however, that there is commonly a looseness and want of definition in the use of the word "ecstasy".[5] Thus Hölscher distinguishes sharply between the older ecstasy and the later. "The utterance of Amos", he says,[6] "bears the characteristics of ecstatic speech—but how far removed from the older prophetic ecstasy! No

weil die ekstatischen Offenbarungen vielmehr nur Mittel für die Ausführung des *besonderen prophetischen Berufs* waren und also nicht der Kern ihrer Religiosität selbst, wollen wir auch nicht die grossen Propheten Israels als Mystiker bezeichnen." Cf. also *id.*, *Profetismen i Israel*, 1934, pp. 121 ff., and in *Festschrift für Alfred Bertholet*, 1950, pp. 325 ff. In the latter place Lindblom distinguishes between two kinds of ecstasy, and maintains that only the latter can legitimately be mentioned in connexion with the Hebrew prophets, who were not absorbed in the deity, but who were supremely aware of the personality and message of God. For a short study of the nature of ecstasy and its varieties, cf. J. Mauchline, "Ecstasy", in *E.T.*, xlix, 1937–38, pp. 295–299.

[8] *Prophet und Gott*, 1923.

[9] "Recherches récentes sur le prophétisme israélite", in *R.H.R.*, civ, 1931, pp. 279–316, and *Les prophètes d'Israël et les débuts du Judaïsme*, 1935, pp. 55 ff. (= *The Prophets and the Rise of Judaism*, E.Tr. by Hooke, 1937, pp. 51 ff.).

[10] "Die geistigen Abnormitäten der alttestamentlichen Propheten", in *N.T.T.*, xxiii, 1934, pp. 26–48.

[1] Cf. *The Hebrew Prophetic Consciousness*, 1947, pp. 53 ff. Here it is argued that while the Hebrew prophets borrowed the forms of manticism current in their environment, they infused them with a new spirit. Knight therefore distinguishes—rightly, it will be argued below—between the form and the substance, and the latter is of greater importance in estimating the essence of prophecy.

[2] *Exp.*, 9th series, i, 1924, p. 358=*S.A.T.*, II, ii, 1923, p. xviii.

[3] *Die Ekstase der at.lichen Propheten*, 1920, p. 4: "Die Ekstase zum Wesen des Propheten gehört."

[4] *Z.A.W.*, N.F. iv, 1927, p. 4.

[5] Cf. J. W. Povah, *The Old Testament and Modern Problems in Psychology*, 1926, pp. 62 f.; N. W. Porteous, *Record and Revelation* (ed. by H. W. Robinson), 1938, p. 228. Cf. too Mowinckel (*Acta Orientalia*, xiii, 1935, p. 273 n.): "What is wrong in Hölscher's treatment of higher prophethood is, mainly, only that he stretches the word 'ecstasis' too far." Mowinckel adds that Micklem's criticism (quoted in *Z.A.W.*, 1934, p. 31, n. 2) does not therefore apply to Hölscher. Had he consulted the passage in N. Micklem's *Prophecy and Eschatology*, 1926, p. 50, he would have seen that Micklem's criticism was precisely his own. "The protagonists of the 'ecstatic' view of prophecy," says Micklem, "would appear to use the term 'ecstasy' in a very wide sense. There is much in Hölscher's description of Isaiah with which it is possible largely to agree, but the use of the term 'ecstasy' and the constant reference backwards to the frenzied *nebi'im* of earlier days seem to me to result in a generally distorted picture. It is Hölscher's psychology that is fundamentally inadequate."

[6] *Die Profeten*, p. 197. Cf. Jacobi, *op. cit.*, p. 14; Lods, *Les prophètes*, pp. 63 f. (=E.Tr., p. 58); also J. Skinner, *Prophecy and Religion*, 1922, pp. 220 f.

stammered, half-intelligible sounds, but clear publication of divine truths. All the outer expedients, dance and music, which were still practised in the guilds of the prophets, all excited behaviour has given place to clear spiritualization." With this may be contrasted Theodore Robinson's vivid portrayal of the process of prophecy:[1] "We can now call before our minds a picture of the prophet's activity in public. He might be mingling with the crowd, sometimes on ordinary days, sometimes on special occasions. Suddenly something would happen to him. His eye would become fixed, strange convulsions would seize upon his limbs, the form of his speech would change. Men would recognize that the Spirit had fallen upon him. The fit would pass, and he would tell to those who stood around the things which he had seen and heard."[2]

Such a view had been rejected in advance by Robertson Smith, when he declared that God "speaks to His prophets, not in magical processes or through the visions of poor phrenetics, but by a clear intelligible word addressed to the intellect and the heart. The characteristic of the true prophet is that he retains his consciousness and self-control under revelation."[3] Similarly M. Buttenwieser, writing before the publication of Hölscher's work, said:[4] "The inspiration of the great literary prophets has nothing in common with the ecstasy of the prophets of the older type."[5] Nor has there been any general acceptance of the extremer ecstatic theory since its formulation. It has been contested, in different ways and to a widely varying extent, by G. Ch.

[1] *Prophecy and the Prophets*, p. 50. Cf. J. Hempel, *Die althebräische Literatur und ihr hellenistisch-jüdische Nachleben*, 1930, pp. 62 ff.; Hackmann, *loc. cit.*, p. 30.

[2] With this compare the view of J. Lindblom (*Die lit. Gattung der proph. Literatur*), who thinks that the prophet presented in literary form what he had learned in "ecstasy". Whereas Robinson divides the prophetic books into very small units, which he believes to have been separately delivered in "ecstasy" and then translated into intelligible terms, Lindblom believes that they were literary compositions in larger units, and not "ecstatic" utterances. He says (*Prophecy in Ancient Israel*, E.Tr., 1962, p. 35): "I prefer to use the term ecstasy where the inspiration has grown so strong that the inspired person has lost full control of himself."

[3] *The Old Testament in the Jewish Church*, 1907 ed., p. 289.

[4] *The Prophets of Israel*, 1914, p. 138.

[5] Cf. also H. Wheeler Robinson, *The Religious Ideas of the Old Testament*, 1913, p. 115: "The prophets who so profoundly transformed the religion of Israel and of the world were assuredly not men of unbalanced mind. But certain features of the prophetic writings do seem to point to an intensity of physical experience, and therefore of temperament, which distinguishes the prophets generally from other men"; and E. König, in Hastings's *E.R.E.*, x, 1918 (written apparently before the publication of Hölscher's work), p. 391b.: "The prophets in question . . . give no hint of any state of ecstasy, i.e. unconsciousness or frenzy. . . . It is clear, accordingly, that the theory of ecstasy finds no support in the passages cited, while we have the positive evidence that the prophets lived an ordered life . . . and that their discourses . . . are the work of sane and sober minds."

Aalders,[1] J. Hänel,[2] W. F. Lofthouse,[3] N. Micklem,[4] H. Junker,[5] A. Causse,[6] P. Volz,[7] S. Mowinckel,[8] A. Heschel,[9] N. W. Porteous,[10] W. A. Irwin,[11] I. P. Seierstad,[12] and J. Ridderbos.[13]

That there were frenzied prophets in Israel is agreed by all,[14] and

---

[1] *De Profeten des ouden Verbonds*, 1918, pp. 49 ff.

[2] *Das Erkennen Gottes bei den Schriftpropheten*, 1923. Cf. "Prophetische Offenbarung" in *Z.S.T.*, iv, 1926–27, pp. 91–112.

[3] "Thus hath Jahveh said", in *A.J.S.L.*, xl, 1923–24, pp. 231–251.

[4] *Prophecy and Eschatology*, 1926, chap. i.   [5] *Prophet und Seher in Israel*, 1927.

[6] "Quelques remarques sur la psychologie des prophètes", in *R.H.P.R.*, ii, 1922, pp. 349–356.   [7] *Der Prophet Jeremia* (in Sellin's K.A.T.), 2nd ed., 1928, p. xxxiv.

[8] "Ecstatic Experience and Rational Elaboration in Old Testament Prophecy", in *Acta Orientalia*, xiii, 1935, pp. 264–291; *Die Erkenntnis Gottes bei den alttestamentlichen Profeten*, 1941, pp. 13 ff. (published also in French, "La connaissance de Dieu chez les prophètes de l'Ancien Testament", in *R.H.P.R.*, xxii, 1942, pp. 69 ff.).

[9] *Die Prophetie*, 1936. Cf. p. 32, where Heschel declares ecstatic prophecy to be a *contradictio in adjecto*. Cf. also *id., The Prophets*, 1962, pp. 324 ff.

[10] "Prophecy", in *Record and Revelation* (ed. by H. W. Robinson), 1938, pp. 216–249.

[11] In J. M. P. Smith's *The Prophets and their Times*, 2nd ed., revised by W. A. Irwin, 1941.

[12] *Die Offenbarungserlebnisse der Propheten Amos, Jesaja und Jeremias*, 1946. For a criticism of Seierstad cf. S. Mowinckel, "Ekstatiske innslag i profetenes oplevelser", in *Nor.T.T.*, xlix, 1948, pp. 129–143, 193–221, and J. Lindblom, in *Festschrift für Alfred Bertholet*, 1950, pp. 325 ff. Cf. also *E.T.*, lx, 1948–49, p. 54a, where I observed: "While the reviewer is unconvinced by the extremer forms of the 'ecstatic' theory, he would not repudiate it so sharply as does Seierstad, or distinguish between these prophets and earlier prophets in quite so clear-cut a way as is here done." See further K. Schjelderup, "Religions-psychologiens anvendelse i profetforskningen," in *Nor.T.T.*, xlviii, 1947, pp. 122–143, for an extended examination of Seierstad's positions.   [13] *Profetie en Ekstase*, 1942.

[14] It has long been recognized that this kind of prophecy was found outside Israel as well as in. T. H. Robinson (*Prophecy and the Prophets*, 1923, pp. 33 f.) suggested that it arose in Asia Minor among the Hittites, and from there spread eastwards to Syria and Palestine and westwards to Greece (cf. *The Classical Quarterly*, xi, 1917, pp. 201 ff.). It is now known that it was found also at Mari. Cf. A. Lods, "Une tablette inédite de Mari, intéressante pour l'histoire ancienne du prophétisme sémitique", in *Studies in Old Testament Prophecy* (T. H. Robinson Festschrift), 1950, pp. 103–110; M. Noth, "History and the Word of God in the Old Testament", in *B.J.R.L.*, xxxii, 1949–50, pp. 194–206, and *Geschichte und Gotteswort im Alten Testament*, 1950 (reprinted in *Gesammelte Studien zum Alten Testament*, 1957, pp. 230–247); F. M. Th. de Liagre Böhl, in *Ned.T.T.*, iv, 1949–50, pp. 82 ff., and in *Opera Minora*, 1953, pp. 63–80; W. von Soden, in *Die Welt des Orients*, i, 1947–52, pp. 397 ff.; and H. Schmökel, "Gotteswort in Mari und Israel", in *Th.L.Z.*, lxxvi, 1950, cols. 54 ff.; N. H. Ridderbos, *Israëls Profetie en "Profetie" buiten Israël* (Exegetica, II, i), 1955; A. Malamat, *Eretz-Israel*, iv, 1956, pp. 74–84, v, 1958, pp. 67–73. In the Bible there are references also to dreams as the source of prophetic illumination (Num. 12: 6, Jer. 23: 25 ff.) and of divine revelation to others (e.g. Gen. 20: 3, 40: 5 ff., 43: 1 ff.). Here once more there is an example from Mari, where divine revelation was given to an ordinary individual through a dream. Cf. G. Dossin, "Une révélation du dieu Dagan à Terqa", in *R.Ass.*, xlii, 1948, pp. 125–134. Th. C. Vriezen (*An Outline of Old Testament Theology*, E.Tr., 1958, p. 262) recognizes the possibility of some Canaanite influence on Israelite prophecy. Cf. J. Lindblom, "Zur Frage des Kanaanäischen Ursprungs des altisraelitischen Prophetismus", in *Von Ugarit nach Qumran* (Eissfeldt Festschrift), 1958, pp. 89–104.

it is frequently allowed that the canonical prophets sometimes had abnormal experiences of the types analysed by the "ecstatic" school.[1] Especially is this agreed in the case of Ezekiel, in whom the older "ecstatic" element is allowed to have become prominent again.[2] But this is far from holding that "ecstasy" was normal, or even typical, of the experiences of the greater prophets.[3] Theodore Robinson, indeed, maintains that in conceding so much the critics of the "ecstatic" view have really conceded all.[4] Yet there is little indication that the extremer view is gaining ground, and in my judgement it is unlikely to do so. Old Testament prophecy is far too complex in nature and origin to be reduced to any single type.[5] Moreover, as Porteous says:[6] "It is a mistake to assume *a priori* that the experience of the great prophets is directly accessible to modern psychological methods."

[1] Cf. J. Skinner, *Prophecy and Religion*, 1922, p. 4 n.: "The fact that the great prophets far surpassed their predecessors in their apprehension of religious truth is no reason for denying the reality of the ecstatic element in their experience, or for explaining it away as a mere rhetorical accommodation to traditional modes of expression"; H. Wheeler Robinson, *Redemption and Revelation*, pp. 143 f. (=*Z.A.W.*, xli, 1923, p. 5): "There was an abnormal element in the experience of the Hebrew prophets which marked them out from their fellows. The evidence for this is well known, and has been emphasized by Hölscher in particular, in his *Die Profeten*. It is not likely that a prophet of the classical period would have dared to prophesy without an inaugural vision such as Isaiah's in the temple, or an audition such as Jeremiah's, or such a characteristically peculiar experience as that of Ezekiel. . . . Moreover, we may expect such experiences to recur from time to time, and our expectation is fulfilled"; J. P. Hyatt, *Prophetic Religion*, 1947, p. 17: "Whether the great prophets from Amos on were subject to ecstatic seizure is uncertain. Old Testament scholars now tend to deny that they were. A reasonable judgment seems to be that, although they were not usually subject to abnormal psychological experiences, the great prophets occasionally experienced mild forms of ecstasy, particularly in the visions in which they were commissioned to prophesy."
[2] Cf. Mowinckel, *Acta Orientalia*, xiii, 1935, p. 277; Porteous, *Record and Revelation*, p. 230.
[3] Cf. H. Wheeler Robinson, *The People and the Book* (ed. by A. S. Peake), 1925, p. 373: "All this does not mean necessarily that every message received and recorded in the Old Testament was given through these abnormal experiences."
[4] *Th.R.*, N.F. iii, 1931, p. 85.
[5] Cf. A. Causse (*R.H.P.R.*, ii, 1922, p. 350): "C'est peut-être un peu trop simplifier les problèmes que de vouloir ainsi ramener à un fait élémentaire les mouvements très complexes qui constituent l'histoire du prophétisme hébreu."
[6] *Record and Revelation*, p. 227. Cf. Causse (*loc. cit.*, p. 351): "Ceux qui prétendent décrire les états mentaux des hommes d'autrefois dans les termes de la psychologie contemporaine doivent prendre garde que ces états ont été exprimés dans une autre langue que la nôtre et dans un autre ordre de pensée. On ne saurait appliquer à la mentalité primitive les catégories de notre logique sans s'exposer à de graves méprises."

(2)

Theodore Robinson claims that the very name *nābhî'* implies ecstatic behaviour, and that it would not have been used if the prophets were not ecstatic.[1] This is inadequate, since (*a*) the philology is more than doubtful, and (*b*) words have a history as well as a derivation. It would be unsafe to argue that the derivation of the word *priest* proves that only an elderly man could be called a priest, and it is equally unsafe to assume that no non-ecstatic person could be called a *nābhî'*.

On the philological side it is incontestable that the verb *nibbā'*, *hithnabbē'*, commonly means "to behave in an uncontrolled manner".[2] And many actions ascribed to *nᵉbhî'îm* were certainly uncontrolled. The verb is used of Saul when he lost control of himself and hurled a javelin at David (1 Sam. 18 : 10), and of the prophets of Baal on Mount Carmel, when they danced about and gashed themselves with knives (1 Kings 18 : 28 f.), and when Saul tore off his clothes and rolled about on the ground, his behaviour is described by this verb (1 Sam. 19 : 24). All of the evidence of this nature contained in the Old Testament—and there is much of it—has been fully and frequently marshalled, and may be accepted without question. But that does not of itself establish the philology of the word *nābhî'*. For the verb *nibbā'*, *hithnabbē'*, is almost certainly a denominative from *nābhî'*, and the original root from which *nābhî'* itself comes is not found in the Old Testament. Hence *nibbā'*, *hithnabbē'*, simply means "to play the *nābhî'* ", and it may well be that the admittedly "ecstatic" connotation of the verb is quite secondary, and is due to the fact that early prophets were of the frenzied type. The fundamental meaning of the word *nābhî'* itself falls still to be considered.

By Gesenius[3] the lost primary stem of the verbal root from which *nābhî'* comes was connected with the Hebrew *nābha'* = *bubble forth*, and this view still has its advocates.[4] At best it is a doubtful hypothesis, itself

---

[1] *Exp., loc. cit.*, p. 224. Cf. J. Pedersen, *Israel: its Life and Culture III–IV*, 1940, p. 111: "The term nābhî' is perhaps derived from the ecstatic incoherent cries."

[2] F. Häussermann (*Wortempfang und Symbol in der alttestamentlichen Prophetie*, 1932, pp. 10 f.) distinguishes between the Niph'al, *nibbā'*, and the Hithpa'ēl, *hithnabbē'*.

[3] *Thesaurus linguæ Hebrææ et Chaldææ Veteris Testamenti*, II, ii, 1840, p. 838a. Cf. B. Stade, *op. cit.*, i, p. 132; A. Kuenen, *The Prophets and Prophecy in Israel*, E.Tr. by A. Milroy, 1877, p. 42.

[4] Cf. Hackmann, *loc. cit.*, p. 42. Mowinckel, too, would seem to make the same connexion, for he says that *nābha'* is a "nabiistic" term, meaning "(ekstatische) Machtwort hervorsprudeln lassen" (*Psalmenstudien*, i, 1921, p. 16). A. R. Johnson (*The Cultic Prophet in Ancient Israel*, 2nd ed., 1962, pp. 24 f. note) rejects this derivation.

deduced from the assumed original meaning of *nibbā', hithnabbē'*.[1]
More usually the lost root is connected with Accadian *nabû = call,
announce*, and Arabic *naba'a = announce*. By W. F. Albright[2] the word
nābhî' is then taken in a passive sense = *one who is called* (by God), while
E. König[3] takes it in an active sense = *an announcer*, and A. Guillaume[4]
finds the form to indicate that the prophet is the passive recipient of
something manifested in his condition as well as in his speech = *one
who is in the state of announcing a message which has been given to him*.[5]
J. Lindblom defines a prophet as "a person who, because he is conscious
of having been specially chosen and called, feels forced to perform
actions and proclaim ideas which, in a mental state of intense inspiration or real ecstasy, have been indicated to him in the form of divine
revelations."[6]

The etymological argument is therefore inconclusive, and there can
be no certainty as to what the primary meaning of the word was.
There is, however, an important passage in Exod. 7 : 1 which reads:
"And the Lord said unto Moses, See, I have made thee a god to
Pharaoh: and Aaron thy brother shall be thy prophet [*nābhî'*]."[7] With
this we may compare the parallel passage in Exod. 4 : 15 f. which
reads: "Thou shalt speak unto him [Aaron], and put the words in his

---

[1] Cf. W. Robertson Smith, *The Prophets of Israel*, 2nd ed., 1912, p. 391: "When Kuenen
selects the notion of *bubbling up*, and regards the prophet as one who bubbles up under
inspiration, this hypothesis has no more value than that of a guess guided by the particular development of the root idea found in *nābhakh* and *nābha'*."

[2] *From the Stone Age to Christianity*, 1940, pp. 231 f. Cf. H. Torczyner, *Z.D.M.G.*,
lxxxv, 1931, p. 322: "Das hebräische Wort bedeutet ... gewiss nicht aktiv den 'Sprecher',
sondern passiv den Verzückten, vielleicht urspünglich den vom Geist 'Berufenen'." Cf.
J. Lindblom, *Prophecy in Ancient Israel*, E.Tr., 1962, p. 102.

[3] *Hebräisches und aramäisches Wörterbuch zum Alten Testament*, 1936 ed., p. 260b. Cf.
H. Zimmern, in E. Schrader's *K.A.T.*, 3rd ed., 1903, p. 400; C. Brockelmann, *Grundriss
der vergleichenden Grammatik der semitischen Sprachen*, i, 1908, §138b (p. 354); Häussermann, *op. cit.*, p. 10; W. Eichrodt, *Theology of the Old Testament*, E.Tr. by J. A. Baker,
i, 1961, p. 312. J. A. Bewer (*A.J.S.L.*, xviii, 1901–2, p. 120) disputed this derivation and
preferred to connect the word with Accadian *nabû = tear away*, and to find its original
significance to be "one who is carried away by a supernatural power".

[4] *Prophecy and Divination*, 1938, pp. 112 f. With this cf. Aalders, *De Profeten des Ouden
Verbonds*, 1918, p. 11: "De naam nabi' beteekent *spreker, die het woord van God vertolkt.*"
R. B. Y. Scott, *The Relevance of the Prophets*, 1944, p. 12, defines the prophets as 'spokes-
men of crisis".

[5] Cf. F. Zorell, *Lexicon Hebraicum et Aramaicum Veteris Testamenti*, Fasc. 5, 1946, p.
493: "ex etymo *annuntiator, præco*, præsertim is qui alterius nomine loquitur." On the
etymology of the word *nābhî'* cf. A. R. Johnson, *The Cultic Prophet in Ancient Israel*,
2nd ed., 1962, pp. 24 f. note.

[6] Cf. *Prophecy in Ancient Israel*, E.Tr., 1962, p. 46.

[7] This passage belongs to P. A. Jepsen (*Nabi*, 1934, p. 195) notes that Jer. 1: 5 is the
earliest passage to use *nābhî'* in the sense of *speaker*.

mouth: and I will be with thy mouth, and with his mouth, and will teach you what ye shall say. And he shall be thy spokesman unto the people: and it shall come to pass, that he shall be to thee a mouth, and thou shalt be to him as God."[1] Here the word *nābhi'* is not used, but the same prophetic relationship would seem to be in mind. These passages can in no sense establish the philological meaning of the word *nābhi'*, but they provide some evidence for the conception of the function of the *nābhi'*, and it is plain that the word carried no necessarily "ecstatic" significance. It is concerned with the essence, not the form, of inspiration, and what it here has quite clearly in mind is one who delivers a message not his own, and not one who falls into a fit. With this we may compare Jer. 15 : 19: "If thou take forth the precious from the vile, thou shalt be as my mouth," where again the essence of prophecy is expressed in terms of spokesmanship, and not of ecstasy.

On the side of the history of the word *nābhi'* we have an interesting and familiar note in 1 Sam 9 : 9, which declares that "he that is now called a prophet [*nābhi'*] was beforetime called a seer [*rō'eh*]."[2] The meaning of this oft-quoted text is far from clear. The Septuagint has a slightly different text, yielding "the people used to call a prophet a seer", and this is preferred by some scholars.[3] In that case all that it means is that *seer* was a popular name for the *nābhi'*. In any case the text could not of itself establish that originally the seer and the *nābhi'* were two distinct types. Aalders maintains that the two terms are fully synonymous, and contests the view that these were ever two separate classes.[4] Nevertheless it is common to distinguish them, and such texts as 2 Kings 17 : 13[5] favour this view, though the word for *seer* is there

---

[1] This passage is usually attributed to J, but O. Eissfeldt (*Hexateuch-Synopse*, 1922, p. 97) assigns it to E.

[2] J. Morgenstern (*Amos Studies*, i, 1941, p. 35 n.=*H.U.C.A.*, xi, 1936, p. 51 n.) believes this verse dates from the period preceding somewhat the time of Amos, or at least of Isaiah. It is to be noted, however, that the term *seers* stands in Is. 30: 10. Dhorme (*Les livres de Samuel*, 1910, p. 77) maintains that 1 Sam. 9: 9 is deuteronomic.

[3] So E. König, in Hastings's *E.R.E.*, x, 1918, p. 385a. W. Caspari, *Die Samuelbücher* (in Sellin's K.A.T.), 1926, p. 106; I. Hylander, *Die literarische Samuel-Saul-Komplex*, 1932, p. 140 n.

[4] *Op. cit.*, pp. 11 f. Cf. E. Dhorme (*R.H.R.*, cviii, 1933, p. 123): "C'était [i.e. the *rō'eh*] le prophète avant la lettre." Cf. too H. Junker, *Prophet und Seher in Israel*, p. 82; A. Jepsen, *Nabi*, pp. 43 ff.

[5] R.V.: "Yet the Lord testified unto Israel and unto Judah by the hand of every prophet and of every seer." This rendering follows the Vulgate in dividing the words differently from M.T.

ḥōzeh and not *rō'eh*.[1] Theodore Robinson holds that "the Nabi' functioned spontaneously, while the Seer worked to order", and that "the Nabi' was ecstatic while the Seer was not."[2] On the other hand, Mowinckel denies any psychological distinction between them.[3] It is frequently assumed that 1 Sam. 9 : 9 means that from now on *seer*, whether *ḥōzeh* or *rō'eh*, and *nābhî'* were interchangeable terms. And there is some ground for the assumption. M. Jastrow[4] and J. Hänel[5] distinguish between the *ḥōzeh* and the *rō'eh*, but it is of interest to note that whereas the Chronicler describes Hanani as a *rō'eh* (2 Chron. 16 : 7), he later speaks of Jehu the son of Hanani the *ḥōzeh* (2 Chron 19 : 2). It is therefore improbable that any distinction is to be drawn,[6] and much more likely, as van den Oudenrijn suggests,[7] that *ḥōzeh* is of Aramaic origin[8] and *rō'eh* of Arabic origin. If, then, these terms are to be equated, we may next observe that there are some cases of the same person being called a *nābhî'* and a *ḥōzeh*,[9] and that Amos, whose work is included amongst the collection of *Nᵉbhî'îm*, is described as a *ḥōzeh* (Amos 7 : 12), while Jehu, the son of the above-mentioned Hanani, is himself described as a *nābhî'* (1 Kings 16 : 7, 12).

[1] Cf. also 2 Sam. 24: 11: "the prophet Gad, David's seer [*ḥōzeh*]". Here the two terms are applied to the same person, who would seem to combine the functions of both, if they are properly to be distinguished.

[2] *Exp., loc. cit.*, p. 220. Cf. A. Causse (*Les plus vieux chants de la Bible*, 1926, p. 214 n.): "Son inspiration [i.e. the seer's] n'est pas extatique et orgiastique comme celle des prophètes, et son langage est généralement intelligible." Cf. also G. Hölscher, *Die Profeten*, pp. 125 f.: "Anders die alte Zeit; für sie ist nābī der erregte Ekstatiker, der, wo er als Vermittler übernatürlicher Offenbarungen auftritt, diese unmittelbar von sich gibt, dagegen rō'ä oder ḥōzä der Seher jeder Art, der ohne Ekstase aus mannigfachen äusseren Beobachtungen und Wahrnehmungen, unter denen die Illusionen des nächtlichen Dunkels, des Halbschlafs und Traumes besonders bevorzugt sind, übernatürliches Wissen gewinnt. . . . Wie sich der 'Seher' der alten Zeit vom 'Profeten' unterscheidet, so hat er auch mit der ekstatischen Vision von Hause aus nichts zu tun." Cf. A. R. Johnson, *The Cultic Prophet in Ancient Israel*, 1944, p. 12: "The evidence adduced is far too vague and circumstantial to justify so nice a distinction, which seems rather artificial." Cf. also I. Engnell, *Religion och Bibel*, vii, 1949, pp. 8 ff.

[3] *Psalmenstudien*, iii, 1923, p. 20.   [4] "Rô'ēh und Ḥōzēh", in *J.B.L.*, xxviii, 1909, pp. 42–56.

[5] *Das Erkennen Gottes*, pp. 7 ff. Cf. F. Häussermann, *op. cit.*, pp. 4 ff.

[6] Cf. M. A. van den Oudenrijn, "De vocabulis quibusdam, termino *nābhî'* synonymis," in *Biblica*, vi, 1925, pp. 294–311, 406–417. Cf. too J. Lindblom, *Die lit. Gattung der proph. Literatur*, p. 39 n.: "Von diesem Gesichtspunkt aus kann ich keinen Unterschied zwischen den beiden Begriffen ḥāzā und rā'ā finden."

[7] *Loc. cit.*, pp. 304 f. Cf. G. R. Driver, *Problems of the Hebrew Verbal System*, 1936, pp. 99. Van den Oudenrijn points out, however, that the root ḥz' is used of mantic vision in ancient Arabic. Cf. J. Wellhausen, *Reste arabischen Heidentums*, 2nd ed., 1897, p. 135 n.

[8] Van den Oudenrijn notes that we find ḥzyn=seers in the Zakir inscription (a: 12; cf. M. Lidzbarski, *Ephemeris für semitische Epigraphik*, iii, 1909–15, p. 3).

[9] So Gad, 1 Sam. 22: 5 and 2 Sam. 24: 11; 1 Chron. 21: 9, 29: 29; 2 Chron. 29: 25; Iddo, 2 Chron. 13: 22 and 9: 29, 12: 15.

Theodore Robinson interprets 1 Sam. 9 : 9 to mean that "during the early monarchy the Seer properly so called disappeared, and that his characteristics and functions were assumed by the Nabi' or Ecstatic."[1] But it is hard to see how this meaning can be attached to the text, and simpler to interpret it to mean that the term *nābhî'* had come to be used indiscriminately for two different classes of men, the original *nābhî'* and the *seer*, if these were once distinct.[2] If the seer had ceased to exist as a type, there would have been no need to restyle him a *nābhî'* or indeed to call him anything at all. Moreover, we actually find the term *rō'îm*, or *seers*, in Is. 30 : 10, used of contemporary persons. Apparently there continued to be religious persons of the type once distinguished from the *nᵉbhî'îm* as *seers*, but a less precise age failed to distinguish them by name. To say this is to say that the mere fact that a person is called a *nābhî'* leaves entirely unsettled whether he properly belonged to the one or to the other variety, and still more whether he was "ecstatic" or "non-ecstatic". Robinson holds that Samuel was a seer and not a *nābhî'*, and declares that there is no suggestion of abnormal behaviour on his part.[3] Yet since Samuel is called a *nābhî'*, this is to admit that the term *nābhî'* cannot be held to prove of itself that the person it denotes was an "ecstatic".

Still less can it establish the "ecstatic" character of the experience that belonged to every prophetic utterance.[4] Theodore Robinson says: "The 'dabar' was not simply a subjective conviction, however strong, as to the will of God. An objective criterion is necessarily demanded both by the speaker and by the hearers, both by the prophet and by his audience. Failure to recognize this essential feature of prophecy is to misunderstand the mind of ancient Israel."[5] Here it is clear from the

---

[1] *Prophecy and the Prophets*, p. 35.

[2] A. van Hoonacker, *Les douze petits prophètes*, 1908, p. 269.

[3] *Exp.*, *loc. cit.*, p. 220. Cf. W. F. Lofthouse, in *The People and the Book*, p. 250. With this contrast S. Mowinckel (*Psalmenstudien*, iii, p. 11), who says the Seer was ecstatic. It is also to be noted that 1 Sam. 19: 20 represents Samuel as the head of a group of "ecstatics", whose frenzied abandon was shared by Saul.

[4] Cf. J. Hempel, *Gott und Mensch im Alten Testament*, 1936, p. 97 n.: "Das anderseits freilich nicht alle profetischen Erlebnisse ekstatischer Natur sind ist ohne weiteres deutlich." Cf. A. Causse, *R.H.P.R.*, ii, 1922, p. 350: "Le prophétisme a bien commencé là [with ecstasy]. Mais s'il en était resté à ces rudiments primitifs et grossiers, il serait à jamais passé sans laisser de souvenir, il n'aurait pas fait vivre le monde."

[5] *E.T.*, xlvi, 1934–35, p. 43. With this cf. K. Marti, *The Religion of the Old Testament*, E.Tr. by Bienemann, 1907, p. 183: "The test of the prophet is therefore not the form in which the divine operation manifests itself—neither ecstasy nor cataleptic attacks, neither trances nor 'hearing words' and 'seeing visions'—but the contents of his message." Cf. too F. Weinrich, *Der religiös-utopische Charakter der prophetischen Politik*, 1932, p. 15: "Die Ekstase als solche ist für das prophetische Bewusstsein nicht das Entscheidende, die Ekstase als solche verbürgt nicht die Echtheit des Propheten und seines Wortes."

context that what is meant is an objective criterion of the prophet's reception of the message, not an objective criterion of the soundness of the contents of the oracle. In the light of this claim we may examine the story of Nathan's interview with David after the adultery with Bathsheba (2 Sam. 12 : 1 ff.). The prophet related the story of the rich man's seizure of the poor man's one ewe lamb. Since the king understood the story to be a literal statement of fact, it is quite unnecessary to suppose that Nathan had to give evidence of prophetic inspiration before he related it. It is equally unnecessary to suppose that the prophet was seized with convulsions before he could say "Thou art the man", since it was now clear that this had been the purpose of the telling of the story from the start.[1] It would, of course, be possible to suppose that it was as the result of some "ecstatic" experience that Nathan set out to interview the king,[2] but that could hardly authenticate his message for his hearer. In short, it is hard to see where there is room for any "ecstatic" experience which could serve as a criterion both to the prophet and to his hearer, to prove that his message was from God.

(3)

Recent study has emphasized the variety of prophets in Israel, and it is no longer possible to be content with just two, *seer* and *nābhî'*.[3] The seer is found, perhaps attached to a shrine, where he may be consulted for a fee about private problems, as in the case of Samuel at Ramah (1 Sam. 9 : 6 ff.), or Ahijah at Shiloh (1 Kings 14 : 1 ff.).[4]

[1] It may be recalled that in another case where a prophet similarly trapped a king into self-judgement by a story (1 Kings 20: 35 ff.), before the oracle was delivered he "took the headband away from his eyes; and the king of Israel discerned that he was of the prophets." Clearly here the prophet had some external mark to distinguish him, and it was essential to conceal it to allay any suspicion, and equally necessary to expose it for the utterance of the oracle. Something similar may have happened in the case of Nathan. But that was an objective criterion that the man was a prophet, not that he had received this particular oracle.

[2] Cf. *Exp.*, 8th series, xxi, 1921, p. 235, where Robinson explains the interviews of Isaiah with Ahaz, and Amos with Amaziah, by the suggestion that the oracles they contain were delivered to the prophet in the "ecstatic" state, and recalled and repeated by him in calmer moments.

[3] Cf. S. A. Cook, *The Old Testament: A Reinterpretation*, 1936, p. 168, and *C.A.H.*, iii, 1925, pp. 458 f.

[4] It is far from certain, indeed, that Ahijah was attached to a shrine at Shiloh. The Danish excavations there have made it practically certain that, as had long been surmised (cf. H. Ewald, *Geschichte des Volkes Israel*, 2nd ed., ii, 1853, p. 540), the city was destroyed in the eleventh century, doubtless when the Philistines captured the Ark (cf. H. Kjaer, "The Danish Excavation of Shiloh", in *P.E.F.Q.S.*, 1927, pp. 202–213, and "Shiloh, a

On the other hand, he may be attached to the Court, as in the case of Gad, David's seer (2 Sam. 24 : 11), or consulted by the king about national problems (2 Kings 3 : 11), or consulted in his own home about private matters (2 Kings 5 : 9). The *nābhî'* may be found alone by the wayside, as when Nathan waylaid David (2 Sam. 12 : 1), or the unnamed prophet waylaid Ahab (1 Kings 20 : 38), or Elijah met Ahab (1 Kings 21 : 17 ff.); or he may be found in company with others, as in the case of the band of prophets who met Saul near Gibeah (1 Sam. 10 : 5, 10), or the band with Samuel at Ramah (1 Sam. 19 : 18 ff.), or those who dwelt at Bethel (2 Kings 2 : 3), or at Jericho (2 Kings 2 : 5), or at Gilgal (2 Kings 4 : 38), or yet again, bodies of *nᵉbhî'îm* may be found attached to the Court, as in the case of the Baal *nᵉbhî'îm*, who were maintained at Jezebel's expense (1 Kings 18 : 19), or the four hundred who encouraged Ahab to go up to Ramoth Gilead (1 Kings 22 : 6), or attached to the Temple (Jer. 23 : 11, 26 : 7, Lam. 2 : 20). Sometimes the oracles were supplied to order, as in the consultation of the seers, or as in the royal consultation of the prophets by Ahab, while on other occasions the initiative lay with the prophets.[1] Sometimes the oracle rested on a dream (Num. 12 : 6; Jer. 23 : 28); sometimes it was induced by music (2 Kings 3 : 15; cf. 1 Sam. 10 : 5); sometimes wine may have been used to induce the "ecstatic" state (cf. Is. 28 : 7; Mic. 2 : 11).

Attention has been drawn in recent years to the probability that there were cultic prophets, attached to the shrines alongside the priests, and that so far from prophet and priest being exponents of opposed types of religion, they long flourished side by side as fellow officials of the cultus.[2] Hölscher drew attention briefly to this question,[3] but it was

---

Summary Report of the second Danish Expedition, 1929", *ibid.*, 1931, pp. 71–88; A. Mallon, "Les fouilles danoises de Silo", in *Biblica*, x, 1929, pp. 369–375). That it was not totally uninhabited is doubtless true, though the archaeological evidence suggests that its occupation was negligible for some centuries, in which case it is unlikely that there was any shrine there. Cf. also Jer. 7: 12; 26: 6, 9.

[1] It is interesting to observe that the document which represents Samuel as a seer ascribes to his divinely inspired initiative the establishment of the monarchy, whereas the other document, which represents him as a figure of national eminence, says that the initiative lay with the people, who merely applied to Samuel to divine for them the right man. It would seem that hard-and-fast lines cannot be drawn between the different prophetic functions, and more than one individual seems to have combined more than one variety of function.

[2] W. Eichrodt (*Theology of the Old Testament*, E.Tr. by J. A. Baker, i, 1961, p. 310) thinks the cultus is the most likely sphere of the emergence of the phenomenon of ecstatic prophecy. He rejects the view, however, that there were cultic prophets in Israel (pp. 313 f.), saying that "it is still quite definitely an unjustifiable simplification of the Old

Mowinckel who first brought it into prominence,[1] and secured the recognition of cultic prophets by a growing number of scholars.[2] Of British scholars A. R. Johnson has especially studied the question, on which he has published a short paper,[3] and a larger monograph,[4] and has announced a further forthcoming monograph.[5] It is pointed out by the advocates of this view that Samuel was found in the shrine of Ramah, where he presided at the sacrificial meal (1 Sam. 9 : 13, 22 f.), and that there are a number of passages which connect the prophet and the priest together in relation to the sanctuary,[6] as though they were joint officials of the shrine (Jer. 23 : 11, 26 : 7; Lam. 2 : 20).

Testament material to classify nabism as a whole as a type of sanctuary officials" (p. 314). Cf. A. R. Johnson, *The Cultic Prophet in Ancient Israel*, 2nd ed., 1962, pp. 22 f. note. I have discussed the question of cultic prophets in my essay "Ritual and the Hebrew Prophets" in *From Moses to Qumran*, 1963, pp. 111–138.
[3] Cf. *Die Profeten*, 1914, p. 143.

[1] *Kultprophetie und prophetische Psalmen* (*Psalmenstudien*, iii), 1923 (cf. *The Psalms in Israel's Worship*, E.Tr. by D. R. Ap-Thomas. ii, 1963, pp. 53 ff.). In *Wisdom in Israel and in the Ancient Near East* (S.V.T., iii), 1955, p. 206, Mowinckel says: "The majority of prophets formed an official class of cult functionaries". Cf. already Jacobi, *op. cit.*, 1920, p. 4: "Dieses alte Sehertum berührte sich nahe mit dem Priestertum." A. Neher (*L'Essence du Prophétisme*, 1955, pp. 207 ff.) identifies "nabism" with cultic prophecy, and propounds the view that the prophets substituted themselves for the priests after the destruction of Shiloh, and assumed priestly functions.
[2] Cf. A. Causse, "L'ancienne poésie cultuelle d'Israël et les origines du Psautier", in *R.H.P.R.*, vi, 1926, pp. 1–37, and *Les plus vieux chants de la Bible*, chap. iii; J. W. Povah, *The Old Testament and Modern Problems in Psychology*, 1926, pp. 67 ff.; H. Junker, *Prophet und Seher in Israel*, 1927; I. Hylander, "War Jesaja Nabi?" in *Le monde oriental*, xxv, 1931, pp. 53–66; G. von Rad, "Die falschen Propheten", in *Z.A.W.*, N.F. x, 1933, pp. 109–120; O. Eissfeldt, *Einleitung in das Alte Testament*, 1934, pp. 115 ff.; A. Jepsen, *Nabi*, 1934, pp. 143 ff., 191 ff.; Graham and May, *Culture and Conscience*, 1936, pp. 170, 217; J. Pedersen, *Israel: its Life and Culture III–IV*, 1940, pp. 115 ff.; R. B. Y. Scott, *The Relevance of the Prophets*, 1944, pp. 42 f.; A. Haldar, *Associations of Cult Prophets among Ancient Semites*, 1945, pp. 90 ff. (cf. J. van der Ploeg, *Bi. Or.*, iii, 1946, pp. 12 ff.); I. Engnell, *S.E.Å.*, xii, 1947, pp. 114 ff., and *Religion och Bibel*, viii, 1949, pp. 10 ff. E. Würthwein, *Z.A.W.*, N.F. xxi, 1950, pp. 10 ff.; A. S. Kapelrud, *St.Th.*, iv, 1951–52, pp. 5 ff.; O. Plöger, *Z.A.W.*, N.F. xxii, 1951, pp. 157 ff.; B. W. Anderson, *Understanding the Old Testament*, 1957, p. 460; W. Eichrodt, *Theology of the Old Testament*, E.Tr. by J. A. Baker, i, 1961, p. 333. P. Humbert (*Problèmes du livre d'Habacuc*, 1944, pp. 296 ff.) holds that Habakkuk was a cultic prophet, and many writers have in recent years held parts of the prophetic books to be liturgies composed for use in the cult. So the book of Nahum by Haldar (*Studies in the Book of Nahum*, 1947). A. S. Kapelrud (*Joel Studies*, 1948) holds that the book of Joel is in part composed in the style of a liturgy, though he does not affirm that it was actually used in the cult. Cf. also below, p. 114, n. 1.
[3] "The Prophet in Israelite Worship", in *E.T.*, xlvii, 1935–36, pp. 312–319.
[4] *The Cultic Prophet in Ancient Israel*, 1944 (2nd ed., 1962).
[5] To be issued under the title *The Cultic Prophet and the Psalter*.
[6] Jepsen (*Nabi*, p. 161) notes that there are thirty passages which refer to priests and prophets in friendly association, all in Jerusalem or Judah.

The prophetic bands, or guilds,[1] are chiefly mentioned in connexion with places where there are known to have been shrines, and may have been attached to these shrines,[2] while the Court prophets of Ahab may have been attached to one of the royal shrines. While there is much evidence of this kind, to suggest that cultic persons of various kinds, referred to under the general term "prophets", were associated with the shrines, for individual or corporate consultation, or for group activity, we must beware of outrunning the evidence, or of forgetting that while it is probable that there were cultic prophets in Israel, the evidence does not enable us to draw hard lines or to define with precision their functions, or their relations with other prophets.[3] For it may be noted that in the narrative which tells us of Samuel's presiding at the sacrificial feast in Ramah (1 Sam. 9 : 1 ff.) the seer or prophet is said to have told Saul to await him in Gilgal, where he would come to offer sacrifices (1 Sam. 10 : 8). This would suggest that he was not necessarily of the personnel attached to the particular shrines where he is found. Since prophets were religious persons, devotees of their God, it is natural to find them in the shrines in which religion centred. But that does not make them members of the staff of the shrines. Elijah offered sacrifice on Mount Carmel on an altar which he built, or rebuilt, but there is no reason to suppose that he belonged to the personnel of that or any other shrine. Similarly we find Amos prophesying in the shrine at Bethel, where it is impossible to suppose him to have been a cultic prophet attached to that shrine. When we find other prophets mentioned in association with shrines, therefore,

---

[1] On these guilds cf. van den Oudenrijn, "L'expression 'fils des prophètes' et ses analogies", in *Biblica*, vi, 1925, pp. 165–171. He notes that the term "sons of the prophets" is only attested for the period *circa* 850–750 B.C., and only for the northern kingdom, and thinks they were members of a specifically northern brotherhood. Cf. also H. Junker, *Prophet und Seher in Israel*, for a study of the cultic significance of these brotherhoods.

[2] Cf. Junker (*op. cit.*, p. 33): "Überhaupt sind alle Orte, die als Sitz von Priestervereinen erwähnt werden, Kultorte, wie ausser Rama noch Gabaa, Jericho und Gilgal."

[3] B. D. Eerdmans (*The Religion of Israel*, 1947, p. 141) roundly denies the existence of cultic prophets in Israel; cf. also J. Begrich, *Einleitung in die Psalmen* (K.A.T.), 1933, 370 ff. At the other extreme Haldar (*Associations of Cult Prophets*) has pressed the theory the farthest, and has interpreted Hebrew prophecy as a whole in terms of Babylonian *bārū* and *maḥḥū* guilds (cf. J. Lindblom, *Festschrift Alfred Bertholet*, 1950, pp. 328 ff.). K. Roubos (*Profetie en Cultus in Israël*, 1956, pp. 4 ff.) rejects the views of Haldar, but uncritically fails to distinguish between the views of A. R. Johnson and Haldar. R. Hentschke (*Die Stellung der vorexilischen Schriftpropheten zum Kultus*, 1957, p. 142) attributes to Johnson the view that the cultic prophets, who are identified with the *nᵉbhî'îm*, were also priests (cf. Johnson's reply, in *J.S.S.*, v, 1960, p. 304).

we must not too hastily conclude that they belonged to their staff.[1] Moreover, where we read of groups of prophets residing at Ramah or at Gilgal, where shrines are known to have existed, or coming down from Gibeah, where there was a shrine, this does not necessarily mean that they were functionaries of these shrines. In the case of Gibeah, the prophets were found exercising their function on the road coming away from the shrine, and not at the shrine itself. Again, a group of prophets resided at Jericho (2 Kings 2 : 5), which had only recently been re-walled (1 Kings 16 : 34). While the site had doubtless been occupied to some extent, it had not been the centre of any important settlement for many years, and there is no reason to suppose that it had an important, and largely staffed, shrine. Hence I would suggest reserve in connecting the prophets as closely with particular shrines as the priests, while welcoming the emphasis on their association with cultic centres.[2]

They were not alone interested in the cultus, however, but in poli-

[1] Cf. Pedersen, *Israel III–IV*, p. 117: "They constituted a stable part of the staff of the temple." Johnson says (*E.T.*, *loc. cit.*, p. 315a): "The evidence points to the fact that their [i.e. the Baal prophets'] rivals held a similar position in the cultus of Jahweh, and were *stationed*, in the form of the so-called guilds, at the different *sanctuaries* throughout the country (cf. 2 Kings 2: 3, 5, etc.)." The words which I have italicized seem to me to go beyond the evidence. I should add that in private correspondence Dr. Johnson agrees that the word "stationed" is too strong, and that the cultic prophets should not be thought of as in any sense resident at the shrines. I should also make it clear that he does not suggest that Elijah was a cultic prophet of the Carmel shrine, or Amos of the Bethel shrine, and that I only adduce these examples to show that prophetic activity at a shrine does not provide sure evidence of cultic prophecy. Jepsen tends to outrun the evidence in a different direction. He says (*Nabi*, p. 162): "Die nordisraelitischen Nabis halten also weder am Hof noch an der Priesterschaft einen Rückhalt." So far as the time of Ahab is concerned this is not true of the Court. J. Lindblom (*Prophecy in Ancient Israel*, E.Tr., 1962, p. 80) says: "There can be little doubt that prophets belonged to the permanent staff of the Jerusalem temple." He adds that "the prophets were not always bound to the sanctuaries and the cult, but lived their own life apart from the sacred places." On the other hand, R. de Vaux (*Ancient Israel: its life and institutions*, E.Tr. by J. McHugh, 1961, pp. 384 ff.) rejects the view that there were cultic prophets on the Temple staff (cf. A. R. Johnson, *The Cultic Prophet in Ancient Israel*, 2nd ed., 1962, p. 74 n.).

[2] In my essay "Ritual and the Hebrew Prophets" in *From Moses to Qumran*, 1963, pp. 111–138, I indicate how far I go in the recognition of cultic prophecy in Israel. I make it quite clear that I do not regard the major canonical prophets as cultic prophets. N. W. Porteous (*E.T.*, lxii, 1950–51, p. 8) suggests that the cultic prophets were priests with an added gift. I am not persuaded that they are rightly thought of as priests. H. F. Hahn (*Old Testament in Modern Research*, 1954, p. 141) says: "With this altered perspective on the prophetic function, it was possible to see the priest and prophet, each in his own sphere, working for the furtherance of religion without being continuously at cross purposes. The priest had the help of the cult-prophet in teaching the significance of ritual actions; the canonical prophet added yet more by infusing religious worship with an ethical content."

tical affairs. For politics and religion were intimately related. When the nation was under the Philistine heel, the national religion was threatened and the national God dishonoured, and therefore the devotees of God and of the cultus through which He was worshipped were behind the national resurgence. It was Samuel, the seer, who encouraged Saul to take the lead, and the bands of frenzied prophets who kindled the ardour of the people. Later it was Ahijah who instigated Jeroboam to head the northern revolt (1 Kings 11 : 29 ff.), and Elisha who sent a member of one of the prophetic bands to promote the revolution of Jehu (2 Kings 9 : 1 ff.).

(4)

The relation of the greater canonical prophets to any of these varieties of prophet provides a further question. Frequently they denounce the prophets as faithless misleaders of the people (Hos. 9 : 7; Is. 28 : 7; Mic. 3 : 5, 11; Jer. 23 : 9 ff., 29 : 21; Ezek. 13 : 17 ff.), and it might be supposed that they did not regard themselves as having any part or lot in them. Amos is commonly understood to say in so many words that he is neither a prophet nor a member of a prophetic guild (Amos 7 : 14).[1] Yet when he describes what God called him to do, he uses the word *nibbā'=play the prophet*. Theodore Robinson argues that his use of this word proves that he was an ecstatic,[2] while J. Morgenstern holds that unless he had coined a new word, which would have been far better, he was bound to use this word, inadequate as it was, since it was the only one available.[3] While I have indicated much reserve on the question of the extent to which "ecstasy" marked prophecy, I wholly agree with Robinson that the difference between the greater prophets and the men they denounced should not be exaggerated. Clearly to the outward eye there was no manifest difference,[4] and "ecstasy" marked the one group as much, as or little, as the other. Nor can it be argued that the non-professional character of the canonical prophets differentiated them from the others. Had it been merely that the canonical prophets were "non-ecstatic", while those they denounced were "ecstatic", or that they were non-professional,

---

[1] On this, however, see below.   [2] *Exp.*, *loc. cit.*, p. 224.

[3] *Amos Studies*, i, pp. 32 ff.=*H.U.C.A.*, *loc. cit.*, pp. 48 ff.

[4] Cf. Robinson, *loc. cit.* Cf. G. Widengren, *Literary and Psychological Aspects of the Hebrew Prophets*, 1948, p. 121: "The so-called scribal prophets must not be unduly isolated and separated from the prophetic associations of an earlier age." On the false prophets, cf. G. von Rad, "Die falschen Propheten", *Z.A.W.*, N.F. x, 1933, pp. 109–120; G. Quell, *Wahre und falsche Propheten*, 1952.

while the others were professional prophets, we should have expected the fact to be far more clearly indicated. Amos prophesied in the Bethel shrine, and Jeremiah not alone prophesied in the Jerusalem Temple, but the exiles in Babylonia wrote to the Jerusalem priests to complain that they did not maintain a proper discipline over him (Jer. 29 :26 f.). Mowinckel, indeed, believes that Jeremiah belonged to the Temple personnel.[1] So far as Isaiah is concerned, we know that he met Ahaz (Is. 7 : 3 ff.), much as Nathan had met David or Elijah Ahab, that Hezekiah sent to consult him (Is. 37 : 2) much as Josiah later sent to consult Huldah (2 Kings 22 : 14), and that he visited Hezekiah in his sickness and brought him a prophetic word (Is. 38 : 1). No difference of status as compared with the prophets from whom it is usual to distinguish them can be established, and Mowinckel[2] and Porteous[3] think they may have come from their ranks. Moreover, the inner cleavage between the prophets first appears with Micaiah (1 Kings 22). Yet there it is clear that Micaiah is a prophet in the same sense as the other four hundred. Similarly when Jeremiah, wearing his wooden yoke, confronts Hananiah in the Temple (Jer. 28 : 1 ff.), it is clearly a conflict between two men who claim a like status.

S. Mowinckel[4] and H. Th. Obbink[5] distinguish between the false prophets and the true by finding the former to be "ecstatic" and the

---

[1] *Acta Orientalia*, xiii, p. 267; also *J.B.L.*, liii, 1934, p. 210, where he adds the suggestion that Isaiah was also probably a member of the same personnel. For the latter cf. I. Hylander, *Le monde oriental*, xxv, 1931, pp. 64 f. Lindhagen (*The Servant Motif in the Old Testament*, 1950, p. 117) holds that a number of the canonical prophets had been cultic prophets, including Isaiah, Joel, Nahum, Habakkuk, Haggai, and Zechariah. Mowinckel (*Psalmenstudien*, iii, 1923, pp. 27 ff.) attributes Joel and Habakkuk to cultic prophets; Humbert (*Z.A.W.*, N.F. iii, 1926, pp. 266 ff.; *A.f.O.*, v, 1928–29, pp. 14 ff.; *R.H.P.R.*, xii, 1932, pp. 1 ff.) holds Nahum to be a prophetic liturgy composed to celebrate the fall of Nineveh; E. Balla (*R.G.G.*, 2nd ed., ii, 1928, cols. 1556 f.) and E. Sellin (*Einleitung in das Alte Testament*, 6th ed., 1933, p. 120) viewed Habakkuk as a liturgy (cf. Th. C. Vriezen, *An Outline of Old Testament Theology*, E.Tr. 1958, pp. 63, 125); G. Gerleman (*Zephanja textkritisch und literarisch untersucht*, 1942) found Zephaniah to be from a cultic prophet, Cf. also above, p. 110, n. 2.

[2] *J.B.L.*, loc. cit., p. 206 n.   [3] In *Record and Revelation*, p. 233.

[4] " 'The Spirit' and the 'Word' in the Pre-exilic Reforming Prophets", in *J.B.L.*, liii, 1934, pp. 199–227. In the course of this paper Mowinckel says that the great reforming prophets had experiences of an "ecstatic" character (p. 214), and that the "ecstatic" element was a criterion of prophecy (p. 215), but he contrasts the "elevated" character of their experience and utterance with the crude "ecstasy" of the *nᵉbhî'îm* (pp. 207 f.). Cf. *J.B.L.*, lvi, 1937, pp. 261–265, where, in a postscript to the above article, Mowinckel says he would then have emphasized the "ecstatic" element in the prophets even less.

[5] "The Forms of Prophetism", in *H.U.C.A.*, xiv, 1939, pp. 23–28, especially p. 26: "These prophets deny any relationship with the so-called nebi'im, the ecstatic bands of Canaanite prophets."

latter not.[1] Jepsen makes a similarly sharp distinction, though he denies that the n^{e}bhî'îm in Israel were "ecstatic" in the frenzied sense. I have already said that I find it difficult to suppose that any such clear-cut distinction could be made between them.[2] The difference between false and true belongs not to the outer conduct, that the eye of any child might discern, but to the realm of the spirit, where even the trained observer is not infallible. The fundamental complaint made against the false prophets by the great prophets whose words have come down to us was that they prophesied smooth things, the things that men wanted to hear, crying Peace and Prosperity when their message sprang but from wishful thinking, and not from divine inspiration. It is not necessary to suppose that they were always insincere, though insincerity is sometimes laid to their charge. When Jeremiah accuses them of stealing one another's oracles (Jer. 23 : 30), a charge of insincerity would seem to be implied, since they were giving second-hand messages in a calling that professed to deal in the first-hand oracles of God.[3] Micah, too, charges them with giving oracles dictated by the fee they received (Mic. 3 : 5 ff.), where again there is a clear implication of insincerity. But insincerity is not always transparent, and such a charge may be more easily believed than proved. And since the differences claimed by the greater prophets belonged to that intangible realm of the spirit, it is gratuitous to assume that there was an obvious difference of behaviour, which yet finds no clear mention.

[1] Cf. O. Grether, *Name und Wort Gottes im Alten Testament*, 1934, p. 102: "Der Kampf Jeremias mit den Nebiim ist formal betrachtet ein Kampf gegen das Ekstatische am Nabitum." W. F. Albright (*From the Stone Age to Christianity*, p. 233) thinks the Yahwistic movement may have arisen partly as a reaction against pagan ecstaticism. Cf. A. Guillaume, *Prophecy and Divination*, p. 293: "There is an obvious parallel between Hebrew and heathen ecstatics. But this is a fact without great significance. . . . The more they resemble one another the greater the difference." On the false prophets cf. K. Harms, *Die falschen Propheten*, 1947, esp. chap. II, "Die fliessenden Grenzen zwischen wahren und falschen Propheten", pp. 9 ff.; also E. Auerbach, *Die Prophetie*, 1920, pp. 17 ff., esp. p. 19: "Die Unterscheidung des wahren und falschen Propheten ist nicht immer so einfach wie in dem Falle des Deuteronomiums."

[2] Cf. N. W. Porteous, *loc. cit.*, p. 233: "It is difficult to believe that Jepsen is right in making the cleavage between *nebi'im* and canonical prophets as absolute as he does." Cf. also A. Lods (*Les prophètes d'Israël*, p. 64=) *The Prophets and the Rise of Judaism*, p. 59: "The new prophets, if they noticed any differences at all between themselves and their predecessors or contemporaries, looked upon them as very slight. The great prophets *knew of no exterior sign by which the genuinely inspired of Jahweh could be distinguished*"; J. Skinner, *Prophecy and Religion*, 1922, p. 188: "In externals there was nothing to distinguish the one kind of prophet from the other."

[3] Cf. Jer. 14: 14, 23: 32, where Jeremiah charges them with prophesying lying visions and the deceit of their own heart.

(5)

Mowinckel maintains that the great pre-exilic prophets do not claim to be possessed by the spirit of God, but to have the word of God,[1] and he attaches considerable significance to this distinction. He says: "That their own prophetic vocation and their possession of Yahweh's wondrous word come of their having Yahweh's spirit in them is never suggested by so much as a syllable."[2] Indeed, he observes, there are passages where they seem to deprecate the spirit as the organ of revelation. Thus Hos. 9 : 7 says: "The prophet is a fool, the man that hath the spirit is mad"; Mic. 2 : 11 describes the prophet as a man walking in wind and falsehood, where there may be some play on the double meaning of *ruaḥ*—the wind or the spirit—and the suggestion that the spirit produces mere windiness; Jer. 5 : 13 declares that "the prophets shall become wind, and the word is not in them", where again there may be some suggestion of the emptiness of the spirit which possesses them; and Zech. 13 : 3 associates the prophets with the spirit of uncleanness.[3] In Mic. 3 : 8, however, as the text now stands, Micah claims the possession of the spirit of Yahweh. The R.V. renders: "But I truly am full of power by the spirit of the Lord, and of judgement and of might." It has, however, long been held that syntax and rhythm alike show that the words rendered "by the spirit of the Lord" do not belong to the text,[4] and there is therefore good ground for ignoring the passage in this connexion.

With Ezekiel Mowinckel finds a return to the thought of the spirit as the medium of revelation. Thus in Ezek. 11 : 5 we have: "And the spirit of the Lord fell upon me, and he said unto me, Speak." In later

[1] *J.B.L.*, loc. cit.; also *Die Erkenntnis Gottes bei den alttestamentlichen Profeten*, 1941, pp. 16 ff. (=*R.H.P.R.*, xxii, 1942, pp. 79 ff.), and *Nor.T.T.*, xlix, 1948, pp. 206 ff. Cf. F. Häussermann (op. cit., p. 24): "Die klassischen Propheten verzichten auf solche Mittel. Überhaupt ist bei ihnen von der *ruaḥ* selten die Rede. Häufiger begegnet uns der Ausdruck wieder bei Ezechiel." Cf. also A. Jepsen, *Nabi*, 1934, pp. 189 f.; R. B. Y. Scott, *The Relevance of the Prophets*, 1944, pp. 85 f.; and I. P. Seierstad, *Die Offenbarungserlebnisse der Propheten*, 1946, pp. 156 ff. For the place of the "Word" in prophecy, and especially in the thought of Jeremiah, cf. H. W. Hertzberg, *Prophet und Gott*, 1923, pp. 83 ff. Cf. too O. Grether, *Name und Wort Gottes im Alten Testament*, 1934, where it is argued that the word of God is a separate category of revelation, to be distinguished from dream, vision, audition, and ecstasy, and that though the word may have been associated with some abnormal experience it was never mediated merely through it, apart from the conscious co-operation of the recipient.

[2] *J.B.L.*, loc. cit., p. 201.   [3] Cf. Mowinckel, ibid., pp. 204 ff.

[4] So J. Wellhausen, *Die kleinen Propheten*, 2nd ed., 1893, p. 138; W. Nowack, *Die kleinen Propheten*, 1897, p. 203; K. Marti, *Dodekapropheten*, 1904, p. 279; E. Sellin, *Das Zwölfprophetenbuch*, 2nd ed., 1929, p. 326.

prophets there is frequently found this thought of the spirit as the medium of revelation, as in Is. 48 : 16: "And now the Lord God hath sent me, and his spirit"; Is. 61 : 1: "The spirit of the Lord God is upon me"; Joel 3 : 1 (E.V. 2 : 28): "I will pour out my spirit upon all flesh; and your sons and your daughters shall prophesy." There are, however, some passages in proto-Isaiah which imply a similar thought, such as Is. 11 : 2: "The spirit of the Lord shall rest upon him, the spirit of wisdom and understanding, the spirit of counsel and might, the spirit of knowledge and of the fear of the Lord"; Is. 28 : 6: "And for a spirit of judgement to him that sitteth in judgement"; Is. 32 : 15: "Until the spirit be poured upon us from on high." All of these passages, however, whose attribution to Isaiah has been questioned in other quarters and on other grounds, Mowinckel assigns to later dates.[1]

How far the sharpness of this distinction can be maintained is doubtful, and I do not think any of the great prophets would have directly repudiated the spirit of God as the medium of their inspiration.[2] In the story of the first cleavage amongst the prophets, Micaiah says, "Hear thou the *word* of the Lord" when he delivers his message (1 Kings 22 : 19), and speaks of a *spirit* that stood before the Lord entering Zedekiah and the other prophets (22 : 21 ff.); but the story begins with Jehoshaphat's request to Ahab: "Inquire, I pray thee, at the *word* of the Lord" (22 : 5). Both sides dealt in what claimed to be the word of the Lord, and it is probable that both claimed to be possessed by the spirit of the Lord. But Micaiah declared the possibility of possession by a lying spirit, sent from God Himself, and what his successors seem to have meant was that it was necessary to test the spirits. They frequently stigmatize prophecies as lies, and it is probable that their complaint was not that they were born of the spirit, but that they were born of a false spirit. Whether possession by the spirit manifested itself in "ecstasy" or merely in earnestness, it was insufficient. That kind of test could only be applied to the reception or delivery of a message, and could not of itself guarantee the truth of its revelation. The truth belonged to the content, and there alone it could be tested and shown to be the veritable word of God. For the true prophets are Yahweh's spokesmen, not His ravers.

It seems to me that this is getting down much more deeply to the nature of Old Testament prophecy than any concern with mere

---

[1] *J.B.L.*, *loc. cit.*, pp. 201 f. note.
[2] Cf. H. Knight, *The Hebrew Prophetic Consciousness*, 1947, pp. 73 ff.

"ecstasy". For whatever divergence of view there may be as to the extent of the abnormality of the greater prophets, there is none as to its prevalence in earlier times, or its manifestation in the prophets of Baal. Hence the essence of true prophecy cannot be sought in something which it has in common with other prophecy.

There are not wanting, however, those who would deny any distinction, so far as "truth" is concerned, between the rival groups of prophets. Thus Graham and May declare that they were but complementary factors in conditioning the flow of the tide of life which swept them all on to destiny, and that the distinction between them was not one of truth or virtue, but something that lay more in the realm of social function than in morals or philosophy,[1] while Hoschander would prefer rather to reverse the rôles usually assigned to the two groups.[2] He divides the prophets into priestly prophets and nonpriestly prophets, and finds the former to be those who are called false prophets by Jeremiah. But these priestly prophets, who included Joel and Ezekiel, are held to be superior to Jeremiah and his like. For the latter were only interested in morals, whereas the priestly prophets were interested in morals and ritual, and instead of striving after the naked truth, in all the indecency of its nakedness, they sought to dress it attractively in a becoming garment of falsehood, and showed altogether more realism than the purely idealistic prophets, whose effectiveness was destroyed by their idealism.[3] Neither of these views seems to me to penetrate deeply enough into the spirit and essence of prophecy.

(6)

Whether or not *nābhî'* means *called*, as Albright holds, every prophet was conscious of a vocation, and this is the first fundamental characteristic of true prophecy.[4] How the members of the prophetic guilds,

---

[1] *Culture and Conscience*, 1936, pp. 214 f. Cf. also W. C. Graham, *The Prophets and Israel's Culture*, 1934.

[2] *The Priests and Prophets*, 1936, chap. ii.

[3] For a criticism of the unpractical idealism of the greater prophets in the realm of statesmanship, cf. F. Weinrich, *Der religiös-utopische Charakter der "prophetischen Politik"*, 1932, and on the other side K. Elliger, "Prophet und Politik", in *Z.A.W.*, N.F. xii, 1935, pp. 3–22.

[4] Cf. W. F. Albright, *Archæology and the Religion of Israel*, 1942, p. 24: "The central fact of the prophet's consciousness remained thenceforth the memory of that transforming experience, as a result of which he was under special commission from Yahweh to preach to his people." Cf. also S. Mowinckel, *Die Erkenntnis Gottes bei den alttestamentlichen Profeten*, 1941, pp. 11 f. (=*R.H.P.R.*, xxii, 1942, pp. 76 f.). Cf. too L. Dennefeld,

whether cultic officials or not, were recruited we do not know. Guillaume believes that membership was hereditary,[1] and this may well be a part of the truth. In the case of the seer Samuel, we are told that he was dedicated by his parents in his infancy to the service of the shrine (1 Sam. 1 : 28), and if there is substance in the view that seers were stationed at shrines, this narrative may not be misleading in its suggestion that parental dedication may have been one source of recruitment. It should be stated, however, that the narrative is held by some to have been transferred from a Saul saga to a Samuel saga.[2] It is commonly connected with the older cycle of Samuel stories, in which Samuel is described as a seer, but we find that in its immediate sequel he is called a prophet (1 Sam. 3 : 20). That sequel is of importance for our purpose, since it is clearly held that what made him a genuine prophet was not parental dedication, but the fact that when he was still a child the word of God came to him by divine initiative. We are not given the account of the "call" of every one of the greater prophets, but we have enough evidence to reach the reasonable conclusion that their careers began in an experience of inescapable constraint.[3]

Moses is in some passages called a prophet (Num. 12 : 6 ff.; Deut. 18 : 15, 34 : 10; Hos. 12 : 14 (E.V. 13)).[4] There is nothing to suggest that he was of the crudely "ecstatic" type, but if we rightly find prophecy to lie in the mediation of the word of God, there are few

---

Introduction à l'Ancien Testament, 1934, pp. 151 f.; "Chaque *nabi'* était appelé directement par Dieu. . . . Le don prophétique était toujours un privilège personnel spécialement accordé par Dieu; il ne reposait pas, comme le sacerdoce, sur un titre héréditaire et ne provenait ni d'une prédisposition naturelle ni d'une préparation scolaire." With this contrast J. Chaine, *Introduction à la lecture des prophètes*, 7th ed., 1946, pp. 11 ff., where it is said that the prophets are of two classes, voluntary and called, and that the former alone bore the name *nābhi'* and from them the false prophets were recruited. This over-simple division breaks down on the simple fact that in the Old Testament the true prophets are called by the name *nābhi'* no less than their rivals.

[1] *Prophecy and Divination*, 1938, p. 124.

[2] Cf. S. A. Cook, in *C.A.H.*, ii, 1924, p. 388; A. Lods, *Israël des origines au milieu du viiie siècle*, 1930, p. 411 (=E.Tr. by S. H. Hooke, 1932, pp. 354 f.); J. Hempel, *Die althebräische Literatur*, 1930, p. 91; I. Hylander, *Der literarische Samuel-Saul-Komplex*, 1932, p. 13; R. Press, *Z.A.W.*, N.F. xv, 1938, p. 189.

[3] Cf. S. Mowinckel, *J.B.L.*, *loc. cit.*, p. 211: "This prophetic call is not merely felt to be a *certainty*, it is upon them and in them as a *compelling force* from which they cannot escape." Cf. *id.*, *Acta Orientalia*, xiii, 1935, p. 270, and J. P. Hyatt, *Prophetic Religion*, 1947, p. 31. See also J. Hempel's valuable study of the call of the prophets, in his *Worte der Profeten*, 1949, pp. 83–189.

[4] Mowinckel (*Psalmenstudien*, iii, p. 10) holds that Moses was really a seer and that the representation of him as a *nābhi'* is late.

Old Testament characters who can lay better claim to the title.[1] For however little of the detail of our knowledge of his work modern critical study may leave us, the prophetic stature of the man who led Israel out of Egypt, and brought them to commit themselves by a voluntarily accepted bond to a God whose name was hitherto unknown to them, is little diminished.[2] And the familiar story of the call of Moses represents it as something he tried in vain to resist (Exod. 3 : 11 ff.). By whatever psychological theory his reported dialogue with God may be interpreted, its substance is an inescapable certainty that God would not take No for an answer.

Amos declares that he had to prophesy because God took him from following the flock, and said, "Go, prophesy" (Amos 7 : 14 f.), and the constraint was as irresistible as the catch of the heart on hearing the roar of the lion (Amos 3 : 8). I do not think Amos really repudiates the title of prophet, as is so often supposed.[3] When Amaziah scornfully

[1] Cf. K. Marti, *The Religion of the Old Testament*, E.Tr. by Bienemann, 1907, pp. 63 f.: "He is the first in the series of those great men of Israel whom we call prophets. . . . He is only rightly understood when he is conceived as a prophet"; C. R. North, *The Old Testament Interpretation of History*, 1946, pp. 170 f.: "The Hebrew estimate of him was that he was a prophet, indeed the greatest of the prophets. If the function of the prophet was to act as interpreter between Yahweh and his people, that estimate does not seem exaggerated."

[2] Cf. my paper, "The Significance of Moses and his Work", in *Religion in Education*, xi, 1943–44, pp. 63 ff., and Lecture III of my Schweich Lectures, *From Joseph to Joshua*, 1950, pp. 109 ff.

[3] Amos 7: 14 is translated by most "I am no prophet or prophet's son [=member of a prophetic guild]," and the verse is taken to be an indignant denial of prophetic status by Amos. The Hebrew is a noun sentence, and some part of the verb *to be* must be supplied. R. S. Cripps (*A Critical and Exegetical Commentary on the Book of Amos*, 1929, p. 233) quite incorrectly says that the insertion of the *present* tense is alone in accordance with Hebrew usage. E. Sellin (*Das Zwölfprophetenbuch*, 1929, p. 254), while himself preferring the present, agrees that the *past* tense, as found in the Septuagint, the Syriac, and R.V., is equally possible grammatically. Actually it is to be preferred on grammatical grounds, for while a noun sentence in itself may be past, present, or future, in this case it is followed by consecutive *waw* and the imperfect. Hence "and the Lord said unto me, Go, prophesy" is most naturally, though not necessarily, taken as following "I no prophet or prophet's son" in the temporal sequence. It should be noted, however, that Ex. 6: 2 f. is a clear case where a noun sentence followed by consecutive *waw* and the imperfect requires the present tense of the verb *to be* to be supplied. Cf. Jerome (Migne, *P.L.*, xxv, 1845, col. 1077): "non sum propheta, sive non eram (quorum alterum humilitatis, alterum veritatis est)"; Ḳimḥi (*ad loc.*, cf. the *Amsterdam Rabbinical Bible*, 1724–27, iii, folio 287b): *nābhî' min-nᵉ'ûray lô' hāyîthî*="I was not a prophet from my youth"; E. F. C. Rosenmüller (*Scholia in Vetus Testamentum*, VII, ii, 2nd ed., 1827, p. 207): "Non propheta ego *fui* (*hāyîthî*) *ab initio*"; W. Riedel (*T.S.K.*, lxxvi, 1903, p. 165): "Ich war kein Prophet." Cf. too Amos 3: 7 f.: "Surely the Lord God will do nothing, but he revealeth his secret unto his servants the prophets. The lion hath roared, who will not fear? The Lord God hath spoken, who can but prophesy?" where Amos would clearly seem to be referring to himself as numbered with the *nᵉbhî'îm*. For a fuller study of this cf.

told him to go and prophesy in Judah, where he could make a living out of it, he indignantly replied that he was not a prophet because he wanted to get a living by it, but because he had to be. "God took me," he says, "a man who belonged to no prophetic order, and compelled me to prophesy." For the authentication of his prophetic status he appeals to his experience of vocation, not to his choice of a profession, or to the fact that he was as susceptible as others to "ecstatic" experiences.

Hosea found his call in an act to which he was inescapably drawn (Hos. 1 : 2). Into the much-discussed question of the marriage or marriages of Hosea, it is unnecessary here to enter,[1] but I think the

my paper, "Was Amos a Nabi?" in *Festschrift Otto Eissfeldt*, 1947, pp. 191–195; also E. Würthwein's observations thereon in *Z.A.W.*, N.F. xxi, 1905, pp. 19 ff.; and on the other side S. Lehming, *Z.Th.K.*, lv, 1958, pp. 145–169. S. Cohen (*H.U.C.A.*, xxxii, 1961, pp. 175–178) adopts the forced rendering of Amos 7: 14: "No! I am indeed a *nābhî'*." J. Morgenstern (*H.U.C.A.*, xxxii, 1961, pp. 296 f., 339 f.) maintains that Amos denied that he was a professional prophet, though he recognized that on this occasion—the only occasion, in Morgenstern's view, on which he did prophesy—he was functioning as a prophet. Cf. also A. Neher, *Amos: contribution à l'étude du prophétisme*, 1950, pp. 20 ff. G. A. Danell, *S.E.Å.*, xvi, 1951, pp. 7–20; J. Lindblom, *Prophecy in Ancient Israel*, E.Tr., 1962, pp. 183 f. I. Engnell (*Studies in Divine Kingship*, 1943, p. 87) held that Amos was a cultic official, and so A. Haldar (*Associations of Cult Prophets among the Ancient Semites*, 1945, pp. 79 n., 112) and A. S. Kapelrud (*Central Ideas in Amos*, 1956, pp. 5 ff.); while M. Bič (*V.T.*, i, 1951, pp. 293 ff.) argued that the term *nōḳēdh* in Amos 1: 1 shows that Amos was a hepatoscoper, or liver diviner (against this cf. A. Murtonen, *ibid.*, ii, 1952, pp. 170 ff.). W. Eichrodt (*Theology of the Old Testament*, E.Tr. by J. A. Baker, i, 1961, p. 302) says: "It is a striking fact that in Israel there is to all intents and purposes no trace of the study of omens". J. J. Glück (*V.T.*, xiii, 1963, pp. 144 f.) maintains that *nōḳēdh* means "shepherd" and that it is philologically to be traced to the same root as *nāghîdh*, or "leader".

[1] By some the story is interpreted as pure allegory (A. van Hoonacker, *Les douze petits prophètes*, 1908; C. H. Toy, "Note on Hosea 1–3", in *J.B.L.*, xxxii, 1913, pp. 75–79; H. Gressmann, *S.A.T.*, II, i, 1910; A. Regnier, "Le réalisme dans les symboles des prophètes", in *R.B.*, xxxii, 1923, pp. 383–408), and by others as historical (P. Cruveilhier, "De l'interprétation historique des événements de la vie familiale du prophète Osée", in *R.B.*, N.S. xiii, 1916, pp. 342–362; H. Schmidt, "Die Ehe des Hosea", in *Z.A.W.*, N.F. i, 1924, pp. 245–272); by some chapter 1 is regarded as historical and chapter 3 as allegorical (P. Volz, "Die Ehegeschichte Hosea's", in *Zeitschrift für wissenschaftliche Theologie*, xli, 1898, pp. 321–335; H. Guthe, in Kautzsch-Bertholet, *H.S.A.T.*, 4th ed., ii, 1923; P. Humbert, "Les trois premiers chapitres d'Osée", in *R.H.R.*, lxxvii, 1918, pp. 157–171), by some chapter 3 is regarded as an account in the first person parallel to the account in the third person of chapter 1 [L. Gautier, *Introduction à l'Ancien Testament*, 1914 (reprinted 1939); O. Eissfeldt, *Einleitung in das Alte Testament*, 1934; T. H. Robinson, "Die Ehe des Hosea", in *T.S.K.*, cvi, 1934–35, pp. 301–313, and in *Prophecy and the Prophets*, 1923, in Oesterley and Robinson's *Introduction to the Books of the Old Testament*, 1934, and in Robinson and Horst, *Die zwölf kleinen Propheten* (H.A.T., I, xiv), 1938; J. Lindblom, *Hosea literarisch untersucht*, 1928], by some chapter 3 is regarded as the sequel to chapter 1, the woman of chapter 3 being either Gomer [J. A. Bewer, *The Literature of the Old Testament in its Historical Development*, 1922; K. Budde, "Der Abschnitt Hosea 1–3 und seine

view that Gomer was a temple prostitute, and that Hosea, who loathed with all his soul the sacred fornication to which she was dedicated, felt an irresistible constraint to marry her, is right.[1] Modern psychologists may find terms for the particular sort of complex Hosea had.[2] But to him the constraint was of God, and that the experience became to him the medium of the word of God was the sufficient vindication of his belief.

Isaiah found his call[3] in an overwhelming sense of the holy presence of God, crushing him with the consciousness of his own uncleanness, yet touching him into the consciousness of a new purity. And when he heard the voice saying, "Whom shall I send?" he could not withhold his service, or refrain from consecrating to the divine word the lips that had been cleansed by the burning touch (Is. 6).

Of all the prophets Jeremiah seems to have been the most conscious

grundlegende religionsgeschichtliche Bedeutung", in *T.S.K.*, xcvi–xcvii, 1925, pp. 1–89; H. Wheeler Robinson, "The Marriage of Hosea", in *Baptist Quarterly*, N.S. v, 1930–31, pp. 304–313; E. Sellin, *Einleitung in das Alte Testament*, 7th ed., 1935; A. Weiser, *Einleitung in das Alte Testament*, 2nd ed., 1949, p. 175, and *Das Buch der zwölf Kleinen Propheten*, i, 1949; J. Lindblom, *Prophecy in Ancient Israel*, E.Tr., 1962, p. 168 n. (though Lindblom holds that chapter 1 is the sequel to chapter 3); N. K. Gottwald, *A Light to the Nations*, 1959, pp. 298 f.; A. J. Heschel, *The Prophets*, 1962, pp. 52 f.], or another woman [Marti—who, however, holds chapter 3 to be allegorical—*Dodekapropheton* (K.H.A.T.), 1904; D. Buzy, "Les symboles d'Osée", in *R.B.*, N.S. xiv, 1917, pp. 376–423=*Les symboles de l'Ancient Testament*, 1923, chap. ii; Smith-Irwin, *The Prophets and their Times*, 1941]. E. Sellin (*Introduction to the Old Testament*, E.Tr. by Montgomery, 1923) and K. Budde (T.S.K., *loc. cit.*,) hold that an original single autobiographical account has been divided into two and part thrown into the third person. Several writers have defended Gomer's reputation against the charge of adultery (J. Fück, "Hosea Kapital 3", in *Z.A.W.*, xxxix, 1921, pp. 283–290; A. Heermann, "Ehe und Kinder des Propheten Hosea", in *Z.A.W.*, xl, 1922, pp. 287–312; P. Humbert, "Osée, le prophète bédouin", in *R.H.P.R.*, i, 1921, pp. 97–118; L. W. Batten, "Hosea's Message and Marriage", in *J.B.L.*, xlviii, 1929, pp. 257–273; E. Sellin, *Einleitung in das Alte Testament*, 7th ed., 1935; R. H. Pfeiffer, *Introduction to the Old Testament*, 1941). J. Coppens [*Alttestamentliche Studien* (Festschrift Nötscher), 1950, pp. 38 ff.] holds that Gomer was a northern Israelite and that she is on that account, and not on account of her personal inchastity, described as "a wife of whoredom". I have discussed the problems of Hosea 1–3 in my essay on "The Marriage of Hosea", in *Men of God*, 1963, pp. 66–97, where fuller reference to the literature will be found.

[1] So T. H. Robinson, *Prophecy and the Prophets*, 1923, and "Die Ehe des Hosea", in *T.S.K.*, cvi, 1934–35, pp. 301–313; H. Schmidt, "Die Ehe des Hosea", in *Z.A.W.*, N.F. i, 1924, pp. 245–272; O. R. Sellers, "Hosea's Motives", in *A.J.S.L.*, xli, 1924–25, pp. 243–247; H. G. May, "The Names of Hosea's Children", in *J.B.L.*, lv, 1936, pp. 285–291; Smith-Irwin, *The Prophets and their Times*, 1941. For a psycho-analytical study of Hosea's attraction to that which he most loathed, cf. A. Allwohn, *Die Ehe des Propheten Hosea*, 1926.

[2] Sellers, *loc. cit.*, describes Hosea as fundamentally a sensualist and sadist, with a martyr complex, and an anti-food complex. This will satisfy whom it will.

[3] Cf. I. Engnell, *The Call of Isaiah*, 1949, for a study of Is. 6.

of the compelling character of his call. When it first came to him he tried to evade it on the grounds of his youth and inexperience, but the word of God was in his mouth, and it banished his fear (Jer. 1 : 4 ff.). Later, when he tried to escape from his vocation and determined never again to utter the prophetic word, he found a fire burning in his very bones, and an inner constraint that he was powerless to control (Jer. 20 : 9 ff.). When he describes the word of God as a fire and a hammer (Jer. 23 : 29), all-consuming and all-shattering, against which a man is helpless, he is but describing it as he has known it in his own inner consciousness.

It is this sense of divine vocation that is more profoundly characteristic of the higher prophecy than frenzy. And relevant to this is Jeremiah's complaint that his contemporaries were stealing one another's oracles (Jer. 23 : 30), and uttering their own thoughts rather than the word of the Lord (23 : 16). Instead of knowing the direct constraint of the spirit of God, they were looking round for their oracles. They were the mere members of a profession, not men of vocation.

(7)

That there was a large element of abnormality in the higher prophets does not seem to me to admit of question.[1] Sometimes it was doubtless quite indistinguishable from that of their rivals, who, at any rate superficially, and probably often actually, expressed in their various forms of "ecstasy" earnestness as well as "madness".[2] The higher prophets may have known experiences of a more refined and spiritual exaltation, which is better known by other names,[3] as not a

---

[1] Causse would admit this, but declares it only an accident of prophecy. Cf. *R.H.P.R.*, ii, 1922, p. 354: "Elle [i.e. ecstasy] est seulement au point de départ historique et elle s'est maintenue chez les grands prophètes comme une survivance à laquelle les contemporains et le prophète lui-même ont pu ajouter une importance plus ou moins grande, mais elle n'est plus qu'un phenomène accidental." Cf. too Mowinckel, *Acta Orientalia*, xiii, 1935, pp. 271 f.: "Manifestly there is an ecstatic element in all this. . . . All this, however, really represents unessentials."

[2] Cf. J. Lindblom, *Festschrift für Alfred Bertholet*, 1950, p. 326: "Der Hauptfehler Seierstads ist aber, dass er in der Ekstase und in den supranormalen Erlebnissen überhaupt etwas sieht, was der echten Religion fremd oder sogar feindlich wäre. Das ist eine grundfalsche Position. Der Wert der Religion ist von ihrem inneren Gehalt abhängig, nicht von den psychischen Formen oder Nebenerscheinungen, die etwa mit den religiösen Erfahrungen verknüpft werden können."

[3] Cf. Mowinckel, *J.B.L.*, liii, 1934, pp. 207 f.: "On the whole little remains of the ecstatic element, apart from that which is the sound psychological substratum and core of religious ecstasy: the all-predominating, all-exclusive consciousness of having been called by Yahweh to deliver a religious and moral message. All external stimuli, such as dancing

few writers have claimed. Micklem interprets it in terms of poetic inspiration,[1] while others prefer to talk of mysticism.[2] No one of these categories will suffice to embrace the whole of the higher prophecy. For the whole should be interpreted neither in terms of its highest nor of its lowest levels. In our idealization of the prophets we should not forget that there were crudities even in the greatest of them. Gunkel observes that if we would understand the prophet Isaiah, we must never forget that he went about naked in the streets for three years.[3]

and music, have been abandoned. True the state in which they deliver that message is "elevated", but it is also characterized by spiritual clarity and reasoned judgment. Their utterances are given in a finished and artistic form; to the solemn words of judgment they generally add a clear, reasoned, moral and religious exposition; and their words do not come to them as a wild stammering glossolaly—as involuntary, unconscious words accompanied by unconscious reflex actions—but as moral and religious apprehensions of inexorable facts, apprehensions which 'rise up' in them from the depths of the subconscious to attain lucidity, merging into their moral and religious personality." Cf. Guillaume, *Prophecy and Divination*, pp. 292 f.

[1] *Prophecy and Eschatology*, chap. i, A. G. Barrois complains that Micklem's prophets "might be the ancestors of a certain Protestantism". He says: "L'auteur va trop loin dans sa comparaison des prophètes avec nos lyriques modernes, et je crains qu'il ne réduise en fin de compte l'inspiration prophétique à une sorte d'inspiration poétique" (*R.B.*, xxxvi, 1927, p. 132). Cf. H. W. Hines, "The Development of the Psychology of Prophecy", in *J.R.*, viii, 1928, pp. 212–224. Cf. also A. Lods (*Les prophètes*, p. 64=) *The Prophets and the Rise of Judaism*, p. 58: "It is also quite likely that the great prophets thought they heard within themselves the 'word of Jahweh', not only when they were really in ecstatic trance, but also when they were in a state of excitement analogous to what we call poetic or artistic inspiration, when words and images seem to crowd of their own accord into the mind and are apparently dictated to it."

[2] Cf. Hines, "The Prophet as Mystic", in *A.J.S.L.*, xl, 1923–24, pp. 37–71; J. Lindblom, *Die literarische Gattung der prophetischen Literatur*, 1924, where the experiences of medieval mystics are cited for comparison. Cf. also his *Profetismen i Israel*, 1934, pp. 50 ff., 64 ff. A. Heschel (*Die Prophetie*, pp. 40 ff., 165 ff.) differentiates the prophetic consciousness from both the poetic and the mystical. Cf. also A. Guillaume, *Prophecy and Divination*, p. 294.

[3] Cf. *Die Propheten*, 1917, p. 111: "Männer, die so wunderliche Handlungen vornehmen, können auch nicht ruhig und besonnen gesprochen haben. Das also muss man sich bei der Erklärung der Worte, auch eines Jesaia immer wieder vor Augen halten: dieser Mann ist einmal drei Jahre lang nackend gegangen!" O. R. Sellers (*A.J.S.L.*, xli, 1924–25, p. 245) says: "Isaiah's going exposed about the streets of Jerusalem is a clear case of exhibitionism, a tendency which may be observed at any bathing-beach or track meet." With this contrast H. W. Hertzberg, *Prophet und Gott*, 1923, p. 41: "Hier ist die Unterordnung unter den Willen Jahves, das Sich-ganz-in-den-Dienststellen, auf die Spitze getrieben. Es könnte eine Absicht der Berichterstattung darin gefunden werden, dass Jesaja hier,—es ist das einzige Mal—von Jahve 'mein Knecht' genannt wird. Der göttliche Wille füllt so sein Inneres, dass der Prophet nicht anders kann, als auch sein äusseres Handeln zum Ausdruck des in ihm Lebenden zu machen. Das Innere schlägt das Aussere in den Bann. Der Leib wird jetzt gleichsam Werkzeug des Geistes, wie der Geist in diesem Augenblicke Werkzeug der Gottheit ist." In the discussion on the present paper, L. H. Brockington observed that in prophetic symbolism the prophet threw his whole self into his prophecy, and made not his lips alone, but his whole personality, the vehicle of the divine "word".

Not infrequently the prophets did odd things.[1] Jeremiah's marching about with a wooden yoke on his shoulders would strike us as childish, and the symbolic names given to Isaiah's and Hosea's children would seem a little hard on the children. But Wheeler Robinson rightly emphasizes that many of these things were potent symbols, not in the sense of illustrations of the prophet's message, but of prophetic messages in themselves.[2] The Hebrew did not distinguish between the word and the act so sharply as we do, and both could be prophetic. Moreover, both could release power. The prophet's word was never merely a forecast of the future. Like the curse and the blessing,[3] it possessed inherent power to work for its own fulfilment.[4] Just because it was the word of God it was alive and active. When it left the lips of the prophet, it was but launched on its career of activity beyond the control of the prophet and beyond that of his enemies. And in the same way the prophetic acts of symbolism released divine power to effect the things symbolized.[5] Superficially this would seem to reduce them to mere examples of magic, but again Wheeler Robinson has distinguished between prophetic symbolism and magic, in that magic is the attempt to control events by a technique which constrains the spiritual powers, whereas prophetic symbolism is the control of events through the technique by the God whose constraint is the source of the symbol.[6]

It has been said that some interpret prophecy in terms of mysticism, and the mystic's union with the deity. S. A. Cook denies the apposite-

[1] G. Widengren (*Literary and Psychological Aspects of the Hebrew Prophets*, 1948, pp. 94 ff.) studies the parapsychic experiences of the prophets.

[2] "Prophetic Symbolism", in *Old Testament Essays*, 1927, pp. 1–17, and "Hebrew, Sacrifice and Prophetic Symbolism", in *J.T.S.*, xliii, 1942, pp. 129–139. Cf. W. F. Lofthouse, *A.J.S.L.*, xl, 1923–24, pp. 239 ff.; D. Buzy, *Les symboles de l'Ancien Testament* 1923; A. Regnier, "Le réalisme dans les symboles des prophètes", in *R.B.*, xxxii, 1923, pp. 383–408; G. Fohrer, *Die symbolischen Handlungen der Propheten*, 1953.

[3] Cf. J. Pedersen, *Israel I–II*, 1926, pp. 182–212, 411–452.

[4] Cf. Is. 45: 23; 55: 10 f.

[5] Cf. A. Lods (*R.H.P.R.*, ix, 1929, p. 173): "Plusieurs des actes 'symboliques' accomplis par les hommes de Dieu israélites ou attribués à tel d'entre eux, ont une affinité évidente avec les rites de magie imitative pratiqués chez les non-civilisés ou dans l'antiquité pour agir, non pas sur les esprits des assistants, mais *sur les événements* eux-mêmes, sur l'avenir; ces actes sont tenus pour 'efficaces', non parce qu'ils sont 'impressionnants', mais dans un sens bien autrement réel, *parce qu'ils produisent eux-mêmes ce qu'ils figurent*."

[6] Cf. *Old Testament Essays*, 1927, p. 14; *Redemption and Revelation*, 1942, p. 250; *J.T.S.*, xliii, 1942, pp. 132 f. Cf. L. H. Brockington, in *Studies in History and Religion* (ed. by E. A. Payne), 1942, p. 41: "Because of his entire submission to the will of God his acts are fully taken up into the divine purpose and become part of the creative process."

ness of this,[1] and W. F. Lofthouse declares that the divine call differentiates the prophet from the mystic.[2] But again mysticism is a wide term, covering experiences which in some of their reaches are not in any sense typical of the prophet. But that the prophet was conscious of a real union with God is not to be doubted. Hölscher drew attention to the prophet's conception of himself as an extension of the divine personality,[3] and Wheeler Robinson has suggested that the concept of corporate personality can explain in what sense the prophet thought of his union with God.[4] A similar view is taken by A. R. Johnson, who, in the course of a study of corporate personality as it appears in the conception of God, gathers much evidence from the Old Testament to show in how vital a sense the prophet regarded himself as the mouthpiece of God, and believed that he was not merely transmitting the message of God, but that in him God was speaking, since He had gathered the prophet's personality into His own.[5] This is something rather different from the mystic's absorption in God, from which Heschel also would differentiate it, while expressing it in other terms than in those of corporate personality. Heschel speaks of the prophet's sharing of the divine *pathos* in a sympathy whereby he enters into the very experience of God Himself,[6] and this Wheeler Robinson finds to be complementary to his own approach,[7] rather than essentially different from it.[8]

(8)

But if the prophet is an extension of the divine personality, he does not cease to be himself, and his message comes through the organ of his personality, and not by its suspension.[9] I have elsewhere used the

[1] *The Old Testament: A Reinterpretation*, pp. 188 f. Cf. also J. Lindblom, "Die Religion der Propheten und die Mystik", in *Z.A.W.*, N.F. xvi, 1939, pp. 65–74, esp. p. 73: "Die Religion der Propheten ist eine Religion der Extramanenz, nicht eine Religion der Immanenz, eine zirkumspektive Religion, nicht eine introspektive Religion"; and p. 74: "Das Wesen der Religion der Propheten ist nicht *unio mystica* und religiöse Introspektion, sondern Glaube und Gehorsam."   [2] *A.J.S.L.*, loc. cit., p. 237; cf. p. 242.
[3] *Die Profeten*, p. 25: "Die Profeten reden nicht nur im Auftrage und nach dem Geheisse Jahwes, wiederholen nicht nur Worte und Offenbarungen, die der Gott ihnen zugeraunt oder in der Vision gezeigt hat, sondern sie reden als Gott selbst und identifizieren sich, solange sie ekstatisch sprechen, durchaus mit ihm." Cf. H. W. Hertzberg, *Prophet und Gott*, 1923, p. 12: "Das Bewusstsein, mit der Gottheit eins zu sein, gibt ihrer Stellung zur Gottheit das Gepräge."
[4] *Z.A.W.*, xli, 1923, pp. 9 f.= *Redemption and Revelation*, pp. 149 f.
[5] *The One and the Many in the Israelite Conception of God*, 1942, especially pp. 36 f.
[6] *Die Prophetie*, pp. 127 ff.   [7] *Redemption and Revelation*, p. 150 n.
[8] Cf. N. W. Porteous, in *Record and Revelation*, (ed. H. W. Robinson), p. 240.
[9] Cf. L. H. Brockington, loc. cit., p. 35: "The word of God to the world was not independent of the personality of the men who heard it and uttered it."

figure of light passing through a piece of coloured glass, where the light is wholly from without the glass, yet wholly modified by it. The prophets believed that they were charged with the word of God, yet that word was everywhere marked by the experience, outlook, and personality of the prophet through whom it was given. Here there is little difference between the more extreme "ecstatic" theorists and others. For the former, though finding the prophet's conscious personality suspended in the trance or fit through which he received the oracle, but go down to his unconscious self, which is yet more truly himself. Theodore Robinson says:[1] "Since in abnormal psychological states it is a man's real nature and opinions that are expressed, it makes little or no difference whether and to what extent men like Hosea and Micah were ecstatic; in any case, they believed profoundly in the truth of what they said, and they were impelled to speak by their own intense convictions." This might seem to suggest that prophetic "ecstasy" was a mere lifting of all restraint, so that the prophet's real self appeared, instead of the imposing of a divine constraint. There are not wanting, indeed, those who would go to this extreme, and who would trace the prophet's inspiration to nothing deeper than himself. Thus H. C. Ackerman regards the prophetic consciousness as a piece of self-deception.[2] He traces the source of his utterance wholly to the prophet himself, and in particular to his interest and meditation. Elijah's still, small voice, he says, was "clearly the result of original meditation."[3] Or again, "The manner in which Jeremiah expresses his inspiration is illustrative of the general prophetic habit to sublimate the facts of their inspiration. This deliberate subtilization of inspirational power . . . tends to cover up the commonplace nature of inspiration, or at any rate, to conceal the prophet's own psychological ignorance of the source of his prophetic calling."[4] That Theodore Robinson would not subscribe to so shallow a view, however, is clear, for he elsewhere declares that the "ecstatic" theory "insists that the real point at which the self-revealing divine impinges on the human soul is to be found in those deeper ranges of spiritual life which lie far below the level of normal consciousness."[5] He therefore recognizes that if the prophet's inspiration comes through his subconscious self, it does not come

[1] In Oesterley and Robinson's *Hebrew Religion*, 2nd ed., 1937, p. 223. Cf. *Prophecy and the Prophets*, pp. 44 f. Cf. also *E.T.*, xl, 1928–29, p. 298: "The prophetic utterances were based directly on the prophet's knowledge of God and man."

[2] "The Nature of Hebrew Prophecy", in *A.Th.R.*, iv, 1921–22, pp. 97–127.

[3] *Ibid.*, p. 103.   [4] *Ibid.*, p. 102.

[5] *E.T.*, xlviii, 1936–37, p. 182.

wholly from it, and that his personality is so profoundly the organ of the inspiration that the content of his message accords with his intense convictions. His conscious as well as his subconscious self would thus appear to be in his utterance, and the source of his inspiration is not traced wholly to himself, nor so wholly to the not-self that he ceases to be more than the passive medium of his message. Here again we have passed to something much more fundamental than the extent of "ecstasy" in the prophetic psychology. That the prophets were real men, with real interests, and minds that functioned, is not to be denied. But that their message came merely from themselves, and was authenticated by an experience precisely similar to that whose authenticating value they denied in others, could not carry us far. Nor could it offer any solution of the problem of prophecy profound enough to account for its phenomena.

(9)

We must distinguish between the occasion, or the medium, of inspiration and its source.[1] Sometimes a chance sight or sound, arising from some ordinary experience, suggested a message.[2] When Amos saw a basket of summer fruit, his thought travelled from the word *summer* (*ḳayiṣ*) to the word *end* (*ḳēṣ*), and thence to the consummation to which the life of Israel was hastening (Amos 8 : 1 ff.). When Jeremiah saw an almond tree in blossom, his mind similarly moved from *almond tree* (*shāḳēdh*) to *waking* (*shōḳēdh*), and he reflected on the awakening activity of God in the affairs of men (Jer. 1 : 11 f.). A seething pot set over a rough fireplace, fed and blown from the northern side, similarly turned his thoughts to the situation of the hour (Jer. 1 : 14 ff.). On another occasion the sight of two baskets of figs of widely contrasted quality set him thinking on the men who had gone into exile and those who had taken their place in the control of the State (Jer. 24 : 1 ff.); and on yet another occasion a potter at his wheel set his mind working (Jer. 18 : 1 ff.). On all such occasions the prophets believed that their minds sprang to the fundamentally unrelated message because God controlled it. There was nothing in the thing seen of itself to dictate the contents of the message. The modern

---

[1] Cf. J. Enciso, "El modo de la inspiración profética según el testimonio de los profetas" in *Estudios Bíblicos*, ix, 1950, pp. 5-37.

[2] Theodore Robinson agrees that these were ordinary experiences of real objects, but supposes that the prophets stared hard at them, until their whirling brain perceived more than others could detect (*Exp.*, 8th series, xxi, 1921, pp. 226 f.). I do not think there is adequate evidence for this supposition.

interpreter may trace it no farther than to the prophet's own mind, or to his unconscious self. But the prophet believed that it was in a flash of divine illumination that he perceived what God was saying to him through the experience. A. Guillaume has collected from Arabic sources a number of parallels, recording accounts of diviners who found their message mediated to them through some simple thing on which their eye happened to light.[1] In the case of the prophets, however, there is a greater spontaneity, in that it was not when applied to for a message that they looked round for some timely omen, but that the sight appears to have prompted the message, either apropos of nothing in particular, or perhaps because it happened to fit in with their train of thought.[2]

Sometimes the message was mediated not through a momentary experience, but through a prolonged one, whose significance may not at once have become clear to the prophet. Thus Hosea's experience of his wife's unfaithfulness brought him first agony before it led him to a deeper understanding of the love of God. Nor did he trace his message no farther than to his suffering when he found it. He traced it to God. There is nothing in that experience of suffering itself to proclaim the love of God to man. Similarly Jeremiah through his deep loneliness found the inner quality of true religion, and just because he was cut off from the observance of the cultus, yet was conscious of God's presence, found religion to be something more profound than the cultus. Yet again he would have repudiated the thought that he had merely meditated on the meaning of his experience. For the experience itself had not this meaning. It was what God was saying to him through the experience, and seeking through him to say to men. For he was the mouthpiece of God, not himself the object of God's message so much as the extension of the divine personality, through whom the message was given to men.

In all this we are therefore brought back to God as the fundamental authenticator of prophecy. It was not because the prophets were "ecstatic" that they knew their message to be true, and not because they were less "ecstatic" than others that they differentiated their message as true from that which they held to be false. It was because

---

[1] Cf. *Prophecy and Divination*, pp. 118 ff., 142 ff.

[2] Cf. L. H. Brockington (*loc. cit.*, p. 36): "The process may probably be explained as one of association: a chance presentation of an object to the eye, or of a sound to the ear or any other sense perception, elicits and makes fully articulate what has been already half-formed or partially realized, just as memory long dormant can be awakened in the same way."

God was so overpoweringly real to them,[1] constraining them irresistibly to deliver a message that often racked their very soul, or speaking to them through an experience of deepest agony, that they knew they had the word of God. Others might claim to be speaking in the name of God a message in direct disagreement with their own, and to the eye of the observer there might be little to mark the one as authentic and the other as false. But the prophets were sure that that other message was mediated through a shallow experience of God, or born of insincerity of spirit, just because they were so sure of their own experience.[2] By its very nature that was not a certainty that could be communicated to others in any undeniable manner. For it was a religious certainty.[3] And religion must ever be something more than an intellectually or scientifically demonstrable proposition.

In this connexion the story of 1 Kings 13 is instructive. The prophet who came from Judah to Bethel delivered his prophecy and set out to return to Judah, in obedience to the word of the Lord that came to him, saying "Thou shalt eat no bread and drink no water there, nor turn again to go by the way that thou camest." Later the old prophet of Bethel went after him and lied to him, alleging a prophetic message cancelling the one on which the other relied. Later in the story the lying prophet becomes the medium of an authentic message to the other, which was duly fulfilled—a message, singularly enough, rebuking him for listening to the bogus message. Clearly there was nothing superficially to distinguish the true message from the false, and so far as the reversal of a prophetic message is concerned, other cases are recorded where both are regarded as genuine. Yet here there is less condemnation for the lying prophet than for his victim, whose fault was just that he allowed a communication received through another, whose authenticity in the nature of the case could never be as certain

[1] Cf. J. Skinner, *Prophecy and Religion*, pp. 195 f.: "This immediate consciousness of having the mind of God is the ultimate secret of true prophetic inspiration, which, being incommunicable, can neither be analysed nor applied as an objective criterion of an alleged revelation. . . . He who has it knows that he has it, though he who lacks it may be deceived in thinking he has it."

[2] Cf. J. Pedersen, *Israel III–IV*, 1940, p. 126: "In the depths of the prophet's soul instinct created a vision of spontaneous certainty which he felt to be infused by God."

[3] Cf. H. Wheeler Robinson, *Redemption and Revelation*, p. 90: "If we go on to say that in this and through this consciousness, by some leap of 'sympathetic' faith on the prophet's part, God was enabled in fulfilment of His purpose to enter human history, then the statement constitutes a leap of faith akin to that made by the prophet himself. We can never eliminate that personal factor, in regard to either the outer or inner event"; cf. p. 139: "In the last resort, we shall know as much or as little of the prophetic consciousness as is the degree to which we share its essential and central experience."

as the authenticity of his own direct message, to override the latter. That lying prophecies should mislead the general public, who had no infallible means of testing them, is not surprising, and the prophets therefore denounce in the strongest terms the iniquity of the lying prophets. But for the prophet who, in his own inner consciousness, has known the certainty of the divine word to defer to a word received through any other, incompatible with it, is disobedience. He is substituting what may be of man for what he is sure was of God.

(10)

It will be observed that I have said nothing of prediction, and nothing of the common view to-day that true prophecy was essentially prophecy of woe, *Unheilsprophetie*.[1] So far as the latter is concerned I do not share the view that woe was of the essence of true prophecy, and that the prophets of weal who opposed the greater prophets stand exposed as false by the fact. It is true that the greater prophets were usually prophets of woe.[2] But Isaiah was just as truly a prophet when he promised deliverance to Jerusalem as when he opposed the anti-Assyrian policy.[3] Nor do I share the view which has long been all too common that prediction is not a mark of prophecy.[4] The common modern antithesis between *foretelling* and *forthtelling* would have had little meaning in ancient Israel.[5] For the prophets were continually predicting the future, though commonly the future as arising out of the present rather than a distant and unrelated future;[6] and Deutero-Isaiah

---

[1] Cf. B. Baentsch, *Z.W.T.*, l, 1908, p. 464; H. Gressmann, *Der Messias*, 1929, pp. 77 ff.; H. Gunkel, in *R.G.G.*, 2nd ed., iv, 1930, cols. 1543 f.; F. Weinrich, *op. cit.*, pp. 24 ff.; S. Mowinckel, *J.B.L.*, *loc. cit.*, p. 219.

[2] Cf. Jer. 28: 8 f.

[3] Cf. A. Jepsen, *Nabi*, p. 252, where, in the closing words of his book, the author summarizes prophecy as "Zeugnis von Gott, seinem Gesetz, seiner Verheissung, seinem Handeln in der Geschichte in Gericht und Gnade". Both *Gericht* and *Gnade* belong to true prophecy.

[4] Cf. H. C. Ackerman, *A.Th.R.*, iv, 1921–22, p. 116: "Prophecy was certainly predictive"; H. Gunkel, *Exp.*, 9th series, i, 1924, p. 433 (= *S.A.T.*, II, ii, 1923, p. xxvi): "There is none among the literary prophets whose first word was not an announcement of a future event"; A. Guillaume, *op. cit.*, p. 111: "There is no prophet in the Old Testament who was not a foreteller of the future."

[5] Cf., e.g., R. H. Charles, *Critical and Exegetical Commentary on the Book of Daniel*, 1929, p. xxvi: "Prophecy is a declaration, a forthtelling, of the will of God—not a foretelling. Prediction is not in any sense an essential element of prophecy, though it may intervene as an accident—whether it be a justifiable accident is another question."

[6] There is no reason to deny that they also spoke of that more distant future, and uttered prophecies of things not causally related to the events of their own day, and the general relegation to a later age of every such prophecy is no longer in vogue amongst scholars.

appeals to fulfilled prediction as the vindication of prophecy[1] no less confidently than Deuteronomy lays down the fulfilment or non-fulfilment of prophecy as the test of its genuineness.[2]

But it was not mere prediction as a brilliant forecast of the future, whether near or distant, that gave to prophecy its deepest content. For Old Testament prophecy is a fundamentally spiritual phenomenon. The prophet's message always bore the mark of the personality of the man through whom it came. But he was always sure it bore the mark of something profounder than his personality, because he was so sure of the One from whom it came. That it was imperfect and fallible is not surprising, since it was mediated through imperfect and fallible men. Yet it mediated some light from Him who is perfect and infallible. For the prophet's message was ever related to his view of God. Through the immediacy of his inner experience of God he perceived the meaning of the events of his own life and of the contemporary affairs of men, and he saw all in the illuminating light of what he had seen of God. As Mowinckel has observed,[3] the word that came to the prophets must accord with what they had known of Yahweh, and by this they were able to test the message that came to them. The prophet's real criterion was therefore not whether he had received the message in some "ecstatic" way, but whether it harmonized with the character of the God he had known.[4] A mere welling up of words from his own heart might be but false prophecy. It was therefore necessary to test it by its content.[5] This means, says Mowinckel, that the prophets'

---

[1] Cf. Is. 45: 21; 46: 9 f.

[2] Deut. 18: 22. That this simple test is not alone adequate is recognized in Deut. 13: 1 ff., but that it should be mentioned at all as a test of prophecy shows beyond a peradventure that prophecy was regarded as dealing essentially in prediction.

[3] *J.B.L.*, liii, 1934, p. 211.

[4] Cf. Mowinckel, *Acta Orientalia, loc. cit.*, pp. 279 f.: "The content is the deciding factor, which makes the prophets' experience an experience of God. The experience of an empty and more or less unutterable *mysterium tremendum et fascinosum* would not make the prophets essentially different from the common nabhi'; the ecstatic nebhi'im had purely 'numinous' experiences, but these were of no value as revelations. What is merely 'numinous' may just as well be 'Ba'al' as Yahweh; it may just as well be a 'lying spirit' as the spirit of Yahweh, and of this the great prophets are fully aware. The content of an experience makes it an experience of Yahweh, or rather proves that it is one. In other words, *the certitude of the experience depends upon whether it has a definite content, capable of being apprehended by the mind and tested by religious and moral standards.*" Cf. *J.B.L., loc. cit.*, p. 217; also Skinner, *Prpohecy and Religion*, p. 195.

[5] Cf. Mowinckel, *Acta Orientalia, loc. cit.*, p. 286: "The great prophets know perfectly well that 'words' can come to them which are nothing but 'visions of their own hearts'. Accordingly they lay down certain criteria of the *true word of Yahweh*. . . . The *content* of the word will afford a more reliable test."

minds were at work, not only in the depths of the unconscious, but in their conscious thought as well.[1]

To say this, of course, is not to revert to the view that the prophet's message has no deeper source than his own heart, and that it was mere self-deception to attribute it to God. It is rather to say that the man who had known God in the immediacy of his own experience, and who under the constraint of that experience addressed himself to the needs of the world which he saw in the light of his knowledge of God, spoke a word which was at once his own and not his own.

That this was true in some measure of the false prophets I see no reason to doubt. For the difference between the true and the false prophets was no clear-cut distinction that contemporaries or successors could easily discern.[2] It was at bottom a difference in the experience of God and in the understanding of His nature and will. With a shallower experience of God the false prophets were less concerned with the sinfulness and unrighteousness of the nation. Because they had not realized that it was an offence to God it was no offence to them. Men who had not known Amos's burning sense of the righteousness of God could not know his horror at the injustice that prevailed; men who had not shared Hosea's perception of the love of God could not share his realization of the demand of that love for the undivided love and loyalty of men in response. Therefore they could not be expected to utter predictions which sprang out of that horror or that realization, or to utter a word of Yahweh summoning men to righteousness and love.

While, therefore, true and false prophets both provided evidence of abnormal psychology, and both forecast the future, the nature of prophecy is not to be defined in terms of these things. What is really vital is the relation of the prophet and of his word to God. The prophet who is properly so called was a man who knew God in the immediacy of experience, who felt an inescapable constraint to utter what he was profoundly convinced was the word of God, and whose word was at bottom a revelation of the nature of God no less than of His will, who saw the life of men in the light of his vision of God, and who saw the inevitable issue of that life, who therefore declared that issue and

---

[1] *Acta Orientalia, loc. cit.*, p. 289.

[2] Cf. J. Lindblom, *Prophecy in Ancient Israel*, E.Tr., 1962, p. 34: "Inspiration has many degrees, according to the force and the intensity of the influx from the other world."

pleaded with men to avoid it by the cleansing and renewing of their lives.[1] He was a true prophet in the measure of his experience of God, and the measure of his experience was the measure of his receptiveness and of his response to it.

[1] Cf. W. F. Albright, *From the Stone Age to Christianity*, p. 232: "The prophet was a man who felt himself called by God for a special mission, in which his will was subordinated to the will of God, which was communicated to him by direct inspiration. The prophet was thus a charismatic spiritual leader, directly commissioned by Yahweh to warn people of the perils of sin and to preach reform and revival of true religion and morality." Cf. also E. O. James, *Religion and Reality* (Henry Myers Lecture, 1950), p. 9: "What differentiated men like Amos, Hosea, Jeremiah, and Isaiah from their predecessors was the character of their message. This was stamped with a genuine originality and urgency in direct opposition to contemporary opinion. They were aware of a constraining purpose behind their proclamations, which they prefaced with the words 'Thus saith Yahweh'; but unlike the ecstatics, they remained in full possession of their rational and moral consciousness."

THE CHRONOLOGICAL ORDER OF
EZRA AND NEHEMIAH

4

The Chronological Order of Ezra and Nehemiah

THE question of the chronological order in which the work of Ezra stood to that of Nehemiah has been a vexed one for the past half-century and more, and there is still no prospect of agreement amongst Old Testament scholars. To these two leaders is ascribed the inauguration of the era of Judaism,[1] which so largely contributed to the heritage of both Christianity and Islam. It is therefore the more surprising that we cannot demonstrate the relations between them, or even the order in which they came to Jerusalem.

The superficial reading of the books of Ezra and Nehemiah would seem to leave the matter in no doubt. Ezra came to Jerusalem in the seventh year of Artaxerxes,[2] while Nehemiah received the royal authority to journey to Jerusalem in the twentieth year of Artaxerxes,[3] and apparently in the same year[4] Ezra publicly read the law in the presence of Nehemiah.[5] It would seem to be clear, therefore, that the work of Ezra lay before that of Nehemiah in the reign of the same monarch. While a few scholars have placed them both in the reign of Artaxerxes II,[6] the usual view has always been that they belonged to

---

[1] Cf., however, A. C. Welch's depreciatory estimate of Ezra in *Post-Exilic Judaism*, 1935, pp. 245 ff.

[2] Ezra 7: 8.   [3] Neh. 2: 1.

[4] It is to be noted that no date is specified, and it is only the position of the narrative that offers any suggestion of date.

[5] Neh. 8: 9.

[6] Cf. D. von Haneberg, *Versuch einer Geschichte der biblischen Offenbarung*, 1850, pp. 381 ff. (4th ed., 1876, pp. 428 ff.); F. de Saulcy, *Étude chronologique des livres d'Esdras et de Néhémie*, 1868, pp. 41 ff.; H. J. Elhorst, *T.T.*, xxix, 1895, pp. 93 ff. (in the course of an extended review of W. H. Kosters, *Het Herstel van Israël in het Perzische Tijdvak*, pp. 77–101); J. Marquart, *Fundamente israelitischer und jüdischer Geschichte*, 1897, pp. 31 ff.; H. P. Smith, *Old Testament History*, 1903, pp. 382, 395. C. C. Torrey, while allowing (*Ezra Studies*, 1910, p. 140 n.) that the Aramaic papyri render it probable that Nehemiah lived in the time of Artaxerxes I, maintained that the Chronicler clearly supposed that the king of Ezra 7 ff. and of Nehemiah was Artaxerxes II (*op. cit.*, pp. 140 n., 249, 333 ff.; cf. *Composition and Historical Value of Ezra-Nehemiah*, 1896, p. 65, and *Second Isaiah*, 1928, pp. 456 ff.). It should be noted that though Marquart placed both Ezra and Nehemiah in the reign of Artaxerxes II, he held that Ezra followed Nehemiah and was to be dated 368 or 365 B.C. (*op. cit.*, p. 36).

the first Artaxerxes, and this is still the view of the majority of scholars. It will be seen below that so far as Nehemiah is concerned the evidence for placing him in the reign of Artaxerxes I now amounts almost to a demonstration.

The closer study of the books of Ezra and Nehemiah, however, raised doubts as to whether the compiler of the work had mistakenly supposed these two men to be contemporaries, and had arranged the material he drew from his sources accordingly, or whether there had been some derangement in the transmission of the text. Of some derangement in this work there is clear evidence. For it is widely, and indeed almost universally,[1] held that Chronicles-Ezra-Nehemiah formed a single work, and the fact that the closing verses of 2 Chronicles stand also at the beginning of the book of Ezra lends some support to this. Yet Chronicles follows Ezra and Nehemiah in the Bible. We cannot therefore rule out the possibility that there have been further dislocations within the rest of the work, and that if we had it in its original form it might create a different impression. Indeed we can go beyond this. For in the Greek we have a variant arrangement of the text of the book of Ezra, together with part of Neh. 8, which is transferred to follow Ezra 10.[2] Here, then, we have indisputable evidence that part of the work circulated in a different arrangement, and neither can be assumed to represent the original order. The question is therefore one for the patient examination of the contents of the traditions of the work of Ezra and Nehemiah, to see what indications of priority they contain.

In 1889 Maurice Vernes ventured the suggestion[3] in a brief footnote that while Nehemiah belonged to the reign of Artaxerxes I, Ezra, if he was indeed a character of history, belonged to that of Artaxerxes II. It was Van Hoonacker, however, who gave the view real currency. In a series of publications, ranging from 1890 to 1924,[4] he expounded and

---

[1] Cf., however, A. C. Welch, op. cit., and The Work of the Chronicler (Schweich Lectures), 1939.

[2] On the problems of 1 Esdras cf. C. C. Torrey, Ezra Studies, pp. 11–36; E. Bayer, Das dritte Buch Esdras und sein Verhältnis zu den Büchern Esra-Nehemia (Biblische Studien, XVI), 1911; B. Walde, Die Esdrasbücher der Septuaginta, ihr gegenseitiges Verhältnis untersucht (Biblische Studien, XVIII), 1913; S. A. Cook in Apocrypha and Pseudepigrapha of the Old Testament (ed. by R. H. Charles), i, 1913, pp. 5 ff.; S. Mowinckel, Statholderen Nehemia, 1916, pp. 1 ff.; W. O. E. Oesterley, Introduction to the Books of the Apocrypha, 1935, pp. 133–141; C. C. Torrey, The Apocryphal Literature, 1945, pp. 43 ff.; and R. H. Pfeiffer, History of New Testament Times, 1949, pp. 233–257.

[3] Précis d'histoire juive, 1889, p. 582 n.

[4] Cf. Néhémie et Esdras, une nouvelle hypothèse sur la chronologie de l'époque de la restauration, 1890 (reprinted from Le Muséon, ix, 1890, pp. 151–184, 317–351, 389–401); Néhémie en l'an 20 d'Artaxerxès I: Esdras en l'an 7 d'Artaxerxès II, 1892; "La question Néhemie et

defended this thesis against the criticisms of A. Kuenen,[1] W. H. Kosters,[2] and F. X. Kugler.[3] At first the view of Van Hoonacker won few converts, but for many years now it has gathered a broad stream of followers, though naturally some have modified details of his view. In a letter to the present writer this statement was challenged, and the view expressed that apart from a few British scholars little support had been won for it, and in E. Kalt's *Biblisches Reallexikon* it is stated[4] that "die durch van Hoonacker aufgestellte These . . . wird jetzt fast allgemein abgelehnt". It may be well, therefore, to record the names of some of those who have adopted this view, and to observe that they include scholars of many countries and schools. Without any attempt to compile an exhaustive list, the present writer has noted the following: G. Klameth,[5] M. J. Lagrange,[6] L. W. Batten,[7] J. Touzard,[8] S. Mowinckel,[9] Zschokke-Döller,[10] L. E. Browne,[11] J. B. Pelt,[12] W. E.

Esdras", in *R.B.*, iv, 1895, pp. 186–192; *Nouvelles études sur la restauration juive après l'exil de Babylone*, 1896; "Notes sur l'histoire de la restauration juive après l'exil de Babylone", in *R.B.*, x, 1901, pp. 5–26, 175–199; *Une communauté Judéo-Araméenne à Éléphantine en Égypte, aux VIe et Ve siècles av. J.-C.* (Schweich Lectures), 1915, pp. 19 ff.; "La succession chronologique Néhémie-Esdras", in *R.B.*, xxxii, 1923, pp. 481–494, xxxiii, 1924, pp. 33–64.

[1] Cf. "Die Chronologie des persischen Zeitalters der jüdischen Geschichte", in *Gesammelte Abhandlungen zur Biblischen Wissenschaft*, 1894, pp. 212–251 (translated by K. Budde from the Dutch text which appeared in 1890).

[2] Cf. *Die Wiederherstellung Israels in der persischen Periode*, 1895 (translated by A. Basedow from the Dutch text which appeared in 1894). Cf. S. Jampel, "Die Wiederherstellung Israels unter den Achämeniden", in *M.G.W.J.*, xlvi, 1903, pp. 97–118, 206–229, 301–325, 395–407, 491–513; xlvii, 1903, pp. 1–23, 97–110, 193–201, 385–399, 481–490. Cf., too, J. Nikel, *Die Wiederherstellung des jüdischen Gemeinwesens nach dem babylonischen Exil* (Biblische Studien, V), 1900, and J. Fischer, *Die chronologischen Fragen in den Büchern Esra-Nehemia* (Biblische Studien, VIII), 1903.

[3] Cf. *Von Moses bis Paulus*, 1922, pp. 215–233.

[4] Cf. 2nd ed., i, 1938, cols. 503 f. R. A. Dyson (*Catholic Commentary on Holy Scripture*, 1953, p. 378a) says that there is today a marked reaction in favour of the traditional view.

[5] Cf. *Ezras Leben und Wirken*, 1908, pp. 124 ff.

[6] Cf. *R.B.*, N.S. v, 1908, pp. 343 ff. Lagrange had earlier championed the view that Nehemiah belonged to the reign of Artaxerxes II and Ezra to that of Artaxerxes III. See "Néhémie et Esdras", *ibid.*, iv, 1895, pp. 193–202.

[7] Cf. *The Books of Ezra and Nehemiah* (I.C.C.), 1913, pp. 28–30.

[8] Cf. "Les juifs au temps de la période persane", in *R.B.*, N.S. xii, pp. 59–133.

[9] Cf. *Ezra den Skriftlærde*, 1916, pp. 65–72.

[10] Cf. *Historia sacra Veteris Testamenti*, 7th ed., 1920, p. 297 (according to H. Höpfl, *Introductio specialis in Vetus Testamentum*, 5th ed., 1946, ed. by A. Miller and A. Metzinger, p. 188; I have had no access to Zschokke-Döller).

[11] Cf. *Early Judaism*, 1920, chapter x; Peake's *Commentary on the Bible*, rev. ed., edited by M. Black and H. H. Rowley, 1962, pp. 374 f.

[12] Cf. *Histoire de l'Ancien Testament*, ii, 8th ed., 1925, pp. 385–387 (according to Höpfl, *loc. cit.*; I have had no access to Pelt).

Barnes,[1] C. F. Kent,[2] V. Coucke,[3] W. F. Lofthouse,[4] W. O. E. Oesterley,[5] A. Thomson,[6] S. Navarro,[7] L. Hennequin,[8] G. Ricciotti,[9] A. Lods,[10] S. A. Cook,[11] S. H. Blank,[12] A. Vincent,[13] H. Wheeler Robinson,[14] W. L. Wardle,[15] Theodore Robinson,[16] N. H. Snaith,[17] J. N. Schofield,[18] Fleming James,[19] J. Pedersen,[20] H. Daniel-Rops,[21] Lusseau-Collomb,[22] W. K. Lowther Clarke,[23] E. G. Kraeling,[24] H. Cazelles,[25]

[1] Cf. *The People and the Book* (ed. by A. S. Peake 1925), pp. 293 f.

[2] Cf. *History of the Jewish People*, i, 1927, pp. 199 ff. In *The Growth and Contents of the Old Testament*, 1926, pp. 79 f., Kent had favoured the suggestion that Ezra's mission fell towards the end of the reign of Artaxerxes I.

[3] Cf. *S.D.B.*, i, 1928, cols. 1269 f.

[4] Cf. *Israel after the Exile* (Clarendon Bible), 1928, p. 198.

[5] Cf. *History of Israel*, ii, 1932, pp. 114–118; and Oesterley and Robinson, *Introduction to the Books of the Old Testament*, 1934, pp. 127–129.

[6] Cf. *A.J.S.L.*, xlviii, 1931–32, pp. 117 f.

[7] Cf. '¿Esdras-Nehemias?' in *Estudios Bíblicos*, v, 1933, pp. 12–19 (according to Höpfl, *loc. cit.*; I have had no access to Navarro).

[8] Cf. *S.D.B.*, ii, 1934, cols. 1018 f.

[9] Cf. *Storia d'Israele*, ii, 1934, pp. 125–130 (= *Histoire d'Israël*, translated by P. Auvray, ii, 1939, pp. 132–138; 2nd ed., 1948, pp. 133–142).

[10] Cf. *Les prophètes d'Israël et les débuts du Judaïsme*, 1935, pp. 336–344 (= *The Prophets and the Rise of Judaism*, E.Tr. by S. H. Hooke, 1937, pp. 296–304).

[11] Cf. *The Old Testament: a Reinterpretation*, 1936, p. 194 n., and *Introduction to the Bible*, 1945, p. 159. Earlier Cook had been less decided whether to follow this view or that of Kosters (see below), or whether to reject Ezra from the page of history with Torrey (see below). Cf. *C.A.H.*, vi, 1927, p. 174: "It is very generally agreed, therefore, that Ezra did not return before Nehemiah, though it is disputed whether to place the priestly scribe between the first and second visits of Nehemiah, or after Nehemiah and under the *Second* Artaxerxes, or even to reject the story of Ezra as a later invention."

[12] Cf. *H.U.C.A.*, xi, 1936, pp. 159 f.

[13] Cf. *La religion des Judéo-Araméens d'Éléphantine*, 1937, pp. 235 f.

[14] Cf. *History of Israel: its Facts and Factors*, 1938, pp. 148–158.

[15] Cf. *Record and Revelation* (ed. by Wheeler Robinson), 1938, p. 127.

[16] Cf. *Companion to the Bible*, (ed. by T. W. Manson), 1939, pp. 257 ff.

[17] Cf. *Studies in the Psalter*, 1934, pp. 11 ff.; *Record and Revelation*, p. 258; *Z.A.W.*, N.F. xxii, 1951, pp. 53 ff.

[18] Cf. *The Historical Background of the Bible*, 1938, pp. 226 f., and *The Religious Background of the Bible*, 1944, pp. 168 ff.

[19] Cf. *Personalities in the Old Testament*, 1939, pp. 462 ff.

[20] Cf. *Israel: its Life and Culture, III–IV*, 1940, p. 607: "Whether Ezra came before or after Nehemiah is difficult to decide, though the arguments for Ezra coming after Nehemiah seem the strongest." It is not clear from this whether Pedersen inclines to Van Hoonacker's view or that of Kosters and Bertholet (see below). But since his footnote says "Thus Mowinckel . . . and Oesterley" it is apparent that it is the former.

[21] Cf. *Histoire sainte: le peuple de la Bible*, 1943, pp. 348–353, 455 (E.Tr. by K. Madge, 1949, pp. 238 ff., 305 f.; American ed., 1949, pp. 319 ff., 412).

[22] Cf. *Manuel d'études bibliques, II, Histoire du peuple d'Israël*, 6th ed., 1945, pp. 1009–1016; but cf. below, p. 144, n. 8.

[23] Cf. *Concise Bible Commentary*, 1952, pp. 452 f.

[24] Cf. *The Brooklyn Museum Aramaic Papyri*, 1953, p. 109.

[25] Cf. *V.T.*, iv, 1954, pp. 113 ff.

R. A. Bowman,[1] K. Galling,[2] P. Lemaire and D. Baldi,[3] O. Eissfeldt,[4] B. M. Pelaia,[5] N. K. Gottwald,[6] J. Gray,[7] J. Mauchline,[8] P. R. Ackroyd,[9] and R. Tournay.[10] Despite this impressive support, this view has never been unchallenged, and there have always been scholars of eminence—even more numerous than its supporters—who have refused to adopt it, but have adhered to the traditional view. R. Kittel,[11] H. H. Schaeder,[12] and E. Sellin[13] have rejected it, as have G. Hoberg,[14] A. Fernández,[15] H. M. Wiener,[16] J. Morgenstern,[17] H. Höpfl,[18] R. de Vaux,[19] A. Médebielle,[20] M. Rehm,[21] P. Heinisch,[22] A. Vaccari,[23] A. van Selms,[24] J. L. Myres,[25]

---

[1] Cf. *I.B.*, iii, 1954, pp. 554, 562 f.

[2] Cf. *Die Bücher der Chronik, Esra, Nehemia* (A.T.D.), 1954, pp. 12 ff.; also *R.G.G.*, 3rd ed., ii, 1958, cols. 693 f.

[3] Cf. *Atlante Storico della Bibbia*, 1954, pp. 164, 167 (French Tr., 1959, pp. 170, 173).

[4] Cf. *Einleitung in das Alte Testament*, 2nd ed., 1956, pp. 684 ff., 3rd ed., 1964, pp. 750 ff. In the 1st ed., 1934, p. 597, Eissfeldt had said: "Die uns überlieferte Folge Esra Nehemia aus historischen Gründen die grössere Wahrscheinlichkeit für sich hat als ihre Umkehrung in Nehemia Esra."

[5] Cf. *Esdra e Neemia* (La Sacra Bibbia, ed. by S. Garofalo), 1957, pp. 10 ff.

[6] Cf. *A Light to the Nations*, 1959, pp. 432 f.

[7] Cf. Peake's *Commentary on the Bible*, rev. ed., 1962, p. 71b.

[8] Cf. Hastings's one-volume *D.B.*, rev. ed., edited by F. C. Grant and H. H. Rowley, 1963, p. 286a.

[9] Cf. T. W. Manson's *Companion to the Bible*, 2nd ed., edited by H. H. Rowley, 1963, p. 318.   [10] Cf. *Le Cantique des Cantiques* (E.B.) 1963, p. 20.

[11] Cf. *Geschichte des Volkes Israel*, iii, 2nd part, 1929, pp. 567–650.

[12] Cf. *Esra der Schreiber*, 1930.

[13] Cf. *Geschichte des israelitisch-jüdischen Volkes*, ii, 1932, pp. 134–163.

[14] Cf. "Die Zeit von Esdras und Nehemias", in *Festschrift G. von Hertling*, 1913, pp. 36–40.

[15] Cf. "Epoca de la actividad de Esdras", in *Biblica*, ii, 1921, pp. 424–447. Fernández concludes: "Nuestra conclusión es que hoy por hoy el orden Esdras Nehemías es al que mejor justifican los textos. . . En tanto no see presenten, tenemos por más científico sostener que Esdras regresó a Jerusalén el año 7 y Nehemias el año 20 del mismo monarca, esto es, de Artajerjes I" (p. 447). Cf. also A. Fernández, *Comentario a los libros de Esdras y Nehemías*, 1950, pp. 196–218 (the quoted words stand repeated on p. 217).

[16] Cf. "The Relative Dates of Ezra and Nehemiah", in *J.P.O.S.*, vii, 1927, pp. 145–158.

[17] Cf. *A.J.S.L.*, lv, 1938, p. 56; *U.J.E.*, x, 1943, p. 356; *H.U.C.A.*, xxii, 1949, p. 401, xxxi, 1960, pp. 24 ff.; *J.S.S.*, vii, 1962, pp. 1 ff. For a discussion of Morgenstern's view that Jerusalem suffered a major disaster in 485 B.C. and its bearing on the question of Ezra's mission, cf. H. H. Rowley, *Men of God.*, 1963, pp. 238 ff.

[18] Cf. *Introductio specialis in Vetus Testamentum*, 5th ed. (edited by Miller and Metzinger), 1946, pp. 186–191.   [19] Cf. *S.D.B.*, iv, 1949, cols. 765 f.

[20] Cf. *Esdras-Néhémie*, in Clamer and Pirot, *La sainte Bible*, iv, 1949, pp. 266–271.

[21] Cf. *Esra-Nehemias*, in *Echter-Bibel, Das Alte Testament*, ed. by F. Nötscher, Lieferung 10, 1950, p. 5 (2nd ed., Altes Testament, ii, 1956, p. 415).

[22] Cf. *Geschichte des Alten Testamentes*, ii, 1950, pp. 285 f. (E.Tr. by W. Heidt, 1952. pp. 326 f.).   [23] Cf. *Biblica*, xxxii, 1951, p. 300.

[24] Cf. *Bi. Or.*, viii, 1951, pp. 185–187.   [25] Cf. *P.E.Q.*, 1953, p. 13.

C. H. Gordon,[1] R. A. Dyson,[2] J. E. Steinmueller and K. Sullivan,[3] H. Bardtke,[4] J. de Fraine,[5] S. Barabas,[6] and the Danish scholar E. Johannesen in his posthumous work.[7] In 1947 two English writers, J. Stafford Wright[8] and W. M. Scott,[9] apparently quite independently, challenged the tendency to reverse the traditional order, and almost simultaneously B. D. Eerdmans' book on *The Religion of Israel* appeared in English to renew the same challenge,[10] while more recently E. J. Young has announced his adhesion to the traditional view.[11] It is therefore clear that bold claims, on the one side or the other, that the question is definitely settled are unjustified. Such claims have been made on both sides. Browne has claimed that the evidence from the Elephantine papyri "makes it quite clear Ezra belongs to the reign of Artaxerxes II . . ., and Nehemiah to the reign of Artaxerxes I",[12] and Oesterley has made a similar claim,[13] while Kugler has stated with equal confidence on the other side that the assignment of Ezra to the reign of Artaxerxes I is now so firmly established that it can no longer be reasonably doubted.[14] It would seem to be wiser, with several of the scholars who have followed Van Hoonacker, to confess that certainty

[1] Cf. *Introduction to Old Testament Times*, 1953, pp. 269 f.

[2] Cf. *A Catholic Commentary on Holy Scripture*, 1953, pp. 377 f.

[3] Cf. *Catholic Biblical Encyclopedia*, Old Testament, 1956, p. 329.

[4] Cf. *Calwer Bibel-lexikon*, 5th ed., edited by K. Gutbrod and R. Kücklich, 1959, col. 288.

[5] Cf. *Esdras en Nehemias* (B.O.T.), 1961, p. 15.

[6] Cf. *The Zondervan Pictorial Bible Dictionary*, edited by M. C. Tenney, 1963, p. 272.

[7] Cf. *Studier over Esras og Nehemjas historie*, 1946, pp. 210–216, 277–289. Cf. also S. Granild, *Ezrabogens literære Genesis*, 1949, pp. 170 f., on which see A. Bentzen, "Ezras Persönlichkeit", in *St.Th.*, ii, 1948, pp. 95–98.

[8] Cf. *The Date of Ezra's Coming to Jerusalem*, 1947 (2nd ed., 1958; cf. review of H. H, Rowley in *J.S.S.*, iii, 1958, pp. 398 ff.); *The New Bible Dictionary*, edited by J. D. Douglas. 1962, p. 408.

[9] Cf. "Nehemiah-Ezra", *E.T.*, lviii, 1946–47, pp. 263–267. Cf. also C. T. Wood, "Nehemiah-Ezra", *ibid.*, lix, 1947–48, pp. 53 f.

[10] Cf. pp. 233 f.

[11] Cf. *An Introduction to the Old Testament*, 1949, pp. 369 ff.

[12] *Op. cit.*, 2nd ed., 1929, p. 179.

[13] Cf. Oesterley and Robinson, *Introduction to the Books of the Old Testament*, p. 129: "There can be no doubt that in the case of Nehemiah it was Artaxerxes I, who came to the throne in 464, so that his twentieth year was 444; in that of Ezra it was Artaxerxes II, who came to the throne in 404, so that his seventh year was 397."

[14] Cf. *op. cit.*, p. 222: "Die Tatsache, dass Esra mit seiner Karawane im 7. Jahre Artaxerxes' I (458 v. Chr.) von Babel nach Jerusalem zog, steht jetzt so fest, dass daran vernünftigerweise nicht gezweifelt kann." Cf., too, G. Hoberg (*Festschrift G. von Hertling*, 1913, p. 40): "Die Frage über die Zeit des Esdras und Nehemias ist daher durch den besprochenen aramäischen Papyrus endgültig gelöst."

is quite unattainable,[1] and that no more than a balance of probability is to be found.[2]

Some have been influenced by Van Hoonacker's views to the extent of dating Ezra after Nehemiah, while keeping both in the reign of Artaxerxes I.[3] This has involved some purely conjectural emendation of the text, and the transfer of Ezra to a much later point in the reign of Artaxerxes than the seventh year of Ezra 7 : 8. This view has been taken by W. H. Kosters,[4] and A. Bertholet,[5] amongst others, while W. F. Albright has wavered between this and Van Hoonacker's view. In 1921 he followed Van Hoonacker,[6] but in 1932 he announced his adhesion to the view of Kosters.[7] In 1940, however, he reverted to the view of Van Hoonacker,[8] only to come back in 1946 to the other,[9]

---

[1] Cf. M. Noth, *History of Israel*, 2nd ed., E.Tr. revised by P. R. Ackroyd, 1960, p. 320: "It must be stressed that it is impossible to reach an absolutely firm decision on this point because there is a lack of reliable and unambiguous evidence, and that all we can hope to attain is a limited degree of probability."

[2] A. Bentzen, *Introduction to the Old Testament*, ii, 1949, pp. 207 f., does not commit himself on the question. So, too, A. Jepsen, *Z.A.F.*, N.F. xxv, 1954, p. 104 ("Solange die Angreifer nicht Schärfere Waffen haben und nicht einheitlicher vorgehen, dürfte m.E. ihrem Angriff kaum Erfolg beschieden sein"); A. van den Born, *Bijbels Woordenboek*, 1954–57, col. 470, and *Dictionnaire encyclopédique de la Bible*, 1960, cols. 558 f.; E. Dhorme, *La Bible de la Pléiade*, L'Ancien Testament, i, 1956, p. cxii; H. Schneider, *Die Bücher Esra und Nehemia* (H.S.A.Tes.), 1959, p. 75, and *Lexikon für Theologie und Kirche*, 2nd ed., edited by J. Höfer and K. Rahner, iii, 1959, cols. 110 f.

[3] B. W. Anderson (*Understanding the Old Testament*, 1957, pp. 450 f.) holds that Ezra followed Nehemiah, but leaves it open whether he came to Jerusalem towards the end the reign of Artaxerxes I or early in the reign of Artaxerxes II. So also *Bibel-lexikon*, ed. by H. Haag, 1951, cols. 433 f.; A. Weiser, *Einleitung in das Alte Testament*, 4th ed., 1957, pp. 282 f., 5th ed., 1963, p. 260 (E.Tr. by D. M. Barton, 1961, p. 322). In the early editions (1st ed., 1939, pp. 264 ff., 2nd ed., 1949, pp. 235 ff.) Weiser had maintained that Ezra's mission fell in the seventh year of Artaxerxes I. M. Noth inclines to a date late in the reign of Artaxerxes I, but is not sure; cf. *History of Israel*, 2nd ed., 1960, p. 320.

[4] Cf. *Wiederhestellung*, pp. 95 ff. Kosters holds the date of Ezra 7: 8 to be without authority, and then assigns Ezra's coming to the thirty-second year of Artaxerxes I (p. 116).

[5] Cf. *Die Bücher Esra und Nehemia* (K.H.A.T.), 1902, pp. 30 f.; and *R.G.G.*, ii, 1910, cols. 636 f.

[6] Cf. "The Date and Personality of the Chronicler", in *J.B.L.*, xl, 1921, pp. 104–124.

[7] Cf. *Archæology of Palestine and the Bible*, 1932, p. 219. Following Kosters and Bertholet, Albright assigned the work of Ezra to the thirty-second year of Artaxerxes.

[8] Cf. *From the Stone Age to Christianity*, 1940, p. 248. Here Albright observes that Van Hoonacker's date "may now be said to be virtually certain".

[9] Cf. "A Brief History of Judah from the days of Josiah to Alexander the Great", in *B.A.*, ix, 1946, pp. 1–16, esp. pp. 10 ff., *From the Stone Age to Christianity*, 2nd ed., 1946, p. 366, and in *The Jews: Their Culture, History and Religion* (ed. by L. Finklestein), 1950, i, pp. 53, 64. Albright here places Ezra in the thirty-seventh year of Artaxerxes I. J. A. Bewer inclines to this date (*Der Text des Buches Ezra*, 1922, p. 68), but admits that its only basis is the theory it serves. J. Marquart had earlier suggested emending Ezra 7: 8

dating Ezra now in the thirty-seventh year of Artaxerxes I. Antoine Baumgartner is unable to reach a decision as between these two views.[1] Several scholars have more recently signified their acceptance of the transfer of Ezra's mission to the thirty-seventh year of Artaxerxes I. These include C. Kuhl,[2] V. Pavlovský,[3] J. Bright,[4] and A. Lefèvre.[5] J. de Fraine[6] rejects this view on the ground that the same error would not be made twice in Ezra 7 : 7 f.

Yet another variety of the view that places Ezra late in the reign of Artaxerxes I assigns his mission to the twenty-seventh year of that reign. This has been advanced by T. K. Cheyne,[7] and H. Lusseau.[8] This would bring Nehemiah and Ezra together in Jerusalem, but would make Ezra's mission abortive. For if, on his arrival in Jerusalem, he persuaded the people to dissolve marriages with foreign wives and to undertake not to contract such marriages in the future (see below), it would be surprising for such a situation as Nehemiah found on his return to have developed within a few years, while Ezra was still in the city.

A further view has been that Ezra's mission fell wholly between the two visits of Nehemiah. This was advanced by R. H. Kennett,[9] and has been renewed by A. Gelin,[10] who assigns Nehemiah's first visit to 445–433 B.C. and his second visit to 424 B.C. with Ezra's visit falling in 427(?)–426(?) B.C.[11] Against this L. E. Browne[12] raises the objection that Ezra would never have allowed the situation which so angered Nehemiah on his return (Neh. 13 : 4–9) to develop.

to read thirty-seventh or fortieth year, but had understood it to refer to Artaxerxes II (*op. cit.*, p. 36). For the reading "thirty-seventh year" in Ezra 7: 8 and the transfer of Ezra to follow Nehemiah in the reign of Artaxerxes I, cf. W. Rudolph, *Esra und Nehemia* (H.A.T.), 1949, pp. 65–71. A. van Selms (*Bi.Or.*, viii, 1951, p. 187a) denies that there is any trace of corruption in Ezra 7: 8.

[1] Cf. "Note complémentaire" (added to the 3rd ed. of L. Gautier's *Introductiun à l'Ancien Testament*, 1939), pp. 51 f.

[2] Cf. *Die Entstehung des Alten Testaments*, 1953, pp. 312 f.; 2nd ed., 1960, p. 303 (E.Tr. by C. T. M. Herriott, 1957, p. 287).

[3] Cf. *Biblica*, xxxviii, 1957, pp. 275 ff., 428 ff., esp. pp. 443 ff.

[4] Cf. *Kaufmann Jubilee Volume*, 1960, pp. 70 ff., and *History of Israel*, 1959, pp. 375 ff.

[5] Cf. *S.D.B.*, vi, 1960, cols. 419 ff.

[6] Cf. *Esdras en Nehemias* (B.O.T.), 1961, p. 151.

[7] Cf. *E.B.*, iii, 1902, col. 3385.

[8] Cf. *Introduction à la Bible*, ed. by A. Robert and A. Feuillet, i, 1957, pp. 713 f.

[9] Cf. *Cambridge Biblical Essays*, ed. by H. B. Swete, 1909, pp. 123 ff., and *Old Testament Essays*, 1928, p. 85.

[10] Cf. *Esdras, Néhémie* (Jerusalem Bible), 1953, pp. 18 ff.

[11] Gelin had earlier assigned Ezra's visit to 428 B.C.; cf. *Lumière et Vie*, No. 7, December 1952, p. 103.

[12] Cf. Peake's *Commentary on the Bible*, revised ed., 1962, p. 374b.

S. Jellicoe has advanced a further variety of this view, and has suggested that the dates of Nehemiah and Ezra have been deliberately reversed by the Chronicler, so that Nehemiah's arrival in Jerusalem should be placed in the seventh year of Artaxerxes I and his second visit twelve years later, and Ezra's visit in the twentieth year of the same king.[1]

Others have taken more radical views still. M. Vernes, though he made the suggestion that Ezra might belong to the reign of Artaxerxes II, preferred to reject the whole story of Ezra as unhistorical.[2] This view has been vigorously championed by C. C. Torrey,[3] who holds that, while the Chronicler's intention was to locate the two leaders in the reign of Artaxerxes II, the historical problem should be liquidated by the elimination of Ezra altogether from the stage of history, and by resolving him into the fictitious creation of the Chronicler.[4] This view has largely influenced G. Hölscher,[5] R. Fruin,[6] A. Loisy,[7] and R. H. Pfeiffer,[8] while others have expressed their sympathy for it without committing themselves to it.

To review all the complexities of a problem on which so much has been written and so little agreement reached is out of the question in a short paper, and all that can be here attempted is to offer a brief examination of arguments put forward in the most recent attacks on the Van Hoonacker view, and to restate in summary form the reasons which still seem to produce a balance of evidence for the Belgian scholar's view. That not all of the indications that have been held to point to the priority of Nehemiah are of equal weight is but natural, and the recent critics of that view have mainly contented themselves with criticism of these less weighty arguments, while ignoring the others. It will therefore be well to see first how far the weakness of the attacked considerations may be admitted, before turning to examine other considerations.

---

[1] Cf. "Nehemiah-Ezra: a reconstruction", in *E.T.*, lix, 1947–48, p. 54.

[2] *Op. cit.*, pp. 572 ff.

[3] Cf. *Composition and Historical Value of Ezra-Nehemiah*, 1896, pp. 51–65, and *Ezra Studies*, pp. 238–248. On this view cf. Batten, *op. cit.*, pp. 51 f.

[4] Cf. J. Meinhold, "Esra der Schriftgeleherte?" in *Vom Alten Testament* (Marti Festschrift, ed. by K. Budde), 1925, pp. 197–206.

[5] Cf. *Die Bücher Esra und Nehemia*, in Kautzsch-Bertholet, *H.S.A.T.*, 4th ed., ii, 1923, pp. 491 ff., esp. pp. 500 f. In the third edition of this work (ii, 1910, pp. 451 f.) Hölscher followed the view of Van Hoonacker.

[6] Cf. "Is Ezra een historisch Persoon?" in *N.T.T.*, xviii, 1929, pp. 121–138.

[7] Cf. *La religion d'Israël*, 3rd ed., pp. 228 f.

[8] *Introduction to the Old Testament*, 1941, pp. 816–830.

It is pointed out that if the Chronicler compiled the books of Ezra and Nehemiah *circa* 300 B.C., then he would be too close in time to an Ezra who arrived in Jerusalem at the beginning of the fourth century to have been able to make so glaring an error as half a century in Ezra's date.[1] It is said that there would doubtless have been people still living who would remember Ezra, and who could expose the error. In this consideration there is little force. In the first place, not all scholars date the work of the Chronicler *circa* 300 B.C. Some bring it down below this,[2] while Albright thinks that Ezra himself was the author of the work.[3] If the composition of the work belongs to a later date, the force of the argument is greatly weakened, while if it belongs to an earlier date, or even comes from the pen of Ezra himself, the argument is completely invalid against the possibility of some dislocation of the text, so that it is not in its original order. To this it is replied that so wholesale a rearrangement would be required that it would be intrinsically improbable, though certainly possible.[4] It should be added that Albright does not think any rearrangement is necessary, if it is recognized that Ezra affixed Nehemiah's memoirs to his work, rather than put them in their chronological order, since that would have deranged his scheme.[5] This does not seem very probable to the present writer. On the other hand, he does not think the theory of a later dislocation of the text is very satisfactory. It seems much more probable that the Chronicler believed, or wished his readers to believe, that Ezra preceded Nehemiah.

This does not add any weight to the consideration advanced against the late date for Ezra, however. For the argument tacitly assumes that the books were "published" in a modern sense, and that they would immediately circulate amongst readers who could check their statements.[6] It is very unlikely that many copies of the Chronicler's work

---

[1] Cf. Wright, *op. cit.*, pp. 14 ff. Cf. also Scott, *loc. cit.*, p. 267. N. H. Snaith (*Z.A.W.*, xxii, 1951, p. 66) assigns the Chronicler's work to a date not later than 395 B.C., within a year or two of the arrival of Ezra in Jerusalem. He postulates a deliberate dislocation of the text.

[2] Cf. Pfeiffer, *op. cit.*, p. 812, where a date *circa* 250 B.C. is maintained. A. Lods (*Les prophètes d'Israël*, p. 339=E.Tr., p. 299) dates the Chronicler after Ben Sira. Cf. R. H. Kennett, *Old Testament Essays*, 1928, p. 221.

[3] Cf. *J.B.L.*, xl, 1921, pp. 119 f., and *B.A.*, ix, 1946, p. 15.

[4] Cf. Wright, *op. cit.*, pp. 16 f.   [5] Cf. *J.B.L.*, *loc. cit.*, p. 123.

[6] J. S. Wright (*The Date of Ezra's Coming to Jerusalem*, 2nd ed., 1958, p. 14) replies to this that the Chronicler's work was surely intended to have readers. While this is, of course, true, they would be very few for a long time, and if the Chronicler wrote half a century or a century after Ezra's mission, very few of those few would have any means of checking its statements, even if they were interested in scientific history (cf. *J.S.S.*, iii, 1958, pp. 398 f.).

would be made for some time, and the chance of those that were made falling into the hands of the oldest inhabitants would not be great. Nor would the Chronicler have been greatly concerned if they did. It is likely that when he wrote, copies of the books of Samuel and Kings were more plentiful than copies of his own book would be for long years, and it may be presumed that few of his readers were without access in some way to these books. For Samuel and Kings must already have been treated with veneration, even though we ought not to think of any strict Canon of the Prophets as having been already fixed. Yet the Chronicler had no hesitation in modifying the statements he found in the earlier books. Few readers would remember Ezra, but many would be able to challenge the price the Chronicler put on the Temple site,[1] or his statements that Asa[2] and Jehoshaphat[3] removed the high places. If then he could boldly modify history where he had an axe to grind, we cannot suppose that he would be unable to do so where he had none. Wright observes[4] that the more a writer wishes to write history with a purpose the more careful he must be not to expose himself to the charge of inaccuracy. In fact, the Chronicler does not seem to have been troubled about this, and had no hesitation in knowingly and wilfully modifying the facts. But if his error were made in ignorance and not with intention, he could not even challenge it himself, and few of his readers would be in a better position than he. For he was not writing a work of scholarship to be read by a learned circle, to be judged by the canons that would apply to a modern work of research.

One of the arguments for the reversal of the traditional order of Ezra and Nehemiah, to which appeal has been made by almost every adherent of the alternative order, has been that when Ezra arrived he found the city wall already built,[5] whereas the building of the walls was the work of Nehemiah. The most recent critics of the argument point to the choice of the word for *wall*,[6] as many earlier writers had

[1] 1 Chron. 21: 25. With this cf. 2 Sam. 24: 24.

[2] 2 Chron. 14: 3, 5. With this cf. 1 Kings 15: 14. It may be noted that here the Chronicler also preserves in 2 Chron. 15: 17 the statement of 1 Kings 15: 14, but adds "out of Israel" to avoid verbal contradiction of 2 Chron. 14: 5. Since Asa was not king over Israel, however, the addition is really meaningless, and it would be far easier to challenge him here from his own work than it would be to challenge him on the date of Ezra on the testimony of someone who remembered Ezra.

[3] 2 Chron. 17: 6. With this cf. 1 Kings 22: 43.

[4] *Op. cit.*, p. 14.

[5] Ezra 9: 9.

[6] Cf. Johannesen, *op. cit.*, pp. 279 f.; Scott, *loc. cit.*, p. 264; Eerdmans, *op. cit.*, pp. 233 f.

already done.[1] For it is not the word used for *wall* in the account of Nehemiah's work, but a word which stands nowhere else in the whole of Ezra-Nehemiah. It is used elsewhere in the Old Testament for a fence round a vineyard,[2] and it is claimed that the rendering of the LXX here by *phragmos*, and the reading *stereōma* in 1 Esdras 8 : 81, suggests that the reference is not to a city wall here.[3]

It may be agreed that this argument for the priority of Nehemiah is not a strong one. On the other hand, it must be recognized to be possible that Ezra's reference is to the city wall which Nehemiah had built. For the word here used stands in Mic. 7 : 11 for a city wall,[4] and if Ezra lived half a century after Nehemiah he would scarcely be bound to use the word for *wall* which stands in Nehemiah's memoirs, but could surely use a less common word which is known to have been capable of the same reference.

J. S. Wright chooses a different way of turning this argument. Instead of questioning the reference to the city wall, he resorts to it, and boldly claims that it was a wall which was going up in Ezra's time,

---

[1] Cf. Jampel, *loc. cit.*, xlvii, 1903, p. 21; Wiener, *loc. cit.*, p. 152; Fernández, "La voz *gādhēr* en Esd. 9. 9", in *Biblica*, xvi, 1935, pp. 82–84, in criticism of H. Kaupel, "Die Bedeutung von *gādhēr* in Esr. 9. 9", in *Biblische Zeitschrift*, xxii, 1934, pp. 89–92. Cf. the subsequent discussion in *Biblica*: H. Kaupel, "Zu *gādhēr* in Esr. 9, 9", *ibid.*, xiv, pp. 213 f.; G. Ricciotti, "La voce *gādhēr* e un passo di Flavio Giuseppe", *ibid.*, pp. 443–445; A. Fernández, "Esdr. 9, 9 y un texto de Josefo", *ibid.*, xviii, 1937, pp. 207 f. Cf. also A. Fernández, *Comentario a los libros de Esdras y Nehemías*, 1950, pp. 205 ff.

[2] Is. 5: 5; Ps. 80: 13.

[3] So Scott, *loc. cit.*, In Ezra 9: 9 there is a variant Greek reading *teichos* (see *The Old Testament in Greek*, edited by Brooke, McLean and Thackeray, II. iv, 1935, *ad loc.*), but this has no serious weight. The verse in 1 Esdras is numbered 78 (82) in the Greek.

[4] Fernández (*Biblica*, xvi, 1935, p. 83) denies that the meaning is a city wall in this text, but Kaupel (*ibid.*, p. 213) adduces many commentators who have so understood it, while Ricciotti (*loc. cit.*) adduces Josephus's use of the walls of Jerusalem as a figure for the wall of the fatherland, and hence concludes that a figurative sense in Ezra 9: 9 does not exclude the material. A. S. Kapelrud, *The Question of Authorship in the Ezra-Narrative*, 1944, pp. 66 f.) strongly insists that "the word means wall in every instance, even if in certain places it can be interpreted figuratively. The usual thing is to interpret this word figuratively here. . . . This is in reality to interpret away the word that is in the text, and there is no foundation for such an interpretation in the text itself. The supposition is founded on the hypothesis that the Ezra-narrative was written by Ezra himself and that he came to Jerusalem in 458 B.C., at a time when the city had no wall. As against this we insist that the word in the present passage means wall, wall of defence, but no more. . . . Mowinckel and Oesterley insist that the word must be understood literally here, as well as elsewhere. This opinion is strengthened if one asks the question negatively: would the word 'gâder' have been used, if, at the time at which it is used, there had *not* been a wall around Jerusalem? Surely not."

but which was broken down before Nehemiah's mission to Jerusalem.[1] Here it may be agreed that the grief of Nehemiah on hearing of the condition of Jerusalem[2] is more likely to have been occasioned by something that had happened recently than by something that had happened nearly a century and a half earlier in the time of Nebuchadrezzar. There would seem, therefore, to have been some recent destruction of the walls of Jerusalem. But in Ezra 4 : 7–23 we read of some building of the walls in the time of Artaxerxes which was violently interrupted after appeal to the Court. The problems of the introduction to that account, and of the inconsequential verse that follows, which has reference to the house of God and not to the walls, cannot be discussed here.[3] That it has reference to operations in the reign of Artaxerxes I prior to the mission of Nehemiah is widely agreed. But Wright argues that this wall was actually going up in Ezra's time, but was then broken down.[4] This failure of Ezra's work, through some tactlessness on his part, is supposed then to have brought discredit on him, so that he fell out of the picture until Nehemiah, moved to grief by the new disaster which had befallen Jerusalem, came and carried through the work successfully, when Ezra's star began to shine again, albeit with the reflected glory of Nehemiah's.[5] Similar attempts to prove Ezra's priority by first discrediting him have been made by others. Thus Fischer held him to have been a young

---

[1] Op. cit., p. 18. It is somewhat surprising to find that Scott, who is at such pains to deny that Ezra 9: 9 refers to the city wall, yet holds that the walls were standing in 457 B.C., and that they were broken down in the period between Ezra's coming and Nehemiah's.

[2] Neh. 1: 1–4.   [3] Cf. H. H. Rowley, Men of God, 1963, pp. 219 ff.

[4] In the second edition of his work, Wright modifies his argument. He now argues (pp. 17 f.) that Ezra 9: 9 refers to the abortive building of the walls, referred to in Ezra 4: 7–23, on which Ezra 9: 9 looks back after some years. It would be strange for Ezra to refer to a wall as a God-given protection some years after it had been destroyed. Nehemiah does not seem to have found much satisfaction in the abortive attempt (Neh. 1: 3 ff.) and it is improbable that Ezra would find any more. Further, Wright now suggests that Ezra may have returned to Babylon soon after dealing with the problem of mixed marriages (pp. 24 f.) and so not have been in Jeruaslem at the time of the abortive building of the walls, but may have been recalled to Jerusalem when Nehemiah was there. At the same time he holds that the failure of the earlier building may have brought discredit on Ezra. It is hard to follow the argument here. If Ezra were absent from Jerusalem and in no way responsible for the abortive attempt to rebuild the walls, it is hard to see why he should be blamed for it. But if he was blamed, his stock would scarcely have been high enough for him to be sent again to Jerusalem, and of a second mission we have no evidence except baseless conjecture.

[5] Op. cit., pp. 25 f. Van Hoonacker (Néhémie en l'an 20 etc., 1892, p. 17) had already pointed out how purely conjectural was a similar supposition of Kuenen's (op. cit., pp. 236 ff.).

hothead who achieved nothing,[1] and Wiener allows his imagination to run away with him to the extent of writing: "By his intemperate and inhuman insistence on his interpretation he brought upon his people the greatest disaster that had befallen them since the fall of the Temple."[2] He then asks: "If Ezra never existed, how came a pious and patriotic Jew like the Chronicler to invent or adopt the story we have which makes him responsible for so great a Jewish catastrophe?"[3] The reader has only to reflect that Wiener and not the Chronicler is the pious Jew who has invented this story, of which there is no hint whatever in the pages of the Chronicler, and he will wonder why Wiener did not supply the answer to his own question. The Chronicler records no disaster which Ezra brought on his people, and the association of Ezra with the wall of Ezra 4 : 7–23 is wholly gratuitous. He is not mentioned at all in connexion with the affair. Granted that there was an unsuccessful attempt to build the walls in the time of Artaxerxes I, there is no reason whatever to connect it with Ezra. It is entirely unrelated to the mission with which he was charged. This was to regulate the religious usage, and he came bearing the book of the Law. The assumption that he ignored the purpose of his commission, for which he was armed with considerable powers by the king, in order to undertake something for which he was not authorized, and that he was then discredited for several years, after which he quietly stepped back to fulfil his original commission may seem an attractive story.[4] But it is entirely fictitious, without a shred of support in the Bible. Not even the merest hint of it is allowed to fall. One might have expected that if Ezra had so abused the confidence of the king the latter would not

---

[1] Cf. *Die chronologischen Fragen in den Büchern Esra-Nehemia* (Biblische Studien, VIII), 1903, pp. 73 f.

[2] Cf. *J.P.O.S.*, vii, 1927, p. 157. Cf. H. E. Ryle, *Ezra and Nehemia* (Camb. B.), 1923 ed., p. xli; A. T. Olmstead, *History of Palestine and Syria*, 1931, p. 587; J. S. Wright, *The Date of Ezra's Coming to Jerusalem*, pp. 25 f.; W. M. F. Scott, *E.T.*, lviii, 1946–47, p. 264a; C. T. Wood, *E.T.*, lix, 1947–48, pp. 53 f.; P. Heinisch, *Geschichte des Alten Testamentes*, 1950, p. 291 (E.Tr. by W. Heidt, 1952, p. 332).

[3] *Loc. cit.*

[4] C. T. Wood (*E.T.*, lix, 1947–48, pp. 53 f.) adopts this view, holding that Ezra came to Jerusalem armed with a religious mandate, but proceeded to rebuild the walls, and so brought about the cancellation of his mandate and lived as a private person in the city, though still enjoying religious prestige among the people. He adds that this is precisely the position he holds under Nehemiah (Neh. 8: 1–9). It may be asked how it came about that Ezra did not read the Law with which he was armed until Nehemiah arrived, when *ex hypothesi* he had forfeited his authority, and how he retained religious prestige among his people during the period before the arrival of Nehemiah, when *ex hypothesi* he had completely neglected his religious mandate and had not even made his Law known.

have contented himself with ordering that the work of building the walls should be stopped, but would have punished Ezra.

Indeed, we may rather turn the argument round. If the events of Ezra 4 : 7–23 were the cause of Nehemiah's grief, they should have taken place but recently at the time of that grief. But if Ezra came to Jerusalem in 457 B.C., and remained in Jerusalem until Nehemiah came, then we should have expected him to have some hand in these events. Yet since his name is unmentioned in this account, we have no reason to associate him with them. It would therefore seem unlikely that he was in Jerusalem at this time. V. Pavlovský[1] holds that political and economic conditions in the early part of the reign of Artaxerxes I preclude the possibility of dating the mission of Ezra then, while H. Cazelles[2] has adduced evidence from the Elephantine Papyri,[3] showing that the Persians lost control of Egypt in 399 B.C., to support the view that the mission of Ezra fell shortly after this date, since it was politically important for Persia to have a friendly Jewish state on its border.

It has always seemed curious that Ezra, who came to Jerusalem armed with authority to put into effect the Law, should not have read it for thirteen years after his arrival in the city. R. Kittel held that he actually read it in 458 B.C., soon after he arrived in Jerusalem.[4] This would loose him from direct public association with Nehemiah as completely as the view that Ezra's mission fell after Nehemiah's. But the significance for the estimating of the work of Ezra is greatly changed. For, as Bright observes,[5] if Ezra read the Law in 458 B.C., his mission must have ended in failure, since the abuses against which he contended persisted and were rampant in Nehemiah's day, so that it is difficult to understand how so frustrated a career could have made the impact on the history and tradition of Judaism that it certainly did.

---

[1] Cf. *Biblica*, xxxviii, 1957, pp. 283 ff.

[2] Cf. *V.T.*, iv, 1954, p. 132. On the other hand, however, F. M. Heichelheim has argued that the political conditions in 458 B.C. made such a mission as Ezra's politically expedient (*Z.R.G.G.*, iii, 1951, pp. 251–253). The story of the abortive rebuilding of the walls of Jerusalem in Ezra 4, however, does not suggest that Artaxerxes I was disposed to win the support of the Jews. Since that incident possibly took place later than 458 B.C. (see p. 149), the King's gesture of friendship would have been short-lived, and the assumption that Ezra was in Jerusalem at that time, as he must have been if he came in 458 B.C. and was still there in 444 B.C., raises, as we have seen (cf. pp. 149f.), serious problems.

[3] Cf. E. G. Kraeling, *The Brooklyn Museum Aramaic Papyri*, 1953, pp. 111 ff.

[4] Cf. *Geschichte des Volkes Israel*, iii, Part 2, 1929, pp. 589 f. Cf. too H. H. Schaeder, *Esra der Schreiber*, 1930, p. 12; J. Morgenstern, *H.U.C.A.*, x, 1935, p. 71 n.; R. de Vaux, *S.D.B.*, iv, 1949, col. 765; P. Heinisch, *Geschichte des Alten Testamentes*, p. 289 (E.Tr., p. 330).

[5] Cf. *Kaufmann Jubilee Volume*, pp. 73 f.; *History of Israel*, 1959, pp. 377 f.

Pfeiffer thinks the whole account of the reading of the Law is unhistorical,[1] whereas Mowinckel believes it comes from an eyewitness.[2] If Ezra came armed with the book of the Law, we should expect him to proclaim it on his arrival, and if this is what he actually did, but at a date subsequent to the mission of Nehemiah, the enduring effect of his work is understandable.

Another of the arguments to which resort has been had is based upon the apparently well-populated state of Jerusalem in Ezra's time[3] compared with its deserted condition in Nehemiah's.[4] Against this it is noted that a population which might be small in relation to a city might yet be adequate to provide a large assembly.[5] Alternatively the value of Ezra 10 : 1 is depreciated as an invention of the Chronicler to exalt his hero Ezra,[6] or attention is called to the statement that the large crowd came not merely from Jerusalem, but from Israel.[7] That it was a local assembly, however, is shown by the fact that it was followed by a summons to the surrounding population of Judah to gather in Jerusalem with the local inhabitants.[8] Moreover, 1 Esdras 8 : 91,[9] which is parallel to Ezra 10 : 1, reads "from Jerusalem" instead of "out of Israel". Wright observes that we do not know which of these readings is correct, and while this is true, it is also true that if the reading of Ezra 10 : 1 is original, it must be understood in the light of the obvious meaning of Ezra 10 : 7.

Nevertheless, it must be agreed that no strong case could be based on these texts. That Ezra 10 : 1 and Neh. 7 : 4 suggest quite different conditions is doubtless true. Both statements could be taken at their face value if Ezra's work fell some years after Nehemiah had rebuilt the walls and gathered a larger population into the city. On the other hand, if some recent disaster had befallen Jerusalem when Nehemiah came, its population might well have fallen considerably below what it had been in 457 B.C.

---

[1] Cf. *Introduction to the Old Testament*, 1941, p. 828.
[2] Cf. *Ezra den Skriftlærde*, 1916, p. 49.
[3] Ezra 10: 1.
[4] Neh. 7: 4.
[5] Cf. Scott, *loc. cit.*, pp. 263 f. Cf. also Kittel, *op. cit.*, p. 19.
[6] Cf. Scott, *loc. cit.*: "It is not legitimate to stress the details of Ezra 10: 1, which comes not from Ezra's memoirs but from the Chronicler's pen. His wish to exalt his hero Ezra would naturally find expression in such touches as this. He felt that Ezra's chief actions were so important that there must be a crowd worthy of the occasion."
[7] So Wright, *op. cit.*, p. 19.
[8] Ezra 10: 7 ff.
[9] Numbered in the Greek 88 (92).

A third argument, to which appeal is often made,[1] rests on the fact that Nehemiah's name precedes Ezra's in Neh. 12 : 26. Albright declares that this is the most conclusive passage.[2] In the present writer's view, little weight can be placed upon it.[3] Scott points out[4] that G. A. Smith once has this order, though he held that Ezra's work preceded that of Nehemiah.[5] A more direct consideration is Wiener's, who says: "The author refers to two periods, each introduced by the expression 'in the days of'. One of them is the epoch of Joiakim, son of Joshua, the other the age of Nehemiah and Ezra, who are therefore regarded as contemporaries",[6] But this tells us no more than we already knew—that the Chronicler supposed they were contemporary. For if Nehemiah and Ezra were not contemporaries, it is probably to the Chronicler that we owe the juxtaposition of these names, and there is no reason to suppose that he either knew or thought that Nehemiah preceded Ezra. It is probable that the words "and of Ezra the priest the scribe" were not found by him in the list of names on which he drew, but were added by him.[7] This is suggested by the fact that they are in such poor syntactical style. For we have here not merely two genitives dependent on a single construct—a usage which is found frequently enough, though it is not normal—but in addition we have a word in apposition with the first standing between the genitives. Hence these words have the appearance of having been tacked on.

It may be agreed that all of these arguments are of slight weight in favour of the order Nehemiah-Ezra, though they offer no support at all to the other view, but must be explained away or discounted. A much stronger argument is based on the consideration that Nehemiah was the contemporary of Eliashib, and Ezra of Eliashib's grandson. For in the account of the work of Nehemiah we find several references to Eliashib, the high priest,[8] while in Ezra 10 : 6 we are told that Ezra went into the chamber of Jehohanan the son of Eliashib. Since "son" is sometimes used for "grandson", and since it would appear

---

[1] Cf. Van Hoonacker, R.B., x, 1901, p. 197. Batten, op. cit., p. 278; Browne, op. cit., p. 179.

[2] Cf. J.B.L., xl, 1921, p. 121.

[3] Cf. Fernández, Biblica, ii, 1921, pp. 435 f.; Johannesen, op. cit., p. 285.

[4] Loc. cit., p. 265.

[5] Cf. Exp., 7th series, ii, 1906, p. 8, in the course of an article on "Ezra and Nehemiah" (pp. 1–18).

[6] Loc. cit., p. 156.

[7] Hölscher (in Kautzsch-Bertholet, H.S.A.T., ii, 1923, p. 556) omits as a gloss "and in the days of Nehemiah the governor, and of Ezra the priest the scribe."

[8] Neh. 3: 1, 20 f.; 13: 4, 7.

from Neh. 12 : 10 f., 22, that Johanan[1] was the grandson of Eliashib, we appear to be carried on two generations.[2]

The shifts that are resorted to in order to get round this consideration are the clearest evidence of its embarrassment to the traditional view. It is claimed that the Jehohanan of Ezra 10 : 6 may have been literally the son of Eliashib, and therefore the brother of Joiada and the uncle of the Johanan who became high priest.[3] But since we find a similar reference to Johanan the son of Eliashib in Neh. 12 : 23, in a context which makes it clear that the Johanan who became high priest is meant, this is not very probable. It is also noted that the name Johanan is a very common one, and there is the less reason to suppose that two people who bore it should be identified.[4] If it were merely a question of a common name, without any context to suggest their identification, this might be agreed. But here there is also a common father's or grandfather's name, and moreover both have important associations with the Temple. For whereas the one became high priest the other has a room in the Temple. To this it is replied that many people had rooms in the Temple, and Johanan might well have been serving in the Temple in some subordinate capacity at the time.[5] Moreover, he is not said to be the high priest, as we should have expected if he were the high priest at the time.[6] Hence, even though it were the same Johanan, this incident might belong to his youth.[7]

---

[1] Jehohanan and Johanan are forms of the same name, just like Jehoash and Joash. It would appear that the Jonathan of Neh. 12: 11 is to be identified with the Johanan of 12: 22. The names, indeed, are not to be equated, and some have held that a link has been accidentally omitted and that Johanan was the father of Jonathan. Since Jaddua was the high priest in the time of Alexander, it is said that this would better bridge the gap, since only Jaddua is mentioned after Johanan who was already high priest *circa* 410 B.C. (see below). But Torrey (*J.B.L.*, xlvii, 1928, p. 383; cf. also *Ezra Studies*, p. 321) observes that Josephus represents Jaddua as of venerable age in the days of Alexander, and there is no reason to postulate another high priest between Johanan and him. Mowinckel (*Ezra den Skriftlærde*, 1916, pp. 65 ff.) thinks Jonathan was the son of Joiada, who succeeded his uncle Johanan in the high-priestly office. But cf. Johannesen, *op. cit.*, pp. 280 f. It is simplest to regard Jonathan of verse 11 as a scribal slip for Johanan. The difference in the Hebrew is very slight. *Ywntn* and *Ywḥnn*. De Saulcy (*Étude chronologique des livres d'Esdras et de Néhémie*, 1868, p. 15 n.) observes that the difference is much slighter in the square character than in the old character, and the substitution must date from after its use.

[2] V. Pavlovský (*Biblica*, xxxviii, 1957, pp. 289 ff.) argues that the mention of Johanan as the contemporary of Ezra makes the date 458 B.C. for his mission impossible.

[3] So Wiener, *loc. cit.*, p. 155. Cf. Wright, *op. cit.*, p. 20; Scott, *loc. cit.*, p. 56.

[4] Cf. Wright, *op. cit.*, p. 20.

[5] Cf. Wiener, *loc. cit.*, p. 155; Wright, *op. cit.*, p. 20; Scott, *loc. cit.*, p. 265.

[6] Cf. Wiener, *loc. cit.*; Wright, *loc. cit.*; Scott, *loc. cit.*

[7] Cf. J. Morgenstern, *J.S.S.*, vii, 1962, p. 8, where it is argued that Johanan "was still quite a young man, probably not more than eighteen years of age, but already functioning as a priest."

All of this is in the highest degree improbable. In the context of events narrated in this chapter Ezra would not be expected to be consorting with subordinate officials and youths, but with the high priest,[1] and since it is known that Johanan the grandson of Eliashib occupied the high-priesthood it is most likely that it was as high priest that Johanan received him into his room.[2] That the Chronicler refers to "Eliashib the high priest", but only to "Jehohanan the son of Eliashib", is curious, but proves little. For, as has been noted, in Neh. 12 : 23 we find the same thing, though there the context shows that he was actually the high priest. It may be recalled that Josephus narrates that this Johanan was a fratricide, who quarrelled with his brother in the Temple and there slew him.[3] Josephus expresses the utmost abhorrence for this unparalleled crime, and it is likely that the Chronicler would be even more shocked. It may well be, therefore, that he withheld the title of high priest from Johanan, though he actually filled the office, because he regarded him as unworthy of his office.[4] It may equally well be that though the Chronicler usually adds "the high priest" when speaking of one who held that office, his sources did not always do so, and his belief that Ezra and Nehemiah were contemporaries in the high-priesthood of Eliashib would sufficiently account for his not concluding that Johanan was the high priest.

It is in this connexion that the evidence of the Elephantine papyri is

---

[1] Cf. Albright, *J.B.L.*, xl, 1921, p. 121. Cf. also H. E. Ryle, *Ezra and Nehemiah* (Camb. B.), 1893, p. 129. Cf. Snaith, *Studies in the Psalter*, 1934, pp. 12 f.: "The fact that Jehohanan had a chamber in the Temple assigned to his own personal use does not in itself prove that he was High Priest at the time (cf. Tobiah, Neh. 13: 4 f.), but it is extremely probable that, according to the Chronicler's sources, this was the case." Cf., further, V. Pavlovský, *Biblica*, xxxviii, 1957, pp. 289 ff.

[2] Ryle (*loc. cit.*) notes the suggestion that in the Chronicler's day the high priest's room was known as Johanan's chamber, and hence he anachronistically used this name. Similarly Bertheau-Ryssel, *Die Bücher Esra, Nechemia und Ester* (Kurzgefasstes exegetisches Handbuch), 1887, pp. 121 f.; F. W. Schultz, *The Book of Ezra* (in Lange's Commentary, translated by Briggs), 1877, p. 96, and J. Nikel, *Wiederherstellung*, p. 159: "Wichtiger dürfte der Umstand sein, dass in dem Ausdruck 'Zelle des Johanan ben Eljashib' eine Modernisierung vorliegen kann, die der Chronist an den Esramemoiren vorgenommen hat, um seinen Zeitgenossen besser verständlich zu sein." Similarly also F. Ahlemann, *Z.A.W.*, N.F. xviii, 1942–43, p. 98. This solution does not seem very probable. It is, in any case, an explaining away of the evidence rather than the use of it.

[3] Cf. *Antiquities*, xi, 297–299 (XI, vii, 1). Snaith (*Studies in the Psalter*, 1934, pp. 23 f.) thinks the murdered brother was no other than the man who had been driven out by Nehemiah because he had married a foreign woman (Neh. 13: 28), and that he was actually the elder brother of Jehohanan. While this is conjectural, and it must not therefore be overstressed in favour of the view which finds Nehemiah to precede Ezra, plausible reasons in its support are presented by Snaith.

[4] Cf. Albright, *J.B.L.*, *loc. cit.*, pp. 121 f.

of interest, though it is going too far to say, as is sometimes claimed, that this evidence establishes the priority of Nehemiah. It brings support, though neither here nor anywhere else in all this vexed question is there any evidence that can be held to amount to proof on one side or on the other.[1] In a letter dated in 408 B.C. the Jews of Elephantine wrote to the governor of Judaea, stating that they had written three years earlier to "Johanan, the high priest, and his colleagues, the priests who are in Jerusalem", and that they had also sent a letter to "Delaiah and Shelemiah, the sons of Sanballat, the governor of Samaria".[2] From this it is clear that Johanan was high priest *circa* 410 B.C., and that Sanballat was still governor of Samaria at that time. We are not told in the Bible that he held the office of governor, though he was clearly a person of influence, and there is nothing inconsistent with his being governor.[3] It would appear that he was now an old man, and that the

[1] J. Bright claims to present evidence that the work of Ezra must have lain before the despatch of the so-called Passover Papyrus to Elephantine in 419 B.C. (A. Cowley, *Aramaic Papyri*, 1923, pp. 60 ff.). For there we find mention of a Hananiah, whom Bright (following Albright, in *The Jews*, ed. L. Finkelstein, i, 1949, pp. 53 f., and C. G. Tuland, *J.B.L.*, lxxvii, 1958, pp. 167 ff.) identifies with Nehemiah's brother Hanani (Neh. 1: 2, 7: 2), and then proceeds to argue that the Priestly Law must have been established in Jerusalem before that Papyrus was despatched. The equation of the two persons is very hazardous, as the name Hananiah or Hanani was a very common one (cf. Cowley, *op. cit.*, p. 62) and there is nothing in the Papyrus to demand the keeping of the Priestly Law. It mentions Unleavened Bread, and may have enjoined the keeping of Passover. though this cannot be established. But both Passover and Unleavened Bread were observed before the mission of Ezra, and it is a curious commentary on the theory that the Papyrus enjoined the keeping of the Priestly Law to find that in the month of Sivan of the same year (i.e. two months after the feast enjoined in the Papyrus was to be observed), if Cowley rightly dates it in the reign of Darius II, the Elephantine community recorded a collection for the funds of their Temple that was in flagrant violation of the Priestly Law (cf. Cowley, *op. cit.*, pp. 65 ff.), in that some of the funds collected were earmarked for Ishumbethel and Anathbethel, and only a part for Yahu. If E. G. Kraeling is right, and the papyrus belongs to the reign of Amyrtaeus (cf. *The Brooklyn Museum Aramaic Papyri*, 1953, p. 62), so late as 400 B.C. the Elephantine community was not observing the Priestly Law.

[2] Cf. A. Cowley, *Aramaic Papyri of the Fifth Century B.C.*, 1923, pp. 108 ff. (AP 30: 18, 29).

[3] In *Ezra Studies*, pp. 334 f. Torrey says: "The book of Nehemiah does not, indeed, refer to its Sanballat as the governor of Samaria, but this fact is of little importance, since 'the Horonite' is doubtless employed as a mere term of contempt. We may regard it as fairly certain, in any case, that Nehemiah's Sanballat was in fact governor of Samaria." In the *J.B.L.*, xlvii, 1928, p. 386, however, he completely reverses this view, on the basis of the same evidence, saying: "It is quite evident that Nehemiah's adversary *was not governor of Samaria at the time of these events*. Nothing in the record implies this, and the actual situation renders the supposition most improbable." It should be added that Torrey believes that Nehemiah's adversary became governor later. He holds, as will be noted below, that there were two Sanballats, of whom one is mentioned in the Papyri and the other in the Bible, the one being the grandfather of the other, and neither being in office in the time of Nehemiah.

administration of affairs was in the hands of his sons.[1] Sanballat's *floruit* must therefore have fallen some time earlier than this, and since the work of Nehemiah clearly lay in the period when Sanballat was actively in charge of affairs, it would seem that the only Artaxerxes under whom Nehemiah could have lived was Artaxerxes I. Further, since Johanan was high priest in 410 B.C., his grandfather's high-priesthood could well have covered the year 444 B.C. We have some indication in the Bible that Eliashib died while Nehemiah was absent from Jerusalem, for Neh. 13 : 4–7 records things that Eliashib had done during Nehemiah's absence, while Neh. 13 : 28 shows that Joiada, the son of Eliashib and the father of Johanan, was now high priest. This is not clear to the reader of the English version, which reads: "one of the sons of Joiada, the son of Eliashib the high priest, was son-in-law to Sanballat." But, as Wiener points out,[2] "in the phrase A, son of B, the high priest, the qualifying words refer to the son, not the father". While this may not invariably be so,[3] it seems likely that it is so here, as frequently. The succession Eliashib, high priest in 444 B.C., Joiada, high priest *circa* 432 B.C., Johanan, high priest in 410 B.C., may therefore be said to be established by the Elephantine evidence taken in conjunction with the Biblical, while the heyday of Sanballat's power may with probability be carried back to the time of Eliashib. If, therefore, Nehemiah's work fell in Sanballat's time, there is every probability that he belonged to the time of Artaxerxes I.

Torrey, who incorrectly says that the mention of Sanballat in the papyri is the sole reason for assigning Nehemiah to the time of Arta-xerxes I,[4] seeks to turn this by holding that there were two Sanballats,[5] and by arguing that Nehemiah's contemporary was not the person whose sons are mentioned in the letter from Elephantine. But this is quite insufficient to turn the argument. For Torrey accepts the evidence of the Elephantine letter that Johanan was high priest *circa* 410 B.C.[6] He omits to show how a Nehemiah who was contemporary with Johanan's grandfather could have flourished in the fourth century B.C. For it is not merely a question of Sanballat, but of Sanballat and Eliashib.

---

[1] N. Messel, *Ezechielfragen*, 1945, pp. 23 f., holds that they were living in Jerusalem, and were friends of Bagoas.

[2] *Loc. cit.*, p. 155.

[3] In the case above cited, from the Elephantine papyri, it is clearly not so with the title "governor of Samaria" in "Delaiah and Shelemiah, the sons of Sanballat, the governor of Samaria". Had a single son been mentioned, there would clearly have been ambiguity.

[4] Cf. *J.B.L.*, xlvii, 1928, p. 380.

[5] Cf. "Sanballat 'the Horonite' ", *ibid.*, pp. 380–389.   [6] *Ibid.*, p. 383.

Torrey makes no claim that there was a second Eliashib who held office as high priest between Johanan and Jaddua, but expressly states that since Jaddua was an old man in the time of Alexander, no other high priest should be interposed between Johanan and Jaddua.[1] It is true that Torrey had earlier[2] rejected the Chronicler's list of high priests as unreliable on the grounds that six high priests were insufficient to cover two hundred years, and that they are represented as in a continuous line. To others there has seemed nothing at all improbable in this,[3] but whether this list is complete and reliable or not, it would seem arbitrary to reject Eliashib from their number. He stands not merely in the genealogy that is dismissed as artificial, but in the tradition as the contemporary of Nehemiah. There can be no reason for rejecting this tradition except its conflict with Torrey's theory. It remains alongside the mention of Sanballat as a further piece of evidence, fully consistent with the evidence of the papyri on Johanan's high-priesthood, and quite fatal to Torrey's transfer of Nehemiah to the following century.

All probability, therefore, points to the reign of Artaxerxes I for Nehemiah, and if Ezra was contemporary with the high-priesthood of Johanan, the only possible Artaxerxes whose seventh year could have seen him come to Jerusalem was Artaxerxes II, If, however, some higher figure is substituted for the seventh year, and the work of Ezra is transferred to the end of the reign of Artaxerxes I, it is possible that by then Johanan had succeeded Joiada. If, on the other hand, Johanan is supposed not to have been high priest in the time of Ezra, and the incident of Ezra 10 : 6 is dated in the seventh year of Artaxerxes I, we have a most improbable situation. It has been noted that Eliashib appears to have died while Nehemiah was absent from Jerusalem, so that Joiada succeeded to the office *circa* 432 B.C. At that time Johanan's brother had but recently married,[4] and he may be presumed to have been a young man. It would be surprising if Johanan were old enough and important enough to have a room in the Temple, to which an

---

[1] *Ibid.*

[2] Cf. *Ezra Studies*, pp. 219 f.

[3] Cf. Batten, *op. cit.*, p. 276: "The list therefore extends through two centuries; as there are six generations, the time covered corresponds very closely to that date." Similarly, Bertheau-Ryssel, *Die Bücher Esra, Nechemia und Ester* (Kurzgefasstes exegetisches Handbuch), 1887, p. 330: "Auf eine der 6 Generationen, welche durch diese Hohenpriester-Reihe von 538–333 v. Chr. repräsentiert werden, kommt etwas weniger als 35 Jahre, was ganz mit der Wahrscheinlichkeit übereinstimmt."

[4] Neh. 13: 28. Clearly the marriage must have taken place while Nehemiah had been absent.

Ezra could resort, twenty-five years earlier than this.[1] Such an assumption not only presupposes great disparity in the ages of these brothers. It also presupposes that in 410 B.C. Johanan must have been at least seventy years of age. Since only one further high priest followed him to the time of Alexander—another eighty years on—we should have to make the further unlikely assumptions that either Jaddua was the son of his father's old age or he was much more than a centenarian. It is surely simpler, and more reasonably consistent with the data, to suppose that Nehemiah was contemporary with Sanballat and Eliashib in 444 B.C., that Eliashib had been lately succeeded by Joiada *circa* 432 B.C., and that Johanan was in the neighbourhood of fifty in 410 B.C., by which time he had succeeded, and that it was to his room that Ezra repaired in the seventh year of Artaxerxes II. Even then Jaddua could easily have been a hundred years old by the time of Alexander, and that would be quite adequate to account for the tradition that he lived to a great age.

More than one writer has argued that the fact that the name of Artaxerxes is spelt in two different ways in Ezra-Nehemiah is an indication that two different kings are referred to. In Ezra 4 : 7 f., where Artaxerxes I is almost certainly intended, we find 'Artaḥshaśtâ, and the same spelling is found in Ezra 6 : 14. On the other hand, in Ezra 7 we find the Artaxerxes of Ezra's time spelt 'Artaḥshastâ, and this spelling is found in the book of Nehemiah. The earliest writer to make this suggestion appears to have been J. Imbert.[2] C. C. Torrey[3] and W. O. E. Oesterley[4] have renewed it, while H. M. Wiener[5] and A. S. Kapelrud[6] have rejected it. To the present writer the suggestion is precarious and improbable.[7] If it were valid, it would confirm Torrey's view that the Chronicler supposed that Ezra and Nehemiah both fell in the reign of Artaxerxes II. If we assume for the Chronicler a date as late as *circa* 250 B.C., this would be a little more than a century after the thirty-second year of Artaxerxes II. It would be surprising if the Chronicler supposed that Eliashib was high priest a century before his time, and that he had been followed by Joiada, Johanan, and Jaddua, as well as the high priests between Jaddua's day and his own—who might be presumed to have been even better known to him. But on Oesterley's view we should have a still more surprising position. For

[1] Cf. Lusseau-Collomb, *op. cit.*, p. 1014.   [2] Cf. *Muséon*, vii, 1888, p. 223.
[3] Cf. *Ezra Studies*, p. 170.   [4] Cf. *History of Israel*, ii, p. 96 n.
[5] *Loc. cit.*, p. 150 n.   [6] *Op. cit.*, p. 19.
[7] Cf. the present writer's *Darius the Mede and the Four World Empires in the Book of Daniel*, 1935, pp. 49 f.

Oesterley dates the Chronicler's work "in the second half of the fourth century, but possibly even later."[1] This means that Oesterley holds that the Chronicler may have written within half a century of that thirty-second year of Artaxerxes II, and yet have recorded this crowded succession of high priests in the recent past. This is vastly more improbable than the assigning of an event of a century earlier to a date a century and a half earlier. For this would involve vigorous confusion about events that were well within his own memory, as well as that of countless people around him.

It is to be noted that neither of the spellings agrees with that found on contemporary texts from the time of Artaxerxes I.[2] If we cannot suppose that they represent an artificial distinction for which the Chronicler was responsible, therefore, neither can we suppose that either represents a genuine contemporary spelling in sources that came from the time of Artaxerxes I. The only difference between the two spellings is the substitution of s for š. This substitution in words generally, which became common in later Aramaic, is found in its beginnings in Biblical Aramaic[3] though only sporadically. It may well have been, therefore, that in the Chronicler's Aramaic source, on which he drew for Ezra 7 : 12–26, the spelling with s appeared. He therefore followed it here, as he had followed his Aramaic sources in his earlier spelling, and harmonized the Hebrew introduction to Ezra 7 : 12–26 with this spelling, which he then continued to use throughout the rest of his work.[4]

More important than any of these considerations, however, is the fact that Ezra is ignored throughout the memoirs of Nehemiah.[5] If he had come to Jerusalem armed with the extensive powers he is said to have had, and if he was still in Jerusalem, it is almost incredible that

[1] Cf. Oesterley and Robinson, *Introduction to the Books of the Old Testament*, p. 112.

[2] Cf. *Darius the Mede*, p. 49.

[3] Cf. the present writer's *Aramaic of the Old Testament*, 1929, pp. 33 ff.

[4] Cf. R. Marcus (in Josephus, Loeb edition, vi, 1937, pp. 505 f.): "The fact that one consonant in the spelling of the name is a phonetic variant of the consonant used in the name Artaxerxes mentioned in the Aramaic documents in the book of Ezra does not necessarily mean that the Chronicler or a later scribe meant to distinguish two Persian kings of that name; and even if it did, the distinction throws no light on the chronology of Nehemiah."

[5] H. Schneider (*Die Bücher Esra and Nehemia*, 1959, p. 68) discounts this by noting that it is equally true that Nehemiah is unmentioned in the Ezra sources, with the exception of Neh. 8: 9, where the name is probably secondary. But the two cases are not parallel. If Ezra and Nehemiah were contemporaries in Jerusalem, we should expect each to mention the other, but if Ezra followed Nehemiah by half a century, there would be nothing surprising in his failure to mention Nehemiah (cf. *Th.Z.*, xvi, 1960, p. 219).

he should be so ignored. It is true that all who hold that Ezra was either a fictitious character, or one whose memoirs come from the Chronicler's hand and reflect his exaggerations, doubt the value of the document with which Ezra is said to have been armed. But this does not touch the problem. For if the Chronicler was prepared to invent Ezra, or to exaggerate his importance, he might have been expected also to make Nehemiah take notice of him. That he does not do so suggests that he is dealing with real sources. Lods observes: "The autobiography of Ezra contains a number of concrete details, whose sobriety, precision and probability forbid us to see in these pages a piece of fiction."[1] In the Chronicler's sources neither of these leaders takes any account of the other, with such possible exceptions as will be examined below.

To Scott the matter is simple. He supposes that Nehemiah based his work on Ezra's, and put into effect Ezra's ideas. He says: "Ezra the scribe and theorist arrived in 457 and introduced a law, but was not able to enforce it. Nehemiah arrived fourteen years later, and being a man of action and an administrator he was able to enforce the law already introduced, or as much of it as he thought practicable."[2] Yet it is surely surprising that he nowhere gives the slightest indication that he is enforcing Ezra's law, or so much as refers to the man whose ideas he is supposed to be putting into practice. Scott apparently transfers the story of Neh. 8 to the time of Ezra's arrival, and so dissolves the slender link between these two men presented by the Chronicler. For he says: "Ezra evidently appeared on the scene as the purveyor of an unknown law. Only so could he arouse the curiosity described in Neh. 8 which made the people demand to hear what its terms were."[3]

Nor does the matter rest there. For we find Nehemiah reviewing the census of the families that returned with Zerubbabel, but completely ignoring those who are said to have returned with Ezra.[4] It would almost look as though he is at pains to slight the man whose work he is supposed to have taken up and brought to fruition. The more natural impression the reading of this chapter would make is that Nehemiah had never heard of the considerable company said to have been led by Ezra.[5]

If Nehemiah and Ezra were together in Jerusalem, in the way the Chronicler would clearly have us believe, the problem is still more acute. For the powers with which Ezra was armed and those which

---

[1] Cf. *Les prophètes d'Israël*, p. 338 (E.Tr., p. 299).   [2] *Loc. cit.*, p. 266.
[3] *Ibid.*   [4] Neh. 7: 5 ff.   [5] Ezra 8: 1 ff.

Nehemiah exercised were so similar that they could hardly be exercised together. Had Ezra addressed himself exclusively to the religious side of the people's life, with which he was charged, and Nehemiah addressed himself exclusively to civil tasks, we might still have expected to find them in closer association than we do. But we find Nehemiah regulating the priesthood,[1] and later regulating tithes and appointing Temple treasurers,[2] and concerning himself with the observance of the sabbath.[3] Moreover, both take action in the matter of mixed marriages. But to this we must return. The fields of their interest and activity so much overlapped, therefore, that they can hardly have exercised authority simultaneously.

Van Hoonacker had already observed[4] that whereas Nehemiah appointed a commission of four to act as treasurers for the Temple,[5] Ezra finds a similar commission already in being when he arrives.[6] There is no indication that Nehemiah's action was the reconstitution of something that had fallen to pieces while he had been absent from Jerusalem. Similarly, in the account of the tithes which is associated with this, there is no suggestion that Nehemiah is simply restoring something which had been regularly observed during the period of his administration before he left Jerusalem—as it ought to have been if Ezra's law was proclaimed in 444 B.C., at the beginning of Nehemiah's administration—but that he is tackling a long-standing abuse.

In the matter of the mixed marriages, we find that Ezra was distressed on his arrival in Jerusalem to find the extent of the problem they created, and he therefore tackled it at once and that in radical fashion by the dissolution of all such marriages, as well as by the stopping of such marriages[7] for the future.[8] Scott supposes[9] that Ezra's drastic tactics were a failure. Of this he produces no evidence. The only evidence we have is that Ezra successfully brought all these marriages to an end. Scott does not say whether he supposes that these divorced wives were brought back again, but there is certainly no reason to suppose that they were. If, on the other hand, he only supposes that Ezra was unsuccessful in preventing new marriages with foreign women from being contracted, his whole theory breaks down. For he holds that Nehemiah was successful because he adopted the gentler line of preventing such marriages in the future. He can hardly assume, therefore, that Ezra's policy failed precisely on its gentler side that was

---

[1] Neh. 7: 64 ff.; 10: 32 ff.   [2] Neh. 13: 10 ff.   [3] Neh. 13: 15 ff.
[4] Cf. *R.B.*, x, 1901, pp. 182 f.   [5] Neh. 13: 13.   [6] Ezra 8: 33.
[7] Ezra 9 and 10.   [8] Ezra 9: 12.   [9] *Loc. cit.*, p. 266.

in harmony with Nehemiah's. Moreover, further difficulties would still remain. For, following Ezra's reading of the law, we find that the people swear that they will not allow their children to intermarry with aliens.[1] Presumably this is what Scott regards as Nehemiah's gentler methods. Yet when Nehemiah returns to Jerusalem on his second visit he finds the problem of mixed marriages confronting him. Clearly then his gentler policy has not been successful. For it is manifest that he is not only thinking of such marriages as have taken place during his absence, since already there are children of these marriages growing up and speaking another tongue. Nehemiah therefore abandons a gentle policy, and resorts to curses, and plucking off of the hair of the offenders, and violent expulsion.[2] This is surely an odd commentary on the thesis of Nehemiah's successful gentleness.

It is more natural to suppose that Nehemiah is dealing with the problem for the first time when he returns to Jerusalem, rather than admitting his own slackness and inefficiency in dealing with it before. It was a problem which had been developing for some time, which was brought to a head by the marriage of the high priest's grandson to Sanballat's daughter[3] while Nehemiah had been absent.[4] Stirred by this marriage with his own arch-enemy's daughter, he reacts violently against all intermarriage. His solution of the problem is not lasting, because he himself does not seem to have remained on the scene long after his return. Hence, if Ezra belongs to the reign of Artaxerxes II, there is nothing surprising in his finding the problem still a real one when he reached Jerusalem.[5] The view that assigns Nehemiah to the reign of Artaxerxes I and Ezra to that of Artaxerxes II finds a gap between the missions of these two men during which the problem could have arisen again; the view that Ezra preceded Nehemiah in the reign of Artaxerxes I offers no gap between their labours, and even though it assumes a period of eclipse for Ezra before Nehemiah arrived, it can provide no adequate gap between 444 B.C., when it

---

[1] Neh. 10: 30. [2] Neh. 13: 25, 28.

[3] On the problems raised by Sanballat and by this marriage, see H. H. Rowley, *Men of God*, 1963, pp. 246 ff.

[4] Neh. 13: 28. Nehemiah's anger would be the more kindled since he found that the high priest had assigned a room in the Temple to Tobiah the Ammonite, who had been associated with Sanballat in hostility to himself (Neh. 13: 4 f.).

[5] N. H. Snaith (*Studies in the Psalter*, 1934, pp. 13 f.) identifies the priest whom Nehemiah expelled with Jeshua, the brother of Johanan, to whom, according to Josephus, Bagoas promised the high-priesthood, and who may well have returned to Jerusalem to claim the office when Johanan slew him. In that case Johanan might be expected to support Ezra's policy with regard to mixed marriages wholeheartedly.

assumes that the problem was dealt with, and Nehemiah's return to Jerusalem, when it was still acute.

There are, however, a few passages where the names of Ezra and Nehemiah stand together, or in contexts that suggest that they were contemporary. In Neh. 8, which tells of Ezra's reading of the Law, we suddenly find the name of Nehemiah introduced alongside that of Ezra.[1] Here it is often noted that Nehemiah's name does not stand in the parallel text in 1 Esdras,[2] and it is widely believed that it is not original to the passage.[3] Its omission leaves no gap in the sense of the passage, and Nehemiah plays no part whatever in the scene. It might perfectly easily have been introduced by one who thought they were contemporary and who therefore supposed that they ought to have appeared together on such an occasion. There is no need to look beyond the Chronicler for such a person. If Nehemiah's name did not stand in his source, he could easily have added it.[4] For unless we resort to the hypothesis of considerable dislocation in the work, accompanied or followed by deliberate editorial activity, we must recognize that the Chronicler, whether rightly or wrongly, did suppose that Nehemiah and Ezra were contemporary. And since he has placed this chapter—which is manifestly about Ezra's fulfilment of the mission with which Ezra 7 : 10, 14, 26 declares him to have been charged— amongst the Nehemiah memoirs, it is not surprising that he has introduced the name of Nehemiah. His economy in adding such touches suggests that he is not wilfully misleading his readers, but arranging his materials according to his view of history, and relying mainly on his arrangement to present that view.

At Neh. 12 : 26 we have already looked, and there is no need to re-examine that passage here. In Neh. 12 : 36, in the account of the dedication of the walls of Jerusalem, we read, "and Ezra the scribe was before them". But here again we have no evidence that these words stood in

---

[1] Neh. 8: 9.

[2] 1 Esdras 9: 49. The text of Neh. 8: 9 has "Nehemiah which was the Tirshatha", while that of 1 Esdras 9: 49 omits the name Nehemiah and understands the title to be a proper name, Attharates.

[3] Cf. Hölscher, in Kautzsch-Bertholet, H.S.A.T., 1923, p. 546. Torrey holds (Ezra Studies, pp. 269, 282) that the text originally had "the Tirshatha" only, both here and in Neh. 10: 1, and that the Chronicler did not know who was the Tirshatha at the time, but that the name Nehemiah has been subsequently added. Kapelrud (op. cit., p. 85) thinks that the words "Nehemiah the Tirshatha" have been added.

[4] Wright (op. cit., p. 27) says the omission of Nehemiah's name in 1 Esdras 9: 49 is natural, since the compiler has not yet introduced the story of Nehemiah. If he knew that it was in fact Nehemiah, there would be no obvious reason for the suppression of this name.

the Chronicler's source. Just as Nehemiah plays no real part on the occasion reported in Neh. 8, so Ezra plays none here. We should have expected him to play a larger part than this on a religious occasion, yet all that we have is the minimum reflection of the Chronicler's belief that these two men were contemporary.

These passages are therefore quite insufficient to convince us that Ezra and Nehemiah were dominant figures living and working side by side in Jerusalem, each acting independently on the same questions. Wherever their names are found together one is a mere passenger, whose name can be dropped without the slightest consequence to the narrative.

Against this it has been frequently claimed that a few of the helpers of Nehemiah are mentioned also in connexion with Ezra.[1] Thus we find a Hattush, the son of Hashabiah, amongst Nehemiah's builders,[2] and also a Hattush amongst those who returned with Ezra.[3] The readiness to identify these two[4] contrasts with the unwillingness to identify Jehohanan, the son of Eliashib, in Ezra 10 : 6, and Johanan, the son of Eliashib, in Neh. 12 : 23. There, as has been said above, there is much supporting reason for the identification, but here we are not even told the name of the father of the Hattush who returned with Ezra. Neither figures in any incident which would be particularly appropriate to the other, and we have here no other fact except the common name without any known common paternal name, to suggest the assumed identification. The case is manifestly of the weakest.[5]

As weak is the case of Hashabiah.[6] Here we find that there was a Hashabiah amongst Nehemiah's builders,[7] and a Hashabiah amongst

---

[1] Cf. Kuenen, *op. cit.*, p. 242; Nikel, *op. cit.*, pp. 154 ff.; Jampel, *loc. cit.*, xlvii, 1903, pp. 20 f.; Wright, *op. cit.*, p. 21; Scott, *loc. cit.*, p. 265.

[2] Neh. 3: 10.

[3] Ezra 8: 2.

[4] Cf. Nikel, *op. cit.*, pp. 155 f.; Jampel, *loc. cit.*, p. 21; Wiener, *loc. cit.*, p. 158; Wright, *op. cit.*, p. 21.

[5] J. Bright argues that since Hattush, who returned with Ezra (Ezra 8: 2), was a fifth-generation descendant of Jehoiachin (1 Chron. 3: 22), he must have been born about 487 B.C., if we allow a liberal $27\frac{1}{2}$ years for each generation (cf. *Kaufmann Jubilee Volume*, pp. 83 f.; *History of Israel*, p. 385). But we have no means of estimating the date of his birth, since we do not know the ages of the parents at the time of the birth of the relevant sons. Moreover, Hattush was at least a sixth-generation descendant: Jehoiachin, Pedaiah, Zerubbabel, Hananiah, Shecaniah, Shemaiah, Hattush. The meaning of 1 Chron. 3: 21 is very obscure and much disputed, and even if Bright's view that it lists six brothers is correct, Shecaniah would be the youngest of the six. This whole argument is very precarious.

[6] Cf. Nikel, *op. cit.*, pp. 154 f.; Jampel, *loc. cit.*, p. 20; Wiener, *loc. cit.*, p. 158.

[7] Neh. 3: 17.

those who returned with Ezra.[1] But of reasons which would point to their identification there are none.

Even weaker is the case of Meshullam.[2] Amongst those who returned with Ezra we find one bearing this name,[3] while amongst Nehemiah's builders there figures a Meshullam, the son of Berechiah.[4] That these cannot be identified with the slightest confidence is proved by the fact that when Ezra divorces foreign wives, there is a Meshullam who assists him,[5] and another whose marriage is dissolved,[6] while another Meshullam, the son of Besodeiah, is found amongst Nehemiah's builders,[7] and yet another Meshullam the son of Joed appears later,[8] while Meshullams of unspecified paternity, who may be different from all of these and from one another, appear in various other places in the book of Nehemiah.[9] Clearly we must know something more than a man's name before we can identify him.

No stronger is the case of Malchijah, the son of Harim.[10] This name figures amongst Nehemiah's builders,[11] while in the list of people who were compelled by Ezra to divorce foreign wives we find a Malchijah among the sons of Harim.[12] Here it is not certain that Harim is the actual father, rather than the name of a much wider family. For in Neh. 7 : 35 we read of three hundred and twenty sons of one Harim, and in Neh. 7 : 42 of a thousand and seventeen sons of another. Even granting that Ezra's Malchijah is the actual son of Harim, his list provides evidence of two families of Harim,[13] the one priestly and the other non-priestly, while in Nehemiah's list of builders we find another Malchijah.[14] Two other persons named Malchijah stand in Ezra's list of divorced persons,[15] while the name stands elsewhere in the book of Nehemiah, where we have no means of identifying with any of the foregoing.[16] Neither name is therefore unique, and there is nothing beyond the names to identify the first two. The incidents in which they figure have nothing in common. In the one Malchijah is censured; in the other a praiseworthy act is recorded. It is, of course, conceivable that in 457 B.C. Malchijah should be censured and in 444 B.C. should help with Nehemiah's building; it is equally possible that one Mal-

---

[1] Ezra 8: 19. [2] Cf. Nikel, *op. cit.*, p. 156; Scott, *loc. cit.*, p. 265.
[3] Ezra 8: 16. [4] Neh. 3: 4, 20. [5] Ezra 10: 15.
[6] Ezra 10: 29. [7] Neh. 3: 6. [8] Neh. 11: 8.
[9] Neh. 8: 4; 10: 7, 20; 12: 25, 33.
[10] Cf. Kuenen, *op. cit.*, p. 242; Nikel, *op. cit.*, p. 156; Wright, *op. cit.*, p. 21.
[11] Neh. 3: 11. [12] Ezra 10: 31. [13] Cf. Ezra 10: 21.
[14] Neh. 3: 14. Cf. also Neh. 3: 31. [15] Ezra 10: 25.
[16] Neh. 8: 4; 10: 3; 12: 42.

chijah should share in the building in 444 B.C. and another should be made to give up his foreign wife nearly half a century later. The one might possibly be the grandson of the other, since it was not uncommon for men to bear their grandfather's names. But he might equally well be quite unrelated.

Much stronger is the case of Meremoth, the son of Uriah.[1] One bearing this name appears amongst Nehemiah's builders,[2] while we find that when Ezra reaches Jerusalem he hands the treasure he has brought to Meremoth, the son of Uriah, and some others.[3] It is probable that Nehemiah's Meremoth is a priest, since we find that he repairs an extra portion of the wall,[4] and that this portion covered the high priest's house. There is every reason to identify the Meremoth of these references. The Meremoth who was selected to act as the chief treasurer was clearly a man of some personality, and the Meremoth of the other incident was equally clearly one who rose above the common level. But there is no likelihood that the building incident came thirteen years after the other. The builder who undertook a double portion of the building was most likely a young man, strong and vigorous; while the treasurer of national funds would be much more likely to be a senior member of the priesthood.[5] If he was already a senior and a man of high authority in the Temple in 457 B.C., his age in 444 B.C. would render it very unlikely that he would be fit for a double portion of building. On the other hand, if he were a youthful enthusiast of twenty in 444 B.C., in 397 B.C., when Ezra found him already at the head of the treasury of the Temple, he would be sixty-seven. In this there is no improbability whatever.

Enough has been said to show that the latest attacks on the priority of Nehemiah and the location of Ezra in the reign of Artaxerxes II have produced no substantially new arguments that their predecessors have not used. While we have not, and are not likely to have, any evidence which can prove that Ezra belonged to the fourth century B.C., still less is there any evidence that he belonged to the fifth century B.C. In the balance of probabilities the scales seem still to come down on the side of Van Hoonacker's view, with the exception that the Belgian scholar needlessly supposed that Ezra had also been in Jerusalem with Nehemiah on the latter's second visit to Jerusalem,

---

[1] Cf. Kuenen, *op. cit.*, p. 242; Nikel, *op. cit.*, p. 156; Wright, *op. cit.*, p. 21; Scott, *loc. cit.*, p. 265.
[2] Neh. 3: 4.   [3] Ezra 8: 33.   [4] Neh. 3: 21.
[5] Cf. Albright, *J.B.L.*, xl, 1921, p. 123.

many years before he began his own mission in 397 B.C. Most of his followers have differed from him here, and have made Ezra's work begin in 397 B.C., thus eliminating the difficulty of the advanced age that Ezra would otherwise have reached when he undertook his mission, and eliminating any overlap in the period of activity of Nehemiah and Ezra.

THE MARRIAGE OF RUTH

5

The Marriage of Ruth[1]

THE simple story of the book of Ruth abounds in problems for which no final solution can ever be found, since the materials for their solution are denied us. On this village scene, so different in character from most of the scenes of those ungentle times, the curtain is half lifted. But only half. Naomi returns from her sojourn abroad, bringing her daughter-in-law with her, and Ruth goes out to glean in the harvest field. Then unexpectedly we find Naomi possessed of land, and we are left to guess how it came into her possession, and what had happened to it during the years of her sojourn in Moab. We are not told the relationship of Boaz to Elimelech, or the relationship of the nearer kinsman;[2] nor are we told why the hand of Ruth went with the property. That the story of Ruth's marriage must be linked with the question of levirate marriage is generally agreed, though this is clearly not strictly a case of levirate marriage, since Boaz is not a brother-in-law or *levir*.[3] There are not wanting, indeed, those who draw a much sharper distinction between Ruth's marriage and levirate marriage, but to this we must return. Of levirate marriage in ancient Israel we know very little, and while the later scholasticism of the Talmud may preserve some ancient traditions, it cannot be implicitly trusted to throw light on customs which were already obsolete when the book of Ruth was written, needing to be explained to the reader as customs that formerly held in Israel.[4] We do not know when the book of Ruth was written, and widely differing dates have been ascribed to it by modern

---

[1] Paper read at the meeting of the Society for Old Testament Study held in Cardiff, September 1946.

[2] Rashi, in his comment on Ruth 3: 12, conjectured that Elimelech was an uncle of Boaz, while the nearer kinsman was the brother of Elimelech. But this is no more than conjecture, found also in the Midrash Rabba.

[3] Cf. M. Burrows (*J.B.L.*, lix, 1940, p. 23): "The marriage of Boaz and Ruth presupposes a custom related to levirate marriage, but not quite the same." On levirate marriage cf. D. R. Mace, *Hebrew Marriage*, 1953, pp. 95 ff.; B. M. Vellas, *Israelite Marriage*, E.Tr. by J. S. Koulouras, 1956, pp. 31 ff.; W. Rudolph, "Levirat und *ge'ullā*", in *Ruth, Hohe Lied, Klagelieder* (K.A.T.), 1962, pp. 60 ff.), where much literature is cited.

[4] Ruth 4: 7.

critical scholars.[1] Nor is there any agreement as to the purpose of the book.[2] Some have regarded it as a tract of the fifth century B.C.,

[1] According to the Talmud "Samuel wrote his own book and Judges and Ruth" (T.B., *Baba Bathra*, 14 b), and this has been followed in modern times by R. Cornely (*Introductio in Veteris Testamenti libros sacros*, II, i, 1897, pp. 233 f.). The book has been ascribed to the period of the early monarchy by C. F. Keil (*Lehrbuch der historisch-kritischen Einleitung in die Schriften des Alten Testamentes*, 3rd ed., 1873, p. 437), C. H. H. Wright (*The Book of Ruth in Hebrew*, 1864, p. xliv—not later than David; modified later in his *Introduction to the Old Testament*, 1890, p. 126, to a date between David and the Exile), L. Fillion (in Vigouroux' *Dictionnaire de la Bible*, v, 1912, cols. 1275 f.), J. E. Steinmueller (*Companion to Scripture Studies*, ii, 1942, p. 82), and E. J. Young (*An Introduction to the Old Testament*, 1949, p. 330—during the reign of David); to a period between David and the Exile by S. Oettli (in Oettli and Meinhold, *Die geschichtlichen Hagiographen und das Buch Daniel*, 1889, pp. 215 f.), S. R. Driver (*Introduction to the Literature of the Old Testament*, 9th ed., 1913, pp. 454 ff.), J. Fischer (in *Echt. B.*, Lieferung 10, 1950, *Rut*, pp. 5 f.), H. W. Hertzberg [*Die Bücher Josua, Richter, Ruth* (A.T.D.), 1953, p. 257—the middle of the monarchical period], S. B. Guriewicz (*Australian Biblical Review*, v, 1956, pp. 53f.), and W. Rudolph [*Das Buch Ruth, Das Hohe Lied, Die Klagelieder* (K.A.T.), 1962, p. 29]; to the period of Hezekiah by S. Davidson (*Introduction to the Old Testament*, i, 1862, pp. 482 ff.) and E. Reuss (*Littérature politique et polémique*, 1879, pp. 26 f.); to the pre-Deuteronomic period by J. Fichtner (*R.G.G.*, 3rd. ed., v, 1961, cols. 1253f.); to the exilic period by H. Ewald (*Geschichte des Volkes Israel*, 3rd ed., 1864, p. 225), E. König (*Einleitung in das Alte Testament*, 1893, p. 287), A. Jepsen (*T.S.K.*, cviii, 1937–38, p. 424), and M. David (*O.T.S.*, i, 1941–42, pp. 55–63); to the post-exilic period by J. Wellhausen (in F. Bleek's *Einleitung in das Alte Testament*, 4th ed., 1878, pp. 204 f.), A. Bertholet (in Budde, Bertholet and Wildeboer, *Die fünf Megilloth*, 1898, pp. 49 ff.), W. Nowack (*Richter, Ruth und Bücher Samuelis*, 1902, pp. 180 f.), C. Cornill (*Introduction to the Canonical Books of the Old Testament*, E.Tr., 1907, pp. 254 f.), C. Steuernagel (*Lehrbuch der Einleitung in das Alte Testament*, 1912, pp. 430 f.), L. Gautier (*Introduction à l'Ancien Testament*, ii, 3rd ed., 1939, p. 150), E. Sellin (*Introduction to the Old Testament*, E.Tr., 1923, p. 226—the first years after the Return; cf. *Einleitung in das Alte Testament*, 7th ed., 1935, p. 147—in fourth century B.C.), P. Jöuon (*Ruth*, 1924, pp. 12 f.), J. Meinhold (*Einführung in das Alte Testament*, 3rd ed., 1932, pp. 336 f.), Oesterley and Robinson (*Introduction to the Books of the Old Testament*, 1934, p. 84), O. Eissfeldt (*Einleitung in das Alte Testament*, 1934, pp. 542 f., 3rd ed., 1963, p. 654; R. H. Pfeiffer (*Introduction to the Old Testament*, 1941, pp. 717 ff.), R. Tamisier (in *La Sainte Bible*, ed. by Pirot and Clamer, iii, 1949, pp. 305–307), A. Vincent [*Le Livre des Juges, Le Livre de Ruth* (Jerusalem Bible), 1952, p. 146], L. Pettibone Smith (*I.B.*, ii, 1953, p. 830a), B. Vellas (*The Book of Ruth and its Purpose*, 1954, pp. 11 f.), and J. P. Hyatt (in Hastings's one-volume *D.B.*, revised ed., 1963, p. 865b). A. Bentzen (*Introduction to the Old Testament*, ii, 1949, p. 85) leaves open the possibility of a date during the later monarchy or the post-exilic period, while A. Penna [*Giudici e Rut* (La Sacra Bibbia, ed. by S. Garofalo), 1962, p. 263] does not decide between an exilic and a post-exilic date. G. S. Glanzman (*C.B.Q.*, xxi, 1959, pp. 201–207) argues for three stages in the composition of Ruth, an old poetic tale of non-Israelite origin, a prose form dating from the ninth or eighth century B.C., and the present form dating from the post-exilic period (for a criticism of this cf. O. Loretz, *C.B.Q.*, xxii, 1960, pp, 397 f. note). On poetic elements in the book of Ruth, cf. J. M. Myers, *The Linguistic and Literary Form of the Book of Ruth*, 1955. B. Ubach [*Josuè-Jutges-Rut* (Montserrat Bible), 1953, p. 334] leaves the date completely open.

[2] Cf. L. B. Wolfenson, "The Purpose of the Book of Ruth", in *Bibliotheca Sacra*, lxix, 1912, pp. 329 ff.; B. Vellas, *The Book of Ruth and its Purpose*, 1954.

written to oppose Nehemiah and Ezra, when they sought to root out foreign marriages from the Jews,[1] though it would be just as easy to read it as a defence of their policy against such as produced David's Moabite ancestress to discredit it.[2] It has little of the flavour of a political tract, however, and I cannot think of it as written for any such purpose.[3] To some its purpose is revealed in its closing verses, containing the genealogy of David,[4] while to others this genealogy is a later addition, inconsistent with the earlier part of the book.[5] To Reuss its

[1] So, e.g., by A. Bertholet (op. cit., pp. 52 ff.), C. Cornill (op. cit., p. 256), E. Sellin (Einleitung, 7th ed., p. 147), J. Meinhold (op. cit., p. 337), J. Hempel (Die althebräische Literatur, 1930, pp. 153 f.), A. Lods (La Bible du Centenaire, L'Ancien Testament, iii, 1947, p. xviii), G. A. F. Knight [Ruth and Jonah (Torch Bible), 1950, pp. 20 f.], M. D. Goldman (Australian Biblical Review, v, 1956, p. 55) and A. Weiser (Introduction to the Old Testament, E.Tr., 1961, p. 304). This view was proposed as long ago as 1816 by L. Bertholdt (Historisch-kritische Einleitung in sämmtlichen Schriften des Alten and Neuen Testaments, 1812–19, pp. 2356 f.; the passage is given in translation in Joüon, op. cit., p. 4).

[2] Cf. my Israel's Mission to the World, 1939, pp. 46 ff. J. J. Slotki, in The Five Megilloth, ed. by A. Cohen, 1946, p. 39a, regards the purpose of the book as being inter alia (a) to protest against intermarriage, unless it occurs in exceptional circumstances, and (b) to check indiscriminate proselytization.

[3] Cf. M. Haller, Die fünf Megilloth (H.A.T.), 1940, p. 2; M. David, O.T.S., i, 1941–1942, p. 63; R. Tamisier, in La Sainte Bible, ed. by Pirot and Clamer, iii, 1940, p. 307; J. de Fraine, Dictionnaire encyclopédique de la Bible, 1960, col. 1632. B. Vellas (op. cit., pp. 7 f.) says: "A book which was written in those troubled times of Ezra and Nehemiah, as a protest against those men, could not possess that beautiful atmosphere and those idyllic surroundings which, so skilfully, the author of Ruth creates, nor could it be possible to possess an unforced, serene and calm tone of style." F. W. K. Umbreit (T.S.K. vii, 1834, pp. 305 ff.) argues that its purpose was religious rather than political: "Der Verf. wollte zeigen, wie selbst eine Fremde aus dem Gebiete der verhassten Moabiter gewürdigt werden konnte, Stammutter des grossen Königs David zu werden, weil sie zum Gotte-Israels ein unbedingtes Vertrauen bewiesen." Vellas (op. cit., pp. 10 ff.) holds that the purpose of the book was to stress family unity and the sacredness of family bonds in an age when, as Mal. 3: 24 shows, such bonds were being relaxed, and J. de Fraine [Richters-Ruth (B.O.T.), 1956, p. 140] believes it was written to exalt pietas; while J. P. Hyatt in Hastings's one-volume D.B., rev. ed., 1963, p. 865b) thinks it was written to plead for a wider interpretation of levirate marriage.

[4] Cf. Keil, op. cit., p. 437; L. Fillion, loc. cit., cols. 1280 f. Cf. O. Loretz, C.B.Q., xxii, 1960, pp. 391–399, where it is argued that the purpose is to show that God's election of David began during the lives of his ancestors.

[5] So, amongst many others, König, op. cit., p. 287; Bertholet, op. cit., pp. 68 f.; S. R. Driver, op. cit., pp. 455 f.; W. R. Smith, E.B., iv, 1907, col. 4169; L. B. Wolfenson, The Book of Ruth, 1911, p. 9=A.J.S.L., xxvii, 1910–11, p. 293; Joüon, op. cit., p. 96; M. Burrows, J.B.L., lix, 1940, p. 450; A. Vincent, Le Livre des Juges, Le Livre de Ruth, 1952, p. 164. Wellhausen, on the other hand, thought that this genealogy was "das wichtigste Merkmal der Zeit" (op. cit., p. 204). G. Gerleman [Ruth (B.K.A.T.), 1960, p. 8] also contests the view that the genealogy is secondary, and argues that it is improbable that anyone would have invented the story that David had a Moabite ancestry unless there was a firmly established tradition behind it.

purpose was to demonstrate that in the line of David the inheritance of Judah and northern Israel became united, since Obed was the legal heir of the Ephraimite Mahlon, as well as the actual issue of the Judahite Boaz.[1] Margaret Crook finds two strands in the book, one coming from the time of the Judges and the other coming from the time of Athaliah and marked by a polemical purpose against her.[2] By most genuine historical worth is credited to the story, while Gunkel roundly declares that it is devoid of historical worth.[3] Into this tangle of problems, where we have so little to guide us, I enter with some diffidence, and can only hope to find a view which is consistent with what we learn elsewhere, and which is therefore possible.[4] Moreover, the questions of the date and purpose of the book must be left undiscussed, since the limits of this paper allow no time for them.

Outside the book of Ruth the only passages in the Old Testament which deal with anything akin to levirate marriage are Gen. 38 and Deut. 25 : 5–10. It is significant that both of these are referred to, explicitly or implicitly, in the book of Ruth. There are specific references to Tamar and her son, while the incident of the drawing off of the shoe when Ruth was declined by her next-of-kin recalls the similar, though not identical, custom of Deut. 25 : 9. It is therefore not without reason that these three passages have been frequently considered together, and all probability is against those who differentiate Ruth's

---

[1] *Op. cit.*, pp. 25 f. The assumption that Mahlon was an Ephraimite rests on the description of him as an Ephrathite in Ruth 1: 2, and the evidence of Judges 12: 5 that an Ephrathite means an Ephraimite, But Ruth 1: 4 shows that Mahlon was of Bethlehem, which in Ruth 4: 11 is equated with Ephrath or Ephrathah, from which the gentilic is here derived. Cf. also Mic. 5: 1 (E.V. 2).

[2] Cf. *J.B.R.*, xvi, 1948, pp. 155–160. Professor Crook regards Is. 9: 1–6 (E.V. 2–7) and 11: 1–9 as composed for the accession of Joash, and believes that Jehoiada was the author of the second strand of the book of Ruth.

[3] In *R.G.G.*, v, 1913, col. 107 (2nd ed., iv, 1930, col. 2181): "Die Erzählung enthält nichts Geschichtliches." Cf. H. Gressmann [*Die Anfänge Israels* (*S.A.T.*) I, ii, 1914, p. 284], who declares that it is "keine Geschichte, sondern Sage" and "Novelle". Gunkel had earlier (*Reden and Aufsätze*, 1913, p. 85) used the term "Novelle" to describe the "Gattung" of this book. So, more recently, M. Haller, *Die fünf Megilloth* (H.A.T.), 1940, p. 2. This view is rejected by G. Gerleman, *Ruth* (B.K.A.T.), 1960, pp. 7 ff. Cf. also H. A. Brongers, "Enkele opmerkingen over het verband tussen lossing en leviraat in Ruth IV", in *Ned.T.T.*, ii, 1947–48, pp. 1–7. For studies of the art and form of the book cf. H. Gunkel, "Ruth". in *Reden und Aufsätze*, pp. 65–92; P. Humbert, "Art et leçon de l'histoire de Ruth", in *R.Th.Ph.*, N.S. xxvi, 1938, pp. 257–286; E. Robertson, "The Plot of the Book of Ruth", in *B.J.R.L.*, xxxii, 1949–50, pp. 207–228.

[4] I am not concerned with the date or historicity of the book, but only with the question of its self-consistency and accord with what we learn elsewhere.

marriage from levirate marriage in kind and not merely in the degree of relationship between Ruth and Boaz.[1]

The Deuteronomic passage says nothing whatever about any more distant kinsman than a brother-in-law.[2] Indeed, it limits the duty of taking the childless widow to a brother who has actually been living with the deceased brother,[3] and *prima facie* this has no relevance to the case of Ruth.[4] On the other hand, Gen. 38 tells how Tamar, when she was denied her brother-in-law, managed to outwit her father-in-law, and become the mother of his children. That story seems to indicate

[1] So S. R. Driver, *Critical and Exegetical Commentary on Deuteronomy*, 2nd ed., 1896, p. 285: "The marriage of Boʻaz and Ruth is not a Levirate-marriage: Boʻaz ... 'purchases' her." L. M. Epstein (*Marriage Laws in the Bible and the Talmud*, 1942, pp. 86 ff.) draws a sharp distinction between levirate marriage and *geʼullāh* marriage, with the latter of which he identifies the marriage of Ruth, the distinction being that whereas in the former the widow remains in the same family household (operating only in the case of brothers living together), in the latter she goes over to another. E. Neufeld (*Ancient Hebrew Marriage Laws*, 1944, pp. 38 ff.) more soundly holds that the levirate duty is one of the Goʻel's (*sic!* for Goʼel's) responsibilities. J. A. Bewer (*A.J.S.L.*, xix, 1902–3, pp. 143 ff.), while holding that the *geʼullāh* and the levirate were combined in the oldest times, thinks that in the book of Ruth the *geʼullāh* is not connected with the levirate. He eliminates the references to the levirate in the book of Ruth as interpolations (*T.S.K.*, lxxvi, 1903, pp. 328 ff., 502 ff.), and is followed by Wolfenson (*The Book of Ruth*, p. 15=*A.J.S.L.*, xxvii, 1910–11, p. 299). Cf. also *A.J.S.L.*, xx, 1903–4, pp. 202 ff., where Bewer maintains that the levirate interpolations were inserted by partisans of Nehemiah and Ezra to neutralize the effect of the book by their skilful suggestion that Boaz only married Ruth because he was by law compelled to do so. Bewer's suggestion is rejected by Burrows (*J.B.L.*, lix, 1950, p. 450). Burrows also rejects the view of Koschaker, Gordon, and Mittelmann that Ruth is inherited as part of the estate (*ibid.*, p. 449). So also A. van Praag, *Droit matrimonial assyro-babylonien*, 1945, p. 110. Of this there is no suggestion whatever. Ruth was in Bethlehem because she had chosen to come, not because she was part of the property at the disposal of another. In contrast to Bewer, H. A. Brongers thinks the purpose of the book of Ruth is to bring together the *geʼullāh* and the levirate, which were really distinct (*Ned.T.T.*, ii, 1947–48, pp. 1–7).

[2] A. Van Praag (*op. cit.*, pp. 108 f.) thinks that the word "brother" in Deut. 25: 5–10 indicates not an individual, but a category of persons larger than that denoted by our word. If that is correct, this passage does not limit the duty to the *levir*, but leaves it wider in its reference.

[3] Cf. G. R. Driver and J. C. Miles, *The Assyrian Laws*, 1935, p. 243; A. van Praag, *op. cit.*, p. 109; A. F. Puukko, *Archiv Orientální*, xvii, 1949 (Hrozný Festschrift), pars secunda, p. 296; D. Daube, *The Juridical Review*, lxii, 1950, pp. 71 ff. Daube thinks that levirate marriage was closely connected with the *consortium*, where brothers instead of dividing an estate on the death of their father, continued to administer it jointly. This would seem to distinguish the marriage of Ruth too sharply from levirate marriage, and would make the references to Deut. 25: 5–10, and Gen. 38 in the book of Ruth hard to explain.

[4] Cf. above, note 1 and Epstein's distinction between *geʼullāh* marriage and levirate marriage. But Deut. 25: 5–10 cannot be treated as basic for the discussion of a usage which has its roots much farther back, and if, as is commonly held, that law restricted levirate marriage, it cannot be held that in earlier days a less restricted usage did not constitute levirate marriage.

that in ancient times the duty of raising children to bear the name of a dead kinsman was not strictly limited to a brother-in-law, but that failing him another kinsman might serve.[1] This would seem to be implied also by the book of Ruth. Neither Boaz nor the other kinsman was a brother of Ruth's husband, nor, apparently, a brother of Naomi's husband, Elimelech, yet some duty to raise children to the dead is implicit. Moreover, here again we find that if the next-of-kin declines the duty, then one farther removed may assume it, while both there and here the widow has some claim on the next-of-kin, or failing him on the next but one. In Deut. 25, on the other hand, nothing whatever is said about anyone else taking over the duty. There only the brother-in-law figures as accepting or declining the duty. Further, nothing is said in that passage of any property complications. That is probably, as will be said below, because ordinarily they would not arise.

That the Old Testament law of the levirate marriage arose out of a wider context is generally agreed, and, indeed, is beyond question. Comparable customs are found widely spread amongst men,[2] and the source and significance of the custom have been much discussed without yielding any agreed solution.[3] That polyandry or group marriage provides the basis of the custom has been maintained by some,[4] while others have connected it with ancestor worship,[5] and yet others have

---

[1] Cf. C. Lattey, *The Book of Ruth*, 1935, p. xxvi: "The principle upon which Tamar acts, and which Judah acknowledges as just, seems to be that since the proper Goel, Judah's third son Shelah, is not allowed her, she has a right to the next Goel after him, Judah himself." J. Morgenstern (*H.U.C.A.*, vii, 1930, p. 163) notes that in the Hittite Code there is a provision that when there is no brother-in-law to perform the levirate duty, this devolves upon the father-in-law. Cf. E. Neufeld, *The Hittite Laws*, 1951, p. 192. G. R. Driver and J. C. Miles (*op. cit.*, p. 242) say: "She (Tamar) was able to vindicate herself by proving that Judah, upon whom the duty of the levirate ultimately lay, was the father of her child. This is the reason why she was acquitted, and not because Judah her judge was *particeps criminis*."

[2] Cf. E. Westermarck, *History of Human Marriage*, iii, 5th ed., 1921, pp. 208 ff. note; J. Scheftelowitz, "Die Leviratsehe", in *A.R.W.*, xviii, 1915, pp. 250 ff.; and, amongst older writers, F. Benary, *De hebræorum leviratu*, 1835, pp. 31 ff.

[3] For recent reviews of the discussion cf. Epstein, *op. cit.*, pp. 77 ff., and Neufeld, *Ancient Hebrew Marriage Laws*, pp. 23 ff.

[4] Cf. J. F. McLennan, *Primitive Marriage*, 1865, p. 204 (= *Studies in Ancient History*, 1886, pp. 112 f.): "the only explanation that can be given . . . is that the law of succession was derived from polyandry" (cf. also *The Patriarchal Theory*, 1885, pp. 330 ff.); J. G. Frazer, *Folklore in the Old Testament*, ii, 1919, p. 304: "the two customs of the sororate and the levirate seem traceable to a common source in a form of group marriage."

[5] Cf. A. Bertholet, *Deuteronomium* (K.H.A.T.), 1899, p. 77; G. Margoliouth, in Hastings's *E.R.E.*, i, 1908, pp. 448 f.

traced it to the conception of the woman as property, in which the family have secured rights which they are entitled to exploit.[1] Into any discussion of this I do not propose to go, save to say that the motives and ideas that gather round any custom are less simple than our tidy minds desire. Customs arise out of a complex situation, for life is always complex, and they are retained for a complex of reasons, though in different areas and ages different elements of the complex may be more prominent. So far as the Old Testament is concerned polyandry or group marriage was no longer practised, ancestor worship survives only in a few disputed traces, and the conception of the woman as property belonging to the relatives nowhere appears.[2] It is the widow's title to motherhood which is here prominent, and that only as the expression of her loyalty to her deceased husband.[3]

The comparison of the Israelite usage with that of Israel's ancient

[1] Cf. I. Benzinger, *E.B.*, ii, 1901, col. 2675: "Hebrew levirate marriage admits of sufficient explanation from the simple fact that in Hebrew baal-marriage wives in general are property that can be inherited." Cf. also P. Koschaker, "Die Eheformen bei den Indogermanen", in *Sonderheft des 11. Jahrgangs der Zeitschrift für ausländisches und internationales Privatrecht*, 1937, pp. 77–140 b (to which I have not had access), and "Fratriarchat, Hausgemeinschaft und Mutterrecht in Keilschriftrechten", in *Z.A.*, xli, 1933, pp. 1 ff. (esp. p. 61); and Epstein, *op. cit.*, p. 79: "the two primitive concepts, that the woman is family property and that the childless person is cut off from the family tree and must be artificially regrafted, are the main motives transmitted to us . . ., and are in themselves sufficient to explain the origin of the levirate custom." Burrows, in contrast to Benzinger, above cited, says: "We may observe that, except among the Hebrews and perhaps the Canaanites, levirate marriage was not in the ancient Near East a means of securing a son for the dead. It was rather a part of the whole system of family relationships, authority, and inheritance" (*B.A.S.O.R.*, No. 77, February 1940, p. 15). Cf. C. H. Gordon, *J.B.L.*, liv, 1935, p. 230.
[2] G. Parrinder, *The Bible and Polygamy*, 1950, p. 23, says: "The root principle of the Levirate marriage is that a man's widow is inherited by his agnates." No Biblical evidence is, or can be, offered in support of this, however true it may be in the wider setting.
[3] The sole *raison d'être* of levirate marriage that appears in the Old Testament is the provision of an heir for the deceased. This has led J. Morgenstern to suggest that the origin of the practice in Israel was independent of that elsewhere. Cf. *H.U.C.A.*, vii, 1930, pp. 161 f.: "This is an altogether new motif, not without occasional, though not frequent, parallels in the marriage practice of other, non-Semitic peoples, but entirely without parallel in Semitic practice, at least so far as present evidence goes. It is this motif which is characteristically Israelite, and which indicates that the institution of levirate marriage must have had an independent development in Israel." The reinterpretation and rationalization of older practice in terms congenial to the culture of the time is by no means uncommon, however. Cf. C. H. Gordon, *J.B.L.*, liv, 1935, p. 230: "In the Old Testament, a secondary, sentimental and purely fictitious phase of levirate marriage, to wit, that of supplying the deceased with an heir, has evolved into its *raison d'être*."

neighbours,[1] of the Arabs of more recent times,[2] and of more widely scattered peoples,[3] as well as the careful study of the Biblical passages

[1] Cf. M. Burrows, "The Ancient Oriental Background of Hebrew Levirate Marriage", in *B.A.S.O.R.*, No. 77, February 1940, pp. 2 ff., and "Levirate Marriage in Israel", in *J.B.L.*, lix, 1940, pp. 23 ff.; also the same writer's *Basis of Israelite Marriage*, 1938; P. Koschaker, *Quellenkritische Untersuchungen zu den "altassyrischen Gesetzen."* (M.V.A.G., xxvi, No. 3), 1921, pp. 46 ff.; P. Cruveilhier, "Le lévirat chez les hébreux et chez les assyriens", in *R.B.*, xxxiv, 1925, pp. 534 ff.; F. Hrozný, *Code Hittite*, 1922, pp. 145 f. (§ 193); Koschaker, "Zum Levirat nach hethitischem Recht", in *Revue hittite et asianique*, ii, 1932-34, pp. 77 ff.; I. M. Price, "The so-called Levirate-marriage in Hittite and Assyrian Laws", in *Oriental Studies dedicated to Paul Haupt*, 1926, pp. 268 ff.; C. H. Gordon, "Parallèles nouziens aux lois et coutumes de l'Ancien Testament", in *R.B.*, xliv, 1935, pp. 34 ff. (esp. p. 37); A. F. Puukko, "Die Leviratsehe in den altorientalischen Gesetzen", in *Archiv Orientálni*, xvii, 1949 (Hrozný Festschrift), pars secunda, pp. 296-299; A. van Praag, *op. cit.*, pp. 115-127. In view of this widespread practice throughout Israel's *milieu*, it is impossible to accept the view of A. Geiger that the levirate was confined to Judah ("Die Leviratsehe, ihre Entstehung und Entwickelung", in *Jüdische Zeitschrift*, i, 1862, pp. 19 ff.). It should be added that in Ras Shamra texts there are found occurrences of the expression *ybmt limm*, where appears the root from which the Hebrew *yābhām*= brother-in-law comes, and where Albright renders *progenitress of the peoples* (cf. *B.A.S.O.R.*, No. 77, February 1940, pp. 6 f.). This is held to show that the original meaning of the root was *procreate*, and hence that *brother-in-law* is a secondary limitation in Hebrew. Cf. Neufeld, *op. cit.*, p. 23 n. C. H. Gordon (*Ugaritic Literature*, 1949, pp. 29, 90) renders the Ras Shamra expression by "sister-in-law of Nations", following Ch. Virolleaud (cf. *La légende phénicienne de Danel*, 1936, p. 235; in *Syria*, xvii, 1936, p. 152 n., however, Virolleaud renders "la protectrice des peuples"). H. E. del Medico (*La Bible cananéenne*, 1950, p. 94) also understands it to mean sister-in-law, since he renders the line "ta femme sera épousée comme concubine étrangère suivant les lois du lévirat". While it is antecedently likely that the levirate existed at Ugarit, the surviving evidence is not very clear; cf. A. van Selms, *Marriage and Family Life in Ugaritic Literature*, 1954, p. 36; M. Tsevat, *J.S.S.*, iii, 1957, pp. 239 f.

[2] Cf. G. Sale's note on Qur'an iv. 23 (*The Koran*, 1838, ed., pp. 57 f.) and Tabari's comment on the passage (cited and translated in W. R. Smith's *Kinship and Marriage in Early Arabia*, 1903 ed., pp. 104 f.). Cf. also Muhammad Ali's comment on the passage (*The Holy Qur-án*, 2nd ed., 1920, p. 205—text numbered iv. 19 in this edition), but contrast R. Bell's note (*The Qur'ān*, i, 1937, p. 71). Cf., too, al-Bukhari's *Ṣaḥīḥ*, lxv, on Sura iv. 6 (in L. Krehl, *Recueil des traditions mahométanes par . . . el-Bokhari*, iii, 1868, p. 220): "(avant l'islamisme) lorsqu'un homme mourait, c'étaient ses heritiers qui avaient un privilège sur sa veuve. Ceux qui le voulaient l'épousaient; d'autres préféraient la marier à un tiers, et ceux qui le voulaient ne les mariaient pas du tout. Ils avaient plus de droits sur cette veuve que leurs propres parents" (tr. of O. Houdas, *Les traditions islamiques*, iii, 1908, p. 295). For more modern times cf. J. J. Burckhardt, *Notes on the Bedouins and Wahábys*, 1830, p. 64: "If a young man leaves a widow, his brother generally offers to marry her; custom does not oblige him or her to make this match, nor can he prevent her from marrying another man. It seldom happens, however, that she refuses; for by such an union the family property is kept together"; or A. Jaussen, *Coutumes des Arabes au pays de Moab*, 1908, p. 48: "En principe, elle [i.e. the widow] doit devenir la femme du frère du mari, qui a droit sur elle, et très souvent l'épouse. Si la veuve ne veut absolument pas, elle retourne chez son père."

[3] The evidence from India contained in the Laws of Manu is frequently cited. There we learn that if a man died after betrothal to a maiden his brother "shall approach her once in each proper season until issue be had" (ix, 69 f.; tr. by E. Bühler in *The Laws*

which are relevant, makes it probable that the law of Deut. 25 : 5–10 reflects a limitation of something that was once wider in Israel, and this view is further supported when we look beyond the question of the childless widow[1] to the wider duties devolving on the next-of-kin.

The duty of blood revenge does not figure in the book of Ruth, but is found elsewhere in the Old Testament, and we find a steady limitation in Israel.[2] What seems in very ancient times to have been a duty falling on any member of the clan of a slain man to slay any member of the clan of the slayer[3] was doubly limited in Israel. It is probable that this obligation always rested with especial weight on the next-of-kin, and was always regarded as particularly fulfilled when it exacted the penalty of the slayer, but in the Old Testament, in the earliest sources of which we have knowledge, the duty of blood revenge was the specific duty only of the next-of-kin, and it was his duty to kill the slayer only.[4] Moreover a distinction is drawn between murder and homicide,

of Manu, in Sacred Books of the East, xxv, 1886, pp. 339 f.), though her consent must be obtained (ix, 97; p. 344). Further, if a man is without issue, his brother or some other relation may be authorized to beget a son for him, but again it is emphatically stated that a single son is permitted (ix, 59 f.; pp. 337 f.). Here it is not clear whether this is permitted while the husband still lives, or only after his death, but the commentators follow the former interpretation. Further, it is laid down that "he who takes care of his deceased brother's estate and of his widow shall, after raising up a son for his brother, give that property even to that son" (ix, 146; p. 356. Cf. ix, 190; p. 369).

[1] It is probable that the Rabbis correctly interpret the Hebrew practice, in the later historical times at any rate, when they say that if the deceased left a child of either sex there should be no levirate marriage (cf. Epstein, op. cit., pp. 96 f.). From the time when a daughter was allowed to inherit this may have become the case and "son" in Deut. 25: 5 may thus have had this wider interpretation. (In T.B., Baba Bathra, 119b, the law permitting daughters to inherit is based on the interpretation of "son" in Deut. 25: 5 in the sense of child of either sex.) In more ancient times it is likely that only a male heir would count (cf. I. I. Mattuck, in Studies in Jewish Literature issued in Honor of Kaufmann Kohler, 1913, p. 211), and beyond the borders of Israel we find that even where there were male children levirate marriage was practised (cf. Joüon, The Book of Ruth, p. 9; and Cruveilhier, R.B., xxxiv, 1925, pp. 533 ff.). But in Israel levirate marriage was limited to the one purpose of raising an heir for the dead. Hence the emphasis is not on the childlessness of the widow, but of the deceased. It is not that she is entitled to motherhood for her own sake, but that her husband is entitled to an heir from her, if he has not already had one from her or from another wife.   [2] Cf. Pedersen, Israel I–II, 1926, pp. 395 ff.

[3] Cf. W. R. Smith, op. cit., p. 25: "If the slayer and slain are of different kindred groups a blood-feud at once arises, and the slain man may be avenged by any member of his own group on any member of the group of the slayer." Cf. too S. R. Driver, in E.B., ii, 1901, cols. 1746 f.; S. Nyström, Beduinentum und Jahwismus, 1946, pp. 11 f.

[4] Exod. 21: 12 makes it clear that the penalty is to be exacted of the slayer only, but does not specify that only the next-of-kin of the slain is required to exact it. The Deuteronomic law (Deut. 19: 6, 12), with its reference to "the avenger of blood" seems to imply that there is only one. 2 Sam. 14: 7, in an account of the time of David, represents "the whole family" as rising up, but this is in a case of fratricide, and therefore within a single family group, and the sequel again, 14: 11, speaks only of "the avenger of blood".

and while the next-of-kin's right to slay the homicide is still allowed, there are areas of sanctuary where it is disallowed,[1] while in the Priestly Law there is a further temporal limitation. For there the death of the high priest dissolves all blood feuds in cases of homicide, so that the homicide need no longer remain within the sanctuary.[2]

It is possible that there was a comparable limitation of the duty of raising an heir to the dead, so that what began as an obligation on the next-of-kin, or failing him on others in order of nearness of kin, was limited to the next-of-kin only, and to him only if he were a full brother.[3] The book of Ruth then preserves an older usage than the book of Deuteronomy prescribed.[4] This, of course, does not mean that the book of Ruth was written before the book of Deuteronomy, though neither does it exclude that possibility. It but means that it may preserve a true tradition of pre-Deuteronomic conditions. And this it ought to do, if it narrates things that happened centuries before Deuteronomy was written.

Another duty of the next-of-kin was the duty of buying property that was in danger of being lost to the family by being sold outside. The law prescribing this duty is found in Lev. 25 : 25 ff., and we find in Jer. 32 : 6 ff., an example of its operation. If the fortune of the original owner should improve, he was expected to recover the property by full purchase, and had the right thus to reclaim it even from an unrelated purchaser, while it was laid down that in any case it should revert to him in the year of jubilee. This law clearly rests on a conception of the wide solidarity of the family, comparable with that which lies behind the earliest form of blood revenge, and of the vicarious begetting of children to the dead. Moreover, the duty here laid down quite clearly comes into the question of Ruth's marriage.

---

[1] The altar in Exod. 21: 14; cf. 1 Kings 1: 50, 2: 28 ff. Deut. 19: 1 ff. appoints cities of refuge, and so Num. 35: 9 ff. The two latter passages lay down provisions for adjudication, so that only the homicide and not the murderer may be given benefit of sanctuary.

[2] Num. 35: 25, 28.

[3] J. A. Bewer (*A.J.S.L.*, xix, 1902–3, pp. 143 ff.) traces four stages in the development of the levirate.

[4] Driver and Miles (*The Assyrian Laws*, 1935, pp. 244 f.) hold that the book of Ruth represents an extension of levirate marriage from the brother-in-law to more distant kinsmen. So J. Morgenstern, *H.U.C.A.*, vii, 1930, pp. 175 f. This seems most improbable. It is far more likely that what was once wider became narrowed to the brother-in-law, just as we know that in later times it was rarely practised at all, and the Talmud hedges the practice round in every way (cf. Epstein, *op. cit.*, pp. 93 ff.).

Presumably the immediate brother was for all these purposes regarded as the normal next-of-kin. Upon him fell the duty of blood revenge; upon him fell the duty of buying in property in danger of being lost to the family; upon him fell the duty of begetting children to his deceased brother. If for any reason he declined any of these duties he incurred dishonour, and a more distant kinsman might then assume the duty.[1] Presumably the measure of stigma would be in direct ratio to the nearness of the relationship, and consequently custom would press less heavily on the more distant relations.[2] It is probable that in the absence of a brother the duty of blood revenge would be more pressing on a more distant relation than the duty of redeeming property, and there was no need to legislate for the case when the next-of-kin, whoever he was, should refuse. It is also probable that the duty of levirate marriage was regarded in historical times as the least pressing of the duties of the next-of-kin. Already when it first comes before us in the story of Judah, we find that it can be disregarded, and Tamar does not appeal to public opinion to bring pressure to bear on Judah, but resorts to her own wits. If it could be disregarded where a brother was concerned, it is improbable that a more distant next-of-kin who disregarded it would suffer much discredit, and it may well be that Deuteronomy's failure to prescribe any alternative to a brother-in-law who should decline the duty was but a simple recognition of the fact that in practice few more distant next-of-kin would accept the duty. Deuteronomy's limitation of the *gō'ēl* to the brother-in-law for this purpose, therefore, may have been less purposeful than a recognition that the custom was already beginning to fall into disfavour, and this is borne out by its prescription of the treatment of the brother-in-law who declines. Evidently refusal here was not regarded as something almost unthinkable.

That the measure of the stigma would be in direct ratio to the nearness of the relationship of the next-of-kin, even in the times when the duty was not regarded as limited to a brother-in-law, seems to me to give the true explanation of the difference of the ceremony of the drawing off of the shoe in Ruth and in Deuteronomy. In the latter the rejected widow publicly draws off the shoe of her brother-in-law and

[1] In the case of the redemption of property this is stated explicitly in Lev. 25: 45 f.

[2] Cf. H. Lesêtre (in Vigouroux' *Dictionnaire de la Bible*, iv, 1908, col. 215): "si les frères avaient à épouser la veuve de leur aîné défunt, l'obligation était étendue, à défaut de frères, aux parents les plus proches. Mais alors l'obligation s'imposait sans doute moins impérieusement."

spits in his face; in the book of Ruth the widow is not even present, and while there is the drawing off of the shoe, there is no spitting. It is sometimes suggested that the book of Ruth reflects a later, and less crude, age than Deuteronomy, when the ceremony had been softened somewhat. This seems to me very improbable. A custom later than Deuteronomy, and yet obsolete before the book of Ruth was written, and needing to be explained, would carry us down far for the composition of the book of Ruth.[1] I think it is much more reasonable to suppose that, long before the Deuteronomic age, the dishonour incurred by a more distant relation would be much less, and its lesser nature would be reflected in the modification of the ignominy of the ceremony.

The book of Ruth interprets the ceremony of the shoe as an ancient attestation in cases of redeeming and exchange, and commentators sometimes treat it as belonging to any contract for the sale of property.[2] It is possible that this was so, but the book of Ruth provides no evidence of it. Its evidence only concerns a case of "redeeming and exchange"—i.e., where a kinsman was involved, and where some measure of duty was being abandoned, and some right was being transferred to another. The drawing off of the shoe did not signify the purchase or sale of any property, for the kinsman neither bought nor sold anything. It was Boaz who bought of Naomi, and Boaz did not draw off a shoe in attestation of the purchase. The drawing off of the shoe here signified the abandonment of the obligation resting on the kinsman in respect of the property and in respect of Ruth, and it clearly opened the way for Boaz to do what he could not else have done.[3]

---

[1] L. Dennefeld (*Introduction à l'Ancien Testament*, 1934, p. 83) regards 4: 7 as a late gloss. The only reason for this supposition is apparently its embarrassment of the theory of the composition of the book in the age of David. In that, as in all matters, it is preferable to seek a theory which fits the facts rather than to bend the facts to a theory.

[2] Cf. A. R. S. Kennedy, *The Book of Ruth*, 1928, p. 57: "It is purely symbolical, representing the transfer of a right, or of property, from one person to another. In Scotland the conveyance of land used to be similarly ratified by the seller handing a piece of turf to the purchaser"; G. A. Cooke, *The Book of Ruth* (Camb.B.), 1918, p. 15: "When *property was transferred*, as in the present case, to take off the sandal and hand it to the person in whose favour the transfer is made gave a symbolic attestation to the act, and invested it with legal validity." But no property was transferred; it remained in the hands of Naomi at this stage.

[3] J. Morgenstern (*H.U.C.A.*, vii, 1930, p. 169; cf. pp. 170 f.) rightly emphasizes that the ceremony of the drawing off of the shoe in Deut. 25: 7–10 had as its purpose the restoration of freedom to the woman from the authority and control of her brother-in-law.

Parallels from India,[1] Egypt,[2] and the Nuzu texts[3] have been gathered to show that the shoe was a symbol of power[4] and of possession, and from Arabia[5] to match the association with a woman. The next-of-kin had not merely some duty towards Naomi and Ruth, however slight its measure might be owing to the distance of his relationship; he had also some rights and some power, until he voluntarily surrendered them.[6]

It is idle to speculate on the amount of the property Naomi had. It has been suggested that it may have been barely sufficient to maintain Naomi, and therefore insufficient to maintain Naomi and Ruth.[7] It may have been less or more than this. But it seems likely that the property was but a counter in the game, and that Boaz skilfully used it to secure his end. It is improbable that the property had been effectively occupied by Naomi since her return. For she arrived back at the beginning of the barley harvest, which had barely been gathered in by the time the story reaches its climax. It is unlikely that the usufruct of the property had been enjoyed by Elimelech and his heirs during the years of Naomi's sojourn in Moab, and probable that it had been

---

[1] Cf. the Ramayana, Book ii, Canto 112 (R. T. H. Griffith, *The Rámáyan of Válmíki*, 1915, pp. 265 f.), where Rama symbolizes his surrender of his authority to Bharat by giving him his sandals.

[2] Cf. J. Scheftelowitz, *A.R.W.*, xviii, 1915, p. 255: "Der Schuh gilt nämlich als Symbol des Rechts, des Besitzes. Schon bei den alten Aegyptern ist die Sandale das Symbol der Macht, der Herrschaft."

[3] Cf. E. R. Lacheman (*J.B.L.*, lvi, 1937, pp. 53 ff.), who explains Ruth 4: 7 f. by a Nuzu text, which shows that in a case of adoption the transfer of real estate was made more valid by lifting the foot from the property and placing the foot of the other party in it. Also E. A. Speiser (*B.A.S.O.R.*, No. 77, February 1940, pp. 15 ff.), who argues that shoes and garments were token payments to validate special transactions by lending them the appearance of normal business practice, and who applies this to Ruth 4: 7 and 1 Sam. 12: 3 (emended text), and also to Amos 2: 6.

[4] Cf. also M. Buttenwieser, *The Psalms*, 1938, pp. 75 f., where Ps. 60: 10 (E.V. 8)= Ps. 108: 10 (E.V. 9) is explained in terms of the shoe as a symbol of domination.

[5] Burckhardt (*op. cit.*, pp. 64 f.) says: "If a man permits his cousin to marry a lover, or if a husband divorces his runaway wife, he usually says, 'She was my slipper. I have cast her off'."

[6] Bewer (*A.J.S.L.*, xix, 1902–3, p. 144) says that the drawing off of the shoe in the case of the levirate signifies his renunciation of his right of inheritance. This is doubtful. As the next-of-kin he would seem to be the heir, but since it is his duty to beget an heir, he would forfeit the inheritance by performing the levirate duty. Since it is improbable that a man who refused to perform the duty would be allowed to have the inheritance, he would lose it either way—unless the levirate union was not fruitful. On the symbolism of the shoe, cf. further S. Nyström, *Beduinentum und Jahwismus*, 1946, pp. 57 f. Cf. also J. Nacht, "The Symbolism of the Shoe with special reference to Jewish Sources", *J.Q.R.*, N.S. vi, 1915–16, pp. 1–22.

[7] Cf. Burrows, *J.B.L.*, lix, 1940, p. 448.

farmed by other members of the family, who had enjoyed its fruits.[1] It may even have been that Naomi was unaware of her title to it, or that she would have been powerless to secure possession but for the support of Boaz. But Boaz knew of her legal right to it, and used it for his purpose. How she came to have this legal right escapes us, since we are not told elsewhere of the inheritance rights of widows without living children.[2] But that she had a title to an unspecified amount of property is quite clear.

The next-of-kin was entitled to the first refusal of this if Naomi for any reason was forced to sell; he was also the person who had the first responsibility to raise children by Ruth.[3] The two responsibilities were

[1] Burrows (*ibid.*, p. 447) suggests that the property had been held in pledge by a friend.

[2] Num. 27: 1–11 shows that daughters could inherit in Israel when there were no sons. In Arabia the rule was anciently otherwise (cf. W. R. Smith, *Kinship and Marriage*, 1903, p. 117). But we are nowhere told of the wife's title to inherit in Israel, though in 2 Kings 8: 1–6 we find a widow in possession—presumably in trust for her son. E. Neufeld (*op. cit.*, pp. 240 f.) suggests that Naomi may have been "merely the executrix or trustee for the regulation of the succession of the legal heirs". This is very improbable. Since there were no children of Elimelech, and even to Naomi a levirate marriage for herself or her daughters-in-law seemed out of the question, unless Naomi had some rights in the property the only heirs were Elimelech's relations. It is improbable that a woman who was, *ex hypothesi*, not herself one of the heirs would be given any authority over the legal heirs. Moreover, if this were all Naomi's right, why should the next-of-kin, who was then presumably the heir, he asked to buy the property of Naomi, and be ready to buy it before the question of taking Ruth arose? Clearly Naomi had some title of her own in the property. A. Jepsen (*T.S.K.*, cviii, 1937–38, pp. 419 ff.) had suggested that the property was received by Naomi from her own family, and merely administered by Elimelech during his lifetime, and since this would mean that the redeemer would have to be of Naomi's family he concludes that Naomi and Boaz were related. A similar view had been advanced by W. Caspari (*N.K.Z.*, xix, 1908, pp. 115 ff.). This view is unlikely, and is not supported by Ruth 4: 3, 9. J. A. Bewer (*A.J.S.L.*, xix, 1902–3, p. 148) finds in Naomi's possession of the property a "very late mode of inheritance". But we have no solid grounds for this assumption. Presumably a widow with minor sons administered the property for them until they were of age. It is unlikely that a widow who had reared sons to manhood would be treated with less honour. While it is improbable that a general title of widows to inherit prevailed in ancient Israel, we cannot assume from the book of Ruth that its author presumed such a title. It merely sets before us a widow of advanced age, who had fulfilled the function of motherhood, and who had outlived her husband and her married sons, inheriting her husband's property. To such a woman custom, which is the maker of law, may well have accorded rights. Nor can we exclude the possibility that Elimelech had willed the life interest in the property to her. For even where a woman had no title to inherit, a husband might have had power to will her a share in his estate. This was done in Nuzu texts (cf. E. A. Speiser, *A.A.S.O.R.*, x, 1930, p. 19: "The wife receives a life interest in whatever share is willed to her, the ultimate heirs being the sons") and its possibility here cannot be excluded.

[3] P. Joüon (*op. cit.*, p. 10) holds that Ruth only replaced Naomi because Naomi was too old to bear children. It is doubtless true that if Naomi had been younger the next-of-kin's first responsibility would have been to her and not to Ruth. But is is more doubt-

in themselves different. The one had relation to the estate of Elimelech; the other had relation to the widow of Elimelech's son. But since the same person was the nearest surviving relative of both, he could hardly accept the one without the other. Either he must play the part of the kinsman or he must not.

So far as the raising of children is concerned, there is no reference to property in the law of levirate marriage in Deuteronomy. But that is because the law did not contemplate the complication of a widowed mother-in-law as well. Where a man left property and a widow, the brother-in-law would not need to buy the property and marry the widow. He would marry the widow and the property would support her, until her child in due course became its heir, as the legal son of the deceased man. If the property were insufficient the brother-in-law might have to supplement it for her support, but he would not have to buy her property from her and then support her as well. No great financial obligations would rest on the brother-in-law therefore,[1] and there was no need to treat of the property in the law of levirate marriage. But when the kinsman was confronted at once with the problem of redeeming Naomi's land and marrying a penniless Ruth, he was unable to face it. These were two separate and distinct responsibilities which fell upon him, either of which he could have contemplated separately, but not both together.[2] Yet he could not choose one and reject the other.

It is clear that Ruth's kinsman would have been ready to discharge

---

ful if Joüon is right in saying that Ruth replaced Naomi legally just as Boaz replaced Elimelech. For Boaz replaced Elimelech as a blood relation, whereas Ruth was not of the same stock as Naomi. We must beware of linking the present case with one such as Leah's and Rachel's giving of their handmaids to bear for them. It was not as Naomi's handmaid that Ruth preserved the line of Elimelech, but as Mahlon's widow. Whoever was next-of-kin to Elimelech was also next-of-kin to Mahlon, but it was only in relation to the younger of these widows that levirate marriage could fulfil its purpose. P. Volz (Th.L.Z., xxvi, 1901, cols. 348 f.) with still less reason suggests that in the original form of the story Naomi married Boaz.

[1] M. Burrows (J.B.L., lix, 1940, p. 29) notes that there is no indication as to what happened to the dead man's estate when the brother-in-law refused to take the widow, and suggests the possibility that the brother-in-law was then the legal heir. It seems inconceivable that he would be rewarded for his dishonour of his brother by the possession of that brother's estate.

[2] Burrows (ibid., p. 449) does not seem to me sufficiently to distinguish between these two things. He observes that Boaz "acquires her along with the field, which he purchases as redeemer". But Ruth was no more part of the property than was Orpah, and she is nowhere spoken of as property to be exploited by a purchaser, but as one to whom the next-of-kin owed a duty; moreover, his "possession" of her was for one purpose and one purpose only—viz., the raising of seed to the dead.

his duty to her if it could have been done without loss, but he could not afford to "spoil his inheritance". Similarly he was prepared to buy Naomi's field, if that were all, since he would not thereby be impoverished. He would have to find the value of the land, but he would receive the land against it. No heir could be born to Elimelech to reclaim the land in due course, for Naomi was now childless, and any child that Ruth might have borne subsequently could not be regarded as Elimelech's heir unless born from a levirate marriage. But if he bought the land and also made Ruth a mother, he would be impoverished. For the land would revert to Ruth's child, as the heir of Elimelech, and he would be left with nothing in return for his outlay on Naomi's land.

It has been suggested that the duty of levirate marriage only fell on an unmarried brother, and that it never involved bigamy.[1] This is highly improbable. The custom goes back to a pre-monogamous state of society, where no problem of this kind would arise.[2] Moreover, it is probable that levirate marriage was not normally thought of as marriage in the full sense. The woman was still considered as the wife of the dead man, and the brother was merely a substitute for him for a single purpose. Again, levirate marriage had reference only to a single birth. The brother-in-law had completed his duty when he had provided the dead with a single heir.[3] The Deuteronomic law says that the first-born reckoned as the heir of the dead man, and it is sometimes supposed that any succeeding children reckoned as those of the actual

[1] So H. Lesêtre (loc. cit., col. 216): "Il est clair que le frère déjà marié était exempt du lévirat, autrement la loi eût prescrit la bigamie." Cf. Lattey, op. cit., p. xxii. With this contrast the view of Cruveilhier (R.B., xxxiv, 1925, p. 544): "Le Deutéronome ne specifie aucunement que le beau-frère doit être célibataire. Un tel silence autorise à croire que le lévir pouvait être marié. Nous pouvons même ajouter que généralement il devait l'être, le mariage étant dans l'antiquité la condition normale de tous les adultes. On conçoit que pour le but à la fois élevé et pieux de procurer des enfants issus d'un sang fraternel, on n'ait point hésité à faire une brèche au principe monogame." It is doubtful, however, if Cruveilhier is right in speaking of a monogamic rule at this time. G. Parrinder, The Bible and Polygamy, 1950, p. 23, says that among the Hebrews levirate marriage was a frequent cause of polygamy. This may have been so, but we have no evidence of it. The cases of levirate marriage recorded in the Old Testament are rare, and there is no proof of polygamy where they occur.

[2] A. Alt (Ursprünge des israelitischen Rechts, 1934, pp. 12–33) argues that the casuistic laws of Israel were of Canaanite origin. The Deuteronomic formulation of the law of levirate marriage is probably so far modified from any assumed Canaanite original that it is doubtful how far its form can be held to be Canaanite, but that the custom of levirate marriage had its roots in pre-Israelite practice is almost certain.

[3] Cf. the Indian practice cited above. Burrows (B.A.S.O.R., No. 77, February 1940, pp. 5 f.) thinks the Hebrew practice was differentiated from the Indian in this respect. To the present writer this seems unlikely.

father.[1] This is very unlikely. Certainly if the brother-in-law were previously unmarried and the widow became his full wife, so that her first child was also his first child and the fruit of a legal marriage, it is almost unthinkable that such a child would not be his own heir. When the law of Deuteronomy speaks of the firstborn child it is not implied that the union would normally continue and that there would be other children who would not take the name of the dead man, but rather that levirate marriage was only concerned with a first birth.[2]

If, now, Elimelech's next-of-kin were a married man with a family of his own,[3] it is easy to see how his own inheritance would be spoiled. He would have to use part of what ought to become his own children's inheritance to buy Naomi's property, and then restore that property to Ruth's child.[4] It may be said that any addition to a man's family would reduce the patrimony of his existing children. Yet that did not ordinarily deter men from accepting family responsibilities amongst a people where a large family was regarded as one of the supreme blessings of life.[5] But here it is a case of a child who would not be reckoned as the real father's own, and the mulcting of his own children's estate for one who would be regarded as the heir of another. To beget children by Ruth without marring his estate the kinsman could have considered; to buy Naomi's land without taking Ruth he could also have considered. It was the bringing of these two things into relation with one another that made both impossible for him. And it was here that Boaz's resource became apparent.

[1] Cf. Lattey, *op. cit.*, p. xxvi. Lattey assumes that in levirate marriage the widow became the full legal wife of the kinsman, but that the first son was reckoned not as his, but as the dead man's, while succeeding sons were regarded as the issue of the second husband. If the woman had but one son by her second husband, this would mean that the latter would be left without legal issue, although he had a child born in legal wedlock. I cannot think this is in any way probable, and it is not supported by the book of Ruth, as will appear below.

[2] Where the levirate bridegroom was not previously married and the widow became his full wife, one would expect the first son to be both the real father's heir and also the legal heir of the deceased, while any succeeding children would be reckoned to the real father alone. Where, however, the levirate bridegroom already had children the case would be different, and an institution whose only *raison d'être* in Israel was to provide an heir for the dead would hardly function beyond the range of its purpose. It is not without significance to observe here that Judah, who was not himself childless, had no further relations with Tamar, after she had once become pregnant.

[3] So Josephus, *Antiquities*, v, 334 (V, ix, 4); also Targum on Ruth 4: 6. So, too, Morgenstern, *H.U.C.A.*, vii, 1930, pp. 174 f.

[4] Cf. J. Fischer, in *Echt. B.*, Lieferung 10, 1950, *Rut*, p. 13: "Das gekaufte Land würde dem Sohn aus dieser Ehe zufallen, aber seiner eigenen Familie verloren gehen. So verzichtet er auf beides, auf das Feld und auf die Heirat."

[5] Cf. Pedersen, *Israel I–II*, 1926, pp. 204 ff.

Neufeld has suggested that from the very beginning Naomi set herself to secure Boaz for Ruth.[1] This is certainly not borne out by the book of Ruth, where it is said that it was Ruth's suggestion that she should go gleaning, and that it was by chance that she lit upon the piece of ground that Boaz's men were reaping. It was not until she returned home and reported to Naomi where she had gleaned that she even knew that Boaz was akin to her late husband, and it was only when Ruth reported the kindness of Boaz that Naomi thought of making a claim on him. Then Ruth was sent to claim the cover of his skirt. Again wider parallels are adduced to explain the symbolism of this act,[2] but it is quite clear that it implied both protection and union.

It is surprising that Naomi did not know at this stage that there was a nearer kinsman,[3] but Boaz knew, and knew also that great caution was necessary if he were to have Ruth. It is clear that he was attracted by her, and flattered that she should come to him. But it is also clear that the nearer kinsman had not alone a prior duty, but prior rights. And if Boaz had responded to Ruth's approach before he were given the first refusal, he would have had grounds of complaint, and perhaps worse. It will be remembered that, in the case of Tamar, Judah proposed that she should be burnt as an adulteress.[4] Although she was a widow, living in her own father's house, she was still regarded as the

---

[1] *Op. cit.*, p. 37 n. Neufeld says "it is clearly indicated that the fact that Ruth went to glean on the field was only the means employed by her to introduce herself to the notice of Boaz . . . in the hope of subsequent marriage with him". He neglects to say where this is "clearly" indicated.

[2] In the Arabic parallels to the levirate marriage above noted, the kinsman established his claim to the widow by throwing his garment over her. J. Lewy (*R.H.R.*, cx, 1934, pp. 31 ff.) cites Assyrian evidence to show that the skirt of the garment stood for the personality of the wearer, and especially for his honour. Hence the symbolic action here invited would signify that Boaz extended the cover of his position and person to her. Cf. Deut. 23: 1 (E.V. 22: 30), Ezek. 16: 8.

[3] W. E. Staples (*A.J.S.L.*, liv, 1937, pp. 62 ff.; cf. L. Pettibone Smith, *I.B.*, ii, 1953, p. 830b) maintains that Naomi knew that Boaz was not her next-of-kin. He translates Ruth 2: 20 "he is not our *go'el*", instead of "he is one of our kinsmen", while Ruth 3: 12 becomes "I am not really your *go'el*". Despite the ingenuity with which these renderings are defended, they are not natural, and no attempt is made to convert Ruth 3: 9 into anything other than a simple statement of Ruth to Boaz that he was her *gō'ēl*. The sincerity of Naomi and Ruth must then be impugned in the interests of these unnatural renderings, and the view is proposed that Ruth's visit to Boaz was to force the next-of-kin to take up his obligations or to renounce his rights. How a visit which had to be kept from his knowledge could force him to do anything is discreetly not shown. The story shows how his hand was forced precisely by suppressing the knowledge of this.

[4] Gen. 38: 24. P. Cruveilhier (*R.B.*, xxxiv, 1925, p. 527) describes Tamar's conduct as incest and a crime. That it was such by the standards of the time is most improbable. In many lands where levirate marriage is found the father-in-law takes the widow, and if in pre-Deuteronomic days the duty was not restricted to the brother-in-law, but

wife of Judah's son, and Judah had power over her. Her defence was that she had gone to the next-but-one-of-kin, since the next-of-kin was withheld from her. But for Ruth to go to the next-but-one-of-kin without first seeking the next-of-kin was to commit a serious mistake, and to infringe his rights. When the Mishnah says that a deceased brother's wife acquires her freedom by *ḥaliṣah* or by the death of her brother-in-law,[1] it implies that to give herself to another before the loosing of the shoe was to commit adultery. In view of the case of Tamar this is probably right, and it would then imply that, in the days before the duty was limited in law or in practice to a brother-in-law, the next-of-kin must first release her or he could charge her with adultery. Presumably this was why Boaz cautioned Ruth to slip home quietly and very early in the morning and to make sure that no one knew whither she had been.[2] If the nearer kinsman had had any idea

extended to the next-of-kin, or failing him the next but one, it is hard to see where incest or crime comes in. This does not mean that we need go all the way with Gunkel in lauding Tamar [*Die Urgeschichte und die Patriarchen* (*S.A.T.*, I, i), 1911, pp. 256 f.].

[1] *Kiddushin*, i, 1.

[2] H. G. May (*J.R.A.S.*, 1939, pp. 75 ff.) holds that Ruth's night interview with Boaz took place at the Bethlehem high place, and that relations between them occurred on that occasion. He finds some evidence of this in the six omers of barley which Boaz gave to Ruth, which he connects with the hire of a sacred prostitute, and believes that our present text has been purged. This reduces the insistence on the importance of seeing that no one knew of Ruth's visit to nonsense, since *ex hypothesi* Boaz would not be the only person celebrating the festal harvest rites at the shrine. It is unnecessary to rewrite a story which is consistent with itself in order to turn it into the account of something which is imposed upon it. In the same way it is entirely without evidence when May observes that "Naomi and Ruth, as the source of the Davidic line, are represented according to the pattern of the mother-goddess who gives birth to a son who rules as divine king and brings prosperity to the land". Of this there is no hint whatever in the book, and it is quite gratuitous to read it into it. Similarly with the further statement that "this historical tradition of David's ancestry proclaimed the divine character of the Hebrew kingship by the mythological patterns which formed its literary structure". W. E. Staples, who also quite gratuitously imposes a cultic interpretation on the book, denies that it has anything at all to do with David. He eliminates every reference to David as secondary, and assigns such historical basis as the book possesses to the period of Nebuchadrezzar. Elimelech is here made the dying god and Naomi becomes the mother-goddess, whose devotee, or *ḳedeshah*, Ruth is (*A.J.S.L.*, liii, 1936-37, pp. 145 ff.). To the present writer this seems completely fanciful, and the evidence offered of the flimsiest. The etymology of the name Bethlehem cannot establish that every incident that happened in the town must be cultic; nor can the etymology of the names of Elimelech and Naomi prove that this is a cultic story. Yet it is on such "evidence" that Staples relies. On such principles much cultic significance could be found in the genealogies in the early chapters of 1 Chron. The unnamed kinsman is useless to Staples, and he therefore regards him as negligible, and says he adds nothing to the story. This neatly evades the issue why a cultic text should be burdened with what is cultically meaningless. Actually the nearer kinsman is anything but unimportant in the story. A. Weiser (*Introduction to the Old Testament*, E.Tr., 1961, p. 304) says the view of Staples is "mere conjecture without any

that Boaz wanted to marry Ruth, he might have been ready to exploit the situation. And Boaz knew enough of human nature to guess what this might have meant. The kinsman might have needed inducing to renounce his claim, or even to withhold a charge of adultery against Ruth for what had already happened, so that his children's patrimony might have been not alone unimpaired, but substantially improved! Also Ruth was in real danger, and it needed all the resource of Boaz to cope with the situation. He kept his own desire for Ruth completely in the background, and appeared primarily as the economic benefactor of Naomi. Indeed, it was his masterstroke to introduce the question of the land into the matter at all. Naomi may well not have thought of selling, but Boaz perceived that by bringing in the property he could place the next-of-kin in a real dilemma. And thus he manœuvred him into a renunciation of his rights and duties,[1] and then dramatically assumed what the other had declined.

David has recently argued that the book of Ruth fails to understand levirate marriage.[2] He relies on Ruth 1 : 12 f., where Naomi says: "Turn again, my daughters, go your way; for I am too old to have a husband. If I should say, I have a hope, if I should even have a husband to-night, and should also bear sons; would ye therefore tarry till they were grown?" David observes that if Naomi had married another husband, any sons she could have borne would not have been Elimelech's sons, and therefore they could not have been looked to to fill the role of brothers-in-law in connexion with levirate marriage.[3] This is to press the passage too far. All that Naomi is saying is that it is beyond the bounds of possibility for her to provide them with substitutes for their dead husbands. She herself is already past child-bearing, and even though she were not, her children could be of no use to them, since they could not afford to wait so many years. Even if Elimelech had

reliable and convincing substance". The cultic interpretation of the book is rejected also by R. H. Pfeiffer (*Introduction to the Old Testament*, 1941, p. 719), B. Vellas (*The Book of Ruth and its Purpose*, 1954, pp. 9 f.), and J. de Fraine (*Rechters-Ruth* (B.O.T.), 1956, p. 140a).

[1] J. Morgenstern (*H.U.C.A.*, vii, 1930, p. 169), after saying (in my view incorrectly) that Ruth 4: 7 shows that the drawing off of the shoe was the symbol of the conclusion of a transfer of property, rightly observes: "By the performance of this particular ceremony . . . she (i.e. the widow) had acquired her freedom and full control of her person from her brother-in-law; no longer did he have any authority over her, but she was now free to dispose of herself as she might choose."

[2] *Het Huwelijk van Ruth*, 1941, pp. 7 f.; and *O.T.S.*, i, 1941–42, p. 58.

[3] It is possible that some reference to the story of Tamar lies in the suggestion of waiting for them to be grown up. Tamar had to wait some years for the brother-in-law who was then denied her; but to wait for unborn sons would be unthinkable!

been still alive, this would have been so. How much more when he was dead, and when to Naomi's years there was added the further handicap of widowhood, and when therefore no levirate fathers of their children were even imaginable! Naomi is not implying that any children she might possibly have borne as the result of a new marriage contract with a husband unrelated to Elimelech could have been looked to, but stressing the complete impossibility of her providing them with fathers of their children. At this moment the idea of a levirate marriage for either herself or her daughters-in-law does not occur to her as a practical proposition. For her it was out of the question by reason of her age, as well as by reason of the fact that she knew of no likely relation, and even though it was not out of the question, it could be of no use to her daughters-in-law. For them, too, she does not contemplate a levirate marriage with a more distant relation than a brother-in-law, and it is obvious that though such a union was possible, it was most uncommon. Similarly the idea of such a thing did not occur to the next-of-kin until Boaz raised it.

By most who have treated of this theme Lev. 18 : 16 and 20 : 21 are brought into the discussion. Not seldom they are cited to show that by the later law levirate marriage was regarded as incest. Thus Bewer says that Lev. 20 : 21 was the final abrogation of the levirate.[1] More usually, however, it is held that that verse expresses the general rule, while Deut. 25 : 5–10 express the special exception.[2] On this view marriage with a sister-in-law is forbidden if she has been divorced, or if the brother has left living issue; it is ordained if he has died childless. It is not certain, indeed, that Lev. 20 : 21 is thinking of marriage at all, and Bertholet maintains that it deals only with extra-marital relations.[3] While some of the provisions of the chapter certainly have to do with extra-marital relations, it is doubtful if this is so here.[4] But while later practice may have excluded marriage with a sister-in-law in general, whether it continued to allow levirate marriage for the specific and limited purpose of raising seed to a childless brother or not, we must beware of confusing levirate marriage ordinarily with full marriage. Apparently it neither required nor excluded full marriage, for whereas in the case of Tamar and Judah there was no marriage, in the case of Ruth and Boaz there clearly was. And these are the only two examples

[1] Cf. *A.J.S.L.*, xix, 1902–3, p. 144.
[2] So Lattey, *op. cit.*, p. xxix; Epstein, *op. cit.*, pp. 93 f. Cf. also B. Wechsler, in *Jüdische Zeitschrift*, i, 1862, pp. 253 ff.
[3] *Deuteronomium*, 1898, p. 78.
[4] Cf. Paterson, in Hastings's *D.B.*, iii, 1900, p. 269b.

of marriage of this type that we have in the Old Testament. While Tamar's connexion with Judah was legitimate for the purpose of obtaining offspring for her husband, it became illegitimate when it had achieved its purpose, and Tamar certainly did not become the full wife of Judah. There is no evidence to show that in the case of the actual brother-in-law it either must have been full marriage, or ordinarily was such. Where it was such it must have functioned far beyond the purpose of providing a single heir for the deceased, yet that is the sole justification of the practice of which we have any record in the Old Testament. Yet in the case of Boaz and Ruth it would seem that there was full marriage. While this again was not strictly marriage with a brother-in-law, we cannot say that in such a case full marriage would have been excluded. Indeed, if in the case of a brother-in-law such marriage would have been excluded, it is hard to see how Ruth's marriage could have been brought within the framework of the levirate custom at all. The scanty evidence we have thus suggests that we ought to recognize a much greater degree of looseness than some writers allow. Levirate marriage was not in early times limited to a brother-in-law; it neither required nor excluded full marriage; it neither required nor excluded the unmarried condition of the levirate partner.

Finally, we come to Boaz himself. He was obviously a man of advancing years. He occupied a position of standing, and was a man of substance, yet he was flattered that Ruth should offer herself to him instead of seeking to attract one of the younger men of the village. Ruth was apparently an attractive young lady, who might be expected to secure a husband without difficulty, and without resorting to anything of the nature of levirate marriage. It was a mark of her loyalty to the family of her late husband that she preferred to bear an heir to Mahlon, rather than to remarry without relation to Mahlon's family, and a compliment to Boaz that she should prefer him to a younger man.

I think it very probable that Boaz was childless. It is improbable that he was a bachelor, since bachelors do not seem to have been common in Israel, and it is apparent that Boaz was well past the usual age of marriage. It is possible that his wife was dead, though the story is laid in an age when polygamy was common enough. But if Boaz was childless, much is clear that were else obscure. When Ruth bears a child Naomi is congratulated, and the child is treated as her child—i.e., as the child of her son Mahlon. This is in full accord with what Boaz had said to the nearer kinsman, when he had reminded him that in buying the field he must also take Ruth,[1] and "raise up the name of the dead upon his inheritance". Ruth's child was manifestly regarded by a legal fiction as Mahlon's. Yet in the genealogy at the end of the book Ruth's child is just as clearly reckoned as the child of Boaz. It is because of this that it is often argued that the genealogy is a later appendix, presenting a point of view in conflict with the preceding narrative.[2] But this is not convincing. If the appendix is really in conflict with the story, it is surprising that the writer who added it was not aware of it. But is it? If Boaz had no child hitherto, then Ruth's first child would be the child of Mahlon by a legal fiction, and also the child of Boaz by actual paternity; and if Boaz had taken Ruth to be his legal wife, and had not merely played the part of kinsman, then the same child would be his heir as well as Mahlon's. Hence, not alone could Boaz afford to accept what the other kinsman had been forced to decline, since Boaz was a man of substance whose patrimony could easily carry the new responsibility; but also there would be no diminishing of that patrimony for any other son, since in Ruth's son the line of Mahlon and Boaz would unite, and he would be the heir of both. There is thus no

[1] Ruth 4: 5. Most editors recognize that the present Hebrew text (="thou must buy it also of Ruth the Moabitess") needs to be corrected by the change of a single letter, to yield "also Ruth the Moabitess thou must acquire". Cf. 4: 9. Th. C. Vriezen (O.T.S., v, 1948, pp. 80–88) rejects this correction and renders the text (p. 81): "What day thou buyest the field of the hand of Naomi, then I maintain with regard to Ruth the Moabitess, the wife of the dead, the rights to raise up the name of the dead upon his inheritance." Vriezen argues that Boaz did not charge the nearer kinsman with the levirate task, but assumed it for himself. He was merely concerned with the settlement of the inheritance of Elimelech. This is quite unconvincing. It offers no explanation of Boaz's insistence that Ruth's night visit should be kept secret, and robs his reference to a nearer kinsman, before any question of the property arose, of any point. Vriezen himself argues that even if the nearer kinsman had bought the property it would have reverted to any child Ruth should bear to Boaz. It is not clear therefore how Boaz secured the property for Ruth's child by needlessly buying it. Moreover, if he could have married Ruth by a levirate marriage, as Vriezen argues, without the consent of the nearer kinsman, it is not clear why it was necessary for Naomi to sell the property at all. Boaz was a man of substance, and since in the event he maintains both Naomi and Ruth there was no need for any sale of the property to him to ensure this. Vriezen rightly says (p. 88): "It is quite impossible to think that Boaz could try to oblige the other $g\bar{o}$'$\bar{e}l$ to marry Ruth." On the contrary, by skilfully bringing the property into the matter he was forcing the nearer kinsman to renounce his rights and his duties. The property was a counter in the plan. To suppose that the nearer kinsman was offered the property, but warned that Boaz did not intend to give him any chance of having Ruth, is to divorce rights and duties. On my view, which seems to me more natural, it was the clever linking of these together which extricated Ruth from the awkward and dangerous position in which she had placed herself by her visit to the threshing floor.

[2] Cf. supra. That the genealogy was appended by another hand is likely enough, but not on this ground.

conflict on this view between the appendix and the preceding verses.

Nor does the case rest there alone. For even without the appendix this view is supported. When Boaz announced his intention to buy the property and to take Ruth, the people in the gate who witnessed his contract said: "The Lord make the woman that is come into thine house like Rachel and Leah, which two did build the house of Israel; . . . and let thy house be like the house of Perez, whom Tamar bare unto Judah, of the seed which the Lord shall give thee of this young woman." What could be clearer evidence that any child that Ruth should bear was regarded in advance as belonging to the family of Boaz? Here then, in the story itself, and not alone in the appendix, Ruth's child appears as belonging both to the family of Mahlon and to the family of Boaz.[1] There is no need to deal surgically with the text to eliminate either of these points of view. Their combination would be both natural and inevitable if Boaz were childless when he married Ruth, so that she was at once his full wife and the widow of a kinsman, whom he was piously serving by taking into his home.

[1] This disproves such a statement as that of W. R. Smith (*E.B.*, iv, 1907, col. 4169): "That the genealogy was borrowed from Chronicles and added to Ruth by a later hand seems certain, for the author of Ruth clearly recognizes that Obed was legally the son of Mahlon, *not of Boaz*" (italics mine). Cf. Burrows (*J.B.L.*, lix, 1940, p. 450): "*Obed* is not regarded as the son of Boaz except in the genealogy"; also Joüon (*op. cit.*, p. 96): "Dans la seconde généalogie, les mots *Boaz engendra 'Obed*, ne sont pas dans l'esprit du récit, car ainsi le nom d'Elimèlek ne serait plus 'prononcé en Israel'." Morgenstern (*H.U.C.A.*, vii, 1930, p. 177) would delete Ruth 4: 11b, 12, as well as the genealogy at the end of the chapter, but no reason for this is offered except its supposed conflict with the point of view of the rest of the book. He thus takes the opposite course to Bewer, who, as above noted, deletes as secondary every reference to levirate marriage for Ruth, in order to leave her child as the heir of Boaz and not of Mahlon, while F. Dijkema (*N.T.T.*, xxiv, 1935, pp. 111 ff.) holds that Ruth 4: 17b is an interpolation, and so abolishes both Obed and David from the book. It seems more satisfactory to seek a solution which can accommodate all the facts presented to us, rather than to impose our theory upon the facts by violence. In the present case such a theory does not seem hard to attain, and there is the less justification for violence.

THE INTERPRETATION OF THE
SONG OF SONGS

6

The Interpretation of the Song of Songs

THERE is no book of the Old Testament which has found greater variety of interpretation than the Song of Songs. Nor can it be said that there is any real agreement amongst scholars to-day as to the origin and significance of the work.[1] In the title it is ascribed to Solomon, but no weight can be attached to that tradition, and writers of all schools now recognize it to be without authority. It is generally believed, however, that it was owing to the fact that it was wrongly ascribed to Solomon that it secured its place in the Canon of Scripture, and owing to the allegorical interpretation it received that it maintained itself there. We know that in the first century A.D. there was some disagreement amongst the Rabbis as to whether it ought to have a place in the Canon,[2] and there is preserved for us the opinion expressed by Rabbi Akiba, that "the world itself was not worth the day on which this book was given to Israel".[3] The very extravagance

---

[1] Cf. Westminster Assembly's *Annotations upon all the Books of the Old and New Testament*, 2nd ed., 1651, i, Introduction to the annotations on the Song of Solomon (the pages are not numbered): "It is not unknown to the learned, what the obscurity and darknesse of this Book hath ever been accounted, and what great variety of Interpreters, and Interpretations have indeavoured to clear it, but with so ill successe many times, that they have rather increased, then removed the cloud."

[2] Solomon Zeitlin (*An Historical Study of the Canonization of the Hebrew Scriptures*, 1933, pp. 10 f.) accepts the statement of Rabbi Akiba (Mishnah, *Yadaim*, iii, 5) that there had never been any dispute about the Song of Songs, and says that according to everyone it was canonical. He interprets the difference of opinion ascribed in the same passage to Rabbi Judah and Rabbi Jose to mean that according to the latter the Song was unanimously accepted, while Ecclesiastes was rejected after a dispute, whereas according to the former Ecclesiastes was unanimously rejected, while the Song was accepted only after a discussion. It is not clear why he should take the same Hebrew word to mean in the one case *rejected* after a dispute, and in the other *accepted* after a discussion, but in any case it is obvious that some must have challenged the canonicity of the Song. Moreover, even though, as he supposes (p. 73), Rabbi Akiba's words imply that the Song was received into the Canon prior to the destruction of the Temple, the fact that a judgement of Rabbi Akiba on the issue should be preserved implies that in his day it was still a living issue, and there was some uneasiness about the Song.

[3] Mishnah, *Yadaim*, iii, 5. Cf. Origen (Migne, *P.G.*, xiii, 1862, col. 37): "Quomodo didicimus per Mosen quædam esse non solum sancta, sed et Sancta sanctorum, et alia non tantum Sabbata, sed et Sabbata sabbatorum; sic nunc docemur scribente Salomone

of this utterance is perhaps an indication of the depth of the division of opinion, and it may well be that the ascription to Solomon turned the scale.

There is little reason to doubt that what caused some to urge its exclusion from the Canon was the sensuousness of its images, and its apparently erotic character. Indeed, we are told that the same Rabbi Akiba pronounced a curse on those who treated this book as a common ditty and sang passages from it at banquets.[1] Clearly, there were some who so treated the Song, and who thereby brought it into discredit.

(1)

How, then, was its credit restored? By the Rabbis it was interpreted allegorically,[2] and this is the first type of interpretation at which we must look, apart from the plain erotic interpretation, to which we shall

esse quædam non solum cantica, sed et Cantica canticorum. Beatus quidem is qui ingreditur sancta, sed beatior qui ingreditur Sancta sanctorum. Beatus qui sabbata sabbatizat, sed beatior qui sabbatizat sabbatorum Sabbata. Beatus similiter et is qui intellegit cantica et canit ea: nemo quippe nisi in solemnitatibus canit: sed multo beatior ille qui canit Cantica canticorum." With this we may compare the utterance of a modern author, D. Buzy (in *Mémorial Lagrange*, 1940, p. 162): "Si on le comprend, on ne peut s'empêcher de la proclamer le chef d'œuvre de la mystique de tous les temps, et nous espérons l'avoir montré, un chef d'œuvre de poésie pure, peut-être aussi de toutes les littératures le plus parfait et le plus beau." Cf. A. Feuillet, *R.B.*, lxviii, 1961, p. 36: "Quelques commentateurs, au nombre desquels nous nous rangeons, continuent de regarder ce poème comme un des sommets de l'Ancien Testament. . . . Le Cantique tire les conséquences ultimes de la foi en un Dieu d'amour, qui a choisi librement Israël." Cf. also D. Buzy, in *Le Sainte Bible*, ed. by L. Pirot and A. Clamer, vi, 1946, p. 296: "Le Cantique est le IVe Évangile de l'Ancien Testament."

[1] Tosephta, *Sanhedrin*, xii, and T.B., *Sanhedrin*, 101a. Cf. Strack-Billerbeck, *Kommentar zum Neuen Testament aus Talmud und Midrasch*, i, 1922, p. 516. The word which I have rendered "banquets" is frequently given as "taverns". Strack-Billerbeck render by "Hochzeitshäuser", and so A. Lods (*R.H.R.*, lxxxii, 1920, pp. 221 f.), who objects to the rendering "banquet" and thinks the meaning is "the house in which a wedding was being celebrated". Similarly, U. Cassuto, *G.S.A.I.*, N.S. i, 1925–28, p. 37. This limitation of the meaning is not necessary, and this passage cannot fairly be used to support the Wetzstein-Budde view of the Song.

[2] It is interesting to observe that one of the Chinese Classics, the *Shih Ching*, or *Book of the Odes*, similarly contains poems for whose preservation we are indebted to the allegorical interpretation that was given to them. Thus the ode (Part I, Book vii, Ode 13), which is rendered by Legge (*The Chinese Classics*, iv, Part 1, 1871, p. 140; cf. S. Couvreur, *Cheu King*, 3rd ed., 1934, p. 96 and B. Karlgren, *The Book of Odes*, 1950, p. 57): "If you, Sir, think kindly of me, I will hold up my lower garments and cross the Tsin. If you do not think of me, is there no other person (to do so)? You foolish, foolish fellow! If you, Sir, think kindly of me I will hold up my lower garments, and cross the Wei. If you do not think of me, is there no other gentleman (to do so)? You foolish, foolish fellow!" or more spiritedly by H. A. Giles (*History of Chinese Literature*, 1923, p. 14):

return. We find a trace of this allegorical interpretation in the Mishnah, where 3 : 11 is quoted, "Go forth, ye daughters of Zion, and behold King Solomon with the crown wherewith his mother crowned him in the day of his espousals, and in the day of the gladness of his heart", and then the strange comment is added, "*In the day of his espousals—* this is the giving of the Law; *and in the day of the gladness of his heart—* this is the building of the Temple."[1] Other traces of an allegorical interpretation are found in the Talmud,[2] and in the Targum[3] the text

> "If you will love me dear, my lord,
> I'll pick up my skirts and cross the ford,
> But if from your heart you turn me out—
> Well, you're not the only man about,
> You silly, silly, silliest lout!"

is thus commented on by Legge: "The Preface understands the piece as the expression of the wish of the people of Ch'ing that some great state would interfere, to settle the struggle between the marquis Hwuh and his brother Tuh. Hwuh succeeded to his father in 700 B.C.; and that same year he was driven from the State by his brother Tuh. In 696, Tuh had to flee, and Hwuh recovered the earldom, but before the end of the year Tuh was again master of a strong city in Ch'ing, which he held till Hwuh was murdered in 694. The old school holds that Tuh is "the madman of all mad youths" in the fifth line; but how an interpretation of the other four lines, according to the view of the Preface, was ever thought of as the *primary* idea intended in them, I cannot well conceive." That allegorical interpretations are very ancient, indeed, is clear from a passage in the *Lun Yü*, or *Confucian Analects* (Book iii, chap. viii), where the reference is to a poem which did not secure admission to the *Shih Ching*, which Legge translates (*The Chinese Classics*, i, 2nd ed., 1893, p. 157): "Tsze-hsia asked, saying, 'What is the meaning of the passage —The pretty dimples of her artful smile! The well-defined black and white of her eye! The plain ground for the colours?' The Master said, 'The business of laying on the colours follows the preparation of the plain ground.' 'Ceremonies then are a subsequent thing?' The Master said, 'It is Shang who can bring out my meaning. Now I can begin to talk about the odes with him'." W. E. Soothill's rendering of the quoted Ode (*The Analects of Confucius*, 1910, p. 191) may be appended:

> "As she artfully smiles
> What dimples appear!
> Her bewitching eyes
> Show their colours so clear,
> Ground spotless and candid
> For tracery splendid!"

[1] Mishnah, *Ta'anith*, iv, 8.

[2] P. Vulliaud (*Le Cantique des Cantiques d'après la tradition juive*, 1925, pp. 53–59) quotes a number of passages.

[3] For a modern edition of the Targum, with supralinear vocalization, see R. H. Melamed, "The Targum to Canticles, according to six Yemen MSS.", in *J.Q.R.*, xii, 1921–1922, pp. 57–117, and for a translation into English see H. Gollancz, *The Targum to "the Song of Songs"*, etc., 1908. Vulliaud (*op. cit.*, pp. 67–103) has translated it into French, and W. Riedel (*Die Auslegung des Hohenliedes in der jüdischen Gemeinde und der griechischen Kirche*, 1898, pp. 9–41), into German.

is expanded by a running commentary, which interprets the whole Song in terms of Israel's history, taking it as an allegory, which under the figures of human love set forth the story of God's dealings with His chosen people.

Along this path Rabbinical scholarship pressed, and ingenuity was strained to find the most unlooked-for of meanings.[1] Thus the verse "A sachet of myrrh is my beloved to me, Between my breasts it lies" (1 : 13) was found by Rashi[2] and Ibn Ezra[3] to be a reference to the Shekinah, between the cherubim that stood over the Ark; the Targum supposed "Come, O my beloved, be thou like a gazelle, Or a young hart on the spicy mountains" (2 : 17) to be a reference to Mount Moriah, and the two breasts of 4 : 5, 7 : 4 (E.V. 3) to be the two Messiahs, ben David and ben Ephraim, while Moses ibn Tibbon[4] saw Moses and Aaron in the two breasts; Rashi thought "On my bed by night I sought him whom my soul loveth, I sought him but I found him not" (3 : 1) referred to the years of wandering in the wilderness; pseudo-Sa'adia[5] believed "Black am I but comely, O daughters of Jerusalem" (1 : 5) to mean that Israel was black by reason of the making of the Golden Calf, but comely by reason of receiving the

---

[1] S. B. Freehof (*J.Q.R.*, N.S. xxxix, 1948–49, pp. 397–402) has recently argued that the whole book is a series of dream experiences, and that the Rabbis knew this, and hence resorted to the allegorical interpretation because dreams were believed to be the medium of divine communication.

[2] The commentary of Rashi may be found in any Rabbinical Bible. It was translated into Latin by J. F. Breithaupt in *R. Salomonis Jarchi commentarius hebraicus in librr. Josuæ . . . et Canticum Canticorum latine versus*, 1714.

[3] Ibn Ezra's commentary has come down to us in two recensions, one of which stands in the Rabbinical Bibles, and the other of which was edited and translated by H. J. Mathews, in *Abraham ibn Ezra's Commentary on the Canticles after the first recension*, 1874, The reference here is to the former.

[4] *Perush 'al Shir Hasshirim*, in Silbermann's *M'Kize Nirdamim*, 1874, p. 16a.

[5] See *Sheloshah Perushim 'al Shir Hasshirim*, by Sa'adia, Joseph Caspi and Jacob Provincial, ed. by Isaac 'Akrish, Constantinople, c. 1577, p. 11b, or *Perush 'al Megillath Shir Hasshirim*, Prague, 1608, p. 3. Sa'adia's commentary has been translated from Arabic into Hebrew and changed (cf. M. Steinschneider, *Catalogus librorum hebræorum in Bibliotheca Bodleiana*, 1852–60, ii, col. 2817). His commentary in Arabic stands in the British Museum MS. Or. 1302, fol. 154*a* ff., and a portion was published by A. Merx in *Die Saadjanische Uebersetzung des Hohen Liedes in's arabische*, 1882, pp. 34 f. On Sa'adia's authorship of the translation and commentary attributed to him, see S. Salfeld in *Magazin für die Wissenschaft des Judenthums*, v, 1878, pp. 125–131; J. Loevy, *ibid.*, x, 1883, pp. 33–41; W. Bacher, *Leben und Werke des Abulwalid Merwân ibn Ġanaḥ*, 1885, p. 93, note 21; H. Malter, *Saadia Gaon: His Life and Works*, 1921, pp. 322 f. It is generally held that, while they are not by Sa'adia in their present form, they are reworkings of his writings.

Ten Commandments,[1] while Moses ibn Tibbon[2] explained the verse to mean black in this world and fair in the world to come; and Ibn Ezra[3] supposed "thy navel" (7 : 3, E.V. 2) to refer to the Great Sanhedrin, and in the "mixed wine" found the Law, while "thy belly is an heap of wheat" he supposed to refer to the Little Sanhedrin.

It is of interest to observe that so recently as 1909 a Roman Catholic scholar of the highest reputation as a philologist and grammarian[4] revived this old Jewish view of the Song and interpreted the book throughout in terms of Israel's history. He finds in the first half the story of Israel from the Exodus to the time of Solomon, and in the second half the story of Israel's defection from God, leading to the Exile, followed by the renewal of the divine favour, and the return from the Exile, with the restoration of the Temple and the walls of Jerusalem. At many points he follows the old Jewish interpreters, but at others he produces fresh flights of fancy. Thus, the verse already quoted, "On my bed by night I sought him whom my soul loveth, I sought him but I found him not", is said to be a reference to the capture of the Ark by the Philistines;[5] while the verses "We have a little sister, and she hath no breasts. What shall we do for our sister, In the day when she shall be spoken for? If she be a wall we will build upon her A battlement of silver; And if she be a door we will fashion upon

[1] Cf. the Targum: "When the Israelites fashioned the Calf, their faces darkened as those of the children of Ethiopia, who dwell in the dwellings of Kedar: when they turned in penitence, and their guilt was pardoned, the brilliant radiance of their countenance increased as that of angels; (this occurred) when they made the curtains for the Tabernacle, and the Divine Presence once again dwelt in their midst; when Moses, their Teacher, went up to Heaven, and brought about peace between them and their King" (Tr. of Gollancz, op. cit., p. 20).

[2] Loc. cit., p. 9b.

[3] Cf. H. J. Mathews, op. cit., Hebrew part, p. 21. This does not stand in the later recension.

[4] P. Joüon, Le Cantique des Cantiques. A. Robert (Mélanges E. Podechard, 1945, p. 211) refers to "la tentative malheureuse du P. Joüon". Vulliaud (op. cit., p. 163 n.) refers to a work issued without date some years before Joüon's, E. A. Fraisse's La clé du Cantique des Cantiques, which maintained that the Song "est une page de l'histoire nationale d'Israël à la fois politique, religieuse et sociale", but I have not had access to this. More recently than Joüon, G. Ricciotti (Il Cantico dei Cantici, 1928, pp. 121–157) has argued for the view that the Song is an allegory of God's dealings with Israel. Cf. also J. Carlebach, "Das Hohelied" in Jeschurun, x, 1923, pp. 97–109, 196–206, 291–295, 355–364, 435–444 (esp. pp. 196–204), and R. Breuer, Lied der Lieder, 1923.

[5] Op. cit., p. 173. One of the least understanding comments of Joüon is on 1 : 2, where he would read "Let him kiss us with the kisses of his lips", on the ground that a single person would have used the singular, kiss (p. 128). An anonymous French Rabbi knew the ways of lovers better, and commented: "Kisses: many kisses, for I was not satisfied with one kiss, or two, but with many kisses" (cf. Festschrift zum 80en Geburtstag Moritz Steinschneider's, 1896, Hebrew part, p. 165).

her A board of cedar. I am a wall, And my breasts are towers" (8 : 8–10) are found to refer to the restoration of the walls of Jerusalem.[1]

(2)

Few, however, have been the Christian scholars who have interpreted the Song in terms of Israel's history. In the fourteenth century the Franciscan Nicolaus de Lyra, whose biblical work so greatly influenced Luther that men sang "Si Lyra non lyrasset, Luther non saltasset", i.e., "If Lyra had not piped, Luther had not danced", and who is said by an unreliable tradition to have been himself of Jewish descent,[2] supposed the first six chapters to recount the history of Israel, and the last two chapters to deal with the Christian Church, humble and weak amongst her enemies prior to Constantine's day.[3]

But, speaking generally, while the Church took over from the Rabbis the allegorical method of interpretation, it was re-applied to fit the Christian interests, and the Song was held to be an allegory of the dealings of Christ with His Church, or of the faithful soul with the Divine Logos.[4] With some important exceptions, which we shall note presently, this view has held the field until modern times, and it is represented in the chapter headings of the Authorized Version. In recent years it has still found some advocates, indeed, and in 1925 it was re-presented by a French writer,[5] who suggests that while it was

[1] Op. cit., p. 319. Cf. Ricciotti, op. cit., p. 282. (For a legal study of these verses, and of the rights of brothers in the disposal of their sisters' hands, see S. Krauss, "Die Rechtslage im biblischen Hohenliede" in M.G.W.J., lxxx, 1936, pp. 330–339.)

[2] Cf. Legacy of Israel (ed. Bevan and Singer), 1927, p. 307. Ricciotti (op. cit., p. 177) quotes a different jingle, "Nisi Lyra lyrasset, totus mundus delyrasset", i.e., "Had Lyra not sung, the whole world had been delirious".

[3] Biblia sacra cum glossa interlineari, ordinaria, et Nicolai Lyrani postilla, iii, 1588, fol. 367 D.

[4] For a most valuable survey of the history of Christian interpretation of the Song to circa A.D. 1200, see F. Ohly, Hohelied-Studien, 1958.

[5] E. Tobac, "Une page d'histoire de l'exégèse" in Revue d'histoire ecclésiastique, xxi, part I, 1925, pp. 510–542 (reprinted in Les cinq livres de Salomon, 1926), Cf. especially p. 524 (Les cinq livres, p. 110, with omission of word here bracketed), "Dans le sens littéral propre, le Cantique est une description de l'amour (humain). Mais l'amour ne figure ici que comme point de comparaison. L'auteur qui a composé les divers chants, ou tout au moins le rédacteur inspiré qui les a réunis, a voulu dans un sens littéral figuré, et au moyen d'une parabole tacite, représenter l'amour de Jahvé pour Israël et d'Israël pour Jahvé. Enfin, il nous semble, en nous basant sur l'exégèse des Pères, que le Saint-Esprit a voulu aussi, dans un sens typique, symboliser l'amour de Dieu pour son Église, pour l'âme fidèle, pour la Sainte Vierge Marie." It should perhaps be added that Joüon holds

God's love for Israel that primarily filled the thought of the writer, the inspiring Spirit intended it equally to set forth the relations with the Church.[1]

Some of the early Fathers of the Church interpreted particular phrases in the Song in relation to the Virgin Mary,[2] and in the twelfth century this became a favourite line of interpretation that was greatly extended.[3] It requires no great powers of imagination to see how, once this principle of interpretation was accepted, the Virgin Mary could be read into many texts. Thus Richard of St. Victor[4] comments on the verse "Thou art all fair, my love; And there is no spot in thee" (4 : 7) with the words "The Blessed Virgin Mary was wholly fair, because she was sanctified in the womb; and also after she was born she committed no sin, either mortal or venial." Needless to say, this particular variety of interpretation has not flourished in Protestant circles, though its influence persists in Roman Catholic works.[5]

There have, however, been many strange extravagances of interpretation in all schools of allegorists, and the bold sensuousness of the figures of the Song has been transmuted in the hands of the allegorists into the vehicle of their own ideas. A few samples may be quoted in

that it is legitimate to interpret the Song also in terms of Christ's relation to His Church, though he finds its primary meaning to deal with Israel's history (*op. cit.*, p. 19). The application to the faithful soul he finds rather less justified, but the application to the Virgin Mary "très légitime" (pp. 19 f.). Cf. H. Höpfl, *Introductio specialis in Vetus Testamentum*, 5th ed., ed. by A. Miller and A. Metzinger, 1946, pp. 340–353.

[1] Cf. also J. Hontheim, *Das Hohelied übersetzt und erklärt*, 1908, p. 4: "Das Hohelied, sage ich, stellt die Vereinigung Jahwes mit seinem Volke dar, folglich auch die Verbindung Christi mit der Kirche, die Verbindung Gottes mit jeder menschlichen Seele, besonders die Verbindung mit einzelnen hochbegnadeten Seelen, z.B. der allerseligsten Jungfrau." Cf. G. Gietmann, in *The Catholic Encyclopedia*, iii, 1908, p. 305b; J. E. Steinmueller, *A Companion to Scripture Studies*, ii, 2nd ed., 1944, p. 205. In one of the most recent Roman Catholic commentaries, the allegorical interpretation is given at the end of each section. Cf. J. Fischer, in *Echt. B.*, Lieferung 10, 1949, *Das Hohelied*.

[2] Cf. Ambrose (in Migne's *P.L.*, xvi, 1845, cols. 326 f.): "Quam pulchra etiam illa quæ in figura Ecclesiæ de Maria prophetata sunt; si tamen nonmem bra corporis, sed mysteria generationis ejus intendas! Dicitur enim ad eam: *Moduli fen.orum tuorum similes torquibus, operi manuum artificis, Umbilicus tuus crater tornatilis non deficiens mixto. Venter tuus sicut acervus tritici muniti inter lilia;* eo quod continens sibi in omnibus Christi ortus ex Virgine, sicut victores solent sæcularium præliorum, strenuorum virorum donatis torquibus honorare cervices; ita jugum nostrum levavit, ut fidelium colla virtutis insignibus coronaret."

[3] It was with Rupert of Deutz that this extension began. F. Ohly (*Hohelied-Studien*, 1958, p. 125) says "Hiermit ist Rupert zugleich der erste christliche Exeget, der in einem Hoheliedkommentar die Deutung der Braut auf Maria folgerichtig und folgenreich mit Entschiedenheit seinem ganzen werk zugrunde gelegt hat."

[4] Cf. Migne, *P.L.*, cxcvi, 1855, col. 482.

[5] Cf. the quotations in the preceding notes.

illustration. Origen[1] held the verse "Black am I but comely, O daughters of Jerusalem" (1 : 5) to mean black with sin but comely through conversion; Philo Carpasius[2] and Cyril of Alexandria[3] believed "A sachet of myrrh is my beloved to me, Between my breasts it lies" (1 : 12) to refer to the Scriptures of the Old and New Testaments, between which stands Christ, while Justus Urgellensis[4] found the breasts to denote the learned teachers of the Church, and pseudo-Cassiodorus[5] thought the verse referred to the Crucifixion of Christ, which the believer keeps in eternal remembrance between his breasts, i.e. in his heart, and which is as myrrh to him; the last-named writer[6] interpreted "The voice of the turtle-dove is heard in the land" (2 : 12) of the preaching of the Apostles, and Philo Carpasius[7] of the preaching of Paul; Cyril of Alexandria[8] took "On my bed by night I sought him whom my soul loveth, I sought him but I found him not" (3 : 1) to refer to the women who sought Christ on the Resurrection morning; Cyril of Jerusalem[9] saw in the words "King Solomon made himself a palanquin" (3 : 9) a reference to the Cross, and in its "silver pillars" an allusion to Judas's thirty pieces of silver, and in "the crown wherewith his mother crowned him in the day of his espousals" a reference to the crown of thorns; Justus Urgellensis[10] referred "A garden enclosed is my sister, my bride; A spring enclosed, a fountain sealed" (4 : 12)

[1] Cf. Migne, P.G., xiii, 1862, col. 43. With this compare Hippolytus's comment that the blackness was due to the sin in Paradise, and the fairness born of the hope that is in Christ [see G. N. Bonwetsch, *Hippolyt's Kommentar zum Buche Daniel und die Fragmente des Kommentares zum Hohenliede*, in *Hippolytus Werke* (Die griechischen christlichen Schriftsteller der ersten drei Jahrhunderte), i, 1897, p. 359]. Migne (*P.G.*, x, 1857) gives only a short fragment of Hippolytus's commentary in Greek, and it has been supposed that his work was lost, save for the Slavonic and other fragments which Bonwetsch has translated [cf. also Bonwetsch, *Studien zu den Kommentaren Hippolyts zum Buche Daniel und Hohen Liede* in Gebhardt and Harnack's Texte und Untersuchungen, xvi (N.F. i), 1897, Heft 2, and *Hippolyt's Kommentar zum Hohenlied auf Grund von N. Marr's Ausgabe des grusinischen Textes, ibid.*, xxiii (N.F. viii), 1902, Heft 2c]. A Sovic, however, has given reasons for supposing that a fragment of an anonymous commentary in Greek, preserved in the Bodleian, is really the work of Hippolytus (*Biblica*, ii, 1921, pp. 448–453).

[2] Cf. Migne, P.G., xl, 1863, col. 56, Cf. W. Riedel, *Die Auslegung des Hohenliedes in der jüdischen Gemeinde und der griechischen Kirche*, 1898, pp. 76–79. Cf. also Hippolytus (Bonwetsch, *Hippolytus Werke*, i, p. 344).

[3] Cf. Migne, P.G., lxix, 1864, col. 1281.   [4] Cf. Migne, P.L., lxvii, 1848, col. 968.
[5] *Ibid.*, lxx, 1847, col. 1060.   [6] *Ibid.*, col. 1065.
[7] Cf. Migne, P.G., xl, 1863, col. 69.   [8] Cf. Migne, P.G., lxix, 1864, col. 1285.
[9] Cf. Migne, P.G., xxxiii, 1857, cols. 1141–1146, 793. This view is erroneously attributed to Cyril of Alexandria by C. D. Ginsburg (*The Song of Songs*, 1857, p. 67), and, following him, by A. Harper (*Song of Solomon*, Camb. B., 1902, p. xliii), G. Luzzi (*Gli Agiografi*, La Bibbia tradotta e annotata, 1925, p. 11), and H. Ranston (*The Old Testament Wisdom Books and their Teaching*, 1930, pp. 212 f.).
[10] Cf. Migne, P.L., lxvii, 1848, col. 978.

to the Virgin Mary, and pseudo-Cassiodorus[1] to the Church; pseudo-Athanasius[2] believed "I have come to my garden, my sister, my bride, I have gathered my myrrh and my spices" (5 : 1) to declare the Incarnation of our Lord; Philo Carpasius[3] and Cyril of Alexandria[4] believed the words "Eat, O friends, and drink, Yea, drink abundantly, O beloved" (5 : 1) to refer to the Last Supper, while "I was asleep" (5 : 2) is then held to mean on the Cross, and "but my heart is waked" to announce the Harrowing of Hell; Philo Carpasius[5] took "Thy navel is a circular goblet, Wherein mixed wine is not lacking" (7 : 3, E.V. 2) to refer to the sanctuary of the Church, and Hengstenberg[6] to the cup from which the Church revives the thirsty with its refreshing draught; Bishop Wordsworth[7] found "There are sixty queens and eighty concubines, And young women without number" (6 : 8) to signify that the sectarians should outnumber the true Church, while Epiphanius[8] found here a reference to the eighty heresies. With this last we may compare J. Durham's view[9] that "Take us the foxes, the little foxes, That spoil the vineyards" (2 : 15) is clear guidance to the secular authorities to co-operate with the Church in stamping out every heresy and schism, however small it might seem.

[1] Cf. Migne, *P.L.*, lxx, 1847, col. 1074.

[2] Cf. Migne, *P.G.*, xxvii, 1887, col. 1356. Ricciotti, *Il Cantico dei Cantici*, 1928, p. 172, says "L'omelia che si trova nelle sue opere, in Migne, *P.G.* 27, 1349–1361, è certamente spuria. Il solo frammento 1348–1349 sembra genuino." For the interpretation cf. Hippolytus (Bonwetsch, *Hippolytus Werke*, i, p. 374).

[3] Cf. Migne, *P.G.*, xl, 1863, col. 100.   [4] Cf. Migne, *P.G.*, xlix, 1864, col. 1289.

[5] Cf. Migne, *P.G.*, xl, 1863, col. 126.

[6] *Das Hohelied Salomonis ausgelegt*, 1853, p. 186. He compares John 7: 38. With this view cf. that of Symon Patrick, *The Books of Job . . . and the Song of Solomon paraphras'd . . . with Annotations*, ed. of 1727 (imprimatur dated 1678), p. 532a: "What is the mystical meaning of this Hieroglyphick Vesture is very hard to say. It may be applied to the two Sacraments, which the Church administers to her children: The Font in Baptism being represented by the former; and the Sacrament of the Lord's Supper by the other part of this Figure"—i.e. the navel represents the Font, and the belly the Lord's Supper. The same idea is found in the Westminster Assembly's *Annotations upon all the Books of the Old and New Testament*, 2nd ed., 1651, i *ad loc.* (the pages are not numbered). For a very different interpretation of the belly cf. J. Dove, *The Conversion of Salomon: a direction to holinesse of life, handled by way of commentary upon the whole booke of Canticles*, 1613, pp. 254 f.: "The swelling of *the belly*, and roundness of the nauell, is an argument that the wombe of the Church is fruitfull to bring foorth many children."

[7] *The Books of Proverbs, Ecclesiastes, and Song of Solomon, with Notes and Introductions*, 1868, p. 148.

[8] Cf. Migne, *P.G.*, xli, 1863, col. 632; xlii, 1858, col. 772.

[9] *Clavis Cantici*, 1669, pp. 143 ff. Durham recognizes, indeed, that the injunction is not addressed to magistrates (p. 145), but to the Church, but adds that "the duty from the force of its argument will also reach him in his station, because he should so far as he can prevent the spoiling of Christ's vinyard in his place."

Enough has been said to indicate what a wide field for fancy the method opened up, and how impossible it is by this means to reach any agreement as to what the Song really meant. The necessity to find a meaning for every detail led to this great variety of forced interpretations, which had to be brought to the Song rather than found in it. To free the interpretation from this necessity the view that the Song is a parable, rather than an allegory, has been advanced.[1] This view has been particularly developed in a series of publications by D. Buzy,[2] who observes that a parable requires only a general correspondence.[3] It is not, therefore, necessary to attach any particular significance to geographical or historical allusions.[4] What the Song describes, according to Buzy, is the bond between Yahweh and Israel, but with a plenary sense which extends to Christ and the Church, to Christ and the individual soul, and to the Virgin Mary.[5] This view is declared to be an evasion by A. Robert,[6] who prefers to describe the Song as an allegorical midrash.[7]

To understand what is meant by this, we need to define the term midrash. Robert defines it as any research into the meaning of Scripture

[1] Cf. F. Ruffenbach, *Canticum Canticorum* 2nd ed., 1932, pp. 20–24; L. Dennefeld, *Introduction à l'Ancien Testament*, 1934, p. 141; R. E. Murphy, *C.B.Q.*, xi, 1949, p. 381; A. Bea, *Canticum Canticorum*, 1953, p. 4. P. P. Saydon (*A Catholic Commentary on Holy Scripture*, 1953, p. 498) favours the parabolic-allegorical interpretation.

[2] Cf. *Mémorial Lagrange*, 1940, pp. 147–162; *R.B.*, xlix, 1940, pp. 169–194; *Vivre et Penser*, iii (=*R.B.*, lii), 1943–44, pp. 77–90; *La Sainte Bible*, ed. by L. Pirot and A. Clamer, vi, 1946, pp. 286–296 (also published separately, with some rearrangement, as *Le Cantique des Cantiques*, 1949); *Mélanges J. Lebreton*, i, 1951–52, pp. 99–114.

[3] *Ibid.*, p. 99. In this article Buzy examines a number of Biblical parables and concludes (pp. 113 f.): "Il existe dans l'Ancien Testament une tradition d'exégèse parabolique. . . . Cette tradition comporte au centre du tableau une métaphore. . . . Cette personne ou personnification centrale est uniformément placée dans un cadre de détails ou de traits dénués de toute intention métaphorique, et qui n'ont de signification que dans leur ensemble. . . . L'allégorisation est un genre artificiel relevant de la pédagogie ou d'un exercice d'école plutôt que de l'enseignement populaire. La présomption biblique ne semble donc pas en faveur de l'exégèse allégorique du Cantique."

[4] Cf. *La Sainte Bible*, vi, pp. 293 f.

[5] Cf. H. Lusseau (*Introduction à la Bible*, ed. by A. Robert and A. Feuillet, i, 1957, p. 662): "Toutefois nous croyons préférable d'opter pour le sens littéral figuré, c'est-à-dire allégorique, compte tenu de l'extension que le sens put acquérir lorsque, les circonstances s'y prêtant, la pensée s'éleva, à partir de l'union de Yahvé et d'Israël, vers celle du Christ et de l' Église, du Christ et de l' âme individuelle, de l'Esprit-Saint et de la Vierge Marie." A. van den Born, in *Bijbelsch Woordenboek*, 1941, col. 675, finds in it a *sensus literalis*, a *sensus typicus*, and a *sensus accommodatus*, of which the first was an allegory of Yahweh's dealings with Israel, the second was a prophecy of Christ's relations with the Church, and the third of His relation to the soul or to the Virgin Mary (cf. *Bibel-Lexikon*, ed. by H. Haag, 1951, cols. 731 f.; *Bijbels Woordenboek*, 2nd ed., 1954–57, cols. 741 f.; and *Dictionnaire encyclopédique de la Bible*, 1960, cols. 254 f.).

[6] Cf. *Mélanges E. Podechard*, 1945, p. 212.   [7] Cf. *E.Th.L.*, xxx, 1954, pp. 283 f.

in the light of the Bible as a whole.[1] He therefore argues that the Song carries its own key and that its figures can be paralleled elsewhere in relation to Yahweh and Israel,[2] though he fails to adduce evidence of Yahweh's concubines elsewhere. He holds that the two heroes of the Song are Yahweh and Israel personified as husband and wife,[3] and holds that the use of such terms as wife, king, shepherd, flock, vineyard, garden, Lebanon, springtime blossoming, night, and dream support this view.[4] Robert is followed by A. Feuillet,[5] who adduces such terms as marriage, shepherd, flock, lost sheep, morning, noon, night, dew, feast, the formula seek-find, the mountain (which is identified with the Temple mount), sleep, awaking, wild beasts as symbols of enemies,[6] and argues that these evoke theological ideas. To these R. E. Murphy[7] replies that while some of these terms have theological implications in their context elsewhere in the Bible, there is

[1] *Ibid.*, p. 283. Cf. R. Bloch, *S.D.B.*, v, 1957, col. 1263: "En réalité, il désigne un genre édifiant et applicatif étroitement rattaché à l'Écriture, dans lequel la part de l'amplification est réelle mais secondaire et reste toujours subordonné à la fin religieuse essentielle, qui est de mettre en valeur plus pleinement l'œuvre de Dieu, la Parole de Dieu." Cf. also A. Robert, *S.D.B.*, v, 1957, cols. 410 f.

[2] Cf. *Vivre et Penser*, iii (=*R.B.*, lii), 1943–44, pp. 192–213. Cf. also *Mélanges E. Podechard*, 1945, pp. 211–223, where he reaches the conclusion (p. 223): "Ainsi le bien-aimé est identifié avec le Temple, et la bien-aimée avec la Terre sainte. . . . Le thème général est bien celui de l'union entre Yahweh et Israël, mais avec des nuances complexes et touchantes qui font de ce beau livre le plus divin et le plus humain de l'Ancien Testament." In "Les appendices du Cantique des Cantiques (8: 8–14)", in *R.B.*, lv, 1948, pp. 159–183, Robert argues that the closing verses of the book are additions from a later date, in part coming from the end of the second century B.C., and referring to the conflict between the Pharisees and Sadducees at that time. E. Jacob goes some way with this view; cf. *Theology of the Old Testament*, E.Tr. by A. W. Heathcote and P. J. Allcock, 1958, p. 177: "The theme of conjugal love was widely diffused to express the relationship between Yahweh and his people. . . . We have proof of it in the Song of Songs, which celebrates conjugal love in terms borrowed from the metaphorical language of the prophets."

[3] *Le Cantique des Cantiques* (Jerusalem Bible), 1951, p. 14. The major work of Robert on the Song of Songs was published posthumously, after being completed by R. Tournay and A. Feuillet [*Le Cantique des Cantiques* (E.B.), 1963]. The approach of this volume was rejected by P. Grelot (*R.B.*, lxxi, 1964, p. 51) and M. A. Dahood (*Biblica*, xlv, 1964, pp. 113–115).

[4] Cf. *Le Cantique des Cantiques* (Jerusalem Bible), p. 13. Cf. *Initiation Biblique*, ed. by A. Robert and A. Tricot, 3rd ed., 1954, p. 198. This is repeated by R. Bloch, *S.D.B.*, v, 1957, col. 1273.

[5] Cf. *Le Cantique des Cantiques* (Lectio Divina, 10), 1953.

[6] *Ibid.*, p. 195.

[7] Cf. *C.B.Q.*, xvi, 1954, pp. 5 f. For other criticisms of Robert and Feuillet, cf. A.M. Dubarle, *R.B.*, lxi, 1954, pp. 72 ff.; J.P. Audet, *R.B.*, lii, 1955, pp 197–221, and *Scripture*, x, 1958, pp. 79 ff.; and J. Winandy, *Le Cantique des Cantiques*, 1960, pp. 17 ff. On the other hand, R. Tournay ends his review in *R.B.*, lx, 1953, pp. 414–417, with the words: "Puisse l'exégèse moderne prendre au sérieux la méthode ici préconisée!"

nothing in the terms themselves to require those implications in a context where nothing suggests it. Moreover, we are soon carried back to the eisegesis of the older allegorists. "Rise up, my love, my fair one, and come away" (2 : 10) is said to be a summons to captive Zion to return from the Babylonian exile; "the flowers appear on the earth" (2 : 12) is interpreted by Hos. 14 : 6–8; "the time of singing is come, and the voice of the turtle is heard in our land" (2 : 12) is held to refer to the time of glad songs so often promised in Is. 40–55;[1] "O my dove, that art in the clefts of the rock" (2 : 14) is explained as an allusion to the Babylonian exiles on the strength of Is. 42 : 7; 49 : 9, and Lam. 3: 7;[2] "Take us the foxes, the little foxes, that spoil the vineyards" (2 : 15) is treated as a reference to the Samaritans, Ammonites, Arabs, and Philistines, who were installed in Judaea in place of the exiles.[3] None of this springs naturally from the passages, and, as Murphy observes,[4] it is incoherent. Equally fanciful is the interpretation of "I said, I will climb up into the palm tree, I will take hold of the branches thereof" (7 : 8) as a reference to the liberties taken by the rivals of Yahweh in Ezek. 23 : 3–21.[5]

It is, indeed, undeniable that the relation between God and His people is often represented in the Old Testament under the figure of marriage, especially in the prophets. Thus Jeremiah, speaking in the name of God, says "I remember your early devotion, The love of your bridal days; How through the wolds you followed me, Through lands unsown"[6] (2 : 2), and Israel's worship of other gods is constantly spoken of under the figure of adultery. Moreover, in the New Testament Christ is spoken of as the Bridegroom, and the Church as His Bride. All of this is readily conceded. But there is nothing on all fours with the allegorical interpretation of the Song of Songs. For wherever the figure is used elsewhere, it is plainly symbolic, whereas here there is no hint whatever of allegory,[7] and the whole Song can

[1] Cf. Le Cantique des Cantiques, 1953, p. 97.
[2] Ibid., p. 98.
[3] Ibid., p. 99.
[4] Cf. C.B.Q., xvi, 1954, p. 7.
[5] Cf. A. Feuillet, op. cit., p. 170; A. Robert, Le Cantique des Cantiques (Jerusalem Bible), p. 55.
[6] Moffatt's rendering.
[7] Cf. La Bible du Centenaire, L'Ancien Testament, iii, 1947, p. xiv b: "Sans doute l'idée de comparer les relations de Dieu avec la nation élue, celles du Christ avec son Église ou avec l'âme fidèle à des fiançailles ou à un mariage est familière à beaucoup d'écrivains de l'Ancien et du Nouveau Testament. Mais ils indiquent alors toujours expressément qu'ils emploient une image. Rien de semblable dans le Cantique."

be read through without of itself suggesting any of the varied meanings the allegorists have read into it.[1]

Some further varieties of allegorical interpretation should perhaps be mentioned, though they have exercised little influence on the stream of interpretation. So far as I know, the medieval Jew Abravanel[2] was the first to advocate the view that the Bride represented Wisdom. He saw in the characters of the Song not God and Israel, but Solomon and Wisdom. He therefore found it necessary to regard only the Bride as an allegorical figure, and supposed that Solomon spoke in his own proper person as the Bridegroom. Abravanel was followed by his son, Leon Hebraeus,[3] who held that Solomon likened Wisdom to a beautiful woman in the Song of Songs. A few others have followed this line of interpretation, including E. F. C. Rosenmüller,[4] and the view has found a new advocate in recent years in the person of G. Kuhn,[5] who, however, while identifying the Bride with Wisdom, finds in the Bridegroom not the Solomon of history, but a type of the seeker after wisdom.[6] In a very different way Luther,[7] who held that Solomon spoke in his own proper person, found the Bride to be symbolical, for in his view she symbolized Solomon's kingdom, and the Song is a hymn of praise for the loyalty of his subjects and the peaceful state of his realm.

[1] Cf. J. W. Rothstein (Hastings's *D.B.*, iv, 1902, p. 589b): "What we hear of is earthly love, that of betrothed or married persons, and nowhere does the natural eye detect a single indication that would call it away from this and compel it to see in the figures presented to it images of a higher love."

[2] See E. I. Magnus. *Kritische Bearbeitung und Erklärung des Hohen Liedes Salomo's*, 1842, p. 26.

[3] *De Amore Dialogi tres*, 1564, p. 280. This is a translation from the Italian, in which the work originally appeared. For a Hebrew translation see Silbermann's *M'kize Nirdamim*, 1871 (p. 87a corresponds to the above reference). An English translation by F. Friedeberg-Seeley and Jean H. Barnes, appeared in 1937 under the title *The Philosophy of Love*. Cf. pp. 422 f.

[4] *Scholia in Vetus Testamentum*, part IX, vol. ii, 1830, pp. 270 ff.

[5] *Erklärung des Hohen Liedes*, 1926 (much of this work appeared also in *N.K.Z.*, xxxvii, 1926, pp. 501 ff., 521 ff.). Kuhn also gives to the book its plain meaning, and observes, "So kann also jede reine Ehe im Hohen Liede zum Teil ihr Spiegelbild finden" (p. 60).

[6] The Cabbalistic view which identified the Bridegroom with the Infinite ('Ên Sôph) and the Bride with the first of the ten emanations (S^ephîrôth) may also be noted (cf. Ricciotti, *Il Cantico dei Cantici*, 1928, p. 78, and, for a fuller account of Cabbalistic interpretations, Vulliaud, *Le Cantique des Cantiques d'après la tradition juive*, 1925, pp. 116–133; cf. also *Encyclopædia Judaica*, viii, 1931, cols. 179–182), though its influence is entirely confined to the literature of the Cabbala. Vulliaud (*op. cit.*, p. 116) claims that the Cabbala but systematized the interpretation of the Targum and the Midrash, and his work is largely devoted to a rehabilitation of its view. But cf. Ricciotti, *op. cit.*, pp. 290 f.

[7] *In Cantica Canticorum brevis enarratio*, 1539 (or *Sämtliche Schriften*, ed. Walch, v, 1741, cols. 2384 ff.).

Yet another type of allegorical treatment is given to the Song by Cocceius,[1] who finds in it a detailed prophecy of the history of the Church, with an anti-papal turn. The divisions of the Song he finds to correspond with the periods of the history of the Church, and his interpretation becomes particularly full and detailed with the pre-Reformation and the Reformation period, and the coming triumph of Protestantism in which he believes the Song culminates. He explains "terrible as bannered hosts" (6 : 10) of John Wiclif,[2] and the Shulammite (7 : 1, E.V. 6 : 13) as that part of Bohemia which made peace with the Roman Church,[3] while 7 : 5 (E.V. 4) he connects with Luther.[4]

It is not surprising that the whole allegorical view, which is so varyingly applied at the impulse of obviously subjective factors, is generally abandoned in modern times, though not a few writers have adopted a modified form of it. They have supposed the Song to have a double meaning. Primarily, they suppose, it deals with human love, but a deeper, mystical meaning also penetrates it.[5] This view must not be confused with that of the older allegorical interpreters, who sometimes treated first of the literal meaning of the text and then of its allegorical meaning. To them the literal meaning belonged merely to the form and not to the essential significance of the work, and they were far from suggesting that a double meaning attached to the text.[6] But here

---

[1] *Cogitationes de Cantico Canticorum Solomonis*, 1665 (or *Opera omnia theologica, exegetica, didactica, polemica*, 3rd ed., 1701, ii, pp. 553 ff.).

[2] *Ibid.*, p. 135 (or *Op. omn.*, p. 604a). [3] *Ibid.*, p. 145 (or *Op. omn.*, p. 607a).

[4] *Ibid.*, p. 153 (or *Op. omn.*, p. 610a).

[5] This is the view presented by A. Miller, *Das Hohe Lied* (H.S.A.Tes.), 1927, pp. 7 ff. It is also the view of M. A. van den Oudenrijn, *Het Hooglied* (B.O.T.), 1962, pp. 10 f., where an allegorical meaning is rejected. An earlier article by van den Oudenrijn expressing the same view (*Divus Thomas*, xxxi, 1953, pp. 257–280) has been accessible to me only through the review of A.-M. Dubarle in *R.S.P.T.*, xxxviii, 1954, pp. 95 f. N. K. Gottwald (*A Light to the Nations*, 1959, p. 491) says: "Mystics such as Bernard of Clairvaux regarded the allegory as bodying forth the relation of Christ and the individual believer. It must be insisted unequivocally, however, that there is no ground whatsoever for an allegorical interpretation. The result of such mitigation of the plain meaning of the poems is a sickly religious eroticism far more objectionable than the healthy emotion expressed by the poet."

[6] This method of interpretation is as old as Origen, who gave a threefold explanation. The first, or literal, he regarded as unworthy of the Holy Spirit, and as merely providing the vehicle for the second, which unfolded the relations between the soul and God, and the third, which treated of Christ and His Church. Cf. P. P. Parente, *C.B.Q.*, vi, 1944, p. 150: "The only sense of the Canticle intended by God is the spiritual or allegorical sense. Those who stop at the literal sense of the text and perceive nothing of the spiritual meaning read something that refers to natural love only and find anything but edification. A carnal man should not read this book. It is the book of perfect souls."

a double meaning is found. Lane[1] compared the Song with some Moslem songs he heard in Cairo, which were full of sensuous images, and which were understood erotically by the common people, but which were really intended to convey a spiritual meaning. Beside this we may place R. A. Nicholson's observation[2] on the medieval poet Ibnu'l-Fáriḍ: "The double character of Islamic mystical poetry makes it attractive to many who are out of touch with pure mysticism. Ibnu'l-Fáriḍ would not be so popular in the East if he were understood entirely in a spiritual sense. The fact that parts of the Díwán cannot be reasonably understood in any other sense would not, perhaps, compel us to regard the whole as spiritual, unless that view of its meaning were supported by the poet's life, the verdict of his biographers and commentators, and the agreement of Moslem critical opinion." On the view that the Song of Songs belongs to this type of poetry, the earthly figures which filled the superficial thought of the writer were also intended to be types of higher and holier things. Just as our Lord found a deeper meaning in the sign of Jonah, or in the Brazen Serpent, so, it is held, may the Song of Songs have a hidden meaning.[3] But this idea rests on some confusion of thought. That we, for our profit, may rightly find in the images of the Song, as in all experience, analogies of things spiritual, does not mean that it was written for this purpose, or that the author had any such idea in mind.[4] That Jesus found an analogy

---

[1] *Manners and Customs of the Modern Egyptians*, ed. of 1898, p. 454. Cf. also Sir Wm. Jones, "On the Mystical Poetry of the Persians and Hindus", in *Asiatick Researches*, iii, 1792, pp. 165–207. M. Stuart (*Critical History and Defence of the Old Testament Canon*, 1845, pp. 370–373) follows this view, but discloses his uneasiness by suggesting that the usefulness of the book is primarily for Orientals and that Occidentals can do better without making use of it in public or private.

[2] *Studies in Islamic Mysticism*, 1921, p. 168. Cf. also pp. 168 f.: "The Odes retain the form, conventions, topics, and images of ordinary love-poetry: their inner meaning hardly ever obtrudes itself, although its presence is everywhere suggested by a strange exaltation of feeling."

[3] Cf. H. Ranston, *The O.T. Wisdom Books and their Teaching*, 1930, p. 217.

[4] I have elsewhere observed (*Baptist Quarterly*, viii, 1937, p. 413) that "we should learn to distinguish between what is devotionally profitable and what is exegetically sound". P. P. Parente, "The Canticle of Canticles in Mystical Theology", in *C.B.Q.*, vi, 1944, pp. 142–158, defends a mystical interpretation of the Song on the ground that the mystical union of the soul with God is a spiritual marriage. That the metaphor of marriage may be used for that union is no evidence that it is so metaphorically used here, where there is no reference to God, and where the so-called metaphor is carried through with a detail that goes far beyond any metaphorical necessity. Cf. J. Winandy, *Le Cantique des Cantiques*, 1960, p. 59: "En affirmant, comme nous le faisons, que le Cantique ne fut primitivement qu'un poème chantant l'amour humain nous ne songeons nullement à contester la légitimité de son application à l'amour réciproque de Yahvé et d'Israël, ou du Christ et de l'Église."

of the Cross in the Brazen Serpent can scarcely be held to prove that the purpose for which the Brazen Serpent was made was to prefigure the Cross. Nor can the fact that Eastern literatures provide other well-authenticated cases of apparently erotic poetry having an esoteric meaning prove that the Song of Songs is such a poem, in the absence of the slightest indication in the poem itself, and in the complete absence of agreement amongst those who find an esoteric meaning in it as to what that meaning is.

(3)

In the nineteenth century the view that the Song is a drama gained wide currency. The idea is older than that century, indeed, for Cornelius a Lapide[1] had already termed it such, and Milton[2] had called it a "divine pastoral drama", while even so anciently as in the third century A.D. Origen[3] had applied the word "drama" to it. It was in the nineteenth century, however, that the view was particularly elaborated, and became especially popular. It still flourishes, indeed, for two of the most recent commentaries,[4] though in wholly different ways, adhere to it.[5]

The dramatic view has taken more than one form, however. Of the various forms it has assumed two have enjoyed especial popularity. According to one of these there are in the drama two characters, Solomon and a Shulammite shepherd girl. The king saw her and fell in love with her, and took her from her country home to make her his bride in Jerusalem, with the result that he was lifted from a merely physical attraction to a true and pure love. The most notable advocate

---

[1] *Commentarius in Ecclesiasten, Canticum Canticorum et Librum Sapientiæ*, ed. 1740, p. 264 F.

[2] *The Reason of Church Government urg'd against Prelaty*, Book II, Introduction: "The Scripture also affords us a Divine pastoral Drama in the Song of *Solomon*, consisting of two Persons, and a double *Chorus*, as *Origen* rightly judges" (*A Complete Collection of the Historical, Political and Miscellaneous Works*, i, 1738, p. 60, or Columbia University Press edition of *The Works of John Milton*, III, i, 1931, pp. 237 f.).

[3] Cf. Migne, *P.G.*, xiii, 1862, col. 61: "Epithalamium libellus hic . . . dramatis in modum mihi videtur a Salomone conscriptus."

[4] Pouget and Guitton, *Le Cantique des Cantiques*, 1934, and A. Hazan, *Le Cantique des Cantiques enfin expliqué*, 1936. For a criticism of the former cf. Dussaud, *R.H.R.*, cxii, 1935, pp. 111–115, or F. Ogara, "Novi in 'Canticum' commentarii recensio et brevis de sensu litterali et typico disceptatio", in *Gregorianum*, xvii, 1936, pp. 132–142. The work of Pouget and Guitton has now been translated into English by J. L. Lilly, as *The Canticle of Canticles*, 1948.

[5] P. Riessler (*Theologische Quartalschrift*, c, 1919, pp. 5–37) regards the Song as a dramatic allegory, with two principal characters, a chorus and a chorus leader associated with the teaching and practice of the Essenes and Therapeutae.

of this view was Delitzsch.[1] Its difficulties, however, were numerous, as its critics were not slow to point out. For it would be surprising to find Solomon acting as a shepherd (1 : 7), and still more so to find the closing scene in the girl's native village. Moreover, while in 3 : 6–11 Solomon is the bridegroom, in other passages he seems to be distinguished from the bridegroom. Thus, in 8 : 11 f. the bridegroom says that Solomon is welcome to his vast estate. To get his thousand pieces of silver he has to expend two hundred, whereas the bridegroom without any such outlay has all he can desire in his bride. Similarly, in the passage "There are threescore queens, and fourscore concubines, And young women without number. But my dove, my perfect one, is alone" (6 : 8 f.), the lover seems to contrast his bride with the royal harem. To these considerations Harper[2] adds the observation "We think few will find themselves able to believe that a voluptuary like Solomon could be raised to the height of pure love by the beauty of the Shulammite."

Hence another form of the dramatic view has been much more popular. This is associated especially with the name of H. Ewald,[3] though it rests on the ideas of Jacobi[4] and S. Löwisohn,[5] and has been worked out by later scholars with some divergence of detail from Ewald's view. He found three principal characters—Solomon, the Shulammite maiden, and her rustic lover. On this view, the maiden resisted the king's advances, and though he carried her off to the royal palace, she was still true to her rustic swain, until the king, failing to win her affection, allowed her to return to her true love. The book is thus turned into the story of the triumph of pure love over the

---

[1] *Biblischer Commentar über die poetischen Bücher des Alten Testaments*, iv, *Hoheslied und Koheleth*, 1875 (E.Tr. by M. G. Easton, as *Commentary on the Song of Songs and Ecclesiastes*, 1877). Cf. also *Das Hohelied untersucht und ausgelegt*, 1851. Delitzsch did not think the Song was written to be acted, however, but remarks: "The Song is certainly not a theatrical piece" (*Bib. Comm.*, p. 10, E.Tr., p. 8). He describes it as a dramatic pastoral (cf. Milton's "pastoral drama"). With this view we may compare that of A. Vaccari (*I Libri Poetici della Bibbia*, 1925, p. 285): "La Cantica è un dramma? È una lirica? È un po' di tutto questo; ma nulla che risponda esattamente alle nostre categorie letterarie. È un dialogo lirico accompagnato qualche movimento drammatico."

[2] *Op. cit.*, p. xxxiii.

[3] *Das Hohelied Salomo's übersetzt mit Einleitung, Anmerkungen und einem Anhang*, 1826.

[4] *Das durch eine leichte und ungekünstelte Erklärung von seinen Vorwürfen gerettete Hohelied*, 1771. (I have not had access to this work. The author's initials are variously given as J. F., J. T., and J. C. I believe the first is correct.)

[5] *Melizas Jeschurun*, 1816, pp. 32–41.

blandishments of a Court.[1] Some of the advocates of this view have turned the Daughters of Jerusalem into a sort of Greek Chorus, and so have still more filled out the dramatic form of the work.[2]

Of other varieties of dramatic view we may note that of Renan,[3] who found a complete cast, consisting of some ten individual performers, and two choruses, one of men and one of women, and that of one of the most recent advocates of a dramatic theory, A. Hazan,[4] who offers a complete rendering for the stage in dramatic verse, and who finds, in addition to the Fair Maid and her Shepherd lover, the King and the favourite lady of his harem, and a number of minor characters.[5]

It must be recognized that scholars of the highest standing have accepted the dramatic view, and Ewald's theory stands in the work that has been regarded for more than a generation as the standard Introduction to the Old Testament in English.[6] Nevertheless, its popularity has greatly declined. So much has to be read between the lines, and such complicated stage directions have to be supplied, that its critics feel almost as much has to be brought to the book on this interpretation as on the allegorical.[7] Despite the fact that analogies for the omission of

---

[1] E. Junès, *Le Cantique des Cantiques de Salomon*, 1932, follows this view of the purport of the Song, but denies that it has dramatic form. He says (p. 9): "On célèbre, dans le Cantique des Cantiques, les amours d'un pâtre et d'une brune paysanne, remarquable par sa beauté. De celle-ci est épris aussi le roi Salomon. Il la convoque dans son palais, lui offre perles et colliers, cherche à l'éblouir par son faste. Peine inutile: l'amoureuse jeune fille retourne irrésistiblement à son modeste soupirant."

[2] R. Dussaud (*Le Cantique des Cantiques*, 1919, p. 16) maintains that there is nothing in the book to suggest that the shepherd and the king are rivals. He supposes the Song to consist of four poems which have been jumbled together by a redactor, and that the poems dealing with Solomon's love and the shepherd's love were originally quite distinct. For a criticism of Dussaud's view see A. Lods, *R.H.R.*, lxxxii, 1920, pp. 217–224.

[3] *Le Cantique des Cantiques*, 1860, pp. 72, 179–210.

[4] *Le Cantique des Cantiques enfin expliqué*, 1836. Hazan entitles his dramatic rendering "La Belle et Le Pâtre."

[5] E. I. Magnus (*Kritische Bearbeitung und Erklärung des Hohen Liedes Salomo's*, 1842) found both dramatic and non-dramatic elements in the book, and largely rearranged it, while Adam Clarke (*Commentary on the Old Testament*, iii, 1836, p. 2563) regarded it as a mask, akin to Milton's *Comus*. He says: "It is rather a composition *sui generis*, and seems to partake more of the nature of what we call a mask, than anything else; an entertainment for the guests who attended the marriage ceremony with a *dramatic cast* throughout the whole, though the *persons* who speak and act are not formally introduced."

[6] S. R. Driver, *Introduction to the Literature of the O.T.*, 9th ed., 1913, pp. 436 ff.

[7] Cf. also W. O. E. Oesterley's argument (*The Song of Songs*, 1936, p. 10a): "Among the Semites generally, and of course this applies to the Hebrews, drama was unknown. In the immense mass of ancient Hebrew and Jewish literature there is no sign of the existence of anything in the shape of drama; and the same applies to all other Semitic literature that is extant. To the Jews of old, dramatic performances were held in horror, because they were regarded as heathenish and irreligious. . . . It is, therefore, quite un-

the stage directions can be found, it is probable that the ingenuity of
the dramatic interpretation belongs rather to the editors than to the
author. Who, for instance, would suppose, as Pouget and Guitton do,[1]
that the dialogue in 1 : 15–2 : 3 is a dialogue at cross-purposes, the king
praising the maiden, and her replies having reference, not to him, but
to her absent lover:

Solomon:	How beautiful art thou, my love, how beautiful!
	Thy eyes are doves.
The Shulammite:	How beautiful art thou, my Beloved, how lovely!
	Our bed is verdant.
Solomon:	The beams of our house are cedar,
	The rafters are cypress.
The Shulammite:	I am a narcissus of Sharon,
	A lily of the valley.
Solomon:	Like a lily among thorns
	Is my beloved among the youthful maidens.
The Shulammite:	Like an apple tree in the midst of the forest
	Such is my Beloved among men.

Surely it is much more natural to see in this passage a dialogue between
two lovers, who are mutually praising each other.

(4)

We have already seen that in the first century A.D. there were some
who sang the Song as an ordinary song, giving it its plain sense as an

thinkable that the Jewish religious authorities would have permitted the performance of
dramatic pieces, and still more so that they would ever have consented to a written
drama figuring among the sacred writings of their Canon." Cf. K. Budde (in *H.S.A.T.*
4th ed., ii, 1923, p. 390b): "Das drama auf rein semitischen Boden nirgendwo Fuss
gefasst hat." Cf. also E. Junès, *op. cit.*, p. 15; J. Fischer, in *Echt. B.*, Lieferung 10, 1949,
Das Hohe Lied, p. 6. Cf. also D. Buzy, in *La Sainte Bible*, ed. by L. Pirot and A. Clamer,
vi, 1946, p. 287: "Le drame est irrecevable comme explication du Cantique. Non pas que
ce genre littéraire répugne au concept d'inspiration. Mais le texte se montre absolument
rebelle à cette interprétation et à ce genre littéraire. Ce n'est qu'à force de prétendus
changements de décors, de sous-entendus et d'apartés, d'artifices et de contrefaçons que
l'on peut faire courir dans cette poésie idéale la trame d'une intrigue ou d'un roman"
(repeated, with the change of one word, from *R.B.*, xlix, 1940, p. 169).

[1] *Op. cit.*, pp. 155 f. (E.Tr. by Lilly, pp. 174 f.). Cf. Ewald's interpretation, which
assigns 1: 15 to Solomon, and 1: 16–2: 1 to the Shulammite, 2: 2 to Solomon and 2: 3
to the Shulammite, and similarly holds that the Shulammite is thinking of her absent lover
(*op. cit.*, p. 67).

erotic poem. At the end of the fourth century this view was taken by Theodore of Mopsuestia,[1] who maintained that when Solomon's subjects criticized his marriage with an Egyptian princess he boldly sang of his love in this Song.[2] More than a century after his death, he was anathematized, and his views were condemned as unfit for Christian ears.[3] In the twelfth century an anonymous French Rabbi[4] revived this view, and held that Solomon sang of his favourite wife. One of the early Reformers, Sebastian Castellio (Châteillon)[5], presented a similar view, and declared that the Song should be excluded from the Canon, since it dealt merely with earthly affections—a view which Calvin strongly reprobated, and which led to Castellio's departure from

[1] See J. D. Mansi, *Sacrorum conciliorum nova et amplissima collectio*, ix, 1763, col. 225. Cf. the Introduction to Isho'dad of Merv's Commentary (see G. Diettrich, *Išô'dâdh's Stellung in der Auslegungsgeschichte des Alten Testamentes*, B.Z.A.W., vi, 1902, pp. xvii–xix), where Theodore's method of approach is contrasted with the allegorical approach of Gregory of Nyssa and Chrysostom, and with the Rabbinical approach. Cf. also W. Riedel, *Die Auslegung des Hohenliedes in der jüdischen Gemeinde und der griechischen Kirche*, 1898, pp. 80–86.

[2] Theodore's brother Polychronius (cf. Theodoret, *Historia ecclesiastica*, V, xxxix, in Migne, *P.G.*, lxxxii, 1859, col. 1277) perhaps adopted the allegorical view. Cf. J. Meursius, *Eusebii, Polychronii, Pselli, in Canticum Canticorum expositiones graece*, 1617, p. 77: "The Bridegroom is our Lord; the Bride is the Church; the friends of the Bridegroom are angels and saints; the maidens are the followers of the Church." But this commentary is of doubtful authenticity. Cf. H. B. Swete, in Smith and Wace, *Dictionary of Christian Biography*, iv, 1887, p. 435b.

[3] See Mansi, *loc. cit.*, Philastrius (cf. Migne, *P.L.*, xii, 1845, cols. 1267 f.) had earlier treated as heretical the view that the Song dealt with human love, but as Calès (*Le Livre des Psaumes*, 1936, i, p. 15) says, Philastrius was "quelque peu enclin à prodiguer l'épithète d'hérétique." On the nature of the condemnation of Theodore, cf. A. M. Dubarle, *R.B.*, lxi, 1954, pp. 68 f.

[4] The commentary of this Rabbi, which is found in the Bodleian MS. Opp. 625, has been edited by H. J. Mathews, in *Festschrift zum 80en Geburtstag Moritz Steinschneider's*, 1896, pp. 238–240, and Hebrew part, pp. 164–185. Cf. another anonymous Rabbinical commentary, published by A. Hübsch in *Die fünf Megilloth nebst dem syrischen Thargum genannt "Peschito" mit einem Kommentare zum Texte aus einem handschriftlichen Pentateuch-Codex der k. k. Univ. Bibliothek zu Prag*, 1866. This author says (p. 9b): "Solomon had one wife who was beloved more than all his wives, and he sang this Song about her." Cf. also S. Salfeld in *Magazin für die Wissenschaft des Judenthums*, v, 1878, pp. 155 f. S. Eppenstein (*R.E.J.*, liii, 1907, pp. 242–254) has published a fragment of another anonymous commentary, preserved in Turin, whose point of view is intermediate between that of these commentaries and the usual Jewish view.

[5] Cf. Calvin's statement issued to Castellio on his departure from Geneva, in which he says, "Our principal dispute concerned the Song of Songs. He [i.e. Castellio] considers that it is a lascivious and obscene poem, in which Solomon has described his shameless love affairs." See *Ioannis Calvini Opera quae supersunt omnia*, ed. G. Baum, E. Cunitz, E. Reuss, xi (*Corpus Reformatorum* xxxix), 1873, col. 675, or F. Buisson, *Sébastien Castellion: sa vie et son œuvre*, 1892, i, pp. 198 f.

Geneva.[1] Later Grotius[2] adopted these views, and maintained that Solomon concealed all the intimacies of love under innocent terms. It is true that Grotius also gave the Song a mystical meaning, but he does not seem to have attached great weight to this, or to have devoted so much pains to the unfolding of this meaning as to the unfolding of the erotic sense. In the eighteenth century Whiston[3] declared that the Song was written by Solomon "when He was become Wicked and Foolish, and Lascivious, and Idolatrous", and thought so immoral a book had no rightful place in the Canon,[4] and in the nineteenth century E. Reuss[5] similarly regarded the work as merely profane poetry, which ought not to be included in the Canon of Scripture.

Not all who have rejected the allegorical view, and found the theme of the Song to be only human love, have felt it to be a thing evil and unworthy of a place in the Bible. The poet Herder[6] found its theme to be pure love, and found beauty and worth enshrined in it. He did not regard it as a single composition, but as a collection of detached and

---

[1] Castellio's disagreement with Calvin was mainly on the question of the Song of Songs and on the Descent of Christ to Hell. It was referred to the Council, but without the full disclosure of the facts, though Calvin wrote to Viret that this was to spare Castellio's reputation (cf. J. Bonnet's *Letters of John Calvin*, E.Tr. by D. Constable, i, 1855, p. 380). It is only fair to Calvin to add that, when Castellio felt he could no longer remain in Geneva, Calvin wrote, in the same letter to Viret: "Do you look after him, and help him to the utmost of your power." Cf. E. Giran, *Sébastien Castellion et la réforme calviniste*, 1914, pp. 65–76.

[2] *Opera omnia theologica*, i, 1732, p. 276a: "Nuptiarum arcana sub honestis verborum involucris hic latent: quæ etiam causa est cur Hebræi veteres hunc librum legi noluerint nisi a jam conjugio proximis."

[3] *A Supplement to Mr. Whiston's late Essay. Towards restoring the true text of the Old Testament, proving that the Canticles is not a sacred book of the Old Testament*, 1723, pp. 5 f. Cf. also p. 13: "I venture to affirm, as to the internal Composition and Contents of this Book itself; that so far as the common Meaning of Words and critical Judgment of the Nature of the Book can guide us, this Evidence is wholly on the other Side [i.e. against the allegorical and mystical view]; and this so certainly and plainly, that 'tis next to a Demonstration against its allegorical Meaning, and consequent Authority."

[4] Cf. also J. Le Clerc (*Sentimens de quelques théologiens de Hollande sur l'Histoire Critique du Vieux Testament, composée par le P. Richard Simon*, 1685, pp. 273 f.): "On croit communément que le Cantique des Cantiques est un Livre Mysterieux, qui décrit l'amour mutuel qui est entre Jesus Christ et son Eglise. Mais on n'en a aucune preuve, ni dans le Vieux, ni dans le Nouveau Testament, ni dans le Livre même. . . . N'ayant aucune preuve des mystéres qu'on cherche dans ce Livre, si nous en jugeons par le Livre même, nous trouverons que ce n'est qu'une Idile, ou une Eglogue, où Salomon s'introduit lui-même en Berger, et l'une de ses femmes (peut-être la fille de Pharaon, comme le croient quelques Savans) en Bergere."

[5] *Le Cantique des Cantiques*, 1879, p. 3: "Ce n'est qu'avec une certaine hésitation que nous abordons le Cantique, pour le joindre aux autres livres bibliques. . . . Nous avons maintenant affaire à une poésie profane."

[6] *Lieder der Liebe*, 1778, pp. 89–106.

separate poems. This view has found a number of followers, of whom we may note J. C. C. Döpke[1] and A. Bernstein.[2] It has also exercised a considerable influence upon many later students of the Song, who have, however, embodied also elements of other theories yet to be examined. To these we shall have occasion to return.

Meanwhile, scholars who themselves retained the allegorical view of the Song were preparing the way for a fresh line of approach. At the end of the seventeenth century Bossuet,[3] who held, like many who had preceded him from the time of Origen,[4] that the occasion of the Song was the marriage of Solomon with Pharaoh's daughter,[5] observed that amongst the Jews the customary period for the celebration of a wedding was seven days. He then found the Song to fall into seven divisions, which he believed to correspond to the seven days of the feast. In this he was followed by Calmet[6] and Lowth,[7] both of whom held firmly that the Song had also an esoteric meaning. Lowth said:[8] "May we not with some shadow of reason suspect that, under the allegory of Solomon choosing a wife from the Egyptians, might be darkly typified that other Prince of Peace, who was to espouse a Church chosen from among the Gentiles?"

In 1860 Renan[9] noted the similarity of the Song to modern Syrian

[1] *Philologisch-critischer Commentar zum Hohen Liede Salomo's*, 1829. Döpke held that all the songs did not come from a single author.

[2] *Das Lied der Lieder, oder das hohe Lied Salomo's*, 1834, published under the pseudonym A. Rebenstein. Bernstein thought the third chapter was a later interpolation.

[3] *Biblia sacra cum commentariis*, xiv, 1751, p. vi. Bossuet divides the days as follows: 1: 1–2: 6; 2: 7–17; 3: 1–5: 1; 5: 2–6: 8; 6: 9–7: 10; 7: 11–8: 3; 8: 4–14. For a completely different division cf. J. W. Lethbridge, *The Idyls of Solomon: the Hebrew marriage week*, 1878.

[4] Cf. Migne, *P.G.*, xiii, 1862, col. 61.

[5] So D. Broadribb, *Abr-Nahrain*, iii, 1963, p. 20. Broadribb thinks the setting of the poem is Solomon's palace in Jerusalem (p. 23).

[6] "Préface sur le Cantique des Cantiques", in *Commentaire littéral sur tous les livres de l'Ancien et du Nouveau Testament*, xii, 1713, pp. 149 ff.

[7] *Lectures on the Sacred Poetry of the Hebrews*, E.Tr., 1847, pp. 335 ff. This view was contested by J. D. Michaelis (*In Roberti Lowth prælectiones de Sacra Poesi Hebrærum notae et epimetra*, 1763, p. 162), who found nothing whatever in the book to suggest allegory, or indeed anything to do with the marriage ceremony, since there is no mention of marriage rites anywhere in the poem (p. 154). He says. "Restat, ut meam profitear sententiam, castos conjugum amores cani, non sponsi et sponsae" (p. 155).

[8] *Loc. cit.*, pp. 347 f.

[9] *Le Cantique des Cantiques*, 1860, p. 86: "Je ne doute pas que le Cantique des Cantiques ne fût le plus célèbre de ces jeux qu'on célébrait à l'époque des mariages", with the footnote "M. Ch. Schefer, qui connaît si bien l'Orient mussulman, m'apprend que les divertissements de ce genre se pratiquent encore, pour les mariages, à Damiette et dans certaines localités de la Syrie. Ils durent sept jours, durant lesquels l'épousée parait chaque fois en costume différent"

wedding poetry, and in 1873 Wetzstein,[1] who was a German consul in Syria, published a study of modern marriage customs in Syria. It is customary for the celebrations to last seven days, during which the bridegroom and his bride are crowned, and treated as king and queen.[2] Poems called *wasfs* are sung in their honour, describing their physical beauty, and also songs of war, while the bride performs a sword dance with a naked sword.[3]

Not for twenty years did this study bear fruit, save for a brief note by B. Stade,[4] until K. Budde[5] presented the theory, with a force and persuasiveness that immediately secured the adhesion of C. Siegfried[6] and dominated the discussion of the book for a quarter of a century, that we have here a collection of poems sung in connexion with the simple wedding ceremonies of the people.[7] Customs are very tenacious, and it is said that the modern marriage customs of Syria may be not very different from those of two thousand years ago, and in

---

[1] "Die syrische Dreschtafel", in *Zeitschrift für Ethnologie*, v, 1873, pp. 270–302; also "Bemerkungen zum Hohenliede", in Delitzsch's *Biblischer Commentar*, 1875, pp. 162–177 (E.Tr. by Easton, 1877, pp. 162–176). Cf. also B. Chémali, "Mariage et Noce au Liban", in *Anthropos*, x–xi, 1915–16, pp. 913–941, where Christian ceremonies are described, and Christian songs are translated; also St. H. Stephan, "Modern Palestinian Parallels to the Song of Songs", in *J.P.O.S.*, ii, 1922, pp. 199–278.

[2] Cf. also E. Littmann (*Neuarabische Volkspoesie*, 1902, A IV 98, 100, pp. 43, 126), who presents a case where the bridegroom is compared with the reigning king, and who remarks: "Zur Zeit Salomos mag man den Bräutigam, den Hochzeitskönig, ebenfalls Salomo genannt haben und nachher, da Salomos Friedenherrschaft auf lange Zeit im Herzen des Volkes weiterlebte, mag man auch seinen Namen für den Friedenskönig der Hochzeitswoche beibehalten haben" (pp. 98 f.).

[3] Cf. also J. G. Wetzstein in *Z.D.M.G.*, xxii, 1868, pp. 105 f., note 45.

[4] *Geschichte des Volkes Israel*, ii, 1888, p. 197. Stade rejected the view that the book was a drama, and held that it sang the union of a bridal pair, adding "Den förderlichsten Beitrag zum Verständniss dieses ganz einzigartigen Buches hat in unserer Zeit J. G. Wetzstein gegeben."

[5] "The Song of Solomon", in *The New World*, iii, 1894, pp. 56–77, later published as "Was ist das Hohelied?" in *Preussische Jahrbücher*, lxxviii, 1894, pp. 92–117. See also Budde's commentary on the Song in K.H.A.T., 1898, and in *H.S.A.T.*, 4th ed., ii, 1923.

[6] See his commentary in Nowack's *Handkommentar*, 1898. So also J. C. Matthes, "Het Hooglied", in *Een Bundel*, 1913, pp. 208–237 (first published in 1895).

[7] This view was hailed by C. Cornill (cf. *Introduction to the Canonical Books of the Old Testament*, E.Tr., 1907, p. 461) as definitely solving the riddle of the book, and it is still presented by E. Sellin (*Einleitung in das Alte Testament*, 7th ed., 1935, p. 146). Cf. also U. Cassuto, "Il significato originario del Cantico dei Cantici", in *G.S.A.I.*, N.S. i, 1925–28, pp. 23–52, and G. Luzzi, *Gli Agiografi* (La Bibbia tradotta e annotata, viii), 1925; also S. Krauss, *Occident and Orient* (Gaster Anniversary Volume), 1936, pp. 323–330, where Cant. 3: 8 is explained in connexion with the supposed activity of evil spirits on the bridal night. It is still preferred by A. Lods, *Histoire de la littérature hébraïque et juive*, 1950, pp. 748–758, and E. Dhorme, *La Bible de la Pléiade*, Ancien Testament, ii, 1959, p. cxliv.

any case they seem to throw much light on this book. For the descriptions of the charms of the bride[1] and the bridegroom found in the Song have much of the character of the *wasfs*, while 6 : 10, 7 : 1-6 (E.V. 6 : 10, 13-7 : 5) may belong to the bride's sword dance.

It is not to be supposed, however, that this view has passed without criticism. While it has gathered to itself a long list of supporters, from the first it has had criticism,[2] and it is now falling somewhat out of fashion. It is pointed out that there are here no war songs, and that the whole collection is insufficient to last for seven days. To this it is replied that we have only a selection of the amorous poems used on such occasions, rather than a complete cycle. O. Gebhardt, however, disputes the relevance of the assumption on which the whole view rests. He observes[3] that the Syrian peasants of Transjordan are a mixed race, the result of frequent invasions, and their customs have no bearing on Jewish poetry.[4] To this we may add that a recent student of marriage conditions in Palestine[5] says that it is uncertain whether the custom described by Wetzstein exists in Palestine, and adds that most

---

[1] We may note, however, that L. Waterman (*J.B.L.*, xliv, 1925, pp. 179 f.) finds these descriptions to be somewhat left-handed compliments. He says: "He compares separate items of her features and form to various objects in a manner that is often either decidedly ugly or manifestly grotesque, e.g. her hair is likened to the dingy, shaggy, and multi-colored effect of a flock of goats, with the figure drawn in such a fashion as to give the impression that she was also partially bald (4: 1b). She is complimented for having all of her teeth, but by a figure that shows them to be horribly uneven (2: 2, *sic*; ?4: 2), while in the very next breath he uses a figure which pictures her mouth as that of an old woman who has lost all her teeth. He likens her eyes to doves but admits that he can't see them because her hair hangs down so as to cover them (4: 1). In the same manner he likens her temple to a cross-section of a pomegranate, but also admits that he can't really see them [*sic*] because her locks obscure them (4: 3b). Her neck is described in a manner to suggest the earliest recorded case of goitre."

[2] Cf. A. Harper, *op. cit.*, pp. 74–93, and W. W. Cannon, *The Song of Songs edited as a Dramatic Poem*, 1913, pp. 28–40. Cannon is himself amongst the followers of Ewald, though he holds that the Song was never intended to be acted, but recited, and that while it is certainly dramatic, it is not scenic.

[3] *Das Lied der Lieder übertragen mit Einführung und Kommentar*, 1931, pp. 12 f. Gebhardt holds that the Song is not a drama, but a bucolic Mimos. The shepherds are only imaginary, and the work is not mere folk-poetry, but a work of art, that can best be understood in the light of the idylls of Theocritus (pp. 17 ff.). Older writers observed the similarity between the Song and Theocritus, and Lethbridge, (*op. cit.* p. 31) even held that the latter was acquainted with the Song.

[4] Cf. Cannon, *op. cit.*, p. 29: "It is an enormous assumption that these wedding ceremonies described by Wetzstein as taking place in Syrian villages near Damascus in 1861, were necessarily the same in weddings in Judea more than 2,000 years earlier, or at any time."

[5] Hilma Granqvist, *Marriage Conditions in a Palestinian Village*, ii, 1935, p. 137 n.

writers on wedding customs in Palestine say nothing of a "king's week", of which she herself saw no sign in the village she describes. Moreover, Rothstein[1] has pointed out that the Shulammite is never called "queen" in the Song, as on Budde's view she ought to have been.

Hence a few writers, while recognizing that the marriage-cycle theory has contributed something to the understanding of the Song, and while finding in the poems it contains songs akin to the *wasfs* already mentioned, hesitate to accept the theory of Budde. The *wasf*, indeed, was not limited to marriage celebrations, and Dalman[2] has adduced some Arabic pre-nuptial *wasfs*. It is therefore held that we have in the Song a collection of love lyrics rather than merely marriage songs. This view, which runs back to the already noted view of Herder, has been adopted by E. Reuss,[3] P. Haupt,[4] M. Jastrow,[5] W. Staerk,[6] O. Eissfeldt,[7] H. Wheeler Robinson,[8] R. H. Pfeiffer,[9] A. Bentzen,[10]

---

[1] See Hastings's *D.B.*, iv, 1902, p. 593a. Cf. also Harper, *op. cit.*, p. xv, and Carlebach, *Jeschurun*, x, 1923, p. 199.

[2] *Palästinischer Diwan*, 1901, pp. xi ff. Cf. also Ricciotti, *Il Cantico dei Cantici*, 1928, pp. 23–52—"Paralleli letterarii al Cantico dei Cantici."

[3] Cf. *Die Geschichte der Heiligen Schriften Alten Testaments*, 1881, p. 223.

[4] *Biblische Liebeslieder*, 1907. Haupt rearranges the Song and divides it into twelve separate poems. He emphasizes the obscene associations which he finds to belong to many of the expressions of the Song.

[5] *The Song of Songs, being a Collection of Love Lyrics of Ancient Palestine*, 1921.

[6] *Lyrik* (S.A.T., III, i), 2nd ed., 1920, p. 293: "Wir haben es also im HL überwiegend mit Liebes- bzw. erotischer Poesie zu tun, und nur weniges lässt sich mit Sicherheit oder Wahrscheinlickheit als Hochzeitspoesie im eigentlichen Sinn nachweisen." E. Suys ("Les Chants d'amour du Papyrus Chester Beatty I", in *Biblica*, xii, 1932, pp. 209–227) suggests, but without developing the idea, that the Song rests on Egyptian lyrical poetry.

[7] Cf. *Einleitung in das Alte Testament*, 1934, p. 534 (2nd ed., 1956, p. 603; 3rd ed., 1963, p. 660).

[8] *The Old Testament: Its Making and Meaning*, 1937, pp. 161 f. Cf. also Meinhold, *Einführung in das Alte Testament*, 3rd ed., 1932, p. 366: "Doch ist's schon möglich, dass manches der im Hohenlied enthaltenen Liebeslieder dort Aufnahme fand, ohne dass es gerade ein Hochzeitslied zu sein brauchte." Cf. too Lods (*R.H.R.*, lxxxii, 1920, p. 223): "J'inclinerais, pour ma part, à croire qu'une partie au moins des poésies du Cantique étaient des chants nuptiaux, les autres étant de simples poèmes d'amour qui ont, du reste, pu être exécutés aussi dans les festins de noces"; A. Weiser (*Einleitung in das Alte Testament* 1939, p. 250): "Diese Sammlung profaner Liebeslyrik" (5th ed., 1963, p. 264; E.Tr. by D. M. Barton, 1961, p. 302); W. Rudolph (*Z.A.W.*, N.F. xviii, 1942–43, p. 191): "Das HL ist eine Sammlung weltlicher Hochzeits- und Liebeslieder, die nichts anderes als die Liebe der Geschlechter zum Gegenstand haben." This view is also adopted by S. Krauss, "The Archaeological Background of some Passages in the Song of Songs", in *J.Q.R.*, N.S. xxxii, 1941–42, pp. 115–137, xxxiii, 1942–43, pp. 17–27, xxxv, 1944–45, pp. 59–78.

[9] *Introduction to the Old Testament*, 1941, p. 711.

[10] *Introduction to the Old Testament*, ii, 1949, p. 182.

W. J. Lowther Clarke,[1] R. Gordis,[2] N. K. Gottwald,[3] J. Winandy,[4] A. S. Herbert,[5] and W. Rudolph.[6]

I am inclined to agree to some extent with this view. I am not persuaded that the marriage-week theory is soundly based, or that the songs as a whole[7] had anything to do with a wedding occasion. They appear rather to be a series of poems in which a lover enshrined the love he gave and the love he received. But, unlike some of those who have treated the book as a collection of amorous poems, I am not able to distribute the poems amongst several authors. W. O. E. Oesterley,[8] for instance, who finds in the book twenty-eight separate songs, some of which may be connected with the marriage week, and some of which are of liturgical origin,[9] says that "unity of authorship is quite out of the question". Of this I am not persuaded.[10] The repetitions that occur leave the impression of a single hand, and there is a greater unity of theme and of style than would be expected in a collection of poems from several hands, and from widely separated ages.[11] It is probable, too, that there is artistry in the arrangement of the

[1] Cf. *Concise Bible Commentary*, 1952, pp. 515 f.
[2] Cf. *The Song of Songs*, 1954, pp. 8 ff.
[3] *A Light to the Nations*, 1959, p. 492; *I.D.B.*, iv, 1963, p. 424.
[4] Cf. *Le Cantique des Cantiques*, 1960, p. 59.
[5] Cf. Peake's *Commentary on the Bible*, revised ed., 1962, p. 469b.
[6] Cf. *Das Buch, Ruth, Das Hohe Lied, Die Klagelieder* (K.A.T.), 1962, p. 105.
[7] They appear to me to express the love of two lovers who married, but not to be written for, or used at, the marriage ceremony. Cf. J. Winandy, *Le Cantique des Cantiques*, 1960, p. 26; "Le poème n'a rien de sensuel au sens péjoratif du terme: il ne chante pas une liaison coupable, mais un amour et une admiration réciproques dont rien ne permet de croire qu'ils ne soient pas légitimes."
[8] *The Song of Songs*, 1936, p. 6b. F. Landsberger (*J.B.L.*, lxxiii, 1954, pp. 203 ff.) argues that the Song consists of a far larger number of separate brief poems. Similarly M. H. Segal (*V.T.*, xii, 1962, p. 477) maintains that the Song is a collection of separate poems of varied character, from many different hands (p. 489). R. Gordis (*The Song of Songs* 1954, p. 24) similarly denies unity of authorship.
[9] See the following section.
[10] M. H. Segal (*V.T.*, xii, 1962, pp. 470–490) maintains that the individual poems of which the Song is composed are from more than one hand. He stresses the secular character of the Song, and holds that though it is not of Solomic authorship it dates from the period of Solomon in its original form, but was transmitted orally until the late Hellenistic period, in which its language securely fixes its present form.
[11] Cf. O. Gebhardt, *op. cit.*, pp. 22 f. Cf. also F. Scerbo ("Note critiche sopra il Cantico dei Cantici", in *G.S.A.I.*, xvii, 1904, pp. 65–111): "Una certa unità regna dal principio alla fine del componimento, comecchè l'intreccio della varie parti non sempre chiaro si scorga. Mal s'avvisano dunque, secondo noi, quelli che considerano la Cantica quale un'accòlta di canti diversi di genere amoroso." R. E. Murphy (*C.B.Q.*, xvi, 1954, p. 2) maintains the unity of the song and says the reasons in favour of unity are strong enough to win general acceptance. Cf. A. Feuillet, *R.B.*, lxviii, 1961, p. 10, where it is argued that the constant return to the same images, expressions, and themes does not favour the

pieces, and it may be, as M. Thilo[1] holds, that they trace the development of love to its consummation in marriage. I am not able, however, with Thilo, to find in the work an ethical or social tract, teaching a loftier view of woman than prevailed in contemporary society.[2] That it presents a high conception of human love I am ready to agree. But I do not believe that it had the slightest didactic purpose.[3] Love is ever content to express itself, and we need ask no other purpose of the Song. Its author was an artist, who created in these poems masterpieces of beauty. It is true that they are bolder in their images than our taste fancies, yet just because the love they sing is the true and pure love of two ardent lovers, they are infused with a spirit which perfects their artistry.[4]

(5)

During the last generation, however, yet another view is gaining ground. This is associated with the name of Professor T. J. Meek, who in 1922 first published his theory.[5] He believes the book was from the beginning a religious composition, but not connected with the

---

view that we have a collection of separate pieces. D. Broadribb (*Abr-Nahrain*, iii, 1963, p. 15) also maintains the unity of the work. On the other hand, C. H. Toy (*J.E.*, xi, 1905, p. 467a) allows the poems unity of emotion only.

[1] *Das Hohelied, neu übersetzt und ästhetisch-sittlich beurteilt*, 1921.

[2] Rothstein, who held the dramatic view, but believed that older wedding songs had been worked up in the Song, thought the purpose of the work was to glorify betrothed love and fidelity (Hastings's *D.B.*, iv, 1902, p. 594b). True and faithful love is so glorious that in its very expression of itself it must glorify itself, though without any such self-conscious purpose.

[3] C. E. De Vries (*The Zondervan Pictorial Bible Dictionary*, ed. by M. C. Tenney, 1963, p. 803b) says: "The Didactic-moral interpretation holds that the book presents the purity and wonder of true love. It regards the book as history and also agrees that the love portrayed does direct us to the greater love of Christ, in accordance with the history of Christian interpretation. The purpose of the Song of Solomon, therefore, is to teach the holiness and beauty of the marriage-love relationship which God Himself ordained."

[4] P. Gilbert (*Chronique d'Égypte*, Nos. 45–46, April 1948, pp. 22 f.) says that the Song recalls collections of Egyptian poems, and that some were probably used for marriage celebrations and others for other festive occasions. The repetitions that are found here may be paralleled there. He thinks some of the poems, particularly at the end, are only represented by their first verses.

[5] Cf. "Canticles and the Tammuz Cult", in *A.J.S.L.*, xxxix, 1922–23, pp. 1–14. Cf. also the same writer's further articles, "The Song of Songs and the Fertility Cult", in *The Song of Songs: A Symposium*, ed. by W. H. Schoff, 1924, pp. 48–79, and "Babylonian Parallels to the Song of Songs", in *J.B.L.*, xliii, 1924, pp. 245–252. Professor Meek has now published a commentary on the Song of Songs in *I.B.*, v, 1956, pp. 91–148. He says that his view has been considerably modified (p. 95b), but there seems to be little specific repudiation of the views presented in this essay. See, however, below, p. 233, n. 2.

worship of Yahweh. Instead he believes it was a liturgy of the Adonis-Tammuz cult. We have surviving texts from Babylonia, where the cult flourished, and these are held to exhibit so marked a similarity to the Song of Songs as to establish its character beyond dispute. The cult is also known to have been widely prevalent in Syria, and the Old Testament contains ample evidence that it existed in Israel.[1] Thus in Ezek. 8 : 14 we read of women weeping for Tammuz, and Is. 17 : 10 f.[2] gives further evidence of the cult.[3]

It was, indeed, a very ancient cult, going back to the time before the Israelites entered Palestine, and it seems to have retained its hold on the common people throughout almost the whole period of the Old Testament. It was linked to the fertility rites which the prophets so often denounced in all their forms. In the Adonis-Tammuz cult someone represented the god and someone the goddess. The death of the god and his descent to the underworld, followed by the descent of the goddess in search of him, with the consequent languishing of Nature, and their subsequent release and return to the upper world, were all represented in a ritual drama. The rites then culminated in the marriage and union of those who represented the god and goddess, to the accompaniment of the ritual dance and much licentiousness. It was not regarded as mere licentiousness, however, but was believed to be an essential factor in the achievement of the annual miracle of reproduction in Nature.[4] For by sympathetic magic all of this human acting was believed to effect the union of the god and goddess represented, and thus to release the powers of fertility in all Nature.[5] The omission

[1] Cf. Beatrice A. Brooks, "Fertility Cult Functionaries in the Old Testament", in *J.B.L.*, lx, 1941, pp. 227–253.

[2] "For thou hast forgotten the God of thy salvation, and has not remembered the rock of thy refuge; therefore thou plantest plantations of Adonis, and settest vine-cuttings of an alien god. On the day thou plantest, thou dost make it grow, and in the morning thou dost make thy seed to blossom." The rendering "thou dost make it grow" follows the A.V., in agreement with Ḳimḥi and Ibn Ezra; so also B. Duhm, K. Marti, and G. B. Gray. O. Procksch objects that a Pilpel from a Lamed He root is improbable. The lexicons of Brown-Driver-Briggs and Gesenius-Buhl both render as in R.V.: "thou hedgest it in".

[3] Cf. my article "The Song of Songs: an Examination of Recent Theory" in *J.R.A.S.*, 1938, pp. 251–276, from which I have incorporated much of the material here.

[4] Cf. Graham and May, *Culture and Conscience*, 1936, p. 122: "By the enactment of the accompanying drama the worshippers felt themselves to be reinforcing the power of the spoken word to influence the forces of nature so that the normal seasonal cycle might be maintained for the preservation and enrichment of human life. The psychology underlying this technique was one of coercion and manipulation."

[5] There were also uglier features. Sidney Smith observes (*J.R.A.S.*, 1928, p. 867): "Fertility cults are often attended by bloodthirsty rites. Natives of those districts where such cults have been practised in modern times have given only scanty information to

of these rites would therefore entail the direst consequences for the whole community.

Meek propounded the view that the Song of Songs is a thinly disguised survival of a liturgy of this cult. There had, indeed, been some anticipations of this view, though Meek was unaware of them when in 1920 he first presented his theory.[1] In 1906 Erbt had given a cultic interpretation to the Song in terms of the astral theory of the Pan-Babylonian school.[2] Its association with the ideas of that school was, however, sufficient to restrict the range of its influence, and little was heard of it.

The next form in which this view appeared connected it with Egypt. This was presented in 1914 by O. Neuschotz de Jassy, who developed the thesis that the Song is a liturgy of the Osiris cult.[3] Again, however, the view commanded no attention. In a letter to its author Loisy expressed his doubt as to whether it would immediately command acceptance, but thought it worthy of discussion. Little discussion was given to it,[4] however, and it left no ripple on the waters of scholarship. In 1919 Ebeling published an Accadian text, or series of fragments of texts, belonging to a liturgy of the Babylonian Tammuz

scientific inquirers. . . . Those rites involved the perpetuation of the life of the king by the god and goddess after a sacred *connubium*, probably enacted by a man and woman representing the deities, a banquet, a setting forth as though to war, and the final result was a number of tombs near the *gigunus* outside the wall of the temenos, in a ditch." The cult involved something more than the mere *joie de vivre*, and the spring rejoicing in the awakening of Nature. It was a ritual to achieve fertility, and the price of that achievement had to be paid. The weeping for Tammuz was no mere pretence, for the gods are not so easily deceived.

[1] To the American Society of Biblical Literature and Exegesis. This was the paper subsequently published in *A.J.S.L.*

[2] Cf. *Die Hebräer: Kanaan im Zeitalter der hebräischen Wanderung und hebräischer Staatengründungen*, 1906, pp. 196–202. Erbt's view was criticized by V. Zapletal, *Das Hohelied*, 1907, pp. 52–56.

[3] Cf. *Le Cantique des Cantiques et le Mythe d'Osiris-Hetep*, 1914. Neuschotz dissolved the Solomon of history into mere myth and legend (pp. 21 ff.), and identified the Solomon of the Song with Osiris (pp. 16 f.) and Jerusalem with Hor-Hetep, holding that the city of *peace* really means the city of the *dead* (pp. 17 f.), while the Shulammite he found to be Hetepith, or Isis (p. 21). He regarded the Song as concerned not with love, but with the resurrection of Osiris, and hence he interpreted the kiss in 1: 2 as the priestly kiss of resurrection, and not the kiss of lovers (p. 32). Similarly he argues that the kiss of Judas was not the kiss of betrayal, but the kiss of resurrection, which has been wrongly changed by tradition, and claims that the fact that the kiss was given in the garden of Gethsemane (=*gê sh^emānîm*; cf. the part played by spices in the Song of Songs) supports this view (p. 34).

[4] J. Halévy devoted a few scornful pages (*R.S.*, xxii, 1914, pp. 248–255) to it, and concluded "Je renonce à répondre aux grossièretés gratuites de l'auteur et lui souhaite une plus grande dose de bons sens et de modestie."

cult,[1] and this was not long in reopening the issue in the new form which Meek gave to it. Many Babylonian liturgies of the Tammuz cult had already been published prior to the appearance of this text,[2] but Meek was at once struck with the similarities between the Song of Songs and passages here.[3] The view of Meek does not depend on this particular text, however, for our knowledge of the Tammuz cult of Babylonia,[4] and of the kindred rites of the Osiris cult of Egypt and the Adonis cult of Syria, is considerable, and it is upon that knowledge, rather than upon the text which directed Meek to it, that the theory rests. It should be added that since Meek's theory was formulated the Ras Shamra texts have been published,[5] and our knowledge of the

[1] Cf. *Keilschrifttexte aus Assur religiösen Inhalts*, i, Heft 4, 1919, No. 158 (pp. 267–276). Cf. p. 352, where the text is described as a "Katalog von Hymnen-Anfängen an verschiedene Götter". Cf. also W. G. Lambert, "Divine Love Lyrics from Babylon", *J.S.S.*, iv, 1959, pp. 1–15

[2] Cf. S. Langdon, *Babylonian Liturgies*, 1913, and more recently M. Witzel, *Tammuz-Liturgien und Verwandtes*, 1935.

[3] The text has been translated in part or in whole by Ebeling (*M.D.O.G.*, No. 58, 1917, pp. 49 f.), Langdon (*J.R.A.S.*, 1921, pp. 183–190), Meek (*J.B.L.*, xliii, 1924, pp. 245–252), and Barton (*Archaeology and the Bible*, 6th ed., 1933, pp. 518–520). It may be noted that Barton's view of the Song of Songs is not quite clear. He quotes (pp. 515 ff.) some Egyptian parallels to the Song, and comments that they "make it clear that in Egypt love . . . was as warmly felt as in Israel, and was likewise poetically and passionately expressed". Since the parallels adduced are not presented as liturgies, it would seem that Barton regarded the Song merely as amorous poetry. The Babylonian parallel he quotes, however, he presents as a cult poem of the Tammuz worship. But since he then defines the theme simply as two lovers' praises for one another's charms, and the delight in love, it is not certain that he attaches himself to the theory of Meek.

[4] Cf. W. W. von Baudissin, *Adonis und Esmun*, 1911; S. Langdon, *Tammuz and Ishtar*, 1914; J. G. Frazer, *Adonis, Attis, Osiris*, 3rd ed., 2 vols., 1914; H. Gressmann, *Tod und Auferstehung des Osiris* (*Der Alte Orient*, xxiii, No. 3), 1923.

[5] Cf. Ch. Virolleaud, "Un poème phénicien de Ras Shamra: la lutte de Mot, fils des dieux, et d'Aleïn, fils de Baal", in *Syria*, xii, 1931, pp. 193–224; *id.*, "The Gods of Phoenicia, as revealed by the Poem of Ras Shamra", in *Antiquity*, v, 1931, pp. 405–414; *id.*, "La naissance des dieux gracieux et beaux", in *Syria*, xiv, 1933, pp. 128–151; R. Dussaud, "La mythologie phénicienne d'après les tablettes de Ras Shamra", in *R.H.R.*, civ, 1931, pp. 353–408; *id.*, "Le mythe de Ba'al et d'Aliyan d'après des documents nouveaux", *ibid.*, cxi, 1935, pp. 5–65; G. A. Barton, "A Liturgy for the Celebration of the Spring Festival at Jerusalem in the Age of Abraham and Melchizedek", in *J.B.L.*, liii, 1934, pp. 61–78; W. C. Graham, "Recent Light on the Cultural Origin of the Hebrews", in *J.R.*, xiv, 1934, pp. 306–349; D. Nielsen, *Ras Šamra Mythologie und Biblische Theologie*, 1936; R. Dussaud, *Les découvertes de Ras Shamra et l'Ancien Testament*, 1937, 2nd ed., 1941; S. H. Hooke, *The Origins of Early Semitic Ritual*, 1938; F. F. Hvidberg, *Graad og Latter i det Gamle Testamente*, 1938 (cf. *Z.A.W.*, N.F. xvi, 1939, pp. 150–152); C. F. A. Schaeffer, *The Cuneiform Texts of Ras Shamra-Ugarit*, 1939; I. Engnell, *Studies in Divine Kingship in the Ancient Near East*, 1943; C. H. Gordon, *The Loves and Wars of Baal and Anat*, 1943; J. Obermann, *Ugaritic Mythology*, 1948; T. H. Gaster, "A Canaanite Ritual Drama", in *J.A.O.S.*, lxvi, 1946, pp. 49–76; *id.*, *Thespis*, 1950; R. Largement, "La naissance de l'Aurore", 1949. Cf. also *Myth and Ritual*, ed. by S. H. Hooke, 1933; *The Labyrinth*, ed. by S. H. Hooke, 1935; and *Myth, Ritual and Kingship*, ed. by S. H. Hooke, 1958.

North Syrian forms of the cult and the mythology on which it rests has been greatly enriched.[1]

Not a few scholars have announced their adhesion to this view.[2] They include M. L. Margolis,[3] W. H. Schoff,[4] E. Ebeling,[5] S. Minocchi,[6] L. Waterman,[7] W. Wittekindt,[8] D. S. Margoliouth,[9] N. H. Snaith,[10] Graham and May,[11] W. O. E. Oesterley,[12] F. Dornseiff,[13] M.

---

[1] The descent of the goddess in search of the dead god, to which reference is made above (cf. also *Myth and Ritual*, ed. by S. H. Hooke, 1933, pp. 80 ff.). figures particularly in the Ras Shamra texts, together with the combat whereby the goddess slew the foe of the dead god, and to this part of the ritual, especially to the descent of Ishtar, many references have been found in the Song (cf. Meek, in *Symposium*, pp. 60 ff.).

[2] J. E. McFadyen, in *The People and the Book* (ed. by A. S. Peake), 1925, p. 214, held it to be probably correct.

[3] Cf. *The Song of Songs: A Symposium*, ed. by W. H. Schoff, p. 16.

[4] Cf. "The Offering Lists in the Song of Songs", in *The Song of Songs: A Symposium*, pp. 80-120.

[5] Cf. *Z.D.M.G.*, lxxviii, 1924, pp. lxviii f. (a brief report of a paper read at Munich).

[6] *Le Perle della Bibbia: Il Cantico dei Cantici e l'Ecclesiaste*, 1924, Cf. pp. 22 f.; "In questo senso il Cantico è tutto quanto poesia mistica. È un inno simbolico in cui si rappresenta una viva realtà naturale ed umana: la fecondata bellezza della terra e del cielo, al rinascere dell'anno, che è poi primavera della vita per la virtù dell'amore nel rinnovarsi delle anime. E i due amanti sono i simboli vivi della universale rinascita, non oscuramente indicati come tali dal poeta medesimo. Però tutto il Cantico è un inno alla primavera, l'esaltazione lirica della nuova creazione attuata dalla potenza divina immanente nelle cose; ed è in pari tempo anche un dramma, l'espressione rituale, in forme umane, delle profonde potenze spirituali che operano, palesi insieme e occulte, nella natura visibile. ... Il Cantico è una poetica celebrazione della primavera e dell'amore, per via di simboli mitici, aventi valore ad un tempo naturale e umano; i due amanti figurano o sostituiscono originariamente due divinità, rappresentano un mito, o, per essere esatti, i residui letterarii di un mito."

[7] Cf. "The Rôle of Solomon in the Song of Songs", in *J.B.L.*, xliv, 1925, pp. 171-187.

[8] Cf. *Das Hohe Lied und seine Beziehungen zum Istarkult*, 1926, esp. pp. 179-217.

[9] Cf. *A New Commentary on Holy Scripture*, ed. by C. Gore, H. L. Goudge and A. Guillaume, 1928, pp. 415 f.

[10] Cf. "The Song of Songs: The Dances of the Virgins", in *A.J.S.L.*, l, 1933-34, pp. 129-142. See also *id.*, *The Jewish New Year Festival*, 1947, p. 54 f.

[11] Cf. *Culture and Conscience*, 1936, pp. 122 f. Cf. also H. G. May, "The Fertility Cult in Hosea", in *A.J.S.L.*, xlviii, 1931-32, pp. 73-98.

[12] Cf. *The Song of Songs*, 1936, pp. 11 ff. Oesterley says (p. 15b): "There is much justification for the interpretation of the Song as being a survival of a number of early liturgies of the fertility cult. What has been said is far from exhausting all that can be urged in favour of this interpretation. It is not to be denied that there is a good deal in the Song which admits of a different interpretation; that there are wedding-songs pure and simple in which there is not necessarily any reference to the Tammuz-myth seems certain; but it is probable that they are based, all unconsciously, on early traditional liturgies of the cult whose meaning had been entirely lost."

[13] Cf. "Ägyptische Liebeslieder, Hoheslied, Sappho, Theokrit", in *Z.D.M.G.*, xc, 1936, pp. 589-601.

Haller,[1] I. Engnell,[2] G. Widengren,[3] H. Schmökel,[4] H. Ringgren,[5] and J. W. Wevers.[6] Not all of these scholars content themselves with merely accepting the views of Meek, indeed. Several of them give some distinct originality of form to their presentation of it. Thus Waterman, instead of holding with Meek that the old Tammuz liturgy has been revised[7] to bring it into accord with Yahwism, believed that it was reduced to the level of folk poetry, and then made into an allegory of the political relations between the two Israelite kingdoms in the period following the Disruption.[8] Again Snaith analysed the

[1] Cf. *Die fünf Megilloth* (H.A.T.), 1940, pp. 21 f.

[2] Cf. "Höga Visan", in *S.B.U.*, i, 1948, cols. 905–908.

[3] Cf. "Hieros gamos och underjordvistelse", in *Religion och Bibel*, vii, 1948, pp. 17–46; *Sakrales Königtum im Alten Testament und im Judentum*, 1955, pp. 78 f. D. Broadribb (*Abr-Nahrain*, iii, 1963, p. 35) ascribes the origin of the Song to some cultic situation which had disappeared by later Jewish times, and which belonged to the New Year Festival.

[4] Cf. *Z.A.W.*, N.F. xxiii, 1952, pp. 148–158, and *Heilige Hochzeit und Hohes Lied*, 1956 (cf. F. Horst's review in *Th.L.Z.*, lxxxiii, 1958, cols. 184–186).

[5] *Das Hohe Lied* (A.T.D.), 1958, pp. 3 f.; "Hieros gamos i Egypten, Sumer och Israel", *Religion och Bibel*, xviii, 1959, pp. 23–51.

[6] Cf. Hastings's one-volume *D.B.*, revised ed., edited by F. C. Grant and H. H. Rowley, 1963, pp. 930 f,

[7] Meek spoke of its reinterpretation and adaptation to meet changing conditions, beliefs, and practices (*A.J.S.L.*, xxxix, 1922–23, p. 13), and also said "it is not to be expected that much of its original character as a Tammuz liturgy has survived" (*ibid.*, p. 9). Schoff, whose article was published together with Meek's second article, and whose article was referred to with satisfaction by Meek, devoted much of his space to the "revision" of the original liturgy (see below). In private correspondence Meek prefers to use the term "absorption" rather than "revision", and says: "Just as Christmas, Easter, and other institutions came down through various religions and finally into Christianity, so the fertility cult came down through various religions and then into the Hebrew religion." Here, however, it is to be observed that Christmas and Easter have been "revised" and christianized, and related to the Christian message. They have not been absorbed into Christianity without the mention of Christ in relation to them. Yet Meek believes the absorption of a Tammuz liturgy into the Hebrew religion was effected without the mention of Yahweh. There is therefore a fundamental dissimilarity, rather than similarity, here. That much was absorbed into the Hebrew religion from the older Canaanite religion, or fertility cult, I fully agree (cf. *The Re-discovery of the Old Testament*, 1946, pp. 49 f., American ed., 1946, pp. 69 f., where I recognize that the feast of Tabernacles goes back to pre-Israelite usage; cf. also above in the present volume, pp. 47 f., where I recognize that much of the Israelite ritual was modelled on older ritual). But whatever was absorbed was integrated into Israel's faith, and made the vehicle of Yahwism. Other elements could not be so absorbed (cf. *The Re-discovery of the Old Testament*, p. 51, American ed., pp. 71 f.), and were therefore opposed by the prophets, though admittedly adopted by many in Israel. The elements which could not be absorbed were precisely the elements with which the Song of Songs is said to be connected.

[8] More recently Waterman has drawn away from Meek's theory, and developed his own original view. In *J.B.L.*, xliv, 1925, p. 172, he said: "The proposal of Meek to find the basic material of the piece in the poetry of the fertility cult of Babylonia and Syria has gone far beyond any previous attempts of this sort not only by adducing an array

Song into alternating passages from two cycles, the one having associations with the spring and the other with the autumn,[1] and brought it into connexion with the stories of the rape of the maidens of Shiloh and the sacrifice of Jephthah's daughter, while Oesterley found in the Song diverse elements, some of which are fragments of the old Tammuz liturgies, and others of which belong to the wedding celebrations of simple peasants. The most detailed working out of the theory in a complete commentary on the Song has been provided by Wittekindt, who believes it is a Jerusalem liturgy prepared for the celebration of the wedding of Ishtar and Tammuz at the spring new moon.

of very attractive analogies and explanations, but more particularly by being able to show convincing philological evidence of Babylonian origin. This hypothesis calls for a certain unity of conception based upon a very definite cycle of motives and aims." In *The Song of Songs translated and interpreted as a Dramatic Poem*, 1948, p. 2, however, he says of Meek's theory: "It is a reversion to the theory that the poem is an allegory, but one whose original significance was unknown to the Hebrews who were responsible for its present form. The objections to the allegorical approach in general are no less applicable here." Instead Waterman now proposes the view that the Song rests on a historical basis, and that after the death of David and Adonijah's fatal request for the hand of Abishag, the Shunammite refused the advances of Solomon through her loyalty to her rustic lover. The Song is held to have been originally of northern origin, and to have hailed this rebuff of Solomon in the early days after the Disruption, but to have been later re-arranged by a southern editor. For a criticism of Waterman, cf. T. J. Meek, in *J.B.L.*, lxviii, 1949, pp. 177–179, to which Waterman replied in a pamphlet *Answers to Questions in a Review*, 1950. Waterman's basic assumption that the heroine was Abishag is shared with many writers, but is devoid of foundation. Cf. my article, "The Meaning of 'The Shulammite'", in *A.J.S.L.*, lvi, 1939, pp. 84–91. The only support Waterman claims for it is the reading of LXXᴮ in Cant. 6: 13, but actually this MS. has *Soumaneitis* (cf. Waterman's pamphlet, p. 3). Even if it had Shunammite, this would be insufficient to overturn the rest of the evidence, as I have shown (*loc. cit.*, pp. 89 ff.). It is, indeed, far more probable that Shulammith is really a feminine formation from Solomon, and means "the Solomoness", as many scholars of various schools have held [*ibid.*, pp. 84–88; a printer's omission occurred in the rendering of the first author (p. 84): "The Shulammite was beloved of Solomon, for she was called after the name of her beloved"; to the list of authors who have adopted this view may be added H. S. Nyberg, *A.R.W.*, xxxv, 1938, pp. 354 f.]. The statement of D. Buzy (*Mémorial Lagrange*, 1940, p. 153) that the Septuagint and the Vulgate have maintained the reading Shunammite is misleading, since he omits to add that this is not the best attested reading of either version. With Waterman's latest view that of H. Torczyner (*Shir ha-Shirim*, written in Hebrew, 1943) may be compared. Here, too, it is argued that Abishag and Solomon figured, and that the king failed to win her from her rustic lover, and the Song is held to come from the days of Solomon. R. Tournay (*V.T.*, ix, 1959, pp. 288 ff.) thinks Shulammite was a deliberate alteration of Shunammite, and similarly Ammi-nadib in 6: 12 was a deliberate change of Abinadab, the reference in the one case being to Abishag the Shunammite (1 Kings 1: 3) and in the other to the Abinadab who gave shelter to the Ark (1 Sam. 7: 1). This does not seem very probable.

[1] Meek (*I.B.*, v, p. 95a) says Snaith carries his thesis too far and divides the book too mechanically between the autumn and the spring festivals.

On the other hand, the critics of this view have been slow to expose its weaknesses. Two, indeed, in the persons of Umberto Cassuto[1] and Nathaniel Schmidt,[2] appeared promptly to enter a caveat, and to expose some of the difficulties of the theory, and later Ricciotti briefly criticized it,[3] while Dürr subjected Wittekindt's work to a very brief critical review.[4] Most of those who have remained unconvinced have been content with rejection rather than reply.[5]

There is, indeed, to-day a growing tendency to find in various parts of the Old Testament ritual survivals,[6] and it is in full harmony with this tendency that the Song of Songs should be ritually interpreted. Moreover, there is a growing recognition of references to the Adonis-Tammuz cult in the Old Testament.[7] But this does not establish the

---

[1] Cf. his review of The Song of Songs: A Symposium, in G.S.A.I., N.S. i, 1925–28, pp. 166–173 (in Fasc. 2, dated Jan.-March, 1926).

[2] Cf. "Is Canticles an Adonis Liturgy?" in J.A.O.S., xlvi, 1926, pp. 154–164. In a private letter, dated in 1938, Professor Meek says: "I think Schmidt will agree with my view now." I am not aware that he published any retractation of his criticisms.

[3] Cf. Il Cantico dei Cantici, 1928, pp. 117–120, 298 f. Cf. also A. Bentzen, Introduction to the Old Testament, ii, 1949, p. 182: "It is not easy to understand how and when poems of this kind have been preserved in the passover ritual in spite of the strong anti-Canaanite reaction of the ninth-sixth centuries. We have here to count upon too many uncontrollable intermediate links."

[4] Cf. O.L.Z., xxxi, 1928, cols. 113–115.

[5] Cf. R. Gordis, J.B.L., lxiii, 1944, p. 263: "This theory has, however, for substantial reasons found few advocates"; T. H. Gaster, Thespis, 1950, p. 233 n.: "This theory is far from proved." R. Gordis further examines and rejects the theory in The Song of Songs, 1954, pp. 4 ff.

[6] Thus Mowinckel (Psalmenstudien, i, 1921) explains many of the Psalms as ritual texts, and argues (Psalmenstudien, iii, 1923, pp. 96–101) that Ps. 45, whose similarity to the Song of Songs has long been recognized, is a ritual psalm of prophetic import, while A. R. Johnson ("The Rôle of the King in the Jerusalem Cultus", in The Labyrinth, ed. by S. H. Hooke, 1935, pp. 73–111) finds many of the Psalms to preserve elements of the ritual in which the king figured (cf. Sacral Kingship in Ancient Israel, 1955, and Myth, Ritual, and Kingship, ed. by S. H. Hooke, 1958, pp. 204 ff.); P. Humbert (Z.A.W., N.F. iii, 1926, pp. 266–280; A.f.O., v, 1928–29, pp. 14–19; R.H.P.R., xii, 1932, pp. 1–15) explains the book of Nahum as a ritual for the autumn festival in Jerusalem in 612 B.C., when the fall of Jerusalem was celebrated; E. Balla (R.G.G., 2nd ed., ii, 1928, cols. 1556 f.), followed by Sellin (Einleitung in das Alte Testament, 7th ed., 1935, p. 119), explains the book of Habakkuk as a ritual text, and Humbert (Problèmes du livre d'Habacuc, 1944) argues that this book was composed as a liturgy for a service of intercession in 602–601 B.C.; Engnell "Joels bok", in S.B.U., i, 1948, cols. 1075–1077) interprets the book of Joel in terms of an ancient liturgy (cf. A. S. Kapelrud, Joel Studies, 1948, where parts of the book are said to be written in the style of a liturgy, but where a historical interpretation is offered).

[7] Meek (A.J.S.L., xxxix, 1922–23, p. 3) notes Is. 17: 10 f., Jer. 22: 18, Ezek. 8: 14, Zech. 12: 11, and elsewhere (Symposium, p. 48 n.) adds to these Joel 1: 8 ff., while Graham (J.R., xiv, 1934, p. 315), following a hint of Meek's (Symposium, p. 67), and claiming support from the Ras Shamra texts, regards Is 5: 1–7 as the prophet's reaction to a vineyard ritual which was a feature of the popular cultus. Most of these references to the

thesis that a Tammuz liturgy is preserved in the Bible. For none of these references recognized the cult as a legitimate one. They are merely the evidence that it was popularly practised, and are on the same footing as the innumerable references to Baal worship in the Old Testament. These amply prove that that worship had a strong hold on the people,[1] without leading us to expect to find a ritual of its practice in the Canon.

Here, indeed, we find the first serious difficulty Meek's theory has to face. The Adonis-Tammuz cult was inextricably connected with the immoral fertility rites, which the prophets so frequently denounced. When, then, can this liturgy be supposed to have been brought into the Canon? It cannot have been brought in in pre-exilic days, for there is no evidence for the existence of a Canon at that time.[2] Nor is it likely to have been received into the sacred corpus until late post-exilic days, for in the first century A.D. there was still some dispute amongst the Rabbis as to whether it was properly to be regarded as canonical, and the seriousness of the doubt may be reflected in Rabbi Akiba's extravagant opinion.[3] It may well be, as Meek points out,[4] that the reference

Adonis-Tammuz cult may be readily recognized, though Schmidt [*J.A.O.S.*, xlvi, 1926, p. 157; but cf. W. W. von Baudissin, *Adonis und Esmun*, 1911, p. 91, and A. Bertholet, in *Abhandlungen zur semitschen Religiongeschichte und Sprachwissenschaft* (Baudissin Festschrift), 1918, p. 52] is not persuaded that Jer. 22: 18 is connected with it, and Joel 1: 8 ff. is not necessarily so connected (cf. however F. F. Hvidberg, *Graad og Latter*, 1938, pp. 122 f., and A. S. Kapelrud, *Joel Studies*, 1948, pp. 31 ff.). Indeed, it may be freely admitted that the Old Testament contains a great many more allusions to the cult. Cf. H. Gressmann's important article "The Mysteries of Adonis and the Feast of Tabernacles", in *Exp.*, 9th series, iii, 1925, pp. 416–432; W. W. von Baudissin, *op. cit.*, pp. 385–510; H. G. May, "The Fertility Cult in Hosea", in *A.J.S.L.*, xlviii, 1932, pp. 73–98.

[1] In recent years there have been many suggestions that Old Testament characters were the offspring of sacred prostitution. Beatrice A. Brooks (*J.B.L.*, lx, 1941, p. 228) gives references for such suggestions in relation to Joseph, Shamgar ben-Anath, Jephthah and his daughter, Samson, Samuel and his parents, Tamar, Jeroboam's mother, Gomer, the mother of Immanuel in Isaiah's prophecy, and Ruth.

[2] In a private letter Professor Meek says: "I believe that Canticles got into the Canon in pre-exilic days. It is true that there was no formal canon in those days, but the makings were there; much of the literature that came to be incorporated into the Canon was of course produced in pre-exilic days." This confuses the question of the date of composition with that of canonicity. There is no evidence that any book in the third division of the Hebrew Canon was regarded as canonical in pre-exilic days, either formally or informally, and few scholars hold that any book of this division was even written in pre-exilic days—though earlier materials may be embodied in Psalms and Proverbs. J. W. Wevers (Hastings's one-volume *D.B.*, revised edn., ed. by F. C. Grant and H. H. Rowley, 1963, p. 931) says the view of Meek best explains the inclusion of the book in the Canon. On the other hand N. K. Gottwald (*I.D.B.*, iv, 1962, p. 423a) says the crowning objection to the view "is that, far from ensuring the book a place in the Canon, its association with pagan religion would have barred it." Cf. H. Gross, *Lexikon für Theologie und Kirche*, ed. by J. Höfer and K. Rahner, v, 1960, col. 441.   [3] Cf. *supra*, pp. 197 f.

[4] Cf. *A.J.S.L.*, *loc. cit.*, p. 3. Cf. also Schoff, *Symposium*, p. 106.

to the Tammuz cult in Deutero-Zechariah shows that the cult retained its hold over the people until a late post-exilic period, but it is highly unlikely that in the age when Judaism was developing its exclusiveness its leaders would recognize as canonical a work associated with the fertility cult.

This difficulty Meek resolves in a diametrically opposite way to that of Neuschotz. The latter boldly maintained[1] that the Rabbis knew full well the character of the Song, and that this explains why they declared its sacredness. This is to meet the difficulty by evading it. That it was sacred to one cult could provide no reason why it should be incorporated in the Canon of another, and vigorously hostile, cult.[2]

Meek, however, supposes that in the Song we have not the Tammuz liturgy in its original and offensive form, but that it has been revised to harmonize it with the Yahweh cultus.[3] Neuschotz had expressly denied any such revision,[4] and had declared that the Song has remained what it was from the beginning. Moreover, Waterman,[5] while holding that we have not the liturgy in its original form, supposed it to have undergone a totally different revision from that assumed by Meek. So far from the revision having been undertaken in the interests of the Yahweh cult, he believed that it secularized all the older religious elements.[6] The Solomon of the Song he held to be not Tammuz, the hero of the liturgy, but the villain of the piece, and would-be destroyer of love,[7] striving to get the maiden into his power and make her forget her lover.[8] But in the secularization of the poem its religious significance was changed for a political meaning, and the struggle between Israel and Judah depicted.[9]

---

[1] *Op. cit.*, p. 71.

[2] It is true that, even in the period of growing exclusiveness, Judaism could and did receive from Zoroastrianism many ideas and beliefs, because they were not fundamentally inimical to the faith of the Jews; but it is hard to suppose that its leaders could so come to terms with the Adonis-Tammuz cult as to include its liturgy in their sacred corpus.

[3] Cf. *Symposium*, p. 53: "As Canticles came to be incorporated into the Yahweh cult, the symbols and material allusions were supplemented by others drawn from the Temple cultus." Cf. also *supra*, p. 218 n.

[4] *Op. cit.*, p. 90: "Le Cantique des Cantiques est resté ce qu'il a été dès le début, le chant funéraire d'Isis-Sulamith ou *hetepith*, cherchant son frère et époux Osiris-Salom ou *hetep*, disparu dans les ombres de l'Amenti."

[5] Cf. *J.B.L.*, *loc. cit.*   [6] *Ibid.*, p. 183.   [7] *Ibid.*, pp. 179 f., 187.   [8] *Ibid.*, p. 183.

[9] *Ibid.*, p. 182. Cf. p. 187: "A fertility cult liturgy reduced to folk poetry and reinterpreted by a political *motif*, that was later partly obscured by a divergent national ideal, would seem to satisfy and explain Solomon's connection with the poem." It has been noted above that Waterman has since modified his view of the Song, though he still holds the Solomon of the Song to have been the villain of the piece in its original form, and that he has developed the political side of his interpretation, while dropping the cultic.

It is clear, therefore, that Meek had failed to convince even one who was largely impressed by his theory of this alleged revision. And in truth we look in vain in the Song for any real indication of the Yahweh cult. Indeed, Meek himself observes:[1] "Rather strikingly Yahweh never once appears in the book. When the liturgy was incorporated into the Yahweh cult, it was deemed sufficient to transfer the titles to him without adding his name." Surely this was a strange procedure, which left traces of the rejected cult everywhere in the book, but which left the new cult into which it was absorbed unmentioned. An intelligent reviser would have taken care that the Yahwism whose interests the book was now to serve would be unequivocally displayed in it, and not left to the reader to supply.[2]

It is true that Schoff attempts to supply Meek's deficiency, and to explain the nature of the alleged revision. The name of David has long been connected with the divine name Dod,[3] and both Meek[4] and Schoff[5] adopt this view, and identify Dod with Tammuz. They also identify Shelem, from whom they hold Solomon to have been named, with the same god.[6] From this Schoff concludes that both David and

---

[1] Cf. *Symposium*, p. 56.

[2] In his most recent treatment of the subject Meek (*I.B.*, v) abandons the view that the Song was revised to bring it into accord with Yahwism, and says that "the transforming influence of later Yahwism has almost completely obliterated the elements of the dying and rising god, the sacred marriage, and the place of the king in the rites; but enough traces remain to show that they were once there, although long since forgotten" (p. 95a). He further adds: "In course of time, however, the early connections of the book were forgotten, and it became so secularised that it appears today as a simple anthology of love poems without any religious connection other than its connection with Passover and its inclusion in the canon" (p. 95b). This would seem to abandon the only possible reason for its inclusion in the Canon. For it is doubtful if the connection with the Passover antedated the inclusion in the Canon (cf. A. Bentzen, *Studia Orientalia Ioanni Pedersen dicata*, 1953, p. 43: "Such poems do not belong to the specifically Israelite tradition in the Old Testament Passover"; see also below, pp. 240 f.). "To have got into the canon," says Meek, "the book at some time must have had some religious function, and that was manifestly the promotion of new life in soil and womb" (p. 96b). If the book had no religious association with Yahwism, it is hard to see how a manifest association with the fertility cult could have brought it into the Canon. W. Baumgartner (*O.T.M.S.*, 1951, p. 234) says: "The greatest difficulty is to see how this interpretation would make the inclusion of Canticles within the canon any easier to understand since, in view of the deeply rooted repugnance to any sexual association with the deity which we find in Israelite religion, the slightest hint of anything in this direction would have the exactly opposite effect."

[3] Cf. A. H. Sayce, *Lectures on the Origin and Growth of Religion as illustrated by the Religion of the Ancient Babylonians*, 1887, pp. 56 f.; H. Winckler, in *K.A.T.*, 1903, p. 225.

[4] Cf. *A.J.S.L.*, loc. cit., pp. 4 ff.; *Symposium*, pp. 54 f. In *I.B.*, v, p. 96a, Meek says that the epithet *Dôdh* would suffice to suggest the name of Yahweh, while on p. 96b he says that we know that *Dôdh* was the name of a fertility god.

[5] Cf. *Symposium*, pp. 88 f.

[6] On the god Shālīm, or Shulmānu, cf. H. S. Nyberg, *A.R.W.*, xxxv, 1938, pp. 352 ff.

Solomon recognized the Tammuz cult, and he suggests that the abortive effort of Adonijah to secure the throne was part of a puritan move to abolish this worship. Naturally, therefore, he holds that when the Temple was built the Tammuz cult found a place in it. He says:[1] "There is nothing intrinsically impossible, therefore, in the presence of the Tammuz cult in the temple or in the survival in some form of its ceremonial."[2]

With all this no fault can be found. For there can be no doubt that many practices found a home in the Temple, though later conscience condemned them,[3] and it is highly probable that the popular Tammuz rites were observed through long periods even in the Jerusalem sanctuary. Nor would the mere survival of a Tammuz liturgy from Jerusalem appear at all incredible. It is its survival in the Canon of the Old Testament which needs to be shown to be probable.

Nor does Schoff's alleged double revision succeed in this task. For the first revision he supposes the Song to have undergone was merely an adaptation to the conditions of the Temple. He has made an elaborate study of the Offering-lists in the Song, and claims that one hundred and thirty-four of the terms have reference to the Tammuz cult, and one hundred and twenty-six to the early sanctuaries. The impressiveness of this conclusion vanishes on examination, however.

We may take as an example his lists for chap. I, where he finds the Tammuz cult in *wine, vineyards, flock, kids, king, vineyard, doves,* and *couch,* and the early sanctuaries in *ointments, chambers, tents, curtains, veil, steed, chariot, circlets, pearls, beads, studs, gold, silver, table, myrrh, beams, cedar, panels, cypress.* It is at once clear that, if this analysis of the reference of the terms is justified, the revision was not to bring the work into accord with the fundamental religious ideas of Yahwism, but merely to adapt the still unchanged fertility rite to the Temple *venue.* It was in no sense a revision that accommodated the Tammuz ritual to

---

[1] *Ibid.*, pp. 94 f. Cf. also W. F. Albright, "The Syro-Mesopotamian God Šulmân-Ešmûn and Related Figures", *A.f.O.*, vii, 1931, pp. 164–169. Albright holds that the Shulammite stands for Shulmânîtu, the female counterpart of Shulmân, the god of war [*Studies in Old Testament Prophecy* (T. H. Robinson Festschrift), 1950, p. 7, and *Hebrew and Semitic Studies* (G. R. Driver Festschrift), 1963, p. 5].

[2] Cf. Graham and May, *Culture and Conscience*, 1936, p. 239: "While it is too daring to affirm that Solomon's temple was oriented as it was with reference to the enactment of some such cycle of nature myths as was in use in the cultus at Ras Shamra, the well-attested place of solar features in the Jerusalem cultus makes such a possibility not unreasonable."

[3] Cf. my article "Zadok and Nehushtan", in *J.B.L.*, lviii, 1939, pp. 113–141, and "Melchizedek and Zadok (Gen. 14 and Ps. 110)", in *Festschrift für Alfred Bertholet*, 1950, pp. 461–472.

Yahwism, or that could for a moment satisfy the objections of the prophets to the fertility cult,[1] and it can hardly be supposed that such a revision would have sufficed to win for the ritual recognition from the later leaders of Judaism.

Nor is the case improved by the second revision which Schoff supposes the work to have undergone, to adapt it to the Second Temple. For here he finds seven terms to indicate the extent of the revision, but as two of them are duplicates, they are reduced to five. These are *spikenard, henna, palanquin, saffron,* and *aloes.* It is hardly fair to ascribe to the supposed reviser such complete incompetence for his task. For not one of the five terms even points to the Second Temple at all.[2] Moreover, four of the five terms of this alleged revision are found only in the Song of Songs, and while the fifth (*aloes*) is found in the Pentateuch, it is in the Balaam oracles.[3] But even if all five terms pointed unequivocally to the Temple, they would still be quite unrelated to the essential ideas of Yahwism. The fundamental *differentiae* between the fertility cult and Yahwism were not to be found in these things, and a revision which consisted merely in rubbing a little ointment on the older ritual, and which failed to bring out the real qualities of the faith

[1] Schoff says (*Symposium*, p. 98): "It began as an early Canaanite ritual. It received additions as that ritual was adapted, under protest by the prophetic party, to the temple services at Jerusalem."

[2] It is true that Schoff adduces evidence from the Talmud and the Jewish Prayer Book to show that amongst the ingredients of the ceremonial incense and the anointing oil were *spikenard* and *saffron* (*ibid.*, p. 85), but since Mark 14: 3 and John 12: 3 show that spikenard had other uses, quite unrelated to the Temple ritual, no necessary connexion with the Temple can be established. A reviser who wished to re-adapt this ritual to accord with the practices of orthodox Judaism would have taken care to use terms that pointed unmistakably to the Law contained in the Pentateuch, not terms that were destined to appear centuries later in the Talmud. For Schoff holds that this second revision took place at a post-Alexandrine date (*ibid.*, p. 82), and we know from the Chronicler's work that when a Jew of that age revised history he left the marks of his revision, and the marks of Pentateuchal law, unmistakably upon it. We have no right to assume that in a revision of ritual for use in the Temple, where it was far more important to secure accord with the sacred Law, the reviser would proceed in so meagre and ambiguous a way. Reference has been made above to Gressmann's view that the Feast of Tabernacles goes back in its origin to Adonis rites (*Exp.*, 9th series, iii, 1925, pp. 416–432)—a view with which I should not disagree. Its assimilation to Yahwism has, however, been altogether more thoroughgoing than this mere pretence of a revision which is assumed for the Song.

[3] Num. 24: 6. The word is found also in Prov. 7: 17 and in Ps. 45: 9. In the two former passages it is masculine in form, but in Ps. 45: 9 it is feminine, as in Cant. 4: 14. Since Meek and Schoff regard Ps. 45 as another surviving fragment of fertility-cult liturgy (cf. *Symposium*, pp. 49 n., 108), it is surprising that this word is not emphasized as a further link between the Song and this Psalm, associated with the cult, instead of finding it to point to the Second Temple.

in whose interest it was carried through, would be left to exist in the mind of the interpreter rather than in the achievement of the reviser.

Nor can we be satisfied that Schoff's analysis rests on any substantial ground. For Meek finds[1] two of the five terms which Schoff regards as marks of the second revision to belong to the old fertility cult—viz., *henna* and *palanquin*—and Wittekindt agrees,[2] so far as *henna* is concerned. And since Schoff is himself doubtful of *aloes*, the marks of this revision become woefully slight to account for the strange acceptance of a Tammuz ritual into the Canon of Judaism.[3]

Furthermore, in Schoff's first list are some terms which Meek regards[4] as marks of the Tammuz cult, viz., *myrrh*, *cedar*, *cypress*, and several which Wittekindt holds to belong to that cult, e.g., *myrrh*,[5] *table*,[6] *steed*,[7] *pearls*,[8] *wall*,[9] *windows*,[10] *lattice*.[11] The alleged revision is therefore both doubtful in itself, and altogether inadequate to give to the Song a definitely Yahwistic character.

The triviality of this alleged revision is the more surprising, since when Hebrew writers elsewhere used material which they had taken over from non-Yahwistic sources, they displayed an altogether greater skill is assimilating it to their own religious ideas. Thus, while there may be some connexion between the Creation story in Gen. 1 and the Babylonian Creation Epic, all the cruder elements have gone, and to the whole there is given a nobility which belongs to the Hebrew writer and not to his source. If Tiamat survives, it is as the innocuous *tᵉhôm*,[12]

---

[1] Cf. *Symposium*, p. 58.   [2] *Op. cit.*, p. 99.

[3] Meek says (*A.J.S.L.*, *loc. cit.*, p. 14): "To make it still more acceptable the panegyric on love (8: 6 f.) crept into the text, and lo, in a generation or two the book had become canonical, 'The Song of Songs'!" It is not clear how this would have helped, and Meek himself subsequently retracted this by implication, and found in 8: 6 a survival of the fertility cult, saying (*Symposium*, p. 62): "This in its original context was manifestly a reference to the power of the love of the goddess to win the god back from the netherworld, despite the floods and other obstacles that lay between this world and the next." Moreover, Schoff (*ibid.*, p. 120) finds in 8: 6 f. one mark of the Tammuz cult and three marks of what he calls the first revision. Cf. also Wittekindt (*op. cit.*, p. 57), who interprets this passage in *sensu obsceno*.

[4] Cf. *Symposium*, p. 58. See also *A.J.S.L.*, *loc. cit.*, p. 9.

[5] *Op. cit.*, p. 99. Cf. also Frazer, *Adonis, Attis, Osiris*, 3rd ed., 1914, i, pp. 227 f.

[6] *Ibid.*, p. 98.   [7] *Ibid.*, p. 29. Cf. Meek, *A.J.S.L.*, *loc. cit.*, p. 11.

[8] *Op. cit.*, p. 30.   [9] *Ibid.*, p. 68.   [10] *Ibid.*   [11] *Ibid.*

[12] It is doubtful whether there is any connection between *tᵉhôm* and Tiamat other than a similarity of sound. No personality is ascribed to *tᵉhôm*, and it figures in no combat. Further, whereas part of Tiamat's body is stretched out to form the firmament of heaven, in the Biblical account the firmament is formed to hold the upper waters from the lower, and at the time of the Flood, the fountains of *tᵉhôm* burst forth.

and the majestic God is not left to the reader's imagination to supply, but is dominant in the story.

Again, the ingenuity with which Tammuz is imported at every point by the advocates of this theory can only cause grave doubts as to the soundness of the theory. If a writer cannot mention such common things of experience as *shepherd, vine, vineyard, dove, gazelle, apple, cedar, palmtree, garden,* or *hyacinth,* to name some things from Meek's list of alleged allusions to the Tammuz cult, without being held to be writing of that cult, the way of letters for all but devotees of Tammuz is made very hard;[1] and when to these we add some further terms from Schoff's list, *flock, kids, king, couch, fruit, flowers, blossoms, bed, lions, leopard, sister, bride, honey, milk, spring, fountain, waters, dew, maidens, moon, sun, nuts,* and *dance,* the poet's case becomes desperate indeed. For how could one write a love lyric in any language if such terms must be excluded from his vocabulary?[2] The fact that these terms occur in relation to the Tammuz cult is no proof that they could only have relation to that cult.[3] If the method of this theory should be applied to the whole of the Old Testament with something of the

[1] It is curious to note that some of the terms to which Robert and Feuillet appeal for the establishment of their view (see above, p. 207) are here claimed to be evidence for a very different view. A. S. Herbert (Peake's *Commentary on the Bible,* revised ed., edited by M. Black and H. H. Rowley, 1962, p. 469b) wisely says: "Varied and considerable though the language of love may be, it is none the less limited. Moreover, the ritual language that would describe the acts of the divine lovers must inevitably draw on the language of human love which, in the experience of man, is prior."

[2] Beatrice A. Brooks (*J.B.L.,* lx, 1941, pp. 231 f.) observes in another connexion: "One wonders whether it is legitimate to interpret so much of the Old Testament phraseology as echoes of the primitive rites which had been practised in the Near East for so long, and which evidence proves were incorporated into the popular cult of the early history of Israel. It is easy to find such phrases if one is looking for them. . . . At least some of these interpretations seem forced, as forced as if one were to claim that the verse 'In the Spring a young man's fancy lightly turns to thoughts of love' should be considered a reflection of the Adonis myth."

[3] I am not persuaded that even the word *dôdh* points necessarily to Adonis. That the word could have a cultic reference may be readily granted, without any acknowledgment that in all periods those who used the word thought of that reference. The English word *jovial* is etymologically connected with the name of a pagan deity, and once denoted the disposition of one born under the planet Jupiter. But it has acquired a sense which is independent of the superstition which lies behind its etymology, and it can today be used without exposing its user to the charge of superstition. In the same way *dôdh= beloved* and *dôdhîm= love* could be used without necessary association with the cult, just as *māweth = death,* though etymologically connected with the name of the god Mot, who is frequently mentioned in the Ras Shamra texts, could be used on the lips of the Hebrews without any reference to this particular god. Love and death are normal experiences of men and women in all ages, and it were unreasonable to deny them the right to mention them without being charged with idolatry.

energy with which Cheyne applied his Jerachmeel theory, or the astral theorists their ideas, there would soon be little of it left without connexion with the Tammuz cult.[1]

Two further points made by Meek in support of his theory have to be examined. The first is his claim[2] that the word *zāmîr* in 2 : 12 is an indication that we have here a liturgy, since this is a technical term for such a liturgy, and the second is the allegedly significant fact that the Song belongs to the Passover liturgy of the Jews. So far as the first is concerned, Schmidt has replied[3] that the word had certainly a wider use, while it is not certain that it means any kind of a song in Cant. 2 : 12.[4] Meek dismisses[5] the suggestion of Ehrlich and others[6] that it here means *the pruning of vines*, on the ground that pruning is not done so late in the spring, and Snaith asks:[7] "Who ever pruned when the flowers were in blossom?" But Snaith finds in the Song two alternating groups of passages, the one having associations with the spring and the other with the autumn. He believes the Song is intimately connected with the two ritual dances of maidens and youths celebrated outside Jerusalem in Mishnaic times, the one on the fifteenth of Ab, and the other on the Day of Atonement.[8] The former group, he says, has associations with the spring, but its setting is in the time of the fruits

---

[1] The process has, indeed, already begun. W. E. Staples (*A.J.S.L.*, liii, 1936–37, pp. 145–157) resolves the book of Ruth into a Tammuz liturgy. W. C. Graham (*J.R.*, xiv, 1934, p. 328) interpreted Ps. 23: 4 in this way, and I. Engnell (*Studies in Divine Kingship in the Ancient Near East*, 1943, pp. 176 f.) finds in the Psalm heading "To David" no more than an original cultic-liturgical rubric inherited from pre-Israelite Jebusite times.

[2] Cf. *Symposium*, pp. 49 f.

[3] Cf. *J.A.O.S.*, *loc. cit.*, p. 159. See also U. Cassuto, *G.S.A.I.*, N.S. i, 1925–28, pp. 169 f. The word stands in the observation of Rabbi Akiba, referred to above (p. 198), where I have rendered "common ditty", and where the meaning is clearly that of a secular song.

[4] R.V. "singing of birds" can claim little justification, for, as J. Bloch says (*A.J.S.L.*, xxxviii, 1921–22, p. 115), wherever this word is used of singing, it refers to human singing.

[5] Cf. *Symposium*, p. 50.

[6] Cf. *Randglossen zur hebräischen Bibel*, vii, 1914, p. 7. The view is, of course, very much older than Ehrlich, for it is represented in the LXX, Peshitta, and Vulgate.

[7] Cf. *A.J.S.L.*, *loc. cit.*, p. 131 n. Cf. also Ibn Ezra: "There are some who say that it is to be explained by 'nor prune thy vineyard' (Lev. 25: 4), but it was not the time for it."

[8] Cf. *A.J.S.L.*, *loc. cit.*, p. 138, and *The Jewish New Year Festival*, 1947, pp. 54 f. Cf. J. Morgenstern, "Two Ancient Israelite Agricultural Festivals", in *J.Q.R.*, N.S. viii, 1917–1918, pp. 31–54, where it is argued that these rites could not have been observed in the post-exilic Day of Atonement, and hence the reference must be to something earlier than the institution of the Day of Atonement. Morgenstern argues that this was the pre-exilic New Year's Day, and the custom related went back to the pre-Israelite fertility cult.

of the gardens in the height of summer.[1] It may then be relevantly recalled that in the Gezer Calendar *yrḥw zmr* follows the month of general harvest, and precedes the harvest of summer fruits. Since all the other items of this calendar are connected with agricultural operations, it is probable that this is also, and that it is to be rendered the two months[2] of vine-pruning,[3] the reference being to the second pruning.[4]

The other point, which is made by both Meek[5] and Schoff,[6] is the claim that it is significant that the Song belongs to the Passover liturgy of the Jews, since the Passover is a spring festival, while the Adonis festival was also observed in the spring.[7] Schoff observes that its incorporation in the Passover liturgy clearly indicates that it has been brought down from the primitive spring festival. Meek, however,

[1] Cf. *A.J.S.L.*, *loc. cit.*, p. 136. It is interesting to set this against the view of Meek, Schoff, and Wittekindt, noted below, that the Passover reading of the Song is evidence that it was a spring ritual. For the connexion with a later season in the year, in relation to Budde's wedding song theory of the origin of the book, cf. G. Dalman, *Palästinischer Diwan*, 1901, p. xii: "Nebenbei sei auch erwähnt, dass nicht der Frühling, sondern der Herbst in ganz Palästina die beliebteste Zeit zu Hochzeiten ist, weil man dann aus dem Ernteertrag das zur Brautzahlung nötige Geld gelöst hat und ausserdem nach Vollendung des Dreschens müssige Zeit besitzt." Cf. too H. Granqvist, *Marriage Conditions in a Palestinian Village*, ii, 1935, p. 32: "There is always a certain air of foolishness attached to those who do not know that summer is the time for weddings. . . . It is a striking fact that although the summer is so long, a wedding is often postponed till the autumn."

[2] Cf. W. F. Albright, *B.A.S.O.R.*, No. 92, Dec. 1943, pp. 22 ff.

[3] So M. Lidzbarski, *P.E.F.Q.S.*, 1909, p. 29, and *Ephemeris für semitische Epigraphik*, iii, 1909-15, p. 41; G. B. Gray, *P.E.F.Q.S.*, 1909, p. 31; S. Ronzevalle, *ibid.*, p. 110; S. R. Driver, *Notes on the Hebrew Text of the Books of Samuel*, 2nd ed., 1913, p. vii; H. Gressmann, *Altorientalische Texte zum Alten Testament*, 2nd ed., 1927, p. 444; D. Diringer, *Le iscrizione anticho-ebraiche palestinesi*, 1934, p. 5; G. R. Driver, *P.E.Q.*, 1945, p. 7; J. G. Février, *Semitica*, i, 1948, pp. 37 f.; and W. F. Albright, in *Ancient Near Eastern Texts relating to the Old Testament* (ed. by J. B. Pritchard), 1950, p. 320a.

[4] So G. Dalman, *P.E.F.Q.S.*, 1909, p. 119: "Zāmîr can, neither here nor in Cant. 2: 12, mean the first pruning of vine, which is done in March, but the second pruning in June or July." It should perhaps be noted that P. Vulliaud (*Le Cantique des Cantiques d'après la tradition juive*, 1925, pp. 38 ff.) defends the meaning *cutting* for zāmîr, but explains it in connexion with the law of Lev. 19: 23 ff. (cf. Mishnah, *Orlah*). In this he follows the interpretation of the Cabbalists. The Targum also found the meaning *cutting* in the word, but interpreted it of the cutting off of the Egyptian firstborn. R. Gordis (*The Song of Songs*, 1954, pp. 6 f. note) rejects the view that the word *zāmîr* can mean "pruning" in the Song, but he equally rejects the view that it means a ritual song. He argues for the meaning "secular song".

[5] Cf. *A.J.S.L.*, *loc. cit.*, p. 4, and *Symposium*, p. 49.   [6] *Ibid.*, p. 86.

[7] It should, however, be observed that M. J. Lagrange (*Études sur les religions sémitiques*, 1905, pp. 305 f.) and W. W. von Baudissin (*Adonis und Esmun*, 1911, pp. 121-133) maintain that the Adonis rites were celebrated in the summer and not in the spring. Cf. M. Jastrow, *Religion of Babylonia and Assyria*, 1898, p. 547: "The Tammuz festival was celebrated just before the summer solstice set in."

admits[1] that this practice was officially adopted only in the Middle Ages, and this admission robs the practice of any evidential value for the original use and purpose of the Song. Against it may be set the statement of Theodore of Mopsuestia[2] that neither Jews nor Christians had ever read the book in public. As Schmidt observes,[3] we can hardly suppose that Ecclesiastes was written as a vintage hymn, or Ruth as a Pentecostal story, and we are therefore scarcely bound to suppose that the Song was written for a spring festival.

It should however, be added that Wittekindt[4] repeats the argument of Meek, but disputes his admission that our evidence for the reading of the book at Passover is only late. He discounts the statement of Theodore of Mopsuestia, and finds significance in the fact that Hippolytus expounded Cant. 3 : 1–4 at Easter, and that the Targum expounds part of the Song in relation to the first Passover and the Exodus from Egypt. That this interpretation cannot naturally be got out of the Song itself is held to point to the fact that behind the Targum lies the already existing custom of reading the book at Passover, and Wittekindt therefore concludes that this practice may go back to the beginning of the Christian era. A very slight study of the history of the interpretation of the Song should suffice to show that innumerable meanings which cannot naturally be got out of the Song have been read into it, and that they are evidence for nothing whatever but the fancy of the interpreters, while for Hippolytus' choice of Easter for the exposition of Cant. 3 : 1–4 we need look no farther than the nature of the interpretation given to the Song in the Early Church.[5] Moreover, even if it were proved conclusively that the Song was read at Passover as early as the beginning of the Christian era, this would not establish any community of origin between Passover and the Song. For, as Dürr points

---

[1] Cf. *A.J.S.L.*, *loc. cit.*, p. 4 n. Cf. also U. Cassuto, *G.S.A.I.*, N.S. i, 1925–28, p. 169: "Ma occorrerebbe prima dimonstrare che quest'uso risale a un'alta antichità, il che non sembra probabile, non trovandosi esso ricordate prima del Masseketh Sôpherîm, che appartiene, come è noto, all'epoca gaonaica." R. Gordis (*The Song of Songs*, 1954, p. 6) also says that the oldest reference to the reading of the Song at Passover stands in the tractate Sopherim, which comes from the sixth century A.D.

[2] "Unde nec Judæis, nec nobis publica lectio unquam cantici canticorum facta est" (Mansi, *Sacrorum Conciliorum nova et amplissima collectio*, ix, 1763, col. 227; cf. Migne, *P.G.*, lxvi, 1864, col. 700). I am informed by Rabbi P. R. Weis that there is reason to think that it was publicly read by the seventh century A.D., but that it is publicly read today in few places except in Lithuania.

[3] Cf. *J.A.O.S.*, *loc. cit.*, p. 156.

[4] *Op. cit.*, pp. 199 f.

[5] Cf. Cyril of Alexandria's view that Cant. 3: 1 refers to the women who sought Jesus on the Resurrection morning (cf. Migne, *P.G.*, lxix, 1864, col. 1285).

out,[1] Passover was kept at the full moon, whereas Wittekindt[2] finds the origin of the Song in the wedding of the Sun god and the Moon goddess that was celebrated at the spring new moon. Whenever the reading of the Song of Songs at Passover began, its choice for reading at that festival was natural, since the Song is full of the springtime, and since the spring is not merely the season of Adonis, but the time of love all the world over.

The case for the Adonis-Tammuz liturgy theory, therefore, does not seem to be adequately supported, and we cannot regard the Song of Song as the liturgy of a pagan cult that was abhorred of the prophets.[3] At the same time, it may be freely allowed that many of the allusions in the Song may genuinely refer to elements of the Adonis-Tammuz cult,[4] whether found in the practice of the poet's contemporaries, or inherited in speech from an earlier age,[5] and we owe a real debt to

---

[1] Cf. *O.L.Z.*, xxxi, 1928, col. 115.   [2] *Op. cit.*, pp. 187 f., 191 f.

[3] Cf. N. K. Gottwald, *I.D.B.*, iv, 1962, p. 423: "In effect, the cultic interpretation is a more sophisticated version of the allegorical approach, but it is no more successful in unlocking the book." W. Baumgartner (*O.T.M.S.*, 1951, p. 234) says: "This theory . . . needs to be convincingly proved if it is to be accepted, That, however, has not yet happened." A. Bentzen (*Studia Orientalia Ioanni Pedersen dicata*, p. 47) says: "There is a ritual background for the canonical status of the Song of Songs. It is not found in ancient Canaanite rites, but in the Synagogue, after the Exile."

[4] Cf. A. Jeremias, *Das Alte Testament im Lichte des Alten Orients*, 4th ed., 1930, p. 670, where Cant. 4: 8 is held to be an allusion to the Tammuz legend. Cf. also A. Bertholet, "Zur Stelle Hohes Lied, iv. 8", in *Abhandlungen zur semitischen Religionsgeschichte und Sprachwissenschaft* (Baudissin Festschrift), 1918, pp. 47–53). Cf. further, A. R. Hulst, *R.G.G.*, 3rd ed., iii, 1959, cols. 429 f.

[5] Cf. O. Eissfeldt, *Einleitung in das Alte Testament*, 1934, pp. 533 f. (2nd ed., 1956, p. 603; 3rd ed., 1963, pp. 662 f.): "Indes bleibt bei genauerer Nachprüfung dieser Theorie [i.e. Wittekindt's] nichts weiter übrig als die freilich sehr beachtenswerte und auch sonst bedeutsame Wahrscheinlichkeit, dass in Israel, wie anderswo in der Welt, die Sprache der Liebenden durch die mythisch-kultische Diktion, insofern sie das Verhältnis von Gott und Göttin zum Gegenstand hat, beeinflusst worden ist, wie auch umgekehrt der Mythus bei der erotischen Poesie Anleihen gemacht hat." Cf. also L. Dürr, *O.L.Z.*, xxxi, 1928, col. 115: "Es dürfte sicher sein, dass manche Züge der Ischtar auch auf die orientalische Liebespoesie eingewirkt haben"; W. Rudolph, *Z.A.W.*, N.F. xviii, 1942–43, pp. 191 f.: "Ebensowenig Zukunftsaussicht hat die neuerdings in Mode gekommene mythologische Auffassung des HL, die in seinen profanen Liedern ursprüngliche heidnische Kultlieder sehen will, in denen die Liebesbeziehungen zwischen Gottheiten im Mittelpunkt stehen. Denn sie vermag auf keine Weise deutlich zu machen, wie solche Lieder bei dem bekannten Abscheu der Jahwereligion vor der Götterliebe und bei der scharfen Polemik der Propheten gegen die Fruchtbarkeitskulte im Kanon Aufnahme gefunden haben sollen, da von der angeblichen jahwistischen Überarbeitung nicht das Geringste zus püren ist. Selbst die erweichte Form, in der diese These heute in die gangbaren Werke über 'Einleitung ins AT' Eingang gefunden hat, ist abzulehnen, dass nämlich jene kultischen Liebeslieder auf Inhalt und Ausdruck der weltlichen Gesänge des HL abgefärbt haben." Cf. also J. Hempel, *Die althebräische Literatur*, 1930, pp. 26 f.; F. F. Hvidberg, *Graad og Latter i det Gamle Testamente*, 1938, pp. 129 f. (E.Tr., *Weeping and Laughter in the Old Testament*, 1962, pp. 148 f.); P. Grelot, *R.B.*, lxxi, 1964, p. 52.

Meek and his associates for the light they have shed on some things in the Song, even though they have failed to carry conviction in their main thesis. For we must distinguish between the finding of allusions to the Tammuz cult and the acceptance of the Song as a cult liturgy. On Budde's view it is a cycle of popular marriage songs, and on the view above adopted it is a series of love lyrics. Now, since it is agreed that Adonis-Tammuz rites were deeply imbedded in the popular superstition, popular songs or lyrical poems, themselves essentially sensuous, would readily contain allusions to those rites. Our own poetry abounds in allusions to a mythology the poets did not seriously accept. An instance taken at random is from Milton's *L'Allegro*:

> But come, thou Goddess fair and free
> In heaven yclept Euphrosyne,
> And by men, heart-easing Mirth,
> Whom lovely Venus at a birth
> With two sister Graces more
> To ivy-crowned Bacchus bore.

If our own poets can thus deck their poems with allusions to an ancient and outgrown mythology, it can occasion no surprise that Hebrew poets should adorn the songs in which they expressed their love with allusions to the mythology that had long flourished in the land, and that doubtless still flourished all around them.[1] For these poems were not composed for the Canon, but to express the warm affection of lovers' hearts.[2]

[1] Already, in 1919, before Meek propounded his theory, Dussaud had recognized this. He wrote (*Le Cantique des Cantiques*, 1919, p. 29): "L'identification de l'amante avec la nature nous place sur un terrain familier au mythe, en particulier au mythe d'Esch-moun-Adonis. En effet, les deux poèmes du bien-aimé comportent non seulement l'iden-tification du jeune homme au printemps et de la jeune fille à la nature, mais encore la fuite de l'amant vers la montagne et sa poursuite par l'amante. Le rapprochement marque à quel point la société israélite était encore imprégnée par les cultes naturistes; mais il n'y a pas lieu de pousser la comparaison plus avant. Après avoir écarté ces poèmes des rites nuptiaux, nous ne songeons nullement à y reconnaître l'écho de la liturgie des Adonies." A. Lods (*R.H.R.*, lxxxii, 1920, p. 223) says that in this view Dussaud "obéit très certainement à un sentiment juste." Cf. also Lods, *Histoire de la littérature hébraïque et juive*, 1950, p. 748: "Il se pourrait fort bien que les poètes israélites aient employé tradi-tionnellement dans leurs pièces érotiques des images et des locutions inspirées des cultes naturistes ou même du mythe d'Adonis-Tammouz, le jeune dieu aimé d'Ichtar, qui meurt et renaît chaque année"; *La Bible du Centenaire*, L'Ancien Testament, iii, 1947, p. xivb: "Pour expliquer ceux des rapprochements signalés entre le Cantique et tel ou tel mythe qui sont réellement plausibles, il suffit peut-être d'admettre que certains traits empruntés à la mythologie étaient chez les Juifs, comme chez nous, entrés dans le langage courant des amoureux et des poètes"; Th. C. Vriezen, *Oud-israëlietischen Geschriften*, 1948, p. 221.

[2] R. Gordis (*J.B.L.*, lxiii, 1944, pp. 262-270) has argued that Cant. 3: 6-11 is the oldest poem in the collection and that this was composed on the occasion of one of Solomon's marriages to a foreign princess.

(6)

From this brief résumé of the history of the exegesis of the Song[1] it will be clearly observed that there is as yet no generally accepted view of the interpretation it should be given. In the present century there have been serious advocates of the old Jewish allegorical view, of the Christian allegorical view, of the dramatic theory, of the wedding-cycle theory, of the Adonis-Tammuz liturgy theory,[2] and of the view that we have a collection of amorous poems, whether from a single author or from several. All interpreters agree in recognizing the high poetic quality of the Song, and in recognizing, too, that its metaphors show a freedom and boldness we should not allow ourselves to-day. The view I adopt finds in it nothing but what it appears to be, lovers' songs, expressing their delight in one another and the warm emotions of their hearts. All of the other views find in the Song what they bring to it.[3]

One question still arises. In adopting a view which has so much in common with the anathematized view of Theodore of Mopsuestia, are we not proposing that which is "unfit for Christian ears",[4] and

[1] I would here acknowledge the help I have received from the following works, each of which contains a useful summary of the history of exegesis up to the date of its publication: C. D. Ginsburg, *The Song of Songs with a Commentary, historical and critical*, 1857; O. Zöckler, *Das Hohelied und der Prediger* (in Lange's *Bibelwerk*), 1868 (E.Tr. by W. H. Green, 1870); S. Salfeld, "Das Hohelied bei den jüdischen Erklärern des Mittelalters", in *Magazin für die Wissenschaft des Judenthums*, v. 1878, pp. 110–178, vi, 1879, pp. 20–48, 129–209; P. Joüon, *Le Cantique des Cantiques*, 1909; M. Jastrow, *The Song of Songs*, 1921; P. Vulliaud, *Le Cantique des Cantiques d'après la tradition juive*, 1925; G. Ricciotti, *Il Cantico dei Cantici*, 1928; H. Ranston, *The Old Testament Wisdom Books and their Teaching*, 1930; D. Lerch, *Z.Th.K.*, liv, 1957, pp. 257–277 (also *R.G.G.*, 3rd ed., iii, 1959, cols. 430 f.); G. Gerleman, *Das Hohelied* (B.K.A.T.), 1963, pp. 43 ff. For an account of recent work on the Song, up to 1928, cf. A. Vaccari, "Il Cantico dei Cantici nelle recenti pubblicazioni", in *Biblica*, ix, 1928, pp. 443–457, and up to 1937 cf. C. Kuhl, "Das Hohelied und seine Deutung", in *Th.R.*, N.F. ix, 1937, pp. 137–167.

[2] The view of L. Waterman ("The Rôle of Solomon in the Song of Songs", in *J.B.L.*, xliv, 1925, pp. 171–187) is an interesting combination of several of these views. He holds that the Song was originally a Tammuz liturgy, which was reduced to folk poetry, and then made the vehicle of allegory, concerning the relations between the northern and southern divisions of the kingdom in the early years of the divided kingdom. He embodies something of the dramatic theory in his supposition that Solomon is seeking to make the maiden forget her lover and yield herself to his power. The later development of his view is referred to above.

[3] Cf. Vulliaud, *op. cit.*, p. 18: "La variété des opinions est telle que l'on pourrait conclure à bon droit que la faculté maîtresse des exégètes n'est point la raison, comme cela devrait être, mais l'imagination."

[4] Cf. the Westminster Assembly's *Annotations upon all the Books of the Old and New Testament*, 2nd ed., 1651, i. Introduction to the annotations on the Song of Solomon (the pages are not numbered): "Both among them [i.e. the Jews], as well as other Readers,

does not this view mean that the Song, as Castellio and Whiston said, in quite unworthy of a place in the Canon?[1] I do not think so. The view that it was written for use in connexion with the fertility rites, and that it has been very thinly disguised, would seem to make it very unworthy of a place there. But if we have songs that express pure human love,[2] and the mutual loyalty of lovers to one another, even though the physical side of their love is expressed with a frankness we should not emulate, I do not think the Song is undeserving of inclusion in the Canon.[3] For there is no incongruity in such a recognition of the essential sacredness of pure human love.[4] The Church has always consecrated

there were some that had lower conceptions of it, and received it as an hot carnall pamphlet, formed by some loose Apollo or Cupid, rather than the holy inspiration of the true God. But this blasphemy hath perished with the fathers of it."

[1] Cf. Ibn Ezra, Preface to his commentary on the Song: "Abhorred, abhorred be the idea that the Song of Songs is in the category of love songs, but rather has it the character of a parable; and were it not for the greatness of its excellence it would not have been incorporated in the corpus of sacred writings." Cf. H. J. Mathews, *Abraham ibn Ezra's Commentary on the Canticles after the first recension*, 1874, Hebrew part, p. 9, for the variant text of that recension. Cf. also Jephet ibn Ali, *In Canticum Canticorum commentarium arabicum*, ed. by J. J. L. Bargès, 1884, on 1: 1, which Bargès (p. 6) renders: "Ne cadat in mentem eorum qui illius sensum non capiunt, sermonem hic haberi alicujus viri meretricem amantis; nullatenus enim computandus est Salomon (cui salus!) inter eos, qui talem januam ingrediuntur; verumenimvero Spiritu Sancto afflatus istud dixit Canticum, verba nimirum dans congregationi Israel, et loquentes inducens Immaculatos viæ, Fortes Israel et germen Davidicum."

[2] J. L. McKenzie (*C.B.Q.*, xv, 1953, p. 243) objects that there is nothing in the text of the Song to indicate that the love is pure. To this R. E. Murphy (*C.B.Q.*, xvi, 1954, p. 9 n.) replies: "Is not the use of the term 'bride' enough to justify Rowley's view? This makes married love the theme and thereby adequately provides for the physical expressions found in the Canticle. It would be no reply to say that marriage is described only at the end of the poem; it is sufficient that the whole poem is written in view of married love." Cf. A. M. Dubarle, *R.B.*, lxi, 1954, p. 82; H. M. Segal, *V.T.*, xii, 1962, p. 470.

[3] Cf. Graham and May, *Culture and Conscience*, 1936, p. 230: "The same appreciation of sheer beauty and of the power of love comes to classic expression in the Song of Songs, which has been designated, and rightly so for the pure in heart, as the 'Holy of Holies' of the Old Testament." This endorsement of an extreme judgement comes indeed somewhat strangely from authors who hold that the Song is a survival from a fertility cult liturgy (p. 123).

[4] L. Dennefeld, *Introduction à l'Ancien Testament*, 1934, p. 140, says: "Cette conception [i.e. that the Song is a collection of love songs] est exclue par le seul fait que le Cantique se trouve dans le canon biblique." Yet on the following page he says: "L'amour naturel, dénué de toute sensualité coupable, est le type le plus parfait de l'amour surnaturel." Why, then, should it be regarded as a thing evil in itself, and patently unworthy of a place in the Canon? Cf. also J. Chaine, in *Initiation Biblique*, ed. by A. Robert and A. Tricot, 2nd ed., 1948, p. 175: "On peut penser à un amour moral, tel que le Créateur l'a voulu, celui qui unit deux jeunes êtres dans le mariage. Cet amour qui est sanctifié par un sacrament dans la nouvelle alliance, a bien pu être chanté dans l'ancienne par un auteur inspiré"; A. Bentzen, *Introduction to the Old Testament*, ii, 1949, p. 182): "Why

the union of man and woman in matrimony, and taught that marriage is a divine ordinance, and it is not unfitting that a book which expresses the spiritual and physical emotions on which matrimony rests should be given a place in the Canon of Scripture.[1]

not thank God, because he among the sacred books has also given us words of love?" Grelot, *R.B.*, lxxi, 1964, p. 46: "L'amour humain correctement compris ne constitue-t-il pas, dans la révélation biblique, une *valeur* réelle dont l'expression serait en elle-même digne de la Parole de Dieu?" Cf. also A. M. Dubarle, *R.B.*, lxi, 1954, pp. 67–86, esp. pp. 81 f., and *Scripture*, x, 1958, pp. 79 ff.; J.P. Audet, *R.B.*, lxii, 1955, pp. 197–221.

[1] Cf. E. J. Young, *An Introduction to the Old Testament*, 1949, p. 327: "The Song does celebrate the dignity and purity of human love. This is a fact which has not always been sufficiently stressed. The Song, therefore, is didactic and moral in its purpose. It comes to us in this world of sin, where lust and passion are on every hand, where fierce temptations assail us and try to turn us aside from the God-given standard of marriage. And it reminds us, in particularly beautiful fashion, how pure and noble true love is. This, however, does not exhaust the purpose of the book. Not only does it speak of the purity of human love, but, by its very inclusion in the Canon, it reminds us of a love that is purer than our own." Cf. J. Winandy, *Le Cantique des Cantiques*, 1960, pp. 56 ff.; also S. M. Lehrman, in *The Five Megilloth*, ed. by A. Cohen, 1946, pp. xii f. D. A. Hubbard, (*The New Bible Dictionary*, ed. by J. D. Douglas, 1962, p. 1206a) says: "The Song, though expressed in language too bold for Western taste, provides a wholesome balance between the extremes of sexual excess or perversion and an ascetic denial of the essential goodness of physical love."

THE UNITY OF THE BOOK OF DANIEL

7

The Unity of the Book of Daniel[1]

WITH imposing unanimity critical scholars seem to be moving away from the once common belief in the unity of the book of Daniel. There are still conservative scholars who maintain the unity of the book and ascribe the whole to a sixth-century author,[2] but of critical scholars who have dealt with the book in recent years few have defended its unity.[3] It is true that the unanimity with which the unity of this book is denied dissolves into a chorus of discordant voices as soon as it is asked what view is to replace it, and there is no positive view which can claim anything like a consensus of opinion. It is also true that none of the divisive theories can offer an answer to the case for the unity, or avoid greater difficulties and embarrassments than those it seeks to remove. It may not be inopportune, therefore, to restate the case for the unity of this book, and to expose the weaknesses, as well as the variety, of the rival views. Since the rival views on this question current to-day all place the completion of the work in the Maccabaean age, as also the present writer does, there would seem to be no need to argue the case for this here. Moreover, the discussion

---

[1] This paper was read as a Presidential Address to the Society for Old Testament Study in London, January 1950.

[2] So E. J. Young, *The Prophecy of Daniel*, 1949, pp. 19 f.; also W. Möller, *Der Prophet Daniel*, 1934, pp. 4 ff.

[3] They include G. Luzzi, *Gli Agiografi*, 1925, pp. 255 ff.; R. H. Charles, *Critical and Exegetical Commentary on the Book of Daniel*, 1929, pp. xxx ff.; H. L. Willett, in *The Abingdon Commentary*, 1929, p. 747; G. H. Box, *Judaism in the Greek Period*, 1932, pp. 210 ff. (but cf. p. 207); H. H. Rowley, *Darius the Mede and the Four World Empires in the Book of Daniel*, 1935, pp. 176 ff.; R. H. Pfeiffer, *Introduction to the Old Testament*, 1941, pp. 760 ff.; B. Balscheit, *Der Gottesbund: Einführung in das Alte Testament*, 1943, pp. 198 ff.; *La Bible du Centenaire*, iii, 1947, p. xxv; *The Westminster Study Bible*, 1948, p. 1236; G. G. Hackman, in Alleman and Flack's *Old Tesyament Commentary*, 1948, p. 779; J. Barr in Peake's *Commentary on the Bible*, revised ed., 1962, p. 591; N. W. Porteous, *Das Danielbnch* (A.T.D.), 1962, pp. 13 f. Oesterley and Robinson do not commit themselves to the maintenance of the unity of the book, though they plainly incline to it. Cf. *Introduction to the Books of the Old Testament*, 1934, p. 366. In *C.Q.R.*, cx, 1930, p. 124, Oesterley had suggested that chapters 1–6 may be somewhat older than the rest of the book, and may have been regarded as canonical before the later chapters were written by the same author.

will be limited to the parts of Daniel which are accepted as canonical by Jews and by all varieties of Christians, and the extra-canonical, or deutero-canonical, parts not preserved in Hebrew or Aramaic will be left out of account.[1]

The *prima facie* grounds for a theory of at least two authors are obvious enough. The first half of the book consists of simple stories about Daniel that any child could remember and repeat in substance, while the second part consists of visions seen by Daniel, becoming increasingly complicated and detailed, and impossible to be similarly repeated after being merely heard. Again, the first part of the book makes no pretence to have been written by Daniel, whereas the second part would appear to have come from his pen. Yet again, the first half of the book, with the exception of the opening chapter and a few verses of the next, is written in Aramaic, while the rest stands in Hebrew.[2] There is thus an inner division within the book on grounds of language, of the character of the sections, and of pseudonymity or anonymity. If only these three tests yielded the same results, the case against unity would indeed be a strong one. Unhappily they do not. For the division of language does not coincide with the division into stories and visions; nor does the transition from anonymity to pseudonymity coincide with either. We have not, therefore, a threefold cord which cannot be broken, drawing us to accept the division of the book, but three separate strands pulling us in different directions. We may proceed, as some have done, to import yet more authors to evade the difficulties; yet we find that the maximum number yet proposed does not escape them all, and involves fresh difficulties that cannot be resolved.

The dissection of the book is no new phenomenon, and before we come to the twentieth-century divisive theories we may glance at some of their predecessors. In the seventeenth century Spinoza[3] already postulated a separate author for the last five chapters, which he held to be earlier than the first seven. In the following century Newton[4] sup-

---

[1] For a magnificently documented survey of recent work on every side of Daniel study, see W. Baumgartner, "Ein Vierteljahrhundert Danielforschung", in *Th.R.*, N.F. xi, 1939, pp. 59–83, 125–144, 201–228. Cf. also *R.G.G.*, 3rd ed., ii, 1958, cols. 26–31.

[2] C. H. Gordon (*Introduction to Old Testament Times*, 1953, p. 73) thinks the Hebrew-Aramaic-Hebrew structure may have been intentional, and thinks it should deter us from hastily dissecting the text.

[3] Cf. B. Spinoza, *Tractatus theologico-politicus*, 1670, p. 130 (E.Tr. by R. Willis, 2nd ed., 1868, p. 209).

[4] Cf. Sir Isaac Newton, *Observations upon the Prophecies of Daniel and the Apocalypse of St. John*, 1733, p. 10 (= *Sir Isaac Newton's Daniel and the Apocalypse*, new ed. by Sir William Whitla, 1922, p. 145).

posed that the last six chapters were the work of Daniel and the first six were a later creation, and a similar view was held by Beausobre.[1] Towards the end of the same century Eichhorn[2] maintained that the first six chapters had a different origin from the last six, which he too assigned to Daniel himself at first, but later[3] to an author in the Maccabaean period. He thought that the section 2 : 4b–6 was drawn from a separate source, and that chapter 1 was written when the two parts of the book were combined.

Bertholdt,[4] at the beginning of the nineteenth century, postulated no less than nine authors, In this he was followed by Augusti.[5] Such a view is declared by Montgomery[6] to indicate a bankruptcy of criticism, and it is not surprising that it secured so little following. When in 1822 Bleek[7] demonstrated the unity of the book he dealt all this criticism what Stuart[8] believed to be a death-blow from which it was unlikely to recover. Throughout most of the nineteenth century, accordingly, the unity of the book continued to be generally held,

---

[1] Cf. I. de Beausobre, *Remarques historiques, critiques, et philologiques sur le Nouveau Testament*, 1742, p. 71.

[2] Cf. J. G. Eichhorn, *Einleitung ins Alte Testament*, 2nd ed., iii, 1790, pp. 316 ff. (The writer has had no access to the first edition.)

[3] Cf. *id., Einleitung in das Alte Testament*, 3rd ed., iii, 1803, p. 421: "Ein früherer Jude zeichnete auf, was die Tradition von Daniel und seinen drey Freunden meldete; ein späterer Jude aus den Zeiten kurz nach Antiochus Epiphanes, der den von seiner Nation erlebten Drangsalen der frühern und spätern Zeit ein prophetisches Gewand umwerfen wollte, stellte sie der Täuschung wegen seiner Kunst-Composition voran, und band sie durch die früheren Lebens-Nachrichten vom Daniel der Geschichte zu einem Ganzen." This is repeated in the 4th ed., iv, 1824, p. 515, save for the correction of "Geschichte" to "Gesichte" at the end.

[4] Cf. L. Bertholdt, *Daniel neu übersetzt und erklärt*, i, 1806, pp. 49 ff., 83 ff. Bertholdt held that chapter 1 was written in the time of Artaxerxes Longimanus, or shortly after; chapter 2 after the death of Ptolemy Philadelphus; chapter 3 appreciably later; chapter 4 at the beginning of the Maccabaean period; chapters 5 and 6 somewhat later; chapter 7 in the time of Antiochus shortly after the desecration of the Temple; chapter 8 after the death of Antiochus; chapter 9 somewhat later, its author being a Jerusalem priest; chapters 10–12 most probably last of all. J. D. Michaelis had earlier hinted at a similar view of a variety of authors (*Orientalische und exegetische Bibliothek*, i, 1771, p. 190), and then proposed the curious division of chapters 3–6 from the rest of the book, holding the remainder to be the authentic work of Daniel and these chapters to belong to the Greek period (*ibid.*, iv, 1773, pp. 28 ff., and *Deutsche Uebersetzung des Alten Testaments*, x, 1781, Anmerkungen zum Propheten Daniel, p. 22).

[5] Cf. J. C. W. Augusti, *Grundriss einer historisch-kritischen Einleiting in's Alte Testament*, 2nd ed., 1827, pp. 319 ff.

[6] Cf. J. A. Montgomery, *A Critical and Exegetical Commentary on the Book of Daniel*, 1927, p. 92.

[7] Cf. F. Bleek, "Ueber Verfasser und Zweck des Buches Daniel", in Schleiermacher, de Wette, and Lücke's *Theologische Zeitschrift*, Heft 3, 1822, pp. 171–294.

[8] Cf. M. Stuart, *A Commentary on the Book of Daniel*, 1850, p. 399.

both by those who maintained the traditional date and by critical scholars who accepted the Maccabaean dating.

Towards the end of the nineteenth century, however, divisive theories were again beginning to appear. Lenormant[1] distinguished between the two parts of the book, and postulated a long and complicated history for it. He supposed the first part to have been composed in the time of the Great Synagogue, and the second part to have been written by an author who was acquainted with the first part. Later, he supposed, part of the text was lost and replaced by an Aramaic translation, into which he believed a number of glosses had crept. Quite different was the view of Havet,[2] who held that the first part of the book was to be differentiated from the second, which dated from Herodian times. He supposed that while the later chapters ostensibly point to Antiochus Epiphanes, he was merely a prudent substitute for Herod.

In a series of publications Meinhold[3] presented the view that the Aramaic part of the book was composed in pre-Maccabaean days by a different author from the writer of the Hebrew sections. He believed that chapters 2 : 4b–6 were written *circa* 300 B.C., and that chapter 7 was later added as an appendix, while the Hebrew beginning and end of the book date from the Maccabaean period. Strack[4] adopted a similar view, though he subsequently expressed it more cautiously.

Shortly after the first of these publications of Meinhold's appeared, Lagarde[5] argued for a theory of the compilation of the book from several disconnected sources, and maintained that some of them were composed as late as the first century A.D., and were unknown to Josephus. He is thus one of the rare advocates of a post-Maccabeaan date for any part of the book.

In view of these new challenges, the defence of the unity of the book

[1] Cf. F. Lenormant, *La Divination et la science des présages chez les Chaldéens*, 1875, pp. 169–227.

[2] Cf. E. Havet, *Le Christianisme et ses origines*, iii, 1878, pp. 304–311; and in *Revue des deux mondes*, xciv, 1889, pp. 825–828.

[3] Cf. J. Meinhold, *Die Composition des Buches Daniel*, 1884, p. 38; *Beiträge zur Erklärung des Buches Daniel*, 1888, pp. 68 ff.; *Das Buch Daniel* (in Strack-Zöckler's Kurzgefasster Kommentar), 1889, p. 262.

[4] Cf. H. L. Strack, in *P.R.E.*, 2nd ed., vii, 1880, p. 419 (cf. 3rd ed., ix, 1901, p. 748); in Zöckler's *Handbuch der theologischen Wissenschaften*, i, 1883, p. 165; and, less confidently, *Einleitung in das Alte Testament*, 4th ed., 1895, pp. 145 f., 5th ed., 1898, p. 150.

[5] Cf. P. de Lagarde, review of Havet's *Études d'histoire religieuse*, in *G.G.A.*, 1891, pp. 497–520.

was once more undertaken, and when in 1895 von Gall[1] published his treatise on the question, the issue appeared once more to be firmly settled. Von Gall allowed, however, as many other advocates of the general unity of the book have allowed,[2] that the prayer of Daniel in 9 : 4–20 was unoriginal.[3] So firmly did the issue appear to be decided that Cornill[4] could declare that hardly any other book of the Old Testament is so uniform or written in so single a strain.

Scarcely was the ink on von Gall's page dry, however, before fresh attempts at dissection were made. Before the century was out Barton[5] postulated a number of authors for the work. In addition to three original authors (responsible for chapters 2, 4, 5, 7, 8; chapters 9 and 6, composed in that order; and chapters 10–12) he distinguished a possible fourth hand in the author of chapter 2, and a redactor who composed chapter 1 and the concluding verses of the book, and who sprinkled editorial additions through the rest of the work. More simply, Dalman[6] argued that the first six chapters were from a different hand from the last six, and that the editor who combined the two parts translated the beginning of each into the language of the other. A similar position was taken up by Preiswerk[7] in a doctoral dissertation at the beginning of the present century.

From all of these challenges no pattern was even beginning to appear, and Bevan[8] had felt it to be unnecessary even to review their arguments, since the discordance between them sufficiently proved their arbitrariness. While it is disconcerting to find so little agreement as to where the book is to be divided, this somewhat contemptuous brushing of these theories aside was an inadequate reply. To-day it is even more inadequate, since the attacks on the unity of the book have continued to be made with fresh zeal during the present century, though with no more agreement. The attackers do, however, fall into groups with a measure of agreement within the group.

[1] Cf. A. Freiherr von Gall, *Die Einheitlichkeit des Buches Daniel*, 1895.

[2] More recently von Gall has weakened his maintenance of the unity of the book. Cf. *Basileia tou Theou*, 1926, p. 266 n.: "Mag der Grundstock des Buches auch im 3. Jahrhundert entstanden sein, sein jetziges eschatologisches Gepräge hat es erst in der Zeit der Religionsverfolgung unter Antiochus IV erhalten."

[3] This question will not be discussed in the present article.

[4] Cf. C. H. Cornill, *Einleitung in die kanonischen Bücher des Alten Testaments*, 1905, p. 243 (E.Tr. by G. H. Box, 1907, pp. 390 f.).

[5] Cf. G. A. Barton, "The Composition of the Book of Daniel," in *J.B.L.*, xvii, 1898, pp. 62–86.

[6] Cf. G. Dalman, *Die Worte Jesu*, 1898, p. 11 (E.Tr. by D. M. Kay, 1902, p. 13).

[7] Cf. H. Preiswerk, *Der Sprachenwechsel im Buche Daniel*, 1902, pp. 115 ff.

[8] Cf. A. A. Bevan, *A Short Commentary on the Book of Daniel*, 1892, pp. 8 f.

Quite early in the century Torrey[1] argued, in a paper which has had great influence on subsequent writers, and which has much in common with the view of Dalman, that the first half of the book dates from the middle of the third century B.C., while the second half was composed in the Maccabaean age, the author of the second half turning the beginning of the earlier work into Hebrew and composing the first part of his own work in Aramaic in order to dovetail the whole firmly together. This view has found a number of adherents who follow it more or less closely. Kent[2] found it quite convincing, and saw a sharp contrast between the first six chapters and the last six, both in literary style and in the representation of Daniel, and held that whereas the first half of the book contained no reference to Antiochus he occupied the central place in the second half. Similarly Montgomery[3] declared Torrey's solution the only one which recommended itself to him, but was doubtful[4] whether chapter 7 should be regarded as a distinct composition standing between the writing of the first six chapters and that of the last five. Eissfeldt[5] similarly believed the first six chapters to have been an older work, dating from the third century B.C., while the last six were written by an author in the Maccabaean period as a continuation of the older work, the first chapter of this half being written in the language of the older work, and the rest in Hebrew. Vriezen,[6] too, adopts a similar view, though without committing himself to a date for the first half of the book. So, again, C. Kuhl[7] holds that the stories of chapters 1–6 circulated independently and singly in the third century B.C. but were extended and brought up-to-date in the second century B.C. by the addition of the visions of chapters 7–12.

An even more influential paper than Torrey's was written by

[1] Cf. C. C. Torrey, "Notes on the Aramaic Part of Daniel", in *T.C.A.*, xv, 1909, pp. 241–282.

[2] Cf. C. F. Kent, *The Growth and Contents of the Old Testament*, 1926, pp. 130 f.

[3] *Op. cit.*, p. 90. Gehman (see J. D. Davis, *The Westminster Dictionary of the Bible*, revised by H. S. Gehman, 1944, p. 129) does not commit himself on Montgomery's view, though he observes that problems of authorship do not disturb the unity of the book, and would seem to reject it. He allows that Daniel "could very easily be assigned to the second century B.C.", but without definitely accepting this date. Cf., however, *Interpretation*, iii, 1949, pp. 479 f., where he more clearly accepts it.

[4] *Op. cit.*, p. 95.

[5] Cf. O. Eissfeldt, *Einleitung in das Alte Testament*, 1934, pp. 574 ff. (cf. 3rd ed., 1963, pp. 708 ff.).

[6] Cf. Th. C. Vriezen, *Oud-israëlietische Geschriften*, 1948, pp. 230 f. (cf. *De Literatuur van Oud-Israël*, 1961, pp. 208 f.).

[7] Cf. *The Old Testament: its Origin and Composition*, E.Tr. 1961, pp. 275, 279.

Hölscher,[1] who argued that the division of the book should be made at the end of chapter 7, the first six chapters dating from the third century B.C., and the seventh being an appendix of slightly later date, while the last five chapters are of Maccabaean date. Hölscher also maintained that Maccabaean glosses had been added to the pre-Maccabaean sections which he distinguished.[2] This view is in substantial agreement with that already briefly presented by Sellin,[3] and Meinhold[4] withdrew his earlier view in its favour. It is followed substantially by Obbink,[5] who thinks the acceptance of the unity of the work would give rise to inexplicable difficulties, and who divides the book at the end of chapter 6, but thinks the author of chapters 7–12 used an older basis for chapter 7. Gressmann,[6] Kuhl,[7] and Bentzen[8] also gave Hölscher's view their adhesion, and Nyberg[9] appears broadly to follow it. He assigns chapters 1–7 to the post-exilic period, but does not specify his adhesion to the view that chapter 7 is to be separated from chapters 1–6, or commit himself to the acceptance of glosses in chapters 2 and 7. His view is closely similar to that advanced many years earlier by Albright,[10] who contented himself with observing that the book of Daniel is obviously composite, and dating the first seven chapters in the first half of the third century B.C., and the last five without question in the Maccabaean period. He thought the first part was written in Babylonia and was unknown in Palestine until the author of the second part wrote the concluding chapters.

Some other writers have contented themselves with dividing the book at the end of chapter 7, without isolating chapter 7 from the preceding chapters. Thilo[11] followed this course, though he recognized

[1] Cf. G. Hölscher, "Die Entstehung des Buches Daniel," in *T.S.K.*, xcii, 1919, pp. 113–138.

[2] In *R.H.P.R.*, ix, 1929, p. 108. Hölscher speaks of "le premier livre des Maccabées, connu et utilisé par Daniel". From this it would appear that he had changed his view and transferred the book of Daniel to a much later date.

[3] Cf. E. Sellin, *Einleitung in das Alte Testament*, 1910, pp. 129 f. In the later editions Sellin observes that Hölscher affords convincing proof of the correctness of his hypothesis. So in the English translation by W. Montgomery, based on the 3rd German ed., 1923, p. 234, and in the 7th German ed., 1935, pp. 152 f.

[4] Cf. J. Meinhold, *Einführung in das Alte Testament*, 3rd ed., 1932, p. 355.

[5] Cf. H. W. Obbink, *Daniël*, 1932, pp. 20 ff.

[6] Cf. H. Gressmann, *Der Messias*, 1929, p. 346.

[7] Cf. C. Kuhl, *Die drei Männer im Feuer*, 1930, pp. 77 ff.

[8] Cf. A. Bentzen, *Daniel*, 1937, pp. vi f.; *Indledning til det Gamle Testamente*, I, i, 1941, p. 176; *Introduction to the Old Testament*, ii, 1949, p. 203.

[9] Cf. H. S. Nyberg, article on "Daniel" in *S.B.U.*, i, 1948, col. 345.

[10] Cf. W. F. Albright, *J.B.L.*, xl, 1921, pp. 116 f.

[11] Cf. M. Thilo, *Die Chronologie des Danielbuches*, 1926, pp. 31 ff.

glosses from the author of chapters 8–12 in the earlier part of the book. So, also, Welch,[1] though with some hesitation as to whether chapter 7 belonged to the earlier or the later part of the book. He assigned the conposition of the first part to a writer in Babylon. Eerdmans,[2] however, who also divided the book at the end of chapter 7, was convinced that the first part could not have been written before the fourth century B.C., though it embodied older traditions, while the closing chapters were Maccabaean.

To this group belongs Weiser[3] also, who holds that the Maccabaean author of chapters 8–12 found chapters 1–7 in an older Aramaic work from which he extracted them, and that he translated the first chapter into Hebrew to give the impression that it was all his own work. Scott,[4] again, held that the division of the book comes at the end of chapter 7, but maintained that chapter 2 is drawn from two variant forms of the story, and that chapter 7 consists of a *Grundschrift* which has been worked over. He thinks that there was first a collection of midrashic stories which consisted of chapters 1–6 substantially, but that only the material from one source then stood in chapter 2, but that later the author of chapter 7 introduced the material from the variant source into chapter 2, glossed chapters 4 and 6, and wrote the *Grundschrift* of chapter 7. Still later another writer glossed chapter 7 and added the closing chapters. E. W. Heaton[5] dates chapters 1–7 before chapters 8–12, but assigns both to the reign of Antiochus Epiphanes, within the space of a few years, But he holds that chapters 2–7 were based on older stories which already had a fairly fixed form.[6]

Haller[7] proposed to modify Hölscher's view by arguing that chap-

[1] Cf. A. C. Welch, *Visions of the End*, 1922, p. 54.

[2] Cf. B. D. Eerdmans, "The Origin and Meaning of the Aramaic Part of Daniel", in *Actes du xviiie congrès international des orientalistes*, 1932, pp. 198–202; *The Religion of Israel*, 1947, pp. 222 ff., 249.

[3] Cf. A. Weiser, *Einleitung in das Alte Testament*, 1939, pp. 262 f.; 2nd ed., 1949, p. 234 (E.Tr., 1961, p. 316).

[4] Cf. R. B. Y. Scott, "I Daniel, the Original Apocalypse", in *A.J.S.L.*, xlvii, 1930–31, pp. 289–296.

[5] Cf. *The Book of Daniel* (Torch Bible), 1956, pp. 47 ff.

[6] J. Barr (*loc. cit.*, p. 591a) thinks it unlikely that the stories existed in written form before the present book was composed. If the Prayer of Nabonidus (see below, p. 277, n. 1) is older than the book of Daniel, then we should have to argue that sources of the stories of Daniel already existed, but this would not support the idea that they had a fairly fixed form. There is no need to suppose that the author of Daniel created all his stories out of nothing, but only that he used tradition, written or unwritten, to serve his purpose.

[7] Cf. M. Haller, "Das Alter von Daniel 7", in *T.S.K.*, xciii, 1920–21, pp. 83–87; *Das Judentum*, 2nd ed., 1925, pp. 272 f.

ter 7 is the oldest in the book, dating from the fourth century B.C., and thus antedating the section containing chapters 1–6. This was carried still further by Noth,[1] who argued that chapters 2 and 7 should both be dated in the fourth century B.C. He thought the former of these chapters was included in the collection of stories made in the course of the third century, but that the latter was glossed and added in the Maccabaean period, after which the remaining chapters were added, still in the time of Antiochus. Baumgartner[2] dated the source that contained chapters 1–6 in the Persian period, but believed that chapter 7 in its earliest form belonged to the time of Alexander. He thus adhered to Hölscher's dissection of the sources, though differently dating the sections.

In one of the most recent studies of Daniel, Ginsberg[3] has developed the view of Hölscher, and attempted further dissection of the book as well as greater precision in the dating of the sections. He postulates a total of not less than six hands in the work. Of these the author of chapters 1–6 wrote between 292 and 261 B.C.,[4] while chapter 2 was glossed between 246 and 220 B.C. He ascribes the composition of chapter 7 to the Maccabaean period, between 175 and 167 B.C., though he finds later glosses in this chapter. Two further authors are postulated in 166 or 165 B.C., responsible for chapter 8 and chapters 10–12 respectively. Chapter 9 is thought to have come from a yet later hand, and the glossing of the other parts of the second half of the book is held to have been done either by the same hand, or by one or two further writers.[5] Here we seem to be getting to the multiplicity of authors demanded by the view of Bertholdt, though Ginsberg's assignment of material to the various hands is quite different. More vaguely, Meyer[6]

---

[1] Cf. M. Noth, "Zur Komposition des Buches Daniel", in *T.S.K.*, xcviii–xcix, 1926, pp. 143–163.

[2] Cf. W. Baumgartner, *Das Buch Daniel*, 1926, p. 9; *Z.A.W.*, N.F. iii, 1926, p. 39; *R.G.G.*, 2nd ed., i, 1927, cols. 1781 f. More recently Baumgartner has assigned the first part of the book to the third century B.C. (cf. *Th.Z.*, i, 1945, p. 22), in closer agreement with Hölscher's position.

[3] Cf. H. L. Ginsberg, *Studies in Daniel*, 1948, pp. 5 ff., 27 ff. Cf. my review in *J.B.L.*, lxviii, 1949, pp. 173–177, and Ginsberg's reply, *ibid.*, pp. 402–407, with my rejoinder, *ibid.*, lxix, 1950, pp. 201–203. In *V.T.*, iv, 1954, pp. 245–275, Ginsberg made a regrettably intemperate reply to the present essay, to which I replied in *V.T.*, v, 1955, pp. 272–276.

[4] More recently changed to *circa* 304 B.C. (cf. *Studies in Koheleth*, 1950, p. 42).

[5] Ginsberg complains (*V.T.*, iv, 1954, pp. 274 f. n.) that I ought to have said "by the same hand; except for viii. 18–29, which is the work of the author of chs. x–xii, and for xii. 13, which may be either by the author of ch. ix or by one or two further hands".

[6] Cf. E. Meyer, *Ursprung und Anfänge des Christentums*, ii, 1925, p. 184.

contented himself with supposing that the book is compiled from very different elements and has had a long history, though he shared with some of the writers noted above the view that the stories were composed within the compass of the third century B.C.[1]

One writer has reverted to the view that the first chapter was written by the author of the closing chapters, and that the Aramaic chapters alone are from an older source. This is the view of Beek,[2] who dates the Aramaic part of the book in the Persian period, and the rest in the Maccabaean period.

Hertlein[3] belonged to the small group of writers who have brought part of the book down to a post-Maccabaean period. But whereas Havet dated the second part of the work in the Herodian age, and Lagarde assigned chapters 7 and 9–12 to the first century A.D., Hertlein assigned the first seven chapters to this late date, and held the remaining chapters to be Maccabaean. His division of the book at the end of chapter 7 agreed with some of the views already noted, though he has nothing else in common with the holders of those views. In his dating of the work he has found a hesitant follower in Stevenson,[4] but so far as the writer is aware he has found no other.

A few Catholic scholars have adopted a divisive theory, though most have belonged to the school that contended for the unity of the book and its composition in the sixth century B.C.[5] Lagrange,[6] Bigot,[7] and Bayer[8] went so far as to ascribe the composition of the whole book to the Maccabaean age. Junker,[9] too, would date the composition of the whole then, but claims to establish that not only in the earlier chapters

---

[1] *Ibid.*, p. 186.

[2] Cf. M. A. Beek, *Das Danielbuch*, 1935, pp. 91 ff.

[3] Cf. E. Hertlein, *Der Daniel der Römerzeit*, 1908, pp. 8 ff. For a criticism of Hertlein's positions, see K. Marti, in E. Kautzsch, *Die Heilige Schrift des Alten Testaments*, 3rd ed., ii, 1910, pp. 417 f.; 4th ed., edited by A. Bertholet, ii, 1923, p. 458.

[4] Cf. W. B. Stevenson, "The Identification of the Four Kingdoms of the Book of Daniel", in *T.G.O.S.*, vii, 1936, pp. 4–8, esp. p. 8.

[5] So still L. Hudal and J. Zeigler, *Précis d'Introduction à l'Ancien Testament*, French Tr. by M. Grandclaudon, 1938, p. 220, and C. Lattey, *The Book of Daniel*, 1948, pp. xxxvii ff., though less decidedly. Cf. also J. Prado, "Carácter histórico del libro de Daniel", in *Sefarad*, iii, 1943, pp. 167–194.

[6] Cf. M. J. Lagrange, *R.B.*, N.S. i, 1904, pp. 494–520; *Le judaïsme avant Jésus-Christ*, 2nd ed., 1931, pp. 62 f. B. Rigaux (*L'Antéchrist*, 1932, pp. 151 ff.) follows Lagrange.

[7] Cf. L. Bigot, in Vacant and Mangenot's *Dictionnaire de Théologie Catholique*, iv, 1911, cols. 63–73. F. E. Gigot (*The Catholic Encyclopedia*, iv, 1908, pp. 623–625) is more non-committal on the date and authorship.

[8] Cf. E. Bayer, *Danielstudien*, 1912, pp. 1 ff.

[9] Cf. H. Junker, *Untersuchungen über literarische und exegetische Probleme des Buches Daniel*, 1932, pp. 101 ff.

but also in the later the writer was reworking older sources. Riessler[1] more conservatively held that chapters 7–12 were the genuine work of Daniel in their original form, while chapters 1–5 were composed by a later hand in the Persian period, on the basis of written or oral traditions, and chapter 6 was subsequently added from a separate source. He thought that in the Maccabaean age glosses were added to chapters 9 and 11 and the Greek words were introduced into chapter 3. Goettsberger's[2] view had much in common with Riessler's, though in some respects simpler. He dated the completion of the book about 300 B.C., but held that it embodied material going back to the time of Daniel himself. He therefore maintained that later glosses had been added to chapter 11. This had long been a popular view amongst those who dated the whole book before the Maccabaean period.[3] Goettsberger's view has been followed by some other Catholic scholars, including Höpfl-Miller-Metzinger,[4] while Linder[5] modified it to the extent of holding that chapters 7–12 in their original form came from the pen of Daniel himself, while chapters 1–6 were written either by Daniel or by another in the same period, but that the editorial combination of the two parts was effected *circa* 300 B.C. Rinaldi[6] adopts a similar position, while Kalt[7] thought the work had had a long history, and that parts remained separate until a late date. Nötscher,[8] again, dates the completion of the book in the Maccabaean age, but believes that it was compiled from many elements which were much older.

[1] Cf. P. Riessler, *Das Buch Daniel*, 1902, pp. xi–xiii.

[2] Cf. J. Goettsberger, *Das Buch Daniel*, 1928, pp. 6 ff.

[3] So J. P. Lange, "Einleitung in das Alte Testament", prefixed to *Genesis* in his Bibelwerk, 2nd ed., 1877, p. xxxv (E.Tr. by T. Lewis and A. Gosman, 1868, p. 38); O. Zöckler, *Der Prophet Daniel*, 1870, pp. 5, 16, 230 (E.Tr. by J. Strong, 1876, pp. 5, 17, 257); J. W. Bosanquet, *Messiah the Prince*, 1866, pp. 110 ff.; Küper, *Das Prophetenthum des Alten Bundes*, 1870, p. 395; C. H. H. Wright, *Daniel and His Prophecies*, 1906, pp. 242 ff.; C. Boutflower, *In and Around the Book of Daniel*, 1923, pp. 3 ff. R. Cornely and A. Merk, while defending the unity and traditional date of the book, vaguely recognize the presence of glosses. See *Manuel d'introduction à toutes les Saintes Ecritures*, French Tr., by Mazoyer, i, 1930, p. 744. The translator of Zöckler will have none of this tampering with the sacred text, and observes that Zöckler is inconsistent in objecting to a pseudonymous work of Scripture, but allowing interpolation. He observes: "The distinction in this respect between a whole work and a part only is too nice to escape the odium of a 'pious fraud' " (*loc. cit.*, p. 5 n.). It should be added that these writers differed widely in their definition of the alleged interpolations.

[4] Cf. H. Höpfl, *Introductio specialis in Vetus Testamentum*, 5th ed., ed. by A. Miller and A. Metzinger, 1946, p. 482.

[5] Cf. J. Linder, *Commentarius in Librum Daniel*, 1939, pp. 56 f.

[6] Cf. G. Rinaldi, *Daniele*, 1947, pp. 12 ff.

[7] Cf. E. Kalt, *Biblisches Reallexikon*, 2nd ed., i, 1938, col. 359.

[8] Cf. F. Nötscher, *Daniel* (in *Echt. B.*, Lieferung 6), 1948, pp. 6 f.

This is substantially the view of Dennefeld,[1] who had earlier been more non-committal.[2] Steinmueller[3] is less definite, and inclines to regard the book as of Danielic origin, but preserved for us in a later redaction.[4]

It therefore appears that while the great majority of these scholars who believe the book of Daniel to be composite date its completion in the Maccabaean age, or think it was glossed in that age, they differ widely as to the date of the earlier parts of the book, and as to the delimitation of its various sections. If there is so little consensus of opinion as to which were the earlier parts, we can have little confidence in the method whereby these varying results were reached.[5] Particularly significant is the inability to decide whether chapter 7 belongs to the earlier or later part of the book, or to neither, or whether to tear it apart and attach some verses to one and some to the other. Some find clear evidence that this chapter is not a unity, but comes from two hands or has been glossed, while others see nothing in it to suggest more than a single hand.

To traverse separately all the arguments advanced in favour of each of these views would be wearisome and would tend to much repetition, especially since the effective answers to many of the arguments can be found in the case for others of these divisive views. It will probably be more satisfactory, therefore, to present anew the case for the unity of the book, and to preface it by saying that none of the challenges has considered the cumulative weight of all these arguments. Account will be taken of the principal critics of the various arguments, and reasons will be offered for considering their attack unsuccessful. At the same time enough will be said to indicate the lines of the reply to all these divergent challenges.

(1) *It is generally agreed that chapters 8–12 come from a single hand, and are to be related to the events of the Maccabaean age.*

[1] Cf. L. Dennefeld, *Les Grands Prophètes*, 1947, p. 638.

[2] Cf. *Introduction à l'Ancien Testament*, 1935, pp. 175 ff. J. Chaine, in A. Robert and A. Tricot, *Initiation Biblique*, 1939, p. 109 (cf. 2nd ed., 1948, pp. 144 ff.), had similarly avoided committing himself, as does the Protestant writer Fleming James (*Personalities of the Old Testament*, 1939, p. 556).

[3] Cf. J. E. Steinmueller, *A Companion to Scripture Studies*, ii, 2nd ed., 1944, pp. 272 f. Cf. B. Alfrink, in *Bijbelsch Woordenboek*, 1941, col. 276.

[4] J. T. Nelis (*Dictionnaire encyclopédique de la Bible*, 1960, col. 415) dates the whole book in the Maccabaean period [cf. *Daniel* (B.O.T.), 1954].

[5] Cf. F. Buhl, in *P.R.E.*, 3rd ed., iv, 1898, p. 451: "Betrachten wir zunächst die Frage nach der Einheit des Buches, so lässt es sich nicht leugnen, dass die total verschiedenen Resultate, zu welchen die Bekämpfer der Einheit gekommen sind, wenig Vertrauen zu dieser Kritik erwecken." Cf. *The New Schaff-Herzog Encyclopedia of Religious Knowledge*, iii, 1909, p. 348 n.

It has been said that some have maintained an earlier date and have resorted to the assumption that these chapters have been glossed in the Maccabaean age. No solid reasons for separating these glosses have been offered, save that the allusions are more specific than an earlier writer might be expected to make. But this is to base the case for the alleged glosses on a theory of the origin of the book and not on the evidence. Accepting, then, the view that the last five chapters come from the Maccabaean age in their present form, and that there is no evidence against their unity, we observe that the Little Horn of chapter 8 took away the continual burnt offering and laid the sanctuary waste.[1] In chapter 9 the climax comes when the sanctuary is destroyed and the sacrifices cease.[2] In chapter 11 the great Antichrist profanes the sanctuary and takes away the sacrifice.[3] All of these indications appear to point to the same time, and this impression is confirmed by the obviously connected, though slightly varying, expressions found in 8 : 13 (hap-pesha‘ shōmēm), 9 : 27 (shikkûṣîm meshōmēm), 11 : 31 (hash-shikkûṣ meshōmēm), and 12 : 11 (shikkûṣ shōmēm). The irregularities in concord and in the use of the article are striking, and the view of Nestle,[4] that we have here an alteration, in part contemptuous and in part punning, of the expression Ba‘al shāmayim, has been widely adopted. On this view pesha‘ or shikkûṣ replaced Ba‘al, while shōmēm or meshōmēm replaced shāmayim. Some years ago the present writer suggested[5] that shōmēm or meshōmēm may have had a double reference, indicating the desolation of the sanctuary by Antiochus and the shock this gave the faithful, and also the madness of the desolator, since the root is associated with both meanings. For it is almost certain that all of these pointed to Antiochus and the heathen image and altar[6] which he erected in the Temple, and especially since 1 Macc. 1 : 54 tells us that what Antiochus erected on the altar in the Temple was known as the "abomination of desolation".[7]

(2) *Chapter 7 is closely bound to chapter 8.*

The Little Horn of chapter 7 had a mouth speaking great things and made war on the saints; he spoke against the Most High and thought

---

[1] Dan. 8: 11.   [2] Dan. 9: 26 f.   [3] Dan. 11: 31.

[4] Cf. E. Nestle, "Der Greuel der Verwüstung", in *Z.A.W.*, iv, 1881, p. 248.

[5] Cf. *Z.A.W.*, N.F. ix, 1932, pp. 264 f.

[6] Cf. my paper "Menelaus and the Abomination of Desolation", in *Studia Orientalia Ioanni Pedersen dicata*, 1953, pp. 303–315.

[7] The Greek phrase βδέλυγμα ἐρημώσεως stands in LXX at 11: 31 and in Theodotion at 12: 11, while LXX has βδέλυγμα τῆς ἐρημώσεως in 12: 11, and both LXX and Theodotion have βδέλυγμα τῶν ἐρημώσεων in 9: 27. In 11: 31 Theodotion has βδέλυγμα ἠφανισμένον, and in 8: 13 both LXX and Theodotion have ἡ ἁμαρτία ἐρημώσεως.

to change times and the law, until he was judged and overthrown and the everlasting kingdom of the saints of the Most High was established.[1] The Little Horn of chapter 8 waxed great, even to the host of heaven, and magnified itself even to the prince of the host; it stood up against the prince of princes, until it was suddenly destroyed without hand.[2] while, if the consummation is rightly associated with the consummation of the following chapters, its end heralded the coming of an enduring order in which the righteous should rise to everlasting glory.[3] In both cases, therefore, the Little Horn is portrayed as of the same character, the enemy of God and of the Law, and in both his swift end is the prelude to the setting up of the everlasting kingdom. The most natural interpretation of these passages found in the same book is in relation to the same events, and strong reasons ought to be provided before we are asked to assign them to different authors.[4] Some of the dividers of the book assign these chapters to the same author, and others hold that the author of chapter 8 was responsible for the parts of chapter 7 to which reference is here made. Hence for the present purpose all of these are allied with the present writer against those who would divide the book at the end of chapter 7, without going on to dissect that chapter.

(3) *Chapter 7 is also closely bound to chapter 2.*

There have been a few interpreters who have differently interpreted the four profane kingdoms of Nebuchadnezzar's vision and the four beastly kingdoms of Daniel's vision,[5] but the great majority of interpreters have held firmly to the unity of the interpretation. Such fundamental differences as are sometimes emphasized belong to the forms of the visions rather than to the substance of their messages. In the first vision the four parts of the image are seen simultaneously, but the interpretation shows that they are successive kingdoms; in the second vision the animals rise successively, and again represent successive kingdoms. Ginsberg[6] has alleged a significant and crucial difference in that the kingdoms of the first vision were simultaneously destroyed

---

[1] Dan. 7: 8, 21, 25-27.   [2] Dan. 8: 11, 12, 25.   [3] Dan. 12: 2 f.

[4] E. W. Heaton (*The Book of Daniel*, p. 49) draws a sharp theological distinction between chapters 1–7 and 8–12, but it is hard to see how any such distinction can be established between them. He says that in chapters 8–12 events move according to plan, but this is no more so in chapter 8 than in chapter 7. He adds (p. 50) that chapters 8–12 are best understood as a theological commentary on chapters 2–7, an observation which I find incomprehensible. It would be interesting to know, for example, which part of chapters 8–12 is thought to be a theological commentary on Nebuchadnezzar's madness.

[5] Cf. H. H. Rowley, *Darius the Mede*, 1935, pp. 64 f.

[6] Cf. H. L. Ginsberg, *op. cit.*, pp. 6 f.

when the image fell, whereas in the second vision the first kingdom was already destroyed, while the second and third survived to share in the destruction of the fourth. Even if this were true, it would have to be remembered that the form of the first vision involved the simultaneous destruction, though it is implied that imperial power had passed from each to its successor. It has, however, to be observed that this difference is one which Ginsberg imports by textual emendation in 7 : 4. He transfers the words "and it was made to stand upon two feet as a man" to verse 5, and then understands "it was lifted up from the earth" to mean that it was destroyed.[1] Since the words cannot possibly have that meaning in the present text, it can hardly be claimed that they *must* have the meaning which Ginsberg desiderates,[2] and in any case the argument for a fundamental difference of conception between the two chapters is here of the weakest, since it confessedly does not rest on the text which has come down to us. Moreover, it may be added that 7 : 12 is most naturally understood to refer to the first three kingdoms as surviving the fourth, though robbed of their dominion.

In both visions the four kingdoms are swept away by superhuman power, and their destruction is the prelude to the establishment of the everlasting kingdom. In the one a stone cut without hands brings the image down, while in the other the judgement of the Ancient of Days was apparently executed by the host of angelic ministrants who attended Him. Here we are reminded of the end of the Little Horn of chapter 8, who should be broken without hand. When we find in the same book two passages describing the establishment of an everlasting kingdom, the presumption is that the same kingdom is intended, and strong reasons are required before they can be differently understood. Here Ginsberg[3] points to what he holds to be significant evidence that chapter 2 is pre-Epiphanian and chapter 7 Epiphanian, in that chapter 2 does not hint at any special position of the Jews in the enduring kingdom, whereas chapter 7 does refer to the position of the

---

[1] *Ibid.*, p. 14.

[2] Ginsberg declares that this phrase "can have only one meaning: it perished" (*ibid.*, p. 65). In *V.T.*, iv, 1954, p. 260, Ginsberg challenges me to produce one instance of the verb *ntl* in any language meaning "to raise to the (hind) feet, or to an erect position." In *V.T.*, v, 1955, pp. 275 f., I accept the challenge and produce several instances from Aramaic in the Targums. Here it may suffice to cite Num. 23: 24 where this verb is used in the reflexive in the phrase "as a lion it lifts itself", where the meaning clearly is of a lion raising itself on its hind legs, and where the context makes it absolutely impossible that it could mean "destroys itself". In Dan. 7: 4 we have the passive form of this verb.

[3] *Ibid.*, p. 6.

saints of the Most High. This consideration, along with others whose weakness has been already exposed or will be exposed in the following sections, is held to *prove* diversity of date and origin. It is unreasonable to demand that an author must say everything he has to say on a subject every time he deals with it. There is nothing here in what is said in chapter 2 that is in the least inconsistent with what is said in chapter 7. No loyal Jew, such as the author of this chapter certainly was, would be likely to think of the Kingdom of God without any relation to the Jewish people and its faith. Least of all could the author of the surrounding chapters—for Ginsberg does not differentiate the author of chapter 2 from the author of the surrounding chapters—be supposed to have thought of that kingdom without relation to the Jewish people and its faith.

(4) *The emasculation of chapter 2 by the removal of alleged glosses rests on no solid evidence, and merely reduces the effectiveness of the story.*

Here it is common to strike out as secondary verses 41b–43, and also the reference to toes in verse 41a, on the ground that here we have elements in the interpretation which did not figure in the vision. It will be shown below that this is an argument for the originality of the verses rather than for their elimination. Torrey,[1] who did not strike out these verses, held them to point to a date in the middle of the third century B.C. for the whole of the first half of the book, whereas Ginsberg accepts Torrey's date for these verses, but dates the rest of this chapter and of the first part of the book earlier in the third century.[2] His reason for the earlier dating is not cogent, as has been already indicated. For it rests on the alleged difference between chapters 2 and 7 as to whether the first kingdom survives until the destruction of the fourth. Ginsberg thinks chapter 2 must have been written during the period 292–261 B.C., during which a Babylonian kingdom existed.[3] Since the interpretation of the vision of chapter 2 plainly says that the empires are successive, it is not legitimate to press the form of the vision in this way. Moreover, since chapter 7 equally represents the first kingdom as continuing to exist, though robbed of *imperium*, yet is dated by Ginsberg in the Maccabaean age, it cannot be argued that chapter 2 *must* have been written a century earlier on this ground. For Ginsberg's groundlessly emended translation has been shown to be insufficient to establish a difference between the chapters.

[1] Cf. *T.C.A.*, xv, 1909, pp. 246 f.   [2] *Op. cit.*, pp. 8 f.
[3] *Ibid.*, p. 9. But cf. *supra*, p. 257, n. 4.

The argument for the dating of verses 41b–43, where Ginsberg is in agreement with Torrey, is that the mingling of seed which failed to unite the iron and the clay must refer to the marriage of Antiochus II with Berenice, which ended in the Laodicean war and the weakening of Seleucid rule.[1] The Ptolemaic power is therefore the iron on this view and the Seleucid the clay. That others who assign chapter 2 to a pre-Maccabaean date hold these same verses to be a Maccabaean interpolation[2] is enough to throw doubt on this contention. For the daughter of Antiochus III, Cleopatra, married Ptolemy Epiphanes early in the second century B.C. This union led to no real solidarity between the two houses, but to war in the time of Antiochus Epiphanes,[3] who was checked by the intervention of Rome. Clearly, then, the Ptolemaic kingdom was weak at this time, whereas in relation to it the Seleucid power was still great.

There is no solid ground for dating either these verses or the rest of the chapter before the Maccabaean age, or for separating these verses from the rest. Without them the chapter is merely vague, and they contain the only reference to the expected time of the awaited climax found in the chapter. No evidence is offered that any Jew in the middle of the third century, when the chapter is held to have been written, or these verses to have been added, would be likely to expect that the consequences of the marriage of Antiochus II would precipitate world-shaking events.[4] Into the consequences of the later intermarriage the Jews were deeply drawn, and it was when Antiochus IV fell back from Egypt on Jerusalem in a mood of chagrin after being humiliated by the Romans that he "thought to change times and the law", and matched himself against the God of the Jews.

---

[1] Already Bertholdt (*op. cit.*, pp. 58 ff.) took this view, and based his dating of this chapter on it.

[2] So Sellin, *loc. cit.*; Hölscher, *T.S.K.*, xcii, 1919, pp. 122 f.; Haller, *Das Judentum*, 2nd ed., 1925, pp. 279 f.; Noth, *T.S.K.*, xcviii–xcix, 1926, p. 155; Thilo, *op. cit.*, pp. 33 f.; Junker, *op. cit.*, p. 17.

[3] Both of these intermarriages are referred to in Dan. 11 (verses 6, 17). It is therefore arbitrary for Torrey to argue that the reference in Dan. 2: 43 *must* be to the former (*loc. cit.*, pp. 246 f.).

[4] Torrey points out (*ibid.*, p. 247) that the sequel to the first of these intermarriages made it appear likely that the Seleucid dynasty would lose its last possession, Northern Syria, before the shattering blows of Ptolemy. But that is not what Dan. 2 has in mind. It speaks not of the crushing of the clay by the iron, but of the destruction of both and the inauguration of the new world power established by God. In the second century B.C., following the second intermarriage, this expectation is known to have existed, and it is recognized by both Torrey and Ginsberg. What neither has produced is the slightest evidence of its existence in 245 B.C.

(5) *The emasculation of chapter 7 by the removal of alleged glosses rests on no more solid evidence, and leaves the story with little identifiable point.*

It has been observed that there is no agreement among the dissectors of the book as to whether this chapter is glossed or not. Even those who hold it to be glossed cannot agree as to which are the glosses.[1] In Stevenson's view[2] the work of the interpolator is to be seen in verses 21 f., since they introduce particulars not already given in the vision, and then he eliminates the reference to the saints in verses 18 and 27. It will be seen below that the reason offered for holding verses 21 f. to be an interpolation is really a strong reason in favour of their originality. Riessler[3] rejects as glosses the four heads of verse 6, and all that relates to the eleven horns, but thinks these glosses were added at different times. That relating to the four heads he supposes to have been introduced by one who thought of the third beast as representing Alexander's divided kingdom,[4] while those relating to the horns he thinks were added by one who thought of Alexander as the first of the horns of the fourth beast. Sellin[5] contented himself with removing verses 8, 20–22, 24 f., while Hölscher,[6] Haller,[7] Thilo,[8] and Scott[9] remove also the end of verse 7, and verse 11a. The purpose of these excisions is to get rid of the reference to the Little Horn, or to all the Horns, and thus to leave the chapter shorn of its strongest link with chapter 8.[10] But the reasons offered for the mutilation will not bear examination. Thus Scott,[11] rejects them because they are the only parts of the chapter which connect it with the Maccabaean period, and because verses 21 f. mix up symbolic and real figures in a way that is unlike anything else in chapter 7, but precisely like what is found in 8 : 9–12. It is not, indeed, surprising that if the parts of chapter 7 which show this feature are removed, the rest does not show it. It is equally true that if the parts of the following chapters which point to the Maccabaean period were removed, the rest would not give any

---

[1] Cf. W. Baumgartner, *Th.R.*, N.F. xi, 1939, p. 77.

[2] Cf. *T.G.O.S.*, vii, 1936, p. 7 f. Cf. also Hölscher, *loc. cit.*, p. 120.

[3] *Op. cit.*, pp. 68 f.

[4] H. Gressmann (*Der Messias*, 1929, pp. 344 f., 366 f.) thought the four beasts of chapter 7 represented the successors of Alexander.

[5] *Loc. cit.* [6] *Loc. cit.*, p. 120. [7] *Op. cit.*, pp. 295 ff., 299.

[8] *Op. cit.*, pp. 34 f. [9] *Loc. cit.*, p. 294.

[10] L. Dequeker (*Le Fils de l'homme et les Saints du Très-Haut en Daniel vii, dans les Apocryphes et dans le Nouveau Testament*, 1961, p. 29) excises as secondary verses 8, 11a, 20, (22a), 24, 25a, which introduce the Little Horn, and also verses 21, 22b, 25b, which introduce the war on the saints, and which are held to come from a second redactor.

[11] *Ibid.*

clear reference to it.[1] It is similarly true to say that if the verses of chapter 8 which mix the symbolic and the real were removed, that chapter could as easily as this be relieved of this feature. But if it is allowed that the author of chapter 8 could mix these up, and also recognized that in chapter 7 they are similarly mixed, it can hardly be claimed that the reasons offered for their excision from chapter 7 are convincing.

Ginsberg[2] differs from the group of scholars just mentioned in retaining verses 7bβ, 20aα, and 24a, while rejecting the rest of the material rejected by Hölscher and Scott. Instead of holding with most of the other dissectors of this chapter that it existed first in a pre-Maccabaean form, and that it was then glossed in the Maccabaean age, he holds that it was first written in the reign of Antiochus Epiphanes and glossed a few years later in the same reign. The original writer, on this view, mentioned the ten horns, intending by them to indicate ten kings from Alexander to Antiochus. The glossator, however, is thought to have differently understood the ten horns, and to have intended the eleventh to be identified with Antiochus. It is highly improbable that the chapter would be misundertood and reinterpreted so soon after its composition, and if it were, it is likely that the interpolator would have made the new meaning much clearer than it is. It should be added that Ginsberg's view of the new meaning is also highly improbable in itself. For he supposes the glossator intended the ten horns to be understood to refer to ten contemporary kings, of whom seven were such kings as those of Cappadocia, Bithynia, Pontus, Commagene, Parthia, Sparta, and Macedonia—though he does not pin himself to this particular list—while the remaining three humbled kings were Artaxias of Armenia, and the two young Ptolemies of Egypt. But Antiochus did not put down the two Ptolemies from the Egyptian kingdom,[3] much as he would have liked to do so, and it is improbable that any contemporary would think of the ruler of the Seleucid kingdom as a Little Horn in comparison with, say, the ruler of Bithynia or Sparta.

---

[1] So, e.g., Lange (loc. cit.) excised as unoriginal 10: 1–11: 44, 12: 5–13, and Zöckler (loc. cit.) excised much of 11: 5–39.

[2] Op. cit., pp. 11 f.

[3] The present writer has argued (Darius the Mede, pp. 112 f.) that Ptolemy Philometor was one of the uprooted horns, but uprooted from the Seleucid line. Jerome tells us that that there were some in Syria who favoured the claim of Ptolemy as against Antiochus (cf. Migne, P.L., xxv, 1845, col. 566), and since Ptolemy was a Seleucid on his mother's side, this is quite credible. But this is very different from Ginsberg's view, for which no evidence is, or can be, presented. It is not merely not known that Antiochus uprooted the Ptolemies from Egypt, but definitely known that he attempted to do this and failed.

Noth is perhaps the most radical of all dissectors in his treatment of this chapter. He ascribes chapters 2 and 7 to the same hand,[1] and holds that they are the oldest parts of the book, dating from the time of Alexander. But he whittles down the chapter far more than Hölscher does, regarding verses 1–7abα as its earliest part.[2] The secondary verses 7bβ, 8 he believes to have been added before 168 B.C., at which time the chapter consisted of 1–8, 11b, 15, (16), 17, 19 f., 23 f., 25aα, 26b.[3] Subsequently verse 25aβb, which is dependent on the more recently appended chapters 8 and 9, is held to have been added, followed successively by verses 21, 22b, verses 9, 10, 13, 14, verses 18, 22a, 26a, 27.[4] It is not clear at what stage the remaining additions are supposed to have come in. This highly complicated literary history of the chapter is supported by no weighty arguments. The fact that 1 Enoch has several connexions with Dan. 7 : 9, 10, 13, but interprets the "Son of Man" differently is held to prove that both books draw from a common source.[5] It is equally simple to suppose that the author of 1 Enoch drew the idea from the book of Daniel, but reinterpreted the term in a manner not at all uncommon in apocalyptic works. The connexion of 7 : 25aβb with the situation presented in the following chapters may be agreed, but that in no way proves that it is less original here than the connected verses there.[6]

None of this can be accepted as convincing analysis.[7] Nor can the chapter when stripped of these alleged interpolations yield a satisfying meaning. Ginsberg leaves the chapter still Maccabaean, but most of the other dissectors hold it to be pre-Maccabaean, and find it to give only a vague picture of four successive kingdoms to be followed by the supernatural establishment of an eternal kingdom. As the chapter stands, it represents the succession of earthly kingdoms as reaching the climax of pride and iniquity in the moment when the divine intervention in history takes place. But the emasculated chapter leaves us with the fourth kingdom continuing for an indefinite period until the dénouement of history takes place apropos of nothing in particular. That there was a widespread expectation of four successive empires, to be followed by the crown of history, long antedating the

---

[1] Cf. *T.S.K.*, xcviii–xcix, 1926, pp. 158 f.
[2] *Ibid.*, p. 158.   [3] *Ibid.*, p. 160.   [4] *Ibid.*, pp. 161 f.
[5] *Ibid.*, p. 150.
[6] Cf. also Junker, *op. cit.*, p. 31.
[7] The great variety of analysis of the chapter is the clearest evidence of the subjective nature of the eliminations, and the multiplication of hands in a single chapter should only be resorted to when convincing objective tests require it.

Maccabaean period, is not to be denied.[1] But that it was expressed by some Hebrew writer with the measure of circumstantiality that marks the emasculated chapter, yet missing all dramatic quality by the omission of any setting for its climax, cannot be established from the fact that it contains precisely the desiderated setting. It is not self-evident that it required an interpolator to improve the chapter, and that the original writer must have told a flat and jejune story.[2]

(6) *Despite the efforts that have been made to prove that the Aramaic of chapter 7 is different from that of chapters 2–6, no real difference can be established.*

Charles[3] has shown more points of contact between the Aramaic of this chapter and that of those which precede it than all the alleged points of difference. Scott[4] objects that the points of contact are all found within what he calls the *Grundschrift* of chapter 7, and not in the alleged interpolations. Even if this were true, it would have to be remembered that these extend to but a few verses, and no writer can be expected to exhibit his characteristics in every line. On the other hand, no differences between the Aramaic of the interpolations and that of the preceding chapters can be established.

It is not, however, the case that the points of contact do not extend to these verses. For Charles notes the use of the feminine form *'oḥ°rî* (for which *'ḥrh* is found in the Elephantine papyri) in 2 : 39 (*bis*) and in 7 : 5, 6, 8, 20, of which the last two stand in supposed interpolations; also the use of *dikkēn* in 2 : 31 and in 7 : 20, 21, of which the last two are held to be in interpolations; and the use of *bē'dhayin* twenty-four times in 2 : 4b–6, and in 7 : 1, 11, of which the last is in an alleged interpolation. Especially significant is the use of *dikkēn* which is peculiar to the Aramaic of Daniel.[5]

The weakness of Scott's case is finally exposed, however, when he notes that "one curious difference between the Aramaic of chapter 7,

---

[1] Cf. J. W. Swain, "The Theory of the Four Monarchies Opposition History under the Roman Empire", in *Classical Philology*, xxxv, 1940, pp. 1–21, and W. Baumgartner, "Zu den vier Reichen von Daniel 2", in *Th.Z.*, i, 1945, pp. 17–22.

[2] H. Kruse (*Verbum Domini*, xxxvii, 1959, p. 155) contests this observation, and says that if we eliminate from the chapter all that connects the fourth beast with Antiochus Epiphanes there remains "prophetia, licet brevis et succincta, tamen digna quae prophetae sexti saeculi, immo Danieli Exilico, ascribatur". To this it may be replied that the elimination of all that now admittedly connects the chapter with Antiochus Epiphanes is not evidence that connects it with any other age.

[3] *Op. cit.*, pp. xl ff.   [4] *Loc. cit.*, p. 294.

[5] The word *dkn* appears in one Palmyrene inscription [cf. *P.E.F.Q.S.*, 1928, p. 101, and *C.I.S.*, ii (III, i, 1926), 4174: 6], but J. B. Chabot (*C.I.S.*, *ad loc.*) is doubtful whether it is to be identified with the demonstrative pronoun here.

and that of the previous chapters is the use of '^{a}rû for '^{a}lû in verses 2, 5, 6, 7, and 13. Here again is a difference from the interpolated 'Horns material', where '^{a}lû occurs in verse 8".[1] After having associated the *Grundschrift* with the previous chapters and having distinguished the alleged interpolations from them by the claim that community of usage was not established, he now seizes on a case where the precise opposite is found to support his case. For here the alleged interpolated material agrees with the preceding chapters, whereas his *Grundschrift* does not. This is surely a singular case of wanting it both ways. No differences between the interpolations and the preceding chapters are pointed out; the only difference that is noted is one between the supposed *Grundschrift* and the preceding chapters. So far as this is concerned, it should be observed that '^{a}rû is apparently a later form than '^{a}lû, since *hlu* is found in earlier Aramaic and *hry* in Mishnaic Hebrew. An interpolator in a document which already employed the later form, therefore, might be himself expected to employ that later form. There is no reason to presume that a single author could not use both forms, however, side by side in a single chapter, if he lived at the time when the transition was taking place. In Jer. 10 : 11 we find '*arḳâ* and '*ar'â* side by side, and the Elephantine papyri provide us with many examples of the same thing. No difference of hand within chapter 7 can be established on this ground, and still less can any difference of hand from the author of the earlier chapters be established.

(7) *Chapter 7 is linked with the earlier chapters in that it is written in Aramaic, and equally with the later chapters, in that it has many links of phraseology with them, despite the fact that they are written in Hebrew.*

The fact that chapter 7 is written in Aramaic has led many to divide the book at the end of that chapter; the links with the following chapters have led others to divide the book at the end of chapter 6. Yet others, as we have seen, make an inner dissection of this chapter in order to distribute the parts according to their connexions. Hölscher[2] declares that there are many lexical correspondences between the verses he wishes to omit from chapter 7 and chapters 8–12. What he omits to note is that there are also correspondences between the rest of that chapter and chapters 8–12. The phrase "the four winds of heaven" is found in 7 : 2 and in 8 : 8, 11 : 4; there is a reference to the "books" of judgement in 7 : 10 and in 12 : 1; the use of "the end" in 7 : 26, 28 may be compared with that in 7 : 17, 19, 11 : 6, 27, 35, 40, 12 : 4, 6,

---

[1] *Loc. cit.* Cf. Hölscher, *loc. cit.*, pp. 120 f.   [2] *Loc. cit.*, p. 121.

9, 13; and "the truth" in 7 : 16, 19 may be compared with the corresponding word in 11 : 2. All of these bind the rest of the chapter as
securely to the later chapters of the book as the links which Hölscher
recognizes bind the alleged interpolations to the later chapters.

(8) *Chapter 7 is linked both with the preceding anonymous chapters and
with the succeeding pseudonymous chapters.*

The first six chapters tell stories about Daniel, or about his friends,
without the slightest indication that they were written by Daniel. The
last five chapters are written in the first person, as though by Daniel
himself. Chapter 7 begins in the third person, and then turns over to
the first person. This transition bears no relation to the alleged glosses,
which are held to stand in this chapter, and their removal would not
affect this feature, which binds this chapter firmly with the chapters on
both sides. This transition similarly bears no relation to the change of
language, and is quite unaffected by the theory that the chapter has
been translated by the author of the later chapters, or written by him
in Aramaic. Since the transition from anonymity to pseudonymity
takes place within the course of this chapter, it is a transition which
was made by a single author, and this feature of the book as a whole
does not therefore demand plurality of authorship.[1]

This chapter also marks a transition in other respects. It presents the
first of Daniel's visions, and is therefore linked with the following
chapters, while by its contents it is tied to chapter 2, with its story of
Nebuchadnezzar's vision. It is still of such a character that it is suitable
for popular recital, though some of its details are less easily remembered with precision than details of the earlier stories. On the other
hand, it has less complexity than the following chapters. It is therefore
essentially a transitional chapter.

(9) *The mental and literary characteristics of the book are the same
throughout.*

In nothing is the unity of the book more clearly seen than here. The
writer of the first six chapters is fond of resounding lists of words,
such as the terms for the various classes of wise men, or the lists of
royal officers, or the instruments of Nebuchadnezzar's band. This same
feature is found in chapter 7, where we find the phrase "peoples,
nations and tongues",[2] which stands also in chapter 3, and the phrase

---

[1] E. Reuss (*La Bible, Ancien Testament*, vii, 1879, p. 211) observes: "La transition de la
troisième personne à la première se fait de manière que le rédacteur passe de l'une à
l'autre comme qui dirait par inadvertance."

[2] Dan. 7: 14.

"dominion and glory and kingship".[1] This feature is effective in popular narration, for which the Aramaic chapters were written, but is less suited for the later chapters, which do not appear to have been written for such a purpose. Hence this feature does not mark the last five chapters in the same way.

Moreover, it is characteristic of the author that in his repetitions or interpretations he introduces new elements which were not mentioned before. It has already been said that some scholars would eliminate some verses of chapter 2 on the ground that they introduce in the interpretation elements which did not stand in the account of the vision. Similarly, in chapter 7, new elements of the vision are introduced in verse 21 to prepare the way for the interpretation. In the same way in 7 : 19 we find an additional touch that did not stand in the previous account, in the nails of brass. This does not stand in one of the alleged interpolations, and it is clear that the supposed canon of dissection cannot apply. Ginsberg therefore proposes to apply it in reverse[2] and to insert the reference to "nails of brass" in 7 : 7 to make it agree with 7 : 19. But in 4 : 30 (E.V. 33), in the account of the fulfilment of Nebuchadnezzar's dream, we similarly find something which did not figure in the account of the dream, in the words "till his hair was grown like eagles' feathers, and his nails like birds' claws". Here there can be no question of an interpolator, since no point could be given to these words to explain their insertion as a reference to some historic situation, and there is no reason to insert them into the earlier account. In all of these cases we find a common mind at work, and parallel treatment should be given to them all. As the present writer has written elsewhere,[3] "Instead of striking out these after-thoughts when they point to the Maccabaean age, and leaving them when they do not, it is better to find in them the authentic evidences of a single mind, which was untroubled by a severely logical discipline. It is the same

---

[1] *Ibid.*

[2] *Op. cit.*, p. 69, following Baumgartner in Kittel, *Biblia Hebraica*, 3rd ed., 1937, *ad loc.* Hippolytus is there doubtfully cited in support of this emendation. It is true that Hippolytus has the phrase here (cf. Hippolyte, *Commentaire sur Daniel*, ed. by M. Lefèvre, 1947, p. 268), and it is possible that he found it in some MS. of Theodotion, but this is very weak evidence for the insertion. Few would argue that Theodotion's omission of the words "in the night visions" in this verse justifies their omission, and a single assumed MS. of Theodotion can hardly be given greater authority here than all our witnesses to the text, especially when it is by no means an uncommon phenomenon for a scribe to harmonize one text with another, and when Hippolytus himself may well be responsible for the harmonization.

[3] Cf. *J.T.S.*, xxxviii, 1937, p. 427.

mind which is revealed in the many inconsistencies of detail which are found in the book."

Similarly, when it is objected to some verses in chapter 7 that the symbolical and the real are confused as in some verses of chapter 8, it should not be forgotten that we find precisely the same feature in chapter 4. There we read, in the account of the vision of the tree: "Hew down the tree . . . nevertheless leave the stump of its roots in the earth . . . and let its portion be with the beasts in the grass of the earth . . . let its heart be changed from a man's and let a beast's heart be given unto it."[1] This is surely as singular confusion as anything that can be produced from chapter 7. As Stuart observed:[2] "It seems to me impossible for any one at all skilled in discerning the characteristics of writing, to read the book through attentively in the original, without an overwhelming conviction that the whole proceeded from one pen and one mind."

(10) *The unhistorical representation of Belshazzar as king figures in chapters 5, 7 and 8.*

That Belshazzar was the king's son, and that he was actually left in administrative control of the kingdom for some years, is beyond dispute; but that he had the title of king is inconsistent with our contemporary evidence, as the present writer has sufficiently shown elsewhere.[3] The overworked Persian Verse Account is insufficient to overturn the evidence of the contract tablets, which were never dated by his years, and the fact that the New Year's festival could not be held because Nabonidus was absent from Babylon. Yet in Dan. 7 and 8 we find events dated by his regnal years. Young[4] endeavours to turn this by arguing that though Belshazzar may not have had the title of king, it was proper for Daniel to date events by his regnal years, since he exercised the functions of king, even though this was not done in official documents. But this fails to meet the point that in the book of Daniel Belshazzar is represented as really king. No one could read Dan. 5 and get the impression that Belshazzar was only acting king. The dating of events by his regnal years in the second part, and the representation of him as really king in the first part, are in full agreement with one another, and carry this historical error into both halves of the book.

---

[1] Dan. 4: 11 ff. (E.V. 14 ff.).   [2] *Op. cit.*, p. 399.
[3] Cf. H. H. Rowley, "The Historicity of the Fifth Chapter of Daniel", in *J.T.S.*, xxxii, 1930–31, pp. 12–31.
[4] *Op. cit.*, pp. 115 ff.

(11) *The unhistorical Darius the Mede also figures in both halves of the book.*

That history allows no place for Darius the Mede, the son of Ahasuerus, between the reign of the uncrowned Belshazzar and that of Cyrus, the present writer has once more demonstrated.[1] Here Young[2] confesses that secular sources are silent concerning him, and can only hope that some future discovery will account for him. This ignores the fact that our evidence against Darius the Mede is positive and not merely negative. Cyrus immediately followed Nabonidus, the father of Belshazzar, whose kingdom was annexed, and there is therefore no room for Darius the Mede, as he is depicted in the book of Daniel. This is frankly recognized by Fabre d'Envieu, one of the doughtiest of the defenders of the traditional view of the book of Daniel.[3] Lattey,[4] with some hesitation, revives the claim that Darius is to be identified with Cyaxares II. For the existence of Cyaxares II our only evidence is Xenophon's romance. Lattey accepts this as sufficient, and suggests that Cyrus may have appointed him to be a puppet king in Babylon. Against this it is to be observed that the book of Daniel does not represent him as a puppet king. And neither does Xenophon. According to Xenophon, it was Cyaxares who appointed Cyrus to be puppet king of Babylon.[5] He can hardly be appealed to, therefore, for authority for Lattey's supposition, which is a mere figment of the imagination without a shred of evidence.[6]

(12) *Just as the later chapters contain a clear reference to Antiochus Epiphanes, so chapter 3 contains a clear indication of the same age in the Greek terms it uses.*

The mere use of Greek words might be expected at any time after Greek influence reached the east, but the particular words which stand here are not so easily accounted for.[7] They are the names of

[1] Cf. H. H. Rowley, *Darius the Mede*, pp. 9 ff.

[2] *Op. cit.*, p. 131.

[3] Cf. *Le Livre du Prophète Daniel*, I, ii, 1888, p. 470. His own theory that Darius the Mede is to be identified with Neriglissar is, however, no more tenable.

[4] *Op. cit.*, pp. 74 ff.

[5] Cf. Xenophon, *Cyropædia*, VIII, v, 17 ff.

[6] Fabre d'Envieu (*loc. cit.*) observes of this hypothesis: "Cette hypothèse n'est donc pas soutenable, et les faits qu'elle implique sont inconciliables avec les témoignages les plus dignes de respect et de foi."

[7] J. Linder (*Z.K.T.*, lix, 1935, p. 544) replies to the present writer's argument on the Greek words in this chapter by saying: "Ein kurzer Hinweis auf die neuesten Veröffentlichungen über die Beziehung der Achämeniden zur griechischen Kultur mag als Antwort hierauf genügen." That it will not suffice is plain to everyone who reads what the writer had said. For his argument, as Linder must have known, since he was familiar with *The*

musical instruments,[1] and one of them is nowhere met in Greek literature as the name of an instrument before the second century B.C., and there it is mentioned in connexion with the festivities of Antiochus Epiphanes.[2] As an allusion to Antiochus, it could therefore be pointed and effective here, but no comparable point of relevance has been shown for any of the earlier dates to which the chapter has been assigned. So strong is this evidence that Riessler[3] held these words to have been introduced by a Maccabaean glossator. To resort to textual surgery wherever evidence is inconvenient is ruthless propaganda for a theory, rather than the scientific study of evidence. Bentzen[4] thought the word *sûmpōnyāh* would be read as a reference to Antiochus in Maccabaean days, but thought this was only accidental. It would surely be passing strange for a pre-Maccabaean work to find more point in Maccabaean days than in its own,[5] and a singular circumstance that it is bound up with writings that admittedly come from the Maccabaean age.

Aramaic of the Old Testament, was not based on general considerations, but on a study of specific terms. If Linder found a work ascribed to a date not earlier than the twentieth century on the ground that it referred to someone as a quisling, it would not suffice to reply by referring to evidence that words of Norwegian origin were found in English at an earlier date. And as little relevant is Linder's prudent avoidance of any attempt to answer the writer's arguments. Of the three Greek words found in the book of Daniel the writer observed: "*Psaltērion* is first mentioned in Greek literature in Aristotle, two hundred years after the alleged occurrence in Daniel, and *sumphōnia* first appears in Greek in Plato, some century and a half after the suggested date of Daniel, but in the proper abstract sense of *harmony*, while as the name of a musical instrument it is first found in Greek literature in Polybius, nearly four hundred years after the supposed date of Daniel. In the absence of any shred of evidence to the contrary, or of any adequate suggestion to account for this remarkable fact, we can only conclude that it is highly improbable that Greek words should appear first in literature in an Aramaic work some centuries before they appear in Greek writers. . . . Moreover, G. R. Driver points out (*J.B.L.*, xl, 1926, p. 119) that not only is *sumphōnia* in the concrete sense of a musical instrument not met with until late, but such a use of the abstract term is a post-classical usage" (*The Aramaic of the Old Testament*, 1929, p. 148). Against this Linder's bland generality is futile. To Fabre d'Envieu these Greek words were so serious an embarrassment that he resorted to the desperate expedient of denying that they were Greek (*op. cit.*, I, i, 1888, pp. 87–102). A. Weiser (*Introduction to the Old Testament*, E.Tr., 1961, p. 316) suggests that the Greek words, *inter alia*, point to the third century B.C. But he does not refer to the curious circumstance that one of these words is first found in the sense it has in Daniel in Greek literature in the second century B.C., and is then used in connection with Antiochus Epiphanes.

[1] Cf. H. H. Rowley, *The Aramaic of the Old Testament*, pp. 146 ff.

[2] Cf. Polybius, *Histories*, xxvii, 10, as cited by Athenæus, *Deipnosophists*, v, 193 e, x, 439 ad.

[3] *Op. cit.*, p. xii.

[4] Cf. Bentzen, *Daniel*, 1937, p. 13.

[5] Cf. H. H. Rowley, *J.T.S.*, xxxviii, 1937, p. 426.

(13) *Point can be found for every story of the first half of the book in the setting of the Maccabaean age to which the latter part is assigned.*[1]

The first chapter is the story of Jews who refused to eat unclean foods. In the time of the Maccabaean crisis, when Antiochus sought to compel the Jews to eat swine's flesh that had been sacrificed to idols, many chose to die rather than defile themselves with unclean foods,[2] and Judas the Maccabee is said to have lived on herbs for fear of pollution.[3] So far as the second chapter is concerned, enough has been said above. It is linked by its climax to chapter 7 and the later chapters of the book, and its hope of the imminent establishment of the everlasting kingdom of righteousness is one that was certainly cherished in Maccabaean days. The third chapter is the story of Jews who refused to worship the great image which Nebuchadnezzar set up. Antiochus Epiphanes turned the Temple into a heathen shrine and set up there an idol or idols.[4] Since the Temple was dedicated to Zeus Olympius,[5] an image of Zeus would be expected, and since the king claimed to be Zeus manifest in the flesh, it is likely that it would take the form of a statue of the king.[6] Jerome tells us, indeed, that an image of Zeus and statues of the king were placed in the Temple.[7] While these may not have been colossal in size, they were monstrous in significance in the eyes of faithful Jews, and this chapter would well stimulate men to resistance

---

[1] Cf. F. Bleek, *loc. cit.*, pp. 232 ff. E. W. Heaton (*The Book of Daniel*, 1956, p. 51) says: "Although H. H. Rowley has demonstrated that point can be found for every story of the first section in the setting of the Maccabaean age, this does not establish the view that it was then that they were originally conceived." This misrepresents me by suggesting that I had argued that this consideration "established" the date of the stories. My argument is cumulative, as the reader will perceive. He will also observe that I hold that the author made use of traditions older than his day, but moulded them to serve his purpose. Moreover, it could be retorted that the fact that the stories as a collection have no known relevance to another age comparable with that which they have in the setting of the Maccabaean age does not "establish" that they were written in another age.

[2] 1 Macc. 1: 47, 62 f.; 2 Macc. 6: 8, 18 ff., 7: 1.   [3] 2 Macc. 5: 27.

[4] Cf. Mishnah, *Ta'anith*, iv, 6, and the Gemara thereon (T.B., *Ta'anith*, 28b). H. Danby (*The Mishnah*, 1933, p. 200 n.) says nothing is known of the Apostomos of the Mishnah passage. But the Gemara makes it plain that the tradition was associated with Dan. 12: 11, and that the reference was believed to be to the "abomination of desolation". L. Ginzberg (*Jewish Encyclopedia*, ii, 1902, pp. 21 f.) identifies Apostomos with Antiochus Epiphanes.

[5] 2 Macc. 6: 2.

[6] Bleek (*loc. cit.*, pp. 259 f.) already thought chapter 3 had in mind the setting up of the abomination of desolation—"sonder Zweifel die Statue des Jupiter"—in Jerusalem.

[7] Cf. Migne, *P.L.*, xxv, 1845, col. 569: *in templo Jerusalem, Jovis Olympii simulacrum et Antiochi statuas ponerent quas nunc abominationem desolationis vocat*. Cf. also the Gemara on *Ta'anith*, iv, 6 referred to above, which preserves the tradition that there were two images.

to the king's commands. The fourth chapter is the story of a king whose overweening pride is punished by madness.[1] It is known that Antiochus who fancied himself a god incarnate, was called by his people Epimanes, madman.[2] This chapter, then, might well be understood in that day as a reference to Antiochus, and bring its promise of humiliation at the hands of God. The fifth chapter tells of a king who profaned the Temple vessels, upon whom the judgement of heaven fell. Antiochus is stated to have removed the sacred vessels of the Temple with his own hands,[3] and to people who were filled with horror at such sacrilege this chapter could bring the hope of the outpouring of divine wrath upon him. The sixth chapter tells of the minions of a king, who both encouraged him to suppress religious freedom and treacherously spied on the loyal and denounced them to the king, only to find their plots recoil upon themselves.[4] In the days of Antiochus

[1] S. Smith (*Babylonian Historical Texts*, 1924, pp. 36, 46; cf. also J. M. Wilkie, *J.T.S.*, N.S. ii, 1951, pp. 36–44) suggested that this story really rested on a tradition about Nabonidus, here transferred to Nebuchnezzar. The finding of the text called "The Prayer of Nabonidus" (see J. T. Milik, *R.B.*, lxiii, 1956, pp. 406–415, and R. Meyer, *Das Gebet des Nabonid*, 1962, where the fullest discussion of this text will be found) among the Dead Sea Scrolls from Qumran has made this more probable. For translations of the Prayer cf. E. Vogt, *Biblica*, xxxvii, 1956, pp. 532 ff.; H. M. I. Gevaryahu, in *Studies in the Dead Sea Scrolls*, ed. by J. Liver (in Hebrew), 1957, pp. 12–23; J. T. Milik, *Ten Years of Discovery in the Wilderness of Judaea*, 1959, pp. 36 f.; R. Meyer, *Th.L.Z.*, lxxxv, 1960, cols. 831–834; A. Dupont-Sommer, *The Essene Writings from Qumran*, E.Tr., 1961, pp. 322 f.; G. Vermes, *The Dead Sea Scrolls in English*, 1962, p. 229. There are obvious differences from Dan. 4 (underlined by Dupont-Sommer, *op. cit.*, pp. 323 ff.), but this does not mean that the author of the book of Daniel did not freely use the tradition which lies behind it, adapting it for his purposes. Cf. M. Burrows, *More Light on the Dead Sea Scrolls*, 1958, p. 169: "The Prayer of Nabonidus makes it probable that the story back of chapter 4 was told originally of Nabonidus"; cf. also Milik, *op. cit.*, p. 37; Vogt, *loc. cit.*; Gevaryahu, *loc. cit.*; Meyer, *loc. cit.*; J. Barr in Peake's *Commentary on the Bible*, revised ed., 1962, p. 595a. Barr points out that if Dan. 4 was originally told about Nabonidus and later transferred to Nebuchadnezzar, Belshazzar, who was actually the son of Nabonidus but who is said in Dan. 5 to have been the son of Nebuchadnezzar, may have been once correctly described. Cf. also W. H. Brownlee, *The Meaning of the Qumrân Scrolls for the Bible*, 1964, pp. 36 ff. D. N. Freedman (*B.A.S.O.R.*, No. 145, Feb. 1957, pp. 31 f.) says the new text favours the view of the composite character of the book of Daniel, and the Babylonian origin of chaps. 1–6. It is hard to see how it can do this. The Prayer of Nabonidus comes from Palestine and it brings evidence of a knowledge there of a tradition about Nabonidus which could have been learned by the author of the book of Daniel and used for his purpose.

[2] Cf. Polybius, *Histories*, xxvi, 10, as preserved in Athenæus, *Deipnosophists*, ii, 45c, v, 193d, x, 439a.

[3] I Macc. 1: 21 ff.

[4] In this story Darius is presented in a much better light than the previous kings. It is true he arrogates the place of God, but this is represented as due to the instigation of his ministers who make him their tool. When he realizes that he has been the victim of a plot against Daniel, he strains every nerve to save him. It is clear that none of this has

there was a section of the Jews who fawned on the king for their own advancement, who encouraged him in all his attacks on the liberties of the loyal, and who were traitors to their own people.[1] This chapter brought its promise that upon them, too, would fall the vengeance of God. At the same time it encouraged the faithful to continue in their faithfulness, and to be unmoved by the threats of a king, or by the malice of his servants.

The view that these stories existed in a collection before the second century B.C. asks us to believe that at some earlier date, apropos of nothing in particular, some one had prepared this collection which would have more point and meaning in Maccabaean days than at any other time of which we have knowledge,[2] and that by singular good fortune the collection was taken up by a Maccabaean author into his own work. This groundless theory can hardly be said to be evidence that a Maccabaean author could not himself have written the stories using traditions which he selected and moulded for his own purpose.[3] It can hardly be denied that he could have written for himself stories which could so well serve his purpose. The materials he used were

any relevance to Antiochus. It belongs, however, to the setting of the story, since here it is the king's counsellors who are being pilloried. Darius is presented as the overthrower of the Babylonian empire and the slayer of the impious son of the hated Nebuchadnezzar. As the overthrower of the oppressor of the Jews, he is not presented as an oppressor. Hence here it is the wicked ministers who are the enemies, and upon them the punishment falls.

[1] Cf. 1 Macc. 1: 11 ff.; 2 Macc. 3: 4 ff., 5: 23.

[2] It is sometimes said that pogroms took place in the Persian period, and that they sufficiently account for these stories (cf. Hölscher, loc. cit., p. 125; Kuhl, op. cit., p. 78). But that is wholly to ignore their character. For here we have no persecution of Jews as Jews. The book of Esther tells the story of a projected pogrom and its sequel, but the book of Daniel tells the story of Jews who were subjected to the test of their faith, and not of their birth. And that is precisely what happened in the days of Antiochus Epiphanes, whose persecution was in no sense a pogrom. Jews who were prepared to accept the religious demands of the king were subjected to no persecution.

[3] It is sometimes objected (cf. C. von Orelli, Old Testament Prophecy, E.Tr. by J. S. Banks, 1885, p. 467) that if the stories were written in Maccabaean days, they should have referred to circumcision and Sabbath observance, which were vital issues in those days (1 Macc. 1: 48, 60 f.; 2 Macc. 6: 10; 1 Macc. 1: 39, 43, 45, 2: 32 ff.; 2 Macc. 6: 6). With a deeper religious instinct our author fastens on the duties of resisting idol worship, of refraining from eating defiling foods (by which he probably means food sacrificed to idols), and of maintaining the life of prayer to God. The author of the visions is no more concerned to introduce these other matters than is the author of the stories. Moreover, it was early found in the struggle against Antiochus that Sabbath observance could be carried too far (1 Macc. 2: 39–41), and it is not surprising that this was not pressed here. Further, circumcision was likely to lead to the death of the babes and their mothers (1 Macc. 1: 60 f.), and the book of Daniel concentrated on those loyalties which men could observe at risk to themselves rather than those which involved such dire penalties on their helpless wives and children.

probably taken from various sources, oral and written, but his skill displayed itself in seizing on them and relating them to the needs of his own day, so that they could convey a message to men.

It has often been denied that the stories can be given any relevance to the age of Antiochus,[1] on the ground that no loyal Jew could enter the service of that monarch in the way Daniel is said to have entered the service of Nebuchadnezzar,[2] and it is certain that Antiochus was never brought to acknowledge the true God in the way that Nebuchadnezzar is said to have done. But a story told to point a message does not have to be an exact parallel in all particulars. The form of the story imposes some limitation on the author, so long as it does not conflict with his purpose; and no one could suppose that the purpose of the stories was to encourage Jews to enter the service of heathen kings. Daniel is represented as one who was compelled to enter such service, but who was continually brought into conflict with his masters by his unbending attitude. It is this which is commended to the reader.

While stories about Nebuchnezzar and Belshazzar and Darius were used, it is not necessary to suppose that these were merely lay figures for Antiochus. In certain particulars they were intended to direct men's thoughts to him; but other elements were derived from tradition. And because they were in themselves other than Antiochus, they were represented as in some respects superior to him, since he was thought of as the great Antichrist, or climax of human wickedness. In each case the particular thing for which the kings are held up to obloquy is something which has its counterpart in Antiochus, while the particular thing for which the pious Jews are held up to honour is something which pious Jews in the days of Antiochus might with peculiar appropriateness be encouraged to imitate. In the same way the scheme of four world empires was taken over and not created by our author. His skill lay in using it for his purpose by references to things which his readers would identify as the prelude to the end.

Many of those who hold the book to be composite regard the latter part as having been composed by an author who was familiar with the first part, or who actually took over the first part. It could therefore be held that the community of error about Belshazzar and Darius the Mede, and others of the links which are here held to bind the two parts

---

[1] Cf. Torrey, *loc. cit.*, p. 245; Hölscher, *loc. cit.*, pp. 123 ff.; Montgomery, *op. cit.*, p. 89.

[2] W. Baumgartner (*Th.R.*, N.F. xi, 1939, pp. 125 f.) says: "Gegenüber Rowley muss ich an der vormakkabäischen Entstehung von c. 1 festhalten, da es Situation und Tendenz (Gesetzestreue auch am heidnischen Hof) mit c. 2 ff. teilt."

together, could be accounted for in this way. It can scarcely be denied that they could be even better accounted for by community of authorship, and when the links of style and outlook, which are so clearly acknowledged that the theories of glossing have been so extensively resorted to, are added to the community of error, the case for the unity of authorship is a strong one. The stock argument against it is just that touch of looseness and inconcinnity which is really the strongest argument for it. Community of error can be accounted for by borrowing; but a quality of mind, or mental habit, is not so easily borrowed. Hence the fact that this is found in the oft-severed parts of the book is of the first significance. Not less so is the difficulty of finding any clear division, since the threefold test of language, form, and presumptive authorship yields different results, while chapter 7 will continue to embarrass the dissectors by its refusal to be assigned to either half alone.

The onus of proof lies upon those who would dissect a work. Here, however, nothing that can be seriously called proof of compositeness has been produced. On the other hand, evidence for the unity of the work that in its totality amounts to a demonstration is available.

RECENT DISCOVERY AND THE PATRIARCHAL AGE

8

Recent Discovery and the Patriarchal Age[1]

IN the early years of the present century it was widely thought that the age of the patriarchs was lost beyond recovery. Whether they ever existed at all was sometimes doubted,[2] while at best they were held by some scholars to be no more than personifications of tribes,[3] whose history was reflected in these pseudo-personal narratives. The dictum of Wellhausen, that the patriarchal narratives could give us no knowledge about the times of the patriarchs, but only about the later age in which they were written down,[4] was accepted as axiomatic in

[1] A lecture delivered in the John Rylands Library on 9 February 1949. For a review of the latest discussions of the historical value of the patriarchal traditions, cf. R. de Vaux "Les Patriarches Hébreux et l'Histoire", in *Studii Biblici Franciscani, Liber Annuus xiii*, 1962–63, pp. 287–297. On the whole question covered by the present article cf. the richly documented article by H. Cazelles on "Patriarches" in *S.D.B.*, Fasc. 36, 1961, cols. 81–156.

[2] Cf. J. Wellhausen, *Prolegomena to the History of Israel*, E.Tr., 1885, p. 320, where it is said that Abraham "might with more likelihood be regarded as a free creation of unconscious art". Cf. also G. A. Barton, "Abraham and Archaeology", in *J.B.L.*, xxviii, 1909, pp. 152–168.

[3] Cf. the discussions of this question in S. R. Driver, *The Book of Genesis*, 1904, pp. lv ff., and J. Skinner, *Genesis*, 1910, pp. xix ff.

[4] Cf. J. Wellhausen, *op. cit.*, pp. 318 f. See also L. Wallis, *The Bible is Human*, 1942, p. 146: "The patriarchal figures reflect the sociology and ideology which became standard in the central highlands during the epochs covered by the books of Judges, Samuel, and Kings." Similarly R. Weill attaches little historical value to the patriarchal narratives. Cf. "La légende des patriarches et l'histoire", in *R.E.S.*, 1937, pp. 145–206. M. Noth is also sceptical of the historical value of the patriarchal narratives. Cf. *History of Israel*, E.Tr., 2nd ed., 1960, p. 123: "We have no evidence beyond what has been said already for making any definite historical assertions about the time and place, presuppositions and circumstances of the lives of the patriarchs as human beings. Even the original tradition of the patriarchs was not, however, much concerned with their human personalities, but rather with the divine promises that had been made to them"; p. 125: "The theme of the patriarchs was evolved from the point of view of the promise that was ultimately fulfilled in the occupation of the land by the Israelite tribes." For later modifications of Noth's position, especially in Oxford *Congress Volume* (S.V.T. vii), 1960, pp. 262–282, cf. A. Soggin, *B.A.*, xxiii, 1960, pp. 95 ff.; R. de Vaux, *Studii Biblici Franciscani, Liber Annuus xiii*, 1962–63, pp. 292 ff. For a criticism of Noth, cf. J. Bright, *Early Israel in recent History Writing*, 1956. Cf. also Noth, *Interpretation*, xv, 1961, pp. 61–66. G. von Rad (*Old Testament Theology*, i, E.Tr. by D. M. G. Stalker, 1962, pp. 3 ff.) adopts a position very similar to Noth's. On von Rad and Noth, cf. G. E. Wright, *E.T.*, lxxi, 1959–60, pp. 292 ff., and von Rad's reply, *ibid.*, lxxii, 1960–61, pp. 213–216.

some quarters. To-day there are few who would defend these positions, and there is a more general respect for the historical quality of the stories.[1] This is not merely because a more conservative mood has descended upon Old Testament scholars, but because new light has been shed on the patriarchal age from many quarters. Sometimes there is a disposition to err on the other side, and to claim that the new sources of knowledge have proved the accuracy of the Old Testament narratives.[2] This is far from being the case, and it can serve no good purpose to make exaggerated and unprovable claims.[3] All that can be said is that in many respects the stories fit into the background of the age, as we can recover it from other sources of knowledge now available, and that customs which appear in the stories prevailed in the

[1] Cf. S. H. Hooke, In the Beginning, 1947, p. 62: "The sagas of Genesis, while they throw light on the religious ideas of the writers who were using this material, also reflect in many ways the customs and social conditions of an age so far removed in time from that of the Hebrew historian who recorded them that he did not always understand what he was recording; so that we may believe him to have faithfully preserved much of the ancient tradition of his people in its early form." Cf. also Hooke, in Record and Revelation, (ed. by H. W. Robinson), 1938, p. 372: "It is safe to say that the general effect of the discoveries of the last decade has been to confirm the substantial accuracy of the picture of life in Canaan in the second millennium B.C., as described in the patriarchal narratives of Genesis"; H. G. May, J.B.L., lx, 1941, p. 113: "Absolute scepticism towards the patriarchal narratives as historical records is difficult to maintain today in the light of the materials contemporary with the patriarchal period made available as a result of archaeological research"; C. H. Gordon, J.B.R., xxi, 1953, p. 241: "The social institutions of the patriarchs are genuine and pre-Mosaic. They cannot have been invented by any post-Mosaic J, E, D or P."

[2] In The New Bible Handbook (ed. by G. T. Manley), 1947, p. 79, it is said that "today Sir Leonard Woolley tells us that the fact of Abraham's existence is 'vouched for by written documents almost, if not quite, contemporary with him'." What Woolley actually says (Abraham: Recent Discoveries and Hebrew Origins, 1936, p. 42) is that there are "good grounds for believing that the fact of Abraham's existence was vouched for by written documents". The words I have italicized indicate the perversion of Woolley's statement. What he argued was that it is probable that the authors of the Biblical narratives worked with older documents, long since lost (cf. pp. 259 ff.). Again Sir Charles Marston (The Bible Comes Alive, 1937, pp. 44 f.) says: "Sir Leonard Woolley's excavations at Ur of the Chaldees, where Abraham spent his youth, have proved that he lived in a city which had an advanced culture." Actually they have produced not the slightest proof that Abraham lived in Ur at all. As will be seen below, I see no reason to doubt the Biblical statement that Abraham once lived in Ur; but it is a gross exaggeration to suggest that there is any external proof of this. Our sole evidence for the existence of Abraham, or for his residence in Ur, is to be found in the Bible.

[3] Cf. M. Burrows, What Mean these Stones? 1941, p. 2: "More serious is the fact that writers fired by zeal without knowledge have rushed into print with inaccurate statements, doubtless intended for the glory of God but none the less misleading and therefore mischievous. . . . Reverence for the Bible cannot be permanently promoted by making claims on its behalf which will later prove untrue." Cf. W. F. Albright, The Biblical Period from Abraham to Ezra, 1963, p. 5: "This does not, of course, mean that oral tradition . . . can be treated by the historian as though it were based directly on written records."

world in which the patriarchs are set. We have no direct reference in any other source to any incident in the lives of the patriarchs as recorded in the Bible; yet of the credibility of the Biblical record we have greater knowledge than was even quite recently available.[1]

At the same time, it should not be forgotten that every advance in knowledge brings new problems, and not a few of the positions taken by the defenders of tradition against the earlier views I have mentioned are in no less need of revision than the theories they combated. In the present lecture it is impossible to survey all the new knowledge or to look at all the new problems, and all that I can attempt is to give some illustration of the light that is shed on the Biblical narratives and the new difficulties created.[2]

Between the two world wars archaeological work throughout the Bible lands brought a bewildering amount of new material into our hands. Much of it is relevant to the discussion of other periods than that of the patriarchs, and will not call for mention here. The excavations at Ur[3] directed attention to the early narratives of Genesis and to the patriarch Abraham,[4] though sometimes the problems were screened and people imagined that the Ur excavations had proved that the Biblical story of the Flood was true[5] and had established Abraham as a

---

[1] Cf. W. F. Albright, *ibid.*, "As a whole, the picture in Genesis is historical, and there is no reason to doubt the general accuracy of the biographical details and the sketches of personality which make the Patriarchs come alive with a vividness unknown to a single extrabiblical character in the whole vast literature of the ancient Near East."

[2] C. P. Auvray, *S.D.B.*, iv, 1948, col. 1138: "L'archéologie ne répond pas à toutes les questions, mais elle est capable d'éclairer utilement ces textes."

[3] Cf. *Ur Excavations*, I: *Al-'Ubaid*, by H. R. Hall and C. L. Woolley, 1927; II: *The Royal Cemetery*, by C. L. Woolley, 1934; III: *Archaic Seal Impressions*, by L. Legrain, 1936; V: *The Ziggurat and its Surroundings*, by C. L. Woolley, 1939; *Ur Excavations. Texts*, I: *Royal Inscriptions*, by C. J. Gadd and L. Legrain, 1928; II: *Archaic Texts*, by E. Burrows, 1935; III: *Business Documents of the Third Dynasty of Ur*, by L. Legrain, 2 vols. 1937–47; IV: *Business Documents of the New Babylonion Period*, by P. H. H. Figulla, 1949; also C. J. Gadd, *History and Monuments of Ur*, 1929, and *Ur of the Chaldees: A Record of Seven Years of Excavation*, 1929; C. L. Woolley, *The Excavations at Ur and the Hebrew Records*, 1929.

[4] Cf. C. L. Woolley, *Abraham: Recent Discoveries and Hebrew Origins*, 1936.

[5] Cf. G. Duncan, *New Light on Hebrew Origins*, 1936, p. 22: "No one dreamed that the Bible story could ever receive such wonderful confirmation." M. Burrows, *op. cit.*, p. 26, says: "Perhaps the most conspicuous instance of confusing interpretation and evidence is the supposed confirmation of the Biblical account of the flood discovered by Woolley at Ur and by Mackay and Langdon at Kish. . . . The excavators were convinced that they had found the deposit left by the flood described in Genesis. The fact is that this interpretation is not only uncertain; it is not even probable." This judgement is supported by cogent reasons (p. 70): "There is no evidence to connect the deposits of mud found at Ur and Kish with the particular flood of Genesis 6–9. . . . None of the inundations at Kish is contemporary with any at Ur, and none at either place marks a division

figure of history.[1] The period of Abraham was commonly believed, until the last few years, to have been about 2000 B.C., and he was thought to have been contemporary with Ḥammurabi, the great Babylonian king. The Patriarchal age was thought to extend from about 2000 B.C. to about 1700 B.C.[2] For reasons which will become apparent as we proceed, I want to extend our survey down to about 1400 B.C.

In 1926 the German Egyptologist Sethe published some execration texts from Egypt, which had been written on jars to be subsequently broken.[3] The texts contained the names of a number of Palestinian and Syrian states and their rulers, and the breaking of the jars had magical significance and was believed to be potent to ensure a curse on those whose names were inscribed.[4] The texts were probably written in the twentieth century B.C., and they give valuable information about the little states which existed in that period.[5] It became known just before the late war[6] that further texts of the same kind, though from a some-

---

between two different civilizations. In Woolley's own excavation at Tell Obeid, only four miles from Ur, there was no silt at the levels corresponding to those at which it was found at Ur. As a matter of fact, representations of Gilgamesh were found at a lower level than the 'deluge' at Kish, showing that the Babylonian flood-story was of more ancient origin than this." Cf. J. Bright, "Has Archaeology found Evidence of the Flood?", in B.A, v, 1942, pp. 55–62; also J. Gray, *Archaeology and the Old Testament World*, 1962, p. 33.

[1] Cf. above, p. 284 n. 2. G. E. Wright, *The Westminster Historical Atlas to the Bible*, 1945, p. 25 a, states the sober truth when he says: "Thus far no contemporary record of Abraham has been found outside the Bible." Cf. C. L. Woolley, *The Excavations at Ur and the Hebrew Records*, 1929, p. 15: "The name of Abraham has never yet occurred in our discoveries"; and pp. 15 f.: "What we have found is illustrative of Hebrew tradition in a very general way."

[2] The entry of Jacob into Egypt has been commonly assigned to the Hyksos period (*circa* 1730 B.C. to 1580 B.C.). Albright has connected the entry of the Hebrews with the *entry* of the Hyksos (cf. *From the Stone Age to Christianity*, 2nd ed., 1946, p. 150). In my view (cf. my Schweich Lectures, *From Joseph to Joshua*, 1950, pp. 116 f.) the entry must be brought down much later.

[3] Cf. K. Sethe, "Die Ächtungstexte feindlicher Fürsten, Völker, und Dinge auf altägyptischen Tongefässscherben des mittleren Reiches", in *A.P.A.W.*, 1926, No. 5.

[4] Cf. L. H. Vincent, *Vivre et Penser*, ii (replacing *R.B.*, li), 1942, p. 206: "Briser l'objet symbolique, ou ensevelir la figure conventionelle auxquels on pouvait attacher ce nom individuel équivalait à la tuer elle-même, ou à sceller dans un tombeau."

[5] On the date of these texts cf. A. Alt, *Z.D.P.V.*, lxiv, 1941, p. 24; M. Noth, *ibid.*, lxv, 1942, p. 13; R. T. O'Callaghan, *Aram Naharaim*, 1948, p. 30 n.

[6] From G. Posener's paper read at the International Orientalists' Congress at Brussels in 1938—subsequently published in *Actes du xxᵉ Congrès International des Orientalistes*, 1940, pp. 82 f.—and from his essay on "Nouveaux textes hiératiques de proscription", in *Mélanges Syriens offerts à M. René Dussaud*, i, 1939, pp. 313–317.

what later date,[1] and differently inscribed and treated,[2] had been found, though their publication did not take place until the war had begun, and it is only since the war that they have become available for study here.[3] Both series of texts have been much discussed, though some of the continental discussions of the second series are very hard of access in this country.[4]

Another accession to our knowledge between the wars, of outstanding importance, came from the ancient city of the kingdom of Arrapḫa, called Nuzu. This city lay east of the Tigris and south-east of Nineveh. It was excavated between 1925 and 1941 and yielded large numbers of texts, giving an intimate picture of social conditions in the city in the fifteenth and fourteenth centuries B.C.[5] Their importance

[1] Cf. G. Posener, *Mélanges Syriens*, i, 1939, pp. 314, 315 f.; B. Couroyer, *Vivre et Penser*, i (replacing *R.B.*, 1), 1941, p. 260; M. Noth, *loc. cit.*, p. 191; R. T. O'Callaghan, *loc. cit.*

[2] These texts were inscribed on small figurines instead of on jars, and many of them represent captives. From the fact that many were undamaged Posener suggested that they were intended for burial (*loc. cit.*, p. 316). Vincent, *loc. cit.*, p. 190, says: "Le fait qu'un certain nombre de figurines sont à peu près intactes et qu'on ne relève sur aucune des 'traces évidentes de mutilations intentionelles' remet en cause l'hypothèse courante d'un massacre rituel." It may be added that Posener has suggested the possibility that the texts were associated with a magic rite directed not merely against the actual enemies of the moment, but against potential enemies. Cf. *Actes du Congrès*, p. 83.

[3] Cf. Posener, *Princes et pays d'Asie et de Nubie*, 1940.

[4] In addition to the works of Sethe and Posener mentioned above, the following are a few of the discussions of these texts that have appeared: R. Dussaud, "Nouveaux renseignements sur la Palestine et la Syrie vers 2000 avant notre ère", in *Syria*, viii, 1927, pp. 216–231; W. F. Albright, "The Egyptian Empire in Asia in the Twenty-first Century B.C.", in *J.P.O.S.*, viii, 1928, pp. 223–256; G. Posener, "Une liste de noms propres étrangers sur deux ostraca hiératiques du nouvel empire", in *Syria*, xviii, 1937, pp. 183–197, and "Nouvelles listes de proscription (Ächtungstexte) datant du Moyen Empire", in *Chronique d'Égypte*, No. 27, Jan. 1939, pp. 39–46; R. Dussaud, "Nouveaux textes égyptiens d'exécration contre les peuples syriens", in *Syria*, xxi, 1940, pp. 170–182; A. Alt, "Herren und Herrensitze Palästinas im Anfang des zweiten Jahrtausends vor Chr.", in *Z.D.P.V.*, lxiv, 1941, pp. 21–39; B. Couroyer, "Les nouveaux textes égyptiens de proscription", in *Vivre et Penser*, i, 1941, pp. 261–264; M. Noth, "Die syrisch-palästinische Bevölkerung des zweiten Jahrtausends v. Chr. in Lichte neuer Quellen", in *Z.D.P.V.*, lxv, 1942, pp. 9–67; L. H. Vincent, "Les pays bibliques et l'Égypt à la fin de la xiiᵉ dynastie égyptienne", in *Vivre et Penser*, ii, 1942, pp. 187–212; B. Maisler, "Palestine at the Time of the Middle Kingdom in Egypt", in *B.E.H.J.*, i, 1946, pp. 33–68. For some of these articles and for not a few of those noted below I am indebted to the kindness of continental scholars who have sent me copies of their works, often otherwise unobtainable here; in several cases where neither offprints nor copies of the journals could be sent I have received photostats of articles, either from the authors or from other scholars. I would acknowledge with gratitude the fine spirit of co-operation in scholarship I have found in so many quarters. (Needless to say, access is much easier now than when these lines were penned.)

[5] Of the very considerable literature dealing with these texts it must suffice to refer to the following: G. Contenau, "Les tablettes de Kerkouk et les origines de la civilisation assyrienne", in *Babyloniaca*, ix, 1926, pp. 69–151, 157–212, and "Tablettes de Kerkouk du Musée du Louvre", *R. Ass.*, xxviii, 1931, pp. 27–39; C. J. Gadd, "Tablets from

to the student of the Old Testament lies partly in the illustration they provide of customs which figure in the patriarchal narratives, and partly in the new light they shed on the people known as the Ḥabiru. From the Tell el Amarna letters we had long had knowledge of the activities of the Ḥabiru in Palestine in the fourteenth century B.C., and by some scholars they had been identified with the invading Hebrews entering the land after the Exodus from Egypt.[1] From other quarters also we have new light on the Ḥabiru question, which proves to be more complex than had been supposed.

Yet another site, which has yielded the most sensational finds of any excavated between the wars, is Ras Shamra, on the Syrian coast, opposite Cyprus.[2] This proved to be the site of the ancient city of Ugarit,

Kerkuk", *ibid.*, xxiii, 1926, pp. 49–161; E. Chiera, *Inheritance Texts*, 1927, *Declarations in Court*, 1930, *Exchange and Security Documents*, 1931, *Proceedings in Court*, 1934, *Mixed Texts*, 1934 (Publications of the Baghdad School, vols. i–v); E. R. Lacheman, *Miscellaneous Texts*, 1939 (Publications of the Baghdad School, vol. vi); E. Chiera, *Texts of Varied Content*, 1929 (Harvard Semitic Series: Excavations at Nuzi, i); R. H. Pfeiffer, *The Archives of Shilwateshub Son of the King*, 1932 (Harvard Series: Nuzi, ii); T. J. Meek, *Old Akkadian, Sumerian and Cappadocian Texts from Nuzi*, 1935 (Harvard Series: Nuzi, iii); R. H. Pfeiffer and E. R. Lacheman, *Miscellaneous Texts from Nuzi*, Part i, 1942 (Harvard Series: Nuzi, iv); E. R. Lacheman, *Miscellaneous Texts from Nuzi*, Part ii, 1950 (Harvard Series: Nuzi, v); E. Chiera and E. A. Speiser, "Selected 'Kirkuk' Documents", in *J.A.O.S.*, xlvii, 1927, pp. 36–60; E. A. Speiser, "New Kirkuk Documents Relating to Family Laws", in *A.A.S.O.R.*, x, 1930, pp. 1–73; R. H. Pfeiffer, *One Hundred New Selected Nuzi Texts*, 1936 (*A.A.S.O.R.*, xvi); E. Porada, *Seal Impressions of Nuzi*, 1947 (*A.A.S.O.R.*, xxiv); C. H. Gordon, "Fifteen Nuzi Tablets Relating to Women", in *Le Muséon*, xlviii, 1935, pp. 113–132, "Parallèles nouziens aux lois et coutumes de l'Ancien Testament", in *R.B.*, xliv, 1935, pp. 34–41, "The Status of Women Reflected in the Nuzi Tablets", in *Z.A.*, xliii, 1936, pp. 147–169, "The Dialect of the Nuzu Tablets", in *Orientalia*, N.S., vii, 1938, pp. 32–63, 215–232, "Biblical Customs and the Nuzu Tablets", in *B.A.*, iii, 1940, pp. 1–12, and *Introduction to Old Testament Times*, 1953, pp. 100 ff.; D. Cross, *Movable Property in the Nuzi Documents*, 1937; E. M. Cassin, "La caution à Nuzi", *R.Ass.*, xxxiv, 1937, pp. 154–168, and *L'adoption à Nuzi*, 1938; E. R. Lacheman, "Nuziana", in *R.Ass.*, xxxvi, 1939, pp. 81–95, 113–219, and "Nuzi Geographical Names", in *B.A.S.O.R.*, No. 78, April 1940, pp. 18–23, No. 81, Feb. 1941, pp. 10–14; F. R. Steele, *Nuzi Real Estate Transactions*, 1943; I. J. Gelb, P. M. Purves and A. A. MacRae, *Nuzi Personal Names*, 1943; N. Liebesny, "The Administration of Justice in Nuzi", in *J.A.O.S.*, lxiii, 1943, pp. 128–144; J. N. Schofield, *E.T.*, lxvi, 1954–55, pp. 315–318; R. J. Tournay, in *S.D.B.*, vi, 1960, cols. 646–674 (where a full bibliography will be found); O. Eissfeldt, *Der Beutel der Lebendigen*, 1960 (also with full bibliography).

[1] Cf. J. W. Jack, *The Date of the Exodus*, 1925, pp. 128 f., 143 f.; H. R. Hall, *The Ancient History of the Near East*, 7th ed., 1927, p. 409; S. L. Caiger, *Bible and Spade*, 1936, pp. 102 f.; J. de Koning, *Studiën over de El-Amarnabrieven*, 1940, pp. 311 ff.

[2] For a bibliography of more than five hundred titles dealing with these texts and covering the years 1929–1938, cf. C. F. A. Schaeffer, *Ugaritica*, i, 1939, pp. 147–203. This may be substantially supplemented by the bibliography in R. de Langhe, *Les textes de Ras Shamra-Ugarit et leurs rapports avec le milieu biblique de l'Ancien Testament*, i, 1945, pp. xvi–lvii. Schaeffer has now published *Ugaritica*, ii, 1949; *Ugaritica*, iii, 1956; *Ugaritica*, iv, 1962.

mentioned in the Amarna texts,[1] and therefore already known, though little was known about it. Here a number of texts were found, of which those written in alphabetic cuneiform in what is believed to have been a Canaanite dialect[2] have attracted most attention. Many of the texts have been generally described as mythological, though it is held by some that they are cultic and ritual.[3] Of their importance for the study of the background of Israelite religion and culture I cannot speak here,[4] but we shall have to look at some views to which currency

[1] Cf. TA 1: 39, 45: 35, 89: 51, 98: 9, 126: 6, 151: 55 (Knudzton, *Die El-Amarna Tafeln*, i, 1908, pp. 62 f., 310 f., 424 f., 446 f., 538 f., 624 f.).

[2] Cf. J. Cantineau, "La langue de Ras Shamra", in *Syria*, xiii, 1932, pp. 164–169, xxi, 1940, pp. 38–61; W. F. Albright, "Notes on the Language and Script of Ugarit", in *J.P.O.S.*, xiv, 1934, pp. 104–115, and "Recent Progress in North Canaanite Research", in *B.A.S.O.R.*, No. 70, April 1938, pp. 20–22; A. Goetze, "The Tenses of Ugaritic", in *J.A.O.S.*, lviii, 1938, pp. 266–309; Z. S. Harris, "Expressions of the Causative in Ugaritic", *ibid.*, pp. 103–111, and *Development of the Canaanite Dialects*, 1939; C. H. Gordon, *Ugaritic Grammar*, 1940, revised and enlarged as *Ugaritic Handbook*, 1947, further revised as *Ugaritic Manual*, 1955. E. Hammershaimb, *Das Verbum im Dialekt von Ras Schamra*, 1941, R. de Langhe, *op. cit.*, i, 1945, pp. 263–330, and *De taal van Ras Sjamra-Ugarit*, 1948. G. D. Young has published a *Concordance of Ugaritic*, 1956, and J. Aistleitner a *Wörterbuch der ugaritischen Sprache*, ed. by O. Eissfeldt, 1962.

[3] Cf. S. H. Hooke, *The Origins of Early Semitic Ritual*, 1938; I. Engnell, *Studies in Divine Kingship in the Ancient Near East*, 1943, pp. 97–173, "The Text II K from Ras Shamra", in *Horae Soederblomianae*, I, *Mélanges Johs. Pedersen*, i, 1944, pp. 1–20; F. F. Hvidberg, *Graad og Latter i det Gamle Testamente*, 1938, pp. 1–63, and *Z.A.W.*, N.F. xvi, 1939, pp. 150 f.; J. Pedersen, "Die Krt Legende", in *Berytus*, vi, 1941, pp. 63–105; T. H. Gaster, "A Canaanite Ritual Drama", in *J.A.O.S.*, lvi, 1946, pp. 48–76, and his important work *Thespis*, 1950.

[4] Cf. J. W. Jack, *The Ras Shamra Tablets: Their Bearing on the Old Testament*, 1935; J. de Groot, "Rās Šamra en het Oude Palestina", in *J.E.O.L.*, No. 3, 1935, pp. 97–99; D. Nielsen, *Ras Šamra Mythologie und Biblische Theologie*, 1936; A. Jirku, "Die Keilschrifttexte von Ras Šamra und das Alte Testament", in *Z.D.M.G.*, lxxxix, 1935, pp. 372–386; R. de Vaux, "Les textes de Ras Shamra et l'Ancien Testament", in *R.B.*, xlvi, 1937, pp. 526–555; R. Dussaud, *Les découvertes de Ras Shamra (Ugarit) et l'Ancien Testament*, 1937, 2nd ed., revised and enlarged, 1941; A. Bea, "Ras Šamra und das Alte Testament", in *Biblica*, xix, 1938, pp. 435–453; R. de Langhe, *Les textes de Ras Shamra-Ugarit et leurs apports à l'histoire des origines israélites*, 1939, and *Les textes de Ras Shamra-Ugarit et leurs rapports avec le milieu biblique de l'Ancien Testament*, 2 vols., 1945; S. Mowinckel, "Rās Sjamrā og det Gamle Testament", in *Nor.T.T.*, xl, 1939, pp. 16–29; W. Baumgartner, "Ras Schamra und das Alte Testament", in *Th.R.*, N.F. xii, 1940, pp. 163–188, xiii, 1941, pp. 1–20, 85–102, 157–183, and "Ugaritische Probleme und ihre Tragweite für das Alte Testament", in *Th.Z.*, iii, 1947, pp. 81–100; J. H. Patton, *Canaanite Parallels in the Book of Psalms*, 1944; H. L. Ginsberg, "Ugaritic Studies and the Bible", in *B.A.*, viii, 1945, pp. 21–58; W. F. Albright, "The Old Testament and the Canaanite Language and Literature", in *C.B.Q.*, vii, 1945, pp. 5–31; J. Coppens, *Les parallèles du Psautier et les textes da Ras Shamra-Ougarit*, 1946; E. Jacob, "Les Textes de Ras Shamra-Ugarit et l'Ancien Testament", in *R.H.P.R.*, xxvii, 1947, pp. 242–258, and *Ras Shamra et l'Ancien Testament*, 1960; G. R. Driver, "Ugaritic and Hebrew Problems", in Archiv Orientální, xvii (Hrozný Festschrift), Pars prima, 1949, pp. 153–157; J. Gray, "Cultic Affinities between Israel and Ras Shamra", in *Z.A.W.*, N.F. xxi, 1950, pp. 207–220, and *The*

has been given. Amongst these is the claim that the Hebrew God Yahweh figures in these texts, and that the father of Abraham is found here
as a moon-god. Certain Israelite tribes are thought by some to be
mentioned in a text to which geographical and historical significance is
attached. One school has held that reflected in the texts we can find
movements that occurred in the Negeb, in the south of Palestine, in
the period before the entry of the Israelites into Canaan. Further, in a
text published in 1940 there is important evidence bearing on the
Ḥabiru question, to which reference has already been made.

In 1935 the distinguished French archaeologist André Parrot undertook excavations at Mari, an ancient city on the Euphrates,[1] somewhat
farther north-west of Babylon, as the crow flies, than Nuzu lay directly
north of Babylon. Here many thousands of tablets were found,[2] and

---

Legacy of Canaan (S.V.T. v), 1957; A. S. Kapelrud, *Ras Sjamra-funnene og det Gamle
Testament*, 1953. C. H. Gordon has now translated many of the texts into English in
Ugaritic Literature, 1949; cf. also T. H. Gaster, *Thespis*, 1950, pp. 115–313; H. L. Ginsberg,
"Ugaritic Myths and Legends", in *A.N.E.T.*, 1950, pp. 129–155; J. Gray, *The KRT Text
in the Literature of Ras Shamra*, 1955, and "Texts from Ras Shamra", in *D.O.T.*, 1958,
pp. 118–137; G. R. Driver, *Canaanite Myths and Legends*, 1956; also J. Aistleitner, *Die
mythologischen und kultischen Texte aus Ras Schamra*, 1959, for a German translation. Cf.
also H. E. del Medico, *La Bible cananéenne découverte dans les textes da Ras Shamra*, 1950,
where very dubious renderings and interpretations are given.

[1] In *A.J.S.L.*, lii, 1935–36, pp. 43 f., I. J. Gelb entered an objection against the identification of Mari with Tell el Ḥarîri.

[2] Cf. amongst many other works, A. Parrot, "Les fouilles de Mari", in *Syria*, xvi,
1935, pp. 1–28, 117–140, xvii, 1936, pp. 1–31, xviii, 1937, pp. 54–84, xix, 1938, pp.
1–29, xx, 1939, pp. 1–22, xxi, 1940, pp. 1–28, *Mari: une ville perdue*, 1936, new ed., 1945,
and "Les Tablettes de Mari et l'Ancien Testament", in *R.H.P.R.*, xxx, 1950, pp. 1–11; xxxv,
1955, pp. 117–120; H. Frankfort, "Mari et Opis: essai de chronologie", in *R.Ass.*, xxxi,
1934, pp. 173–179; A. Parrot, "La civilisation mésopotamienne", *ibid.*, pp. 180–189;
F. Thureau-Dangin, "Textes de Mari", *ibid.*, xxxiii, 1936, pp. 169–179, "Inscriptions
votives de Mari", *ibid.*, xxxiv, 1937, pp. 172–176, and "Tablettes ḫurrites provenant de
Mari", *ibid.*, xxxvi, 1939, pp. 1–28; W. F. Albright, "Western Asia in the Twentieth
Century B.C.: The Archives of Mari", in *B.A.S.O.R.*, No. 67, Oct. 1937, pp. 26–30;
G. Dossin, "Les archives épistolaires du palais de Mari", in *Syria*, xix, 1938, pp. 105–126,
"Les archives économiques du palais de Mari", *ibid.*, xx, 1939, pp. 97–113, "Benjaminites
dans les textes de Mari", in *Mélanges Syriens offerts à M. René Dussaud*, ii, 1939, pp.
981–996, *Archives royales de Mari*, I. *Lettres*, 1946, and *Archives royales de Mari*, I. *Correspondance de Šamši-Addu*, 1950; C. F. Jean, "La langue des lettres de Mari", in *R.E.S.*,
1937, pp. 97–112, *Archives royales de Mari*, II. *Lettres*, 1941, *Archives royales de Mari*, II.
Lettres diverses, 1950, "Lettres de Mari", in *R.Ass.*, xxxix, 1942–44, pp. 63–82, "Autres
lettres de Mari", in *R.E.S.-B.*, 1942–45, pp. 9–32, and "Lettres de Mari", in *J.E.O.L.*,
x, 1945–48, pp. 425–431; F. M. Th. Böhl, "Brieven uit het archief van Mari", in *Bi. Or.*,
i, 1944, pp. 55–58, 76–79, 101–105; G. E. Mendenhall, "Mari", in *B.A.*, xi, 1948, pp.
2–19; J. R. Kupper, *Archives royales de Mari*, III. *Lettres*, 1948, *Archives royales de Mari*,
III. *Correspondance de Kibri-Dagan, Gouverneur de Terqa*, 1950; W. von Soden, "Das
altbabylonische Briefarchiv von Mari", in *Die Welt des Orients*, i, Heft 3, 1948, pp. 187–
204; A. Lods, "Une tablette inédite de Mari, intéressante-pour l'histoire ancienne du

important evidence was brought to light bearing on ancient chrono-logy.[1] From other sites, too, evidence on this subject has appeared,[2] and anything written before 1940 on the chronology of the first half of the second millennium B.C. is in need of revision.

It will be remembered that we read in the Bible that Abraham sprang originally from Ur,[3] and that his family first migrated from Ur to Harran in northern Mesopotamia, and later the patriarch left Harran for the land of Canaan.[4] It has long been known that Ur was the great centre of the worship of the moon-god Sin, and that Harran was second only in importance to Ur as a centre of worship of the same god. There would thus seem to have been some ancient connexion between these cities, so that it would not be unnatural for a family to leave the one city for the other.[5] Hence verisimilitude had long been allowed to the story, whether it was accepted as historical or not. More, however, cannot be said. We have no direct evidence for the migration outside the Bible itself, and so conservative a scholar as Albright has suggested that the localization of Abraham's home at Ur was secondary.[6]

prophétisme sémitique", in *Studies in Old Testament Prophecy* (T. H. Robinson Festschrift), 1950, pp. 103–110; M. Noth, "History and the Word of God in the Old Testament", in *B.J.R.L.*, xxxii, 1949–50, pp. 194–206, and *Geschichte und Gotteswort im Alten Testament*, 1950 (reprinted in *Gesammelte Studien zum Alten Testament*, 1957, pp. 230–247) and also "Mari und Israel" in *Geschichte und Altes Testament* (Alt Festschrift), 1953, pp. 129–152; *Studia Mariana*, ed. by A. Parrot, 1950 (containing a bibliography of more than 200 items); H. Schmökel, "Gotteswort in Mari und Israel", in *Th.L.Z.*, lxxvi, 1951, cols. 54–58; J. N. Schofield, *E.T.*, lxvi, 1954–55, pp. 250–252; C. F. Jean, *S.D.B.*, v, 1957, cols. 883–905; and J. C. L. Gibson, *J.S.S.*, vii, 1962, pp. 44–62.

[1] Cf. F. Thureau-Dangin, "Iasmaḫ-Adad", in *R.Ass.*, xxxiv, 1937, pp. 135–139; C. F. Jean, " 'Hammurapi' d'après des lettres inédites de Mari", *ibid.*, xxxv, 1938, pp. 107–114; W. F. Albright, "An Indirect Synchronism between Egypt and Mesopotamia, c. 1730 B.C.", in *B.A.S.O.R.*, No. 99, Oct. 1945, pp. 9–18.

[2] Especially from Atchana. Cf. S. Smith, "A Preliminary Account of the Tablets from Atchana", in *The Antiquaries Journal*, xix, 1939, pp. 38–48, and *Alalakh and Chronology*, 1940.

[3] Gen. 11: 28, 31; 15: 7.   [4] Gen. 12: 4.

[5] Cf. P. (E.) Dhorme, *R.B.*, xxxvii, 1928, pp. 379 ff. (= *Recueil Édouard Dhorme*, 1951, pp. 205 ff.). On Abraham and history, cf. the whole article "Abraham dans le cadre de l'histoire", *R.B.*, xxxvii, 1928, pp. 367–385, 481–511, xl, 1931, pp. 364–374, 503–518 (= *Recueil Édouard Dhorme*, pp. 191–272); also A. Parrot, *Abraham et son temps*, 1962; N. Glueck, "The Age of Abraham in the Negeb", *B.A.*, xviii, 1955, pp. 2–9 (also *B.A.S.O.R.*, No. 149, Feb. 1958, pp. 8–17, No. 152, Dec. 1958, pp. 18–38).

[6] Cf. *From the Stone Age to Christianity*, 2nd ed., 1946, p. 179. See also his *Archaeology of Palestine and the Bible*, 1932, p. 209. So also G. E. Wright, *Biblical Archaeology*, revised ed., 1962, p. 41a. J. Bright (*A History of Israel*, 1959, pp. 80 f.) is more cautious. A. Lods (*Israel from its Beginnings to the Middle of the Eighth Century*, E.Tr. by S. H. Hooke, 1932, pp. 162 ff.) rejects the identification of the Biblical Ur with the Sumerian city and argues for its location in northern Mesopotamia; cf. also C. H. Gordon, *J.N.E.S.*, xvii, 1958, pp.

On the question of the date of Abraham the whole discussion has been greatly changed by recent discoveries. A study of certain verses in the Old Testament, which gave the date of the Exodus in relation to the foundation of Solomon's Temple,[1] the date of the entry into Egypt in relation to the Exodus,[2] and the years of the patriarchs from the departure from Harran to the entry into Egypt,[3] would lead to the conclusion that the departure from Harran was to be dated *circa* 2092 B.C.[4] The only passage in the narratives about Abraham which seemed to offer any help in fixing his date in relation to world events was Gen. 14, which tells how Amraphel of Shinar, Arioch of Ellasar, Chedorlaomer of Elam, and Tidal of Goim together came against Sodom and its neighbouring towns. It was a common assumption that Amraphel was to be identified with Ḥammurabi, the great king of Babylon, and this seemed to fit well into the scheme of Biblical chronology to which I have referred. For forty years ago the *Cambridge Ancient History* gave as the date of Ḥammurabi 2123–2081 B.C.[5] The identification of Amraphel with Ḥammurabi was not without difficulties, however, and many scholars refused to accept it.[6] It is probable, as de Vaux says,[7] that this identification only enjoyed such favour as it commanded because it appeared to place Abraham in the setting of world history.

The other names of the chapter were even more intractable. Arioch

28–31, *Before the Bible*, 1962, pp. 27, 34, 288 f., and in *Hebrew and Semitic Studies* (Driver Festschrift), 1962, pp. 77–84. Gordon's view is rejected by H. W. Saggs in *Iraq*, xxii, 1960, pp. 200–209. Cf. also H. Cazelles, *S.D.B.*, Fasc. 36, 1961, cols. 99 f.; W. F. Albright, *B.A.S.O.R.*, No. 163, October, 1961, p. 44 n.; D. J. Wiseman, in *The New Bible Dictionary*, ed. by J. D. Douglas, 1962, p. 1305. J. C. L. Gibson (*J.S.S.*, vii, 1962, pp. 58 f.) advances the view that Abraham's home was at Harran, and that he went to the Sumerian Ur for a temporary visit, and returned to Harran before he set out for Canaan.

[1] 1 Kings, 6: 1.

[2] Exod. 12: 40. The Septuagint and the Samaritan texts halve the length of the Sojourn in Egypt by the addition of some words in this verse, but the fact that they stand in different places in these texts is held by most scholars to be against their originality.

[3] Gen. 12: 4, 21: 5, 25: 26, 47: 9.

[4] Reckoning the foundation of the Temple as *circa* 967 B.C. While there are slight differences of dating amongst scholars, few would go more than a decade from this date, either forwards or backwards.

[5] Cf. *C.A.H.*, i, 2nd ed., 1924, p. 154. See also L. W. King, *History of Babylon*, 1919, pp. 106–111; Albright, *R.Ass.*, xviii, 1921, p. 94.

[6] Cf. Albright, *J.P.O.S.*, i, 1921, pp. 70 f.; E. A. Speiser, *A.A.S.O.R.*, xiii, 1933, p. 45 n.; R. de Vaux, *Z.A.W.*, N.F. xv, 1938, p. 231; J. T. Meek, in *The Haverford Symposium on Archaeology and the Bible*, 1938, p. 184, n. 78; S. H. Hooke, *In the Beginning*, 1947, p. 72; R. T. O'Callaghan, *Aram Naharaim*, 1948, p. 31.

[7] Cf. *R.B.*, lv, 1948, p. 331.

of Ellasar was held to be Rim Sin or Arad Sin of Larsa,[1] whose name might be written Eri-agu, and a late document containing the form Eri-aku was put forward, though there was no evidence to connect this individual with Larsa.[2] Chedorlaomer was believed to be Kudur-lagamur, a possible Elamite name, though one which is not actually found. Moreover, though Babylon acknowledged the suzerainty of Elam at the time of Ḥammurabi's accession, he revolted against Elam, and difficulty was felt about the activity of Elam at this time so far in

[1] Cf. S. R. Driver, *The Book of Genesis*, 1904, p. 156, W. H. Bennett, *Genesis*, p. 187, and H. E. Ryle, *The Book of Genesis*, 1914, p. 167, where Arioch is identified with Rim Sin; H. Gunkel, *Genesis*, 1901, p. 256, where he is identified with Arad Sin, the brother of Rim Sin. Cf. J. Skinner, *Genesis*, 1910, p. 258, and O. Procksch, *Die Genesis*, 1924, p. 503. On Arad Sin and Rim Sin and their relation to the story of Gen. xiv, cf. G. A. Barton, *J.B.L.*, xxviii, 1909, pp. 155 ff.

[2] Cf. Skinner *loc. cit.* Many older scholars regarded Gen. 14 as itself of late origin, and of little historical worth. Cf. J. Wellhausen, *Die Composition des Hexateuchs*, 3rd ed., 1889, pp. 311–313; H. P. Smith, *Old Testament History*, 1911, p. 37; J. Morgenstern, *A Jewish Interpretation of the Book of Genesis*, 1920, p. 119 ("This is a legend pure and simple, without the slightest historical basis"). W. F. Albright formerly subscribed to this view (cf. *J.B.L.*, xxxvii, 1918, p. 136: "The fourteenth chapter must be regarded . . . as a political pamphlet designed to strengthen the hands of the patriotic Jews who were supporting the rebellion of Zerubbabel against the Persian monarch. As we now know that Warad-Sin of Larsa, who, under the mask of Eriaku-Arioch, was long the comfort of the traditionalists, died about thirty years before Ḥammurabi-Amraphel acceded to the throne, the historical view has no foundation"), but later abandoned it (cf. *J.P.O.S.*, vi, 1926, p. 227: "Gen. 14 is a genuine historical document, perhaps somewhat embellished with saga"). R. Dussaud also subscribes to the view that this chapter is a worthless midrash. He says (*L'art phénicien du IIᵉ millénaire*, 1949, p. 32 n.): "Quant au chap. xiv de la Genèse, nous sommes assez renseignés sur les événements de l'époque pour lui refuser toute valeur historique; les efforts déployés à ce propos ne fut que démontrer qu'il ne dépasse pas le cadre d'un simple *midrash*. L'abaissement de la date d'Hammourabi est un nouveau coup qui lui est porté. Pour la thèse contraire, voir H. H. Rowley, dans *Bibliotheca Orientalis*, 1948, p. 139, qui s'oppose à l'avis fort justifié de C. A. Simpson." What none of those who hold this view has done is to show what relevant purpose this late midrash could have had, or to establish any intelligible connexion between this chapter and Ps. 110, where Melchizedek again figures. In my view the chapter is aetiological but early, dating from the time of David, and transferring to Abraham an old tradition [cf. "Melchizedek and Zadok (Gen. 14 and Ps. 110)", in *Festschrift für Alfred Bertholet*, 1950, pp. 461–472]. This view is quite unaffected by any shifting of the date of Ḥammurabi. Cf. also S. H. Hooke, *In the Beginning*, 1947, p. 76: "Thus it may be said that the old view that Genesis 14 is a late midrash is no longer tenable. It suggests a dependence upon written sources and presents a political situation which is not historically impossible. Hence we may legitimately use the story to form some idea of the historical setting of Abraham's activities." This goes somewhat farther than I would go. I accept Gen. 14 as embodying an old tradition, though probably not originally about Abraham. I can therefore subscribe to the statement of M. Noth (*History of Israel*, E.Tr., 2nd ed., 1960, p. 124: "The story contained in Gen. xiv is in every respect so isolated within the whole tradition of the patriarchs that the question is whether it can be included among the authentic basic material of this tradition at all." C. H. Gordon (*J.N.E.S.*, xiii, 1954, p. 57) has suggested that this chapter may have had a Ḥurrian literary background.

the west.[1] For Tidal it was even more difficult to suggest a suitable identification, until Böhl proposed to identify him with the Hittite king Tudḫalia.[2] This, however, led to an approach to the question from the other end. For the first Tudḫalia reigned in the seventeenth century B.C. Hence it was now suggested that Abraham belonged to that century,[3] and that the doubtful equation of Amraphel with Ḫammurabi should be abandoned.[4]

Ḫammurabi himself can no longer be dated at anything like the date I have already mentioned, however. One of the items of evidence which had led to the adoption of that date was the year formula of Ammiṣaduqa in terms of the risings and settings of the planet Venus. Ammiṣaduqa was the tenth monarch of the dynasty of which Ḫammurabi was the sixth king, and hence if the date of Ammiṣaduqa could be fixed, the date of Ḫammurabi would at the same time be determined. Elaborate astronomical calculations were made,[5] but by the nature of the case they could not by themselves fix the chronology. The same cycle of risings and settings of Venus recurs at long intervals, and hence these calculations could only fix the precise date when the approximate date was decided on other grounds.[6]

For the approximate dating we now have several lines of evidence, which have come to light during the last thirty years. There was first evidence that Shamshi Adad I of Assyria was contemporary with the early part of the reign of Ḫammurabi,[7] while Shamshi Adad's approximate period can be fixed by the help of the Khorsabad King list, which was first published during the war.[8] A further general check came from the pottery brought to light at Mesopotamian sites, where some

[1] Cf. S. A. Cook, in *C.A.H.*, i, 2nd ed., 1924, p. 236; F. M. Th. Böhl, *King Ḫammurabi of Babylon in the Setting of his Time*, 1946, p. 18.

[2] Cf. "Tud'alia I, Zeitgenosse Abrahams, um 1650 v Chr." in *Z.A.W.*, N.F. i, 1924, pp. 148–153. In an earlier paper Böhl had identified Tidal with a later Tudḫalia and so had come down even later. Cf. "Die Könige von Genesis 14", *ibid.*, xxxvi, 1916, pp. 65–73.

[3] This date was advocated on different grounds by E. G. Kraeling, *Aram and Israel*, 1918, p. 32; A. Jirku, *Z.A.W.*, xxxix, 1921, pp. 152–156, 323 f.; W. F. Albright, "Shinar-Šangar and its Monarch Amraphel", in *A.J.S.L.*, xl, 1923–24, pp. 125–133.

[4] Cf. W. F. Albright, *J.P.O.S.*, i, 1921, pp. 70 ff.

[5] Cf. S. Langdon and J. K. Fotheringham, *The Venus Tablets of Ammizaduga*, 1928.

[6] Cf. B. L. van der Waerden, *J.E.O.L.*, x, 1945–48, p. 415: "If the historians can fix definite limits, between which the reign of Ammiṣaduqa must lie, astronomy can tell which years between these limits are more or less compatible with the Venus observations recorded in the tablets; and if an exact date is proposed, astronomy can tell whether this date is possible or not."

[7] Cf. F. Thureau-Dangin, "Iasmaḫ-Adad", in *R.Ass.*, xxxiv, 1937, pp. 135–139.

[8] Cf. A. Poebel, "The Assyrian King List from Khorsabad", in *J.N.E.S.*, i, 1942, pp. 247–306, 460–492; ii, 1943, pp. 56–90.

tablets of the time of Shamshi Adad I were found in levels that could be approximately dated at about three centuries earlier than other levels which could be dated by evidence from Nuzu in the fifteenth century B.C.[1] Again, the Mari evidence brought important material, amongst which may be mentioned the evidence that Zimri-lim, the king of Mari, was defeated by Ḥammurabi in the thirty-second year of his reign,[2] while there was some interlocking evidence from Ras Shamra, which led Schaeffer to suggest for Ḥammurabi an eighteenth- or seventeenth-century date.[3]

By almost all scholars such a date would now be agreed, though there is still a measure of disagreement as to the precise fixation of the regnal years of Ḥammurabi. In the year 1940, Sidney Smith[4] and Ungnad,[5] working quite independently on either side of the barrier created by the war, reached almost identical results. Sidney Smith dated Ḥammurabi 1792–1750 B.C.,[6] and Ungnad dated him one year later, 1791–1749 B.C. In the following year Neugebauer observed[7] that "if historical evidence places Ḥammurabi around 1800, then the Venus observations require for his reign either the years 1792–1750 or an interval of 56 (or even 64) years earlier or later". In the following year, 1942, Albright moved down the sixty-four years later, and argued for the date 1728–1686 B.C.[8] Again, by a surprising coincidence, in the

---

[1] Cf. M. B. Rowton, "Mesopotamian Chronology and the 'Era of Menophres' ", in *Iraq*, viii, 1946, pp. 94–110.

[2] Cf. F. Thureau-Dangin, "Sur les étiquettes de paniers à tablettes provenant de Mâri", in *Symbolae Paulo Koschaker dedicatae*, 1939, pp. 119 f.

[3] Cf. C. F. A. Schaeffer, *Ugaritica*, i, 1939, p. 18 n. Cf. also *id.*, *Syria*, xxv, 1946–48, pp. 185 ff., esp. p. 187: "le règne d'Hammourabi tombe entre 1800 et 1700 avant notre ère."

[4] Cf. *Alalakh and Chronology*, 1940, See also the same writer's "A Preliminary Account of the Tablets from Atchana", in *The Antiquaries Journal*, xix, 1939, pp. 38–48, and "Middle Minoan I–II and Babylonian Chronology", in *A.J.A.*, xlix, 1945, pp. 1–24; also *The Statue of Idri-mi*, 1949, pp. 66 ff.

[5] Cf. *Die Venustafeln und das neunte Jahr Samsuilunas*, 1940. Similarly Hrozný, *Histoire de l'Asie Antérieure*, 1947, pp. 211, 125.

[6] In *The Journal of the British Astronomical Association*, lvii, 1947, p. 208, A. G. Shortt criticizes the astronomical argument of Brigadier-General J. W. S. Sewell, on which Smith relied, and claims that Fotheringham would not have agreed with Sewell's results. This not only leaves all other considerations out of account, but takes no account of criticisms of Fotheringham's results (cf. O. Neugebauer, "Zur Frage der astronomischen Fixierung der babylonischen Chronologie", in *O.L.Z.*, xxxiii, 1929, cols. 913–921, "Chronologie und babylonischer Kalender", *ibid.*, xlii, 1939, cols. 403–414), or of other recent discussions of the astronomical side of the problem (cf. the works cited in the preceding and following notes).

[7] Cf. *J.A.O.S.*, lxi, 1941, p. 59.

[8] Cf. "New Light on the History of Western Asia in the Second Millennium B.C.", in *B.A.S.O.R.*, No. 77, Feb. 1940, pp. 20–32; No. 78, April 1940, pp. 23–31.

same year there was published in Germany a completely independent study along entirely different lines, reaching the same conclusion as Albright.[1] While there is no final agreement as to which of these two dates is correct,[2] there can be little doubt to-day that Ḥammurabi must be brought down to one or other of them, and that his reign belonged to the eighteenth century B.C., if not to the seventeenth, and more probably the latter.[3]

This means that if Amraphel is identified with Ḥammurabi and Abraham is made contemporary with Ḥammurabi of Babylon, those chronological verses of the Old Testament to which I have referred must be given up. Actually there is other chronological material in the Bible which cannot be reconciled with them,[4] and the historical value of the traditions is in no sense dependent on the chronological framework in which they are set. It is probable, however, that just as the equation of Amraphel with Ḥammurabi has been clung to in the past by defenders of the Biblical chronology, in the future this always doubtful equation[5] will be rejected by them.

[1] Cf. F. Cornelius, "Berossus und die altorientalische Chronologie", in *Klio*, xxxv, 1942, pp. 1–16. B. L. van der Waerden (*J.E.O.L.*, x. 1945–48, p. 421) after an independent re-examination of the evidence, says: "Cornelius' hypothesis is by far more likely to be true than Ungnad's."

[2] J. Paterson (*Presentation Volume to William Barron Stevenson*, 1945, p. 103) gives as "a fairly definite date" for Ḥammurabi *circa* 1746–1688 B.C., but offers no evidence for this date.

[3] Of many recent discussions of this question the following may be noted: O. Neugebauer, "The Chronology of the Ḥammurabi Age", in *J.A.O.S.*, lxi, 1941, pp. 58–61; F. Weidner, "Die Königsliste aus Chorsabad", in *A.f.O.*, xiv, 1941–44, pp. 362–369; F. Thureau-Dangin, "La chronologie de la première dynastie babylonienne", in *Mémoires de l'Académie des Inscriptions et Belles Lettres*, xliii, 2e partie, 1942, pp. 229–258; P. van der Meer, "Chronologie der assyrisch-babylonische Koningen", in *J.E.O.L.*, ix, 1944, pp. 137–145, *The Ancient Chronology of Western Asia and Egypt*, 1947, and "At what Time has the Reign of Menes to be placed?" in *Orientalia Neerlandica*, 1948, pp. 23–49; W. F. Albright, "An Indirect Synchronism between Egypt and Mesopotamia, *circa* 1730 B.C.", in *B.A.S.O.R.*, No. 99, Oct. 1945, pp. 9–18, and *Bi.Or.*, v, 1948, pp. 125–127; F. M. Th. Böhl, *King Ḥammurabi of Babylon in the Setting of his Time*, 1946; C. Kern, "Primum monumenta, deinde chronologia", in *J.E.O.L.*, x, 1945–48, pp. 481–490; B. L. van der Waerden, "The Venus Tablets of Ammiṣaduqa", in *J.E.O.L.*, x, 1945–48, pp. 414–424; G. Goossens, "La revision de la chronologie mésopotamienne et ses conséquences pour l'histoire orientale", in *Le Muséon*, lxi, 1948, pp. 1–29, esp. pp. 12 f., 23; R. T. O'Callaghan, *Aram Naharaim*, 1948, pp. 6–11; S. N. Kramer, "New Light on the Early History of the Ancient Near East", in *A.J.A.*, lii, 1948, pp. 156–164; R. de Vaux, *R.B.*, lv, 1948, pp. 328–336; J. Vernet, "La cronologia de la primera dinastia babilonica", in *Sefarad*, viii, 1948, pp. 428–434. E. Dhorme (*Les premières civilisations*, new ed., 1950, p. 134) gives the date of Ḥammurabi provisionally as 1848–1806 B.C.

[4] I discuss these passages in my Schweich Lectures, *From Joseph to Joshua*, 1950, pp. 57 ff.

[5] Cf. E. Dhorme, *La Bible de la Pléiade*, L'Ancien Testament, i, 1956, p. 42: "L'identification de ce roi (Amraphel) au fameux Hammourabi de Babylone ne peut être maintenue: elle soulève trop de difficultés du point de vue philologique et historique."

We now know that there were three, if not four, approximately contemporary kings who bore the name Ḥammurabi.[1] There was a Ḥammurabi ruling in Aleppo, and another in Kurda, and some scholars have argued that if Amraphel is indeed to be identified with any one of them, it should be with the king of Aleppo.[2] It is, however, significant that while all our evidence is doubtful, such as it is it seems to be steadily pointing to the seventeenth century B.C. for the period indicated by Gen. 14 : 1. If Albright's date for Ḥammurabi is accepted —and he has produced an interesting supporting argument for it in the form of a Mari reference to a prince of Byblos named Yantin-ḥamu, who is probably to be equated with one Entin referred to in an Egyptian inscription which is to be dated 1740–1720 B.C.[3]—then part of his reign falls in the seventeenth century B.C., to which the Hittite king Tudḫalia I belonged. Böhl, who prefers to identify Amraphel with Amut-pi-el, the king of Qaṭna,[4] has suggested that Arioch is to be equated with Arriwuk, the son of Zimri-lim of Mari,[5] who again would belong to the same century. For Chedorlaomer Albright has proposed the identification with the Elamite king Kuter-Naḫḫunte,[6] whose reign would fall, however, towards the end of the seventeenth century B.C., and therefore later than Ḥammurabi's. Albright does not accept the identification of Amraphel with Ḥammurabi, but relied on this identification of Chedorlaomer to bring down Abraham to a date late in the seventeenth century B.C., after the time of Ḥammurabi.[7]

More recently, however, Albright has abandoned these identifications and returned to an earlier date for Abraham. He now says: "In the writer's present opinion the Terachid movement from Ur to

---

[1] For the fourth cf. *Actes du XXe Congrès international des Orientalistes.* 1940, pp. 116 f.

[2] Cf. F. M. Th. Böhl, *King Ḥammurabi of Babylon,* 1946, p. 17; J. J. Dougherty, *Scripture,* iii, 1948, p. 99.

[3] Cf. *B.A.S.O.R.*, No. 99, Oct. 1945, pp. 9–18. Cf. also *B.A.S.O.R.*, No. 163, Oct. 1961, pp. 49 ff.

[4] Cf. *King Ḥammurabi of Babylon,* pp. 17 f. Böhl thinks Amur-pi-el is a possible corruption of Amut-pi-el, and Dougherty (*loc. cit.*) is inclined to agree. O'Callaghan (*Aram Naharaim,* 1948, p. 31 n.) is more doubtful, finding the suggestion attractive but hazardous, while C. F. Jean (*Bi.Or.*, v, 1948, p. 128) is more critical, and finds it hard to accept the shift from Amut-pi-el to Amur-pi-el. It may be added that Gelb had earlier thought Aleppo a more likely home for Amraphel than Babylon (cf. *A.J.S.L.*, liii, 1936–37, pp. 253 ff.), while some forty years ago Albright had thought of northern Mesopotamia as a more likely home (cf. *ibid.*, xl, 1923–24, pp. 125 ff.).

[5] Cf. *King Ḥammurabi of Babylon,* 1946, p. 17.

[6] Cf. *B.A.S.O.R.*, No. 88, Dec. 1942, pp. 33–36; R. T. O'Callaghan, *Aram Naharaim,* 1948, p. 31; R. de Vaux, *R.B.*, lv, 1948, p. 334.

[7] Meek, who follows Albright's date for Ḥammurabi, places Abraham *circa* 1750 B.C., (*Hebrew Origins,* rev. ed., 1950, pp. 14 f.).

Harran and westward may have taken place in the twentieth and nineteenth centuries."[1] This cuts Gen. 14 entirely loose from all history that can be ascertained from non-Biblical sources, and Albright observes that "Genesis 14 remains an enigma which only the future can solve".[2] De Vaux also rejects the linking of Abraham with the age of Ḥammurabi, and places him *circa* 1850 B.C.[3] This, he observes, at least sets the story of Gen. 14 in an age when Transjordan was occupied by a sedentary population, whereas the researches of Nelson Glueck have established that there was a long break in that occupation from the nineteenth century B.C.[4] It leaves Gen. 14 : 1, however, quite unrelated to general history.

It is clear that none of the proposed identifications is conclusive, and we cannot rely with confidence on Gen. 14 to fix the age of Abraham.[5] In so far as the chapter is relied on it would lead us to a date in the seventeenth century B.C.,[6] and an earlier date can only be defended by disregarding Gen. 14 : 1, or by denying the identification of the names with those of known persons.

Abraham is called "the Hebrew" in the Bible, and this name has long been associated with the name Ḥabiru which is found in the Amarna letters. In those letters, written in the fourteenth century B.C. from the Palestinian princes to the Egyptian chancellery, we find appeals for help against people who are called by the ideogram SA-GAZ in many of the letters, but by the name Ḥabiru in the letters of Abdi-Ḥiba, the king of Jerusalem. The equation of the names Ḥabiru and Hebrews is not quite so simple as it seems to the English reader, and it has always been opposed by a number of scholars.[7] Others claimed

---

[1] Cf. *The Archaeology of Palestine*, 1949, p. 83. Albright has since explained (*Gnomon*, xxiii, 1951, p. 397) that in assigning "the Terachid movement" to the twentieth and nineteenth centuries B.C., he does not carry Abraham back to that time. He holds that Abraham is to be dated relatively late in the Terachid movement, and that his period is *circa* 1650 B.C.

[2] Cf. *ibid.*, p. 237.   [3] Cf. *S.D.B.*, v, 1949, col. 733.

[4] Cf. N. Glueck, *The Other Side of the Jordan*, 1940, p. 114.

[5] Cf. what I wrote in *B.J.R.L.*, xxii, 1938, p. 285: "For myself, I am not disposed to try to fix the age of Abraham. I would merely urge that there is no strong evidence to point to the age of Ḥammurabi, and that the evidence of Gen. 14: 1 is both obscure in itself and of doubtful value even if it were clear." I have more recently discussed Gen. 14 in relation to Ps. 110 in *Festschrift für Alfred Bertholet*, 1950, pp. 461–472.

[6] F. Cornelius (*Z.A.W.*, N.F. xxxi, 1960, pp. 1–7) accepts the identification of Amraphel with Ḥammurabi of Babylon, and assigns the incident recorded in Gen. 14 to *circa* 1650 B.C., and accordingly dates Abraham in that period.

[7] Cf. F. Hommel, in Hastings's *D.B.*, i, 1898, p. 228a; P. (E.) Dhorme, *R.B.*, N.S. vi, 1909, pp. 68 f., and *L'évolution religieuse d'Israël*, i, *La religion des Hébreux nomades*, 1937, pp. 79 ff.; E. G. Kraeling, *Aram and Israel*, 1918, p. 34.

that not only were the names to be equated, but that the Amarna letters gave us the story of the entry of the Israelites under Joshua after the Exodus from Egypt.[1] It is a curious fact that while the Bible speaks of Hebrews before the descent into Egypt and during the sojourn in Egypt, it never uses the term in connexion with the people who were brought out of Egypt by Moses and who entered the land under Joshua. There are some later references to Hebrews at the time of the Philistine oppression and the foundation of the monarchy, but none in connexion with the Settlement in Canaan. This would be curious if the Amarna letters gave the story of their entry under Joshua.

From Egyptian sources we had references to some people called 'Aperu,[2] who were set to hard labour, and these again were identified by some with the Hebrews in Egypt. There was a reference to 'Aperu in a text which told of the activity of Thothmes III in Palestine, but the text itself is of a later date and is not regarded as a historical source.[3] Other texts, of a historical character, came from the reigns of Seti I and Rameses II, and even later, and since, on the view that the Amarna letters give the story of the entry into Palestine after the Exodus, all of these come from a time after the Exodus from Egypt, the equation of 'Aperu with Hebrews has been denied by some of those who have stoutly maintained the equation of Ḥabiru with Hebrews.[4]

Here again we have more evidence to-day than we had but a few years ago.[5] Between the wars further mention of the 'Aperu was found at Bethshan, in the Jordan valley.[6] We now know that there

[1] Cf. J. W. Jack, *The Date of the Exodus*, 1925, p. 143; H. R. Hall, *The Ancient History of the Near East*, 7th ed., 1927, p. 409; S. L. Caiger, *Bible and Spade*, 1936, pp. 102 f.

[2] Cf. H. F. Heyes, *Bibel und Ägypten*, i, 1904, pp. 146 ff.; S. R. Driver, *The Book of Exodus*, 1911, pp. xli f.; A. Jirku, *Die Wanderungen der Hebräer*, 1924, pp. 23 ff.; J. A. Wilson, "The 'Eperu of the Egyptian Inscriptions", in *A.J.S.L.*, xlix, 1923–33, pp. 275–280; B. Gunn, *apud* E. A. Speiser, *A.A.S.O.R.*, xiii, 1933, p. 38; T. J. Meek, *Hebrew Origins*, 1936, p. 11 (rev. ed., 1950, p. 12).

[3] Cf. Jirku, *op. cit.*, p. 24: "An erster Stelle, weil uns dieselbe noch nach Palästina führt, ist da eine Angabe aus einem geschichtlichen Romane zu nennen, der von der Eroberung der palästinensischen Stadt Jaffa durch Thutmosis III handelt."

[4] Cf. K. Miketta, *Der Pharao des Auszuges*, 1903, p. 55; A. H. Breasted, *Ancient Records of Egypt*, iv, 1906, p. 150 n.; F. M. Th. Böhl, *Kanaanäer und Hebräer*, 1911, p. 83.

[5] For a full survey of the evidence, cf. J. Bottéro, *Le Problème des Ḥabiru*, 1954; and M. Greenberg, *The Ḥab/piru*, 1955.

[6] Cf. A. Rowe, *The Topography and History of Beth-shan*, 1930, pp. 29 f. It has been frequently and unwarrantably stated that at Bethshan an inscriptional reference to the 'Aperu as being engaged on the building of Pi-Ramesse in the time of Rameses II was found. Cf. C. S. Fisher, *M.J.U.P.*, xiv, 1923, p. 234; L. H. Vincent, *R.B.*, xxxiii, 1924, p. 429 n.; H. R. Hall, *P.E.F.Q.S.*, 1925, p. 117; J. W. Jack, *The Date of the Exodus*, 1925, p. 22; J. N. Schofield, *The Historical Background of the Bible*, 1938, facing p. 110. Cf. A. Rowe, "The Two Royal Stelae of Beth-shan", in *M.J.U.P.*, 1929, pp. 88–98.

were 'Aperu in the Transjordan in the time of Seti I, and that they were engaged in fighting, though there are obscurities in the text and it is not certain on whose side they were fighting.[1] In 1943 a further reference to no less than 3600 'Aperu prisoners who were taken by Amenhotep II in fighting in Palestine became known.[2] At this time, if the Biblical chronology is correct, and if the view that the Amarna letters tell of Joshua's campaign after the Exodus is correct, the Hebrews ought to have been wandering in the wilderness and not fighting in Palestine.

Again, in 1940 a Ras Shamra text was published which offered evidence for the equation of the names 'prm and SA-GAZ.[3] Since we already had Hittite evidence which made it plain that the terms Ḥabiru and SA-GAZ referred to the same people, it now became clear that 'prm and Ḥabiru should be equated. It was at once claimed, however, that Ḥabiru could no longer be connected with Hebrews.[4] For the word written Ḥabiru could be read Ḥapiru, and it was claimed that the new evidence meant that it should be so read, and the apparent connexion with Hebrews be accordingly weakened. Actually, it is once more not quite so simple as that, and the equation of both Ḥabiru and 'Aperu with Hebrews is still possible, though it is not, and never has been, very secure.[5]

[1] Cf. W. F. Albright, A.A.S.O.R., vi, 1926, p. 36 n.; A. Mallon, Biblica, vii, 1926, p. 109; G. Grdseloff, B.E.H.J., i, 1946, p. 77 n., and Une stèle scythopolitaine du roi Séthos I (Études égyptiennes, Fasc. 2), 1949.

[2] Cf. A. M. Badawi, A.S.A.E., xlii, 1943, pp. 21 ff. See also B. Grdseloff, B.E.H.J., i, 1946, p. 75; E. Drioton and J. Vandier, Les peuples de l'orient méditerranéen, II, L'Égypte, 2nd ed., 1946, pp. 653 ff.; A. H. Gardiner, Ancient Egyptian Onomastica, i, 1947, p. 184* n.; A. Alt, "Amenophis II in Syrien und in Palästina", in F.u.F., xxvi, 1950, pp. 85–87.

[3] Cf. E. G. Kraeling, B.A.S.O.R., No. 77, Feb. 1940, p. 32; Ch. Virolleaud, Syria, xxi, 1940, pp. 125 (II: 7), 132 (VIII: 1), 134 (X: 12), 143, and R.E.S.-B., 1940, pp. 74–76; J. W. Jack, P.E.Q., 1940, p. 97; R. de Vaux, R.B., lv, 1948, pp. 339 f.; B. Couroyer, R.B., lvii, 1950, p. 484.

[4] Cf. Ch. Virolleaud, C.R.A.I., 1939, p. 329; E. G. Kraeling, loc. cit. So also E. Dhorme, Les premières civilisations, new ed., 1950, p. 317, where it is held that Ḥabiru or Ḥapiru may be equated with 'Aperu, but neither has any connexion with 'ibrim. For the latter Dhorme has now abandoned his earlier derivation, and adopted the common view that this gentilic has developed from the preposition 'ēber=beyond. E. Taeubler, in Alexander Marx Jubilee Volume, English Section, 1950, pp. 581 ff., maintains that Ḥabiru and 'Ibrim both mean "those who dwelt beside a river", and that there is no necessary connexion between the peoples known by the name, while W. F. Albright (The Jews, ed. by L. Finkelstein, i, 1949, p. 57) connects 'Aperu with Egyptian 'pr="ship's complement, crew, gang of labourers".

[5] Cf. the present writer's "Ras Shamra and the Ḥabiru Question", in P.E.Q., 1940, pp. 90–94; "Ḥābiru and Hebrews", ibid., 1942, pp. 41–53. See also J. W. Jack, "New Light on the Ḥābirū-Hebrew Question", ibid., 1940, pp. 95–115; and on the other side, E. G. Kraeling, "The Origin of the Name 'Hebrews' ", in A.J.S.L., lviii, 1941, pp. 237–

Evidence from the Nuzu texts brought a much greater complication into the discussion of this question. For there a number of references to Ḥabiru or Ḥapiru are found. Many of them are described as voluntary slaves, and the term by which they are called appears to have a social rather than an ethnic connotation.[1] It is then observed that in the Pentateuch we have legislation that required a Hebrew slave to be set free after six years of service, unless he voluntarily chose to remain in his master's service.[2] Further, there is a nuance of depreciation about most of the uses of the word Hebrews in the Old Testament. Hence, it is claimed, the word had reference primarily to status and not to race, and in so far as it ever has a racial meaning, that is a secondary development in Israel, where it became associated with their

253. B. Maisler (B.A.S.O.R., No. 102, April 1946, p. 9) and B. Grdseloff (Une stèle scytho-politaine du roi Séthos I, 1949, pp. 29 ff.) still accept the equation, while H. L. Ginsberg (B.A., viii, 1945, p. 48) thinks the Ras Shamra evidence has dealt it the severest blow. Cf. R. de Vaux, R.B., lv, 1948, p. 344: "On peut donc maintenir qu'une relation existe entre les Hébreux et les Ḥapiru-'Apiru. Il est vraisemblable qu'Abraham et ses descendants ont été comptés parmi les Ḥapiru en Canaan, parmi les 'Apiru en Égypte"; also R.B., lxiii, 1956, p. 266: "Le problème des Ḥabiru n'est donc pas résolu et cette incertitude rend difficile la comparaison des Ḥabiru avec les Hébreux de l'Ancien Testament, car on ne peut comparer utilement que deux quantités connues", and again (ibid.): "Il n'y a donc pas d'objection décisive au rapprochement des deux noms." Mary P. Gray (H.U.C.A., xxix, 1958, pp. 195 f. note) reproaches me for my unwillingness to decide on this question. Where the evidence is insufficient, it is wiser to refrain from a decision. Miss Gray quotes my observation (P.E.Q., 1942–43, p. 53) that "it seems wiser to refrain from offering an etymology for 'ibrim, since any suggestion must assume either the admittedly doubtful equation or the equally doubtful lack of equation" and she proceeds "If one must 'refrain' from offering an etymology lest it solve a problem in favour of one of two alternatives, then scholarship can be used never to decide questions." The gentle twist given to my words will not pass unnoticed. If a solution rests on an assumption it is inadequately based, since assumption is not evidence. It is always easy to assume what one wishes to establish, but it is not the way of sound scholarship and I still refrain from taking it. A. Haldar (I.D.B., ii, 1962, 506) says: "The volume published by J. Bottéro (see p. 299, n. 5) . . . shows how completely scholarly opinion diverges on practically every point, also on the question of etymology" (for the review of scholarly opinion on the question see Bottéro, pp. v–xxxii). What Miss Gray regards as my unscholarly indecision is shared by M. Greenberg (The Ḥab/piru, 1955, p. 96): "The proposed 'Apiru-Hebrew equation faces thus at present a series of objections. None of these is decisive, but their cumulative effect must be considered to diminish its probability." Cf. J. R. Kupper, Les Nomades en Mésopotamie au temps des rois de Mari, 1957, p. 208: "Toutes les étymologies proposées ont été contestées; aucune, on peut le dire, n'est parvenue à s'imposer."

[1] Cf. E. A. Speiser, A.A.S.O.R., xiii, 1933, p. 35; Cf. also E. Chiera, "Ḥabiru and Hebrews", in A.J.S.L., xlix, 1932–33, pp. 115–124; J. Lewy, "Ḥābirū and Hebrews", in H.U.C.A., xiv, 1939, pp. 587–623, "A New Parallel between Ḥābirū and Hebrews", ibid., xv, 1940, pp. 47–58.

[2] Cf. J. Lewy, ibid., xiv, 1939, p. 609, xv, 1940, pp. 47 ff.; C. H. Gordon, B.A., iii, 1940, p. 12; R. de Vaux, R.B., lv, 1948, p. 343.

national consciousness.[1] On the whole it seems to me more likely that the term began with a racial significance which it lost in such a community as that of Nuzu, where large numbers of them sank into a condition of slavery, until their name became used for their class, whether members of their race or not.[2] In the same way in the Roman world the term Chaldaean, originally of racial significance, came to mean a soothsayer because numbers of soothsayers came from the east.

On this question new evidence has now been published. For in the Mari texts there are references to the Ḥabiru, and here they are no social class of voluntary slaves, but condottieri who raid cities to plunder and kill. A. Parrot has published a translation of a hitherto unpublished text[3] in which we learn of a raid which they made on a town, seizing 500 sheep and killing or capturing ten persons. This tablet is said to be typical of many others, and Parrot observes that the reputation of the Ḥabiru here seems to be similar to that of the Ḥabiru of Palestine in the Amarna age.[4]

It is of importance to observe that not all the Ḥabiru of the ancient

---

[1] Cf. E. A. Speiser, *A.A.S.O.R.*, xiii, 1933, pp. 37 ff.; E. G. Kraeling, *A.J.S.L.*, lviii, 1941, p. 246. Cf. also M. Noth, *Vetus Testamentum*, i, 1951, pp. 78 f.; G. E. Wright, *Biblical Archaeology*, revised edition, 1962, p. 42b. J. Bottéro (*Le Problème des Ḥabiru*, 1954) and M. Greenberg (*The Ḥab/piru*, 1955) favour the view that the term is an appellative and not an ethnic term, the former (pp. 187 ff.) favouring the general sense of refugee, though he would not render it universally by this word, and the latter (pp. 85 ff.) regarding the Ḥabiru as indigent have-nots who sold their services in various ways or organized themselves in bands. R. de Vaux (*R.B.*, lxiii, 1956, pp. 261–267) offers carefully reasoned criticisms of this view in the light of the evidence the authors assemble. More recently Mary P. Gray has argued (*H.U.C.A.*, xxix, 1958, pp. 135–202) for an appellative sense, though she recognizes such a wide variety of usage that it is hard to see what common meaning for the appellative can be suggested. She describes them as "a social group who fulfilled a function" (p. 173), and describes that function (pp. 166 ff.) as supplying soldiers, messengers, scribes, unskilled labour, vineyard workers, general servants or as hirers of servants, with power to control political changes, and to welcome refugees. This would appear to be a somewhat wide "function". As is pointed out by de Vaux (*R.B.*, lxiii, 1956, p. 265) and A. Haldar (*I.D.B.*, ii, 1962, p. 506b) there are passages where the term is more naturally understood as a gentilic. Cf. also H. Cazelles, "Hébreu, Ubru et Hapiru", in *Syria*, xxxv, 1938, pp. 198–217.

[2] J. R. Kupper (*Les Nomades en Mésopotamie au temps des rois de Mari*, 1957, p. 249) recognizes that the term has passed through different meanings at different stages of its history, though he accepts the appellative sense as the primary one (p. 258). A Haldar (*I.D.B.*, ii, 1962, p. 506b) also prefers the view that an originally appellative word developed into an ethnic term. The difficulty is to define what the appellative signified, if all the occurrences are to be brought within its compass.

[3] Cf. *R.H.P.R.*, xxx, 1950, p. 4.

[4] *Ibid.*, p. 5. Cf. also the text on the statue of Idri-mi, line 27 (S. Smith, *The Statue of Idri-mi*, 1949, pp. 16 f.), where there is a reference to a warrior band of SA-GAZ in Northern Syria.

world were in Palestine. The name is found in Babylonia as well as in Nuzu,[1] and if Ḥabiru and ʿAperu are identified, also in Egyptian and Ras Shamra texts, as has been said. It is therefore of much wider significance than to denote the Israelite people in certain periods of their history. This, however, is in full accord with what we read in the Bible. For Eber is the eponymous ancestor of the Hebrews, who therefore include more than Abraham and his descendants through Isaac and Jacob.[2] Some were left in Babylonia when Terah migrated with his family, and some were left in northern Mesopotamia when Abraham migrated from Harran. The putting of the Ḥabiru in a much wider context by archaeological discoveries, therefore, is not an embarrassment to the Biblical student.[3]

If, however, Abraham is placed in the seventeenth century B.C., and it is held that he migrated from Harran to Palestine in that age, there is no room for all the period that separated him from the Exodus if the Exodus is placed in the fifteenth century B.C. Albright associates Jacob and the entry into Egypt with the establishment of the Hyksos power there[4] about 1730 B.C.[5] This seems to me very doubtful,[6] and I think it is more probable that the age of Jacob should be brought down much lower to the Amarna age. Instead, therefore, of finding the campaigns of Joshua reflected in the Amarna letters, I find that age to provide the appropriate setting for a number of the incidents

[1] Cf. V. Scheil, R.Ass., xii, 1915, pp. 114 f.; A. Jirku, Die Wanderungen der Hebräer, 1924, pp. 14 ff.; E. Chiera, A.J.S.L., xlix, 1932–33, pp. 115 ff.

[2] Gen. 11: 16 ff.

[3] Cf. R. de Vaux, R.B., lxiii, 1956, p. 267: "Je continue de penser que ressemblances et différences pourraient s'expliquer si les Israélites-'Hébreux' ne sont qu'une fraction des Ḥabiru-'Hébreux', comme la Bible elle-même paraît l'indiquer."

[4] Cf. J.P.O.S., i, 1921, pp. 65 f.; J.S.O.R., x, 1926, p. 268; B.A.S.O.R., No. 58, April 1935, p. 15; J.P.O.S., xv, 1935, p. 227; From the Stone Age to Christianity, 2nd ed., 1946, p. 150.

[5] This is the date usually given for the establishment of the Hyksos. Cf. K. Sethe, Z.Ä.S., lxv, 1930, p. 83; R. M. Engberg, The Hyksos Reconsidered, 1939, p. 9; E. Drioton and J. Vandier, Les peuples de l'Orient méditerranéen, II: L'Égypte, 1946, pp. 282 f. Albright, however, who formerly dated it circa 1675 B.C. (cf. J.S.O.R., x, 1926, p. 268), dates it 1720 B.C. (cf. J.P.O.S., xv, 1935, p. 225 f.). With this latter date cf. H. Stock, Studien zur Geschichte und Archäologie der 13. bis 17. Dynastie Ägyptens, 1942, p. 70, where the beginning of the Hyksos period is placed at 1720–1710 B.C.

[6] It is improbable for the following reasons: (1) The Hyksos are not likely to have been particularly tender towards Egyptian sensitiveness (Gen. 46: 34); (2) the Hyksos promoted the worship of Set and not of Ra, and therefore it would have been no honour in that age for Joseph to have been given the daughter of the priest of On to wife; (3) the location of the Hyksos capital scarcely fits the Biblical data. Cf. my Schweich Lectures, From Joseph to Joshua, 1950, pp. 24 ff.

recorded in the book of Genesis, dealing with the time before the entry into Egypt.[1]

It has long been known that one of the Hyksos leaders was named Jacob-hr or Jacob-el,[2] and another Jacob-baal, and it has been improbably suggested that they were named after the patriarch Jacob.[3] Such a view would seem to be ruled out if Abraham is to be placed in the period of the Hyksos decline. Further, it has been known for more than half a century that there are Egyptian references coming from *circa* 1479 B.C. to Palestinian place-names Jacob-el and Joseph-el,[4] though the latter name is but doubtfully so read.[5] There is no reason whatever to suppose that any of these names had anything to do with the Biblical characters. We have already seen that there were at least three contemporary kings named Ḥammurabi, and there is no reason why more than one person should not bear the name Jacob or Joseph, or why the place-names should not be connected with a non-Biblical holder of the name. It would in any case be surprising for Joseph, who was carried into Egypt while still a youth, to have left his name in a Palestinian place-name during the period of the sojourn in Egypt; and even on the earliest chronology the year 1479 B.C. would fall within the period of the Egyptian sojourn.[6]

These are not the only Israelite names which are found in non-Biblical texts of the period we are studying, according to the view of

[1] Cf. *ibid.*, pp. 115 ff. D. J. Wiseman (*Illustrations from Biblical Archaeology*, 1958, p. 25) assigns the age of the Patriarchs to *circa* 1750–1550 B.C. C. H. Gordon (*J.N.E.S.*, xiii, 1954, pp. 58 f.) goes farther than I do, and locates the patriarchal period in the Amarna age.

[2] Cf. H. R. Hall, *The Ancient History of the Near East*, 7th ed., 1927, p. 217; H. Stock, *op. cit.*, p. 67; Albright reads Ya'kob-hr, which he interprets as: May the mountain god protect (cf. *From the Stone Age to Christianity*, 2nd ed., 1946, p. 184). Cf. R. de Vaux, *R.B.*, liii, 1946, p. 324; J. R. Kupper, *Les nomades en Mésopotamie au temps des rois de Mari*, 1957, pp. 47–81.

[3] Cf. J. W. Jack, *The Date of the Exodus*, 1925, p. 231.

[4] Cf. A. Mariette, *Les listes géographiques des pylônes de Karnak*, 1875, pp. 36, 40; A. Jirku, *Die ägyptischen Listen palästinensischer und syrischer Ortsanamen*, 1937, pp. 14 f. The former name is found again in a list of the time of Rameses II, and the latter in a later list (cf. Jirku, *op. cit.*, pp. 38, 50).

[5] Cf. C. F. Burney, *Israel's Settlement in Canaan*, 3rd ed., 1921, pp. 89 f.; H. Gressmann, in *Eucharistērion* (Gunkel Festschrift), i, 1923, p. 4; J. W. Jack, *The Date of the Exodus*, 1925, p. 231. The equation of the names is defended by H. F. Heyes, *Bibel und Ägypten*, i, 1904, pp. 104 f., following W. M. Müller, *O.L.Z.*, ii, 1899, cols. 396 ff.

[6] It is true that the view of Josephus [*Contra Apionem*, 103 (i, 16)] that the Exodus is to be identified with the expulsion of the Hyksos, has found some modern following (cf. H. R. Hall, *C.A.H.*, i, 2nd ed., 1924, p. 311, and *The Ancient History of the Near East*, 7th ed., 1927, pp. 213 n., 408 n.; A. H. Gardiner, *J.E.A.*, v, 1918, pp. 36 ff., xix, 1933, pp. 122 ff.). But it is decisively rejected by the great majority of scholars.

some scholars. Leaving out of account the name Abram, which is found in Babylonia, where no one connects it with the Biblical patriarch,[1] and the name Israel, which is doubtfully claimed to be found on a cylinder from the period of Agade,[2] where again it could not possibly refer to the Biblical Israel, we may note that in Mari texts there are references to Benjamites,[3] and it has been suggested that they are to be connected with the Biblical Benjamites.[4] This does not seem very likely.[5] The name Benjamin means "son of the south", and there is no reason why it should not be given to tribes in more than one locality. In Mari we find the corresponding name "sons of the north". If the Mari Benjamites should be connected with the Biblical Benjamites, then the tribe was in existence already at about 2000 B.C., and therefore earlier than the birth of Benjamin on any Biblical chronology. Further, in the Biblical story Benjamin is said to have been born in Palestine, after Jacob's return from Laban, and never to have been in Mesopotamia at all. Clearly the tribe carried no memory of any history of theirs stretching back to the period before their entry into Palestine.

In the earlier collection of execration texts from Egypt, assigned to

---

[1] Cf. W. F. Albright, *J.B.L.*, liv, 1935, p. 194; R. de Vaux, *R.B.*, liii, 1946, p. 323.

[2] Cf. V. Scheil, *R.Ass.*, xii, 1916, pp 5 ff.

[3] Cf. G. Dossin, "Benjaminites dans les textes de Mari", in *Mélanges Syriens offerts à M. René Dussaud*, ii, 1939, pp. 981–996. See also Dossin, *Syria*, xix, 1938, pp. 111 n., 116 n.

[4] A. Alt (*P.J.B.*, xxxv, 1939, p. 52) allows for the possibility of this connexion. Cf. also G. Dossin, in *Mélanges Syriens*, ii, p. 996; W. von Soden, *Die Welt des Orients*, i, 1947–52, pp. 197 f.; A. Parrot, *R.H.P.R.*, 1950, pp. 5 ff. Parrot observes that he does not go so far as to suggest a connexion with the Biblical Benjamites, but only observes that *before* the patriarch Jacob and *before* the birth of his son Benjamin, a tribe bore the name of Benjamites (p. 5 n.). This is undeniable. It is to be observed, however, that Parrot believes it is legitimate to conclude that the Mari Benjamites belonged to the group that migrated with Terah from Ur (p. 6), and thinks Gen. 49: 27 may be an echo of the reputation of the Mari Benjamites (p. 6). He also thinks the Benjamite use of fire signals (Jer. 6: 1) is significant in view of the use of a related term in connexion with the Mari Benjamites (pp. 8 ff.). It is improbable that the use of fire signals was peculiar to the Benjamites, and the terms of Gen. 49: 27 could well fit many peoples. Indeed, according to the quotation which Parrot gives from a Mari text (p. 4), they could be used of the whole of the Ḫabiru group in the neighbourhood of Mari, and not merely of the Benjamites. Cf. also Parrot, *R.H.P.R.*, xxxv, 1955, pp. 117 f. M. Astour (*Semitica*, ix, 1959, pp. 5–20) has argued most strongly for the equation of the Mari Benjamites and the Biblical tribe. Cf. H. Cazelles, *S.D.B.*, Fasc. 36, 1961, col. 108; *Syria*, xxxv, 1958, p. 217 n.

[5] Cf. A. Pohl, *Biblica*, xx, 1939, p. 200; W. F. Albright, *J.B.L.*, lviii, 1939, p. 102; J. J. Dougherty, *Scripture*, iii, 1948, p. 100; R. de Vaux, *R.B.*, liii, 1946, p. 344; M. Noth, *History of Israel*, E.Tr., 2nd ed., 1960, p. 63 n. [less definitely in *Geschichte und Altes Testament* (Alt Festschrift), 1953, p. 144 n.].

the twentieth century B.C., the name 'Ijsipj stands,[1] while in the collection that probably comes from the following century a similar name 'Isipi is found.[2] Dussaud identifies both of them with the already mentioned Joseph-el,[3] but other scholars are unconvinced.[4] If Dussaud is right, we should still not be able to connect the name with the Biblical Joseph, who on any chronology was not born until after the date of the earlier of these texts.

Similarly, in the Posener collection of execration texts, which was published in 1940, the name of Simeon has been found by some scholars,[5] though the identification is denied by others.[6] Once more we should have to recognize, if the identification were established, that the Simeon referred to could with little probability be connected with the Biblical Simeon. In the Sethe collection, coming from an even earlier date, the name of Zebulun has been found,[7] and here Albright accepts the identification of the name.[8] On the other hand, he denies the claim to find the name of Zebulun in the Ras Shamra texts.

Both Asher and Zebulun are alleged to occur there,[9] though for the former Albright finds a verb meaning "march"[10] and Ginsberg the meaning "after",[11] while for the latter Albright finds the meaning "patricians"[12] and Ginsberg "sickness".[13] The view of Albright has a substantial following,[14] and it is clear that the alleged occurrences of

[1] Cf. K. Sethe, A.P.A.W., 1926, No. 5, pp. 54 f., 58.

[2] Cf. G. Posener, Princes et pays d'Asie et de Nubie, 1940, p. 71.

[3] Cf. Syria, viii, 1927, p. 231, xxi, 1940, p. 172.

[4] Cf. W. F. Albright, J.P.O.S., viii, 1928, p. 249. L. H. Vincent, Vivre et Penser, ii, 1942, p. 195, thinks 'Isipi has the value of a divine name.

[5] Cf. Posener, Princes et pays, p. 91. Cf. also Posener, Syria, xviii, 1937, p. 191; Chronique d'Égypte, No. 27, Jan. 1939, p. 44; and L. H. Vincent, Vivre et Penser, ii, 1942, pp. 200 f.

[6] Cf. A. Alt, Z.D.P.V., lxiv, 1941, p. 35; W. F. Albright, B.A.S.O.R., No. 81, Feb. 1941, p. 19 n., No. 83, Oct. 1941, p. 34; B. Maisler, B.E.H.J., No. 1, 1946, pp. 60 f.

[7] Cf. K. Sethe, A.P.A.W., 1926, No. 5, p. 47.

[8] Cf. The Vocalization of the Egyptian Syllabic Orthography, 1934, p. 7.

[9] Cf. Ch. Virolleaud, R.E.S., 1934, No. 1, pp. vi, xi, and La légende de Keret, 1936, pp. 38, 44; R. Dussaud, Les découvertes de Ras Shamra et l'Ancien Testament, 2nd ed., 1941, p. 163; R. Weill, J.A., ccxxix, 1937, pp. 16, 18; G. A. Barton, in Mémorial Lagrange, 1940, p. 30 (=J.B.L., lx, 1941, p. 215).

[10] Cf. B.A.S.O.R., No. 63, Oct. 1936, p. 29 n., No. 71, Oct. 1938, p. 39.

[11] Cf. The Legend of King Keret, 1946, pp. 16–18.

[12] Cf. B.A.S.O.R., No. 63, p. 27 n., No. 71, p. 38.

[13] Cf. The Legend of King Keret, pp. 14, 34.

[14] Cf. A. Goetze, J.A.O.S., lviii, 1938, p. 277 n.; R. de Langhe, Les textes de Ras Shamra-Ugarit et leurs apports à l'histoire des origines israélites, 1939, pp. 76 ff., 79 ff., and Les textes de R. S.-U. et leurs rapports avec le milieu biblique de l'Ancien Testament, ii, 1945, pp. 472

the names of the Israelite tribes are too insecure to build on.[1] On the other hand, there is reason to believe that the name of Asher stands in Egyptian texts coming from the reigns of Seti I and Rameses II in the form 'Asaru.[2] It would then appear that this tribe was already in Palestine in those reigns, and the view that they entered the land in the Amarna age more than a century earlier than the reign of Seti I gains in probability. Nevertheless the identification is not accepted by all scholars, and it cannot be regarded as certain.

On the whole, therefore, it is improbable that in any texts coming from the period 2000 B.C. to 1400 B.C. references to the Biblical tribes or persons are really to be found. A like improbability attaches to the "Negebite" theory of the Ras Shamra texts, associated particularly with the names of Virolleaud and Dussaud.[3] According to this view there are a number of references to the district in the south of Palestine standing in these texts, connecting the history of the Ras Shamra people with that district. Evidence of a great battle with the Terahites has been read into the texts, and the Terahites are then thought to be the ancestors of the Hebrews. All of this is speculative and doubtful, and to-day the Negebite hypothesis commands prac-

---

ff., 477 ff.; C. H. Gordon, *Ugaritic Grammar*, 1940, pp. 34, 36; J. Pedersen, *Berytus*, vi, 1941, p. 68; W. Baumgartner, *Th.R.*, N.F. xiii, 1941, p. 17; I. Engnell, *Studies in Divine Kingship in the Ancient Near East*, 1943, pp. 150, 157 f. G. A. Barton, *loc. cit.*, protests that "The root *ašr* (or *atr*) does not mean 'march' in any Semitic language or in Hittite. So far as Hurrian is yet known to us that tongue furnishes no basis for such a meaning. Egyptian has a verb '*šr*, but it means 'broil', 'roast'." He further observes: "Similarly to translate *zblnm* 'patricians' instead of 'Zebulonites'. in order to get rid of a definite Palestinian reference, appears to be motivated more by a preconceived theory than by philology."

[1] R. de Vaux formerly accepted these references to the Israelite tribes (cf. *R.B.*, xlvi, 1937, pp. 446, 542), but appears to have abandoned this view (cf. *ibid.*, lv, 1948, pp. 326 f.). Cf. also J. P. Lettinga, *J.E.O.L.*, ix, 1944, p. 120; A. Herdner, *Syria*, xxv, 1946–1948, p. 137b.

[2] Cf. W. M. Müller, *Asien und Europa nach altägyptischen Denkmälern*, 1893, pp. 236–239; S. A. Cook, *C.A.H.*, ii, 1924, pp. 319, 326 f.; T. H. Robinson, *History of Israel*, i, 1932, pp. 75 f. See also C. F. Burney, *Israel's Settlement in Canaan*, 3rd ed., 1921, p. 82. Here R. Dussaud denied any reference to the Biblical tribe. Cf. *Syria*, xix, 1938, p. 177b, and *Les découvertes de Ras Shamra et l'Ancien Testament*, 2nd ed., 1941, p. 163 n. So also M. Noth, *V.T.*, i, 1951, p. 78.

[3] Cf. R. Dussaud, "Les Phéniciens au Négeb et en Arabie, d'après un texte de Ras Shamra", in *R.H.R.*, xviii, 1933, pp. 5–49, and *Les découvertes de Ras Shamra et l'Ancien Testament*, 2nd ed., 1941, pp. 160–168; Ch. Virolleaud, *La légende de Keret roi des Sidoniens*, 1936, pp. 4–6. See also T. H. Gaster, "The Ras-Shamra Texts and the Old Testament", in *P.E.F.Q.S.*, 1934, pp. 141–146; R. Weill, "Le poème de Keret et l'histoire", in *J.A.*, ccxxix, 1937, pp. 1–56; "La légende des Patriarches et l'histoire", in *R.E.S.*, 1937, pp. 145–206; G. A. Barton, "Danel: a pre-Israelite Hero of Galilee", in *Mémorial Lagrange*, 1940, pp. 29–37 (=*J.B.L.*, lx, 1941, pp. 213–225).

tically no following.[1] The texts are quite differently understood by most scholars, and where a geographical interpretation is given, it is associated with quite different districts.[2] By some, however, it is held that the texts are of ritual significance, and not of geographical and historical significance.[3]

The mention of Terah, however, raises the question of the mention of the father of Abraham in these texts. It has already been said that Ur and Harran were connected with moon worship. The name Terah appears to be connected with the Hebrew word for moon,[4] and this would not be surprising. It has been claimed, however, that in the Ras Shamra texts the name stands, not as the name of a man, but as that of a divinity, and here the father of Abraham occurs as a moon deity.[5] Again, however, the text is susceptible of a very different interpretation, and it is improbable that the name of Terah stands at all,[6] and

[1] W. F. Albright, "Was the Patriarch Terah a Canaanite Moon-God?" in B.A.S.O.R., No. 71, Oct. 1938, pp. 35–40, and "L'hypothèse négébite des origines cananéennes", in Actes du XXᵉ Congrès International des Orientalistes, 1940, pp. 253–256. On p. 256 Albright speaks of the "mirage enchanteur de Negeb", and in Bulletin, No. 71, p. 40, he says: "There is no reason to give it"—i.e. the literature of Ugarit—"a factitious value by spinning webs of Negebite gossamer and substituting them for honest linen." In Archaeology and the Religion of Israel, 2nd ed., 1946, p. 60, he observes that the entire negebite hypothesis "is now virtually extinct in serious scholarly circles."

[2] Cf. R. de Vaux, "Le cadre géographique du poème de Krt", in R.B., xlvi, 1937, pp. 362–372, and "Les textes de Ras Shamra et l'Ancien Testament", ibid., pp. 526–555 (esp. 535–545); A. Bea, Biblica, xix, 1938, pp. 437–443; R. de Langhe, Les textes de Ras Shamra-Ugarit et leurs apports à l'histoire des origines israélites, 1939, pp. 53–70, and Les textes du R.S.-U. et leurs rapports avec le milieu biblique de l'Ancien Testament, ii, 1945, pp. 488–504; O. Eissfeldt, "Zum geographischen Horizont der Ras-Schamra Texte", in Z.D.M.G., xciv, 1940, pp. 59–85; W. Baumgartner, Th.R., N.F. xiii, 1941, pp. 18 f.; H. L. Ginsberg, The Legend of King Keret, 1946, pp. 7 f.

[3] Cf. F. F. Hvidberg, Graad og Latter i det Gamle Testamente, 1938, pp. 1–63, and Z.A.W., N.F. xvi, 1939, pp. 150 f.; I. Engnell, Studies in Divine Kingship in the Ancient Near East, 1943, pp. 143–173, and Horae Soederblomianae, i, Fasc. 1, 1944, pp. 1–20. S. Mowinckel holds the text to be of a mythological rather than a historical character (cf. Nor.T.T., xlii, 1941, pp. 142–147, xliii, 1942, pp. 24–26), and so Albright (cf. B.A.S.O.R., No. 63, Oct. 1936, pp. 23–32, No. 70, April 1938, pp. 22 f.).

[4] Cf. P. Joüon, Biblica, xix, 1938, pp. 280 f.

[5] Cf. Ch. Virolleaud, Syria, xiv, 1933, p. 149, xvii, 1936, pp. 214, 217, 219 f., La légende de Keret roi des Sidoniens, 1936, pp. 18–33; J. W. Jack, The Ras Shamra Tablets, 1935, pp. 41 f.; C. F. A. Schaeffer, The Cuneiform Texts of Ras Shamra-Ugarit, 1939, pp. 73–76; R. Weill, J.A., ccxxix, 1937, pp. 35–49; R. Dussaud, Les découvertes de Ras Shamra et l'Ancien Testament, 2nd ed., 1941, pp. 141, 143, 156 f., 160–162.

[6] Cf. C. H. Gordon, B.A.S.O.R., No. 65, Feb. 1937, pp. 29–33, J.B.L., lvii, 1938, pp. 407–410; R. de Vaux, R.B., xlvi, 1937, pp. 543–545, liii, 1946, p. 322; W. F. Albright, B.A.S.O.R., No. 71, Oct. 1938, pp. 35–40, Actes du XXᵉ Congrès International des Orientalistes, pp. 253–256; A. Bea, Biblica, xix, 1938, pp. 437 f.; R. de Langhe, Les textes de Ras Shamra-Ugarit et leurs apports à l'histoire des origines israélites, 1939, pp. 71–75, and Les textes de R.S.-U. et leurs rapports avec le milieu biblique de l'Ancien Testament, ii, 1935,

therefore still more improbable that we have any reference to the ancestor of the Israelites.[1]

Of the importance of all the texts I have referred to for other sides of Old Testament study it would be beyond our present subject to speak, and the relatively negative results we have reached so far as any direct references to the Israelite tribes are concerned should not create the impression that they are without value to the Biblical student. In particular, the Ras Shamra texts offer a most valuable contribution to our knowledge of Canaanite thought and practice. And when we remember the evidence of the Old Testament that the Israelites settled amongst the Canaanites, intermarried with them, and often took over their beliefs and practices, we are not surprised to find these texts of the highest importance. There is insufficient evidence, however, to sustain the claim that the name of Israel's God, Yahweh, stands in the texts in the form of Yw, where he is represented as the son of El.[2] The text where the name is said to stand is fragmentary and its interpretation is very doubtful, and until we have clearer and unequivocal evidence it is wiser to treat the claim with caution.[3] Even if the name should be established there, we should have to recognize that this God plays no prominent part in the mythology of Ras Shamra,[4]

pp. 488–519; J. Pedersen, *Berytus*, vi, 1941, pp. 65 f.; E. Hammershaimb, *Das Verbum im Dialekt von Ras Schamra*, 1941, pp. 29 f.; A. Goetze, *J.B.L.*, lx, 1941, pp. 362 f.; J. P. Lettinga, *J.E.O.L.*, ix, 1944, pp. 119–122; A. Herder, *Syria*, xxv, 1946–48, pp. 137 f. Cf. A. Parrot, *R.H.P.R.*, xxx, 1950, p. 4: "Aujourd'hui nul n'accepte plus cette interprétation fondée sur une mauvaise et trop hâtive lecture."

[1] It has been held that the name Terah is found in Safaitic inscriptions and that it there long maintained itself (cf. R. de Vaux, *R.B.*, lv, 1948, p. 324), but G. Ryckmans (*ibid.*, lvi, 1949, pp. 579–582) denies that we have a proper name in these inscriptions.

[2] Cf. R. Dussaud, *R.H.R.*, cv, 1932, p. 247, *C.R.A.I.*, 1940, pp. 364 ff., *Les découvertes de Ras Shamra et l'Ancien Testament*, 2nd ed., 1941, pp. 171 f., and *Syria*, xxxiv, 1957, pp. 232–242; H. Bauer, *Z.A.W.*, N.F. x, 1933, pp. 92–94; O. Eissfeldt, *J.P.O.S.*, xiv, 1934, pp. 298 f.; A. Vincent, *La religion des Judéo-Araméens d'Eléphantine*, 1937, pp. 27 f.; Ch. Virolleaud, *La déesse 'Anat*, 1938, p. 98; A. Bea, *Biblica*, xx, 1939, pp. 440 f.; A. Dupont-Sommer, *C.R.A.I.*, 1947, p. 177.

[3] Cf. R. de Vaux, *R.B.*, xlvi, 1937, pp. 552 f.; C. H. Gordon, *Ugaritic Grammar*, 1940, p. 100 (but cf. *Ugaritic Manual*, 1955, p. 272); W. Baumgartner, *Th.R.*, N.F. xiii, 1941, pp. 159 f.; R. de Langhe, *Un dieu Yahweh à Ras Shamra?* 1942; W. F. Albright, *From the Stone Age to Christianity*, 2nd ed., 1946, pp. 197, 328; T. J. Meek, *Hebrew Origins*, 2nd ed., 1950, p. 105 n.; J. Gray, *The Legacy of Canaan*, 1957, pp. 133 f. (cf. *J.N.E.S.*, xii, 1953, pp. 278–283); G. R. Driver, *Canaanite Myths and Legends*, 1956, p. 12 n.; E. Jacob, *Ras Shamra et l'Ancien Testament*, 1960, pp. 107 f.

[4] Recent studies on the pantheon of the Ras Shamra texts include J. Obermann, *Ugaritic Mythology*, 1948; O. Eissfeldt, *El im ugaritischen Pantheon*, 1951; A. S. Kapelrud, *Baal in the Ras Shamra Texts*, 1952; M. H. Pope, *El in the Ugaritic Texts*, 1955; R. de Langhe, "Myth, Ritual and Kingship in the Ras Shamra Tablets", in *Myth, Ritual and Kingship*, ed. by S. H. Hooke, 1958, pp. 122–148.

and we could hardly trace to the people of Ugarit the influence which led the Israelites to make him the only God whose worship was recognized as legitimate for them.[1]

Despite exaggerated and often doubtful claims, we can at least say that some of the names borne by Biblical characters in the patriarchal age are now known to have been used in that age.[2] Our evidence comes from various localities, and even though none of it refers to Biblical persons, it is still valuable as evidence of verisimilitude in the Biblical accounts, which use these names in that period.

Further, in the Bible we read of a number of different races being found together in Palestine at the time of the Israelite entry into the land. Of the Hittites our knowledge has increased enormously during the present century through the important discoveries of texts at Boghaz Köi in Asia Minor, where the Hittites had their capital. Even before that we had much knowledge from Egyptian sources of their influence in Syria and in Palestine, and their conflicts with Egypt and diplomatic relations with the Egyptian Court. But of another of the races mentioned our knowledge has grown rapidly in much more recent years. It had often been supposed that the Horites were cave dwellers, since their names had been etymologically connected with the Hebrew word for *cave*. To-day they are connected with the Hurrians, who were a powerful people in Mesopotamia, and who were found in Nuzu and Mari, and who are also known from Ras Shamra texts written in the Hurrian language.[3] They were a non-Semitic people, of whose origin we have little knowledge, but of whose activities in the Mesopotamian world we have knowledge from texts written in Babylonian.[4] Texts written in Hurrian are now

---

[1] Cf. A. Bea, *Biblica*, xx, 1939, p. 441.

[2] Cf. R. de Vaux, *R.B.*, liii, 1946, p. 324: "Ainsi les noms des Patriarches appartiennent à des types onomastiques connus dans les milieux d'où sont sortis les ancêtres des Hébreux."

[3] Cf. W. F. Albright, *From the Stone Age to Christianity*, 2nd ed., 1946, p. 109: "The Hurrians (*Biblical Horites*) have only been known to scholars for the past twenty years and most of our information about them is less than ten years old." Already in 1939 R. de Vaux felt it necessary to "opposer des barrières à cette 'invasion hurrite' dont la Bible est menacée" (*R.B.*, xlviii, 1939, p. 621 n.).

[4] Of the considerable literature dealing with the Hurrians only a few titles can be given here: E. Burrows, "Notes on Harrian", in *J.R.A.S.*, 1925, pp. 277–284; E. Chiera and E. A. Speiser, "A New Factor in the History of the Ancient East", in *A.A.S.O.R.*, vi, 1926, pp. 75–92; E. A. Speiser, "Ethnic Movements in the Near East in the Second Millennium B.C.", *ibid.*, xiii, 1933, pp. 13–54; A. Goetze, *Hethiter, Churriter und Assyrer*, 1936; J. Lewy, "Influences hurrites sur Israël", in *R.E.S.*, 1938, pp. 49–75; F. Thureau-Dangin, "Tablettes hurrites provenant de Mâri", in *R.Ass.*, xxxvi, 1939, pp. 1–28; J. Paterson, "The Hurrians", in *Presentation Volume to William Barron Stevenson* (Studia

being read, and a first study of Ḥurrian grammar has been published.[1]

A few years ago it was thought that the Ḥurrians were to be identified with the Subarians,[2] who figure in cuneiform texts as Subartu. Recent study of this question has yielded the view that they were quite separate peoples, and the Subarians have now to be added to the list of peoples who are known to have been in Mesopotamia in the patriarchal age.[3] There was, indeed, quite a mixture of races in Mesopotamia in the first half of the second millennium B.C.,[4] as well as in Palestine, and the migrations that are recorded in the patriarchal narratives were probably connected with wider migrations that marked the age.

I have already noted that Ur and Harran are linked by their common worship of the moon-god Sin. It is now known that there was a temple to the same god at Mari,[5] which lay on the route from Ur to Harran, and more than half way between them. It has been conjectured that it was through Amorite influence that the cult of this god was spread from Ur to the north-west.[6] On the other hand, there is little trace of moon worship at Nuzu.[7] From Harran it spread farther west and south

---

Senitica et Orientalia, ii), 1945, pp. 95–115; I. J. Gelb, *Hurrians and Subarians*, 1944; R. T. O'Callaghan, *Aram Naharaim*, 1948, pp. 44–49; and works mentioned in the following note.

[1] Cf. E. A. Speiser, *Introduction to Hurrian*, 1941 (*A.A.S.O.R.*, xx). Cf. also C. H. Gordon, "Evidence for the Horite Language from Nuzi", in *B.A.S.O.R.*, No. 64, Dec. 1936, pp. 23–28; J. Friedrich, "Der gegenwärtige Stand unseres Wissens von der churritischen Sprache", in *J.E.O.L.*, vi, 1939, pp. 90–96; E. A. Speiser, "Progress in the Study of the Hurrian Language", in *B.A.S.O.R.*, No. 74, April 1939, pp. 4–7, "Notes on Ḥurrian Phonology", in *J.A.O.S.*, lviii, 1938, pp. 173–201, and "Studies in Hurrian Grammar", *ibid.*, lix, 1939, pp. 298–324; R. de Vaux, "Études sur les Ḥurrites", in *Vivre et Penser*, i, 1941, pp. 194–211.

[2] Cf. A. Ungnad, *Subartu*, 1936, pp. 129 ff. See also R. de Vaux, *Vivre et Penser*, i, 1941, pp. 195–200.

[3] Cf. I. J. Gelb, *Hurrians and Subarians*, 1944; R. T. O'Callaghan, *Aram Naharaim*, 1948, pp. 37–44.

[4] Cf. O'Callaghan, *op. cit.*, *passim*.   [5] Cf. O'Callaghan, *ibid.*, p. 28.

[6] Cf. P. (E.) Dhorme, "Abraham dans le cadre de l'histoire", in *R.B.*, xxxvii, 1928, pp. 367–386, 481–511, xl, 1931, pp. 364–374, 503–518, where it is argued that the moon was the god of the nomads, who spread the cult, and that it was worshipped under the name Sin by the Sumerians and Accadians, Warah by the Amorites, and Sahar by the Aramaeans. Cf. also O'Callaghan, *loc. cit.*, where the spread of the cult is associated more particularly with the Amorites, whereas Dhorme had associated it more particularly with the Aramaeans. On Amorite influence at Mari, cf. G. E. Mendenhall, *B.A.*, xi, 1948, p. 12. G. E. Wright (*The Study of the Bible Today and Tomorrow*, ed. by H. R. Willoughby, 1947, pp. 81 f.) thinks it is probable that the "Fathers of Israel were one small branch of the Amorite movement".

[7] Cf. O'Callaghan, *op. cit.*, p. 28.

to Syria and Palestine, where such a place-name as Jericho is connected with the word for moon.[1] In the story of the patriarchs also we find some moon names. It has already been said that the name of Abraham's father, Terah, has been found by some as a divine name at Ras Shamra. While this is improbable, it is not at all improbable that the name Terah is due to moon worship amongst Abraham's ancestors. Similarly the name Laban is another name for the moon deity,[2] and the names Sarah and Milcah may also be associated with moon worship.[3] All of this fits excellently into the fuller background which we now have of this period. As O'Callaghan says: "The Biblical narrative which traces the journey of Abraham ... from Ur to Harran ... could fit in perfectly with the migrations of nomadic or seminomadic peoples of the entire first half of the second millennium B.C."[4]

Finally we may see how some of the customs referred to in the stories of the patriarchal age find their illustration in recently found evidence from Nuzu.[5] Many of the documents found there relate to adoption. Sometimes a childless man or woman legally adopted a free-born person or slave, thus securing someone whose duty it would be to look after them and to bury them, and who in return became the heir of the adopter.[6] The practice was liable to abuse, and indeed became a means of evading one of the laws of the land. For in addition to genuine adoptions, there were what are called sale

[1] Cf. Dhorme, R.B., xxxvii, 1928, pp. 509 ff.; O'Callaghan, op. cit., p. 29 n. See also J. Lewy, "The Late Assyro-Babylonian Cult of the Moon and its Culmination at the time of Nabonidus", in H.U.C.A., xix, 1945–46, pp. 405–489.

[2] Cf. Dhorme, loc. cit., p. 511, and L'évolution religieuse d'Israël, i, La religion des Hébreux nomades, 1937, p. 71. J. Lewy (R.H.R., cx, 1934, p. 45) identifies the Biblical Laban with this moon deity, much as others have identified Terah with the same deity under another name. Cf. Dhorme, loc. cit., p. 74.

[3] Cf. Dhorme, R.B., xxxvii, 1928, p. 511, and La religion des Hébreux nomades, p. 71; O'Callaghan, op. cit., p. 29 n.

[4] Ibid., p. 29.

[5] Illustrations of Biblical customs are noted in many of the works that treat of the Nuzu texts, and in particular in the following: E. A. Speiser, Ethnic Movements in the Near East in the Second Millennium B.C., 1933 (A.A.S.O.R., xiii, pp. 13–54); C. H. Gordon, "Parallèles nouziens aux lois et coutumes de l'Ancien Testament", in R.B., xliv, 1935, pp. 34–41, "Biblical Customs and the Nuzu Tablets", in B.A., iii, 1940, pp. 1–12, The Living Past, 1940, pp. 156–178, and J.N.E.S., xiii, 1954, pp. 56–59, R. T. O'Callaghan, "Historical Parallels to Patriarchal Social Custom", C.B.Q., vi, 1944, pp. 391–405. Cf. also G. E. Wright, Biblical Archaeology, revised ed., 1962, pp. 43 f.; A. Parrot, Abraham et son temps, 1962, pp. 90 ff.

[6] Cf. C. H. Gordon, The Living Past, 1940, pp. 159 f., and B.A., iii, 1940, p. 2. See also E. A. Speiser, A.A.S.O.R., x, 1930, pp. 7–13; E. M. Cassin, L'adoption à Nuzi, 1938, pp. 285 ff.

adoptions.[1] A man who was financially embarrassed would adopt as his son a wealthy man who would help him out of his difficulties and who would become the heir to his land. The law provided that land was inalienable and must be kept within the family, but by the fiction of adoption this was evaded. One man, who appears to have been the richest man in the community, was adopted by very many men.[2] In the deeds of adoption it is specified what gift he gave to each of his "fathers", but there is no mention of any duty to care for them during life and to mourn for them when dead, as there is in genuine cases of adoption.[3]

It will be remembered that in Gen. 15 : 2 Abraham, who has no hope of any children of his own, refers to Eliezer as his heir, and further calls him "one born in my house"—i.e., a slave who had been born in slavery. Presumably Abraham had adopted him in accordance with this custom, to the mutual advantage of them both. But God says to the patriarch, "This man shall not be thine heir."[4] If he had been a legally adopted heir, how could his rights be set aside so long as he fulfilled his filial duties? Here again we find illustration in the Nuzu texts, where it is provided that if the adopter should subsequently beget a son, the adopted son must yield to him the place of chief heir.[5]

Again we find that Sarah, when she had given up hope of motherhood, gave her maidservant Hagar to her husband to be her substitute, saying: "It may be that I shall obtain children by her."[6] Later we find that Rachel does the same thing with Bilhah, and her example is followed by Leah without the same reason.[7] In marriage contracts from Nuzu it is specified that if the wife should prove childless she must provide her husband with a slave wife.[8] It is curious to observe

[1] Cf. E. A. Speiser, loc. cit., pp. 13–18; Cassin, op. cit., pp. 51 ff.; C. H. Gordon, Z.A., xliii, 1936, p. 151, and The Living Past, 1940, pp. 164 f. Some examples of deeds of sale-adoption are given in A.A.S.O.R., xvi, 1936, pp. 82 ff. (translations by E. A. Speiser, the texts transliterated by R. H. Pfeiffer on pp. 21 ff.).

[2] Cf. C. H. Gordon, The Living Past, p. 164: "Tehiptilla, for instance, had himself adopted as the son of several hundred people in the town, and accordingly obtained the right to inherit their property. He thus became the son of many fathers."

[3] Cf. E. A. Speiser, A.A.S.O.R., x, 1930, pp. 30 ff., where some examples of deeds of adoption are given. Cf. C. J. Gadd, R.Ass., xxiii, 1926, p. 94; E. Chiera and E. A. Speiser, J.A.O.S., xlvii, 1927, p. 40.

[4] Gen. 15: 4.   [5] E. A. Speiser, loc. cit., where this provision stands in the texts given.
[6] Gen. 16: 2.   [7] Gen. 30: 3, 9.

[8] Cf. C. H. Gordon, R.B., xliv, 1935, p. 35; E. A. Speiser, loc. cit., pp. 31 f. With this cf. the Code of Ḥammurabi, § 145, where it is laid down that if a man has married a wife who does not bear him children, he shall be free to bring a concubine into his house, but not to put her on an equality with his wife. It will be seen that the Nuzu contracts offer a closer parallel to the Biblical story.

that a foreign slave may be specified in these texts,[1] and that Hagar was a foreign slave. In the Nuzu texts it is specified that the slave must come from Lulluland, whence the best slaves were obtained,[2] while in the case of Hagar she was an Egyptian. Later, when Sarah had herself borne Isaac, she demanded that Hagar and her child should be driven forth, and the patriarch was reluctant to comply with her demand.[3] Indeed, it was only as the result of divine instruction that he complied. Here again the Nuzu documents come to our help, for we find it specified that if the slave wife should bear a son he must not be expelled.[4] In the light of this we can understand Abraham's reluctance to agree to Sarah's illegal demand, until a divine dispensation overrides the law.

There is a parallel to Esau's sale of his birthright. For we learn of a legal arrangement whereby the rights of the first-born are transferred to another.[5] In one case they are transferred to one who was not really a brother, but who was adopted as a brother.[6] In another case actual brothers were involved and the one who renounced his rights received three sheep in return.[7] He seems at any rate to have received more than the single meal which Esau got.

Another tablet offers a parallel to the story of Jacob and Laban. Here a man adopts another as his son, giving him his daughter to wife, and making him and his children heirs unless the adopter should subsequently beget a son, when the adopted son should take an equal share of the estate with the actual son, but the children of the adopted son would forfeit any right.[8] It is further laid down that the adopted

---

[1] As in the text indicated in the preceding note, where we read: "If Gilimninu bears (children), Shennima shall not take another wife; and if Gilimninu does not bear, Gilimninu a woman of the Lullu as wife for Shennima shall take" (translation of Speiser, *loc. cit.*, p. 32).

[2] Cf. C. H. Gordon, *The Living Past*, 1940, pp. 160 f.

[3] Gen. 21: 10 f.

[4] Cf. the text transliterated and translated by Speiser, *loc. cit.*, pp. 31 f. Here again we have a closer parallel than can be provided by the Code of Ḥammurabi, where § 146 lays it down that a slave concubine who has borne children and made herself equal with her mistress must not be sold for money, but reduced to a position among the maid-servants.

[5] Cf. E. A. Speiser, *A.A.S.O.R.*, xii, 1933, p. 44: "Another interesting analogue from Nuzi is a legal arrangement as to the disposition of the birthright: one of the parties acquires the rights of the firstborn, while the other, whose claims to the privilege would have been actually justified by reason of birth, is satisfied to accept a minor share in his father's estate."

[6] Cf. C. H. Gordon, *B.A.*, iii, 1940, p. 5.

[7] Cf. C. H. Gordon, *The Living Past*, 1940, p. 177; *B.A.*, iii, 1940, p. 5.

[8] Cf. C. J. Gadd, *R.Ass.*, xxiii, 1926, pp. 126 f.; C. H. Gordon, *B.A.*, iii, 1940, p. 5.

son would not be entitled to take another wife beside the daughter of his adopted father.[1] While the parallel is not complete, it is sufficiently close to shed light on the Biblical story.

Again, Rachel's theft of the teraphim of Laban[2] is better understood in the light of Nuzu evidence. There we find that in law the possession of such idols by the woman's husband ensured for him the succession to the father-in-law's property.[3] It has been conjectured that Laban had no son at the time of Jacob's marriage of Leah, but that he subsequently became the father of sons, who were therefore now superior in legal standing to Jacob.[4] By carrying off the teraphim, however, Rachel preserved for Jacob the chief title to Laban's estate.

In all of these cases we have customs which do not recur in the Old Testament in later periods, and which therefore are not likely to reflect contemporary society in the age when the documents were written. Their accurate reflection of social conditions in the patriarchal age and in some parts of the Mesopotamia from which the patriarchs are said to have come, many centuries before the present documents were composed, is striking.[5] Speiser conjectures that the true significance of these incidents had probably been lost even before the time of David.[6] It is in any case significant that if these stories had been carried in oral tradition they correctly reflect obsolete customs, and it is not surprising that to-day there is a disposition to treat them with more respect than some of the earlier scholars accorded them. To quote Speiser again: "It follows that we cannot afford to disregard lightly the information contained in the patriarchal stories, no matter what we may think about the historicity of the individual heroes. Since the minor incidents are demonstrably in keeping with the times, not to say conditioned by them, it is likely that the accounts of the migrations of Abraham and his descendants have some foundations in fact."[7]

It may be asked how it comes about that such close parallels can be

---

[1] *Ibid.* [2] Gen. 31: 19.

[3] Cf. S. Smith, *apud* C. J. Gadd, *R.Ass.*, xxiii, 1926, p. 127; C. H. Gordon, *R.B.*, xliv, 1935, pp. 35 f.

[4] Cf. C. H. Gordon, *B.A.S.O.R.*, No. 66, April 1937, p. 26.

[5] Cf. W. F. Albright (*From the Stone Age to Christianity*, 2nd ed., 1946, p. 180): "Since the publication of the Nuzian documents of the fifteenth century B.C. it has become increasingly evident that the customary law reflected by the patriarchal stories of Genesis fits better into the framework of Nuzian social and legal practice than it does into that of later Israel or into that of the Babylonian laws and economic documents of the nineteenth century or the similar Assyrian material of the twelfth century B.C."

[6] Cf. *A.A.S.O.R.*, xiii, 1933, p. 44.

[7] Cf. *A.A.S.O.R.*, xiii, 1933, p. 45.

found at Nuzu, which was a Ḥurrian centre, when it has been said that it was Amorite influence which prevailed at Mari and which may have carried moon worship along the road to Harran. To this the reply is that there was an amalgam of cultures throughout Mesopotamia, and while moon worship does not seem to have taken the same hold at Nuzu, there was certainly Ḥurrian influence there, and also at Mari,[1] and indeed throughout the whole Mesopotamian area.[2] If the Horites of the Bible are equated with the Ḥurrians, then that influence reached Palestine. It certainly reached Ras Shamra on the Mediterranean coast, where some tablets in Ḥurrian have been found.[3] Moreover, there is reason to believe that even Babylonian myths reached the Hebrews through a Ḥurrian *milieu*. For in the Babylonian flood story the hero bears a name which shows little likeness to that found in the Bible. For the Babylonian hero is called Ut-napishtim[4] and the Biblical hero Noah. Here, however, we find that a Ḥurrian fragment of the Gilgamesh epic contains a name related to the Biblical name Noah,[5] and it has therefore been suggested that there was a Ḥurrian source for the traditions of Genesis.[6] Further, in the presence of important bodies of Ḥabiru at Nuzu and in Palestine we have a further link between these two societies that is beyond conjecture, whether Harran provided a bridge between them or not. If the Ḥabiru were of a common stock, they may well have kept in some touch with one another for some time after they broke off into separate groups, just as we are told that the family of Abraham kept in touch with their northern kin for two generations. Later these links would tend to be lost, especially with groups that became absorbed in the

---

[1] Cf. I. J. Gelb, *Hurrians and Subarians*, 1944, pp. 62–65. Some Hurrian texts have been found at Mari, indeed (cf. F. Thureau-Dangin, "Tablettes ḥurrites provenant de Mari", in *R.Ass.*, xxxvi, 1939, pp. 1–28), and these are at least three centuries older than the Ḥurrian texts of Boghaz Köi and Ras Shamra (so A. Bea, *Biblica*, xxi, 1940, p. 193), while Speiser estimates them to be four or five centuries older (cf. *Introduction to Hurrian*, 1941, p. 6) and Thureau-Dangin several centuries older (*loc. cit.*, p. 27).

[2] Cf. W. F. Albright, *From the Stone Age to Christianity*, 2nd ed., 1946, pp. 109 f.; also *B.A.S.O.R.*, No. 67, Oct. 1937, p. 29, and *J.B.L.*, lviii, 1939, p. 101.

[3] Cf. R. de Langhe, *Les textes de Ras Shamra-Ugarit et leurs rapports avec le milieu biblique de l'Ancien Testament*, i, 1945, p. 98. See also H. L. Ginsberg and B. Maisler, "Semitised Ḥurrians in Syria and Palestine", in *J.P.O.S.*, xiv, 1934, pp. 243–267.

[4] P. (E.) Dhorme (*R.B.*, xxxix, 1930, p. 487) maintained that the name should be read Um-napishtim, but most continue to read Ut-napishtim.

[5] Cf. E. Burrows, *J.R.A.S.*, 1925, p. 281. See also J. Lewy, "Nāḫ et Rušpān", in *Mélanges Syriens offerts à M. René Dussaud*, i, 1939, pp. 273–275.

[6] Cf. E. Burrows, *loc. cit.* Cf. W. F. Albright, *The Archaeology of Palestine and the Bible*, 1932, pp. 139 f., *J.B.L.*, lvii, 1938, p. 231; also G. E. Mendenhall, *B.A.*, xi, 1948, p. 16, where an Amorite source is preferred.

culture that surrounded them, or that sank into a normal condition of slavery.

The results of our study, of whose incompleteness I am fully conscious, may seem more meagre than some eager advocates have claimed. Yet they are not inconsiderable; and a sober recognition of the limits of our evidence is less harmful to the cause of truth than any exaggerated claims. Of the events of the patriarchal story we have no confirmation from any external source; of any mention of the patriarchs or of Israelite tribes in non-Biblical sources of the first half of the second millennium B.C. there is no solid evidence; of any external evidence for the soundness of the Biblical chronology which would put Abraham in the twenty-first century B.C. there is none, and he must either be placed in the eighteenth or seventeenth century B.C. or completely loosed from known external history. On the other hand, if the reasonable probability that Gen. 14 : 1 reflects the conditions of the early seventeenth century is recognized much more is gained than is lost by the sacrifice of the chronology, which is, in parts at any rate, late and inconsistent with other Biblical statements. For if a sound tradition lay behind the synchronism of Gen. 14 : 1, it is likely that in other respects the chapter rests on ancient tradition.[1] Further, the evidence that the names borne by persons in the patriarchal stories are known to have been borne by persons in the second millennium B.C., and in some cases borne by several persons, helps to increase our respect for the traditions. For a modern writer to compose historical fiction, with large libraries at his disposal, is one thing; but for an ancient writer it was not so easy. Yet even a modern writer can be guilty of anachronisms. While there are undoubted anachronisms in the book of Genesis, however, such as the use of the name Dan in Gen. 14 : 14[2] and the references to the Philistines in the time of Abraham,[3] they do not concern the names of persons or the conditions of the times. Moreover, the patriarchal stories cannot be classed with modern historical fiction, since they undoubtedly rest on traditions handed down from the past. If they were traditions which came into existence without basis long after the times they purport to describe,

[1] Cf. above, p. 293, n. 2, where I express the view that it was not originally a tradition about Abraham, but one transferred to him.

[2] Cf. Judges 18: 29, where it is said that the city was not called Dan until long after the time of Abraham, and after the days of Moses and Joshua.

[3] Cf. Gen. 21: 32, 34, 26: 8, 14, 15, 18. The Philistines did not enter the land until the beginning of the twelfth century B.C., and therefore long after the Biblical chronology would put Abraham and Isaac, and after that chronology would put Moses.

the close accord with the conditions of those times would be remarkable. For, as Albright says, and as has been made clear in what I have said in this lecture, "It is now becoming increasingly clear that the traditions of the Patriarchal Age, preserved in the book of Genesis, reflect with remarkable accuracy the actual conditions of the Middle Bronze Age, and especially of the period between 1800 and 1500 B.C."[1] It is, therefore, as I said at the outset, not because scholars of to-day begin with more conservative presuppositions than their predecessors that they have a much greater respect for the patriarchal stories than was formerly common, but because the evidence warrants it.[2] That the evidence concerns the background of the stories and not their content does not make it less significant; and in any case it is the only contemporary evidence that we have.

[1] Cf. *Proceedings of the American Philosophical Society*, lxix, 1930, pp. 466 f. Cf. also G. E. Mendenhall, *B.A.*, xi, 1948, p. 16; G. E. Wright, *Biblical Archaeology*, revised ed., 1962, p. 40b. Already in 1938 S. H. Hooke wrote (*Record and Revelation*, ed. by H. W. Robinson, pp. 372 f.): "It is safe to say that the general effect of the discoveries of the last decade has been to confirm the substantial accuracy of the picture of life in Canaan in the second millennium B.C. as described in the patriarchal narrative of Genesis, and to provide some ground for the view that written sources for this period may have existed at a much earlier date than has been commonly supposed." Cf. also H. Cazelles, *S.D.B.*, Fasc. 36, 1961, cols. 155 f.

[2] For a long and valuable study of the subject of the present paper cf. R. de Vaux, "Les patriarches hébreux et les découvertes modernes", in *R.B.*, liii, 1946, pp. 321–348, lv, 1948, pp. 321–347, lvi, 1949, pp. 5–36. Cf. also R. Gyllenberg, *Sinuhe och Abraham: patriarkernas värld i arkeologisk belysning*, 1948, for an account of recent discovery as a background to a comparison of the stories of Sinuhe and Abraham.

Indexes

(a) *Subjects*

(b) Authors

346

(c) Texts

355